OBJECT RECOGNITION

Edited by **Tam Phuong Cao**

Object Recognition
Edited by Tam Phuong Cao

Published by InTech
Janeza Trdine 9, 51000 Rijeka, Croatia

Publishing Process Manager Katarina Lovrecic

Technical Editor Teodora Smiljanic

Cover Designer InTech Design Team

Additional hard copies can be obtained from orders@intechopen.com

Object Recognition, Edited by Tam Phuong Cao
p. cm.
ISBN 978-953-307-222-7

For EU product safety concerns:
IN TECH d.o.o., Prolaz Marije Krucifikse Kozulić 3, 51000 Rijeka, Croatia,
info@intechopen.com or visit our website at intechopen.com.

Meet the editor

Tam Phuong Cao received his Bachelor of Engineering Degree with first class honors from Swinburne University of Technology, Australia, in 2005. He was awarded his Ph.D by La Trobe University, Australia in 2010. From 2009 to 2010, he worked as a research engineer specialised in computer vision applications at Sentient Vision Systems Pty Ltd, Australia. His research interests include computer vision algorithms and implementation techniques, real-time application of computer vision and image processing on FPGA.

Contents

Preface

Vision-based object recognition tasks are very familiar in our everyday activities, such as driving our car in the correct lane or obeying traffic rules posted by road signs. We are usually not paying attention to the process of how we perceive images with our eyes and give feedbacks in terms of action, such as slowing down to the speed limit. We do these tasks effortlessly in real-time. Computer vision and image processing field has been trying to mimic the human's capability in visually recognising objects which will allow machine to replace human in performing boring or dangerous tasks. Many applications have been deployed such as removing defects from a conveying belt in a factory. Many other advanced applications are being improved or developed. These applications require researchers and application developers to gain advanced, broad, in-depth and up-to-date understanding of object recognition.

This book, Object Recognition, offers a closer look at the concepts and techniques being used in computer vision. It covers topics related to object recognition from both biological and technological point of view. These topics include, but are not limited to:

- the process of object recognition in human brain
- some diseases affecting object recognition capability of a body
- image features or descriptors for object recognition
- techniques for improving recognition speed
- object recognition for real-world applications
- object recognition and registration in 3-D domain

This book is suitable for both novice and expert readers. The book provides readers with a vision-based object recognition techniques and enables them to develop advanced, state-of-the-art technique for their applications.

Tam Phuong Cao
Sentient Vision Systems Pty Ltd,
Australia

Part 1

Biological Inspiration and Analysis of Vision-based Object Recognition

1

On the Future of Object Recognition: The Contribution of Color

David J. Therriault
University of Florida
USA

1. Introduction

Cognitive theories of object recognition have traditionally emphasized structural components (Biederman, 1987; Grossberg & Mingolla, 1985). The idea that object recognition is largely driven by shape was advantageous to theory building because of its economy (i.e., only a single dimension needed to be attended and there are a finite number of mutually exclusive components). However, recent work provides evidence that surface level information (e.g., object color) is readily used in object recognition (Rossion & Pourtois, 2004; Tanaka & Presnell, 1999; Therriault et al., 2009; & Naor-Raz et al., 2003). The purpose of this chapter is two-fold: to present results from experiments that more closely examine color's influence on object recognition and to reconcile these results with traditional theories of object recognition.

Section 2 contains a historical overview of the claims made between strucutral (i.e., edge) and view-point dependent (i.e., surface + edge) characterizations of object recognition. Although the debate may be subsiding over the status of viewpoint invariance, many open questions remain concerning how color contributes to the processing and recognition of objects.

Section 3 reviews conflicting research on the role of color in object recognition. Some studies fail to find any effects of color upon recognition, others find evidence for only high color diagnostic objects, and still others find that color readily influences recognition. This section concludes by offering some explanations for differences in obtained results.

Section 4 presents a recent set of experiments from my lab exploring the role of color in recognition, conceptualization, and language use. Most striking, the results from four different experiments are identical with respect to color. The presentation of correctly colored items always enhanced recognition and conceptualization of the objects.

In Section 5, the early conceptual analogy used in object recognition (i.e., speech segmentation) is reviewed and updated. I propose that object recognition is more anlagous to word recognition in reading. This is a more apt analogy because it can accomodate both structural and view-point evidence.

Finally, Section 6 argues that evidence calls for a more nuanced, flexible and integrated theory of object recognition, one that includes both bottom-up and top-down processing. The chapter concludes that the study of color vision is a fruitful area from which to gain a deeper understanding of object recognition generally; and that this pursuit would benefit greatly from the contribution of disciplines beyond cognition (e.g., neuroscience, biology, and linguistics).

2. Structural and view-based accounts of object recognition

Research examining human object recognition has historically been polarized between two views (Hayward, 2003; Hummel, 2000; Tarr & Bülthoff, 1995). The first view, and still the predominant one, argues that a structural approach best characterizes how we recognize objects in our environment. A quick review of three introductory cognitive textbooks confirms the solid footing of structural approaches in the field (i.e., all of these textbooks' coverage of object recognition ends with example figures of structures). The most prominent structural theory remains Beiderman's (1987) RBC (i.e., recognition by components) theory. According to this theory, a finite set of mutually exclusive structural components called geons are the mainstay of object recognition and representation (Biederman, 2007; Biederman, 1987; Biederman and Bar, 2000, Biederman and Gerhardstien, 1995; Biederman and Ju, 1988). Geons are volumetric structures created from the contrasts of two dimensional edges based upon symmetry, curvature, parallelism, and co-termination. Figure 1 contains a sample of geons.

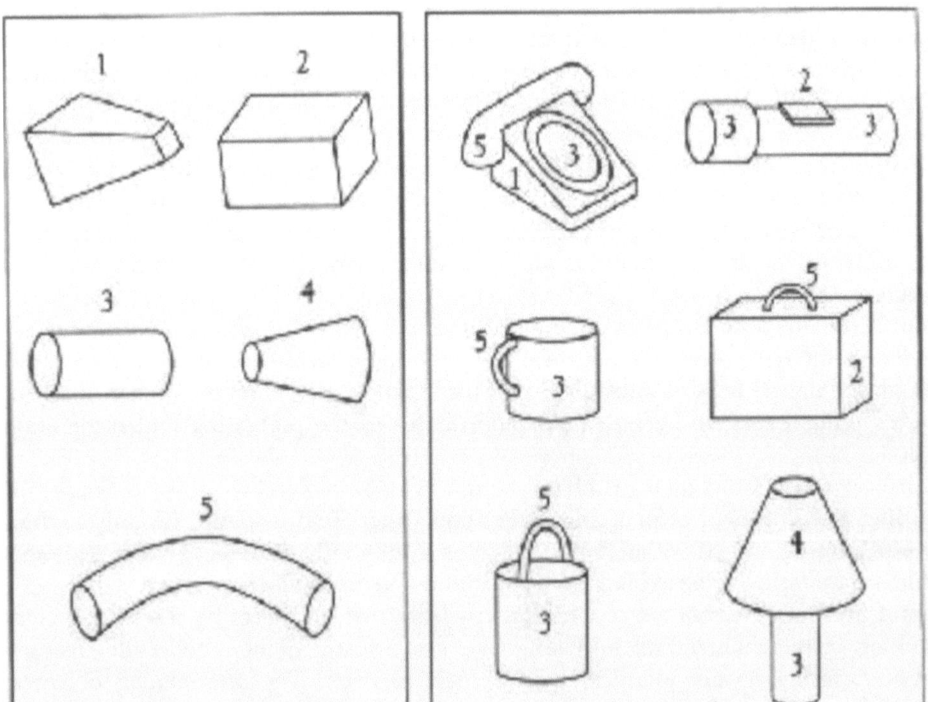

Fig. 1. A sampling of geons (left panel) and common objects with their constitute geons labelled (right panel). (From Biederman, 1990).

These structures are thought to underpin our ability to represent objects, in that, to recognize an object we must first decompose it into its constituent parts and "build" our representation. Geons are the smallest unit upon which elements of an object can be differentiated. One of the stronger claims of RBC theory is that these structures are processed without respect to surface features (they are said to be *invariant* to viewpoint, size, texture, or color). Evidence suggests that these structures are also fairly resistant to occlusion and interference from visual noise. Researchers who adopted the strong version of this theory typically documented the contribution of edge-based information in recognizing objects.

In a view-dependent or an edge + surface account of object perception, elements other than geons contribute in meaningful ways to object recognition. Some structural approaches, for example, Marr (1982) and Marr and Nishihara (1978) argue that surface level information is a necessary step in the process of recognition but only in the service of shape. Perhaps the most well researched aspect of surface level is our understanding of an observer's perceived viewpoint of objects. The impetus for research on this topic probably came from the strong claims of viewpoint invariance in the early RBC model. Hayward and Williams (2000), Tarr and Bülthoff (1995), and Tarr and Pinkert (1989) all provided evidence for recognition costs (i.e., decreased reaction times) associated with rotating the viewpoint of an object from its original presentation, casting doubt upon the invariance built into the RBC model. The more an object is rotated from its original studied view, the longer recognition takes. There are also models of object recognition that make explicit use of surface features. For example, Poggio and Edelman (1990) created a computer model of a neural network that learned to recognize 3-dimensional images in different orientations using a view-based matching algorithm (i.e., geons were not included in the model).

The 90's debate surrounding interpretations of viewpoint was largely a matter of degree. Structuralists first argued for invariance, later conceding that viewpoint could aid object recognition (under very specific conditions). Those exploring edge + surface explanations documented elements of recognition that could not be accommodated in a structuralist framework. The role of color in object recognition remains an open question, but it appears to be following the same research trajectory as viewpoint.

3. Contributions of color research

3.1 Color information is ancillary to object recognition

Beiderman and Ju (1988) first argued that structural (edge-based) properties of objects are theoretically preferred over viewpoint, texture, and color information. It is not the case that these features can't be used, but that they are only useful in certain circumstances when object shape is compromised or extremely variable (e.g., sorting laundry, Biederman & Ju, 1988). Beiderman and Ju (1988) assessed color contribution by measuring participants' naming times of simple line drawings of objects compared to the fully-detailed color pictures of those objects. Beiderman and Ju (1988) failed to obtain any significant differences between the naming times of the two versions of the objects. If surface and color information contributed to recognition, then the fully detailed color versions of the pictures should have been named more quickly. Beiderman and Ju concluded that color and texture were not the primary means to object recognition.

Similarly, Ostergard and Davidoff (1985) examined the contribution of color to object recognition. They provided evidence that color pictures elicited faster naming times, but that presenting the objects in their correct color didn't matter. They explained this result indirectly as a function of shape. That is, color provided extra luminance or contrast that aided in shape extraction. In a follow-up experiment, Davidoff and Ostergard (1988) produced evidence that color did not impact reaction time (in a semantic classification task). They concluded that color is not part of the semantic (i.e., meaningful) representation of objects. They left open that there may be some other representation of objects that includes color information (e.g., ancillary verbal information). Cave, Bost, and Cobb (1996) explored color and pattern manipulations of pictures in repetition priming. They demonstrated that changes in color did not influence repetition priming; whereas, shape did. Cave et al. concluded that repetition priming is insensitive to physical attributes that are not attended (i.e., color or size).

3.2 Color information is an inherent property of objects

In contrast to these results presented above, evidence for the importance of color information has been compounding. Price and Humphreys (1989), Tanaka and Presnell (1999) and Wurm et al. (1993) all had participants engage in some form of an object classification task (i.e., does a picture match a previously presented word). They found that color information facilitated the recognition of objects, but only those with very strong color associations. For example, an orange colored carrot (i.e., high color diagnostic HCD object) was named more quickly than its grayscale compliment; but there were no differences in reaction time between color and grayscale versions of a sports car (i.e., low color diagnostic LCD object). These studies provide evidence that color is an important component in object recognition, but *only* for highly color diagnostic objects. Naor-Raz et al. (2003) also explored color diagnosticity in a Stroop task where participants named objects or words that were matched or mismatched with their appropriate color. They found that response times were significantly faster for objects in their typical color (e.g., a yellow banana) than atypical (e.g., a purple banana). This pattern was reversed when colored words were used to describe the objects (i.e., seeing the word banana in either yellow or purple ink). Naor-Raz et al. (2003) concluded that their results provide evidence that color is encoded in object representation at different levels (i.e., perceptual, conceptual, and linguistic).

Evidence also implicates color processing in recognition of everyday objects that are not color diagnostic. Rossion and Pourtois (2004) revisited the naming times of the Snodgrass and Vanderwart object picture set (260 objects) in which they created three conditions: line drawings (the original set), gray-level detailed drawings, or color detailed drawings. They found that color aided recognition, and that while this was more pronounced for color diagnostic items, color also aided the recognition of low color diagnostic or variable colored items (e.g., man-made objects).

3.3 Explaining the conflicting findings

There are several explanations for conflicting results with respect to color. Probably the most pronounced is the fact that researchers have disagreed on the nature of color diagnosticity (and which items are most appropriate). For example, color diagnostic items tend to be vegetables, fruits, animals, and man-made objects. Studies emphasizing shape often use only man-made items, while those emphasizing color include more natural objects. Nonetheless, the distinction of category has recently been excluded as the predominant reason for conflicting findings, as suggested by Nagai and Yokosawa (2003) and Therriault et al. (2009). Of greater concern is that studies that argue that color is not important in object recognition often do so from a null result. That is, these studies report an *absence* of evidence as evidence that color is not utilized (Biederman & Ju, 1988). Simply put, it is problematic to accept the null hypothesis; it does not provide a solid base to build theory.

4. Our contribution to understanding the role of color in object recognition

4.1 On developing color object stimuli

In a recent article, Therriault, Yaxley, and Zwaan (2009) explored a range of recognition and object representation tasks using color stimuli. We made use of highly detailed photographs of objects. There are several important points to note about our selection of stimuli and their development. First, we only selected high color diagnostic items, most were concepts adapted from Naor-Raz et al. (2003). As noted by Tanaka and Presnell (1999), color diagnostic items used in earlier studies were later found to be problematic (e.g., camera or flowerpot). Consequently, we excluded any objects that were identified as problematic from earlier studies. Once we obtained quality photos, the pictures went through a washing process where we removed all color information (i.e., we transformed them to grayscale using Adobe Photoshop). This insured that once we re-colored the objects they would only contain one color and that we could directly control this color (i.e., all red object colors used the exact same red).

Three different color versions of the objects were created: grayscale, appropriately colored (congruent), and inappropriately colored (incongruent). This departs from previous studies that typically employ two conditions (a grayscale image compared to the appropriate colored version or studies that pit an appropriate colored object against an inappropriately colored version). Experimentally, our design allows comparison of the relative contribution of color (appropriate and inappropriate) to a control (the grayscale image).

Each picture occupied a 3 inch square space (72 pixels per inch) presented on a white computer background controlled using the software program E-Prime (Schneider et al., 2002). Also included in our design were 72 filler items that were not color diagnostic and were randomly colored. The filler items were incorporated to de-emphasise the likelihood that participants would become aware of the color diagnostic nature of our experimental items. The final 24 experimental objects were created in one the following range of colors: brown, green, red, and orange and were repainted with the appropriate translucent color (using the standard RGB code values for each of our colors).

Figure 2 presents two example stimuli in each of the three conditions (for demonstration simplicity, I only included red items). One potential criticism against using color diagnostic items as stimuli is that they are all either food items or animals, and that these could be treated differently than man-made objects. In our study, more than a third of our experimental pictures were man-made objects (see figure 3 for two example man-made items).

4.2 Experimental tasks and results

Therriault et al. (2009) created a set of 4 experiments using the stimuli described above. In Experiment 1, participants were asked to name objects and their time to respond was measured. Experiment 1b used the same stimuli but queried participants if a presented word matched a subsequent picture (while measuring reaction time). Experiment 2 used a rebus paradigm (i.e., participants read sentences with inserted pictures). A critical noun in a sentence was replaced by its picture and reading time was recorded (Potter, et al., 1986). Experiment 3 mirrored Experiment 2 but used an earlier contextual sentence in an attempt to override the congruent color of the object (e.g., a pumpkin is described as painted green in the sentence prior to the presentation of the target sentence with the pictured object).

Fig. 2. Example natural stimuli demonstrating color conditions: incongruent, black and white, and congruent; respectively (From Therriault, et al., 2009).

Fig. 3. Example man-made stimuli demonstrating color conditions: incongruent, black and white, and congruent; respectively (From Therriault, et al., 2009).

Experiment 1 provided a measure of pure recognition. Our results indicated that images presented in congruent color facilitated naming time, whereas incongruent color information actually interfered with naming time (when compare with the control gray-scale image). Experiment 1b provides information on the conceptualization/visualization of the object, as participants had to verify if a presented word matched its picture. Again, congruent color facilitated verification decisions, whereas incongruent color information interfered with verification. Experiments 2 and 3 provided a test of object recognition in which the task was to use the information in the context of comprehending a sentence. In both cases, the same pattern emerged: congruent stimuli aided recognition processes and incongruent stimuli harmed recognition processes. The consistency in color processing across different methods is striking. Below, Figure 4 presents the reaction time data for all of our experiments (error bars depict standard error).

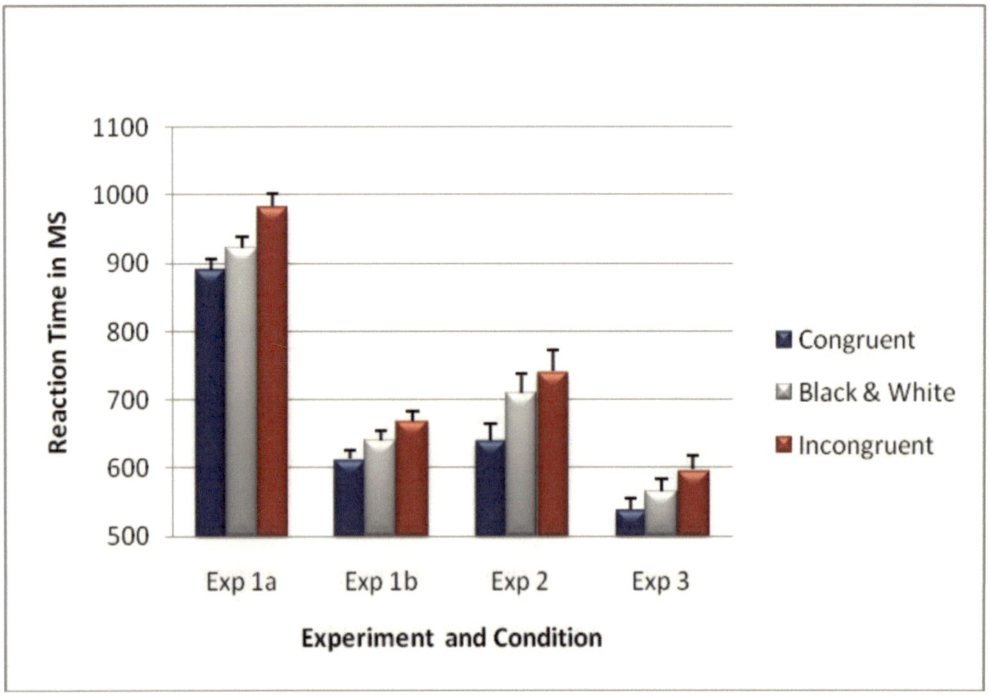

Fig. 4. Reaction time results of all experiments (From Therriault et al., 2009)

We would argue that the experimental bar is set high for our color items. In isolating color we had to present stimuli that were not completely natural. For example, notice that the stems of both the apple and strawberry are incorrectly colored. However, we can be certain that a single color was responsible for differences in reaction time. Results from our experiments consistently demonstrate that object recognition is much more flexible than relying on simple shape extraction from brightness, depth, and color. Knowing that a strawberry is red contributes to recognizing that object in a fundamental way, above and beyond its shape.

5. On finding the right conceptual analogy in object recognition

5.1 The original speech segmentation analogy

Biederman's (1987) article was a landmark paper; to this day it remains a highly cited and informative guide to those interested in object recognition. In that piece, Biederman enlisted research on speech perception. In short, he argued that object recognition is akin to speech segmentation (i.e., the idea that although speech is a continuous sound wave, the listener splits these sounds into primitives in their mind). For example, a novice learning a new language will often complain that it is difficult to tell where one word begins and another stops. Often, comunication at this stage is characterized as gibberish. With skill, the learner begins to make the proper segmentations in the soundwave to distinguish words. In English, all of the words we can create are formed on a small set of primitives or in linguistics called phonemes (there are roughly 46). From these primitives we can form thousands of words and even create new ones. So too, geons are the primitives that we can combine in a multitude of ways to help us recognize and distinguish objects in our environment.

5.2 A proposed analogy: word recognition and the word superiority effect

One could argue that we do not need to stray too far from the visual domain to find an appropriate analogy that captures the nature of both structural and view-based approaches to object recognition. A good candidate would be the recognition processes employed during reading (i.e., word identification). Considerable research in cognitive psychology has documented the contribution of individual letters (bottom-up) and word knowledge (top-down) in word recognition. A fairly well known demonstration is the word superiority effect (Rayner & Pollatsek, 1989; Reicher, 1969). In a typical experiment exploring this effect, participants are presented with a single word, a single letter, or a pseudo-word (on a computer screen) and asked if the display contained a critical letter. For example, given one of the following stimuli (*cork*, *o*, or *lork*), the participant would be asked if the display had an *o* in it. At first blush, one would assume that the letter *o* in isolation would lead to the fastest verification times. This is not the case. Participants were significantly faster to verify the letter *o* in the word *cork* than the *o* in isolation or the pseudo word *lork*. These counter-intuitive results are easily explained as a confluence of bottom-up (i.e., the processing of the individual letters) and top-down processing (i.e., knowledge of the word cork and our experiences with it as a whole unit). Word recognition isn't discriminatory; any activation that helps in the recognition process will be used. In this example case, there are two levels of potential activation with a word that we know (and, incidentally, why we don't see the effect with non-words). In the same fashion, geons represent the parts, bottom-up approach to object recognition; whereas, view-based information and surface features are often better characterized as top-down. Object recognition mirrors word recognition; any activation that helps in the recognition process will be used.

6. Synthesis and concluding remarks

Similar to the word superiority effect, Therriault et al.'s data (2009) can be taken to provide evidence for a *color superiority effect*--the stimuli from our study easily map onto reading (i.e., an incongruent colored object is equivalent to a pseudo-word; a congruent colored object is equivalent to a known word; and a grayscale image is equivalent to a letter in isolation). Our reactions times also mirror the pattern obtained in reading research on the word superiority effect.

Structural accounts of object recognition provide a solid base to ground the shape component of recognition, but they are simply not sufficient to accommodate color. Color is an intrinsic property of many objects and is represented at all levels of the cognitive system as reviewed in this chapter and even in low-level categorization of scenes (e.g., Goffaux et al., 2005; Olivia & Schyns, 2000). Structuralists argued that those who examine surface features (e.g., color) are essentially arguing for a view-based template theory (Biederman, 2007; Hummel, 2000). At the heart of this debate was an either-or-approach, pitting features against templates. Current views on object recognition are much more integrative and pragmatic. Foster and Gilson (2002), Hayward (2003), and Tanaka et al. (2001) all provide examples of how research benefits from the integration of structural and view-based approaches. I would offer that the research presented in this chapter provides an opportunity to build a more complete, albeit less economical, explanation of object recognition.

So, where is the future of color research in object recognition heading? The tent exploring elements of object recognition is large enough to accommodate a more diverse group of disciplines beyond perception (and we would all benifit from it). For example, research in biology suggests that the brain has evolved to separate brightness, depth, color, and movement (Livingston & Hubel, 1987). This begs the question, what ecological advantage does color vision provide? Is it a surprise that color diagnostic items are often natural items (e.g., food or animals)? Primate research provides evidence that vision has optimized to differentiate edible fruits from background colors (Summer & Mollon, 2000). Similarly, Changizia, Zhang, and Shimojo (2006) provide evidence that primate vision has also optimized for colors associated with skin and blood. In the area of cognition, Stanfield and Zwaan (2001), and Zwaan et al. (2002, 2004) all demonstrate rapid interactions between language and visual representations. Connell (2007) and Richter and Zwaan (2009) point out that text color can make use of (interfere) with the representation of object color. There remain challenges with respect to the timing of recognition and its integration (modularity), but research in these varied disciplines will bring us a more complete picture of the role of color in object recognition.

7. References

Biederman, I. (1987). Recognition-by-components: A theory of human image understanding. *Psychological Review, 94,* 115-147.

Biederman, I. (1990). Higher-Level Vision, In *Visual Cognition and Action,* D. N. Osherson et al., The MIT Press, MA.

Biederman, I., & Bar, M. (1999). One-shot viewpoint invariance in matching novel objects. *Vision Research, 39,* 2885-2899.

Biederman, I., & Gerhardstein, P. C. (1993). Recognizing depth-rotated objects: Evidence and conditions for 3D viewpoint invariance. *Journal of Experimental Psychology: Human Perception and Performance, 19,* 1162-1182.

Biederman, I., & Gerhardstein, P. C. (1995). Viewpoint-dependent mechanisms in visual object recognition: Reply to Tarr and Bülthoff (1995). *Journal of Experimental Psychology: Human Perception and Performance, 21,* 1506-1514.

Biederman, I., & Ju, G. (1988). Surface vs. Edge-Based Determinants of Visual Recognition. *Cognitive Psychology, 20,* 38-64.

Cave, C. B., Bost, P. R., & Cobb, R. E. (1996). Effects of color and pattern on implicit and explicit picture memory. *Journal of Experimental Psychology: Learning, Memory, and Cognition, 22 (3),* 639-653

Connell, L. (2007). Representing object color in language comprehension. *Cognition, 102,* 474-485.

Davidoff, J. and Ostergaard, A. (1988) The role of color in categorical judgments. *Quarterly Journal of Experimental Psychology, 40,* 533–544

Foster, D. H., & Gilson, S. J. (2002). Recognizing novel three-dimensional objects by summing signals from parts and views. *Proc. R. Soc. Lond. B. Biol. Sci. 269,* 1939-1947

Goffaux, V., Jacques, C., Mouraux, A. Olivia, A., Schyns, P. G, & Rossion, B. (2005). Diagnostic colors contribute to the early stages of scene categorization: Behavioral and neurophysiological evidence. *Visual Cognition, 12 (6),* 878-892

Grossberg, S. and Mingolla, E. (1985). Neural dynamics of form perception: Boundary completion, illusory figures and neon color spreading. *Psychological Review,* 2 (2), 173-211.

Hayward, W. G. (2003). After the viewpoint debate: Where next in object recognition. *Trends in Cognitive Sciences, 7,* 425-427.

Hayward, W. G., & Williams, P. (2000). Viewpoint costs and object discriminability. *Psychological Science, 11,* 7-12.

Lacey, S., Hall, J., & Sathian, K. (2010). Are surface properties integrated into visuohaptic object representations? *European Journal of Neuroscience, 31*(10), 1882-1888.

Livingston, M. S., & Hubel, D. H. (1987). Psychophysical evidence for separate channels for the perception of form, color, movement, and depth. *Journal of Neuroscience, 7,* 3416-3468.

Marr, D. (1982). *Vision.* San Francisco, CA: W. H. Freeman.

Marr, D. & Nishihara, H. K. (1978). Representing and recognition of the spatial organisation of three-dimensional shapes. *Proceedings of the Royal Society, London, B200,* 269-294.

Naor-Raz, G., Tarr, M. J., & Kersten, D. (2003). Is color an intrinsic property of object representation? *Perception, 32,* 667-680.

Oliva, A. and Schyns, P. (2000) Diagnostic colors mediate scene recognition. *Cognitive Psychology, 41,* 176–210

Ostergaard, A. and Davidoff, J. (1985) Some effects of color on naming and recognition of objects. *Journal of Experimental Psychology: Learning, Memory, & Cognition, 11,* 579-587

Potter, M., Kroll, J. F., Yachzel, B., Carpenter, E., & Sherman, J. (1986). Pictures in sentences: Understanding without words. *Journal of Experimental Psychology: General, 115,* 281-294.

Price C. J., Humphreys, G. W. (1989). The effects of surface detail on object categorization and naming. *Quarterly Journal of Experimental Psychology A, 41,* 797-828.

Rayner, K., & Pollatsek, A. (1989). *The Psychology of Reading.* Hillsdale, NJ: Lawrence Erlbaum Associates, Inc.

Reicher, G. M. (1969). Perceptual recognition as a function of meaningfulness of stimulus material. *Journal of Experimental Psychology, 81 (2),* 275–280

Richter, T. & Zwaan, R.A. (2009). Processing of color words activates color representations. *Cognition*, 111, 383-389.

Rossion, B., & Pourtois, G. (2004). Revisiting Snodgrass and Vanderwart's object pictorial set: The role of surface detail in basic-level object recognition. *Perception, 33,* 217-236.

Schneider, W., Eschman, A., & Zuccolotto, A. (2002). *E-Prime User's Guide.* Pittsburg: Psychology Software Tools Inc.

Stanfield, R.A. & Zwaan, R.A. (2001). The effect of implied orientation derived from verbal context on picture recognition. *Psychological Science, 12,* 153-156.

Summer, P., & Mollon, J. D. (2000). Catarrhine photopigments are optimized for detecting targets against foliage background. *Journal of Experimental Biology, 203,* 1963-1986.

Tanaka, J. W., & Presnell, L.M. (1999) Color diagnosticity in object recognition. *Perception & Psychophysics, 61,* 1140–1153

Tanaka, J. W., Weiskopf, D. & Williams, P. (2001). Of color and objects: The role of color in high-level vision. *Trends in Cognitive Sciences, 5,* 211-215.

Tarr, M. J., & Bülthoff, H. H. (1995). Is human object recognition better described by geon-structural-descriptions or by multiple-views? *Journal of Experimental Psychology: Human Perception and Performance, 21(6),* 1494-1505.

Wurm, L. H., Legge, G. E., Isenberg, L. M., & Luebker, A. (1993). Color improves object recognition in normal and low vision. *Journal of Experimental Psychology: Human Perception and Performance, 19,* 899-911.

Zwaan, R.A., Madden, C.J., Yaxley, R.H., & Aveyard, M.E. (2004). Moving words: Dynamic mental representations in language comprehension. *Cognitive Science, 28,* 611-619.

Zwaan, R.A., Stanfield, R.A., Yaxley, R.H. (2002). Language comprehenders mentally represent the shapes of objects. *Psychological Science, 13,* 168-171.

2

Object Recognition - The Role of Hormones Throughout the Lifespan

Alicia A. Walf[4] and Cheryl A. Frye[1-4]
Departments of Psychology[1], Biological Sciences[2], and The Centers for Neuroscience[3] and Life Sciences[4] Research, The University at Albany-SUNY U.S.A.

1. Introduction

There are several tasks that are used in behavioral neuroscience to reveal the neurobiological underpinnings of learning and memory processes. A task which has been gaining even more widespread use in recent years is the spontaneous object recognition task. The spontaneous object recognition task (heretofore referred to as the object recognition task) was developed for rats over 20 years ago, and has since been modified for use in mice (Dodart et al., 1997; Ennaceur and Delacour, 1988; Messier, 1997; Steckler et al., 1999). The background on this task, typical methods and methodological issues, and representative data obtained, when using this task to assess learning and memory processes in rodent models, will be reviewed in the following sections.

The object recognition task is considered a non-spatial working, declarative memory task. Performance in this task relies upon a functioning cortex and hippocampus. For a thorough review of the brain regions and neurotransmitters involved in object recognition task performance, readers are referred to recent papers on this topic (Dere et al., 2007; Winters et al., 2008). Unlike other tasks that typically rely on aversive stimuli or food rewards, the object recognition task takes advantage of the natural affinity of rodents for novelty (and see review on other methodological and theoretical considerations by Ennaceur, 2010). Although the typical stimuli used in this task are objects of different shapes and complexity, our laboratory has also begun to assess rodents' behavior using more socially-relevant stimuli, such as cagemates and novel conspecifics. In this review, data are presented demonstrating typical patterns of investigation when objects of different complexity, or conspecifics, are utilized as target stimuli in this task. The objective of this report is to review the utility of this task to assess socially- and non-socially relevant stimuli to reveal neurobiological underpinnings (e.g. hormones being of the greatest interest for us) for cognitive processes across the lifespan. The typical methods used in training and testing and assessing performance in this task will be reviewed and are as follows.

2. Training trial

Training in the object recognition task typically involves one training trial. In the case of object recognition memory, as a measure of declarative memory, acquisition is thought to occur with less exposure to the stimuli to be learned/recognized than in the case of non-declarative memory (e.g. procedural memory for a skill). Training in the object recognition task involves exposing rodents to two stimuli. In a typical training trial in this task, rats or mice are trained in a bright open field (for rats: 45 × 24 × 21 cm; for mice: 39 × 39 × 30 cm) with two identical objects as the target stimuli in each of the corners of task that are furthest from where the rodent is introduced to the chamber. Another approach that our laboratory has been using to investigate socially-relevant cognitive processes is to use conspecifics as the training stimuli in this task. Rodents readily explore these novel objects, or other rodent conspecifics, during the training session and the amount of time spent exploring the objects is recorded.

Objects are readily approached and then explored (touching, manipulating, sniffing, climbing/rearing upon) by rodents (Aggelton, 1985). Exploration is operationally defined as the rodent directing its nose at the object at a distance of no greater than 1 cm and/or touching, or climbing on, the object. Rodents typically spend equal amounts of time exploring both objects, or conspecifics, during training. It is important to take into account any preference for one object over another in the training trial. Further discussion of the importance of assessing preferences for objects utilized in the object recognition task is in Section 6 below.

The length of the training trial that we have used with consistent results to be able to assess cognitive performance and mnemonic effects of hormones of rats and mice is three-minutes. Other laboratories have utilized 2-10 minutes for the training trial (reviewed in Dere et al., 2007). Another variation in training trials is that the length of the training trial is based upon animals reaching a pre-set criterion for duration spent investigating the objects (e.g. 30 seconds total exploration time; Frick & Gresack, 2003). A typical inclusion criterion is that subjects spend time exploring each stimuli during training. Valid interpretations cannot be made if rodents do not explore both objects sufficiently during training.

3. Retention Interval

As with the training trial length, the retention interval is an important consideration to make when using the object recognition task. Although the typical retention intervals that are utilized are between 3 and 24 hours, some studies have used retention intervals spanning days (Dere et al., 2007). Rodents' performance in the task is better with shorter retention intervals (Bertaina-Anglade et al., 2006; Dere et al., 2007; Obinu et al., 2002; Schiapparelli et al., 2006), but with intervals shorter than 3 hours, it has been argued that it is not possible to make any attributions about rodents' cognitive performance beyond that they are able to perform the task and investigate the objects (Baker and Kim, 2002; Winters and Bussey, 2005b). Furthermore, forgetting in this task is dependent not only on the retention interval, but other factors, such as the length of the training trials and rodent species and strain used. In our laboratory, we utilize a 4 hour retention interval. This is done because in studies of natural cyclical variations in ovarian or other steroids (glucocorticoids, etc), it can be important to train rodents in the same hormone state as they will be tested in. For example, with respect to female rodents, the estrous cycle phase is 4 days long. In other studies using different learning tasks, we found that it was important to have a short enough retention trial so that they are trained in the same hormone state as when they are tested in (Frye, 1995; Rhodes and Frye, 2004). Indeed, the object recognition task assesses memory for a unique episode or event, and has been argued to be more sensitive to pharmacological or other manipulations that are amnestic (Dere et al., 2007). However, the nature of training and retention trials can be modified so that the effects of amnestic as well as memory-enhancing effects of manipulations can be determined (Ennaceur & Meliani, 1992a; Ennaceur et al., 1989). As such, we have found valid and reliable results utilizing a three-minute training trial with a four-hour retention interval in the object recognition task.

4. Testing trial

Testing in the object recognition task involves assessing whether rats or mice spend more time exploring the novel stimuli, compared to the familiar stimuli they were exposed to during training. After a retention interval, subjects are placed in the same open field, which contains one of the stimuli encountered during training and one novel stimuli. The side of the open field that the novel object, or conspecific, is placed is counterbalanced across subjects in the event of a side bias of the subjects. The testing session is typically the same length as the training session, which is three-minutes in our laboratory. During the testing session, the duration of time rats or mice spend exploring the familiar and novel stimuli are recorded.

An assessment of performance in this task is done by comparing the amount of time exploring the novel object versus the familiar stimuli. This is often calculated as a percentage of total time spent exploring to take into account differences between subjects in exploration of the stimuli during testing. Chance levels of performance in this task are 50% of time spent exploring the novel stimuli during testing. Improved performance in this task is supported by greater than 50% time spent exploring the novel stimuli in this task.

5. Subjects

The object recognition task was developed in rats and can be used with mice with only modest modifications (Dodart et al., 1997; Ennaceur and Delacour, 1988; Messier, 1997; Steckler et al., 1999). As with other learning tasks (Frick et al., 2000; Whishaw and Tomie, 1996), there are differences between mice and rats in the object recognition task. Few studies have directly compared performance of rats and mice in the object recognition task. In one, both male Sprague-Dawley rats and C57Bl/6J mice were sensitive to the amnestic effects of scopolamine, but there were differences in the length of the retention trial in which this became apparent (Bertaina-Anglade et al., 2006). Generally, mice spend less time exploring the objects and approach the objects less (Dere et al., 2007). It is argued that this may be due to greater neophobia of objects among mice (Dere et al., 2004). One way to increase exploration of the objects in this task is to introduce a habituation phase so that rodents have been exposed to the open field prior to testing. This may reduce neophobia as well as reduce the time rodents spend exploring the testing chamber, rather than the stimuli. Thus, rats and mice can be used in object recognition, but there are species characteristics to consider when using this task and interpreting the results gained from it.

Another characteristic of subjects to consider is the strain of rodents utilized. For example, we have primarily utilized Long-Evans rat and mice on a C57Bl/6 background in our laboratory. These strains are pigmented and, thus, likely have greater visual abilities in this task, which may increase time spent exploring and/or improve recognition in the object recognition task. Few studies have systematically investigated strain differences among mice. In one, BALB/C, C3H/He, DBA/2, C57BL/6J, CBA/Ca, and 129S2/Sv mice were compared (Brooks et al., 2005). Mice were able to perform this task with a 1 and 4, but not 24 hour, retention interval, with the BALB/c and DBA/2 strains spending a greater percentage of time exploring the novel object during testing. Of note, there were no differences between strains when the absolute amount of time exploring the novel object was compared. Other studies have noted that C57Bl/6 mice perform better than DBA/2 mice in object recognition (Podhorna & Brown, 2002; Voikar et al., 2005). Thus, strain of mice and rats must be considered with respect to experimental design and interpretation of results using the object recognition task.

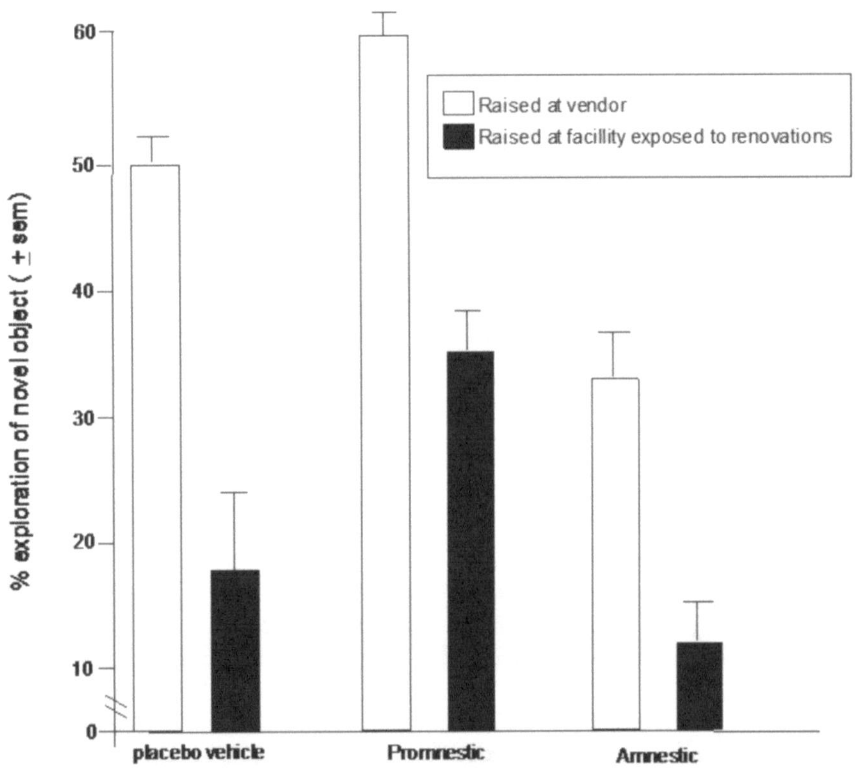

Fig. 1. Behavioral data in the object recognition task of ovariectomized female mice from two sources- raised at a vendor, or purchased from vendor and raised in brand-new facility with noise from renovations. Mice were administered placebo vehicle or a promnestic (estradiol) or an amnestic (scopolamine).

Another question to consider is the source and experiential effects of subjects. We have recently found differences among substrains of C57Bl/6 mice in that those that were raised by a vendor (C57Bl/6Tac) outperformed those that had been purchased from a vendor and raised in our facility (C57Bl/6J) that had renovations ongoing (e.g. frequent fire alarms unintentionally sounding, drilling, etc.), that can be typical of brand-new buildings (Figure 1). As well, the magnitude of effects when mice were injected systemically with a promnestic (estradiol) or an amnestic (scopolamine) was different between these substrains of mice. We are currently investigating these effects and the role of hormones further. Thus, sources and experiential effects must be considered for object recognition.

6. Non-socially-relevant stimuli- objects

A critical aspect of the object recognition task is the stimuli that are utilized (i.e. objects). Rodents must have some preference for the objects used and readily investigate them during training and testing trials. They need to be washable to remove extraneous olfactory stimuli. Likewise, the same type of material should be used (plastic, metal, etc). Similar size objects that differ on shape, color, texture, and/or height are preferable so that objects are different enough so that they can be discriminated. However, it is important that during training and testing objects of similar valence are used so that results are not confounded by a clear preference for one object over another (irrespective of recognizing the novelty or familiarity of the object). In our laboratory, we have analyzed the preference of rats and mice for several objects so that objects are ones those subjects readily investigate for equal amounts of time. A description of these data in mice is as follows.

The objects that we use in our laboratory are made of plastic and are similar size, but have different shapes, colors, and textures. We investigated the average amount of time (seconds) that mice spent exploring objects for three minutes in the open field box. Table 1 depicts the objects analyzed and the mean time spent by groups of mice exploring the objects. These data show that the amount of time mice spend exploring these objects varies across the types of objects assessed. In this example, it would not be preferable to use either the objects that the mice spent a the shortest or longest duration exploring, but rather those objects that mice explored similarly explored for a moderate time so that comparisons between novel and familiar objects could be assessed. By systematically investigating the amount of

Objects	Average Time Explored (seconds)
Apples (toy)	1.9
Blocks	5.0
Buoys (toy)	13.2
Cakes (toy)	7.8
Caps	24.2
Chilies (toy)	6.0
Funnels	8.1
Hydrants (toy)	16.2
Ketchup bottles (toy)	6.7
Lego- large (toy)	0.1
Lego- medium (toy)	0.5
Lego- small (toy)	0.9
Mice	10.2
Oranges	5.5
Pears (toy)	5.3
Pipes	39.1
Soda bottles (toy)	1.4
Water Bottles (toy)	24.8

Table 1. Time spent investigating objects of different complexity by mice.

exploration for all objects to be used for object recognition, it can be determined whether or not objects are ideal to use in an experiment. The ideal objects for use elicit a reliable exploratory response from the mice that can be differentiated from each other. It is advisable to have a catalogue of validated objects for rats and mice. If more objects are needed, they should approximate the characteristics of these existing objects, and be validated. Thus, when setting up the object recognition task to assess cognitive performance of rodents, it is essential to validate and catalogue a number of different objects to utilize.

7. Cognitive performance across the lifespan- role of hormones

Object recognition performance using the methods described above is influenced by hormones. There is evidence for sex differences, and effects of hormone extirpation/removal and replacement for object recognition performance, which suggests that hormones influence performance in this task. There are sex differences in that females typically outperform males in object recognition performance, but males outperform females when the objects are moved to different locations in the testing chamber (spatial version of object recognition referred to as the object placement task; Bowman et al., 2003; Ceccarelli et al., 2001; Sutcliffe et al., 2007). A question that has been of interest in our laboratory is the extent to which some of these effects may be related to effects of ovarian steroids. When rats or mice are tested during the estrous cycle, performance is best when there are natural elevations in estradiol and progestogens (progesterone and its neuroactive metabolites), as compared to their counterparts with low levels of these steroids (Walf et al., 2006; Walf et al., 2009). Ovariectomy (which removes the main peripheral source of estradiol and progestogens) impairs object recognition performance, and this is reversed with replacement back with physiological levels of estradiol or progestogens immediately after training (Walf et al., 2006). Interestingly, these steroids need to be "on-board" during the consolidation phase of memory formation, which occurs within the 1 or 1.5 hours post-training. If steroid administration is delayed to 1-1.5 hours post-training, then performance is not enhanced when rodents are tested 4 hours after training (Frye & Walf, 2008a). Thus, these data support a role of ovarian steroids for object recognition performance.

Performance of rats administered different pharmacological treatments, or mice that are genetic knockouts for steroid targets of interest, in the object recognition task has been used to investigate the mechanisms of steroids for learning and memory in the object recognition task. Data suggest that the traditional target of progesterone, the intracellular progestin receptor, is not required for progestogens' mnemonic effects, but metabolism may be (Frye & Walf, 2010; Frye et al., 2010). Similarly, there may be non-traditional targets of estrogens for object recognition performance. Although selective estrogen receptor modulators that act at estrogen receptor β and the traditional target of estrogens, estrogen receptor α, can improve performance in this task, estrogens do not improve performance of mice that have had estrogen receptor β knocked out (Jacome et al., 2010; Luine et al., 2003; Walf et al. 2008; 2009). Thus, there may be non-traditional actions of steroids for object recognition performance.

The subjects of these studies, discussed above, were young rodents. A question is the extent to which there are age-related changes in performance in object recognition that occur concomitant with decline in ovarian steroids. First, of interest is whether prior hormonally-relevant experiences may alter later effects of hormones for cognitive performance. To investigate this, age-matched rats with different breeding histories (no, one, or multiple past pregnancies) are compared. We, and others, have demonstrated that middle-aged rats that have experienced past pregnancies have improved performance in the object recognition task compared to those that have not experienced such breeding history (Macbeth et al. 2008; Paris & Frye, 2008). Second, of interest is whether older subjects, with reductions in natural variations in steroids, can respond to hormone replacement. We have found that middle-aged rats with declining reproductive status, and lowered capacity to metabolize natural steroids, have worse performance than age-matched rats that have maintained reproductive status (Paris et al. 2010). Further, administration of the hormone therapy, conjugated equine estrogens, to middle-aged rats improves performance in the object recognition task (Walf & Frye, 2008). Among aged mice, administration of progesterone acutely after training improves object recognition performance (Frye & Walf, 2008b). As well, long-term administration of progesterone to transgenic mice with an Alzheimer's Disease-phenotype, or their normative age-matched controls, improved performance in the object recognition task (Frye & Walf, 2008c). Together, these data demonstrate that there is a role of hormones across the lifespan for object recognition performance.

8. Socially-relevant stimuli- conspecifics

Given the clear role of ovarian steroids for object recognition performance, described above, as well as their well-known actions to mediate socially-relevant behaviors (reviewed in Frye, 2009), of interest is designing a one-trial learning task to assess memory for socially-relevant stimuli, such as conspecifics. We have recently been using a modified version of the object recognition task, where, instead of objects as stimuli, novel and familiar conspecifics are utilized. All other aspects of the protocol are the same in terms of the testing chamber utilized, and lengths of the training trial, retention interval, and testing trial. Rodents are trained with two of their cagemates in each corner of the open field. The cagemates are placed under separate screened chambers. The experimental subject can then see and smell, but not touch, the conspecifics. The operational definition of exploring in this case is defined as the rodent touching or directing its nose at the chamber containing the conspecific at a distance of no greater than 1 cm. Rodents typically spend equal amounts of time exploring both cagemates during training. Table 2 describes average duration spent investigating cagemates during training of young adult (virgin, nulliparous) and middle-aged (retired breeder, multiparous) adult male and female mice. Of note, mice spend considerably more time investigating cagemates during training than is observed with objects described in the previous section, irrespective of age or sex.

Condition	Average Total Time Spent Exploring Cagemates During Training (seconds)
Young Female	57.7
Young Male	55.1
Middle-aged Female	58.4
Middle-Aged Male	56.3

Table 2. Time spent by young and middle-aged male and female mice exploring cagemates as training stimuli in a modified version of the object recognition task.

Rodents are then tested after a four hour retention trial. During testing, one cagemate is replaced with a novel conspecific. A typical process is utilized to assess performance in this version of the object recognition task. That is, the duration spent exploring the novel conspecific versus familiar cagemate is compared. It is calculated as a percentage of total time spent exploring both conspecifics during testing to take into account differences between subjects in exploration of the stimuli during this trial. Chance levels of performance in this task are 50% of time spent exploring the novel conspecific during testing and improved performance in this task is described as more than 50% time spent exploring the novel conspecific in this task.

A pilot study using this protocol was conducted. Performance of young, nulliparous (virgin) male and female mice to middle-aged, multiparous (retired breeders) was compared, and results are depicted in Figure 2. We found that males outperformed females (in diestrus with low endogenous levels of estrogens and progestogens). Performance of young and middle-aged males was similar, but performance of females with extensive breeding history was improved compared to their young, virgin counterparts. These data demonstrate that conspecifics may be used as socially-relevant stimuli to investigate hormonal effects for learning and memory processes. Thus, substituting novel and familiar cagemates as stimuli in an object recognition task may be a means to investigate neurobiological mechanisms underlying learning of socially-relevant stimuli.

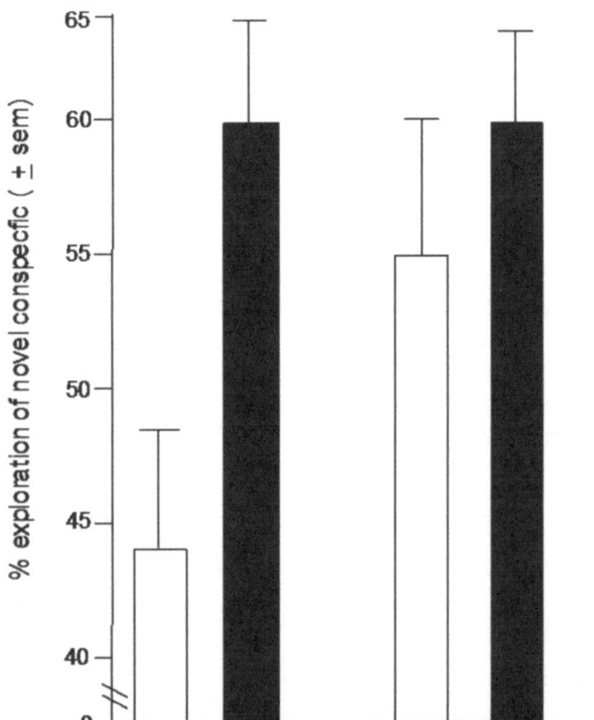

Fig. 2. Cognitive performance of young, nulliparous and middle-aged multiparous female and male mice in the object recognition task using conspecifics as target stimuli.

9. Advantages of using the object recognition task to study cognitive performance across the lifespan

Many aspects of the object recognition task are advantageous to conducting the types of aging and hormone studies described above, as well as studies investigating brain targets and mechanisms underlying these processes. The object recognition task does not require pre-training as it measures spontaneous behavior, exploiting the innate proclivity of rodents to explore novel stimuli. This is a one-trial learning task that does not require multiple, or lengthy, training sessions. This is advantageous to studies of hormonal effects because of the cyclical nature of hormones and we have found that it is important to train and test rodents in the same hormonal state to be able to discriminate the enhancing effects of hormones in object recognition and other tasks (Frye, 1995; Rhodes and Frye, 2004; Walf et al., 2006). As well, object recognition does not rely upon explicit reinforcement with rewarding or noxious stimuli so motivational aspects during training can be minimized. It is advantageous that the target stimuli in this task are not food-based or aversive. This is important in studies of hormones and aging because hormones can influence responses to aversive stimuli (e.g. sensitivities to footshock; Drury & Gold, 1978; Hennessy et al., 1977), as well as food intake (Bell & Zucker, 1971; Frye et al., 1992; Tarttelin & Gorski, 1973). Object recognition is not considered a task that promotes high levels of stress or arousal (Ennaceur & Delacour, 1998). This is advantageous to studies of aging and hormones because hormones alter general arousal (Pfaff et al., 2008). Furthermore, there are interactions of the hypothalamic-pituitary-adrenal and -gonadal axes to influence behavioral responses (reviewed in Frye, 2009; Solomon & Herman, 2009). As such, interpretations of effects may be more straightforward in the object recognition task, in comparison to tasks utilizing aversive stimuli and/or those that influence arousal and stress responding. Another major advantage to using the object recognition task to determine the effects and mechanisms of neuromodulators, such as hormones, is that there is little test-decay in this task when different objects, or conspecifics, are used as target familiar and novel stimuli. This is true as long as there are intervals (days to weeks) between assessments and different objects are utilized (Mumby et al., 2002a). This may be one of the most important factors justifying its use in aging and hormone research. Repeat testing allows for longitudinal studies across the lifespan as well as within-subjects assessments across different natural hormonal milieu (i.e. pregnancy; Paris & Frye, 2008). Thus, there are clear advantages to using the object recognition task to assess the role of hormones across the lifespan.

10. Conclusion

The object recognition task is widely-used to assess non-spatial working, declarative memory task which relies upon a functioning cortex and hippocampus. The typical methods (training, retention interval, and testing) used by our laboratory and others were reviewed with focused consideration on how to use the object recognition task to assess the role and mechanisms of hormones, throughout the lifespan. In addition, there are subjects' variables (e.g. species, strain) that need to be considered in designing experiments and interpreting results using the object recognition task. Another major consideration is the nature and complexity of target stimuli utilized in the object recognition task. The use of objects in object recognition, and findings with regard to aging and hormone studies using the object recognition methods described, were reviewed. Furthermore, a modification to the object recognition protocol using socially-relevant conspecifics, instead of non-socially-relevant objects, was described. Representative data obtained, when using this task with conspecifics to assess learning and memory processes in rodent models, was discussed. Several advantages to using the object recognition task were discussed with respect to training requirements and interpretations. As well, the major advantage to using the object recognition task to determine the effects and mechanisms of neuromodulators, such as hormones, is the absence of test-decay when different target stimuli are used was discussed. This allows for within-subjects designs and longitudinal assessments, which can be particularly important for studies of changes in natural hormonal milieu with aging. Thus, the object recognition task may be particularly suited to assess changes across the lifespan in cognitive performance to reveal mechanisms in the cortex and hippocampus.

11. References

Aggleton, J.P. (1985). One-trial object recognition by rats. *Quarterly Journal of Experimental Psychology*. 37, 279-294

Baker, KB; Kim JJ. (2002). Effects of stress and hippocampal NMDA receptor antagonism on recognition memory in rats. *Learning and Memory 9 (2),* Mar-Apr, 58-65

Bell, D.D.; Zucker, I. (1971). Sex differences in body weight and eating: organization and activation by gonadal hormones in the rat. *Physiology & Behavior*, 7(1), Jul, 27-34

Bertaina-Anglade, V.; Enjuanes, E.; Morillon, D.; Drieu la Rochelle, C. (2006). The object recognition task in rats and mice: a simple and rapid model in safety pharmacology to detect amnesic properties of a new chemical entity. *Journal of Pharmacology and Toxicology Methods*. 54(2), Sep-Oct, 99-105

Dere, E,; Huston, J.P.; De Souza Silva, M.A. (2007). The pharmacology, neuroanatomy and neurogenetics of one-trial object recognition in rodents. *Neuroscience & Biobehavioral Reviews* 31(5), 673-704

Dodart, J.C.; Mathis, C.; Ungerer, A. (1997). Scopolamine-induced deficits in a two-trial object recognition task in mice. *Neuroreport* 8(5), Mar 24, 1173-8

Drury, R.A.; Gold, R.M. (1978). Differential effects of ovarian hormones on reactivity to electric footshock in the rat. *Physiology & Behavior* 20(2), Feb, 187-91

Ennaceur, A. (2010). One-trial object recognition in rats and mice: methodological and theoretical issues. *Behavioural Brain Research* 215(2), Dec 31, 244-54

Ennaceur, A.; Cavoy, A.; Costa, J.C.; Delacour, J. (1989). A new one-trial test for neurobiological studies of memory in rats. II: Effects of piracetam and pramiracetam. *Behavioural Brain Research* 33(2), Jun 1, 197-207

Ennaceur, A.; Delacour, J. (1988). A new one-trial test for neurobiological studies of memory in rats. 1: Behavioral data. *Behavioural Brain Research* 31(1), Nov 1, 47-59

Ennaceur, A.; Meliani, K. (1992). A new one-trial test for neurobiological studies of memory in rats. III. Spatial vs. non-spatial working memory. *Behavioural Brain Research* 51(1), Oct 31, 83-92

Frick, K.M.; Gresack, J.E. (2003). Sex differences in the behavioral response to spatial and object novelty in adult C57BL/6 mice. *Behavioral Neuroscience* 117(6), Dec, 1283-91

Frick, K.M.; Stillner, E.T.; Berger-Sweeney, J. (2000). Mice are not little rats: species differences in a one-day water maze task. *Neuroreport* 11(16), Nov 9, 3461-5

Frye, C.A. (1995). Estrus-associated decrements in a water maze task are limited to acquisition. *Physiology & Behavior* 57(1), Jan, 5-14

Frye, C.A. (2009). Neurosteroids—from basic research to clinical perspectives. In: R.T. Rubin and D.W. Pfaff, Editors, *Hormones/Behavior Relations of Clinical Importance*, 395-416, Academic Press, San Diego

Frye, C.A.; Walf, A.A. (2008a). Progesterone to ovariectomized mice enhances cognitive performance in the spontaneous alternation, object recognition, but not placement, water maze, and contextual and cued conditioned fear tasks. *Neurobiology of Learning and Memory* 90(1), Jul, 171-7

Frye, C.A.; Walf, A.A. (2008b). Progesterone enhances performance of aged mice in cortical or hippocampal tasks. *Neuroscience Letters* 437(2), May 30, 116-20

Frye, C.A.; Walf, A.A. (2008c). Effects of progesterone administration and APPswe+PSEN1Deltae9 mutation for cognitive performance of mid-aged mice. *Neurobiology of Learning and Memory* 89(1), Jan, 17-26

Hennessy, J.W.; Levin, R.; Levine, S. (1977). Influence of experiential factors and gonadal hormones on pituitary-adrenal response of the mouse to novelty and electric shock. *Journal of Comparative Physiological Psychology* 91(4), Aug, 770-7

Macbeth, A.H.; Scharfman, H.E.; Maclusky, N.J.; Gautreaux, C.; Luine, V.N. (2008). Effects of multiparity on recognition memory, monoaminergic neurotransmitters, and brain-derived neurotrophic factor (BDNF). *Hormones and Behavior* 54(1), Jun, 7-17

Messier, C. (1997). Object recognition in mice: improvement of memory by glucose. *Neurobiology of Learning and Memory* 67(2), Mar, 172-5

Mumby, D.G.; Gaskin, S.; Glenn, M.J.; Schramek, T.E.; Lehmann, H. (2002). Hippocampal damage and exploratory preferences in rats: memory for objects, places, and contexts. *Learning and Memory* 9(2), Mar-Apr, 49-57

Obinu, M.C.; Reibaud, M.; Miquet, J.M.; Pasquet, M.; Rooney, T. (2002). Brain-selective stimulation of nicotinic receptors by TC-1734 enhances ACh transmission from frontoparietal cortex and memory in rodents. Progress in neuro-psychopharmacology & biological psychiatry 26(5), Jun, 913-8

Paris, J.J.; Frye, C.A. (2008). Estrous cycle, pregnancy, and parity enhance performance of rats in object recognition or object placement tasks. *Reproduction* 136(1), Jul, 105-15

Pfaff, D.; Ribeiro, A.; Matthews, J.; Kow, L.M. (2008). Concepts and mechanisms of generalized central nervous system arousal. *Annals of the New York Academy of Sciences* 1129, 11-25.

Rhodes, M.E.; Frye, C.A. (2004). Estrogen has mnemonic-enhancing effects in the inhibitory avoidance task. *Pharmacology, Biochemistry, and Behavior* 78(3), Jul, 551-8

Schiapparelli, L.; Simón, A.M.; Del Río, J.; Frechilla, D. (2006). Opposing effects of AMPA and 5-HT1A receptor blockade on passive avoidance and object recognition performance: correlation with AMPA receptor subunit expression in rat hippocampus. *Neuropharmacology* 50(7), Jun, 897-907

Solomon, M.B.; Herman, J.P. (2009). Sex differences in psychopathology: of gonads, adrenals and mental illness. *Physiology & Behavior* 97(2), May 25, 250-8

Steckler, T.; Weis, C.; Sauvage, M.; Mederer, A.; Holsboer, F. (1999). Disrupted allocentric but preserved egocentric spatial learning in transgenic mice with impaired glucocorticoid receptor function. *Behavioural Brain Research* 100(1-2), Apr, 77-89

Tarttelin, M.F.; Gorski, R.A. (1973). The effects of ovarian steroids on food and water intake and body weight in the female rat. *Acta Endocrinology* 72(3), Mar, 551-68

Walf, A.A.; Frye, C.A. (2008). Conjugated equine estrogen enhances rats' cognitive, anxiety, and social behavior. *Neuroreport* 19(7), May 7, 789-92

Walf, A.A.; Rhodes, M.E.; Frye, C.A. (2006). Ovarian steroids enhance object recognition in naturally cycling and ovariectomized, hormone-primed rats. *Neurobiology of Learning and Memory* 86(1), Jul, 35-46

Winters, B.D.; Bussey, T.J. (2005). Glutamate receptors in perirhinal cortex mediate encoding, retrieval, and consolidation of object recognition memory. *Journal of Neuroscience* 25(17), Apr 27, 4243-51

Winters, B.D.; Saksida, L.M.; Bussey, T.J. (2008). Object recognition memory: neurobiological mechanisms of encoding, consolidation and retrieval. *Neuroscience and Biobehavioral Reviews* 32(5), Jul, 1055-70

3

The Object Recognition Task: A New Proposal for the Memory Performance Study

Valeria Paola Carlini
Physiology Institute, Medicals Science School, Córdoba National University, Córdoba Argentina

1. Introduction

In the last few decades, there has been extensive research in the cognitive neurophysiology of learning and memory. Most relevant experimental studies were focused on the possible role of neuropeptides on memory performance and the neurobiological bases of their actions. In general, scientists believe that the answers to those questions relies in understanding how the information about new events is acquired and coded by neurons, how this information is modulated and if it is possible to revert age-related or diseases associated cognitive to failures.

Memory is broadly divided into declarative and nondeclarative forms. The formation of declarative memory depends on a neural system anatomically connected in the medial temporal lobe that recruits hippocampus, dentate gyrus, the subicular complex, and the adjacent perirhinal, entorhinal, and parahippocampal cortices) (Squire & Zola-Morgan, 1991; Eichenbaum & Cohen, 2001). In both, animals and humans, declarative memory supports the capacity to recollect facts and events and can be contrasted with a collection of nondeclarative memory abilities: habits and skills, simple forms of conditioning, and other ways that the effects of experience can be expressed through performance rather than recollection (Squire, 1992; Schacter & Tulving, 1994).

Numerous tests have been used for studying memory; they differ in several ways other than just the type of information that must be remembered. Other differences include the nature of the motivation or reward, the reinforcement contingencies, and the amount of training required. The behaviors that are measured to assess memory also vary considerably and include conditioned reflexes (e.g., Pavlovian fear conditioning), speed or accuracy of spatial navigation (which can involve either swimming -water maze- or running -radial maze-). The object recognition test (e.g., novel object recognition -NOR- or novel object preference -NOP-), also known as the visual paired comparison task in studies with humans and monkeys, is a non-spatial and non-aversive procedure extensively applied to study neuronanatomical and molecular mechanism involves in recognition memory process, a form of declarative memory (Ennaceur & Delacour, 1988; Puma et al., 1999; Bizot et al., 2005).

Recognition memory is a fundamental facet of our ability to remember. It requires a capacity for both identification and judgment of the prior occurrence of what has been identified (Mandler, 1980). This memory includes two components, a recollective (episodic) component that supports the ability to remember the episode in which an item was encountered, and a familiarity component that supports the ability to know that an item was presented (Mandler,

1980; Tulving, 1985; Quamme et al., 2002; Yonelinas, 2002). An important question concerns whether the brain structures that comprise the medial temporal lobe memory system differ in their contributions to recognition memory, or if they differ in how they support its recollective and familiar components. The first possible interpretation was that recognition memory is supported by the cortical areas along the parahippocampal gyrus (for example, the perirhinal cortex) and that the hippocampus itself is needed only for more complex tasks of declarative memory such as forming associations and conjunctions among stimuli (Aggleton & Shaw, 1996; Vargha-Khadem et al., 1997; Tulving & Markowitsch, 1998; Rich & Shapiro, 2009). Good recognition performance has been described following restricted hippocampal lesions in a case of developmental amnesia (Vargha-Khadem et al., 1997; Baddeley et al., 2001). A second possible interpretation was that the hippocampus is essential for normal recognition memory but that the hippocampus itself supports only the recollective (episodic) component of recognition. Under this view, judgments based on familiarity can be supported by adjacent cortex in the medial temporal lobe or perhaps by other structures important for nondeclarative memory (Yonelinas et al., 1998; Eldridge et al., 2000; Brown & Aggleton, 2001; Verfaellie & Keane, 2002; Yonelinas, 2002).

Single-cell recordings in humans and experimental animals also suggest a role for the hippocampus in recognition memory performance. For example, neurons recorded from the hippocampus during visual or olfactory recognition tasks can convey stimulus-specific information as well as an abstract match-nonmatch signal—that is, a response that signals the outcome of the recognition process rather than a signal about the stimulus itself (Fried et al., 1997; Wood et al., 1999; Suzuki & Eichenbaum, 2000). Perhaps, it should not be surprising that recognition memory, including the component of recognition memory that supports familiarity judgments, depends on the integrity of the hippocampus. The hippocampus is the final stage of convergence within the medial temporal lobe, receiving input from both the perirhinal and parahippocampal cortices, as well as the entorhinal cortex. The entorhinal cortex receives about two-thirds of its cortical input from the perirhinal and parahippocampal cortices and originates the major cortical projections to the hippocampus (Suzuki & Amaral, 1994). Anatomical considerations alone suggest that the hippocampus is positioned to combine and extend the operations of memory formation that are carried out by the more specialized structures that project to it.

The Object Recognition Task and the memory performance study

The capacity for recognition memory has been particularly well documented in mice, rats, and monkeys, as well as in humans. **Object recognition** is the ability to perceive some object's physical properties (such as shape, color and texture) and apply semantic attributes to the object, which includes the understanding of its use, previous experience with the object and how it relates to others (Enns, 2004). One of the models for object recognition, based on neuropsychological evidence, provides information that allows dividing the process into four different stages (Humphreys et al., 1999; Riddoch & Humphreys, 2001; Ward, 2006):

Stage 1 Processing of basic object components, such as colour, depth, and form.

Stage 2 These basic components are then grouped on the basis of similarity, providing information on distinct edges to the visual form. Subsequently, figure-ground segregation is able to take place.

Stage 3 The visual representation is matched with structural descriptions in memory.

Stage 4 Semantic attributes are applied to the visual representation, providing meaning, and thereby recognition.

When a subject sees an object, it knows if the objet was seen in a past occasion, this is called recognition memory. Every day we recognize a multitude of familiar and novel objects. We do this with little effort, despite the fact that these objects may vary somewhat in form, color, texture, etc. Objects are recognized from many different vantage points (from the front, side, or back), in many different places, and in different sizes. Objects can even be recognized when they are partially obstructed from view. Not only do abnormalities to the ventral (what) stream of the visual pathway affect our ability to recognize an object but also the way in which an object is presented through the eyes. The ventro-lateral region of the frontal lobe is involved in memory encoding during incidental learning and then later maintaining and retrieving semantic memories (Ward, 2006). Familiarity can induce perceptual processes different to those of unfamiliar objects which mean that our perception of a finite amount of familiar objects is unique. Deviations from typical viewpoints and contexts can affect the efficiency for which an object is recognized most effectively. It is known that not only familiar objects are recognized more efficiently when viewed from a familiar viewpoint opposed to an unfamiliar one, but also this principle applies to novel objects. This deduces to the thought that objects representations in the brain are probably organized in a familiar fashion of the objects observed in the environment (Bulthoff & Newell, 2006). Recognition is not only largely driven by object shape and/or views but also by the dynamic information (Norman & Eacott, 2004). Familiarity then can benefit the perception of dynamic point-light displays, moving objects, the sex of faces, and face recognition (Bulthoff & Newell, 2006). Recollection shares many similarities with familiarity; however it is context dependent, requiring specific information from the inquired incident (Ward, 2006).

The distinction between category and attribute in semantic representation may inform the ability to assess semantic function in aging and disease states affecting semantic memory, such as in Alzheimer's disease (AD) (Hajilou & Done, 2007). The semantic memory is known to be used to retrieve information for naming and categorizing objects (Laatu et al., 2003), individuals suffering from Alzheimer's disease have difficulties in recognizing objects because of semantic memory deficits. In fact, it is highly debated whether the semantic memory deficit in AD reflects the loss of semantic knowledge for particular categories and concepts or the loss of knowledge of perceptual features and attributes (Hajilou & Done, 2007).

It has been widely demonstrated that spontaneous exploratory activity in the rat can be used to provide a valid measure of memory function (Ennaceur & Delacour, 1988; Ennaceur & Meliani, 1992a,b; Ennaceur & Aggleton, 1994; Ennaceur et al., 1996; Hirshman & Master, 1997). In animals the "Object Recognition Task" has been the method more used to measure exploratory activity. It can be conducted on mice and rats, and the recognition memory is assessed by measuring animal's ability to recognize an object previously presented. The novel object recognition task was introduced by Ennaceur & Delacour in 1988, in order to assess the ability of rats to recognize a novel object in an otherwise familiar environment.

Since then, the test has become popular for testing object recognition memory in rodents in general, and the effects of amnesic drugs on exploratory activity in particular (Hammonds et al., 2004). The main advantages of this test are, first: each animal can be tested repeatedly with new stimuli in the same session, thus permitting comparisons between subjects in different conditions; and, second: animals do not require extended training or habituation. Other advantages are that the familiarization phase is identical for all the four versions of the test (with the exception that there are two familiarization phases on the context-memory task); the test does not require external motivation, reward or punishment, and the task can be completed in a relatively short period of time. For these reasons, the "Novel Object

Recognition task" is an excellent option for testing animals which have received previous treatments which might alter the reward system, food and water intake or general stress levels. The object recognition task includes two-trials, the first is an acquisition phase or sample phase, also called training phase, and the second one is known as testing phase. Each of them usually has a duration that can vary between 2 to 5 minutes. In the training phase, in order to get familiarized with the objects, a rodent is placed in an enclosure and exposed for a set length of time to two identical objects that are located in a specified distance from each other (Figure 1 panel a). The animal is then removed from the environment, according to the memory type to assess, and a predetermined amount of time is allowed to pass. The rodent is then retested in the same environment except that one of the two previously used (familiar) objects is replaced with a novel one, that differs from the familiar object in shape (Figure 1 panel b), texture and appearance (e.g., a plastic block is replaced with a metal ball). In each phase, the time spent exploring each of the objects is quantified. Usually, exploration of an object is defined as time spent with the head oriented towards and within two centimeters of the object (Benice & Raber, 2005). Turning around or sitting on the object is not considered as an exploratory behavior. This test gives information on **working, short-term** or **long term memory** depending on elapsed time between the training and the testing phase. Additionally, this test provides information about the exploratory behavior, which is related to attention; anxiety and preference for novelty in rodents. Memory acquisition occurs when the animal perceive the object's physical properties and apply semantic attributes to the object. During consolidation, which can last from minutes to days, this memory is moved from a labile to a more fixed state. During retrieval, the animal supports the ability to know that an item was presented. Then, this test allows evaluating acquisition, consolidation and retrieval, depending on the time course of the manipulations. Pharmacological or physical manipulations such us drug administration or stress, before the training phase can affect both, the early acquisition stage and the consolidation memory stage. If manipulations are performed immediately after training phase affects the late acquisition and consolidation stage. Oppositely, if manipulations are done before the test phase only the retrieval stage is affected. The different stages of memory can be quite difficult to isolate experimentally, because behavioral techniques potentially affect two or more stages of memory. Short-lived treatments, however, can isolate consolidation stage independently of acquisition or retrieval.

The novel object recognition task depends on preference for novelty and also requires more cognitive skills from the subject to explore of novel environments or a single novel object. In order to discriminate between a novel and a familiar object, two identical objects are presented to the subject and then it has to recall the two objects (process known as working memory). Upon replacement of one of the familiarized objects by a novel object, if the animal can recognize that one object as novel, the animal will typically display differential behavior directed towards the novel object. The task scoring has often involved the experimenter recording of the time spent around a novel object versus time spent with a familiar object, and calculation of a novelty or "discrimination index" is based on these measurements (Haist & Shimanura, 1992; Ennaceur et al., 1997; Donaldson, 1999).

Behavioral observation of each animal in the "Novel Object Recognition Task" is time-consuming, and can hinder the ability to use many subjects, particularly in studies requiring exact timing (such as following a pharmaceutical or lesion treatment or a developmental exposure) or many treatment groups (such as dose-response studies). Then, in order to fully describe behavior and to collect all variables of interest, the test session must be recorded by

using videotaping and/or computer software to assist the experimenter observation (Belcher et al., 2005; Ennaceur et al., 2005; Belcher et al., 2006; He et al., 2006). Also, the novel object preference dependent upon strain, sex, and age.
The analysis of the results obtained indicates that non-amnesic animals will spend more time exploring the novel object than the familiar one. An absence of any difference in the exploration of the two objects during the second phase can be interpreted as a memory deficit or, in case of testing an amnesic drug, a non-functioning drug.
The preference for novelty is also influenced by factors such as training phase duration and the inclusion of common features in the familiar object and the novel object (Ennaceur & Delacour, 1988; Ennaceur & Aggleton, 1994; Ennaceur et al., 1996). Advantages associated with this class of measure include the fact that performance does not depend on the retention of a rule, nor is it influenced by changes in responsive to reward. Furthermore, because the test uses a forced choice design it is less likely to be affected by changes in impulsivity or activity. As a consequence such tasks can provide a relatively pure measure of "working memory" (Honig, 1978; Olton & Feustle, 1981).
The experimental conditions are crucial when this behavioral protocol is applied to aged animals. It has been known that aging is associated whit memory impairments. The recognition memory has been recently investigated in aged rats using the object recognition task (Platano et al., 2008). In this regard, it has been demonstrated that the object recognition did not occur in rats older than 18 months (Bartolini et al., 1996). However, in different experimental conditions aged rats (25-27 months old) showed a good object recognition memory performance. Since no effective tasks are reported in the literature for aged rats, a new training protocol was developed (Platano et al., 2008), in this protocol a combination of the repetition of five training sessions in 3 days and smaller area exploration resulted in the establishment of the object recognition memory that persisted for at least 24 h for in both adult and aged rats. On the other hand, the older animals training the small area showed a higher synaptic density and a lower synaptic average area, indicating that the use of the smaller area is very important, because this non-anxiogenic environment induced a good plastic reactivity and memory performance. The authors suggested that this new protocol may be useful to compare functional and structural change associated with the memory formation in adulthood and the physiopathological aging (Platano D et al, 2008).

Apparatus

The apparatus consisted of an open box (100×100×50 cm high) made of aluminum with the inside painted in matt grey. The floor was covered with woodchip bedding which was moved around between trials/days to stop build-up of odor in certain places. The objects to be discriminated were available in four copies and made of an inert material such as glass; plastic or metal Figure 1. The weight of the objects ensured that they could not be displaced by the rats. To achieve this, some objects were filled with water or sand.

Behavioral Testing procedure

Pre-training. The animals are handled for 1 week and then all animals are given one habituation session in which they are allowed 5 min to explore the arena without stimuli (without objects). This habituation is especially important for the animal to become familiar with the environment, increasing the interest of the animal by the objects presented in the training phase.
Training Phase: the animals are placed into the arena facing the center of the opposite wall and exposed for a set length of time to two identical objects (A1 and A2) that are located in

the corner a specified distance from each other (15 cm from each adjacent wall) and allowed to explore for 3 min (Figure 1panel a). The time that the animal explored each object is measured. The rats are then removed to its home cage.

Test phase: this phase is different depending on the NOR variant. The same is done 5 min, 2 h or 24 h after the training phase in order to measure working memory, short-term memory or long-term memory.

There are four versions of this task, Novel object preference task, Object location task, Temporal order task and Object-in-place task. The following describes this phase in the different NOR:

Novel object preference task. The procedure comprised a training phase (acquisition), followed by a test phase (consolidation). In test phase the animal is re-placed in the arena, presented with two objects in the same positions: one object (A1) that is used in the training phase and the other object is a novel object (B) (Figure 2A). The positions of the objects in the test and the objects used as novel or familiar are counterbalanced between the animals.

Object location task. In this test, the rat's ability to recognize that an object that it had experienced before had changed location is assessed. In the test phase, one object (A1) is placed in the same position had occupied in the training phase. Object A2 is placed in the corner adjacent to the original position, so that the two objects A1 and A2 are in diagonal corners. Thus, both objects in the test phase are equally familiar, but one is in a new location (Figure 2B). The position of the moved object is counterbalanced between rats.

Temporal order task. This task comprised two training phases and one test trial. In each training phase, the subjects are allowed to explore two copies of an identical object. Different objects are used for training phases 1 (A1 and A2) and 2 (B1 and B2), with a delay between the training phases of 1 h. The test trial is given 3 h after training phase 2. During the test trial, an objects from training phase 1 (A1) and an objects from training phase 2 (B1) are used (Figure 3). The positions of the objects in the test and the objects used in training phase 1 and 2 are counterbalanced between the animals. If temporal order memory is intact, the subjects will spend more time exploring the object from training 1 (i.e., the object presented less recently) compared with the object from training 2 (i.e., the "new" object).

Object-in-place task. This task comprised a training phase and a test phase separated by a 5 min delay. In the training phase, the subjects are presented with four different objects (A, B, C, D). These objects are placed in the corners of the arena 15 cm from the walls. Each subject is placed in the center of the arena and allowed to explore the objects for 5 min. During the delay period, all of the objects are cleaned with alcohol to remove olfactory cues and any sawdust that had stuck to the object. In the test phase, two of the objects (e.g., B and D, which were both on the left or right of the arena), exchanged positions, and the subjects are allowed to explore the objects for 3 min (Figure 2C). The time spent exploring the two objects that had changed position is compared with the time spent exploring the two objects that had remained in the same position. The objects moved (i.e., those on the left or right), and the position of the objects in the sample phase are counterbalanced between rats. If object-in-place memory is intact, the subject will spend more time exploring the two objects that are in different locations compared with the two objects that are in the same locations.

The following parameters are analyzed: the time spent exploring each objects A1 and A2 in the training phase, the time spent exploring each objects B and A2 (object recognition) or objects A1n (A1in its new location) and A2 (object location) in the test phase. The data are expressed as the percentage (%) of time that the animals explore identical objects ($t_{A2}/[t_{A1} + t_{A2}] \times 100$) during training and the % of time that the animals explore the novel object ($t_B/[t_B$

+ t_{A2}] x 100) in the retention test (Novel Object Exploration -% Time) and total exploration time. The time percentage used for the novel object exploration is considered as an index of memory retention.

In publications by Carlini et al, it was represent the treatment or peptide effect on memory performance in the object recognition test, in a graph in which the percentage time exploration of one object in the training phase and the novel object in the test phase were indicated. As it can be seen, the Figure 4 shows that the animals explore 50% of time in each object in the training phase (these not show preference for one object), while the control animals explore 70 - 80 % of time in the novel object in the test phase under normal experimental condition. In this case it was measured the peptide effect upon short and long-term memory retention. It should be noted that two novel objects were used, and two tests were carried out. The first test was performed one hour after training, the animal was placed in the box for the retention test and allowed to explored for 3 min the objects: one of them was the same as the one used for training (1-familiar object) and the other one was a novel object (3-novel object), them the animal returned to its home cage. The second test was carried out twenty four hours later, the animal was tested in the box but object 3 was changed for another novel object (4-novel object) that the rat had never encountered before (Carlini et al., 2008).

In addition, it can also analyzed: *d1* the index of discrimination, i.e. the difference in time spent exploring the two objects in the training phase (e.g. B–A2 in the object recognition task and A1n–A2 in the object location task), *d2* the discrimination ratio, i.e. the difference in exploration time (i.e. d1) divided by the total time spent exploring the two objects in the training phase (e.g. B–A2/B+A2) in the object recognition task and A1n–A2/A1n+A2 in the object location task) (see Table 1).

The data are evaluated with repeated measures analysis of variance, including training and test phase.

Numerous authors have long been interested in the factors and neuropeptides that modulate the memory retention, particularly in different conditions such as stress, depression, chronic food restriction and undernutrition and examine these issues in an experimental paradigm commonly known as NOR or NOP (Souza, 1992; O´Dell & Marshall, 2005; Hopkins & Bucci, 2010; Kertész, S et al., 2010). In this paradigm, the animal is first allowed to explore a matching set of two identical objects. At some point later, the animal encounters one of the original objects and a novel object with which it has had no prior experience. Berlyne (1950) first demonstrated that animals will spend more time exploring the novel object than the original (i.e., familiar) one when given equal access to both, thus displaying a preference for novel stimulation. If a delay is added between training and test, NOR can also become a useful measure of retention across time (e.g., Ennaceur & Delacour, 1988; Anderson et al., 2004; Anderson, 2006a,b).

It should be noted that object recognition and object location tasks are based on spontaneous exploratory activity, and as a consequence they do not exclude the possibility of individual animals having a preference for a specific object or place that is independent of the familiarity/novelty of that item. In our lab, we use the NOR to examine the different neuropeptide effects on memory performance (Carlini et al., 2007; 2008) and we also examined the motivational behavior in this test, because it is reasonable to believe that the diminished performance in the object recognition test induced by a memory impairment drug, could be a consequence of a motivational deficit; i.e. animals would be not interested in exploring novel objects. In order to explore the above mentioned hypothesis, we quantified during each experiment (1) t1, the total time spent in exploring the two identical objects in the training phase; (2) t2, the total time spent exploring the two objects in the test phase.

Particularly, the object recognition test is very interesting because it is a non aversive test. It has been demonstrated that the effects of pharmacological agents that impair or enhance memory retention for an aversive stimulus as the footshock can be investigated using the step down test (Barros et al., 2001).

In publications by Carlini et al., it was reported the that the obestatin peptide caused increase in a dose-related manner in the latency time in the step down test, when given immediately post training (0 h), suggesting an increase in memory retention. It is known that in several memory aversive paradigms (as step down), the amygdala has also a critical role. Thus, the results from the step-down experiments, showing memory facilitation, suggest that the amygdala may also play an important role in the central effects of this peptide. However, the obestatin effect on memory retention using other behavioral paradigm, the object recognition task, also was studied. It is reasonable to believe that enhanced memory performance induced by obestatin in the step down paradigm could be test dependent. Nevertheless, the result shown that obestatin affects the performance of the animals in the two memory paradigm used (step down and object recognition test) indicates that these effects were not test dependent. Furthermore, in both memory tests, the hippocampus seems to be the principal structure involved (Carlini et al., 2007).

In the paper by Carlini et al, the step down paradigm was not used because the animals were under chronic food restriction. In this experimental condition the animal exhibit anxiety-like behavior and is more sensitive to footshock, showing decreased latency to escape from footshock. It has been demonstrated that undernutrition during suckling caused hyperreactivity to 0.2 mA footshocks in the step down test (Vendite et al., 1987) and that in the shock threshold test the malnourished animals are more sensitive to electric shock (Rocinholi et al., 1997). Footshock escape latency for undernourished rats was less than for well-nourished rats (Souza et al., 1992). Maybe the hyperreactivity or anxiety-like behavior observed in this nutritional condition could be the cause for the improved memory performance showed by these animals, and this can explain some of the interpretations reported in the literature (Souza et al., 1992). Thus, by using the step down test the chronic food restricted animals may show an apparent increase in memory performance. In consequence, under this experimental condition, the object recognition task is more abdicated than the step down, because in it there are not punishment o pain threshold.

Actually, there are some companies that offer several features designed to automate the test procedure and automatically measure and analyze behavioral parameters related to the novel object recognition test. These computational programs automatically record the position of the rodent's nose, relative to spatial zones or objects, measuring the time the animal spends with its nose towards and within a short distance of these zones and, thus, the time the animal spends exploring the separate objects. In addition, the system can also automatically measure elongation of the rodent's body, a parameter frequently used to investigate exploratory behavior. By setting elongation thresholds, you can define different degrees of this behavior as 'stretched, 'normal', or 'contracted' (Benice & Raber, 2005)

Without a doubt, this test, which is frequently applied, could provide new and original insights about physiological processes of learning and memory.

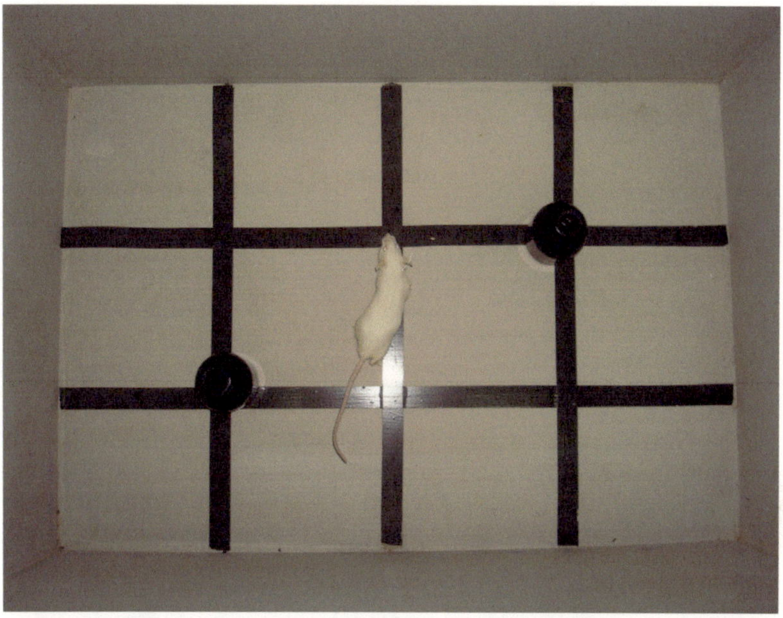

(a)

(b)

Fig. 1. Mouse exposed to two identical objects (A1 and A2) in training phase (panel a) and mouse exposed to novel and familiar object (B and A2) of Novel object preference task (panel b).
Mouse exploring novel object in test phase. It should be noted that exploration of an object is defined as time spent with the head oriented towards and within two centimeters of the object.

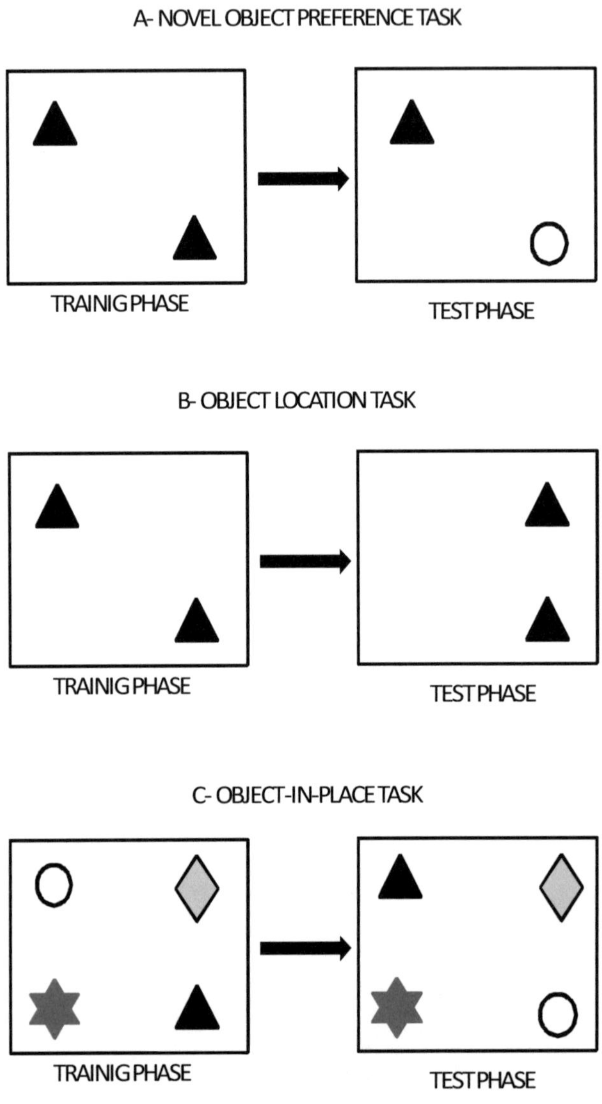

Fig. 2. Diagram of the three object recognition memory tasks. ***A-*** Novel object preference task: Left (training phase), animals are exposed to two identical objects (A1 and A2). Right (test phase), animal are exposed to two different objects, the sample previously explored in the training phase which is now familiar (A1) and a new object (B), never seen before. ***B-*** Object location task: Left (training phase), animals are exposed to two identical objects (A1 and A2). Right (test phase), animals are exposed to two objects, previously explored in the training phase which are now familiar (A1 and A2), but one object (A1) is re-localizated in relation to training phase. ***C-*** Object-in-place task. Left (training phase), animals are exposed to four different objects (A, B, C and D). Right (test phase), animals are exposed to four objects, previously explored in the training phase which are now familiar, but two object (A and B) are re-localizated in relation to training phase.

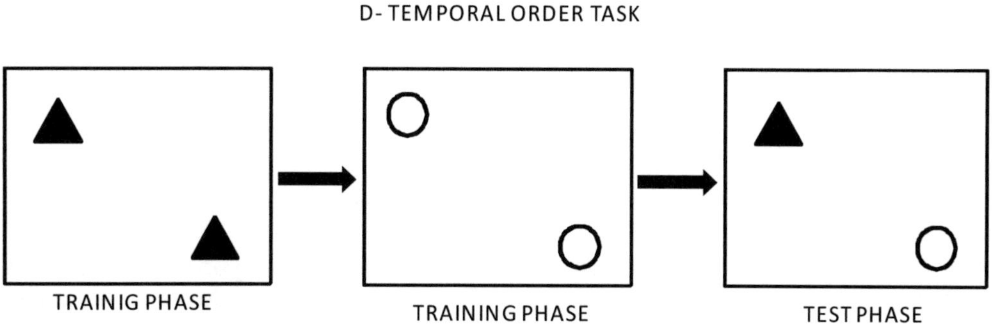

Fig. 3. Diagram of the *Temporal order task.* This task comprised two training phases: Left (first training phase), animals are exposed to two identical objects (A1 and A2); middle (second training phase), animals are exposed to two identical objects (B1 and B2) but these are different to first training phase; right (test phase), animal are exposed to two different objects, both previously explored, one object of the first training phase and other of the second training phase.

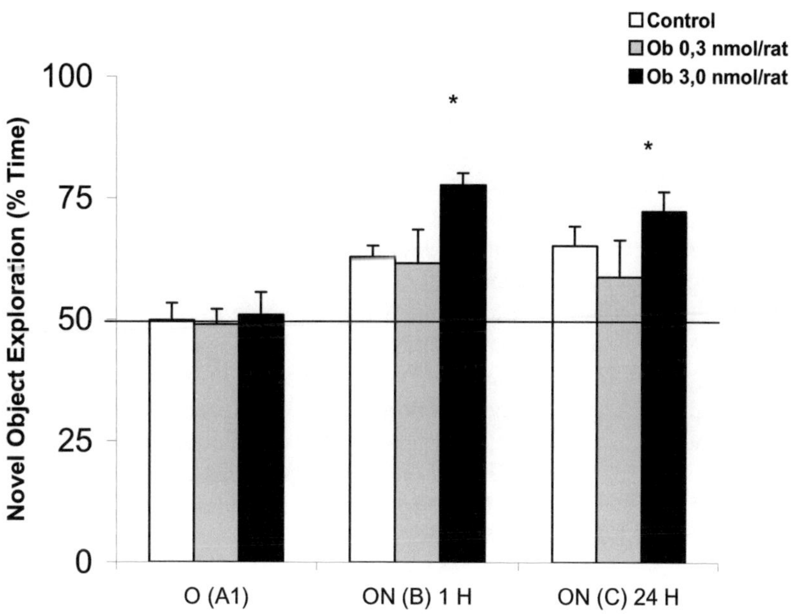

Fig. 4. Representative graphic of the parameters showed about the object recognition test. The figure show the Obestatin effect on memory performance in object recognition test. The animals received Obestatin (Ob) or ACSF (Control). The results are expressed as percentage of novel object exploration (time percentage = $t_{novel}/[t_{novel} + t_{training}] \cdot 100$) ± SEM. Training: the rat was placed with two identical objects (1 and 2). Test 1 and 24 h after training the rat was placed in the box with the object 1-3 and 1-4 respectively. *Significant differences with control animals, $p \leq 0.05$ (The graphic correspond to the figure shown in the paper published by Carlini et al. in Biochem Biophys Res Commun., 2007).

Test	Variable measured					
	% Time Training Object Exploration	% Time Nobel Object Exploration	t1	t2	d1	d2
A. Novel Object Preference	$t_{A2}/[t_{A1} + t_{A2}] \times 100$	$t_B/[t_B + t_{A2}] \times 100$	A1 + A2	B + A2	B–A2	B–A2/B+A2
B. Object location	$t_{A2}/[t_{A1} + t_{A2}] \times 100$	$t_{A1n}/[t_{A1n} + t_{A2}] \times 100$	A1 + A2	A1n + A2	A1n–A2	A2/A1n+A2

Table 1. Index of the different measures involved in the spontaneous recognition memory task for objects and location of objects.
t1 the total time spent exploring two objects A1 and A2 in the sample phase, t2 the total time spent exploring objects B and A2 (object recognition) or objects A1n (A1in its new location) and A2 (object location) in the test phase, *d1* the index of discrimination, i.e. the difference in time spent exploring the two objects in the training phase (e.g. B–A2 in the object recognition task and A1n–A2 in the object location task), *d2* the discrimination ratio, i.e. the difference in exploration time (i.e. d1) divided by the total time spent exploring the two objects in the training phase (e.g. B–A2/B+A2 in the object recognition task and A1n–A2/A1n+A2 in the object location task).

2. References

Aggleton, J.P., and Shaw, C. (1996). Amnesia and recognition memory: a re-analysis of psychometric data. *Neuropsychologia* 34, (Jan, 1996), 51-62. ISSN: 0028-3932.

Anderson, M.J., Barnes, G.W., Briggs, J.F., Ashton, K.M., Moody, E.W., Joynes, R.L., Riccio, D.C. (2004). Effects of ontogeny on performance of rats in a novel object-recognition task. Psychol Rep. 94(2), (Apr, 1994), 437-43. ISSN: 0033-2941

Anderson, M. J. (2006a). Novel object recognition: Assessing memory through exploratory responses. In M. J. Anderson (Ed.), *Tasks and Techniques: A Sampling of Methodologies for the Investigation of Animal Learning, Behavior, and Cognition.* (pp. 39-48). Hauppauge, NY: Nova Science Publishers, Inc.

Anderson, M. J. (2006b). Object Exploration: A non-aversive measure of object recognition, spatial memory, and context familiarity. In S. N. Hogan (Ed.), *Progress in Learning Research.* (pp. 35-47). Hauppauge, NY: Nova Science Publishers, Inc.

Baddeley, A., Vargha-Khadem, F., and Mishkin, M. (2001). Preserved recognition in a case of developmental amnesia: implications for the acquisition of semantic memory? *J. Cogn. Neurosci.* 13, (Apr, 2001), 357–369. ISSN: 0898-929X.

Barnes CA, Nadel L, Honig WK. (1980) Spatial memory deficit in senescent rats.*Can J Psychol.* 34(1), (Mar, 1980), 29-39. ISSN: 0008-4255

Barros DM, Mello e Souza T, de Souza MM, Choi H, DeDavid e Silva T, Lenz G, Medina JH, Izquierdo I. (2001). LY294002, an inhibitor of phosphoinositide 3-kinase given into rat hippocampus impairs acquisition, consolidation and retrieval of memory for one-trial step-down inhibitory avoidance. *Behav Pharmacol.* 12(8), (Dec, 2001), 629-34. ISSN: 0955-8810.

Bartolini L, Casamenti F, Pepeu G. (1996). Aniracetam restores object recognition impaired by age, scopolamine, and nucleus basalis lesions. *Pharmacol Biochem Behav.* 53(2), (Feb, 1996), 277-83. ISSN: 0091-3057.

Belcher A.M., O'Dell S.J. and Marshall J.F. (2006). A sensitizing regimen of methamphetamine causes impairments in a novelty preference task of object recognition. *Behav Brain Res* 170, (Jun, 2006), 167–172. ISSN: 0166-4328.

Benice, T.; Raber, J. (2005). Using EthoVision for studying object recognition in mice. *Proceedings of Neuroscience 2005 Satelite symposium, 14 November 2005, Washington DC, USA.*

Bizot JC, Herpin A, Pothion S, Pirot S, Trovero F, Ollat H. (2005). Chronic treatment with sulbutiamine improves memory in an object recognition task and reduces some amnesic effects of dizocilpine in a spatial delayed-non-match-to-sample task. *Prog Neuropsychopharmacol Biol Psychiatry.* 29(6), (Jul, 2005), 928-35. ISSN: 0278-5846.

Brown, M.W., and Aggleton, J.P. (2001). Recognition memory: what the roles of the perirhinal cortex and hippocampus? *Nat. Rev. Neurosci.* 2 (Jan, 2001), 51–61. ISSN: 1471-003X.

Bulthoff, I., & Newell, F. (2006). The role of familiarity in the recognition of static and dynamic objects. *Progress in Brain Research* . 154, (Sep, 2006), 315-325. ISSN: 0079-6123.

Carlini VP, Martini AC, Schiöth HB, Ruiz RD, Fiol de Cuneo M, de Barioglio SR. (2008) Decreased memory for novel object recognition in chronically food-restricted mice is reversed by acute ghrelin administration. *Neuroscience.* 153(4), (Jun, 2008), 929-34. ISSN: 0306-4522.

Carlini VP, Schiöth HB, Debarioglio SR. (2007) Obestatin improves memory performance and causes anxiolytic effects in rats. *Biochem Biophys Res Commun.* 352(4), (Jan, 2007), 907-12. ISSN: 0006-291X.

Donaldson, W. (1999). The role of decision processes in remembering and knowing. *Mem. Cogn.* 26, (Jul, 1999), 523–533. ISSN: 0278-7393.

Eichenbaum, H., and Cohen, N.J. (2001). *From Conditioning to Conscious Recollection: Memory Systems of the Brain.* (New York: Ox- University Press).

Eldridge, L.L., Knowlton, B.J., Furmanski, C.S., Bookheimer, S.Y., and Engel, S.A. (2000). Remembering episodes: a selective role for the hippocampus during retrieval. *Nat. Neurosci.* 3, (Nov, 2000), 1149–1152. ISSN: 1097-6256.

Ennaceur A, Delacour J (1988) A new one-trial test for neurobiological studies of memory in rats. *Behav Brain Res* 31, (Nov, 1988), 47–59. ISSN: 0166-4328.

Ennaceur A, Meliani K. (1992a). A new one-trial test for neurobiological studies of memory in rats. III. Spatial vs. non-spatial working memory. *Behav Brain Res.* 51(1), (Oct, 1992), 83-92. ISSN: 0166-4328.

Ennaceur A, Meliani K. (1992b). Effects of physostigmine and scopolamine on rats' performances in object-recognition and radial-maze tests. *Psychopharmacology (Berl).* 109(3):321-30. ISSN: 0033-3158.

Ennaceur A, Aggleton JP (1994) Spontaneous recognition of object configurations in rats: effect of lesions of the fornix. *Exp Brain Res* 100: 85–92. ISSN: 0014-4819.

Ennaceur A, Neave N, Aggleton JP (1996) Neurotoxic lesions of the perirhinal cortex do not mimic the behavioural effects of fornix transection in the rat. *Behav Brain Res* 80, (Oct, 1996), 9–25. ISSN: 0166-4328.

Ennaceur A., Neave N. and Aggleton J.P. (1997). Spontaneous object recognition and object location memory in rats: the effects of lesions in the cingulate cortices, the medial prefrontal cortex, the cingulum bundle and the fornix. *Exp Brain Res* 113, (Mar, 1997), 509–519. ISSN: 0014-4819.

Ennaceur A., Michalikova S., Bradford A. and Ahmed S. (2005). Detailed analysis of the behavior of Lister and Wistar rats in anxiety, object recognition and object location tasks. *Behav Brain Res* 159, (Apr, 2005), 247–266. ISSN: 0166-4328.

Enns, J. T. (2004). The Thinking Eye, The Seeing Brain: Explorations in Visual Cognition. New York: W. W. Norton & Company.

Fried, I., MacDonald, K.A., and Wilson, C.L. (1997). Single neuron activity in human hippocampus and amygdala during recognition of faces and objects. *Neuron* 18, (May, 1997), 753–765. ISSN: 0896-6273.

Haist, F. & Shimamura, A. P. (1992). On the relationship between recall and recognition memory. *J. Exp. Psychol. Learn. Mem. Cogn.* 18, (Jul, 1992), 691–702. ISSN: 0278-7393.

Hajilou, B. B., & Done, D. J. (2007). Evidence for a dissociation of structural and semantic knowledge in dementia of the alzheimer type (DAT). *Neuropsychologia* 45(4), (Mar, 2997), 810-816. ISSN: 0028-3932.

Hammonds, R.; Tull, L.; Stackman, R. (2004). On the delay-dependent involvement of the hippocampus in object recognition memory. *Neurobiology of Learning and Memory*, 82, (Jul, 2004), 26-34. ISSN: 1074-7427.

He, Y. Yang, Y. Yu, X. Li and X.M. Li (2006). The effects of chronic administration of quetiapine on the methamphetamine-induced recognition memory impairment and dopaminergic terminal deficit in rats. *Behav Brain Res* 172, (Sep, 2006), 39–45. ISSN: 0166-4328.

Hirshman, E. & Master, S. (1997). Modeling the conscious correlates of recognition memory: reflections on the remember–know paradigm. *Mem. Cogn.* 25, (May, 1997), 345–351. ISSN: 0278-7393.

Hopkins, M.E., Bucci, D.J. (2010). BDNF expression in perirhinal cortex is associated with exercise-induced improvement in object recognition memory. Neurobiol Learn Mem. 94(2), (Sep, 2010), 278-84. ISSN: 1074-7427.

Humphreys, G., Price, C., & Riddoch, J. (1999). From objects to names: A cognitive neuroscience approach. *Psychological Research.* 62, (Jul, 1999), 118-130. ISSN: 0340-0727.

Kertész, S., Kapus, G., Gacsályi, I., Lévay, G. (2010). Deramciclane improves object recognition in rats: potential role of NMDA receptors. Pharmacol Biochem Behav. 94(4), (Feb, 2010), 570-4.

Laatu, S., A, R., Jaykka, H., Portin, R., & Rinne, J. (2003). Visual object recognition in early Alzheimer's disease: deficits in semantic processing. *Acta Neurologica Scandinavica.* 108, (Aug, 2003), 82-89. ISSN: 0001-6314.

Mandler, G. (1980). Recognizing: the judgment of previous occurrence. *Psychol. Rev.* 87, (May, 1980), 252–271. ISSN: 0033-295X.

Norman, G., & Eacott, M. (2004). Impaired object recognition with increasing levels of feature ambiguity in rats with perirhinal cortex lesions. *Behav. Brain Res.* 148, (Jan, 2004), 79-91. ISSN: 0166-4328.

O'Dell and Marshall J.F. (2005). Impaired object recognition memory following methamphetamine, but not *p*-chloroamphetamine- or *d*-amphetamine-induced neurotoxicity. *Neuropsychopharmacology* 30, (Nov,2005), 2026–2034. ISSN: 0893-133X.

Olton DS, Feustle WA. (1981). Hippocampal function required for nonspatial working memory. Exp Brain Res. 41(3-4), (Feb , 1981), 380-9. ISSN: 0014-4819

Platano D, Fattoretti P, Balietti M, Bertoni-Freddari C, Aicardi G. (2008). Long-term visual object recognition memory in aged rats. *Rejuvenation Res.* 11(2), (Apr, 2008), 333-9. ISSN: 1549-1684.

Puma C, Deschaux O, Molimard R, Bizot JC. (1999). Nicotine improves memory in an object recognition task in rats. *Eur Neuropsychopharmacol.* 9(4), (Jun, 1999), 323-7. ISSN: 0924-977X.

Quamme JR, Frederick C, Kroll NE, Yonelinas AP, Dobbins IG. (2002). Recognition memory for source and occurrence: the importance of recollection. *Mem Cognit.* 30(6), (Sep, 2002), 893-907. ISSN: 0090-502X.

Rich EL, Shapiro M. (2009). Rat prefrontal cortical neurons selectively code strategy switches. *J Neurosci.* 29(22), (Jun, 2009), 7208-19. 0270-6474.

Riddoch, M., & Humphreys, G. (2001). *Object Recognition.* In B. Rapp (Ed.), Handbook of Cognitive Neuropsychology. Hove: Psychology Press.

Rocinholi LF, Almeida SS, De-Oliveira LM. (1997). Response threshold to aversive stimuli in stimulated early protein-malnourished rats. *Braz J Med Biol Res.* 30(3), (Mar, 1997), 407-13. ISSN: 0100-879X.

Schacter, D.L., and Tulving, E., eds. (1994). Memory Systems 1994 (Cambridge, MA: MIT Press).

Souza DO, Vendite D, Mello CF, Rocha JB. (1992). Effects of undernutrition during suckling on footshock escape behavior and of post-training beta-endorphin administration on inhibitory avoidance task test behavior of young rats. *Braz J Med Biol Res.* 25(3):275-80. ISSN: 0100-879X.

Squire LR, Zola-Morgan S. (1991). The medial temporal lobe memory system. Science. 253(5026), (Sep, 1991), 1380-6. Review. ISSN: 0193-4511.

Squire LR. (1992). Memory and the hippocampus: a synthesis from findings with rats, monkeys, and humans. *Psychol Rev.* 99(2), (Apr, 1992), 195-231. Review. Erratum in: Psychol Rev 99(3):582. ISSN: 0033-295X.

Suzuki, W.A., and Amaral, D.G. (1994). Topographic organization of the reciprocal connections between the monkey entorhinal cortex and the perirhinal and parahippocampal cortices. *J. Neurosci.* 14, (Mar, 1994), 1856–1877. ISSN: 0270-6474.

Suzuki, W.A., and Eichenbaum, H. (2000). The neurophysiology of memory. *Ann. N Y Acad. Sci.* 911, (Jun, 2000), 175–191. ISSN: 0077-8923.

Tulving, E. (1985). Memory and consciousness. *Canadian Psychology.* 26 (Jan, 1985), 1-12. ISSN: 0008-4832.

Tulving, E., and Markowitsch, H.J. (1998). Episodic and declarative memory: role of the hippocampus. *Hippocampus* 8, (Dec, 2998), 198–204. ISSN: 1050-9631.

Vargha-Khadem, F., Gaffan, D., Watkins, K.E., Connelly, A., Van Paesschen, W., and Mishkin, M. (1997). Differential effects of early hippocampal pathology on episodic and semantic memory. *Science* 277, (Jul, 1997), 376–380. ISSN: 0193-4511.

Vendite, D., Rocha J.B., Mello, C.F., Souza, D.O. (1987). Effect of undernutrition during suckling and of post-training beta-endorphin administration on avoidance performance of adult rats. *Braz J Med Biol Res* 20(6), 731-40. ISSN: 0100-879X.

Verfaellie, M., and Keane, M.M. (2002). Impaired and preserved memory processes in amnesia. In The Neuropsychology of Memory, second edition, L.R. Squire and D. Schacter, eds. (New York: Guilford Press), pp. 35–46.

Ward, J. (2006). The Student's Guide to Cognitive Neuroscience. New York: Psychology Press.

Wood, E.R., Dudchenko, P.A., and Eichenbaum, H. (1999). The global record of memory in hippocampal neuronal activity. Nature *397*, (Feb, 1999), 561–563. ISSN: 0028-0836

Yonelinas, A.P., Kroll, N.E., Quamme, J.R., Lazzara, M.M., Sauvé, M.J., Widaman, K.F., Knight, R.T. (2002). Effects of extensive temporal lobe damage or mild hypoxia on recollection and familiarity. Nature Neurosci. 5, (Nov, 2002), 1236–1241. ISSN: 1097-6256.

Yonelinas, A.P., Kroll, N.E.A., Dobbins, I., Lazzara, M., and Knight, R.T. (1998). Recollection and familiarity deficits in amnesia: convergence of remember-know, process dissociation, and receiver operating characteristic data. *Neuropsychology* 12, (Jul, 1998), 323–339. ISSN: 0894-4105.

4

Object and Scene Recognition Impairments in Patients with Macular Degeneration

Muriel Boucart[1] (PhD) and Thi Ha Chau Tran[1,2] (MD)
[1]*Laboratoire de Neurosciences et Pathologies Fonctionnelles, CNRS, université Lille Nord de France*
[2]*Service d'Ophtalmologie, Hôpital Saint Vincent de Paul, Lille France*

1. Introduction

1.1 Macular degeneration: clinical aspects

Age-related macular degeneration (AMD) is the leading cause of irreversible blindness. (Klaver, et al 1998, Klein 2007). The disease adversely affects quality of life and activities of daily living, causing many affected individuals to lose their independence in their retirement years. It is estimated that, in the USA, over 8 million people have some stage of AMD, with hundred of thousands of people aged 75 or over developing some stage of AMD over any 5-year period. (Klein, et al 1997) Preventive measures are needed to reduce the burden of this disease. AMD affects the region with the highest density of photoreceptors: the macula, about 6 mm in diameter, covering the central 15-20° of the visual field. International classification and grading system for AMD proposes to separate features termed either early, and late age-related macular degeneration (Klein, et al 1992) with the term age-related macular degeneration (AMD) being reserved for late AMD. Early AMD is defined as degenerative disorder in individuals over 50 years of age. Ophthalmoscopy reveals yellow subretinal deposits called soft drusen (large, ≥ 63μm), or retinal pigment epithelial irregularities including hyperpigmentation or hypopigmentation changes. (Bird, et al 1995). Many aspects of visual function, not just visual acuity, show a decline with normal aging, including dark adaptation, stereopsis, contrast sensitivity, sensitivity to glare, and visual field tests. Late AMD is associated with visual loss, and divided into a non-neovascular atrophic type (dry AMD, geographic atrophy), and a neovascular (wet) type.

In atrophic AMD, gradual disappearance of the retinal pigment epithelium results in one or more patches of atrophy that slowly enlarge and coalesce. Geographic atrophy is defined as any sharply delineated round or oval area of hypo or hyperpigmentation or apparent absence of the retinal pigment epithelium, in which choroidal vessels are more visible than the surrounding areas and which is ≥ 1mm in diameter in funduscopy.(Sarks, et al 1988). An illustration is shown in Figure 1. Geographic atrophy involving the center of the macula leads to progressive visual loss. Development of geographic atrophy is associated with subsequent further growth of atrophy. For instance, a study by Lindblad et al (2009) showed that from a median initial lesion size of 4.3 mm^2, average change from baseline geographic atrophy was 2.03 mm^2 at 1 year, 3.78 mm^2 at 2 years, 5.93 mm^2 at 3 years (1.78 mm^2 per year). Average visual acuity decreased by 22 letters after 5 years. Affected areas have no visual function since loss of the retinal pigment epithelium is associated with fallout of photoreceptors. The only proven treatment available for the dry forms of the disease, compassing 85% of cases, is an antioxidants/mineral supplement that can slow the progression of the disease by 25% over 5 years (Age-Related Eye Disease Study Research Group 2001)

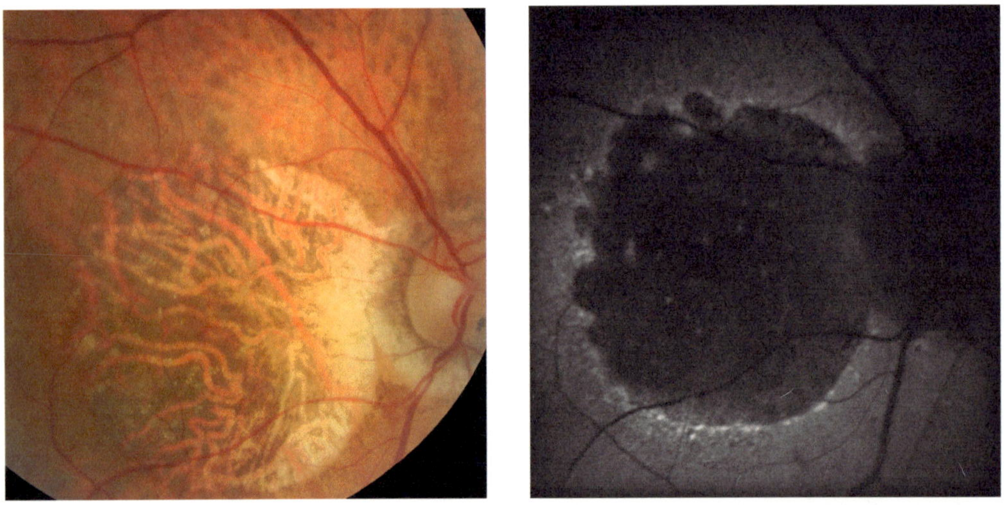

Fig. 1. Fundus photography (left) and fundus autofluorescence (right) of a patient suffering from advanced atrophic AMD. Visual acuity was reduced to "counting fingers" at 1m.

In the wet AMD (or exsudative or neovascular), vision loss appear suddenly, when a choroidal neovascular membrane leaks fluid or blood into the subpigment epithelial or subretinal space. Approximately 10% to 15% of AMD manifest the neovascular form of the disease (Ferris, *et al* 1984). Patients complain of decreased vision, micropsia, metamorphopsia, the presence of a scotoma, see a simulation on Figure 2.

Macular degeneration is associated with severe vision loss at advanced stages. If the advanced stage of both types of AMD is noted in one or both eyes, then rehabilitation with a low-vision department should be considered to determine which activity or device will help the individual to cope with the visual loss. At advanced stage, once the spatial resolution of the fovea cannot be used, and fixation is controlled, a preferred retinal location (PRL) is developed. The location of the PRL depends upon the geographic distribution of the lesion although it tends to develop in a functional retinal area near the edge of the scotoma (Crossland et al 2004; 2005; Cheung & Legge, 2005 for a review). At the end of its evolution, AMD affects all the functions of central vision: acuity, color vision, high spatial resolution, contrast sensitivity, posture and mobility (Wood et al 2009; Hassan et al., 2002).

AMD leads to a central scotoma, a region of diminished vision within the visual field, which can be absolute or relative depending on the degree of central vision loss. The scotoma may cause centrally presented images to appear darker, blurred, and even contain black or grey holes (see Figure 2) (Schumacher et al. 2008). As the macula is responsible for high spatial resolution the patients' ability to obtain information about the environment is reduced. Patients with visual loss resulting from AMD often report AMD as the worst medical problem and have a diminished quality of life (Alexander, *et al* 1988, Mangione, *et al* 1999). The lower quality of life in patients with AMD is related to greater emotional distress, worse self reported general health, and greater difficulties carrying out daily activities. These people report increased difficulty for everyday tasks like reading, driving, cooking, watching TV, recognizing faces and facial expressions, pictures and finding objects especially when the illumination level is low and during the transition from bright to dim illumination (Hart et al., 1999; Brody et al., 2001; Holzschuch et al 2002; Hassan et al., 2002; Bullimore et al 1991; Peli et al 1991; Tejeira et al., 2002; Boucart et al 2008a). Vision-related Quality of Life questionnaires (Mangione et al 2001; Cahill et al 2005) report that patients suffering from AMD also encounter more difficulties than do age matched normally sighted individuals when shopping (i.e., finding objects on shelves), managing money and performing light housework. Therefore, understanding the visual processes impaired, and those spared, is critical for efficient cognitive re-habilitation and for maintaining a relative autonomy in this population.

Fig. 2. Simulation of a view of a scene : (left) a scene as viewed by a person with normal vision. Middle: a scene as viewed by a person with metamorphopsia. Right: a scene as viewed by a person with central scotoma. Picture taken from: www.canadian-health.ca

In the present chapter we will focus on the cognitive aspects of the visual impairments encountered by people with low vision consecutive to macular degeneration, and particularly on visual object and scene perception. Indeed, with only few exceptions (Hogervorst & van Damme 2008; Boucart et al 2008b), research on people with AMD has been focused on investigations of low-level processes with simple static stimuli like gratings, shapes, letters and in word perception and reading (Legge et al., 1985; 1992; Wang et al 2002). Yet, the natural environment is made of dynamic scenes, which put different requirements on the observer in terms of selecting relevant features (colors, contours, texture, spatial layout, figure/ground discrimination,...) that are necessary to quickly understand the meaning of a scene (gist) as well as object search for instance. How do people with central vision loss recognize objects and scenes? Is central vision necessary for scene gist recognition? Does color and context (the surrounding of objects) facilitate or impair object and scene recognition? We summarize three studies (Boucart et al., 2008b; Tran et al 2010; Tran et al 2011) addressing these questions.
Visual acuity is not uniform across the visual field. Neurophysiological studies show that the density of cone photoreceptors, responsible for high resolution perception, decreases considerably as eccentricity increases. The fovea contains the highest density of cones. Their number drops to about 50% at 1.75° from the fovea and to less than 5% at 20° from the fovea (Curcio et al, 1991). The receptive fields are larger in periphery leading to loss of spatial resolution. As a consequence of its low spatial resolution, peripheral vision is far less capable of fine discrimination even after its low spatial resolution has been compensated for

by increase in size (M-Scaling, Saarinen, et al. 1987; Näsänen & O'Leary 1998), contrast enhancement (Makela et al, 2001) and increased temporal integration (Swanson et al. 2008). Moreover, crowding is known to be more pronounced in the periphery (Pelli et al 2004). Crowding refers to the decreased visibility of a visual target in the presence of nearby objects or structures (Levi 2008; Pelli 2008). It impairs the ability to recognize objects in clutters. This has been demonstrated with letters, digits, bars and gabor stimuli (Bouma 1970; Strasburger et al 1991; Fellisbert et al 2005). Figure/ground segregation is also impaired in peripheral vision (Thompson et al 2007). In daily life normally sighted people are not aware of the limitations in spatial resolution in peripheral vision because eye movements place the high resolution of foveal vision in different parts of the visual field. In people with AMD the central scotoma follows eye movements and only the low resolution of peripheral vision remains.

We (Tran et al 2010) examined whether scene gist recognition can be accomplished by low resolution peripheral vision in people with central vision loss. The question of the contribution of central versus peripheral vision on scene gist recognition has been addressed by Larson and Loschky (2009) in normally sighted observers. They presented participants with photographs of real world scenes (27 X 27° of visual angle) for 106 ms each. Each scene was followed by a name (e.g., river). Participants were asked to decide if the scene matched the name. Performance was compared in two conditions: a window condition showing the central portion of the scene and blocking peripheral information and a scotoma condition blocking out the central portion and showing only the periphery. The radii of the window and scotoma were 1, 5, 10.8 and 13.6°. Performance was barely above chance in the 1° window condition suggesting that foveal vision is not useful for recognizing scene gist. Accuracy increased as the radius of the window increased. Conversely, when participants had information from everything but not foveal vision (in the 1° scotoma condition), performance was equal to seeing the entire image. Based on these data the authors suggested that peripheral (and parafoveal vision) is more useful than high resolution foveal vision for scene gist recognition.

We investigated scene categorization in people with central vision loss. Performance was compared for two spatial properties: a categorization based on naturalness (natural versus urban scenes) and a categorization in terms of indoor versus outdoor scenes. Though these two properties are considered as holistic or global (i.e, the categorization can be based on the overall layout; Greene & Oliva 2009a; 2009b), studies on young normally sighted observers have shown longer categorization times for indoor vs outdoor scenes than for naturalness (Joubert et al 2007); likely due to the fact that a more local (object) analysis is required to discriminate between indoor and outdoor scenes whilst a coarse perception based on orientation and color is sufficient to decide if a scene is natural or urban.

27 patients with a confirmed diagnosis of wet and dry AMD and 17 age matched controls were recruited. Inclusion and exclusion criteria and clinical and demographic data are detailed in Tran et al (2010). Participants were tested monocularly, on the best eye for patients and on the preferred eye for controls.

The stimuli were photographs of natural scenes. Two scene properties were selected: naturalness (natural/urban scenes) and indoor/outdoor scenes. Examples are shown in Figure 3. The angular size of the photographs was 15° X 15° at a viewing distance of 1 m. A black fixation cross (5°) was centrally displayed for 500 ms and followed by a single photograph of a scene centrally displayed for 300 ms. Participants were given a target for each categorization task. For naturalness, urban scenes were chosen as target for half of the participants and natural scenes for the other half of the participants. The same procedure was used for indoor/outdoor scenes. A scene appeared every 3 seconds. Participants were asked to press a key as soon as they saw a picture corresponding to the pre-defined target. There were 100 trials/category (50 targets (e.g. natural scenes) and 50 distractors (e.g., urban scenes).

Fig. 3. Examples of indoor/outdoor scenes and natural/urban scenes used in the scene categorization task.

The percentage of correct detections of the target is displayed in Figure 4. The results show that patients with AMD were on average more accurate for natural/urban scenes than for indoor/outdoor scenes whilst performance did not differ significantly between the two categories for age matched controls. False alarms were higher in the indoor/outdoor category than for natural/urban category in both groups of participants but, on average, did not exceed 11%. A detailed description of the results can be found in Tran et al (2010).

The results indicate that scene gist recognition can be accomplished with low resolution peripheral vision as patients with central vision loss were able to recognize scenes with high accuracy in two types of categorization : natural vs urban scenes and indoor vs outdoor scenes. The results therefore confirm Larson and Loschky's (2009) data with artificial scotomas in normally sighted people, and extend them to real scotomas varying from 5° to 30° eccentricity in our patients. The head was not fixed in our study. As the stimuli always appeared at the same spatial location patients with a large scotoma might have moved their head to place the image in their preferred retinal location which is adjacent to the scotoma in AMD (see Cheung & Legge 2005 for a review). This means that scene gist is available at low spatial resolution (in peripheral vision) and even when local information, object identification, might help to distinguish between the two categories (i.e., a bed is more likely to be found indoor and a bike is more likely to be found outdoor). No correlation was found between performance and clinical variables such as the size of the lesion, visual acuity and the type of AMD. Performance is usually found to be related to the size of absolute scotoma when high spatial resolution is required to perform a task, in reading speed and in reading acuity for instance (Ergun et al 2003).

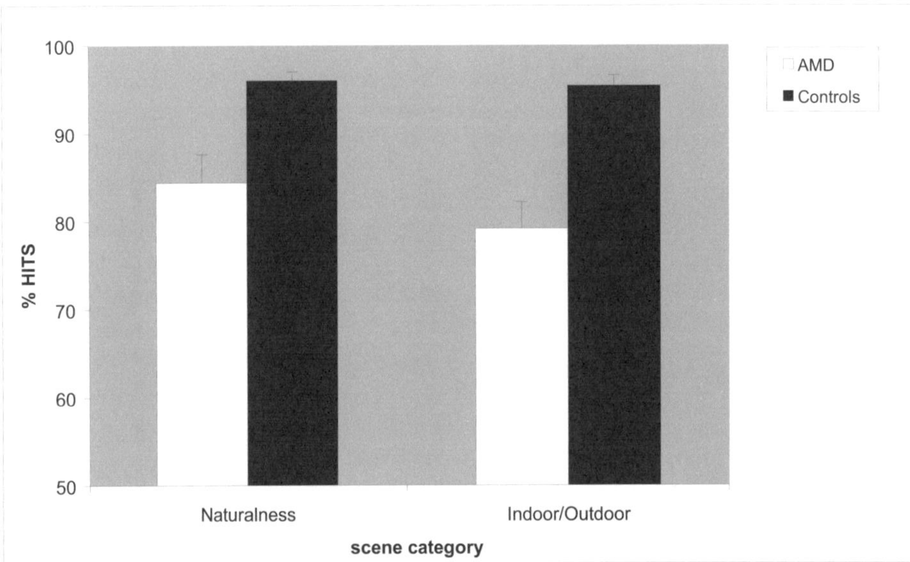

Fig. 4. Percentage of correct detections (Hits) of the target scenes as a function of the category of scene (natural/urban and indoor/outdoor) for patients with AMD and age matched normally sighted controls (adapted from Tran et al 2010).

The scene-centered approach (Oliva, 2005; Greene and Oliva 2009a; 2009b) suggests that the initial visual representation constructed by the visual system is at the level of the whole scene and not at the level of objects. Instead of local geometric and part based visual primitives this account posits that global properties reflecting scene structure, layout and function act as primitives for scene categorization. Processing is considered as global if it builds a representation that is sensitive to the overall layout and structure of a visual scene. Many properties in the natural environment can be global and holistic in nature. For instance, the processing of orientation is sufficient to discriminate a urban from a natural landscape. Consistent with this proposal modelling work has shown success in identifying complex photographs of real world scenes from low level features, such as orientation, and color, or more complex spatial layout properties such as texture, mean depth and perspective (Oliva & Torralba, 2001, Torralba & Oliva, 2002, 2003 Fei-Fei et al 2005; Vogel & Schiele 2007).

Greene and Oliva (2009a) suggested the possibility that the brain is able to rapidly calculate robust statistical summaries of features like the average orientation of a pattern in an automatic fashion and outside the focus of attention. This might explain the advantage observed, in patients with AMD, for naturalness as compared to indoor/outdoor scenes, and also that, within naturalness, urban scenes were categorized faster and more accurately than natural scenes. Indeed, urban scenes (cities with high buildings in our set of images cf Figure 3) were more homogeneous than natural scenes which included rivers, mountains, deserts, forests, beach.... An advantage for naturalness, over indoor/outdoor scenes, has been reported in other studies. Naturalness classification had the fastest categorization threshold in Greene and Oliva's (2009b) study and the fastest response times in Joubert et al. (2007) study. An explanation for this difference is that a low resolution is sufficient to discriminate between natural and urban scenes but a higher resolution is needed for basic level scene categorization such as discrimination between sea, mountain, forests, indoor and outdoor scenes. Our results are consistent with the notion that the initial scene representation is based on global properties and not on the objects it contains as central vision is reduced in AMD and object recognition is impaired.

2. The effect of color on object and scene perception

In normally sighted people there is disagreement about whether color facilitates object recognition or not. Ostergaard and Davidoff (1988) reported that objects were recognized equally fast irrespective of whether they were properly colored or not. Biederman and Ju (1988) failed to find any advantage of color over black and white outline drawings of objects in a naming task and an object verification task, thus supporting edge-based models of object recognition. Delorme et al. (2000) asked normally sighted young participants to make a rapid categorization (animal/non animal or food/non food objects) of briefly displayed (32 ms) colored or achromatic grey level photographs of natural scenes. They found no effect of color leading to the suggestion that the first wave of visual information is essentially coarse and achromatic. Other studies have attempted to determine the conditions in which color information might help object recognition. Three main factors have been investigated: structural similarity, color diagnosticity and degraded shape information. Price and Humphreys (1989) reported that object naming and categorization were facilitated by color, as compared with grey levels, when objects were structurally similar in shape (e.g. orange vs. grapefruit). Rossion and Pourtois (2004) also found that the advantage provided by color was larger for objects structurally similar in shape and for natural objects with a diagnostic color (e.g., a red strawberry) but they reported that man-made objects also benefited from color irrespective of whether they had a single diagnostic color (e.g. a fire engine) or not. The effect of color diagnosticity has been demonstrated in several other studies both with objects (Tanaka & Presnell, 1999; Therriault et al 2009) and with photographs of natural scenes (Oliva & Schyns, 2000), but Gegenfurtner and Rieger (2000) found that recognition accuracy was higher for colored images than for luminance-matched grey level images for all categories: natural scenes and scenes including man-made objects such as cities. Color has been found to help object recognition or object categorization under degraded visual conditions. For instance, at 60° eccentricity where spatial resolution is very low Naili et al (2006) reported a better performance for colored than for grey level photographs of objects in a task requiring participants to decide whether an object was edible or not. Other studies have reported that observers profit from color for recognizing photographs of natural scenes degraded by low pass filtering (Oliva & Schyns, 2000) or by visual noises made by combining the Fourier phase spectra of the natural images with a random phase spectrum using the inverse Fourier transform at different coherence levels (Liebe et al 2009).

Few studies have examined how people with low vision perceive and recognize objects and scenes. Ebert et al. (1986) examined functional visual performance in 52 patients with low vision. The participants were tested with practical tasks such as currency discrimination, color recognition, reading a clock and reading large prints. They found a correlation between Snellen acuity and functional vision. Owsley and Sloane, (1987) measured contrast thresholds for gratings varying on spatial frequencies and contrast thresholds for both the detection and identification of three categories of stimuli (faces, road signs and various common objects). Participants increased the contrast by key pressing until something was just detectable on the screen, and then, they were asked to continue to increase the contrast until identification. The pictures had been seen at optimal contrast before threshold measurement. They found that, for real world targets, acuity was poorly correlated to threshold performance. In contrast the best predictors of contrast thresholds were age and decreased contrast sensitivity at middle-to-low spatial frequencies (i.e., 0.5 to 6 cpd). Wurm et al (1993) examined whether people with low vision benefit from color in object recognition. They compared performance in a naming task for isolated colored vs achromatic pictures of objects in normally sighted people and in people with various types of retinopathies including macular degeneration, cataract, glaucoma and diabetic retinopathy. They reported that people with low vision exhibit a greater advantage in terms of accuracy and response times than normally sighted participants for colored objects, showing that color improves object recognition in low vision. This result was confirmed, and extended to photographs of natural scenes by Boucart et al (2008b). Patients with AMD (including wet and dry AMD) and age matched controls were tested in a categorization task in which they were asked to press a response key when they saw either a target animal or a target face (faces and animals were presented in separate blocks of trials). The stimuli were displayed centrally for 300 ms each. Target animals or faces appeared randomly within photographs containing neither animals nor faces. Performance was compared in four experimental conditions: colored versus grey level photographs of natural scenes and colored versus grey level photographs of isolated object extracted from the photographs of scenes. As can be seen from Figure 5 normally sighted people were not affected by whether the stimuli were colored or not. In contrast, people with low vision benefited significantly from color for both faces and animals.

Wurm et al (1993) used food objects for which color is diagnostic (e.g., to discriminate a tomato from a peach). Our results show that color facilitated the detection of both types of targets (faces and animals) in participants with low vision whilst it had less effect on performance in normally sighted people.

Color perception is classically considered as a function of central vision because the highest density of cones is located in the fovea. However, several studies (Newton & Eskew, 2003: Sakurai et al., 2003; Naili et al 2006) have shown that, at large eccentricities (above 20°) color perception is better than what should be expected from the distribution of L, M and S cones in the retina, likely due to post-receptoral cortical processes. Psychophysical, electrophysiological and histopathological findings indicate that the loss of rods is greater than the loss of cones in the macula of patients with AMD (Curcio et al 2000; Owsley et al, 2000) and post mortem examination of the retina of patients with AMD show that only cones remained at a late stage (Curcio et al. 1996; Jackson et al. 2002). This might explain why patients with AMD benefited from color in our experiment.

It has been reported that the visual system tends to perceive chromatic information at coarser scales better than luminance information. For instance, Oliva and Schyns (2000) measured the gain in categorization performance that arose from the addition of color cues to luminance information at different spatial scales. Normally sighted young participants were asked to categorize filtered (0.5 to 8 cycles per degree) color-diagnostic scenes (e.g.,

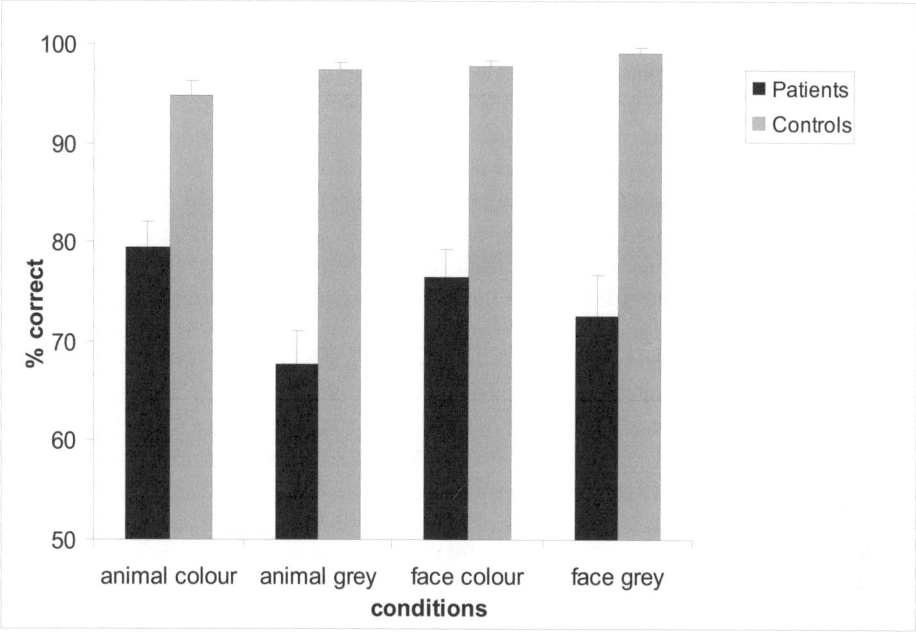

Fig. 5. Performance of patients with AMD and age matched controls for colored and grey level target animals and faces. From Boucart et al (2008b) with permission from Visual Neuroscience.

forest, desert, canyon…), non diagnostic color scenes (e.g., highway, shopping area, bedroom…) and grey levels scenes. They found that color enhances categorization at coarse spatial scales suggesting that color facilitates the initial segmentation of the image. Segmentation refers to the process of segregating a complex scene into its constituent regions, surfaces and objects. Two mechanisms have been suggested to underlie the advantage of color for image recognition: at early stages color helps define spatial contours, surfaces and boundaries, irrespective of what the exact color of the object is (Fine et al 2003; Hansen & Gegenfurtner 2006). The role of color for segmentation is particularly important in cases in which contours and regions are poorly defined by variations in luminance alone, as when visual noise is added (Liebe et al 2009). At a later stage of visual processing it has been proposed that color can act as an additional retrieval cue (Gegenfurtner & Rieger 2000; Wichmann et al 2002; Spence et al 2006).

Our results are consistent with Oliva and Schyns (2000) and Liebe et al (2009) suggestion. As perception of shapes, and particularly perception of detailed information conveyed by high spatial frequencies is degraded in AMD (Sjostrand & Friseu, 1977; Kleiner et al., 1988; Midena et al., 1997; Faubert & Overbury, 2000) people with AMD seem to rely more on color than normally sighted people for contour extraction and scene segmentation.

3. The effect of background on object recognition

As mentioned above some studies have examined object perception in people with low vision (e.g., Wurm et al, 1993; Ebert et al, 1986; Owsley & Sloane 1987) but with pictures of objects in isolation on a white background. Yet, objects in the world rarely appear without some background. Objects are always located within a setting and within other objects. Boucart et al (2008b) explored how low vision affects perception of objects in scenes. They compared performance for photographs of isolated objects and for the same objects in their natural environments in patients with AMD and age-matched normally sighted people. Photographs were presented for 300 ms each and observers were asked to press a key when they saw an animal or a face in separate sessions. The results showed that people with AMD were more accurate for isolated objects, or faces, than for the same objects, or faces, in their natural setting. Normally sighted people were equally accurate for the two versions of images but they were faster for objects in their natural setting than for isolated objects. This better performance for isolated objects in people with AMD was interpreted in terms of a higher sensitivity to crowding in people with central vision loss who must rely on their peripheral vision as the detrimental effect of crowding is more pronounced in peripheral vision (Bouma 1970, Leat el al 1999, Levi 2008; Pelli et al 2004).

We (Tran et al. 2011) explored further the nature of the impairment in discriminating a figure from its background in patients with AMD. Crowding has been suggested as a contributor to slow and difficult peripheral reading in previous studies on people with central vision loss. However, two studies (Chun et al. (2008) and Calabrese et al (2010)) in which line spacing was increased reported little benefit in patients with AMD, as long as line separation is approximately 1 to 1.25X the standard line separation. We examined whether introducing a space between an object and its background would reduce crowding, as it does in reading, and help figure/ground discrimination in people with low vision. To this aim we compared performance for detecting a target object in a photograph of a scene, for detecting a target object when it is isolated on a white background and for detecting a target object when it is separated from the background by a white space.

It has been reported that the magnitude of crowding is affected by the configural properties of the surrounding. For instance, Livne and Sagi (2007) found that crowding was reduced, and even disappeared, when the flankers of a target stimulus were arranged in a continuous complete circular configuration as compared to the same configuration without closure. Based on this finding we compared performance for a target object located in a structured background (a natural setting) versus for a target object located in a non-structured shapeless background. Studies on normally sighted young observers have shown that an object is more easily detected on a structured background that is consistent with the object (e.g., a toaster in a kitchen) than when the object is located on a non structured meaningless background (Biederman et al, 1972; Boyce et al 1989; Boyce & Pollatsek, 1992). If the background, appearing in peripheral vision, is processed efficiently in people with AMD then we expected a better performance for a target located on a structured background than for the same object in a noise background. We also examined whether exploration time facilitates object recognition and figure ground segregation in patients with central vision loss in manipulating the exposure time of the stimuli (300 ms versus 3000 ms).

The participants were 17 patients with a confirmed diagnosis of neovascular AMD and 17 normally sighted age-matched controls. The inclusion and exclusion criteria and the clinical and ophthalmologic examination are described in Tran et al (2011). Both patients and controls were tested monocularly on the eye with the best corrected visual acuity for patients and the preferred eye for controls.

The stimuli were colored photographs of natural scenes taken from a large commercial CD database (Corel) displayed on a light gray background. Half of the scenes contained an

animal (the target) and the other half contained no animal. At a viewing distance of 1 meter, the angular size of the pictures was 20° horizontally and 15° vertically. The original photographs (called "scene" condition) were manipulated with the software Adobe Photoshop CS (version 8.01) to generate three new versions of each image: one in which the target animal or a distractor object was extracted from the scene and presented at the same spatial location on a white background (called "isolated» condition), one in which the target or the distractor object was surrounded by a white rectangle in the scene (called "structured background"), and one in which the target or the distractor object was surrounded by a white rectangle and placed in a modified disorganized version of the original background (called "non structured background"). Examples are shown in Figure 6.
A black (5°) central fixation cross was displayed for 500 ms, followed by a blank interval of 500 ms, and followed by a centrally presented stimulus. A Go/Nogo paradigm was used. Participant were asked to press a key when they saw an animal and to refrain from responding when a non animal object was present. Responses were given on a box containing two keys connected to the computer. They were told that an animal would be present in 50% of the images. Participants were tested in two sessions separated by a pause of 10 minutes: one short exposure duration session in which each stimulus was displayed for 300 ms and one long exposure duration session in which the stimulus was displayed for 3000ms. Half of the participants in each group started with the short duration exposure and the other half started with the long duration exposure session. Each session was composed of 200 trials determined by 50 scenes (25 animals and 25 non animal objects).
The percentage of correct detections of the target is displayed in Figure 7. Performance was lower for patients with AMD than for controls at both exposure durations but, except for photographs of real world scenes at the short exposure time, target detection was highly above chance (> 70% correct) for patients. Patients with AMD detected more easily the target when it was separated from the background by a white rectangle or when it was isolated than when it was located in a scene. The background condition did not significantly affect performance in normally sighted controls whose performance was at ceiling. The number of errors (false alarms) was higher in the non structured background than in the structured background for people with AMD, but remained very low on average (maximum: 6.1%). Performance improved with the increase in exposure time for patients with AMD but remained lower than that of normally sighted controls. Correlations were found between visual acuity, lesion size, and sensitivity in all conditions and at both short and long exposure times. A more detailed description of the results can be found in Tran et al (2011).
In contrast to normally sighted people, patients with AMD benefited significantly from the separation of the target from its background as compared to objects in scenes. This was more pronounced when the exposure time did not allow exploration (300 ms) but the same tendency was present when exploration was possible (3000ms). This result replicates previous data (Boucart et al, 2008b) and extend them in showing that the target object does not have to be completely isolated on a white background. A white space surrounding the object is sufficient to improve its detection and to facilitate figure/ground discrimination. The detrimental effect of scene background (without white space surrounding the object) likely reflects impaired figure/ground segregation in patients with AMD. A higher sensitivity to crowding does not necessarily affect figure/ground segregation. Levi (2007) reported that people with amblyopia, who showed strong crowding, performed nearly normally in a figure/ground segregation task in which they had to discriminate the

Fig. 6. Example of the four background used in a categorization task in which participants were asked to detect and animal and ignore pictures without animals.

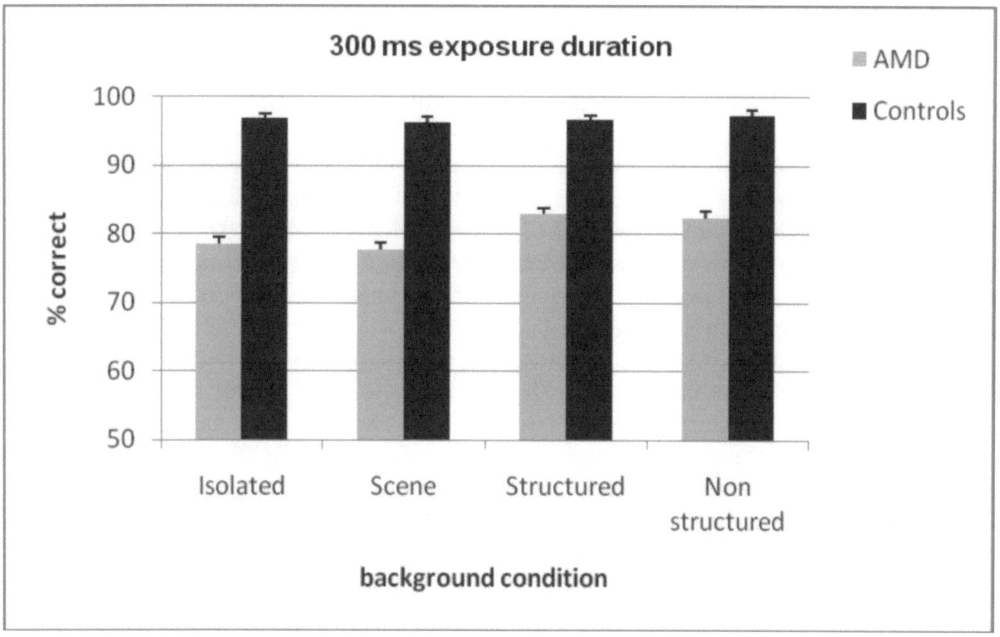

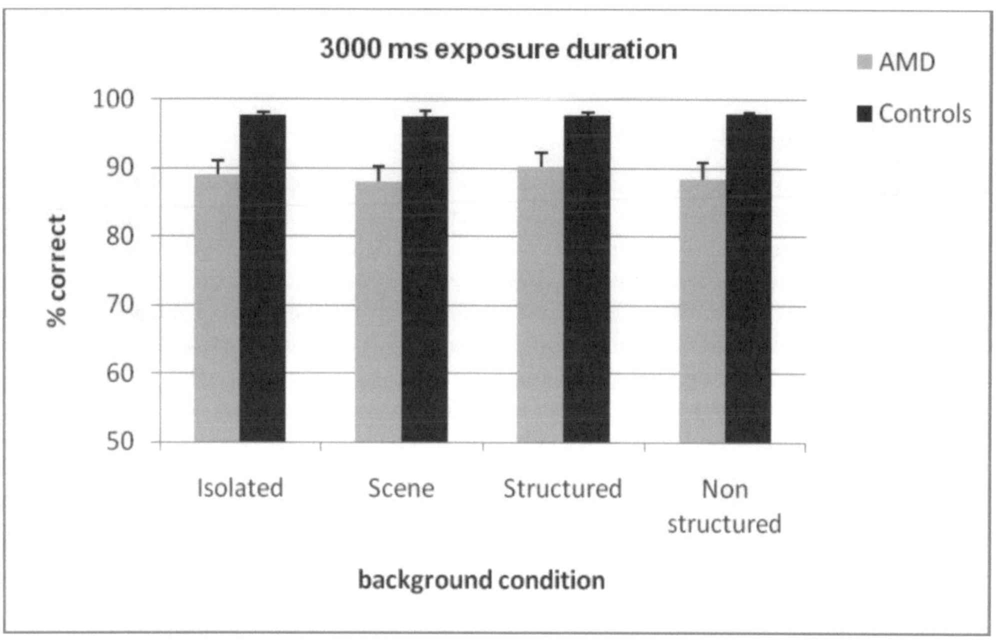

Fig. 7. Accuracy (hits and correct rejections) for the detection of a target animal in various background conditions as a function of exposure time for patients with AMD and age matched controls (adapted from Tran et al 2011).

orientation of a figure (an E made of horizontal gabor patches embedded in a variable number of distracters which were vertical gabor patches).
The visual system arranges the elements of a visual scene into coherent objects and background. Objects are formed by grouping elements and by segregating them from surrounding elements. For something to be identified and represented as a figure its contours need to be identified. Therefore figure/ground segregation is associated with efficient perception of contours which do not have to be physically present. Indeed, brain imaging studies show that the lateral occipital cortex (LOC) responds to real contours and to illusory contours with a similar level of activation (Mendola et al 1999, Stanley & Rubin 2003). The neural mechanisms underlying figure/ground segregation are still unclear. The traditional view is that low level areas (e.g., the primary visual cortex) extract simple features and that the binding of these features into objects occurs at higher level areas (i.e., in the LOC). In monkeys response modulations related to figure/ground segregation are observed in the primary visual cortex but in the late part of the stimulus response (contextual modulation starts approximately 80 ms after stimulus onset whilst in the primary visual cortex the classical response starts about 30 ms after stimulus onset; Supèr & Lamme 2007). For other authors figure/ground segregation involves higher level processes in which an object has to be identified (i.e., access its representation in memory) to be identified as figure. Peterson et al (1991; Peterson & Gibson 1994) showed that changing the orientation of the figure (from upright to upside down) changes the quickness with which figure/ground segregation can be accomplished suggesting contributions to figure assignment from memories of object structure. Other behavioral and neuroimaging studies need to be conducted to understand the level of processing impaired in figure/ground segregation in people with AMD (contour perception, binding processes, impaired structural representations ....).

4. Conclusion and future research

As reading and face perception are the most common clinical complaints of patients with AMD seeking visual rehabilitation few investigations have been conducted on how these people perceive objects and scenes. We have reported a series of studies showing that people with central visual field loss are able to categorize scenes and objects embedded in scenes with high accuracy. Though scene categorization on the basis of global properties (e.g., natural or urban) and detection of an animal in a scene do not reflect common daily activities, the results may be considered for adaptation of the environment of people with low vision, in order to improve their object recognition capacity. Indeed, our results indicate that contrast enhancement (Tran et al submitted), colour (Boucart et al 2008b) and the introduction of a white space between the picture of an object and its surrounding (Tran et al 2011) improve performance in patients with macular degeneration, even at a duration allowing a single fixation. The studies presented in this chapter are only the beginning of investigations on the perception of natural environments in people with low vision in general, and in people with macular degeneration in particular. A lot of questions remain to be investigated like, for instance, what are the mechanisms underlying impaired recognition of an object in a scene by people with AMD: figure/ground segregation, the association of an object to its proper context, object identification? What level of representation is impaired in the ventral stream? Would the deficit be stronger in a task requiring recognition rather than detection or categorization? Are spatial representations impaired in people with central vision loss? Answers to these questions will require both behavioral and brain imaging studies. Studies of functional cortical remapping in people with maculopathy have produced inconsistent results with some works (Nguyen et al 2004; Sunnes et al 2004) reporting a lack of reorganization and others (Baker et al. 2005; Schumacher et al 2008) reporting a functional reorganization. Alterations of visual stimulation may also result in modifications of the cortical structure (Johansson, 2004; Merzenich et al., 1984). Indeed, there is evidence that developmental visual disorders such as amblyopia (Mendola et al., 2005) and albinism (von dem Hagen et al., 2005) affect the structure of the human occipital cortex. A reduced size of the lateral geniculate nuclei has been reported in patients with glaucoma (Gupta et al. 2009) and reduction in grey matter density was found in the retinal lesion projection zones of the visual cortex in patient with age-related macular degeneration (Boucard et al. 2009).

As the proportion of individuals over the age of 65 increases, institutions serving the housing needs of people with degenerative diseases are becoming more numerous. Research on how people with central vision loss perceive objects and scenes can serve as the basis for developing new strategies for adapting the physical environment in which individuals with impaired spatial vision live and interact.

5. Acknowledgements

Parts of the chapter refers to articles published in Investigative Ophthalmology and Vision Science. The authors are grateful to ARVO for permission to use the reprinted material.

6. References

Age-Related Eye Disease Study Research Group. (2001a) A randomized, placebo-controlled, clinical trial of high-dose supplementation with vitamins C and E, beta carotene, and zinc for age related macular degeneration and vision loss: AREDS report no. 8. Arch Ophthalmol, 119, 1417-1436.

Alexander, M.F., Maguire, M.G., Lietman, T.M., Snyder, J.R., Elman, M.J. & Fine, S.L. (1988) Assessment of visual function in patients with age-related macular degeneration and low visual acuity. *Arch Ophthalmol,* 106, 1543-1547.

Baker CI, Peli E, Knouk N & Kanwisher N (2005) Reorganization of visual processing in macular degeneration. The Journal of Neuroscience, 25(3), 614-618.

Biederman I. (1972) Perceiving real-word scenes. Science.;177 :77-80.

Biederman I, Ju G. (1988) Surface versus edge-based determinants of visual recognition. Cogn Psychol; 20:38–64.

Bird, A.C., Bressler, N.M., Bressler, S.B., Chisholm, I.H., Coscas, G., Davis, M.D., de Jong, P.T., Klaver, C.C., Klein, B.E., Klein, R. & et al. (1995) An international classification and grading system for age-related maculopathy and age-related macular degeneration. The International ARM Epidemiological Study Group. Surv Ophthalmol, 39, 367-374.

Boucard CC, Hernowo AT, Maguire RP, Jansonius NM, Roerdink JB, Hooymans JM, Cornelissen FW. (2009) Changes in cortical grey matter density associated with long-standing retinal visual field defects. Brain. 132(Pt 7):1898-906.

Boucart M, Dinon JF, Despretz P, Desmettre T, Hladiuk K, & Oliva A. (2008a) Recognition of facial emotion in age related macular degeneration (AMD): a flexible usage of facial features. Visual Neuroscience, 25(4):603-9.

Boucart M, Despretz P, Hladiuk K, & Desmettre T (2008b) Does context or color improve object recognition in patients with macular degeneration? Visual Neuroscience, 25, 685-91.

Bouma H. (1970) Interaction effects in parafoveal letter recognition. Nature ;226(5241):177-8.

Boyce SJ, Pollatsek A, Rayner K. (1989) Effect of background information on object identification. J Exp Psychol Hum Percept Perform. 15(3):556-66.

Boyce SJ, Pollatsek A.(1992) Identification of objects in scenes: the role of scene background in object naming. J Exp Psychol Learn Mem Cogn. 18(3):531-43.

Bullimore, MA, Bailey, IL, & Wacker, RT (1991) Face recognition in age-related maculopathy. Invest Ophtalmol Vis Sci., 32, 2020-29.

Brody, B. L., A. C. Gamst, et al. (2001) Depression, visual acuity, comorbidity, and disability associated with age-related macular degeneration. Ophthalmology 108(10): 1893-900; discussion 1900-1.

Cahill MT, Banks AD, Stinnett SS, Toth CA (2005): Vision-related quality of life in patients with bilateral severe age-related macular degeneration. Ophthalmology;112:152-158.

Calabrèse A, Bernard JB, Hoffart L, Faure G, Barouch F, Conrath J, Castet E (2010) Small effect of interline spacing on maximal reading speed in low-vision patients with central field loss irrespective of scotoma size. Invest Ophthalmol Vis Sci. 51(2):1247-54

Chung, S.T., Mansfield, J.S., & Legge, G.E. (1998). Psychophysics of reading. XVIII. The effect of print size on reading speed in normal peripheral vision. Vision Res, 38 (19), 2949-2962.

Crossland, M.D., Sims, M., Galbraith, R.F., & Rubin, G.S. (2004). Evaluation of a new quantitative technique to assess the number and extent of preferred retinal loci in macular disease. Vision Res, 44 (13), 1537-1546.

Crossland, M.D., Culham, L.E., Kabanarou, S.A., & Rubin, G.S. (2005). Preferred retinal locus development in patients with macular disease. Ophthalmology, 112 (9), 1579-1585.

Cheung, S.H. & Legge, G.E. (2005). Functional and cortical adaptations to central vision loss. Visual Neuroscience 22, 187–201.

Chung ST, Jarvis SH, Woo SY, Hanson K, Jose RT. (2008) Reading speed does not benefit from increased line spacing in AMD patients. Optom Vis Sci. 85(9):827-33

Curcio CA, Kimberley AA, Sloan KR, Lerea CL, Hurley JB, Klkock IB, (1991) et al. Distribution and morphology of human cone photoreceptors stained with anti-blue opsin. J Comp Neurol 312:610–624.

Curcio CA, Medeiros NE & Millican CL (1996) Photoreceptor loss in age related macular degeneration. Invest Ophthalmol Vis Sci. , 37, 1236-49.

Curcio CA, Owsley C & Jackson GR (2000) Spare the rods, save the cones in aging and age related maculopathy. Invest Ophthamol Vis Sci. , 41(8), 2015-18.

Delorme A, Richard G & Fabre-Thorpe M (2000) Ultra-rapid categorization of natural scenes does not rely on color cues: a study in monkeys and humans. Vis Res, 40, 2187-2200.

Ebert EM, Fine AM, Markowitz J, et al. (1986) Functional vision in patients with neovascular maculopathy and poor visual acuity. Arch Ophthalmol.;104(7):1009-12.

Ergun E, Maar N, Radner W, et al. Scotoma size and reading speed in patients with subfoveal occult choroidal neovascularization in age-related macular degeneration. Ophthalmology. 2003;110(1):65-9.

Faubert, J., & Overbury, O. (2000) Binocular vision in older people with adventious visual impairment: Sometimes one eye is better than two. JAGS, Vol 48, N°. 4, 375-380.

Fei-Fei, L., Iyer, A., Koch, C., & Perona, P. (2007). What do we perceive in a glance of a real-world scene? Journal of Vision, 7(1), 1-29.

Felisbert FM, Solomon JA, Morgan MJ. (2005) The role of target salience in crowding. Perception.;34(7):823-33.

Ferris, F.L., 3rd, Fine, S.L. & Hyman, L. (1984) Age-related macular degeneration and blindness due to neovascular maculopathy. Arch Ophthalmol, 102, 1640-1642.

Fine I, MacLeod DI, & Boynton GM (2003) Surface segmentation based on the luminance and color statistics of natural scenes. J of the Optical Soc of America, 20, 1283-91.

Gegenfurtner KR, Rieger J. (2000) Sensory and cognitive contributions of color to the recognition of natural scenes. Curr Biol; 10:805–808.

Greene, M. R. and A. Oliva (2009a). Recognition of natural scenes from global properties: seeing the forest without representing the trees. Cogn Psychol 58(2): 137-76.

Greene MR, Oliva A. Recognition of natural scenes from global properties: seeing the forest without representing the trees. Cogn Psychol. 2009b;58(2):137-76.

Gupta N, Greenberg G, de Tilly LN, Gray B, Polemidiotis M, Yücel YH. (2009) Atrophy of the lateral geniculate nucleus in human glaucoma detected by magnetic resonance imaging. Br J Ophthalmol.;93:56–60.

Hansen T & Gegenfurtner KR (2006) Higher level chromatic mechanisms for image segmentation. Journal of Vision, 6(3) 239-59.

Hart, P.M., Chakravarthy, U., Stevenson, M.R. & Jamison, J.Q. (1999). A vision specific functional index for use in patients with age related macular degeneration. British Journal of Ophthalmology 83, 1115–1120.

Hassan, S.E., Lovie-Kitchin, J.E. & Woods, R.L. (2002). Vision and mobility performance of subjects with age-related macular egeneration. Optometry and Vision Science 79, 697–707.

Hogervorst MA & van Damme WJM (2008) Visualizing the Limits of Low Vision in Detecting Natural Image Features. Optometry and Vision Science, 85(10), E951–E962

Holzschuch, C., Mourey, F. & Manie`re, D. (2002). Geriatrie et basse vision: Pratiques interdisciplinaires. Paris, Edition Masson.

Jackson GR, Owsley C, Curcio CA (2002) Photoreceptor degeneration and dysfunction in aging and age-related maculopathy. Ageing Res Rev. 1(3):381-96.

Johansson BB. (2004) Brain plasticity in health and disease. Keio J Med.;53:231–46.

Joubert OR, Fize D, Rousselet GA, Fabre-Thorpe M. (2007) Early interference of context congruence on object processing in rapid visual categorization of natural scenes. J Vis.;8(13):11 1-8.

Klaver, C.C., Wolfs, R.C., Vingerling, J.R., Hofman, A. & de Jong, P.T. (1998) Age-specific prevalence and causes of blindness and visual impairment in an older population: the Rotterdam Study. Arch Ophthalmol, 116, 653-658.

Klein, R., Klein, B.E. & Linton, K.L. (1992) Prevalence of age-related maculopathy. The Beaver Dam Eye Study. Ophthalmology, 99, 933-943.

Klein, R., Klein, B.E., Jensen, S.C. & Meuer, S.M. (1997) The five-year incidence and progression of age-related maculopathy: the Beaver Dam Eye Study. Ophthalmology, 104, 7-21.

Klein, R. (2007) Overview of progress in the epidemiology of age-related macular degeneration. Ophthalmic Epidemiol, 14, 184-187.

Kleiner, R. C., Enger, C., Alexander, M. E., & Fine, S. L. Contrast sensitivity in age-related macular degeneration. Arch Ophtalmol, 1988, Vol 106, N°. 1, 55-57.

Larson AM, Loschky LC. The contributions of central versus peripheral vision to scene gist recognition. J Vis. 2009;9(10):6 1-16.

Leat SJ, Li W, Epp K. (1999) Crowding in central and eccentric vision: the effects of contour interaction and attention. Invest Ophthalmol Vis Sci.;40(2):504-12.

Legge, G.E., Rubin, G.S., Pelli, D.G., & Schleske, M.M. (1985). Psychophysics of reading--II. Low vision. Vision Res, 25 (2), 253-265.

Legge, GE, Ross, JA, Isenberg, LM, & LaMay, JM (1992) Psychophysics of reading.XII. Clinical predictors of low vision reading speed. Invest Ophtalmol Vis Sci., 33, 677-87.

Levi DM. (2007) Image segregation in strabismic amblyopia. Vision Res. 2007;47(13):1833-8.

Levi DM. (2008) Crowding--an essential bottleneck for object recognition: a mini-review. Vision Res. ;48(5):635-54.

Liebe S, Fischer E, Logothetis NK & Rainer G (2009) Color and shape interactions in the recognition of natural scenes by human and monkey observers Journal of Vision, 9(5) :14, 1-16

Lindblad, A.S., Lloyd, P.C., Clemons, T.E., Gensler, G.R., Ferris, F.L., 3rd, Klein, M.L. & Armstrong, J.R. (2009) Change in area of geographic atrophy in the Age-Related Eye Disease Study: AREDS report number 26. Arch Ophthalmol, 127, 1168-1174.

Livne T, Sagi D. Configuration influence on crowding. J Vis. 2007;7(2):4 1-12.

Makela, P., Nasanen, R., Rovamo, J., & Melmoth, D. (2001) identification of facial images in peripheral vision. Vision Research, 41, 599-610.

Mangione, CM Gutierrez PR., Lowe, G, Orav EJ & Seddon JM. (1999) Influence of age-related Maculopathy on visual functioning and health-related quality of life. Am J Ophthalmol 128: 45-53.

Mangione CM, Lee PP, Gutierrez PR, Spritzer K, Berry S, Hays RD (2001) Development of the 25-item National Eye Institute Visual Function Questionnaire. Arch Ophthalmol;119:1050-1058.

Mendola JD, Dale AM, Fischl B, et al. (1999) The representation of illusory and real contours in human cortical visual areas revealed by functional magnetic resonance imaging. J Neurosci.;19(19):8560-72.

Merzenich MM, Nelson RJ, Stryker MP, Cynader MS, Schoppmann A, Zook JM. Somatosensory cortical map changes following digit amputation in adult monkeys. J Comp Neurol. 1984;224:591–605.

Midena, E., Degli Angeli, C., Blarzino, M. C., Valenti, M., & Segato, T (1997) Macular function impairment in eyes with early age-related macular degeneration. Invest Ophtalmol Vis Sci, Vol 38, N°. 2, 469-477.

Näsänen R, O'Leary C. (1998) Recognition of band-pass filtered hand-written numerals in foveal and peripheral vision. Vision Res. 38(23):3691-701.

Naïli F., Despretz P & Boucart M. (2006) Color recognition at large visual eccentricities in normal observers and patients with low vision Neuroreport, 17, 1571-74.

Newton JR, Eskew RT Jr. (2003) Chromatic detection and discrimination in the periphery: a postreceptoral loss of color sensitivity. Vis Neurosci. ;20(5):511-21.

Nguyen TH, Stievenart JL, Saucet JC, Le Gargasson JF, Cohen YS, Pelegrini-Issac M, Burnod Y, Iba-Zizen MT, Cabanis EA. (2004) Cortical response in age-related macular degeneration (part I). Methodology and subject specificities. J Fr Ophtalmol. 27(9 Pt 2):3S65-71.

Oliva, A. (2005). Gist of the scene. In the Encyclopedia of Neurobiology of Attention. L. Itti, G. Rees, and J.K. Tsotsos (Eds.), Elsevier, San Diego, CA (pages 251-256)

Oliva A, Schyns P. (2000)Diagnostic colors mediate scene recognition. Cognitive Psychology.;41:176-210.

Oliva A, Torralba A. (2001) Modeling the shape of the scence: A holistic representation of the spatial enveloppe. International of Computer Vision.;42:145-75

Owsley, C & Sloane, ME (1987) Contrast sensitivity, acuity, and the perception of « real-world » targets. Britisch Journal of Ophtalmology, 71, 791-96.

Ostergaard AL, Davidoff JB. (1985) Some effects of color on naming and recognition of objects. J Exp Psychol Learn Mem Cogn ; 11:579–587.

Owsley C, Jackson GR, Cidecyyan AV et al. (2000) Psychophysical evidence for rods vulnerability in age related macular degeneration. INVEST OPHTHALMOL VIS SCI. , 41, 267-73.

Peli, E., Goldstein, R.B., Young, G.M., Trempe, C.L. & Buzney, S.M. (1991). Image enhancement for the visually impaired. Invest Ophthalmol Vis sci. 32, 337–2351.

Pelli DG, Palomares M, Majaj NJ. (2004) Crowding is unlike ordinary masking: distinguishing feature integration from detection. J Vis.;4(12):1136-69.

Pelli DG (2008) Crowding: a cortical constraint on object recognition. Current Opinion in Neurobiology, 18, 445-451.

Peterson MA, Harvey EM, Weidenbacher HJ. . (1991) Shape recognition contributions to figure-ground reversal: which route counts? J Exp Psychol Hum Percept Perform.17(4):1075-89.

Peterson MA, Gibson BS. (1994) Object recognition contributions to figure-ground organization: operations on outlines and subjective contours. Percept Psychophys.;56(5):551-64.

Price CJ, Humphreys GW. (1989) The effects of surface detail on object categorization and naming. Q J Exp Psychol A; 41:797–827.

Righart R, de Gelder B. (2006) Context influences early perceptual analysis of faces--an electrophysiological study.Cereb Cortex 16(9):1249-57.

Rossion B, Pourtois G. (2004) Revisiting Snodgrass and Vanderwart's object pictorial set: the role of surface detail in basic-level object recognition. Perception; 33:217–236.

Saarinen, J., Rovamo, J., & Virsu, V. (1987) Texture discrimination at different eccentricities. Investigative Ophtalmology and Vision Science, 30, 293-296.

Sakurai M, Ayama M, Kumagai T. (2003) Color appearance in the entire visual field: color zone map based on the unique hue component. J Opt Soc Am A Opt Image Sci Vis; 20:1997–2009.

Sarks, J.P., Sarks, S.H. & Killingsworth, M.C. (1988) Evolution of geographic atrophy of the retinal pigment epithelium. Eye (Lond), 2 (Pt 5), 552-577.

Schumacher EH, Jacko JA, Primo SA, Main KL, Moloney KP, Kinzel EN, Ginn J. (2008) Reorganization of visual processing is related to eccentric viewing in patients with macular degeneration. Restor Neurol Neurosci.;26(4-5):391-402.

Spence I, Wong P, Rusan M, & Rastegar N (2006) How color enhances visual memory for natural scenes. Psychological Science, 17, 1-6.

Strasburger, H., Harvey, L.O., & Rentschler, I. (1991) Contrast threshold for identification of numeric characters in direct and eccentric view. Perception & Psychophysics, 49, 495-508.

Stanley DA, Rubin N. (2003) fMRI activation in response to illusory contours and salient regions in the human lateral occipital complex. Neuron.;37(2):323-31.

Sjostrand, J., & Friseu, L. (1977) Contrast sensitivity in macular report. A preliminary report. Acta Ophtalmol (copenh), , Vol 55, N°. 3, 507-514.

Sunnes JS, Liu T & Yantis S (2004). Retinotopic mapping of the visual cortex using functional magnetic resonance imaging in a patient with central scotomas from atrophic macular degeneration. Ophtalmology, 111, 1595-98.

Supèr H, Lamme VA. (2007) Altered figure-ground perception in monkeys with an extra-striate lesion. Neuropsychologia. 45(14):3329-34.

Tanaka JW, Presnell LM. (1999) Color diagnosticity in object recognition. Percept Psychophysiol; 61:1140–1153.

Tejeria, L., Harper, R.A., Artes, P.H. & Dickinson, C.M. (2002). Face recognition in age related macular degeneration: Perceived disability, measured disability, and performance with a bioptic device. British Journal of Ophthalmology 86, 1019–1026.

Therriault DJ, Yaxley RH & Zwaan RA (2009) The role of color diagnosticity in object recognition and representation. Cogn Process, 10(4) : 335-42.

Thompson B, Hansen BC, Hess RF, Troje NF. (2007) Peripheral vision: good for biological motion, bad for signal noise segregation? J Vis.7(10):12.1-7.

Torralba, A., & Oliva, A. (2002). Depth estimation from image structure. IEEE Pattern Analysis and Machine Intelligence, 24,1226-1238.

Torralba A, Oliva A. Statistics of natural image categories. Network: Computational in Neural Systems. 2003;14(3):391-412.

Tran THC, Guyader N , Guerin A, Despretz P, & Boucart M (2011) Figure/ground discrimination in age related macular degeneration. Invest Ophthalmol Vis Sci. 2010 Nov 18.

Tran THC, Rambaud C, Despretz P, & Boucart M (2011) Scene perception in age-related macular degeneration. Invest Ophthalmol Vis Sci. 2010 Dec;51(12):6868-74.

Vogel, J., & Schiele, B. (2007). Semantic scene modeling and retrieval for content-based image retrieval. International Journal of Computer Vision, 72(2), 133–157.

von dem Hagen EA, Houston GC, Hoffmann MB, Jeffery G, Morland AB. (2005) Retinal abnormalities in human albinism translate into a reduction of grey matter in the occipital cortex. Eur J Neurosci.;22:2475–80.

Wang YZ, Wilson E, Locke KG, & Edwards AO (2002) Shape discrimination in age-related macular degeneration. Invest Ophthalmol Vis Sci., 43(6), 2055-62.

Wichmann FA, Sharpe LT, & Gegenfurtner KR (2002) the contribution of color to recognition memory for natural scenes. Journal of Experimental Psychology: Learning, Memory & Cognition, 28, 509-20.

Wood JM, Lacherez PF, Black AA, Cole MH, Boon MY, Kerr GK. (2009) Postural stability and gait among older adults with age-related maculopathy. Invest Ophthalmol Vis Sci.;50(1):482-7

Wurm LH, Legge GE, Isenberg LI, Luebker A. (1993) Color improves object recognition in normal and low vision. J Exp Psychol Hum Percept Perform; 19:899–911.

Part 2

Object Recognition Techniques in 2-D Domain

5

Chord Context Algorithm for Shape Feature Extraction

Yang Mingqiang[1], Kpalma Kidiyo[2] and Ronsin Joseph[2]
[1]ISE, Shandong University, 250100, Jinan
[2]Université Européenne de Bretagne,
France - INSA, IETR, UMR 6164, F-35708 RENNES
[1]China
[2]France

1. Introduction

The emergence of new technologies makes it easy to generate information in visual forms, leading everyday to an increasing number of generated digital images. At the same time, the rapid advances in imaging technologies and the widespread availability of Internet access motivate data browsing into these data bases. For image description and retrieval, manual annotation of these images becomes impractical and inefficient. Image retrieval is based on observation of an ordering of match scores obtained by searching through a database. The key challenges in building a retrieval system are the choice of attributes, their representations, query specification methods, match metrics and indexing strategies.

A large number of retrieval methods using shape descriptors has been described in literature. Compared to other features, for example, color or texture, object shape is unique. It enables us to recognize an object without further information. However, since shapes are 2D images that are projections of 3D objects, the silhouettes may change from one viewpoint to another with respect to objects and non-rigid object motion (e.g., walking people or flying bird) and segmentation errors caused by lighting variations, partial occultation, scaling, boundary distortion and corruption by noise are unavoidable. As we know, while computers can easily distinguish slight differences between similar objects, it is very difficult to estimate the similarity between two objects as perceived by human beings, even when considering very simple objects. This is because human perception is not a mere interpretation of a retinal patch, but an active interaction between the retinal patch and a representation of our knowledge about objects. Thus the problem is complicated by the fact that a shape does not have a mathematical definition that exactly matches what the user feels as a shape. Solutions proposed in the literature use various approaches and emphasize different aspects of the problem. The choice of a particular representation scheme is usually driven by the need to cope with requirements such as robustness against noise, stability with respect to minor distortions, and invariance to common geometrical transforms or tolerance to occultation, etc. For general shape representation, a recent review is given in [1] [2].

In this chapter, a shape descriptor based on chord context is proposed. The basic idea of chord context is to observe the lengths of all parallel and equidistant chords in a shape, and to build their histogram in each direction. The sequence of vector features extracted forms the feature matrix for a shape descriptor. Because all the viewpoint directions, considered with a certain angle interval, are chosen to produce the chord length histogram, this representation is unlike conventional shape representation schemes, where a shape descriptor has to correspond to key points such as maxima of curvature or inflection points, for example, Smooth Curve Decomposition [3], Convex Hull [4], Triangle-area representation (TAR) [5] and Curvature Scale Space (CSS) [6][7] etc. The proposed method needs no special landmarks or key points. There is also no need for certain axes of a shape. The proposed descriptor scheme is able to capture the internal details, specifically holes, in addition to capturing the external boundary details. A similarity measure is defined over chord context according to its characteristics and it confirms efficiency for shape retrieval from a database. This method is shown to be invariant under image transformations, rotations, scaling and robust to non-rigid deformations, occultation and boundary perturbations by noise thus it is well-adapted to shape description and retrieval. In addition, the size of the descriptor attribute is not very great; it has low-computational complexity compared to other similar methods.

2. Chord context

This section details the proposed method, chord context, for extracting attributes from the contour or silhouette of a shape. It then proposes a method of measuring similarities between two shapes.

2.1 Feature extraction

Chord context analysis corresponds to finding the distribution of all chord lengths in different directions in a given shape. For discrete binary image data, we consider each object point as one and the background as zero. In the shape recognition field, it is common to consider the case where the general function $f(x, y)$ is

$$f(x,y)=\begin{cases}1 & \text{if } f(x,y)\in D\\ 0 & otherwise,\end{cases}$$

where D is the domain of the binary shape.

In each direction, we can find all the chords in the shape. Fig. 1 shows an example of chords in direction θ.

A set of lines $T(\rho,\theta)$ is defined by

$$\rho = x\cos(\theta-\pi/2)+y\sin(\theta-\pi/2),\ \theta\in[0,\ \pi], \text{ and } \rho\in(-\infty,\ \infty).$$

The chords are defined by the parts of these lines within the domain of the binary shape. So a shape can be represented by a discrete set of chords sampled from its silhouette. Considering different angles θ, the number and length of chords obtained in different directions may not be the same, except in the case of a circle. One way to capture this information is to use the distribution of chord lengths in the same direction in a spatial histogram.

Concretely, let us assume that the set of chords in directions θ_i are represented by $C=\{c_{i,n} \mid n\in[1,N_i]\}$, where N_i is the number of the chords in direction θ_i. Let $L(c_{i,n})$ be the length of chord $c_{i,n}$. So we can compute a histogram h_i in direction θ_i by

$$h_i^l = \#\{L(c_{i,n}) \in bin(l)\} \quad l \in [1, L_{i,\max}] \tag{1}$$

where $L_{i,max}$ is the longest chord in direction θ_i.

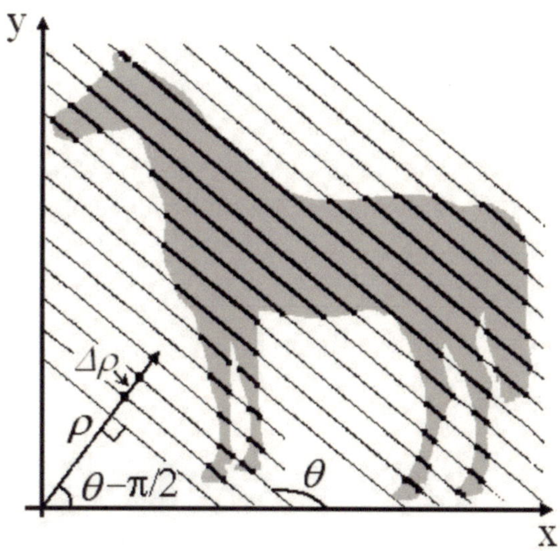

Fig. 1. Representation of chords in direction θ with the interval $\Delta\rho$. The bold lines are the chords of the shape.

In order to capture the details of a shape, the interval $\Delta\rho$ of ρ, i.e. the distance between two parallel chords, should not be great. In practice, $\Delta\rho = L_{max}/(50\sim100)$, where L_{max} is the length of the longest axis of the shape. The histogram h_i of Fig. 1 in direction θ_i is shown in Fig. 2.

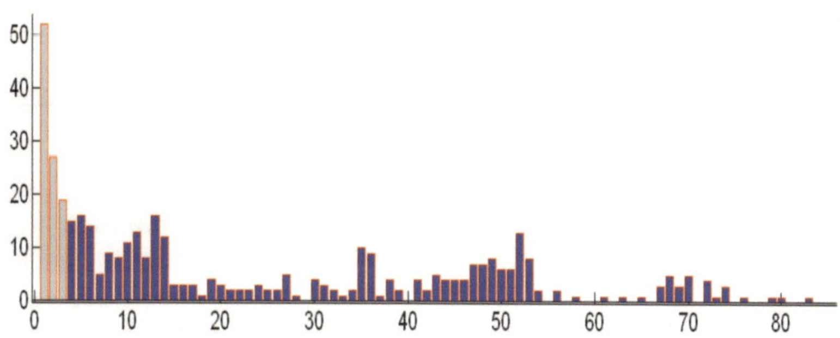

Fig. 2. Histogram of chord lengths in direction θ_i for the shape shown in Fig. 1

An excessive number of too short chords is counted when line T is close to a tangent along the edge of the shape (see Fig. 3). This is because a scraggy edge is produced by the minor disturbances resulting from digitization noise or normalization of the image to a certain size. In fact, these uncertain short chords are harmful to our shape descriptor, so we remove these too short chords directly: this could be seen as a low-pass filtering of the shape contour. Empirical tests show that, if we normalize a shape in an image with 128×128 pixels, i.e. the largest size of the shape is 128 pixels, and the shorter size transforms in proportion, then we can consider the set of chords whose length is shorter than 4 to be too short chords. So they should be discarded. In Fig. 2, the first 3 bins, plotted in gray, should be removed.

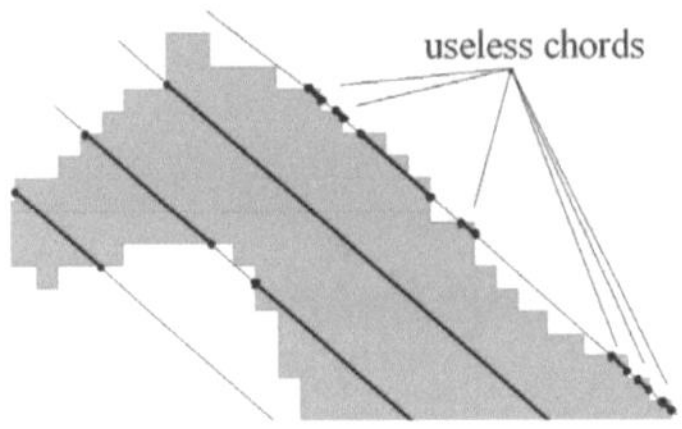

Fig. 3. Illustration of producing very short chords

With θ increasing from 0 to 179 degrees, all the chords in different directions in the silhouette can be recorded. If we divide the orientation range [0, 179] into D', then we can obtain D' histograms h_i, $i \in [0, D'-1]$. They can form a matrix M arranged by a set of histograms with column vector h_i according to the order of angles:

$$M = [\mathbf{h}_0, \mathbf{h}_1, \cdots \mathbf{h}_{D'-1}]$$

The matrix M of Fig. 1 is shown in Fig. 4.

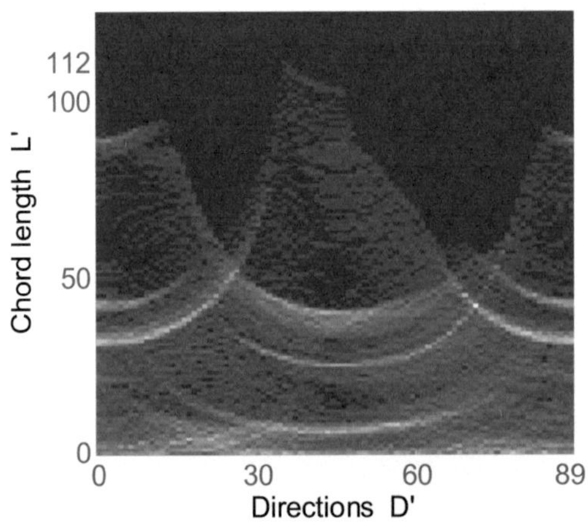

Fig. 4. The matrix M of the shape in Fig. 1 with all orientations.

The matrix element is the number of equal-length chords whose direction and length are given by the value of abscissa and y-axis, respectively. The abscissa is the orientation angle θ, and the y-axis is the length of the chords. The value in each row of the matrix M is the number of the chords with same length in different directions; and each column is the chord length histogram in the same direction.

Due to its very great size, it is unreasonable to use this matrix directly as a shape attribute. For example, in an image with 128×128 pixels, the longest possible chord in the shape is $128 \times \sqrt{2} \approx 181$. So, if D'=90, the size of the matrix will be 181×90=16290. Clearly, it is not appropriate as a direct feature of a shape.

In order to reduce the size of the matrix M and, at the same time, make the extracted feature invariant to scale transforms, we normalize this matrix M as follows:

First, find the maximum of non-zero bin L' for all the histograms in the matrix M. In Fig. 4 for example, L'_{max}=112. Then remove all the bins that are greater than L'_{max}, and form a matrix M' with dimension $L'_{max} \times D'$:

$$M' = [\mathbf{h}'_0, \mathbf{h}'_1, \cdots \mathbf{h}'_{D'-1}]$$

And then, for the next normalization, we expand the matrix M' to matrix M'', using a wrap-around effect, so that to eliminate border effects:

$$M'' = [\mathbf{h}'_{D'-2}, \mathbf{h}'_{D'-1}, \mathbf{h}'_0, \mathbf{h}'_1, \cdots \mathbf{h}'_{D'-1}, \mathbf{h}'_0, \mathbf{h}'_1]$$

Finally, the matrix M'' is subsampled down to a new matrix F with the dimension $L \times D$, after a 4×4 bicubic interpolation algorithm. For convenience, D is even. The bicubic interpolation algorithm means that the interpolated surface is continuous everywhere and also continuous in the first derivative in all directions. Thus, the rate of change in the value is continuous. Each value of matrix F contains a synthesis of its 4×4 neighbouring point values. The feature matrix F can be represented by:

$$F = [\mathbf{f}_0, \mathbf{f}_1, \cdots \mathbf{f}_{D-1}]$$

where $\mathbf{f}_i$, $i \in [0, D-1]$, is a L dimensions column vector given by $\mathbf{f}_i = [f_{i,0}, f_{i,1}, \cdots f_{i,L-1}]^T$.

The feature matrix F is the attribute of a shape. We call this feature matrix F of a shape the "chord context" descriptor.

For L=30 and D=36, the chord context of Fig. 1 is shown in Fig. 5.

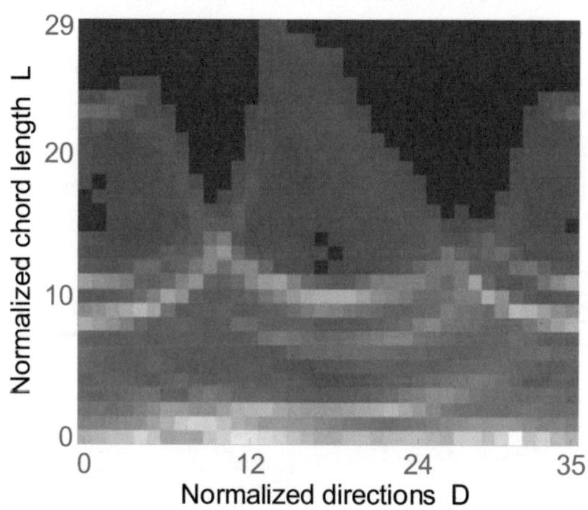

Fig. 5. Chord context of Fig. 1 with 30 rows and 36 columns.

The experiment in section 3 shows that chord context as the feature of a shape can retain the visual invariance to some extent.

2.2 Similarity measure

In determining the correspondence between shapes, we aim to meet the distance between two feature matrices. Such matching combines two criteria: one is the calculation of the minimum value of the distances between histograms of two feature matrices, *e.i.* the *Character Matrix Distance (CMD)*, and the other is a comparison of the *Perpendicular Chord Length Eccentricity (PCLE)*.

In the first criterion, we calculate all the distances between the query feature matrix and the model feature matrix while shifting its histograms one by one. Similar shapes have similar histograms in a same direction, and the rearranged order of these histograms is also similar. To calculate the distance between two attributes of shapes, we first calculate the distance between each corresponding histogram, according to their arrangement orders, and, then calculate the sum of all these distance values. Regarding rotation invariance, we shift the model feature matrix by one histogram, i.e. change the direction used to obtain the histograms, and repeat the same step to calculate the sum of all the values of these distances between the two feature matrices.

We assume that the query feature matrix is F_Q and the model feature matrix is F_M. F_Q and F_M are given by

$$F_q = [\mathbf{fq_0}, \mathbf{fq_1}, \cdots \mathbf{fq_{D-1}}] \text{ and } F_m = [\mathbf{fm_0}, \mathbf{fm_1}, \cdots \mathbf{fm_{D-1}}]$$

According to subsection 2.1, $f\alpha_i$, where α is q or m, $i \in [0, D-1]$, is an L dimensions column vector $\mathbf{f\alpha_i} = [f\alpha_{i,0}, f\alpha_{i,1}, \cdots f\alpha_{i,L-1}]^T$.

So the set of similarity distance is given by

$$DistF_{F_q,F_m}(n) = \sum_{i=0}^{D-1} DistH(\mathbf{fq_i}, \mathbf{fm_j}), \; j = \text{mod}(i+n, D) \tag{2}$$

where $n \in [0, D-1]$ is the number of shifts applied to each histogram in the model feature matrix. The formula shows that the set of similarity distances is the sum of the distances *DistH* between the two corresponding normalized histograms in two feature matrices.

To quantify the similarity between two histograms, there are many methods being reported: Minkowski-form, Kullback-Leibler Divergence, Jeffrey Divergence, Quadratic-form, Earth Mover's Distance, χ^2 statistics, Hausdorff distance, etc. Because of the properties of the chord context histogram:

- they have the same number of bins.
- the value in each bin has great variances; some of values are even zeros, cf. Fig. 2.

We compare χ^2 statistics distance

$$DistH_{\chi^2}(\mathbf{fq_i}, \mathbf{fm_j}) = \frac{1}{2L} \sum_{k=0}^{L-1} \frac{\left(fq_{i,k} - fm_{j,k}\right)^2}{(fq_{i,k} + fm_{j,k})} \tag{3}$$

and our proposed distance formula defined here by

$$DistH(\mathbf{fq_i}, \mathbf{fm_j}) = \begin{cases} 0, & fq_{i,k} = 0 \; and \; fm_{i,k} = 0, \forall k \in [1, L-1] \\ \frac{1}{L} \sum_{k=0}^{L-1} \frac{\left| fq_{i,k} - fm_{j,k} \right|}{\max(fq_{i,k}, fm_{j,k})}, & otherwise \end{cases} \tag{4}$$

on the database of Kimia silhouettes with 216 shapes [8] (see section 3.4). For convenience, we consider the minimum value of the distance set as the similarity distance and call it the *Character Matrix Distance (CMD)*.

$$CMD_{F_q,F_m} = \min_{n=0}^{D-1} DistF_{F_q,F_m}(n) \tag{5}$$

The comparison result of precision vs. recall is shown in Fig. 6. Precision is the ratio of the number of relevant shapes retrieved to the total number of retrieved shapes, while recall is the ratio of the number of relevant shapes retrieved to the total number of relevant shapes in the database.

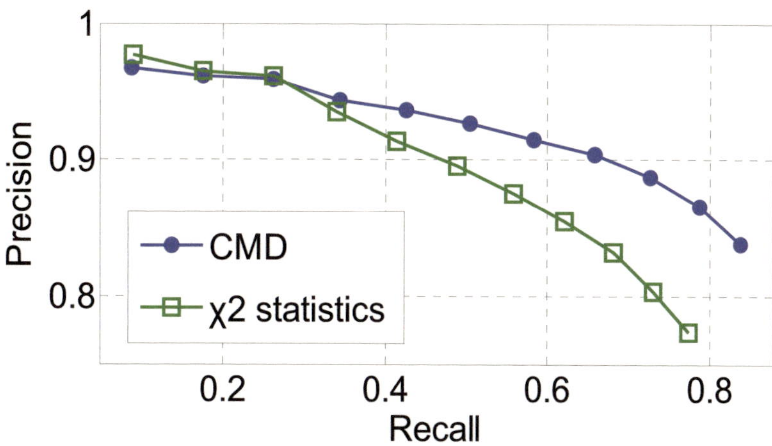

Fig. 6. The precision-recall diagrams for indexing into the database of Kimia silhouettes with 216 shapes.

It is clear from Fig. 6, that our proposed distance formula is better than χ^2 statistics on this similarity measure.

In the second criterion, we propose a new concept, the *Perpendicular Chord Length Eccentricity (PCLE)* as following:

$$PCLE(i) = \begin{cases} \left\| \mathbf{f}_i - \mathbf{f}_{i+(\mathbf{D}/2)} \right\| & i \in [0, \frac{D}{2} - 1] \\ \left\| \mathbf{f}_i - \mathbf{f}_{i-(\mathbf{D}/2)} \right\| & i \in [\frac{D}{2}, D-1] \end{cases} \tag{6}$$

Where $\|\bullet\|$ is the norm; $\mathbf{f}_i$, $i \in [0, D-1]$ (D is even) are vectors of the feature matrix. So (6) is the Euclidean distance between any two histograms of perpendicular directions of chord lengths. Since the norm is symmetric, we have

$$PCLE(i + \frac{D}{2}) = PCLE(i), \quad i \in [0, \ \frac{D}{2} - 1] \tag{7}$$

Clearly, *PCLE* represents the perpendicular directions chord feature in a shape. To compare the query's *PCLE* P_q and the model's *PCLE* P_m, we define the distance between P_q and P_m as follows:

$$D\_PCLE_{P_q, P_m}(n) = \sum_{i=0}^{D-1} \frac{\left| P_q(i) - P_m(j) \right|}{\max(P_q(i), P_m(j))}, \ j = \mathrm{mod}(i+n, D) \tag{8}$$

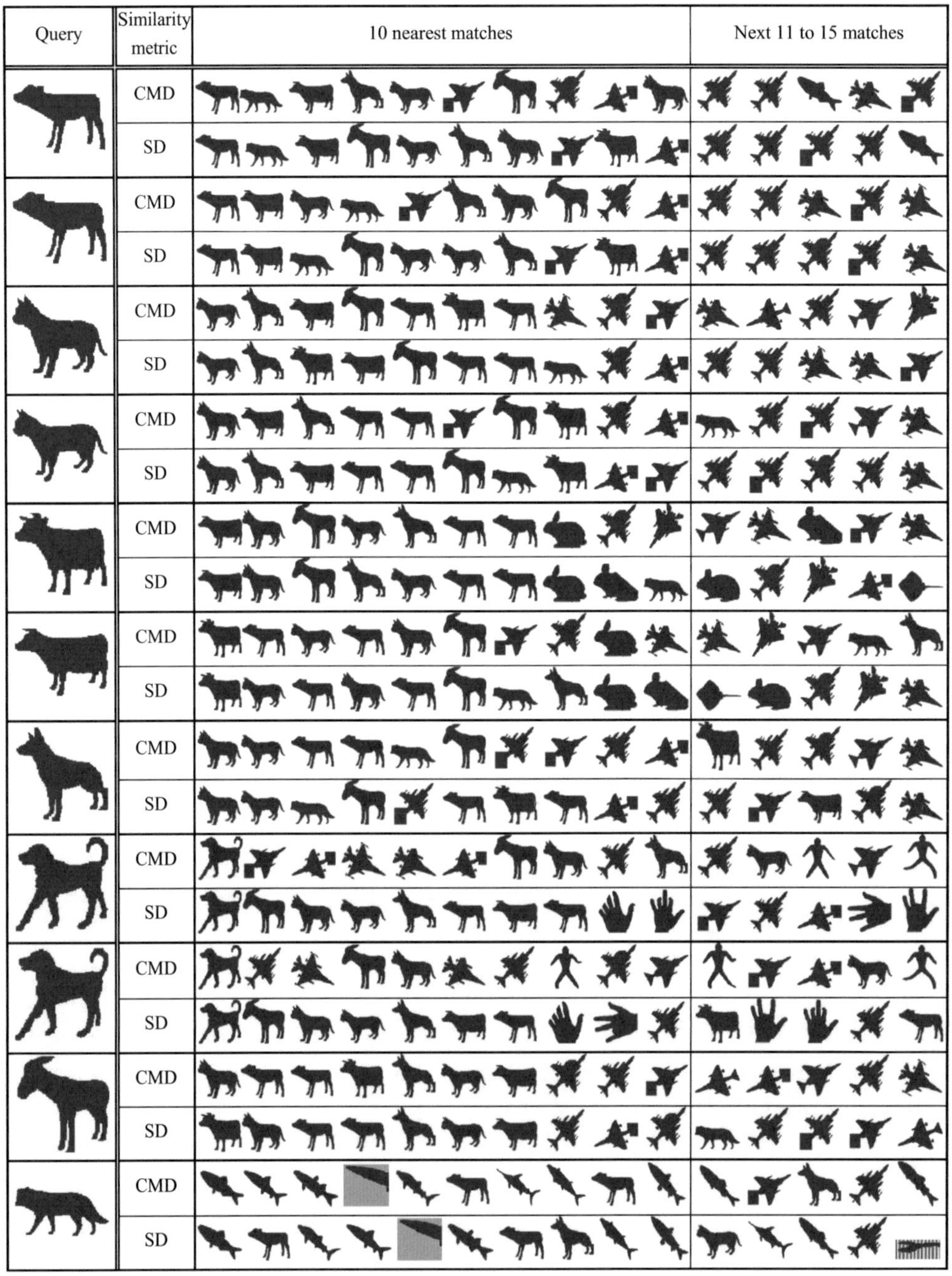

Fig. 7. Illustration of retrieval results from the 'Quadruped' category in Kimia silhouettes set of 99 shapes. The 11 quadruped shape queries in the dataset are shown in the first column. The 10 nearest retrieved shapes for each query are shown in order (from small similarity distance to large similarity distance) in the 3rd column by their similarity metric *CMD* and SD. The next five matches are shown in the 4th column for completeness.

As in (2), n is the number of shifts applied to each histogram in the *PCLE*.
Intuitively, we assume that, in general, if shape S_1 is more similar to shape S_2 than shape S_3, then the smallest value of $D\_PCLE_{P_{S_1},P_{S_2}}$ is less than the smallest value of $D\_PCLE_{P_{S_1},P_{S_3}}$.

So we can use *D_PCLE* to adjust the similarity distance of the *Character Matrix Distance (CMD)* to improve retrieval precision and recall. The combined similarity metric of shape Query and shape Model is computed using a weighted sum:

$$SD_{Q,M} = \alpha CMD_{F_q,F_m} + (1-\alpha)\min_{n=0}^{D-1}(D\_PCLE_{P_q,P_m}(n)) \tag{9}$$

where $\alpha \in [0, 1]$.
Let us explain this hypothesis by the following experiments, where we have used α=0.85. First let us look at the experiment running on the Kimia silhouettes set of 99 shapes [8]. Fig. 7 shows the two retrieval results from querying the 'Quadruped' category. One shows the retrieval results only with the similarity distance of *Character Matrix Distance (CMD)* and the other with the combined similarity metric weighted sum *SD*. As there are 11 shapes in the 'Quadruped' category, each shape is matched against all the other shapes in the database. As there are 11 shapes in each category, up to 10 nearest neighbors can be retrieved from the same category. We count in the *n*th (*n* from 1 to 15) nearest neighbors the number of times that the test image is correctly classified. The best possible result is 110 matches (except the query itself) in all 10 nearest matches. With the similarity metric *CMD*, we found 63 matches

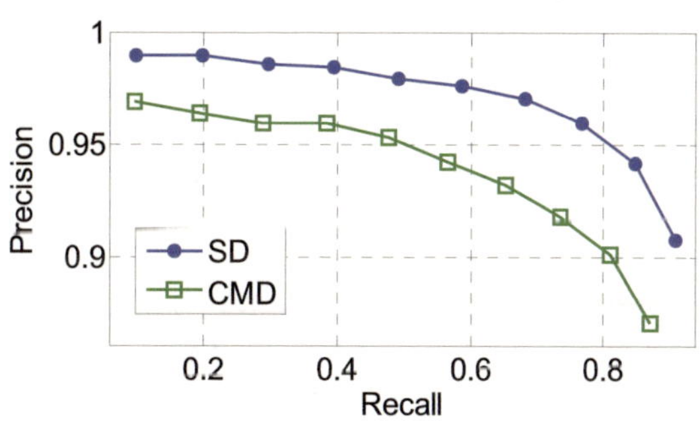

(a)

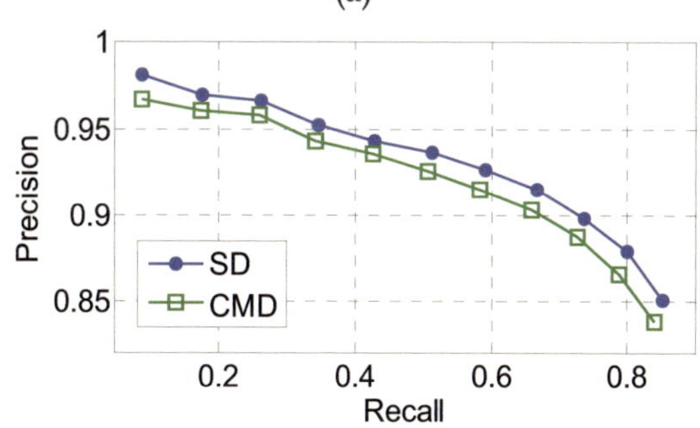

(b)

Fig. 8. The precision-recall diagrams for indexing into the database of Kimia silhouettes with (a) 99 shapes and (b) 216 shapes.

in the first ten retrieved shapes, recall is 63/110=57.3%, and there were 70 matches in the first fifteen retrieved shapes. Whereas with the similarity metric *SD*, we found 80 matches in the first ten retrieved shapes, recall is 80/110=72.7%, and there were 85 matches in the first fifteen retrieved shapes. The result shows that the recall rate in the first ten retrieved shapes was improved by 15.4 percentage points for the 'Quadruped' cluster when we used the similarity metric *SD* instead of *CMD*. It also shows a good performance rate when compared with [9], [10] and [11] which have the same retrieval results of 51 matches in the first ten retrieved shapes.

Let us look at the statistical results. We compare the retrieval results using Character Matrix Distance (*CMD*) to the retrieval results when using the similarity metric *SD* by calculating precision vs. recall in the Kimia silhouette datasets of 99 and 216 shapes [8]. The results are shown in Fig. 8. It is evident that similarity metric *SD* outperforms *CMD.*

3. Experimental evaluations of chord context matching

In this section, we present the results obtained during a more realistic shape recognition process in presence of different possible visual deformations to study the comparative performances of the proposed algorithm. We show that the chord context matching is effective in the presence of commonly occurring visual transformations like scale changes, boundary perturbations, viewpoint variation, non-rigid transform and partial occultation. We also compare its results with ten other well-known algorithms. All the experiments are conducted on the standard database: MPEG-7 CE-shape-1 database (1400 shapes) [12], Columbia University Image Library Coil-100 database (7200 images) [13], and 3 databases of Kimia silhouettes [8]. In all the experiments, the feature matrix was normalized to 30 bins and 36 directions; the similarity measure uses formula (9) with α=0.85 : these values are found to be the most efficient, during various experiments.

3.1 Scale and rotation transforms

Scale and rotation transforms are the important intuitive correspondences for a variety of shapes. They can be regarded as a necessary condition that every shape descriptor should satisfy. In order to study retrieval performance in terms of scale changes and image rotations, we use the test-sets Part A, from CE-Shape-1 database that was defined during the standardization process of MPEG-7, consisting of 1400 shapes semantically classified into 70 classes [12].

For robustness to scaling during the test, i.e. Part A-1, we created a database in which there were 70 basic shapes taken from the 70 different classes and 5 shapes derived from each basic shape by scaling digital images with factors 2, 0.3, 0.25, 0.2, and 0.1. Thus in the database, there were 420 shapes. Each of the 420 images was used as a query image. A number of correct matches were computed in the top 6 retrieved images. Thus, the best possible result was 2520 matches.

For robustness to rotation during the test, i.e. Part A-2, we again created a database including 420 shapes. The 70 basic shapes were the same as in part A-1 and 5 shapes were derived from each basic shape by rotation with angles: 9, 36, 45, 90 and 150 degrees. As in Part A-1, each of the 420 images was used as a query image. The best result was 2520 matches.

The similarity rate in each experiment was calculated by taking the ratio of correct matches to the maximum number of possible matches. Table 1 indicates the similarity rate of comparison of the chord context descriptor with the reported results of certain studies. Note that the proposed descriptor has the best performance in all the experiments.

Data Set	Tangent Space [14]	Curvature Scale Space [15]	Zernike Moments [16]	Wavelet [17]	BAS [18]	Chord context
Part A-1	88.65	89.76	92.54	88.04	90.87	**99.37**
Part A-2	100	99.37	99.60	97.46	100	**100**
Part A	94.33	94.57	96.07	92.75	95.44	**99.69**

Table 1. Comparison of the Retrieval Results of Different Methods in the MPEG-7 CE-Shape-1 Part A Test

The results show that chord context is very invariant to scale and rotation transforms. Reviewing the extracted attribute algorithm in section 2, we are not surprised by the almost perfect results. The attribute matrix is obtained by the statistic of all the chord lengths of a shape in all directions. The rotation of the shape affects the attribute matrix only when shifting the chord length histograms. In the similarity measure, we have considered this point and compared the two attribute matrices by shifting the histograms of either matrix. The rotation of plane shapes does not affect the retrieval result. Since we normalize all the images to a certain size before extracting their features, the scale transform of a shape does not significantly affect the retrieval result.

3.2 Boundary perturbations by noise

The query shape can be perturbed by different noises. It may simply result from digitization. As a reminder, to fight perturbations resulting from shape digitization, and in order to alleviate the influence of boundary perturbation, we have removed the very short chords from attribute matrices. To evaluate the performance of chord context when boundary perturbations are present, we use noisy images with different noise powers as queries to retrieve the relevant image in a database. We generated a 20 sub-database test-set based on MPEG-7 CE-Shape-1. In each sub-database, there were 70 shapes from the 70 different classes according to their orders in the database. The query shapes were all 70 shapes in each sub-database subjected to noise with 4 different noise powers. Thus, the best possible result in each sub-database was 70 matches for each noise power. Suppose the average distance of all the points on the edge of a shape to its centroid is *D*. We then define the signal-to-noise ratio (*SNR*) as follow:

$$\mathrm{SNR} = 20\lg\frac{\mathrm{D}}{\mathrm{r}}(\mathrm{dB})$$

where *r* is the largest deviation of the points on the edge. Fig. 9 shows an example of an original shape and its contaminated shapes produced by random uniform noise with *SNR* equal to 30dB, 25dB, 20dB and 15dB.

Table 2 shows the average similarity rates of the 20 sub-databases at 4 *SNRs*.

SNR(dB)	30	25	20	15
Average Similarity Rate (%)	99.9	99.8	99.1	82.9

Table 2. Average Similarity Rates of the 20 Sub-Databases at *SNR* of 30dB, 25dB, 20dB and 15dB

Fig. 9. Examples of noisy shapes from a model in MPEG-7 CE-Shape-1. From left to right, the original and the resulting noised shapes at an *SNR* of 30dB, 25dB, 20dB and 15dB.

From the results in Table 2, we notice that using noise to impair boundaries does not produce significant differences between similar shapes. As the chord context descriptor utilizes the edge as well as the region feature of a shape, it can bear boundary disturbances due to noise to certain extent.

3.3 Partial occultation

In general, a global descriptor is not robust when a shape is partially occulted. Since the chord context descriptor has the statistical information for a shape, this drawback is alleviated to some extent. To evaluate robustness to partial occultation we ran experiments using the same sub-databases as mentioned in subsection 3.2. We occulted the shapes, applying 4 different percentages of occultation from the left, Fig. 10(a), or right, Fig. 10(b), respectively to them, in raster-scan order. The occultation percentages were 5%, 10%, 15% and 20%. Each occulted shape is retrieved in its sub-database as a query. Thus, the best result in each sub-database is 70 matches for one occultation.

(a)

(b)

Fig. 10. Examples of occulted shapes from a model in MPEG-7 CE-Shape-1. (a) From left-occulted objects; they are occulted by 5%, 10%, 15% and 20%. (b) From right-occulted objects; they are occulted by 5%, 10%, 15% and 20%.

Table 3 shows the average similarity rate of the 20 sub-databases on the 4 partial examples of occultation.

Occultation (%)		5	10	15	20
Average Similarity Rate (%)	Left	99.5	91.3	78.6	58.7
	Right	98.9	94.1	80.7	64.6
	Average	99.2	92.7	79.7	61.7

Table 3. Average similarity rates of the 20 sub-databases at shape occultation of 5%, 10%, 15% and 20%

It is clear from Table 3, that small occultations do not affect chord context significantly. However, the problem of significant occultation remains to be explored. The results show that chord context is robust to minor occultation.

3.4 Similarity-based evaluation

The performance in similarity-based retrieval is perhaps the most important of all tests performed. In order to demonstrate the performance of chord context when deformed parts are present, we turn to three shape databases. All three databases were provided by Kimia's group [8] [19].

The first database is Kimia's data set 1 which contains 25 images from 6 categories (Fig. 11).

Fig. 11. Kimia's data set 1: 25 instances from six categories. Each row shows instances of a different object category.

This property has been tested by shape contexts [20], Sharvit et. al [19], Gdalyahu et. al [21] and Ling et. al [22]. The retrieval results are summarized as the number of first, second, and third closest matches that fall into the correct category. The results are listed in Table 4. It shows that the proposed method outperforms the first 3 reported methods. For the fourth approach, chord context is slightly better than it in the Top 2 closest matches.

Method	Top 1	Top 2	Top 3
Sharvit et. al [19]	23/25	21/25	20/25
Gdalyahu et. al [21]	25/25	21/25	19/25
Belongie et. al [20]	25/25	24/25	22/25
Ling et. al [22]	25/25	24/25	25/25
Chord context	**25/25**	**25/25**	**23/25**

Table 4. Comparison of the Retrieval Results of Different Methods on the Kimia Data Set 1 (Fig. 11)

The second database contains 99 images from nine categories with 11 shapes in each category [8]. It has been tested by D.S. Guru [10], Shape contexts [20], Bernier [9] and Tabbone [11]. Each shape was used as a query to which all other shapes were compared and thus 9801 shape comparisons were made. Ideal results would be that the 10 closest matches (except the query itself) belong to the same category. The results are summarized by precision-recall diagrams in Fig. 12. The proposed method shows better precision and recall rate than the other methods.

The third database contains 216 images from 18 categories with 12 shapes in each category [8]. All the shapes were selected from the MPEG-7 test database [8]. It has been tested by shape contexts [20]. As in the case of second database, a comparison of the results of our

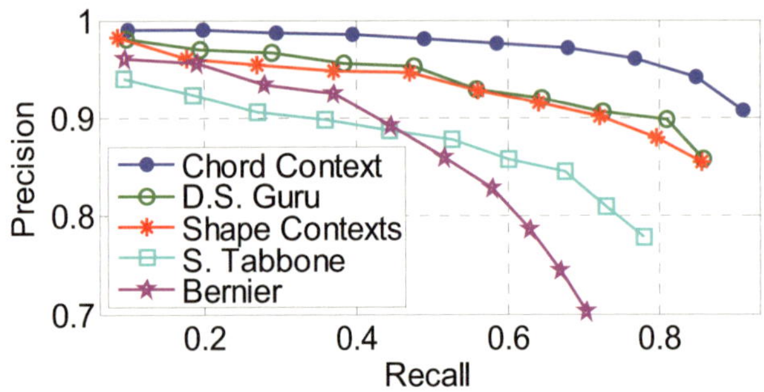

Fig. 12. Comparison of precision and recall rates of different methods on the Kimia Data Set of 99 shapes.

approach to the shape context method is given in Fig. 13. As we see in Fig. 13, the two precision/recall curves cross. This means that the shape contexts [20] method performs better for small answer sets, while our proposed method performs better for larger answer sets. According to [24], the method achieving highest precision and recall for large answer sets is considered to be the best one, so the proposed method is better than shape contexts' method.

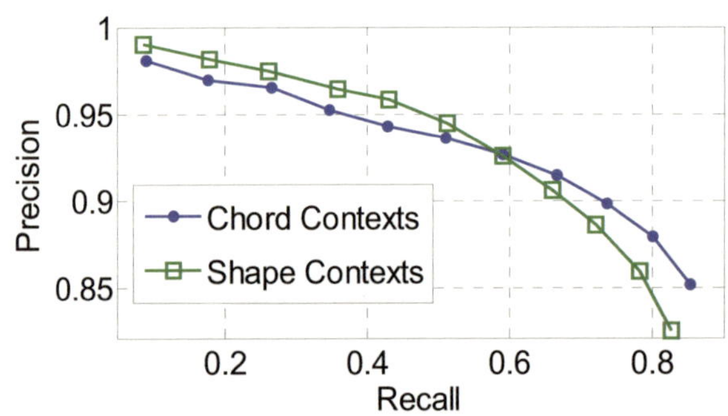

Fig. 13. Comparison of precision and recall rates of different methods on the Kimia Data Set of 216 shapes.

From the above results, it appears that chord context produces outstanding performance in the presence of non-rigid deformations.

3.5 Viewpoint variations

For a better evaluation in the realistic context of image retrieval with industrial vision where the picture of an object from real world is observed from different viewpoints, we have performed tests on shapes extracted directly from these pictures. To test the retrieval performance of the proposed method in the presence of viewpoint changes, the Columbia University Image Library Coil-100 3D object dataset is used. This dataset contains 7200 color images of 100 household objects and toys. Each object was placed on a turntable and an image was taken for every 5 degrees of rotation, resulting in 72 images per object. We converted the color images to grayscale, and then into shapes by using the same gray-value threshold settings for the whole set (e.g., Fig. 14). Since the shapes are projections of 3D objects by a simple gray-value threshold, not only may their silhouettes change from one viewpoint to another; the lighting and object textures may also differ.

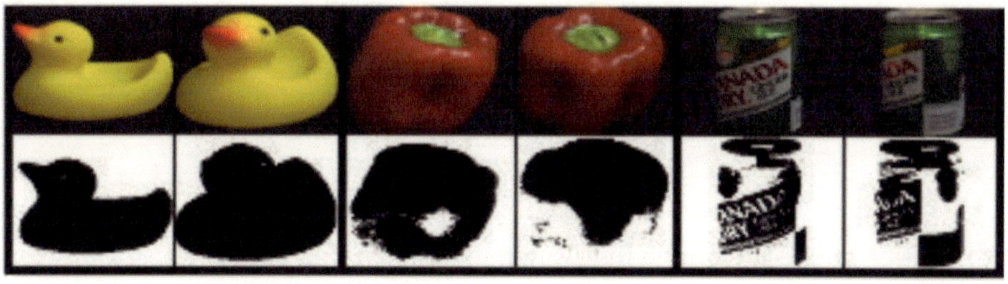

Fig. 14. 6 images taken as an example from the COIL-100 3D object dataset. The first row shows the original images and the second row shows their corresponding silhouettes as produced by gray-value thresholding. In 1st and 2nd columns, the duck's silhouettes change significantly due to a change of viewpoint. In the 3rd and 4th columns, the red pepper's silhouettes change significantly due to a difference in lighting. In 5th and 6th columns, the tin's silhouettes change significantly due to a change in textures.

In the following subsections we present two experiments showing the performance of the proposed method on these test sets. First we compare the new approach to the shape contexts [23]. We converted the color images into shapes, then selected 3 images per object with a 15° viewpoint interval, for example 0°, 15° and 30°. To measure performance, we counted the number of times the closest match was a rotated view of the same object. Our result was 285/300. The result reported in [23] is 280/300.

In the second experiment, we generated 7 sub-databases in which we selected 5 to 17 consecutive viewpoints per object for a total from 500 to 1700 images respectively (cf. Table 5). We use the middle view images in a sub-dataset as a query to retrieve in them. For each query, the number of the best possible matches is 5 to 17 in the 7 sub-databases, respectively. The results are shown in Table 5 and Fig. 15.

	Models in Sub-database (view angle)	Query (view angle)	The best retrieved number	Retrieved results	Retrieved precision
Sub-database1	0, 5, **10**, 15, 20	10	500	**490**	**98.0%**
Sub-database2	0, 5, 10, **15**, 20, 25, 30	15	700	**679**	**97.0%**
Sub-database3	0, 5, 10, 15, **20**, 25, 30, 35, 40	20	900	**827**	**91.9%**
Sub-database4	0, 5, 10, 15, 20, **25**, 30, 35, 40, 45, 50	25	1100	**958**	**87.1%**
Sub-database5	0, 5, 10, 15, 20, 25, **30**, 35, 40, 45, 50,55, 60	30	1300	**1062**	**81.7%**
Sub-database6	0, 5, 10, 15, 20, 25, 30, **35**, 40, 45, 50,55, 60, 65, 70	35	1500	**1149**	**76.6%**
Sub-database7	0,5, 10, 15, 20, 25, 30, 35, **40**, 45, 50,55,60,65, 70,75,80	40	1700	**1211**	**71.2%**

Table 5. The Components of 7 Sub-Databases with Different Viewpoints on Coil-100 3D Object Dataset and Their Retrieval Results

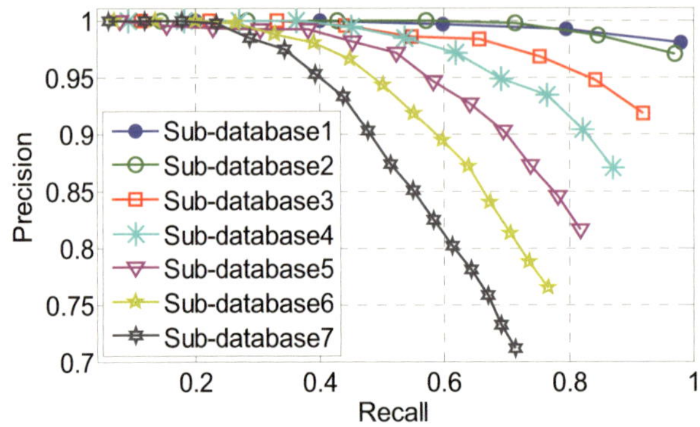

Fig. 15. Precision and recall rates in the 7 sub-databases on Coil-100 3D object dataset.

These results are very encouraging, since they indicate that we can perform satisfactory retrieval with mean average precision of more than 91% for view angle differences of under 20°: see the results of Sub-database1-3. For viewpoint difference of less than 40°, the retrieved precision is more than 71%. Note that this is done exclusively on shape images (without using any intensity information). Clearly, if other information and a more specialized feature set were used, even higher precision scores could be achieved.

4. Conclusions

We have presented a new approach which is simple and easy to apply in the context of shape recognition. This study has two major contributions: (1) defining a new algorithm which can capture the main feature of a shape, from either its contour or its region; (2) proposing an assistant similarity measure algorithm *Perpendicular Chord Length Eccentricity (PCLE)* which can help to improve retrieval precision and recall to some extent.

In various experiments we have demonstrated the invariance of the proposed approach to several common image transforms, such as scaling, rotation, boundary perturbations, minor partial occultation, non-rigid deformations and 3D rotations of real-world objects.

The particular strengths of the proposed descriptor for retrieving images are summarized in the following points:

- **Flexibility:** Chord context can handle various types of 2D queries, even if it has holes or separates itself into several parts. It is robust to noise and minor occultation. So we can use this simple method to segment objects from images.
- **Accuracy:** the proposed method has the advantage of achieving higher retrieval accuracy than the other methods in the literature based on MPEG-7 CE-1 database, Coil-100 database and the Kimia silhouettes datasets retrieval test.

Currently we have not considered the effect of an affine transform of a shape. The chord context method has no special operations that resist affine transforms. We consider this to be the main weakness of this approach and, to achieve more accuracy and have more applications; further work will be carried out on invariance to affine transforms.

5. References

[1] R.C. Veltkamp, M. Hagedoorn, "State of the Art in Shape Matching," *Principles of Visual Information Retrieval,* 2001, pp. 89-119.

[2] D. Zhang, G. Lu, "Review of shape representation and description techniques," *Pattern Recognit.*, vol. 37, 2004, pp. 1–19.

[3] S.Berretti, A.D.Bimbo, and P.Pala, "Retrieval by shape similarity with perceptual distance and effective indexing," *IEEE Trans. Multimedia*, vol. 2, no. 4, 2000, pp. 225–239.

[4] O. El Badawy, M. Kamel, "Shape Retrieval using Concavity Trees," *Proceedings of the 17th International Conference on Pattern Recognition*, vol. 3, 2004, pp. 111-114.

[5] N. Alajlan, Mohamed S. Kamel and George Freeman, "Multi-object image retrieval based on shape and topology," *Signal Processing: Image Communication*, vol. 21, 2006, pp. 904–918.

[6] F. Mokhtarian, A. K. Mackworth, "A Theory of Multiscale, Curvature-Based Shape Representation for Planar Curves," *IEEE Trans. Pattern Analysis and Machine Intelligence*, vol. 14, no. 8, 1992, pp. 789–805.

[7] F. Mokhtarian, Abbasi S and Kittler J, "Robust and efficient shape indexing through curvature scale space," *Proceedings British Machine Vision Conference, Edinburgh, UK*, 1996, pp. 53-62.

[8] T.B. Sebastian, P.N. Klein and B.B. Kimia, "Recognition of Shapes by Editing Their Shock Graphs," *IEEE Trans. Pattern Analysis and Machine Intelligence*, vol. 26, no. 5, 2004, pp. 550-571.

[9] T. Bernier, J.-A. Landry, "A new method for representing and matching shapes of natural objects," Pattern Recognit., vol. 36, issue 8, 2003, pp. 1711-1723.

[10] D.S. Guru, H.S. Nagendraswamy, "Symbolic representation of two-dimensional shapes," *Pattern Recognit. Letters*, vol. 28, 2007, pp. 144–155.

[11] S. Tabbone, L. Wendling and J.-P. Salmon, "A new shape descriptor defined on the Radon transform," *Computer Vision and Image Understanding*, vol. 102, issue 1, 2006, pp. 42-51.

[12] S. Jeannin, M. Bober, "Description of core experiments for MPEG-7 motion/shape," *MPEG-7, ISO/IEC JTC1/SC29/WG11/MPEG99/N2690*, Seoul, March 1999.

[13] Dataset available on the website: http://www1.cs.columbia.edu/CAVE/software/softlib/coil-100.php.

[14] L. J. Latecki, R. Lakamper, "Shape Similarity Measure Based on Correspondence of Visual Parts," *IEEE Trans. Pattern Analysis and Machine Intelligence*, vol. 22, no. 10, 2000, pp. 1185-1190.

[15] F. Mokhtarian, S. Abbasi, and J. Kittler, "Efficient and robust retrieval by shape content through curvature scale space", *In image databases and multi media search, proceeding of the first international workshop IDB-MMS'96*, Amsterdam, the Netherlands, 1996, pp. 35-42.

[16] A. Khotanzan, Y. H. Hong, "Invariant Image Recognition By Zernike Moments," *IEEE Trans. Pattern Analysis and Machine Intelligence*, vol. 12, 1990, pp. 489-497.

[17] G. C.-H. Chuang, C.-C. J. Kuo, "Wavelet Descriptor of Planar Curves: Theory and Applications," *IEEE Trans. Image Processing*, vol. 5, no. 1, 1996, pp. 56-70.

[18] N. Arica, F. T. Yarman-Vural, "BAS: a perceptual shape descriptor based on the beam angle statistics Source," *Pattern Recognit. Letters*, *v*ol. 24, issue 9-10, 2003, pp. 1627-1639.

[19] D. Sharvit, J. Chan, H. Tek and B. Kimia, "Symmetry-Based Indexing of Image Database," *J. Visual Comm. and Image Representation*, vol. 9, no. 4, 1998, pp. 366-380.

[20] S. Belongie, J. Malik and J. Puzicha, "Shape Matching and Object Recognition Using Shape Context," *IEEE Trans. Pattern Analysis and Machine Intelligence,* vol. 24, no. 4, 2002, pp. 509-522.

[21] Y. Gdalyahu, D. Weinshall, "Flexible Syntactic Matching of Curves and Its Application to Automatic Hierarchical Classification of Silhouettes," *IEEE Trans. Pattern Analysis and Machine Intelligence,* vol. 21, no. 12, 1999, pp. 1312-1328.

[22] Haibin Ling, David W. Jacobs, "Shape Classification Using the Inner-Distance," *IEEE Trans. On Pattern Analysis and Machine Intelligence,* 2007, vol. 29, no. 2, pp. 286-299.

[23] S. Belongie, J. Malik, "Matching with shape contexts," Content-based Access of Image and Video Libraries, Proceedings IEEE, 2000, pp. 20-26.

[24] E. Petrakis, A. Diplaros, and E. Milios, "Matching and Retrieval of Distorted and Occluded Shapes Using Dynamic Programming," *IEEE Trans. Pattern Analysis and Machine Intelligence,* vol. 24, no. 11, 2002, pp. 1501-1516.

6

Occluded Image Object Recognition using Localized Nonnegative Matrix Factorization Methods

Ivan Bajla[1], Daniel Soukup[2] and Svorad Štolc[3]
[1,2]*Austrian Institute of Technology GmbH, Seibersdorf*
[3]*Institute of Measurement Science, Slovak Academy of Sciences, Bratislava*
[1,2]*Austria*
[3]*Slovakia*

1. Introduction

In the nineties, appearance-based methods for image object detection/recognition have evoked a renewed attention in computer vision community thanks to their capability to deal with combined effects of shape, illumination conditions, and reflectance properties in the scene (Beymer & Poggio, 1995; Mel, 1997; Murase & Nayar, 1995; Turk & Pentland, 1991; Yoshimura & Kanade, 1994). The major advantage of these methods is that both learning and recognition stage of image processing utilize only two-dimensional brightness images without an intermediate processing. On the other hand, the most severe limitation of these approaches (in their conventional form) consists in problems with object occlusions and varying background. The basic characteristic of the appearance-based approaches is as follows.

They consist of the two stages: the off-line training (learning) stage and the on-line recognition stage. In the first stage a set of sample images (templates) are available which encompass the appearance of a single object under various conditions (Yoshimura & Kanade, 1994), or multiple instances of a class of objects, e.g., faces (Turk & Pentland, 1991). The images in sample sets are chosen to be correlated, thus enabling efficient compression using Principal Component Analysis (PCA) (Jolliffe, 2002). In the second recognition stage, given an unknown input image, we project this image (of identical size as the training images) to the eigenspace generated in the first stage. The recovered coefficients indicate the particular instance of a class to which the given input image belongs. This process can equally be applied to sample objects and subimages of an image in which the existence and/or position of a template object should be detected.

Leonardis & Bischof (1994) modified the PCA space representation method with the goal to improve recognition rates for cases with occlusions. Their robust method extended the domain of applicability of the appearance-based methods towards more complex scenes which contain occlusions and background clutter. The basic novelty of their approach consists in the way the coefficients of the eigenimages are calculated. Instead of computing them by a standard projection of the input data onto an eigenspace, they calculate the coefficients of linear combinations of eigenimages using an objective function and hypotheses on object point subsets. Indeed, this method provides a reduction of occlusion problems. However, this improvement is reached at the expense of significant increase of the computational cost of operations exactly in the on-line stage of the PCA method. The method requires tuning eight specific parameters and a number of additional procedures to be implemented within the on-line recognition stage, thereby reducing the main advantage of PCA data representation for on-line recognition applications: a simple projection on an eigenspace and the nearest neighbor search.

Regardless of the weak points of PCA and its more robust modifications, subspace data representation methods are still a challenging branch of object recognition methods used in computer vision and pattern recognition. In particular, these methods find applications in the fields of face identification, recognition of digits and characters occurring at various labeled products. Therefore we were interested in exploration of other possibilities of object recognition that would be robust to occlusions and could parallely provide an acceptable solution for applications requiring high-performance on-line image processing.

Lee & Seung (1999) showed for the first time that for a collection of face images an approximative representation by basis vectors, encoding the mouth, nose, and eyes, can be obtained using a Nonnegative Matrix Factorization (NMF). It is a method for generating a linear representation of data using nonnegativity constraints on the basis vector components and encoding coefficients. The nonnegative matrix decomposition can formally be described as follows:

$$\boldsymbol{V} \approx \boldsymbol{W} \cdot \boldsymbol{H}\,, \tag{1}$$

where $\boldsymbol{V} \in \mathcal{R}^{n \times m}$ is a positive image data matrix with n pixels and m image samples (templates, which are usually represented in lexicographic order of pixels as column-vectors), $\boldsymbol{W} \in \mathcal{R}^{n \times r}$ are basis column vectors of an NMF-subspace, and $\boldsymbol{H} \in \mathcal{R}^{r \times m}$ contains coefficients of the linear combinations of the basis vectors needed for reconstruction of the original data (called also encoding vectors). Usually, r is chosen by the user so that $(n+m)r < nm$. Then each column of the matrix $\boldsymbol{W}$ represents a basis vector of the generated NMF-subspace. Each column of $\boldsymbol{H}$ represents the weights needed to linearly approximate the corresponding column in $\boldsymbol{V}$ (image template) by means of the vector basis $\boldsymbol{W}$. Various error (cost) functions were proposed for NMF (Lee & Seung, 2001; Paatero & Taper, 1994). The most frequently used is the Euclidean distance:

$$E(\boldsymbol{W},\boldsymbol{H}) = \|\boldsymbol{V} - \boldsymbol{W} \cdot \boldsymbol{H}\|^2 = \sum_{i,j} (V_{i,j} - (\boldsymbol{WH})_{ij})^2\,. \tag{2}$$

The main difference between NMF and other classical factorization models relies in the nonnegativity constraints imposed on both the basis vectors of $\boldsymbol{W}$ and encoding vectors of $\boldsymbol{H}$. In this way, only additive combinations are possible:

$$(\boldsymbol{V})_{i\mu} \approx (\boldsymbol{WH})_{i\mu} = \sum_{j=1}^{r} W_{ij} H_{j\mu}\,.$$

Increasing interest in this factorization technique is due to the intuitive nature of the method that provides extraction of additive parts of data sets interpretable as real image parts, while reducing the dimensionality of the input data at the same time. In the recent years several modifications of NMF schemes applied to various types of image data have been proposed and explored. Also mathematical issues of optimization of objective functions defined for NMF have been addressed and improved numerical algorithms have been developed. We only mention the best-known of them:

1. Local Nonnegative Matrix Factorization (Feng et al., 2002)
2. Nonnegative Matrix Factorization (Liu et al., 2003)
3. Nonnegative Sparse Coding (Hoyer, 2002)
4. Nonnegative Matrix Factorization with Sparseness Constraints (Hoyer, 2004)
5. Discriminant Nonnegative Matrix Factorization (Buciu, 2007; Buciu et al., 2006; Buciu & Pitas, 2004)
6. Nonsmooth Nonnegative Matrix Factorization (Pascual-Montano et al., 2006)
7. Learning Sparse Representations by Nonnegative Matrix Factorization and Sequential Cone Programming (Heiler & Schnörr, 2006).

In our previous research we focused on studying the influence of the matrix sparseness parameter on recognition rates, in particular in images with occluded objects (Bajla & Soukup, 2007). In the recognition experiments, carried out with this goal, we also studied four types of metrics used in the nearest neighbor search. We proposed a weaker alternative of NMF (the so-called semi-NMF) based on Hoyer's NMF algorithm (Soukup & Bajla, 2008) that is numerically more stable.

2. Parts-Based methodology of NMF

In the seminal paper Lee & Seung (1999), the methodology of nonnegative matrix factorization was applied for the first time to the task of image representation. Lee and Seung motivated their approach by psychological and physiological evidence for *parts-based* representation in the brain, and by certain computational theories. However, the notion of *parts-based* representation was not introduced as a formal term. They stated that the NMF algorithm is able to learn parts of the face images and the core of this ability stems from the nonnegativity constraints included in NMF. They also compared the proposed NMF basis vectors to conventional PCA bases with holistic structure and claimed that NMF bases better correspond with intuitive notion of the parts of a face. Moreover, they argued that "PCA allows complex cancellation between positive and negative terms in the linear combination of basis vectors (eigenimages) and therefore it lacks the intuitive meaning of adding parts to form a whole". In the paper of Lee and Seung, an illustration is given of the NMF basis face images (matrix $\boldsymbol{W}$) and face image encodings (matrix $\boldsymbol{H}$). The sparseness of basis images is explained by their non-global nature (they contain several versions of mouths, noses, eyes, etc.), while the sparseness of the encoding coefficient matrix is attributed to the ability of the method to include some basis images and to cancel others from the linear combinations given by the product $\boldsymbol{W} \cdot \boldsymbol{H}$. On the basis of the Lee and Seung methodological statements related to the intuitive notion of the parts-based representation of images (in particular, faces), we can summarize that some characteristic regions of the input image, occurring in certain geometrical locations, are understood as image parts which are represented by image basis vectors (columns of the matrix $\boldsymbol{W}$) only in indirect way.

The results of Lee and Seung encouraged researchers to apply the NMF approach to various image object recognition problems, especially to those affected by local deformations and partial occlusions. In the papers Hoyer (2004); Kim et al. (2005); Li et al. (2001); Pascual-Montano et al. (2006), the use of NMF in recognition tasks has been further explored. In Li et al. (2001) the concept of NMF that non-subtractive combining of NMF basis vectors results in forming the whole (image) was confirmed to some extent. However, the authors showed that additive parts learned by NMF are not necessarily localized. On the basis of recognition experiments they also showed that original NMF representation yields low recognition rates for occluded images. Thus, the results of Li et al. made the justification of the parts-based principle of NMF and its use for the object recognition task questionable. Although they proposed an improved modification of NMF (the so-called local NMF (LNMF)), for learning a spatially more localized parts-based image representation, they did not perform a sufficient number of recognition experiments which could prove better performance of the LNMF method in practical tasks of object recognition.

Buciu & Pitas (2004) developed a novel Discriminant NMF (DNMF) algorithm by introducing two additional constraints on the coefficients. The first constraint is based on the within-class scatter matrix of the class samples (input images) around their mean. The second constraint reflects the between-class variance and it is given by the scatter of the class mean around the global mean. The constraints were incorporated into the divergence cost function of NMF that was applied to the problem of recognizing six basic facial expressions from face images of Kanade et al. (2000) AU-coded facial expression database. The influence of partial occlusions on recognition rates has not been explored systematically neither in this paper, nor in the paper of Li et al.

Kim et al. (2005) explored efficient image representation using Independent Component Analysis (ICA) in the task of face recognition robust to local distortion and partial occlusions. They included in the research also the LNMF method and proved that additional constraints of Li et al. (2001) involved into this method only focused on locality and they do not guarantee localization of meaningful facial features in their basis images.

The next attempt to assign a more accurate meaning to the parts-based methodology of the NMF subspace representation was made in Hoyer (2002; 2004). Hoyer pointed at the most useful property of NMF that is generation of a sparse representation of the data. He stated that such a representation encodes much of the data using few "active" components which make the encoding easy to interpret. Hoyer also claimed that sparseness of basis vectors and encoding coefficients of NMF is reached as a side effect rather than a goal. He proposed a novel NMF modification in which the sparseness of the column vectors in the matrix $\boldsymbol{W}$, as well as the sparseness of the column vectors of the matrix $\boldsymbol{H}$ are explicitly controlled in the course of optimization of the objective function.

We recall here the concept of the vector or matrix sparseness and its measure as was used in Hoyer (2004). The concept of the sparse encoding refers to the data representation task in which only several units are efficiently used to represent typical data vectors. In practice this implies most entries having values close to zero while only few take significantly non-zero values. Various sparseness measures have been used in the literature as mappings from $\mathcal{R}^n \to \mathcal{R}$, quantifying the amount of energy of a vector packed into a few components. On a normalized scale, the sparsest vector with a single non-zero component should have the sparseness measure equal to one, whereas a vector with no element equal to zero should have a sparseness of zero.

Applying the concept of the sparseness to the NMF task leads to the basic question: what actually should be sparse? The basis vectors of $\boldsymbol{W}$ or the encoding coefficients represented by the matrix $\boldsymbol{H}$? According to Hoyer's claim, such a question cannot be answered in a general way, it all depends on the specific application. E.g., when trying to learn useful features from a database of images, it makes sense to require both $\boldsymbol{W}$ and $\boldsymbol{H}$ to be sparse, signifying that any given object is present in a few images and affects only a small part of the image. Hoyer (2004) derived a projected gradient descent algorithm for NMF with sparseness (the details are given in his paper). It can be briefly described in the following way.

Given any vector $\mathbf{x}$, find the closest (in the Euclidean sense) nonnegative vector s with a given L_1 norm and a given L_2 norm. We start by projecting the given vector onto the hyperplane $\sum s_i = L_1$ by assigning $s_i := x_i + (L_1 - \sum x_i)/\dim(\mathbf{x}), \forall i$. Next, within this space, we project to

the closest point on the joint constraint hypersphere. This is done by moving radially outward from the center of the sphere (the center is given by the point where all components have equal values). If the result is completely nonnegative, we have arrived at our solution. If not, those components that attained negative values must be fixed zero, and a new point is found in a similar fashion under those additional constraints.
Thus, using the sparseness concept, the following modified NMF problem can be formulated in which the sparseness of the factor matrices $\boldsymbol{W}$ and $\boldsymbol{H}$ is explicitly controlled during the optimization process. Given a nonnegative data matrix $\boldsymbol{V}$ of size $n \times m$, find the nonnegative matrices $\boldsymbol{W}$ and $\boldsymbol{H}$ of sizes $n \times r$ and $r \times m$, respectively, such that

$$E(\boldsymbol{W},\boldsymbol{H}) = \|\boldsymbol{V} - \boldsymbol{W} \cdot \boldsymbol{H}\|^2 \tag{3}$$

is minimized, under optional constraints

$$s(\mathbf{w}_i) = s_W\ ,\ \ \forall_i,\ i = 1,\cdots,r,$$
$$s(\mathbf{h}_i) = s_H\ ,\ \ \forall_i,\ i = 1,\cdots,r,$$

where $\mathbf{w}_i$ is the i-th column of $\boldsymbol{W}$, $\mathbf{h}_i$ is the ith row of $\boldsymbol{H}$. Here r denotes the dimensionality of an NMF subspace spanned by the column vectors of the matrix $\boldsymbol{W}$, and s_W and s_H are their desired sparseness values. The sparseness criteria proposed in Hoyer (2004) use a measure based on the relationship between L_1 and L_2 norm of the given vectors $\mathbf{w}_i$ or $\mathbf{h}_i$. In general, for the given n-dimensional vector $\mathbf{x}$ its sparseness measure $s(\mathbf{x})$ is defined by the formula:

$$s(\mathbf{x}) = \frac{\sqrt{n} - \|\mathbf{x}\|_1 / \|\mathbf{x}\|_2}{\sqrt{n} - 1}\ . \tag{4}$$

This measure quantifies how much energy of the vector is packed into a few components. This function evaluates to 1 if and only if the given vector contains a single non-zero component. Its value is 0 if and only if all components are equal. It should be noted that the vector scales w_i or h_i have not been constrained yet. However, since $w_i \cdot h_i = (w_i\lambda) \cdot (h_i/\lambda)$, we are free to arbitrarily fix any norm of either one. In Hoyer's algorithm the L_2 norm of h_i is fixed to unity. In this study we have re-run computer experiments with Hoyer's NMF method. The computer experiments, including partially occluded face parts, yielded recognition rates similar to the previously published versions of NMF. In spite of the advantages of the explicit sparseness control in the NMF optimization algorithm proposed by Hoyer, we do not see any direct relation of the sparseness to image parts, as we intuitively understand them. Although it ensures basis vectors with many zeros and local non-zero components, these have not any clear relation to locally defined image parts (regions).
Recently, Spratling (2006) investigated how NMF performs in realistic environments where occlusions take place. As a basic benchmark task he chose a bars problem that consists of a system of elementary bar patterns. He tested NMF algorithms also on the face images from the CBCL and ORL face databases. Based on the results obtained in a comprehensive set of comparative computer experiments he claimed that NMF algorithms can, in certain circumstances, learn localized image components, some of which appear to roughly correspond to parts of the face, but others of which are arbitrary, but localized blobs. According to Spratling, the NMF algorithms essentially select a subset of the pixels which are simultaneously active across multiple images to be represented by a single basis vector. In the case of faces, large subsets of the training images contain virtually identical patterns of the pixel values (eyes, nose, mouth, etc.). The NMF algorithms form distinct basis vectors to represent pieces of these recurring patterns. Spratling concludes that the separate

representation of sub-patterns is due to constraints imposed by the algorithms and is not based on evidence contained in the training images. Hence, while these constraints make it appear that NMF algorithms have learned face parts, these algorithms are representing arbitrary parts of larger image features.

Summarizing the above mentioned results and statements of several authors on the NMF representation of occluded images, we claim that

- the notion of "local representation" is not identical to the notion of "parts-based representation",
- the "sparse representation" does not automatically yield "parts-based representation", and
- the "parts-based representation" of images, as proposed in the published papers, provides no guarantee of achieving satisfactory recognition rates in cases with object occlusions.

3. A modification of the NMF for more efficient application to the problem of object detection in images

For a particular recognition task of objects represented by a set of training images (*V*) we need: (i) to calculate (in off-line mode) projection vectors of the training images onto the obtained NMF vector basis (*W*) (feature vectors), and (ii) for each unknown input vector $\boldsymbol{y}$ to calculate (in on-line mode) a projection vector onto the obtained vector basis (*W*). Guillamet & Vitrià (2003) proposed to use the feature vectors determined in the NMF run, i.e., the columns of matrix $\boldsymbol{H}$. The problem of determining projected vectors for new input vectors in a way that they are comparable with the feature vectors is solved by the authors by re-running the NMF algorithm. In this second run they keep the basis matrix $\boldsymbol{W}$ constant and the matrix $\boldsymbol{V}_{test}$ contains the new input vectors instead of the training image vectors. The results of the second run are the searched projected vectors in the matrix $\boldsymbol{H}_{test}$. However, this method has some weakness, that we described in Soukup & Bajla (2008) using an example of 3D point data instead of high-dimensional images. The points have been divided into two classes A, B, based on point proximity. We ran NMF to get a two dimensional subspace spanned by two vectors w_1 and w_2, which together build matrix $\boldsymbol{W}$. For each class, it can be observed that the projection rays are all non-orthogonal w.r.t. the plane and that their mutual angles significantly differ (even for feature vectors belonging to the same class). Thus the feature vectors of the set A and set B are not separated clusters anymore. We suspect that a reliable classification based on proximity of feature vectors could be achieved in this case (Soukup & Bajla, 2008).

A second possibility to determine proper feature vectors for an NMF subspace, which is conventionally used (e.g., mentioned in Buciu (2007)), is to re-compute entirely new training feature vectors for the classification phase by orthogonally projecting the training points (images) onto to NMF subspace. Unknown input data to be classified are similarly orthogonally projected to the subspace. It can be noticed that the feature vectors determined in this way preserve a separation of the feature vector clusters, corresponding to the cluster separation in the original data space. In view of these observations, we proposed to favor the orthogonal projection method (Soukup & Bajla, 2008).

Nonetheless, *both* methods have their disadvantages. The method of Guillamet and Vitrià operates with non-orthogonally projected feature vectors that directly stem from the NMF algorithm and do not reflect the data cluster separation in the subspace. On the other hand, the conventional method does not accommodate the optimal data approximation result determined in NMF, because one of the two optimal factor matrices is substituted by a different one in the classification phase. In Soukup & Bajla (2008), we proposed to combine the benefits of both methods into one, i.e., benefits of orthogonal projections of input data and

preservation of the optimal training data approximation of NMF. We achieve this by changing the NMF task itself. Before a brief presentation of this modification, we recall in more details how the orthogonal projections of the input data are computed.
As the basis matrix $\boldsymbol{W}$ is rectangular, matrix inversion is not defined. Therefore one has to use a pseudo-inverse of $\boldsymbol{W}$ to multiply it from the left onto $\boldsymbol{V}$ (compare with Buciu (2007)). Orthogonal projections of data points y onto a subspace defined by a basis vector matrix $\boldsymbol{W}$ are realized by solving the following overdetermined equation system:

$$\boldsymbol{W} \cdot \boldsymbol{b} = \boldsymbol{y} \tag{5}$$

for the coefficient vector $\boldsymbol{b}$. This can, for instance, be achieved via the Moore-Penrose (M-P) pseudo-inverse $\boldsymbol{W}^{\dagger}$ giving the result for the projection as

$$\boldsymbol{b} = \boldsymbol{W}^{\dagger} \cdot \boldsymbol{y}. \tag{6}$$

Similarly, for the NMF feature vectors (in the off-line mode) we determine $\boldsymbol{H}_{LS} = \boldsymbol{W}^{\dagger}\boldsymbol{V}$, where $\boldsymbol{H}_{LS}$ are projection coefficients obtained in the least squares (LS) manner. These coefficients can differ severely from the NMF feature vectors implicitly given by $\boldsymbol{H}$. It is important to state that the entries of $\boldsymbol{H}_{LS}$ can contain negative values.
If one has decided to use the orthogonal projections of input data onto the subspace as feature vectors, the fact that the matrix $\boldsymbol{H}$ is not used anymore in the classification phase and that the used $\boldsymbol{H}_{LS}$, that is a substitute for $\boldsymbol{H}$, is not nonnegative anymore, gives rise to the questions whether matrix $\boldsymbol{H}$ is necessary in NMF at all and whether the corresponding encoding coefficient necessarily has to be nonnegative. Moreover, using the orthogonal projection method, we do not make use of the optimal factorization achieved by NMF, as the coefficient matrix is altered for classification. Consequently, we proposed the following modification of the NMF task itself: *given the training matrix* $\boldsymbol{V}$, *we search for a matrix* $\boldsymbol{W}$ such that

$$\boldsymbol{V} \approx \boldsymbol{W} \cdot (\boldsymbol{W}^{\dagger} \cdot \boldsymbol{V}). \tag{7}$$

Within this novel concept (modified NMF), $\boldsymbol{W}$ is updated in the same way as in common NMF algorithms. Even the sparseness of $\boldsymbol{W}$ can be controlled by the standard mechanisms, e.g., those of Hoyer's method. Only the encoding matrix $\boldsymbol{H}$ is substituted by the matrix $\boldsymbol{W}^{\dagger} \cdot \boldsymbol{V}$ to determine the current approximation error. The modified NMF method with Hoyer's sparseness scheme (henceforth we will speak about the Modified Hoyer NMF method) is used in Section 5 for comparison to the proposed NMF method and to Lee-Seung NMF method.

4. A particular concept of the parts-based NMF subspace representation using subtemplates

4.1 Conceptual considerations

In the description of the recent results achieved in the area of NMF methods, provided in the introduction, the emphasis was put on problems occurring in applications of these subspace representation methods to image recognition tasks with occluded objects. We see these problems at two basic levels, (i) in methodological lack of the parts-based principle definition, and (ii) in insufficient systematic evaluation (in the relevant literature) of recognition of images with occlusions. In this section we will address the first point, whereas Section 5 is devoted to the second one.
In the papers dealing with applications of NMF to image recognition tasks, the concept of parts-based representation is considered on an intuitive level, some analogy to the results of neurology is only mentioned. Therefore we based our reasoning about applicability

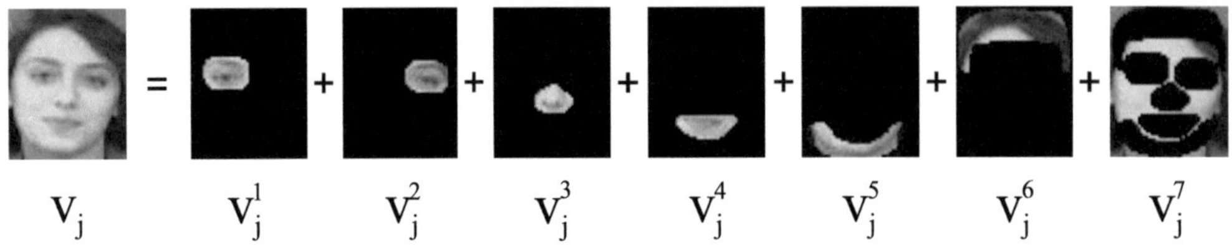

Fig. 1. Illustration of subtemplates for a face template with $p = 7$ parts defined.

of this principle to the NMF tasks on Hoyer's claims and Spratling's arguments. Both authors expressed a critical view to published statements that NMF subspaces follow a parts-based principle. They showed that single positive linear combination of NMF basis vectors obtained by conventional methods (considered as an analogy to combination of image parts) is not sufficient for achieving acceptable recognition rates in cases with occluded objects. They proposed some improvements; Hoyer by the introduction of a mechanism of explicit controlling of the matrix sparseness into the NMF scheme, Spratling by the development of an alternative dendritic inhibition neural network. The analysis of their results lead to the question: what property should NMF vector basis have, in order to really reflect the parts-based principle? We concluded that such a vector basis, in which the groups of vectors would uniquely correspond to individual image parts, could yield truly parts-based representation.

For his argumentation of discrepancy between the unsatisfactory results of application of the NMF to image recognition tasks with object occlusions and expectations of the parts-based representation bounded to the NMF methods, Spratling used a benchmark task of "bars-problem" with simple elementary image parts (bars). If the parts-based principle is tractable within the NMF representation of images with occlusions, then for any case of images with intuitively clear parts, the separate representation of parts by the corresponding NMF basis vectors should provide better approximation than the single nonnegativity of vector combinations. Such an NMF image representation should consequently lead to an improvement of occluded object recognition. Thus, our goal is to propose a benchmark task comprising real complex images which are composed of intuitively clear parts and to derive an NMF vector basis with basis vectors separately encoding these image parts.

4.2 Modular NMF

Intuitively clear understanding of *parts* of an image I_m can be based on the notion of set partition, namely, the partition of a set of raster points into a system of disjunctive subsets, the union of which is the whole raster. Similarly to the requirements used in image segmentation, we should consider only such subsets which give unique correspondence to individual objects or semantically unambiguous parts of an imaged reality (e.g., for face image we can consider as parts: left eye, right eye, nose, mouth, chin, and forehead with hair). In Fig. 1 an example is illustrated with the partition of a face into six parts and the face background as an extra part. For an image matrix I_m representing this face image (template) and subsets $P_1, P_2, \ldots, P_p$ which represent its individual parts we can write $I_m = P_1 + P_2 + \ldots + P_p$. Our intention is to formulate separate NMF tasks for the given parts of an image I_m that, however, would have data structure consistent with the initial NMF task. This means to preserve matrix size (n, m) of the initial image matrix I_m. We propose to do it by definition of matrices with the size (n, m) identical to the size of I_m in which all entries, except those corresponding to the given subset P_j, $j = 1, 2, \ldots, p$, are set to zeros. In accordance with the notation used in the domain of NMF methods, for the input matrix V with the columns $\mathbf{v}_1, \mathbf{v}_2, \ldots, \mathbf{v}_m$, which represent template images, we denote individual subtemplates of the j-th part as $\mathbf{v}_1^j, \mathbf{v}_2^j, \ldots, \mathbf{v}_m^j$. Thanks to the identical sizes of subtemplate image matrices we can express m templates from the input matrix $\boldsymbol{V}$ as the sums of the corresponding subtemplates:

$$\begin{aligned} \mathbf{v}_1 &= \mathbf{v}_1^1 + \mathbf{v}_1^2 + \ldots + \mathbf{v}_1^p, \\ \mathbf{v}_2 &= \mathbf{v}_2^1 + \mathbf{v}_2^2 + \ldots + \mathbf{v}_2^p, \\ &\vdots \\ \mathbf{v}_m &= \mathbf{v}_m^1 + \mathbf{v}_m^2 + \ldots + \mathbf{v}_m^p \,. \end{aligned} \tag{8}$$

Instead of one NMF problem for the input template matrix $\boldsymbol{V}$ of type $(n \times m)$, the basis vector matrix $\boldsymbol{W}$ of type $(n \times r)$, and the matrix $\boldsymbol{H}$ of encoding coefficients of type $(r \times m)$,

$$\boldsymbol{V} = [\mathbf{v}_1, \mathbf{v}_2, \ldots, \mathbf{v}_m] \approx \boldsymbol{W} \cdot \boldsymbol{H} \,, \tag{9}$$

we formulate p separate NMF tasks, each for the separate j-th part (i.e., for all subtemplates representing this part):

$$\boldsymbol{V}^j = [\mathbf{v}_1^j, \mathbf{v}_2^j, \ldots, \mathbf{v}_m^j] \approx \boldsymbol{W}^j \cdot \boldsymbol{H}^j \,. \tag{10}$$

The dimensions $r^\star$ of subspaces generated by each of p separate NMF tasks are identical and we define them as the integer part $r^\star = [r/p]$. For the j-th separate NMF task, $j = 1, 2, \ldots, p$, we express the $(n \times r^\star)$- matrix $\boldsymbol{W}^j$ of $r^\star$ basis column vectors as

$$\boldsymbol{W}^j = [\mathbf{w}_1^j, \mathbf{w}_2^j, \ldots, \mathbf{w}_{r^\star}^j] \,, \tag{11}$$

and, similarly, the $(r^\star \times m)$-matrix $\boldsymbol{H}^j$ of encoding coefficients -column vectors as

$$\boldsymbol{H}^j = [\mathbf{h}_1^j, \mathbf{h}_2^j, \ldots, \mathbf{h}_m^j] \,. \tag{12}$$

The individual components of the z-th column vector of this matrix are denoted as follows:

$$[\mathbf{h}_z^j]' = [h_{z1}^j, h_{z2}^j, \ldots, h_{zr^\star}^j] \,. \tag{13}$$

Assume we have solved all separate NMF tasks for p sets of subtemplates of image parts. Thus we have obtained p NMF subspaces described by the matrices $\boldsymbol{W}^1, \boldsymbol{W}^2, \ldots, \boldsymbol{W}^p$ of basis column vectors. For the j-th separate NMF task we can express the $z-$th column vector of the input data matrix $\boldsymbol{V}^j$ as an NMF-approximated linear combination of basis vectors:

$$\mathbf{v}_z^j \approx h_{z1}^j \mathbf{w}_1^j + h_{z2}^j \mathbf{w}_2^j + \ldots + h_{zr^\star}^j \mathbf{w}_{r^\star}^j \,. \tag{14}$$

In matrix notation we get:

$$\mathbf{v}_z^j \approx [\mathbf{w}_1^j, \mathbf{w}_2^j, \ldots, \mathbf{w}_{r^\star}^j] \cdot \mathbf{h}_z^j \,. \tag{15}$$

We would like to express the z-th template, i.e., z-th column vector $\mathbf{v}_z$ of the input matrix $\boldsymbol{V}$ of the initial NMF task using the results of the separate NMF tasks. First, according to our partition scheme (8), we can express the column vector $\mathbf{v}_z$ as

$$\mathbf{v}_z = \mathbf{v}_z^1 + \mathbf{v}_z^2 + \ldots + \mathbf{v}_z^p \,. \tag{16}$$

Using the results of the solution of p separate NMF tasks (using e.g., the Lee and Seung optimization scheme for the L_2-norm as a cost function) given in (15), we obtain the following (NMF) approximation of the given template

$$\mathbf{v}_z \approx [\mathbf{w}_1^1, \mathbf{w}_2^1, \ldots, \mathbf{w}_{r^\star}^1] \cdot \mathbf{h}_z^1 + [\mathbf{w}_1^2, \mathbf{w}_2^2, \ldots, \mathbf{w}_{r^\star}^2] \cdot \mathbf{h}_z^2 + \\ \ldots + [\mathbf{w}_1^p, \mathbf{w}_2^p, \ldots, \mathbf{w}_{r^\star}^p] \cdot \mathbf{h}_z^p \,. \tag{17}$$

The latter formula can be re-written in matrix notation

$$\mathbf{v}_z \approx [\mathbf{w}_1^1 \ldots \mathbf{w}_{r^\star}^1, \mathbf{w}_1^2 \ldots \mathbf{w}_{r^\star}^2, \ldots, \mathbf{w}_1^p \ldots \mathbf{w}_{r^\star}^p] \cdot \begin{bmatrix} \mathbf{h}_z^1 \\ \mathbf{h}_z^2 \\ \vdots \\ \mathbf{h}_z^p \end{bmatrix},$$

where components of the subcolumns in the matrix $\boldsymbol{H}$ are given in (13). For the whole input matrix $\boldsymbol{V}$ of templates we obtain as an approximative equality, the result of an optimization task of the NMF problem:

$$\begin{aligned} V &= [\mathbf{v}_1, \mathbf{v}_2, \ldots, \mathbf{v}_m] \approx \\ &\approx [W^1, W^2, \ldots, W^p] \cdot \begin{bmatrix} \mathbf{h}_1^1, \mathbf{h}_2^1, \ldots, \mathbf{h}_m^1 \\ \mathbf{h}_1^2, \mathbf{h}_2^2, \ldots, \mathbf{h}_m^2 \\ \ldots \\ \mathbf{h}_1^p, \mathbf{h}_2^p, \ldots, \mathbf{h}_m^p \end{bmatrix} = \\ &= [W^1, W^2, \ldots, W^p] \cdot \begin{bmatrix} H^1 \\ H^2 \\ \vdots \\ H^p \end{bmatrix} = \boldsymbol{W}^\star \cdot \boldsymbol{H}^\star \,. \end{aligned} \tag{18}$$

The approximate factorization of the input image template matrix $\boldsymbol{V}$ obtained in this way comprises basis vectors which uniquely correspond to the individual image parts defined in terms of a set of subtemplates of these parts. A remaining question is: what is the relation between our separated factorization $\boldsymbol{W}^\star \cdot \boldsymbol{H}^\star$, based on the Modular NMF, and any original factorization $\boldsymbol{W} \cdot \boldsymbol{H}$?

Let us denote $reserr_k$ the residual L_2-error of the k-th separate NMF task:

$$reserr_k = \sum_{i,j} \left\| V_{i,j}^k - (\boldsymbol{W}^k \boldsymbol{H}^k)_{ij} \right\|^2 .$$

Since in each individual NMF problem we solve the separate optimization problem (in L_2 norm) which differs from that formulated for the entire image, the residual error of the separated factorization of the entire image is not equal to the sum of the residual errors for the individual NMF tasks:

$$\|W^{\star}H^{\star} - V\|^2 \neq \sum_k reserr_k =$$
$$= \sum_k \sum_{i,j} \left\| V^k{}_{i,j} - (W^k H^k)_{ij} \right\|^2 .$$

Neither the equality between the residual error of an NMF solution of the original entire image $||WH - V||^2$ and the residual error of our separated factorization $||W^{\star}H^{\star} - V||^2$ is valid. What we can do is to formulate a modified optimization NMF problem in L_2 norm, as it is given in Eq. (2), with the initial matrices $W^{\star}$ and $H^{\star}$ instead of the matrices W, H, initialized by random entries. According to Lee & Seung (1999), the convergence property is maintained with all initial values of W and H, only resulting optimum may be altered. Thus, in our case, we use $W^{\star}$ and $H^{\star}$ to drag the NMF algorithm into the desired direction of the parts-based representation.

5. Computer experiments – a comparative study

5.1 Goals

Our analysis and exploration in the previous sections can be summarized in the following way. We have documented that the application of the conventional NMF method of Lee and Seung to image recognition problems with object occlusions does not provide expected parts-based representations. The further attempts to improve applicability of NMF to the recognition of occluded image objects, resulted in various NMF modifications. The semi-NMF approach, we proposed in Soukup & Bajla (2008) as a modification of Hoyer's NMF algorithm, manifested higher recognition rates for some occluded cases of the ORL face database. However, due to the acceptance of negative terms in the linear combination of the obtained NMF basis vectors, the method is even more distant to the parts-based principle. Based on this finding, our next intention was to modify the NMF scheme towards a vector subspace representation that is more compatible with the parts-based principle. The novel Modular NMF algorithm, we have proposed in the previous section, represents a possible improvement in this direction. The basic goal of the computer experiments was to explore behavior of these three NMF algorithms under various conditions. A detailed comparative study should contribute to the explanation of several unclear aspects we encountered in the papers on NMF in which the suitability of the NMF for image object recognition with occlusions was advocated. Moreover, as during some preliminary tests, reported in this Section, it appeared that using the conventionally used face databases suffers from some methodological drawbacks, we decided to analyze first the correctness of the test images and thereby to ensure the unified reference basis for comparisons. The details will be given below.

5.2 Testing conditions and our revisions of input data

There are five key aspects (variables, parameters) which can affect the recognition rate of the NMF algorithms applied to the given problem:

1. type and resolution of the images used for recognition,
2. type of partial object occlusions and the method of their detection and suppression,
3. classification method used,
4. metric of the NMF vector subspace used,
5. dimension of the NMF vector subspace chosen.

Fig. 2. Examples of face images selected from the ORL and YALE face databases.

5.2.1 Image databases

In our computer experiments we needed appropriate image databases with images containing intuitively clear parts. The public databases with faces satisfied this requirement. As in our computational study (Bajla & Soukup, 2007) we used 222 training images, and 148 testing images, selected from 370 faces of the Cambridge ORL face database[1] (Fig. 2, left). These two sets of images were chosen as disjunctive sets in a standard ratio of 60% for the training set and 40% for the testing set. The gray-level images with resolution 92×112 have been downsampled to the resolution $46 \times 58 = 2668$ pixels. For these face images, we defined four intuitively apparent parts of the face: left eye, right eye, nose, and mouth. The fifth part was determined as a complement of the union of all four face parts.

The second gray-level image database of faces we have selected is the YALE B face database[2] (Fig. 2, right). The database contains 5760 single light source images of 10 subjects, each seen under 576 viewing conditions (9 poses and 64 illumination conditions). For our experiments we have limited the number of illumination conditions to 5 representative cases, so that each subject was represented by 45 images. For each person, we have selected 31 images as training and 14 as testing, getting altogether the training set with 310 face images and the testing set with 140 face images. The resolution of the images is $62 \times 82 = 5084$ pixels.

In our preceding computer experiments (the study Bajla & Soukup (2007) and the paper Soukup & Bajla (2008)), also the CBCL face image database, comprising gray-level images with resolution of $19 \times 19 = 361$ pixels has been used[3]. Since the resolution of this database is much lower than in case of images from the two previously mentioned databases, for preserving approximately equivalent conditions, we have decided not to consider this database in the experiments reported in this study.

In the field of image object recognition, in particular, in the tasks in which the face image databases are standardly used, recently in Ling et al. (2006); Shamir (2008) a suspicion appeared that various classifiers, explored in these tasks, exploit not only the relevant information (face pixels), but they considerably utilize also an additional information contained in object background, implicitly comprised in most of the face images. If so, it should have significant consequences on correctness of a unified reference basis of testing image data for evaluation of performance of classifiers in image object recognition. Therefore, it was necessary to examine this suspicion on the selected two face image databases.

To address this question, we introduced alternative training and testing data sets (called "cropped") that contain no background pixels. The background was eliminated by cropping each image tightly around all the known face parts (i.e., left eye, right eye, nose, mouth).

[1] `http://www.cl.cam.ac.uk/research/dtg/attarchive/facedatabase.html`
[2] `http://cvc.yale.edu/projects/yalefacesB/yalefacesB.html`
[3] `http://cbcl.mit.edu/cbcl/software-datasets/FaceData2.html`

Later on, the cropped images were resampled to their original size by a bilinear interpolation. A result of such a cropping operation is shown in Fig. 3 (middle row). Note that, besides the apparent background elimination, this operation partly also normalizes positions of individual face parts.
Related to our analysis of the role of the parts-based principle used in applications of the NMF approaches to image object recognition, we made in Section 2, another aspect had to be investigated, namely, a possibility of how to transform input data in order to normalize geometrical location of the face parts in training and testing images. It can be shown that the NMF method may arrive at the parts-based representations only when distinguished image parts (i.e., principal building blocks) either reside at approximately stable positions or their shape does not vary too much. Otherwise the NMF optimization algorithm is not capable of finding a low dimensional subspace basis that would capture both shape and position variations of possibly occurring image patterns. In case of the face images from the ORL and YALE databases, one can observe significant differences between shapes of multiple parts of the same kind (e.g., eyes of different individuals), as well as variability in their placement within an image (Fig. 3, top row). This is an additional evidence supporting the idea that the raw facial data without any initial adjustment are not suitable for the NMF processing.
To answer this question, we proposed yet another training and testing data sets (called "registered") which contain faces with normalized positions of the face parts. Every image was transformed by an affine transformation so that centroids of its parts approximate the predefined positions as much as possible (Fig. 3, bottom row). Note that the centroid distribution here spreads much less than in the cases of the original and cropped data.

5.2.2 Occlusions

The topic of modeling image object occlusions has not been yet systematically addressed in the NMF literature. In computer experiments with various NMF methods applied to images from three image databases (Bajla & Soukup, 2007), we observed that recognition rates are, in general, sensitive to the location of occlusions. In order to examine the parts-based principle within the NMF scheme, the following aspects of object occlusions are of our interest:

- occlusions should have unique relations to natural facial parts,
- images containing artificial occlusions should be still recognizable by a human observer.

Our preliminary experiments showed that the exact geometrical shape of an occlusion does not influence the obtained RR values as much as its position. Consequently, we have decided for two alternatives, simple rectangles and more detailed polygonal regions covering the individual facial parts. The regions were defined manually by hand for both training and testing data within both ORL and YALE databases, however, only in the case of the Modular NMF, this information was used within the training process. To characterize behavior of projections of occluded faces in NMF subspaces and to evaluate the recognition results on a systematic basis, we have generated a system of four elementary facial occlusions: left eye, right eye, nose, and mouth (Fig. 4, 1-4). Additionally, four complex occlusion types have been defined as combinations of some of the four elementary occlusions (Fig. 4, 5-8).
To simulate a severe facial occlusion we have decided to replace original pixel intensities by zero values. As the assumed face parts have typically a higher brightness, their unoccluded pixel intensities range normally in higher values. Thus, in L_2 sense, the zero values within the occlusions tend to shift the occluded images far from their original unoccluded version (here the images are represented as vectors). Furthermore, such occlusions simulate presence of typical real world occlusions such as mustache or sunglasses, etc (Fig. 4, left). Hereinafter we call this occlusion type as "black occlusion".

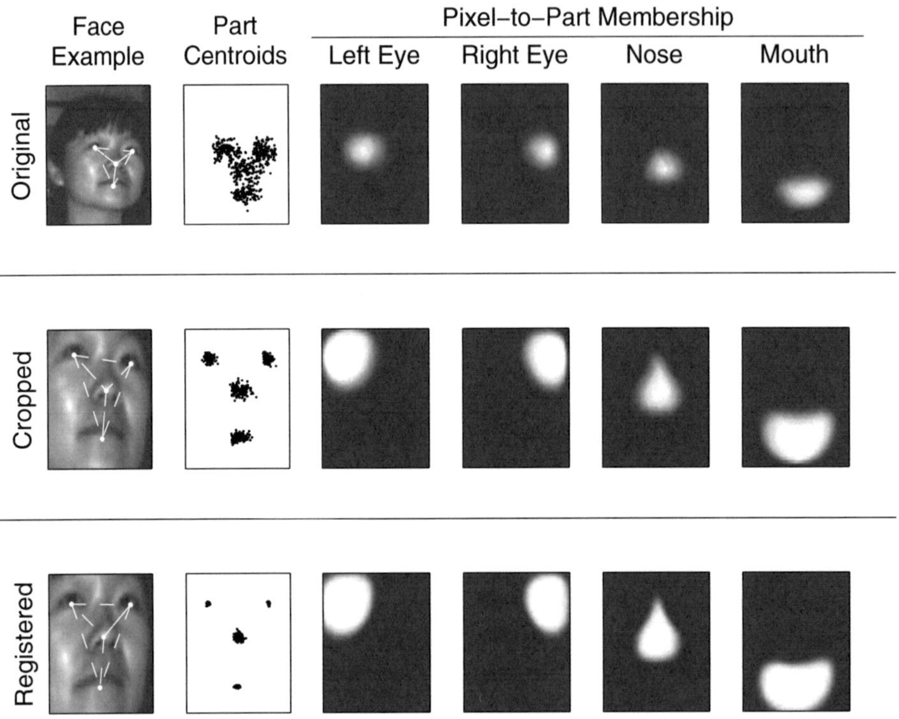

Fig. 3. An example of the original, cropped and registered face from the YALE database. The plots in the leftmost column contains original and transformed face images with centroids of individual face parts (i.e., left eye, right eye, nose, mouth) marked by white points. The second column comprises plots of distributions of the part centroid positions. The remaining four columns show plots of the pixel-to-part membership functions for different face parts. These functions express an estimated probability that particular pixel belongs to the certain face part.

If there exists a method for detecting the area associated with an occlusion, one may pose a question how to incorporate this a priori information into the NMF algorithms. In general there are two possible approaches to this problem: i) to suppress intensities belonging to the occlusion and replace them with values from the normal facial range, or ii) completely exclude the occluded image pixels from NMF calculations.

As for the first approach, we have implemented the occlusion suppression idea by filling the occluded image pixels by values interpolated from the nearest unoccluded pixels (Fig. 4, right). Such corrected images were treated the same way as occluded images and no further modifications of the NMF algorithms were required. Hereinafter we call this occlusion type as "interpolated occlusion".

As mentioned above, the second method for suppressing known occlusions is based on elimination of the occluded image pixels from the entire NMF calculations. Since the occlusion can only occur in the classification (testing) phase (i.e., the training data cannot be disturbed by any occlusions), the NMF training algorithms remain the same, however, a slight modification of the NMF classification procedure is required. Assuming that the exact position and extent of the occlusion is a priori known for every classified image, one can mask out (replace by zeros) all the occluded pixels in the classified image, as well as in all the training images. Only then these images are projected onto the NMF subspace and the classification algorithm is

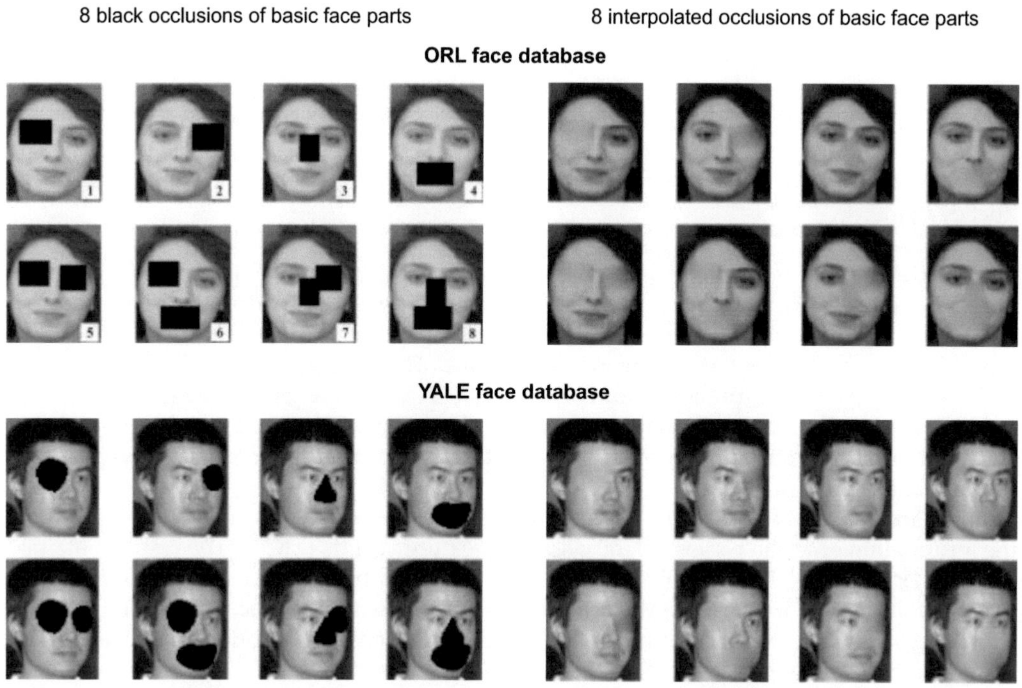

Fig. 4. Test face images with various types of partial occlusions - the left column - full black occlusions, and the right column - interpolated occlusions. The first row of images in each database example represents the elementary occlusions, while in the second row combined occlusions are displayed.

applied to the obtained feature vectors. Hereinafter, we call this occlusion type as "masked occlusion".

Understanding the essence of the mentioned three occlusion types (i.e., black, interpolated, and masked) and their connection to the NMF principles, one can make several assumptions about the performance of NMF applied to such data. Since the black occlusions represent the case where invalid pixels belonging to an occlusion have most severe impact on the final classification decision, the lowest performance should be expected here. In the case of the interpolated occlusions, where the impact of the occluded pixels is already partially suppressed, the classification performance should be significantly better than with the black occlusions. The best performance should be expected in the case of the masked occlusions where all disturbing image pixels are correctly excluded from the calculation and only the remaining valid information is used for making classification decision. Nevertheless, the need of having available all the original training data during the testing phase and the necessity of their masking and projecting along with every new classified image makes this approach highly memory and computationally demanding and, thus, rather difficult to apply in real situations.

5.2.3 Metrics

For the vector subspace methods of image object recognition a metric should be specified first. It measures the distance between the projection of the image being processed onto the subspace and the projections of the training images onto the same subspace (these are usually called feature vectors). In Bajla & Soukup (2007) we reported the results of vast experiments with various types of metrics: Euclidean, Riemannian (Guillamet & Vitrià, 2003), "diffusion-like" (Ling & Okada, 2006), and our modified Riemannian metric, carried out for various image databases and for several NMF methods. These results showed that Recognition Rates (RR) for Euclidean metric are comparable to those obtained for Riemannian metric and that they are much higher than expected in the paper of Guillamet & Vitrià (2003), and Liu & Zheng (2004). Therefore in our experiments with occluded faces we have used only Euclidean metric.

5.2.4 Classifiers

For recognition experiments with subspaces generated by the individual NMF approaches, it is necessary to classify each projection of a test image onto a NMF subspace in classes represented by feature vectors of the given subspace. The classification can be accomplished by means of various approaches, but usually the Nearest Neighbor Classifier (NNC) is used. The NNC is a standard stable non-parametric classifier providing good results having sufficient number of training examples. Some of the good properties of NNC are summarized in Duda et al. (2001).

In preliminary experiments with both face databases we tested also the classifier that utilizes the information on mean centers of the classes of feature vectors (MCC). The results obtained showed that for all three NMF methods, and for both basic types of occlusions (black or interpolated), as well as for all individual cases of partial occlusions (elementary and combined), the RR values achieved for the MCC have been significantly lower than the RR values for the NNC.

Testing more sophisticated classifiers in our experiments of NMF was beyond our interest, but more importantly, the main reason of the application of the NNC exclusively, was to ensure the unified methodological basis of comparison used in most of the papers published in this area (see References).

Subspace dimensions

For both face image databases, we have varied the dimensions of the NMF-subspaces from $r = 25$ up to 250. Elementary and combined types of occlusions have been applied to all test images. The recognition rates have been calculated separately for each set of testing faces with one occlusion type.

For each of the training face images we determined regions of the defined parts by hand (using approximate curvilinear boundaries) which served as subtemplates of the given database used in the Modular NFM algorithm. The sets of training subtemplates have been used for learning the basis image vectors of the individual separate NMF tasks which have been accomplished using Hoyer's algorithm with the controlled sparseness s_W. For solving the Modular NMF problems for the entire image we have used again the algorithm of Hoyer.

In Fig. 5 examples of basis vectors of 140-dimensional NMF subspaces are illustrated. These have been generated by solving two conventional NMF methods for the ORL face image database: Lee-Seung NMF method (Fig. 5, left), and the localized Modular NMF method (Fig. 5, right). Whereas the global nature of the conventional NMF basis vectors is apparent from Fig. 5, left, the vector bases of the Modular NMF method with separated vectors of individual face parts, clearly manifest locality of basis vectors (Fig. 5, right).

5.3 Benchmarking of three NMF methods applied to two face databases and using two types of image partial occlusions

The inclusion of the three above mentioned NMF variants pursued the basic goal to demonstrate their different performances in recognition tasks with occluded image objects.

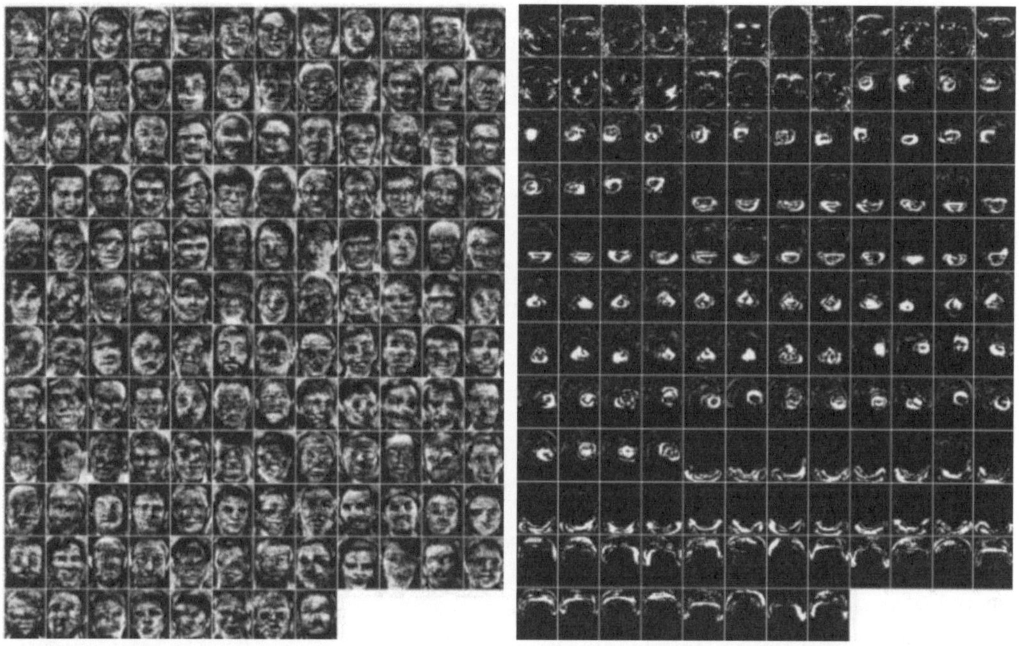

Fig. 5. Visualization of the vector bases of the 140-dimensional image subspaces for the ORL database: i) for the conventional Lee-Seung NMF method (left), ii) for the localized Modular NMF method (right).

The algorithmic versions differ in the following methodological characteristics: (i) the Lee-Seung NMF algorithm provides strictly nonnegative matrix factorization, however, its application to images reveals a discrepancy between the motivating parts-based principle and the real shape of subspace vector basis, and moreover, its expected overall superiority in recognition rates was not confirmed in practice, (ii) the Modified Hoyer NMF algorithm is not strict nonnegative (it is a semi-NMF method), it manifests no apparent relation to the parts-based principle, (iii) the proposed Modular NMF algorithm provides strictly nonnegative matrix factorization and it very closely reflects the parts-based principle. Thus each individual experiment includes the RR values (ordinate) for these three NMF versions which are graphically discriminated in the plots. As the basic variable parameter (abscissa) of the recognition, the NMF subspace dimension is used (Fig. 6).

5.3.1 Evaluation

As a basis for comparison, the NNC of the face images has been performed in the original data space without application of the NMF methods. In Table 1 we document the obtained RR values which confirm the claim of some researchers that questioned the suitability of using raw images contained in standard public domain face image databases. As mentioned above, we have examined this problem on two databases, i.e., ORL and YALE. First of all, a decrease of the RR values should be noted for cropped and registered unoccluded data (numbers listed in the parentheses in the second row of the table) in comparison to RR obtained for the nontransformed original input data. Further, the results obtained for occluded images show that for the raw input data, only minor RR differences between black and interpolated occlusion types are observed (about 9%). In contrast to these characteristics, the RR values achieved for the cropped and registered data manifest a radical change (about 42%). The most

	Original data				Cropped data				Registered data			
	ORL (.958)		**YALE** (.956)		**ORL** (.791)		**YALE** (.713)		**ORL** (.813)		**YALE** (.802)	
Occlusion	*Black*	*Interp.*	*Black*	*Interp.*	*Black*	*Interp.*	*Black*	*Interp.*	*Black*	*Interp.*	*Black*	*Interp.*
Left Eye	.895	.965	.889	.926	.194	.736	.279	.588	.201	.715	.308	.669
Right Eye	.909	.951	.926	.933	.319	.750	.500	.691	.298	.763	.522	.750
Mouth	.854	.951	.882	.948	.138	.770	.323	.705	.145	.770	.264	.742
Nose	.923	.951	.941	.955	.361	.763	.698	.757	.416	.777	.713	.823
LE+RE	.826	.958	.772	.911	.111	.631	.139	.441	.138	.534	.176	.485
LE+Mo	.798	.958	.772	.926	.118	.687	.117	.558	.097	.694	.114	.588
No+Mo	.756	.951	.852	.955	.076	.687	.338	.705	.083	.666	.294	.742
RE+No	.854	.944	.867	.955	.152	.729	.367	.705	.131	.701	.470	.727

Table 1. The RR values obtained by NNC operating in the original image space (i.e., no NMF applied). Different occlusion types, as well as no occlusions (numbers in parentheses) have been considered.

significant decrease of RR values (up to 10 times in the case of the occlusion combination of the nose and mouth) can be observed for cropped ORL images with black occlusions. RR decrease for the same types of occlusions in the case of YALE images is not so extreme. RR obtained for the interpolated types of occlusions are for both databases with cropped face images significantly higher than for the black occlusions. Some improvement in RR increasing is reached for the registered input images in all tested cases.
A set of plots of RR values versus NMF subspace dimensions are depicted in Fig. 6. In these figures we outline a complex picture of the research results on image data representation and reduction using the NMF methods. The ensemble of plots reflects the individual aspects of how the parts-based principle is reflected in each particular combination of parameters. We addressed these aspects in the previous sections. Using the mean RR values, calculated over all elementary types of occlusions (represented in the plots by circles), we intend to express tendencies prevailing in the tested face image recognition. Moreover, this information is completed by gray stripes depicting intervals between minimum and maximum RR values obtained for the elementary occlusions. Fig. 6a shows the results obtained for the ORL face image database, whereas Fig. 6b shows the results for the YALE database. For each database, square blocks of nine plots are related to different NMF approaches (i.e., Lee-Seung NMF, Modified Hoyer NMF, Modular NMF). Nine plots ordered in a single row summarize the RR values achieved for one type of input data (as explained above, we used original, cropped, and registered data). As for three basic types of occlusions (i.e., black, interpolated, and masked) included in our experiments, the plots belonging to one of these types are always collected into a single column. Based on the detailed analysis of relations between the RR plots given in Figs 6, the following findings can be formulated:

- When using the original data, comprising the additional information on the face background, small differences in the mean RR values obtained for all NMF methods and occlusion types, are observed. These values are very close to the RR values obtained for unoccluded image objects (marked as thick gray curves). Apparent differences can be observed only for the representative case of the combined occlusions (marked as thin gray curves). This finding relates equally to ORL and YALE databases.

- As for the cropped face images from both databases, which represent a correct reference basis for benchmarking the individual NMF methods applied to various situations in our research, significant differences are observed. The decrease of RR can be observed already for unoccluded data.

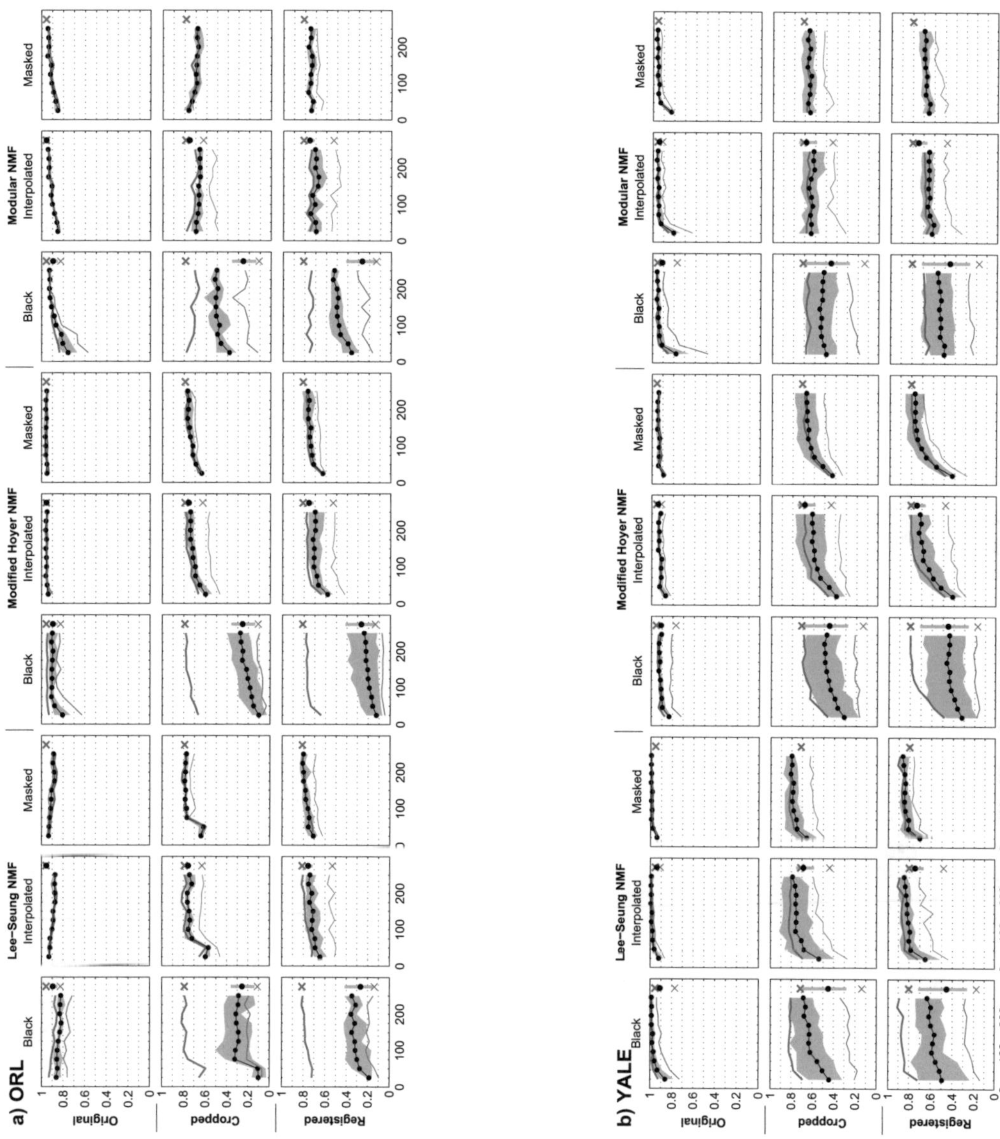

Fig. 6. Integrated presentation of RR for all aspects of NMF methods explored in the course of this study. Two basic blocks of plots are displayed for the face images from ORL (a) and YALE (b) databases. Each individual plot represents the RR values (ordinate) for one NMF method, one basic type of occlusion and ten dimensions of NMF subspaces used in the experiments (abscissa). In the plots, the circles represent the mean RR values calculated over all elementary occlusions, while the gray stripes depict intervals between relevant minimum and maximum recognition rates. The thick gray curves stand for RR values obtained for unoccluded images, while the thin gray curves show recognition rates for representative case of the combined occlusions (LE+RE). The detached bar on the right side of each plot (cross-circle-cross) represent RR values for NNC operating in the original image space.

- The goal of the registration transformation of face image data was to preserve an approximate constant position of face parts over the sets of training, as well as testing images and thereby to provide data suitable for building a parts-based representation. To preserve the correct basis for benchmarking, we applied the registration transformation to the cropped input face images, then, the contribution of this transformation to the improvement of RR can be characterized by a slight increase of RR for both databases, both basic occlusion types and for all three NMF methods explored.
- Focusing our attention only to the registered input data and to the results related to black occlusions, which reflect a real recognition of the raw face images occluded by objects comprising strongly disturbing intensities (approximately zeros), the ability to recognize the face image differs for the individual NMF methods explored. Namely, in the case of the ORL data, the lowest RR mean values are reached for the Modified Hoyer method, and the highest RR mean values are obtained for the Modular NMF method, moreover, this method is characterized by the narrowest stripe of RR variance over elementary occlusion types. RR obtained for the worst combined occlusion case (LE+RE) are also maximal for the Modular NMF. In the case of YALE data, the lowest RR mean values, with apparently widest variance stripes, are achieved again by the Modified Hoyer method. The slightly higher RR mean values than for the Modular NMF method are obtained for the conventional Lee-Seung NMF method, note that considerably higher RR values than in the case of ORL data have been obtained.
- In the plots, it can be seen that considering the interpolated occlusions, representing real situations when intensities belonging to face parts are closer to their normal range (unoccluded), leads to significant improvement of RR for all NMF methods explored and for both image databases (here, we still limit our focus on the registered input data).
- It is worth mentioning that for the registered data, and the maximum data reduction (i.e., subspace dimensions 25-50), the highest RR values are reached for the Modular NMF method – independently on black or interpolated occlusions,
- As for the masked occlusions, the plots confirm our expectation about a maximum improvement of RR for all three NMF methods. In this case almost no difference can be seen between occluded and unoccluded face images.

The explicit particular RR values obtained for all recognition situations included in the computer experiments, from which plots in Fig. 6 have been constructed, are given in Tables 2 and 3. Due to space limitations we made a selection of the most representative RR values (subspace dimensions 25, 250, and Original space).

6. Conclusions

In this research study, using the relevant papers published in the given area, we have analyzed the relation of the parts-based principle to the methodology of NMF data representation when applied to computer vision tasks of image object recognition under partial object occlusions. Beginning by the conventional Lee-Seung NMF method (Lee & Seung, 1999), that does not comprise any explicit concept of a vector sparsity, neither yields subspaces with the vector bases corresponding to natural image parts, the NMF algorithm development in the NMF literature proceeded towards the explicit incorporation of the vector sparsity constraints into the NMF optimization problem, and towards more locally specified vector bases of the NMF representation. After the short description of the NMF algorithm, that we developed in Soukup & Bajla (2008), as a more numerically efficient modification of Hoyer's NMF algorithm (Hoyer, 2004), we have proposed the novel Modular NMF approach that preserves

Subspace dimension	No occ.	Black occ. Max	Mean	Min	LE+RE	Interpolated occ. Max	Mean	Min	LE+RE	Masked occ. Max	Mean	Min	LE+RE
Lee-Seung NMF – Original (top) / Cropped (middle) / Registered (bottom) images													
25	.932	.891	.862	.816	.762	.932	.930	.925	.925	.939	.934	.925	.952
250	.871	.843	.821	.802	.715	.884	.872	.864	.884	.904	.887	.864	.898
Orig. space	.958	.923	.895	.854	.826	.965	.955	.951	.958	–	–	–	–
25	.655	.162	.100	.027	.068	.618	.596	.554	.463	.666	.638	.619	.622
250	.790	.385	.286	.144	.191	.802	.742	.694	.627	.788	.772	.755	.703
Orig. space	.791	.361	.253	.138	.111	.770	.755	.736	.631	–	–	–	–
25	.723	.210	.185	.162	.096	.700	.645	.581	.511	.754	.709	.668	.625
250	.805	.418	.346	.279	.150	.775	.738	.682	.559	.823	.801	.763	.688
Orig. space	.813	.416	.265	.145	.138	.777	.756	.715	.534	–	–	–	–
Modified Hoyer NMF – Original (top) / Cropped (middle) / Registered (bottom) images													
25	.932	.883	.806	.735	.627	.959	.939	.898	.898	.965	.950	.939	.966
250	.945	.931	.899	.850	.837	.952	.948	.945	.959	.952	.952	.952	.952
Orig. space	.958	.923	.895	.854	.826	.965	.955	.951	.958	–	–	–	–
25	.668	.162	.101	.027	.068	.625	.602	.540	.470	.659	.639	.628	.642
250	.783	.400	.274	.202	.097	.802	.740	.714	.566	.802	.767	.736	.737
Orig. space	.791	.361	.253	.138	.111	.770	.755	.736	.631	–	–	–	–
25	.642	.216	.125	.074	.048	.639	.582	.533	.422	.652	.629	.614	.604
250	.777	.406	.239	.121	.077	.761	.699	.614	.518	.822	.767	.729	.688
Orig. space	.813	.416	.265	.145	.138	.777	.756	.715	.534	–	–	–	–
Modular NMF – Original (top) / Cropped (middle) / Registered (bottom) images													
25	.837	.808	.755	.673	.572	.863	.852	.843	.836	.884	.852	.836	.858
250	.939	.932	.928	.925	.925	.945	.94	.938	.945	.952	.943	.938	.939
Orig. space	.958	.923	.895	.854	.826	.965	.955	.951	.958	–	–	–	–
25	.783	.509	.381	.319	.118	.741	.696	.632	.491	.815	.764	.743	.723
250	.709	.530	.502	.476	.239	.686	.663	.632	.551	.700	.684	.655	.662
Orig. space	.791	.361	.253	.138	.111	.77	.755	.736	.631	–	–	–	–
25	.758	.448	.361	.291	.171	.781	.696	.648	.551	.768	.743	.723	.653
250	.738	.557	.522	.479	.314	.755	.706	.659	.518	.768	.752	.702	.694
Orig. space	.813	.416	.265	.145	.138	.777	.756	.715	.534	–	–	–	–

Table 2. A subset of the RR values for individual cases of NMF subspace representations of the ORL face images selected from the set of all results used for the construction of the plots mentioned above.

explicit vector sparsity constraints introduced by Hoyer and simultaneously provides a truly parts-based vector basis of the NMF subspace. The main goal of the comparative computer experiments included in this study was to benchmark the results of the image object recognition with occlusions achieved by the above mentioned three NMF methods for a variety of recognition conditions. We decided to choose for these experiments the facial image data from public databases, since these data are freely available for other experimenters, and are most suitable for studying the algorithmic efficiency of the parts-based principle within the area of NMF data representation and reduction approaches to image object recognition under occlusions.

During the preparation of the extensive set of computer experiments, several methodological issues have revealed which had not been addressed in the existing papers. We have analyzed these issues and based on the results we modified the organization of our experiments. First of all, we have confirmed the published information about using the raw facial image data for benchmarking that suffers from the fact that, besides the relevant face-related pixels,

Subspace dimension	No occ.	Black occ. Max	Black occ. Mean	Black occ. Min	Black occ. LE+RE	Interpolated occ. Max	Interpolated occ. Mean	Interpolated occ. Min	Interpolated occ. LE+RE	Masked occ. Max	Masked occ. Mean	Masked occ. Min	Masked occ. LE+RE
Lee-Seung NMF – Original (top) / Cropped (middle) / Registered (bottom) images													
25	.926	.903	.861	.779	.727	.940	.922	.882	.867	.948	.940	.933	.941
250	.992	1.00	.986	.977	.941	.999	.99	.985	.977	1.00	.994	.985	.985
Orig. space	.956	.941	.909	.882	.772	.955	.941	.926	.911	–	–	–	–
25	.691	.635	.441	.316	.205	.695	.539	.391	.272	.754	.655	.551	.485
250	.808	.813	.683	.595	.338	.873	.788	.725	.595	.858	.798	.772	.625
Orig. space	.713	.698	.450	.279	.139	.757	.685	.588	.441	–	–	–	–
25	.720	.709	.493	.235	.139	.806	.65	.514	.439	.813	.704	.623	.588
250	.889	.739	.631	.507	.279	.910	.846	.822	.705	.903	.863	.808	.764
Orig. space	.802	.713	.452	.264	.176	.823	.746	.669	.485	–	–	–	–
Modified Hoyer NMF – Original (top) / Cropped (middle) / Registered (bottom) images													
25	.875	.844	.833	.814	.720	.903	.870	.830	.823	.911	.893	.875	.867
250	.933	.933	.905	.882	.808	.933	.917	.904	.875	.948	.939	.919	.933
Orig. space	.956	.941	.909	.882	.772	.955	.941	.926	.911	–	–	–	–
25	.463	.444	.310	.176	.169	.459	.388	.310	.264	.473	.430	.404	.338
250	.691	.665	.475	.345	.213	.777	.615	.502	.352	.784	.674	.588	.507
Orig. space	.713	.698	.450	.279	.139	.757	.685	.588	.441	–	–	–	–
25	.485	.465	.321	.176	.183	.495	.413	.330	.290	.503	.423	.382	.286
250	.801	.671	.439	.294	.191	.828	.716	.639	.462	.858	.769	.682	.698
Orig. space	.802	.713	.452	.264	.176	.823	.746	.669	.485	–	–	–	–
Modular NMF – Original (top) / Cropped (middle) / Registered (bottom) images													
25	.852	.873	.780	.660	.485	.851	.805	.748	.632	.851	.829	.807	.808
250	.963	.970	.959	.941	.889	.970	.954	.941	.919	.970	.959	.948	.933
Orig. space	.956	.941	.909	.882	.772	.955	.941	.926	.911	–	–	–	–
25	.683	.665	.491	.397	.183	.754	.638	.568	.316	.725	.650	.595	.507
250	.654	.665	.515	.404	.301	.725	.615	.514	.426	.710	.657	.622	.522
Orig. space	.713	.698	.45	.279	.139	.757	.685	.588	.441	–	–	–	–
25	.676	.628	.504	.411	.227	.710	.620	.570	.343	.717	.652	.610	.514
250	.698	.680	.563	.441	.264	.717	.646	.600	.483	.754	.696	.644	.602
Orig. space	.802	.713	.452	.264	.176	.823	.746	.669	.485	–	–	–	–

Table 3. A subset of the RR values for individual cases of NMF subspace representations of the YALE face images selected from the set of all results used for the construction of the plots mentioned above.

each image contains also the pixels from the background. These pixels can be in some sense even more informative than the facial pixels. The results of our experiments showed that classification of the face images significantly depends on the background presence. For ensuring a correct benchmark reference we proposed to crop all training and testing face images. Furthermore, for the sake of adapting the facial data for NMF parts-based representations, we proposed to normalize the positions of the explicit face parts (i.e., left eye, right eye, etc.) by the geometrical registration.

As for the issue of simulation of the partial object occlusion in images, besides usually used full (black) occlusions, we have introduced also interpolated and masked occlusions. The goal of the interpolated occlusions was to simulate a situation in which the intensities in occluded areas are being reconstructed by interpolation from nearest unoccluded facial pixels. The masked occlusions tried to simulate a situation in which the occluded image pixels were correctly excluded from the NMF calculations.

The detailed evaluation of the influence of various aspects on the Recognition Rates achieved by three NMF methods compared is given in the previous sections. The following general conclusions can be drawn on the basis of this evaluation. For the NMF benchmark studies, it is recommended to use cropped and registered facial image data. For recognition cases with full (nonsuppressed) occlusions and needing to maximally reduce dimension of the data representation, the Modular NMF method is recommended. For cases with other types of occlusions and without restriction on data dimension, the conventional Lee-Seung NMF algorithm slightly overcomes the two others. When the situation allows application of the masked approach to the NMF recognition, there is no apparent advantage of preferring particular one of the compared NMF methods.
It should be noted that the application of the interpolated and masked occlusion compensation method is completely dependent on the existence of an algorithm which is capable to identify the locations of the image pixels belonging to occlusions. Not to mention that the masking procedure is extremely computationally demanding, since it requires all original training data to be available during classification.

7. Acknowledgements

The research has been partially supported by the Slovak Grant Agency for Science VEGA (grant no. 2/0019/10).

8. References

Bajla, I. & Soukup, D. (2007). Non-negative matrix factorization – a study on influence of matrix sparseness and subspace distance metrics on image object recognition, *in* D. Fofi & F. Meriaudeau (eds), *SPIE*, Vol. 6356 of *Proc. 8th International Conference on Quality Control by Artificial Vision*, pp. (635614)–1 – (635614)–12.

Beymer, D. & Poggio, T. (1995). Face recognition from one example view, Proc. 5th ICCV'95, pp. 500–507.

Buciu, I. (2007). Learning sparse non-negative features for object recognition, Proc. 3rd IEEE Int. Conference on Intelligent Computer Communications and Processing, ICCP 2007, Romania, pp. 73–79.

Buciu, I., Nikolaidis, N. & Pitas, I. (2006). A comparative study of nmf, dnmf, and lnmf algorithms applied for face recognition, Proc. 2nd IEEE-EURASIP Int. Symposium on Control, Communications, and Signal Processing, ISCCSP 2006, Morocco.

Buciu, I. & Pitas, I. (2004). A new sparse image representation algorithm applied to facial expression recognition, Proc. IEEE Workshop on Machine Learning for Signal Processing, Sao Luis, Brasil, pp. 539–548.

Duda, R., Hart, P. & Stork, D. (2001). *Pattern classification*, John Wiley and Sons, Inc., New York.

Feng, T., Li, S., Shum, H. & Zhang, H. (2002). Local nonnegative matrix factorization as a visual representation, *Second Int. Conf. on Development and Learning*, Proc. ICDL '02.

Guillamet, D. & Vitrià, J. (2003). Evaluation of distance metrics for recognition based on non-negative matrix factorization, *Pattern Recognition Letters* 24: 1599–1605.

Heiler, M. & Schnörr, C. (2006). Learning sparse representations by non-negative matrix factorization and sequential cone programming, *Journal of Machine Learning Research* 7: 1385–1407.

Hoyer, P. (2002). Nonnegative sparse coding, *Neural Networks for Signal Processing XII*, Proc. IEEE Workshop on Neural Networks for Signal Processing, pp. 557–565.

Hoyer, P. (2004). Nonnegative matrix factorization with sparseness constraints, *Journal of Machine Learning Research* 5: 1457–1469.

Jolliffe, I. (2002). *Principal Component Analysis, Second Edition*, Springer-Verlag, Inc., New York.

Kanade, T., Cohn, J. & Tian, Y. (2000). Comprehensive database for facial expression analysis, Proc. IEEE Int. Conference on Face and Gesture Recognition, pp. 46–53.

Kim, J., Choi, J., Yi, J. & Turk, M. (2005). Effective representation using ICA for face recognition robust to local distortion and partial occlusion, *IEEE Trans. on PAMI* 27(12): 1977–1981.

Lee, D. & Seung, H. (1999). Learning the parts of objects by non-negative matrix factorization, *Nature* 401: 788–791.

Lee, D. & Seung, H. (2001). Algorithms for non-negative matrix factorization, *Advances in Neural Information Processing*, Proc. NIPS 2000.

Leonardis, A. & Bischof, H. (1994). Robust recognition using eigenimages, *Computer Vision and Image Understanding* 78(1): 99–118.

Li, S., Hou, X., Zhang, H. & Cheng, Q. (2001). Learning spatially localized, parts-based representation, *Computer Vision and Pattern Recognition*, Vol. 1 of *Proc. IEEE Computer Society Conference on Computer Vision and Pattern Recognition CVPR'01*, pp. I–207 – I–212.

Ling, H. & Okada, K. (2006). Diffusion distance for histogram comparison, Proc. IEEE Conference on Computer Vision and Pattern Recognition CVPR I, pp. 246–253.

Ling, H., Okada, K., Ponce, J., Berg, T. & Everingham, M. (2006). Dataset issues in object recognition, *Toward Category-Level Object Recognition*, Vol. LNCS 4170 of *Proc. IEEE Conference on Computer Vision and Pattern Recognition CVPR I*, pp. 29–48.

Liu, W. & Zheng, N. (2004). Non-negative matrix factorization based methods for object recognition, *Pattern Recognition Letters* 25: 893–897.

Liu, W., Zheng, N. & Lu, X. (2003). Nonnegative matrix factorization for visual coding, *2nd Int. Conf. on Development and Learning*, Proc. IEEE Int. Conf. Acoustics, Speech, and Signal Processing ICASSP 2003.

Mel, B. (1997). Combining color, shape, and texture histogramming in neurally inspired approach to visual object recognition, *Neural Computation* 9(4): 777–804.

Murase, H. & Nayar, S. (1995). Visual learning and recognition of 3-D objects from appearance, *International Journal of Computer Vision* 14: 5–24.

Paatero, P. & Taper, U. (1994). Positive matrix factorization: A non-negative factor model with optimal utilization of error estimates of data values, *Environmetrics* 5: 111–126.

Pascual-Montano, A., Carazo, J., Kochi, K., Lehman, D. & Pascual-Marqui, R. (2006). Nonsmooth nonnegative matrix factorization (nsNMF), *IEEE Trans. on PAMI* 528(3): 403–415.

Shamir, L. (2008). Evaluation of face datasets as tools for assesing the performance of face recognition methods, *International Jornal of Computer Vision* 79: 225–230.

Soukup, D. & Bajla, I. (2008). Robust object recognition under partial occlusions using nmf, *Computational Intelligence and Neuroscience* 2008: ID 857453; DOI 10.1155/2008/857453.

Spratling, M. (2006). Learning image components for object recognition, *Journal of Machine Learning Research* 7: 793–815.

Turk, M. & Pentland, A. (1991). Eigenfaces for recognition, *Journal of Cognitive Neuroscience* 3(1): 71–86.

Yoshimura, S. & Kanade, T. (1994). Fast template matching based on the normalized correlation by using multiresolution eigenimages, Proc. IROS'94, pp. 2086–2093.

7

Combination of Sparse Scan and Dense Scan for Fast Vision-based Object Recognition

Tam Phuong Cao
Department of Electronic Engineering, La Trobe University, Bundoora, Vic 3086 Australia

1. Introduction

Real-time processing speed is desirable for most vision-based object recognition systems. It is critical in some applications such as driver assistant systems (DAS). In DAS, the vision-based system is expected to operate on a moving platform and the system is required to inform the driver in a timely manner. Therefore, real-time frame rate is very important.
Much improvement has been made over the years to improve the speed of computer-vision systems. The cascaded classifier architecture and the integral image Viola & Jones (2001) are two of those major improvements in recent years. Following this approach many vision based systems, including face detection Viola & Jones (2001), can process images at high frame rate. However, with increasing tasks' complexity and image size, real-time processing speed for object detection systems remains a challenge.
Hardware platforms such as field programmable gate array (FPGA) have been employed to speed up the system performance. Cao Cao & Deng (2008) has shown that vision system can achieve real-time frame rate (60fps) with FPGA. However, the development time for an FPGA system is significantly longer than a system on computers. Hence, it is helpful to have real-time or close to real-time systems on computers as a proof of concept before porting them to hardware platform(s).
Frintrop Frintrop et al. (2007) proposed a visual attention system which combines bottom up and top down approaches to guide the search to interested regions. The bottom-up approach computes contains saliency maps based on image features such as intensity, colour and orientation. The top-down approach computes features specific to the target objects. Test results showed that using integral images Viola & Jones (2001) significantly improve system speed compared to the original method by Itti Itti et al. (1998). However, due to the complexity of the system, the processing frame rate reported (with optimized implementation) was only about 5.3 fps with 800×600 images or equivalent of about 7 fps with 752×480 images.
Zhang Zhang et al. (2007) proposed a method for detecting objects using multi-resolutions. In this method, multiple down sampled copies of the original image are used for detection purpose. The lowest scale is first computed, and then the detection process progresses to higher (resolution) scale. This method improves the speed of the processing system while maintaining or even marginally improve the system's accuracy compared to using only one (original) scale approach. By process a pixel in every 64 (8×8) pixels, the system reported

a frame rate of 25fps with image size of 320×240, or equivalent of about 6fps at 752×480. The proposed method, however, may not work well on small target objects where excessive down sampling may deteriorate the clarity of the target object, thus making it harder to detect. Another potential issue with this method is the large amount of memory required to store multiple copies of the original image, this memory usage could create a bottle neck when this method is used for large images.

Forssen Forssen et al. (2008) also used multi-resolution to detect and track objects. Due to the complexity of the search algorithm, this system could not achieve fast detection speed, only about 5 frames per minute or 0.08 fps. This approach also requires complex and expensive camera system to operate. Other multi-resolution approaches including Ma's Ma & Staunton (2005), Walther's Walther et al. (2005), Meger's Meger et al. (2008) and Cho's Cho & Kim (2005) are either too computational costly or not built to reduce system's computational cost.

From a different point of view, part-based object detection has been investigated for applications such as human detection Mohan et al. (2001); Wu & Nevatia (2007) or car detection Agarwal et al. (2004). The main purpose of these methods are searching for different parts of the target object and their relative relationship to detect the target object. The object's parts are either hand picked (by a trained person) Mohan et al. (2001); Wu & Nevatia (2007) or automatically selected Agarwal et al. (2004). In these part-based algorithms, searching for parts of target object is not to improve detection speed but to detect the target object itself.

In this paper, we propose a vision-based object detection method that combines part-based and multi-resolution approaches. This method detects target object based on the appearance of some of its parts as a result of sparsely scan through the original image. A finer scan in the image only happens at promising locations obtained from the previous sparse scan stage. This method does not require any down sampling of the original image. This method is similar to the cascaded classified in that it quickly processes easy features in simple stage (spare scan) then difficult features are processed by more powerful (but high computational cost) stage.

The remainder of this paper is organised as follows. Section II introduces the general dense scan and describe the proposed method. Section III describes the example systems employing the proposed method. Experiment results and discussions are also included in Section III. Finally, some conclusions are made in Section IV.

2. Proposed method

2.1 Conventional dense scan

As a common approach, to detect the target object in an image, a detection window at a specified size is scanned across the image. After pixels within that window are processed, the window is moved to the next location and the process repeats. The space between two windows' locations determine how many windows are to be processed in an image. Given the same algorithm and computing platform, an increased number of detection window to be processed will increase the computational cost, therefore increase the processing time required for an image. The most popularly used scanning methods is the dense scan (DS) method where the detection window is scanned pixel by pixel within the image. To process a large image, the DS method needs to process a very large number of detection windows, resulting in long processing time.

A simple idea that has been widely used to reduce computational cost in many practical applications is skipping pixels, i.e. a certain number of rows and/or columns of pixels or certain areas in the image are ignored, leaving a smaller number of pixels being processed normally. As a result the amount of data to be processed per image is reduced. However the detection performance of the algorithm may be degraded. The amount of accuracy reduction depends on the robustness of the algorithm and the size of the target object. For example, in a pedestrian detection system proposed by Dalal Dalal & Triggs (2005), the 64×128 pixel detection window is sparsely scanned (every 8th rows and columns) to achieve faster processing. It was reported that the detection performance of the system increased by 5% when the detection window scanned the image more densely (every 4th rows and columns) while computational time increased significantly. This indicates that some accuracy has been sacrificed for speed by skipping pixels. In the example system Dalal & Triggs (2005), the target object is large, hence the small increase in the scan step did not significantly affect the detection performance. The effect of skipping pixels to the system's performance is expected to be larger when a small object is to be detected within a high resolution image.

2.2 Sparse scan

In this paper a combined scanning method is proposed to improve speed while maintaining accuracy of the detection algorithm. In the SS part of the combined scanning method, detection window is moved multiple rows and columns every time the detection window finishes processing at a location. This is similar to the case of skipping pixels. The major difference between the SS, DS scanning (and pixel skipping) methods is in how positive and negative samples are defined during the training process. During the training process, positive samples used for DS and pixel skipping method assume full appearance of the target object while the SS method assumes only some parts of target object are presented. This is similar to detecting parts of the object in the image.

In the case of the DS method, a positive detection window contains an image of the target object together with some noise. In the some transform feature space, such as HoG Dalal & Triggs (2005), the positive detection window is an input vector $\mathbf{x_d}$ which is made up of:

$$\mathbf{x} = \mathbf{x_d} + \mathbf{n} \tag{1}$$

where $\mathbf{x} = \{x_1, x_2, ..., x_p\}$ is a p-dimensional vector generated from a detection window, $\mathbf{x_d} = \{x_{d1}, x_{d2}, ..., x_{ds}\}$ is p-dimensional input vector from the target object, $\mathbf{n}$ is noise in the image such as lighting variations, rotation, skew or white noise.

In the DS method, the detection window passes through every location in the image. Therefore, if there is a target object of the right size in the image, it will fully appear in the detection window and be detected at some point. An example of a possible positive example for the DS classifier is shown in Fig.1.(a) and Fig.1.(c) where a full stop sign or a person appears in the detection window.

For the SS classifier, a positive detection window contains an image of major parts of the target object, image of random background and noise. In some transformed feature space, such as HoG Dalal & Triggs (2005), a positive input vector $\mathbf{x_s}$ is made up of:

$$\mathbf{x_s} = \mathbf{u} + \mathbf{t} + \mathbf{n} \tag{2}$$

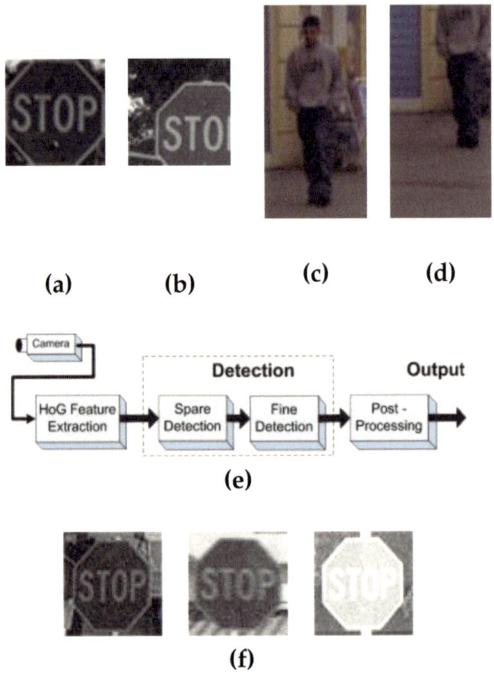

Fig. 1. Positive samples. (a) A positive sample for DS method. (b),(c)Positive sample for SS method which contains majority of stop sign and some random background.

where $\mathbf{u} = \{u_1, u_2, ..., u_p\}$ is a p-dimensional input vector generated from the visible parts of target object within the detection window; $\mathbf{t}$ is another p-dimensional vector that is generated from the random background in the detection window; $\mathbf{n}$ is noise as in (1), which caused by lighting variations, rotation and/or white noise. Equation (1) is a special case of (2) when $\mathbf{t} = \mathbf{0}$, which means the entire stop sign appear inside the detection window. Examples of positive detection windows for the SS classifier are shown in Fig.1(b) and Fig.1.(d) where only some parts of the target object (stop sign or pedestrian) appear in the detection windows.
With the SS technique, a detection window is scanned block by block across the image instead of pixel by pixel. Each block is selected to have certain size such as 3×3 or 6×6 pixels. There is no prior information regarding which parts of the target object are visible or missing, and what type and size of background $\mathbf{t}$ and noise $\mathbf{n}$ in the image. Compared to (1) which has only one random variable $\mathbf{n}$ to be estimated in the training. Therefore (2) is harder to estimate during training process and different training data is required for SS classifiers.

We propose a combined method containing different SS classifiers and DS classifier. With this method, the SS classifiers quickly and roughly process the image then output a map of interested regions that may contain the target object. This map is then used by the DS method to thoroughly process the interested regions to detect whether the target object is actually presented. This combination is similar to multi-resolution approach where the sparse scan (larger block size) acts as processing low resolution image. The finer (smaller) SS and the final DS classifiers act as subsequent higher resolution images. The algorithm of this combined method is shown in Fig.2. This method can speed up the detection process as most of the

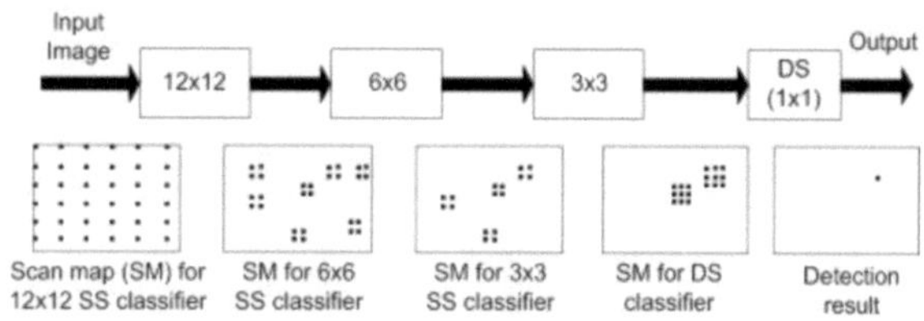

Fig. 2. Detection algorithm using combined SS and DS classifiers. Input image is first processed by the 12×12 classifier using initial scan map (SM). Then new SMs are generated, in which positive entries are at interested regions and their neighbours indentified by previous SS classifier. Final DS produces the detection result.

required processing is handled by the fast SS classifiers which sparsely scan through the image. Only small amount of processing is handled by the DS classifier. This method has another advantage of not requiring to perform resampling and store them in memory. In addition, because only the full resolution image is used, the target object is large hence easier to detect or lower FPPW rate.

3. Example system

3.1 Training data

To compare the performance of different approaches, SS and DS classifiers together with multi-resolution classifiers Zhang et al. (2007) are trained and analysed. Stop signs are chosen to be the target objects. For other target objects, the implementation process is similar but the performance is likely to differ.

Data for training as well as for testing were collected with an automotive grade camera, the Micron MT9V022, mounted near the rear view mirror of a car, as shown in Fig.3. This camera has native resolution of 480×752 pixels. A database of positive and negative sample images is built to train different classifiers. The positive sample set contains 225 extracted images at size of 36×36 pixels containing stop signs. These signs may be affected by size variations, rotation, skew, motion blur or added white noise. The stop signs in the positive sample set have the size of 36 ± 2 pixels across. Three of the positive examples are shown in Fig.1(f). It should be noted that the noise appear in those positive examples are actual noise recorded in the image. Added random noise (with maximum amplitude of 20 for 8-bit grayscale pixels) further degrades the quality of the image. This is done to improve the systems' robustness against noise in different lighting conditions and camera settings.

Different classifiers are trained with different positive and negative examples extracted from the training database. The positive examples of SS classifiers (3×3, 6×6, 9×9, 12×12 and the combination of 12×12, 6×6 and 3×3) were extracted from the positive sample set by using appropriate portion of stop sign (the u portion of e.q.(2)) and randon values (the t portion of e.q.(2)). For example, one member of the positive sample set can generate 9 positive examples when training the 3×3 SS classifier because the t portion in the positive examples of 3×3 SS classifier can range from 0 to 2 pixels in vertical and horizontal directions.

The negative sample set contains 195 negative images mostly at the resolution of 480×752 pixels. These negative images capture scenes of roads, buildings people, and road signs (other than stop sign). Negative examples are collected by moving a detection window within

Fig. 3. Camera used to collect data for training and testing. The camera is powered by USB cable connected to a laptop PC.

the negative images. Due to the resolution difference between positive and negative sample images, the total number of negative examples is much higher than those of positive examples. A test set consists of about 9700 images extracted from the 29 video sequences are used to test the performance of classifiers.

Different stop sign detectors were trained on a PC using Matlab following the DS only, combined SS and DS, and multiresolution approaches. These detectors employ AdaBoost and cascaded of classifiers techniques by Viola Viola & Jones (2001). The detection algorithms in these system were based on a variant of the HoG Dalal & Triggs (2005) feature set where only gradient angle is used (pixel's gradient magnitude was disregarded for faster computation of HoG features) similar to Cao & Deng (2008). The overview of detection system using the proposed SS and DS methods is shown in Fig.1.(e). Detection system that employs only the conventional DS technique is similar to the system shown except that the sparse scan step is by passed. The sparse scan block is equivalent to the low resolution processing in the detection system using the multi-resolution approach following Zhang's Zhang et al. (2007) approach.

3.2 Performance of classifiers

To compare computational cost of the DS, SS and simple multiresolution methods, we quantify computational cost of an algorithm as the total number of detection windows processed. According to the training results of different classifiers, shown in Fig.4.(a), it can be said that the smaller the block size, the lower FPPW the classifier can achieve. This is expected because the random portion t of (2) decreases with the reducing block size. Fig.4.(b) compares detection results based on the low resolution (resampled) images with those of the proposed SS methods. The Half-DS and Quarter-DS classifiers represent classifiers that process resampled images at half or quarter respectively of the number of rows and columns compared to the original image. This was to implement the multi-resolution detection where low resolution image is processed first. Interestingly, the Half-DS classifier performed worse (higher FPPW) than the 3×3 SS classifier and the Quarter-DS was much worse. This may be attributed to the difficulty of detecting the target object in low resolution images. Our proposed combined SS, whose structure is shown in Fig.2, has the FPPW approaching that of Half-DS (at lower computational cost). The 3×3 SS classifier aas the best performance with FPPW of 3.37×10^{-3}. Some example outputs of different sparse detection classifiers are shown in Fig.5. This figure clearly shows that full scan in low resolution produce a lot of false positive.

To compare the cost between different classifiers, let's assume that the total number of

Factors	SS Cost	DS Cost	Total Cost
3×3	34808	1058	35866
6×6	8702	15287	23989
9×9	3867	37587	41454
12×12	**2175**	74043	76218
Combined SS	6833	**192**	**7025**
Half-DS	78320	7894	86214
Quarter-DS	19580	17896	37476
DS only	0	313280	313280

Table 1. Cost of Different Block Size

Factors	**Detection**	**FPPW**	**Processing Time**
3×3	97.74%	8.82×10^{-7}	6.24 sec
6×6	96.22%	9.93×10^{-7}	4.10 sec
Half-DS	97.59%	9.16×10^{-7}	19.66 sec
Quarter-DS	97.60%	1.69×10^{-6}	8.57 sec
Proposed	97.44%	7.99×10^{-7}	1.98 sec

Table 2. Overall Performance of Different Classifiers

detection windows in a 480×752 image is 313,280 windows (excluding border pixels). When the DS only approach is taken, the total cost is simply 313,280 windows. When the system uses both SS and DS classifiers, with the structure shown in Fig.2, the number of windows processed is made up of the initial number of window processed by the SS classifier(s) (SS cost) and the number of windows need to be processed by the DS classifier (DS cost) as resulting from a positive output of the SS module. The SS cost is fixed and depends only on the block size of the SS classifier. The SS cost of different block sizes for the SS classifier is shown on Table.1. The DS cost depends on the performance of the SS classifiers. For example, if an SS classifier with block size of 3×3 accepts 100 windows as positive windows, then the DS cost is $100 \times 3 \times 3 = 900$ windows. As one would expect, the larger the block size, the less powerful the classifier will be, resulting in a higher DS cost. Based on training result, it is shown on Table.1 that the proposed combined SS and DS method has the least total computational cost. The Half-DS classifier has the second highest computational cost, behind the full DS.

3.3 Experimental results

After training, different classifiers were used to implement completed detection systems including the verification module following structure shown in Fig.1.(e). The same DS classifier is shared mong those systems. These system were tested against the test data set and the test results on a 2.6 GHz PC are summarised in Table.2. It is shown in Table.2 that the combined SS and DS systems have the lowest processing time which is about 20 times faster than the conventional method using only DS scanning technique. This speed improvement is due to the low computational cost of the combined SS classifiers, as shown on Table.1. It should be noted that the systems implemented on Matlab did not implement the integral images for each angle bin of the HoG features as used in Zhu et al. (2006). Using integral images is expected to further improve systems' speed without affecting the accuracy.

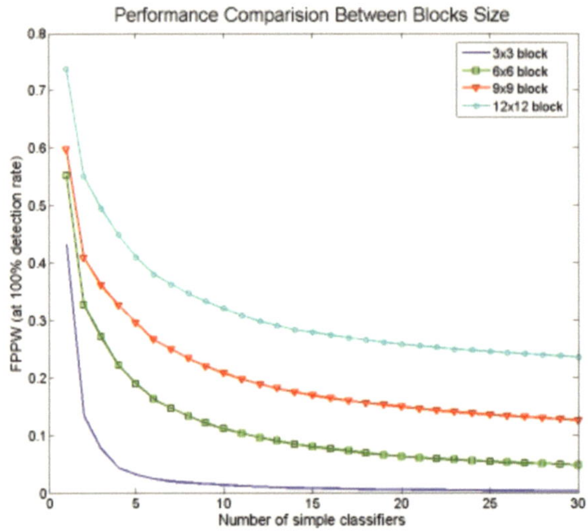

(a)

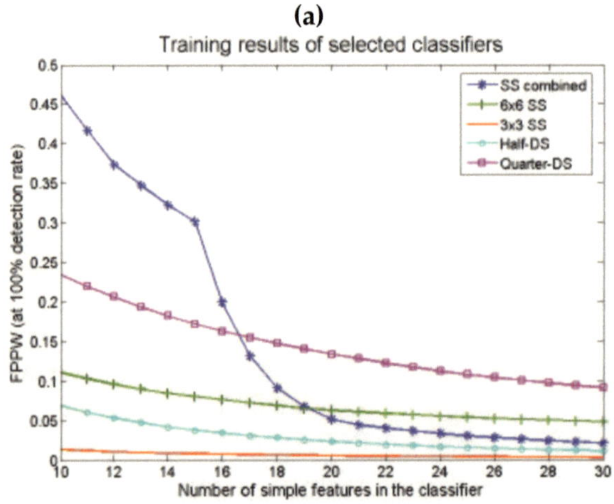

(b)

Fig. 4. Training results of Different Block Sizes for different classifiers. (a). Different SS classifiers. (b). Compare some SS classifers with other multi-resolution classifiers.

In terms of detection rate, all systems have similar detection performance because all of them share the last DS classifier. This similarity may change if different DS classifiers were trained and used for each system. The overall FPPW rate of each systems depends on the number of windows that passed the SS classifier(s) which is represented by the DS cost on Table.1. The combined different SS method has the least DS cost, hence it has the lowest FPPW as shown on Table.2. The false positive rate is greatly affected by the variations of the stop sign's size when the video sequences are manually annotated.

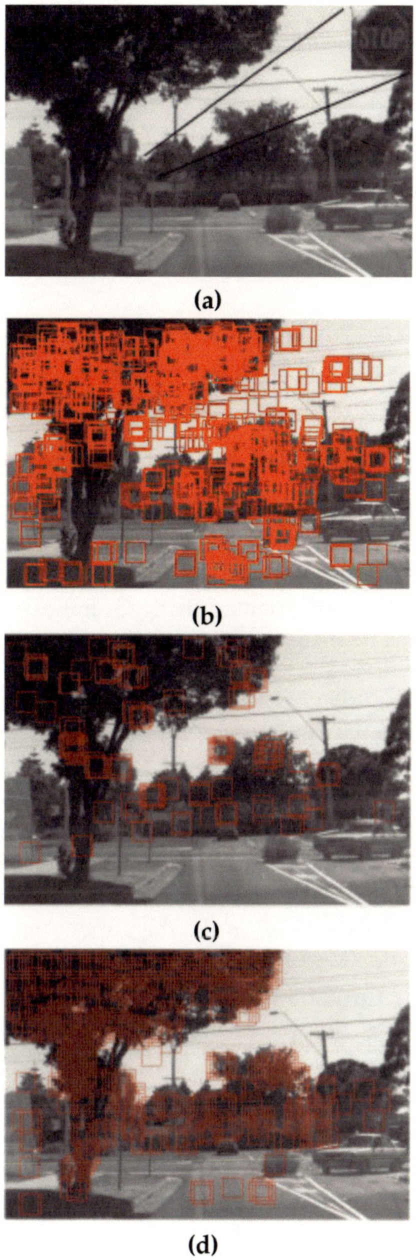

Fig. 5. Example output of SS and Half-DS classifier (a). Original Image. (b). Output of Half-DS classifier. There are a lot of false positives because there are 78320 windows to be processed per 376×240 image. (c). Output of 3×3 SS classifier. (d). Output of 6×6 Classifiers

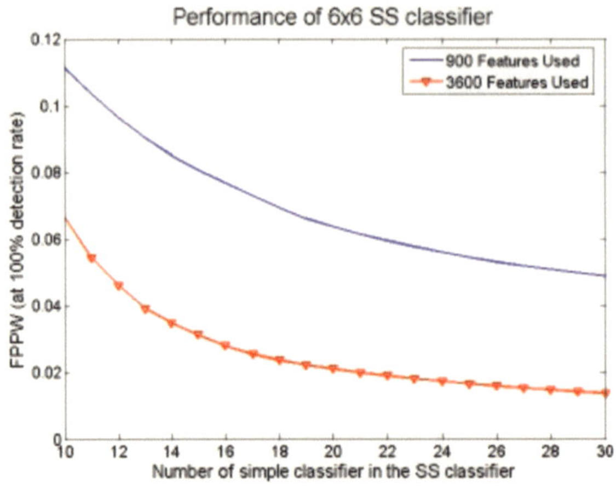

Fig. 6. Performance comparision of 6×6 classifier when using different feature sets

Classifier	DS	6×6 SS-DS	3×3SS-DS
Processing Time	216 ms	77ms	108ms

Table 3. Processing time of classifiers implemented using C : initial result

3.4 Discussions and future work

The performance of the systems studied in this paper can be further improved. The first technique could be used is to use a large more comprehensive feature set in training the classifiers. Generally, the SS and DS classifiers have a better performance ,i.e. lower FPPW rate, when more features are used in the training process. For example the 6×6 SS classifier can improve the performance to 0.014 FPPW when training the classifier with a feature set that contains 3600 HoG features, as shown in Fig.6. It is expected that increasing number of simple features in a classifier also decreases the FPPW rate. With the larger target object, larger sizes of the SS classifiers could be used. In our example, the target object is rather small 36×36, therefore the maximum scan step size considered was 12×12. With larger target object, it is possible to use larger block size to further reduce the computational cost.

The detection systems described in this paper are in the process of being ported to a C implementation. As shown on Table.3, with the initial C implementation using integral images Viola & Jones (2001), the 6×6 SS-DS classifier takes about 77ms to process a 752×480 image on a 2.6GHz PC (not including time for reading and writing input and output files). With those classifiers implemented in C, the time taken to construct four IMaps (one for each angular bin) is about 55ms. The amount of time for constructing IMaps is the major computing time required in the 6×6 and 3×3 SS-DS classifiers. If not taking to account the time taken for the IMaps construction, the 6×6 SS-DS classifier runs about 7 times faster than the original DS only method.

4. Conlcusion

In this paper, a combined SS and DS method for fast vision-based object recognition is proposed. This method is based on the combination of part-based and multi-resolution object detection. The processing of the image starts by sparsely scan the image to find parts of the target object. Finer scan is performed at those locations where positive output was detected at sparse scale. This method shows significant improvement in terms of speed while system's comparable accuracy compared to previously proposed multi-resolution methods. With the use of integral map and optimized software implementation, this method expected to be suitable for real-time applications.

5. References

Agarwal, S., Awan, A. & Roth, D. (2004). Learning to detect objects in images via a sparse, part-based representation, *IEEE Journal of Pattern Analysis and Machine Intelligent* **26**: 1475–1490.

Cao, T. P. & Deng, G. (2008). Real-time vision-based stop sign detection system on fpga, *Proc. 2008 Digital Image Computing: Techniques and Applications*, Canberra, Australia, pp. 465–471.

Cho, J.-H. & Kim, S.-D. (2005). Object detection using multi-resolution mosaic in image sequences, *Signal Processing: Image Communication* **20**(3): 233–253.

Dalal, N. & Triggs, B. (2005). Histograms of oriented gradients for human detection, *2005 IEEE Computer Scociety conference on Computer Vision and Pattern Recognition*, Vol. 1, pp. 886–893.

Forssen, P.-E., Meger, D., Lai, K., Helmer, S., Little, J. J. & Lowe, D. G. (2008). Informed visual search: Combining attention and object recognition., *Procs. IEEE International Conference on Robotics and Automation*, pp. 935–942.

Frintrop, S., Klodt, M. & Rome, E. (2007). A real-time visual attention system using integral images, *Proc. 2007 International Conference on Computer Vision Systems*, Germany, pp. 3385–3390.

Itti, L., Koch, C. & Niebur, E. (1998). A model of saliency-based visual attention for rapid scene analysis, *IEEE transactions on Pattern Analysis and Machine Intelligence* **20**: 1254–1259.

Ma, L. & Staunton, R. (2005). Integration of multiresolution image segmentation and neural networks for object depth recovery, *Pattern Recognition* **38**(7): 985–996.

Meger, D., Forssén, P.-E., Lai, K., Helmer, S., McCann, S., Southey, T., Baumann, M., Little, J. J. & Lowe, D. G. (2008). Curious george: An attentive semantic robot, *Robot and Autmation System* **56**(6): 503–511.

Mohan, A., Papageorgio, C. & Poggio, T. (2001). Example-based object detection in images by components, *IEEE transactions on Pattern Analysis and Machine Intelligence* **23**: 349–361.

Viola, P. & Jones, M. (2001). Rapid object detection using a boosted cascaded of simple features, *2001 IEEE Computer Society Conference on Computer Vision and Pattern Recognition (CVPR'01)*, Vol. 1, pp. 511–518.

Walther, D., Rutishauser, U., Koch, C. & Perona, P. (2005). Selective visual attention enables learning and recognition of multiple objects in cluttered scenes, *Computer Vision and Image Understanding* **100**(1-2): 41–63.

Wu, B. & Nevatia, R. (2007). Improving part based object detection using unsupervised, online boosting, *Proc. IEEE Computer Society conference on Computer Vision and Pattern Recognition*, Minnesota, USA, pp. 1–8.

Zhang, W., Zelinsky, G. & Samaras, D. (2007). Real-time accurate object detection using multiple resolutions, *Proc. 2007 IEEE International Conference on Computer Vision*, Vol. 1, Rio De Janeiro, Brazil, pp. 1–8.

Zhu, Q., Avidan, S., Yeh, M.-C. & Cheng, K.-T. (2006). Fast human detection using a cascade of histogram of oriented gradients, *Proc. IEEE computer society conference on computer vision and pattern recognition*, New York, USA, pp. 683–688.

8

An Approach for Moving Object Recognition Based on BPR and CI

Li Wang, Lida Xu, Renjing Liu and Hai Hong Wang
School of Economics and Management, Beihang University
China

1. Introduction

In the discipline of information science and technology, as one of the information systems frontiers, computer vision enables computers to interpret the content of pictures captured by cameras (Turban et al. 2005). A considerable interest in computer vision has been witnessed in past decades (Li et al. 2007; Xu 1999, 2006; Zhou et al. 2003, 2007). Examples of applications of computer vision systems include systems controlling processes, event detection, information organizing, objects modeling, etc (Bennett et al. 2008; Juang and Chen 2008; Kerner et al. 2004; Wei et al. 2006). Object recognition is one of sub-domains of computer vision. Accurate moving object recognition from a video sequence is an interesting topic with applications in various areas such as video monitoring, intelligent highway, intrusion surveillance, airport safety, etc (Hsu and Wallace 2007). In recent years moving object recognition has been considered as one of the most interesting and challenging areas in computer vision and pattern recognition.

In last few years, researchers have proposed a variety of methodologies for moving object detection and classification, most of them are based on shape and motion features. For example, an end-to-end method for extracting moving targets from a real-time video stream has been presented by Lipton et al. (1998). This method is applicable to human and vehicle classification with shapes that are remarkably different. Synergies between the recognition and tracking processes for autonomous vehicle driving have also been studied (Foresti et al. 1999). The attention on object recognition has been focused on specific parts of the visual signal and assigning them with symbolic meanings. Vehicles are modeled as rectangular patches with certain dynamic behavior (Gupte et al. 2002). The proposed method is based on the establishment of correspondences between regions and vehicles as the vehiclesmove through the image sequence. An object classification approach that uses parameterized 3-D models has been described by Koller et al. (1993). The system uses a 3-D polyhedral model to classify vehicles in a traffic sequence. Petrovic and Cootes (2004) extract gradient features from reference patches in images of car fronts and recognition is performed in two stages. Gradient-based feature vectors are used to produce a ranked list of possible candidate classes. The result is then refined by using a novel match refinement algorithm. There are many other moving objects classification methods based on multi-feature fusion (Lin and Bhanu 2005; Sullivan et al. 1997; Surendra et al. 2006; Takano et al. 1998; Zanin et al. 2003).

In our captured traffic scenes, moving objects are typically vehicles or pedestrians which can be mainly divided into four categories as trucks, cars, motorcycles, and pedestrians. The traffic conditions in certain areas may be quite complex and mixed traffic often appears. As a result, a traffic flow detection system may mistakenly recognize a pedestrian for a vehicle. In general, it is considered meaningful to categorize moving objects in realtime from a camera video stream in the intersection. It is expected that the difference of the area, the shape and the velocity can be distinguished among moving objects. However, under certain circumstances, due to possible occlusions, the characteristics of the objects can be more complex. Lighting, weather conditions, occlusions, shadows, camera calibration, and the importance level of the recognition are factors to be taken into consideration.

Artificial Neural Networks and Choquet (fuzzy) Integral (CI) have been used to solve recognition problems in recent years (Li et al. 2003a, b; Sok et al. 1994; Zhu et al. 2008; Zhou and Xu 1999, 2001). Some researchers have integrated the results of several neural network classifiers and/or fuzzy integral to obtain higher quality recognition (Cho and Kim 1995). We use a high-order neural network (HNN) based on Biomimetic Pattern Recognition (BPR) to model the input data and then extract features from the model. BPR was first proposed by Wang (2002). This new model of pattern recognition is based on "matter cognition" instead of "matter classification"; therefore, BPR is rather closer to the functions that human used to than traditional statistical pattern recognition using "optimal separating" as its main principle. The method used by BPR is called High-Dimensional Space Complex Geometrical Body Cover Recognition Method, which studies types of samples' distribution in terms of feature space, thus samples can be "recognized". BPR has been used in many fields such as in rigid object recognition, multi-camera face identification, and speech recognition, and the results have shown its superiority (Wang et al. 2003, 2005, 2006). Feature spaces have been studied in existing literature (Li and Xu 2001; Li et al. 2003a, b).

This paper mainly focuses on a recognition and classification method for multiple moving objects on a real-time basis. In performing classification tasks, observations from different sources are combined. Firstly, moments, area, and velocity of an object are extracted through classic background subtraction techniques. Secondly, BPR is used to classify the invariants obtained at the first step. Finally, CI is adopted for multi-features fusion purpose based on the area and velocity of the object extracted during the first step and the moments classified at the second step all together. A multi-stage classification procedure is realized thus the accuracies can be further improved. An experiment has been conducted for a mixed traffic intersection. Experimental results indicate that the learning ability and the accuracy of the proposed method are satisfactory.

The rest of the paper is organized as follows. Moving object detection and feature extraction are presented in Section 2. A multi-stage recognition model is discussed in Section 3. The experimental results are presented and discussed in Section 4. Finally, in Section 5, a conclusion is provided.

2. Moving objects detection and feature extraction

Detection of moving objects from image streams is one of our main concerns in this study. Although numerous studies have been conducted, many problems remain outstanding such as the changes of appearance caused by motion of an object or camera, occlusion of a target, and overlapping of objects. In this study, velocity, area and invariant features are used as features for classification purpose.

2.1 Moving objects detection

Segmentation of moving objects in traffic scenes requires the background estimate to evolve over the weather and time as lighting conditions change. We address the problem of moving object segmentation using background subtraction.

Optical flow is a powerful image processing tool for measuring motion in digital images. The optical flow algorithm provides an estimate of the velocity vector at every pixel from a pair of successive images. The traffic background is estimated through optical flow methods (Horn and Schunck 1981; Ji et al. 2005, 2006), and every frame (image) is analyzed to segment the moving objects from background, and a fusion algorithm is used that is based on background segmentation flow field and edge extracted by Cannyąŕs operator in the image sequences acquired by a fixed camera (Canny 1986).

2.2 Complex Zernike moments

Moments and functions of moments have been utilized as pattern features in a number of applications to achieve invariant recognition of two-dimensional image patterns. One advantage of complex Zernike moments is the ability to easily reconstruct the original signal from the moment values (Teague 1980). We first extract the area, shape and velocity of the moving object. Then we may take the first four order Zernike moments as shape parameters as the input of the HNN classifier based on BPR.

Complex Zernike moments are constructed using a set of complex polynomials which form a complete orthogonal basis set defined on the unit disc $x^2 + y^2 \leq 1$. They are expressed as A_{pq}. Two dimensional Zernike moment is,

$$A_{mn} = \frac{m+1}{\pi} \int_x \int_y f(x,y)[V_{mn}(x,y)]^* dxdy \tag{1}$$

where $x^2 + y^2 \leq 1$, $m = 0, 1, 2, ..., \infty$, $f(x,y)$ is the function being described and $*$ denotes the complex conjugate. n is an integer (that can be positive or negative) depicting the angular dependence or rotation, subject to the conditions:

$$m - |n| = even, |n| \leq m \tag{2}$$

and $A^*_{mn} = A_{m,-n}$ is true. The Zernike polynomial $V_{mn}(x,y)$ (Wang and Lai 2005) expressed in polar coordinates are

$$V_{mn}(r,\theta) = R_{mn}(r) exp(jn\theta) \tag{3}$$

where (r,θ) are defined over the unit disc and $R_{mn}(r)$ is the orthogonal radial polynomial, defined as

$$R_{mn}(r) = \sum_{s=0}^{\frac{m-|n|}{2}} (-1)^s \frac{(m-s)!}{s!(\frac{m+|n|}{2} - s)!(\frac{m-|n|}{2} - s)!} r^{m-2s} \tag{4}$$

To calculate the Zernike moments of an image $f(x,y)$, the image (or region of interest) is firstly mapped to the unit disc using polar coordinates, where the center of the image is the origin of the unit disc. Those pixels falling outside the unit disc are not used in calculation.

Translation and scale invariance can be obtained by shifting and scaling the image prior to the computation of the Zernike moments. The first-order regular moments can be used to find the image center and the 0th order central moment gives a size estimate.

2.3 Extraction of area features

The area feature can be obtained after each moving object is segmented. For region R, we assume that the area of each pixel is 1, the area of A can be easily obtained.

Since the scene to be monitored may be far away from the camera, assuming the world coordinate system and the image coordinate system is the same and the coordinate of the target point is $\{\alpha, \beta, \gamma\}$, then the projection on the image plane is

$$\alpha_1 = \frac{f\alpha}{\gamma}, \beta_1 = \frac{f\beta}{\gamma} \tag{5}$$

Generally, a truck has the largest three-dimensional size, and its projected area is the largest also. A car is smaller than a truck, and its projected area is next large. Motorcycles and pedestriansąŕ projected area are the smallest ones. However, the above assumption is not always correct since the projected area of an object is not only related to the objectąŕs actual area, but also the distance between the object and the camera lens. Therefore, objects of different categories may have similar project areas. Other recognition features besides area and shape must be taken into consideration.

2.4 Extraction of velocity features

The velocity of a moving object is denoted by the velocity in images and it can be obtained by classical block-matching algorithm. The match template is obtained during the moving object extraction process.

In general, the velocities in images are in proportional to the real velocities; therefore, we can differentiate different moving objects according to the velocities in images. The velocity of a car or a motorcycle is faster than the pedestrians. The speed range of various moving objects is different. Thus we can estimate the classes of the moving objects with velocities exceed certain values.

However, as an object moves along the camera optical axis, or in the intersections, or in jams, the above conclusion may not hold. As a result, multiple features are required to recognize a moving object.

3. Multi-stage object classifier

After detecting regions and extracting their features such as area, shape, and velocity, the next step is to determine whether or not the detected region is a vehicle. In order to obtain a reliable conclusion, information from several sources is to be integrated. A multi-stage object classifier system for classifying the detected objects has been developed. We first perform a quick classification by BPR using the first forth order Zernike moments obtained as input. CI is then used to perform a second classification of the results of BPR and the extracted results of velocity and area features.

3.1 Classification based on BPR

BPR intends to find the optimal coverage of the samples of the same type. An HNN which covers the high dimensional geometrical distribution of the sample set in the feature space based on BPR is used as a fast classifier (Wang et al. 2005; Wang and Lai 2005). The input layer has nine neurons ($A = \{A_{00}, A_{11}, A_{20}, A_{22}, A_{31}, A_{33}, A_{40}, A_{42}, A_{44}\}$) and the output linear layer has four neurons.

A moving scene can be seen as made up of regions with different motion parameters. We assume that each frame can be segmented into L subsets, forming moving regions, denoted as $\{Z_1, ..., Z_L\}$ The moving objects are considered as compact moving entities, consisting of one or more moving regions. Each moving object is assigned to a class. Each subset Z_k is associated with a nine-dimensional representative vector μ_k, describing the Zernike moment information of a certain moving region.

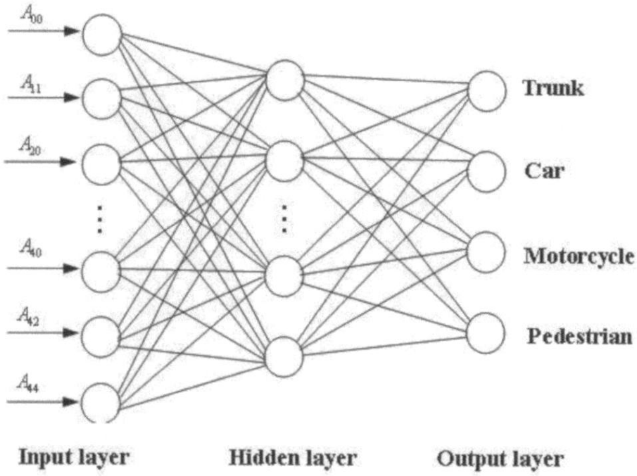

Fig. 1. A three layer high-order neural network

The architecture of a three-layer HNN is shown in Fig. 1. Each of these input units is fully connected with K hidden layer units. Again, all the hidden layer units are also fully connected with the four units of the output layer. Let $\{Y_1, Y_2, Y_3, Y_4\}$ denote the object recognition category, which represents trucks, cars, motorcycles, and pedestrians, respectively. The number of hidden layer units is determined experimentally. For an input vector, the output of j-th output node produced by an HNN is given by

$$\Phi(W, X) = \sum_{i=1}^{n} (\frac{W_{ij}}{|W_{ij}|})^S |W_{ij}(X_i - W'_{ij})|^P - \theta \tag{6}$$

where W_{ij} denotes the direction weight which connects the j-th input and the neuron, and it determines the direction of the neuron. W'_{ij} is the core weight which connects the j-th input and the neuron, it can determine the center position of the neuron; x_j is the j-th input. θ is the threshold, S and P are the power exponents. As parameter S and P change, the hyper-surface of the high-order neuron changes accordingly. If $W'_{ij} = 0$, $S = 1$, $P = 1$, in Eq. 6 holds, Eq. 6 is transformed into a classic neural network. If $W_{ij} = 1$, $S = 0$, $P = 2$ in Eq. 6 holds, Eq. 6 is transformed into a radial basis function neural network. Here three weight neurons are used to construct the high dimensional space geometry region.

The network is trained with HNN and 840 samples collected under various weather conditions used as training set. According to the principle of BPR, determining the subspace of a certain type of samples is based on the type of samples itself. If we are able to locate a set of multiweights neurons that covering all training samples, the subspace of the neural networks will represent the sample subspace. When an unknown sample is in the subspace, it will be determined if it belongs to the same type of training samples. Moreover, if a new type of samples is added, it is not necessary to retrain any trained types of samples. The training of a certain type of samples has nothing to do with the other ones.

4. Recognition based on CI

After the first stage classification, CI is used as the second stage classifier. Fuzzy integral is an effective means to solve complicated pattern recognition and image segmentation (Xu 1988). Recently, since CI has been found useful in data fusion, it has been enjoying successes in image sequence analysis (Cho and Kim 1995; Li et al. 2002; Murofushi and Sugeno 1991; Tahani and Keller 1999). The differences of the shape features of different moving objects is not distinguished under certain circumstances as occlusions happen, the recognition accuracy may not satisfy the requirements. Therefore, combining the area and the velocity to perform further fusion by CI is intended. With this approach, the information sources are given grades of compatibility, and the evidence is weighted and combined accordingly. From three features including area, shape, and velocity, we compute the CI. The definition is as follows,
Fuzzy measure over X is a function g defined on the power set of X, $g : \Omega \to [0,1]$, such that

1. $g(\Phi) = 0, g(X) = 1, g(A) \le g(B)$, if $A \subset B \subset \Omega$
2. if $A, B \subset X$ and $A \cap B = \phi$, then $g(A \cup B) = g(A) + g(B) + \lambda g(A)g(B)$, where λ is the unique root greater than -1 of the polynomial $\lambda + 1 = \Pi_{i=1}^{n}(1 + \lambda g(\{x_i\}))$;
3. if $\lambda > 0$, we must have $\sum g(\{x_i\}) < 1$

Denote $g(\{x_i\})$ by g^i which is called fuzzy density and is interpreted as the importance of the individual information source. For a sequence of subsets of $X : X_i = X_{i-1} \cup \{x_i\}$, $g(X_i)$ can be determined recursively from the densities as follows,

$$g(X_1) = g^1 \tag{7}$$

$$g(X_i) = g(X_{i-1}) + g^i + \lambda g(X_{i-1})g^i \tag{8}$$

CI (Murofushi and Sugeno 1991) $C_g(h)$ is defined as follows:

$$C_g(h) = \int_x h(x) \circ g = \int_0^1 g(h_\partial)d_\partial \tag{9}$$

where $h_\partial = \{x : h(x) \ge \partial\}$.
For $h(x_1) \le h(x_2) \le \cdots \le h(x_n)$,

$$C_g(h) = \sum_{i=1}^{n} g(X_i)[h(x_i) - h(x_{i+1})] = \sum_{i=1}^{n} h(x_i)[g(X_i) - g(X_{i-1})] \tag{10}$$

where $h(x_{n+1}) = 0, g(x_0) = 0$
Let $T = \{t_1, t_2, t_3, t_4\}$ be the object recognition category, which represents trucks, cars, motorcycles and pedestrians, respectively. A is the object to be recognized, and $X = \{x_1, x_2, x_3\}$ be a set of elements, which represents the recognition result of BPR, the area and the velocity of the object, respectively. Let $h_k : X \to [0,1]$ denote the confidence value of the target A belonging to class t_k The flow chart of target recognition algorithm based on CI is shown in Fig. 2

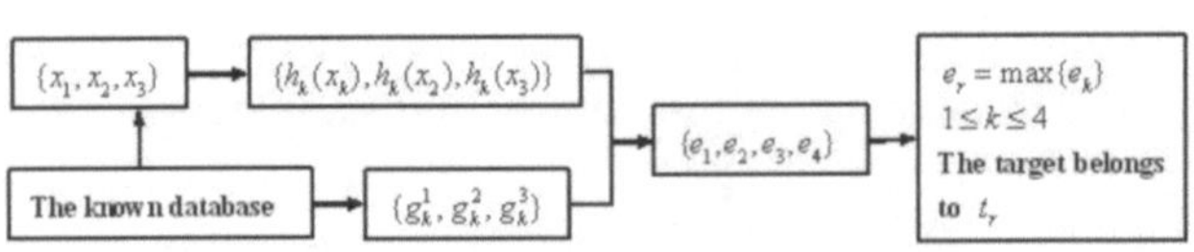

Fig. 2. Flow chart of target recognition algorithm based on CI

In our approach, we let $g_k^1 = 0.7$, $g_k^2 = 0.3$, $g_k^3 = 0.3$, $1 \leq k \leq 4$ (Cho and Kim 1995). We first treat each feature (property) as fuzzy variables and then assign fuzzy density to all possible values. $h_k(x_i)$ represents the degree. A belongs to class t_k according to x_i Figure 2 shows the flow chart of target recognition algorithm based on CI, and Fig. 3 shows the curves of the functions for confidence obtained by experiments.

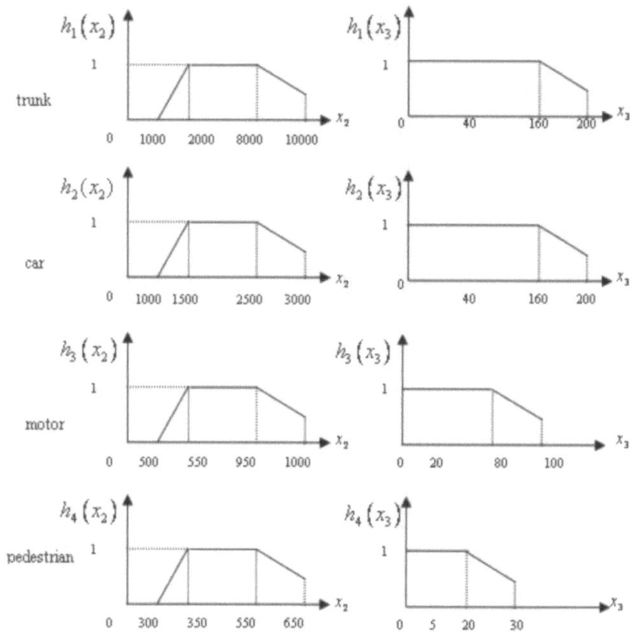

Fig. 3. Curves of the functions for confidence

5. Experiment

The videos used in our work are from the website (http://i21www.ira.uka.de) maintained by KOGS-IAKS Universitaet Karlsruhe. Traffic sequence showing the intersection Karl-Wilhelm-/ Berthold-Straβe in Karlsruhe that is recorded by a stationary camera under various weather conditions. In Fig. 4, we give a typical example of what we might obtain by moving object detection using the above method. After analyzing the traffic image such as shown in Fig. 4a, the current background is obtained as Fig. 4b shows. Figure 4c shows the detected moving object region, and Fig. 4d shows the foreground objects. We extract the moving objects and obtain the first fourthorder moments and set up the training image set by the algorithm proposed in Section 2.1. Four groups of experiments are conducted for normal conditions, heavy fog, heavy snowfall, and snow on lanes, respectively. Under each condition, we select 60 traffic frames to train the HNN, and then classify the other 30 moving objects. The results show that there exists misclassification between cars and trucks, and pedestrians and motorcycles. If we combine the first classification results by BPR, the area and the velocity as the input of CI classifier, the results can be improved. The comparisons are shown in Table 1 and Table 2. The proposed algorithm was able to classify trucks, cars, motorcycles and pedestrians. It can be concluded that the approach proposed in this paper has better recognition ability.

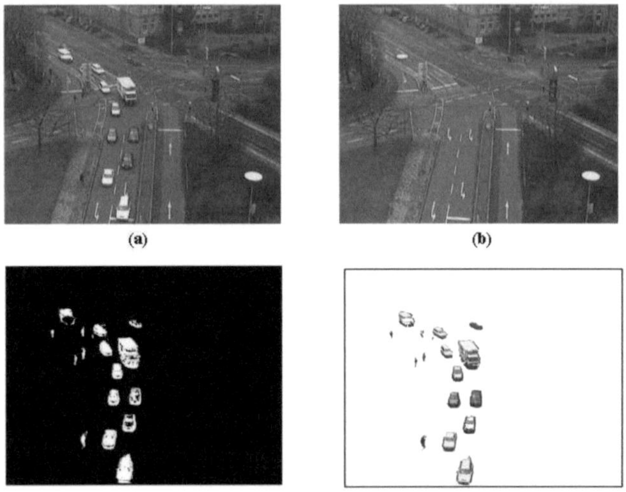

Fig. 4. a A sample frame in video sequence in normal condition; b current background; c detected moving object region by the background subtraction; d foreground

	Recognition result (%)				
	Truck	Car	Motorcycle	Pedestrian	Average
High-order Neural network	90.2	91.8	88.4	82	88.6
Combined with CI	94.3	94.1	92.9	92.8	93.5

Table 1. Recognition results in normal conditions

In this paper, the image size is 768 $\times$ 576 and we have conducted our experiments on a personal computer with an INTEL Celeron 2.4G CPU using Microsoft Visual c++ 6.0. The computation time per frame is around 0.1 s, depending on the image quality and the number of moving objects. For most applications, this can be considered as real-time.

	Recognition result (%)				
	Truck	Car	Motorcycle	Pedestrian	Average
High-order Neural network	90.8	91.2	88.5	82.3	88.7
Combined with CI	93.7	94.2	92.5	91.3	92.9

Table 2. Recognition results in normal conditions

6. Conclusion

In this paper, a multi-stage moving objects recognition approach is presented and applied to mix traffic environment. Area, velocity and invariant feature of the moving object were extracted firstly and BPR and CI techniques have been integrated to perform the multi-stage classification. The experimental results show that the proposed approach is effective.

7. References

Bennett, B., M. D. C. A. . H. D. (2008). Enhanced tracking and recognition of moving objects by reasoning about spatio-temporal continuity, *Image and Vision Computing* 26: 67–81.

Canny, J. (1986). A computational approach to edge detection, *IEEE Transactions on Pattern Analysis and Machine Intelligence,* 8(6): 679–698.

Cho, S., . K. J. H. (1995). Combining multiple neural networks by fuzzy integrals for robust classification, *IEEE Transactions on Systems, Man, and Cybernetics Part C* 5(2): 380–384.

Foresti, G. L., M. V. . R. C. (1999). Vehicle recognition and tracking from road image sequences, *IEEE Transactions on Vehicular Technology* 48(1): 301–318.

Gupte, S., M. O. M. R. F. K. . P. N. P. (2002). Detection and classification of vehicles, *IEEE Transactions on Intelligent Transportation Systems* 3(1): 37–47.

Horn, B., . S. B. (1981). Determining optical flow, *Artificial Intelligence* 17: 185–203.

Hsu, C., . W. W. (2007). An industrial network flow information integration model for supply chain management and intelligent transportation, *Enterprise Information Systems* 1(3): 327–351.

Ji, X. P., W. Z. Q. . F. Y. W. (2005). A moving object detection method based on self-adaptive updating of background, *Acta Electronica Sinaca* 33(12): 2261–2264. in Chinese.

Ji, X. P., W. Z. Q. . F. Y. W. (2006). Effective vehicle detection technique for traffic surveillance systems, *Journal of Visual Communication and Image Representation* 17: 647–658.

Juang, C., . C. L. (2008). Moving object recognition by a shapebased neural fuzzy network, *Neorocomputing* . in press.

Kerner, B., R. H. A. M. . H. A. (2004). Recognition and tracking of spatial-temporal congested traffic patterns on freeways, *Transportation Research Part C* 12: 369–400.

Koller, D., D. K. . N. H. (1993). Model-based object tracking in monocular image sequences of road traffic scenes, *International Journal of Computer Vision* 10(3): 257–281.

Li, H., . X. L. (2001). Feature space theory-a mathematical foundation for data mining, *Knowledge-Based Systems* 14(5-6): 253–257.

Li, H., L. L. . W. J. (2003a). Interpolation representation of feed-forward neural networks, *Mathematical and Computer Modeling* 37: 829–847.

Li, H., X. L. W. J. . M. (2003b). Feature space theory in data mining: transformations between extensions and intensions in knowledge representation, *Expert Systems* 20(2): 60–71.

Li, L., W. J. G. S. G. W. . Q. J. (2007). Advances in intelligent information processing, *Information Systems* 32(7): 941–943.

Li, X. B., L. Z. Q. . L. K. M. (2002). Detection of vehicles from traffic scenes using fuzzy integrals, *Pattern Recognition,* 35(4): 967–980.

Lin, Y., . B. B. (2005). Evolutionary feature synthesis for object recognition, *IEEE Transactions on Systems, Man and Cybernetics Part C* 35(2): 156–171.

Lipton, A., F. H. . P. R. (1998). Moving target classification and tracking from real-time video, *Proceedings Fourth IEEE Workshop on Applications of Computer Vision*, pp. 8–14.

Murofushi, T., . S. M. (1991). A theory of fuzzy measures: representations, the choquet integral, and null sets, *Journal of Mathematical Analysis and Applications* 159: 532–549.

Petrovic, V., . C. T. (2004). Vehicle type recognition with match refinement, *Proceedings of the 17th International Conference on Pattern Recognition*, pp. 95–98.

Sok, G. L., M. A. C. J. . Y. A. (1994). Moving objects classification in a domestic environment using quadratic neural networks, *Neural Networks for Signal Processing* pp. 375–383.

Sullivan, G., B. K. W. A. A. C. . R. P. (1997). Model-based vehicle detection and classification using orthographic approximations, *Image and Vision Computing* 15(8): 649–654.

Surendra, G., O. M. . R. F. K. (2006). Context-based object detection in still images, *Image and Vision Computing* 24(9): 987–1000.

Tahani, H., . K. J. (1999). Information fusion in computer vision using the fuzzy integral, *IEEE Transactions on Systems, Man and Cybernetics* 32(9): 1433–1435.

Takano, S., M. T. . N. K. (1998). *Moving object recognition using wavelets and learning of eigenspaces*, Springer, London.

Teague, M. R. (1980). Image analysis via the general theory of moments, *Journal of the Optical Society of America*, 70(8): 920–930.

Turban, E., R. R. . P. R. (2005). *Introduction to information technolog*, Wiley, New York.

Wang, S. J. (2002). Bionic (topological) pattern recognition-a new model of pattern recognition theory and its applications, *Acta Electronica Sinica* 30(10): 1417–1420. in Chinese.

Wang, S. J., C. X. . L. W. (2005). Object-recognition with oblique observation directions based on biomimetic pattern recognition, *Proceedings of International Conference on Neural Networks and Brain*, Vol. 3, pp. 389–394.

Wang, S. J., S. S. Y. . C. W. M. (2006). A speaker-independent continuous speech recognition system using biomimetic pattern recognition, *Chinese Journal of Electronics* 15(3): 460–462.

Wang, S. J., X. J. W. X. B. . Q. H. (2003). Multi-camera human face personal identification system based on the biomi-metic pattern recognition, *Acta Electronica Sinica* 30(1): 1–3. in Chinese.

Wei, Z., J. X. . W. P. (2006). Real-time moving object detection for video monitoring systems, *Journal of Systems Engineering and Electronics* 17(4): 731–736.

Xu, L. (1988). A fuzzy multi-objective programming algorithm in decision support systems, *Annals of Operations Research* 12: 315–320.

Xu, L. (1999). Artificial intelligence applications in china, *Expert Systems with Applications* 16(1): 1–2.

Xu, L. (2006). Advances in intelligent information processing, *Expert Systems* 23(5): 249–250.

Zanin, M., M. S. . M. C. M. (2003). An efficient vehicle queue detection system based on image processing, *Proceedings of the 12th International Conference on Image Analysis and Processing*, Vol. 3, pp. 232–237.

Zhou, S., . X. L. (1999). Dynamic recurrent neural networks for a hybrid intelligent decision support system for the metallurgical industry, *Expert Systems* 16(4): 240–247.

Zhou, S., . X. L. (2001). A new type of recurrent fuzzy neural network for modeling dynamic systems, *Knowledge-Based Systems* 14(5-6): 243–251.

Zhou, S., G. J. X. L. . J. R. (2007). Interactive image enhancement by fuzzy relaxation, *International Journal of Automation and Computing* 4(3): 229–235.

Zhou, S., L. H. . X. L. (2003). A variational approach to intensity approximation for remote sensing images using dynamic neural networks, *Expert Systems* 20(4): 163–170.

Zhu, X., W. H. X. L. . L. H. (2008). Predicting stock index increments by neural networks: the role of trading volume under different horizons, *Expert Systems with Applications* 34(4): 3043–3054.

9

Vehicle Recognition System Using Singular Value Decomposition and Extreme Learning Machine

Zuraidi Saad, Muhammad Khusairi Osman,
Iza Sazanita Isa, Saodah Omar, Sopiah Ishak[1],
Khairul Azman Ahmad and Rozan Boudville
Faculty of Electrical Engineering &
[1]Department of Computer Science and Mathematic,
Universiti Teknologi MARA
Malaysia

1. Introduction

The purpose of this research is to develop a system that is able to recognize and classify a variety of vehicles using image processing and artificial neural network. In order to perform the recognition, first, all the images containing the vehicles are required to go through several images processing technique such as thresholding, histogram equalization and edge detection before obtaining the desired dataset for classification process. Then, the vehicle images are converted into data using singular value decomposition (SVD) extraction method and the data are used as an input for training process in the classification phase. A Single Layer Feedforward (SLFN) network trained by Extreme Learning Machine (ELM) algorithm is chosen to perform the recognition and classification. The network is evaluated in terms of classification accuracy, training time and optimum structure of the network. Then, the recognition performance using the ELM training algorithm is compared with the standard Levenberg Marquardt (LM) algorithm.

2. Related study

Extreme learning machine (ELM) was proposed in Huang, *et al.* (2004) to provide the best generalization performance at extremely fast learning speed. Compared to ELM, the traditional implementations shown that the learning speed of Feedforward neural networks is in general far slower than required and it has been a major bottleneck in their applications for past decades. These are due to the slow gradient-based learning algorithms are extensively used to train neural networks, and all the parameters of the networks are tuned iteratively by using such learning algorithms. There are many researches have been conducted to compare the performance of ELM training algorithm for training a SLFN network with the other types of neural network training algorithms. Proposed research by Huang and Siew (2004) has extended to single layer feedforward (SLFNs) networks with radial basis function kernels of RBF networks with the implementation of ELM learning algorithm to easily achieve good generalization performance at extremely fast learning speed. This method allows the centers and impact widths of the RBF kernels to be randomly generated and the output weights to be simply analytically calculated instead of iteratively tuned. The experimental results show that the ELM algorithm for RBF networks is able to complete learning at extremely fast speed and produce generalization performance almost similar to SVM algorithm in function approximation and classification problems. Wang and Huang (2005) have evaluated the performance of training the ELM algorithm and the Backpropagation (BP) training algorithms to classify an identified protein sequence and unseen protein sequence in feature patterns extraction of biological data. The study has indicated that the ELM training algorithm needed up to four orders of magnitude less training time as compared to BP algorithm. The ELM algorithm has given better classification accuracy performance as compared to BP algorithm. Moreover, the ELM does not has any control parameters to be manually tuned and hence can be implemented easily. . Evolutionary ELM (E-ELM) algorithm has been proposed by Zhu *et al.* (2005) as an extended research from Huang and Siew (2004). The hybrid learning algorithm of E-ELM algorithm is preferably considered since the ELM algorithm may need higher number of hidden neurons due to the random determination of the input weights and hidden biases. The E-ELM algorithm uses the differential evolutionary algorithm to select the input weights and Moore-Penrose (MP) generalized inverse to analytically determine the output weights. This approach achieved a good generalization performance with much more compact networks as compared to other algorithms including BP, GALs (Ghosh and Verma, 2002) and the original ELM. In the conjunction of the above researches, this study is conducted to develop a different approach for classification task which relating between image processing method and artificial neural network Liang *et al.* (2006) has shown that the ELM training algorithm performance needs an order of magnitude less training time for the Support Vector Machines (SVM) and two orders of magnitude less training time for the BP algorithm. However, classification accuracy performance of ELM algorithm is similar as the SVMs and BP algorithms. From the study, it also shown that classification accuracies can be improved by smoothing of classifiers' outputs. This research has been implemented to classify mental tasks from EEG signals to provide communication and control capabilities to people with severe or complete motor paralysis. Terrain reconstruction in path planning problem for supporting multiresolution terrain access has lead to the study by Yeu *et al.* (2006). The ELM training algorithm has been implemented to speed up the rate for the network learns a priori available maps. From the results, it is shown that the ELM algorithm used during the query stage has performed better than BP, Delaunay Triangle (DT) and SVMs. Furthermore, the ELM training algorithm utilized far less memory for queries on large maps as compared to DT to achieve the same levels of MSE errors. Zhang *et al.* (2007) has quoted that the ELM is able to avoid the problems of local minima, improper learning rate and overfitting commonly faced by iterative learning methods and completes the training very fast. The research has been conducted to classify multicategory cancer based on microarray data sets of cancer diagnosis. The ELM algorithm classification accuracies have been compared with several training algorithms that are BP, Linder's SANN and SVMs of SVM-OVO and Ramaswamy's SVM-OVA. From the study results, it is indicated that when the number of categories for the classification task is large, the ELM algorithm achieves higher classification accuracy than the other algorithms with less training time and a smaller network structure. It can also be seen that ELM achieves better and more balanced classification for individual categories as well.

3. The proposed recognition system

The methodology used to develop the vehicle recognition system includes image acquisition, image processing, image extraction, image training and image testing using a SLFN network trained by the ELM and LM algorithm. To determine the suitability of the SLFN network in recognizing the images, it needs to go through training and testing phase. The training phase is chosen to be 96 dataset and 119 dataset for the testing phase. Once the network has learned the information in the training set and has converged, the test data is applied to the network for verification. The sigmoidal function is used for the hidden node activation function, for both the SLFN trained by the ELM and the BP training algorithms.

3.1 Image acquisition

Image acquisition device is set up as shown as in Figure 1 to obtain the best result in capturing vehicle images. The camera is placed above the bridge for a wider and better capturing area. A set of 119 data sample were captured in video format includes 52 images of motorcycle, 19 images of bus and 48 images of lorry. The image samples are then edited using Gretech Online Movie (GOM) Player to obtain the specific region and format needed for the training purposes. The Gom Player is able to play the majority of media files without the need to obtain a codec as well as play some broken media files. These will gives advantages over the traditional player, like Windows Media Player. Figure 2 shows samples images of motorcycle, bus and lorry that is used as data set in this research.

3.2 Image processing

Image processing is one of the major parts in this research due to the function of the images itself as the input for the training and testing process. All the possible noise, background or any other unwanted data in the images are removed to gain a stable system with high accuracy. In this process, firstly the original input image is cropped to create an interactive Crop Image tool associated with the image displayed in the current figure, called the target image which forms the input to the recognition system by using MATLAB. Sample of images after cropping process are shown in Figure 3. Figure 4 shows the images after converted to gray scale format. Next, the process of thresholding is applied to remove the background as illustrates in Figure 5. The qualities of the images are then enhanced by applying histogram equalization technique as shown in Figure 6.

The edge detection block by using Canny operator finds edges by looking for the local maxima of the gradient of the input image. It calculates the gradient using the derivative of

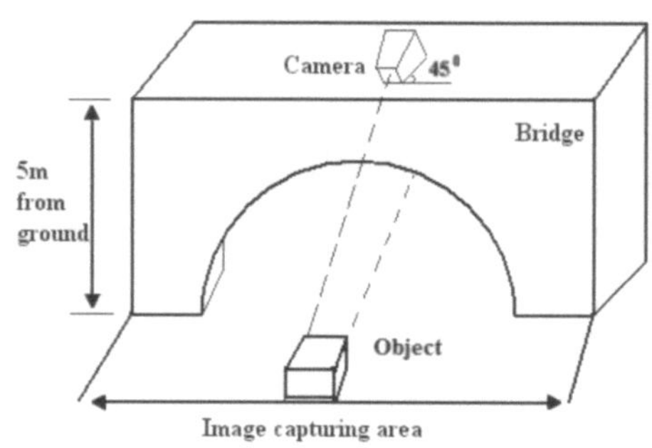

Fig. 1. Image acquisition set up

Fig. 2. Original input images

Fig. 3. The cropped images

Fig. 4. Gray image

Fig. 5. Thresholded images

Fig. 6. Vehicle images after applying histogram equalization

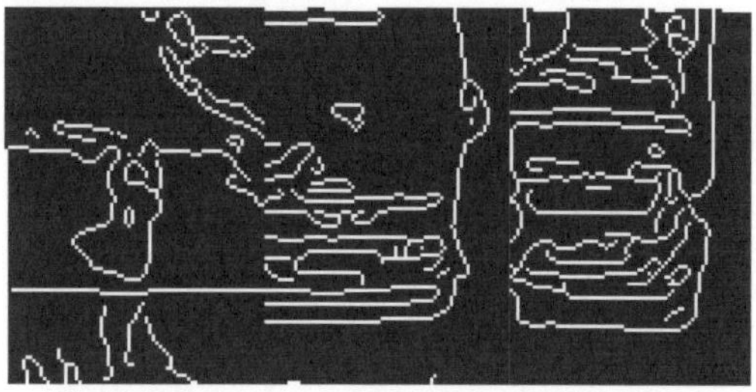

Fig. 7. Vehicle images after applying Canny edge detection

the Gaussian filter. The Canny method uses two thresholds to detect strong and weak edges. It includes the weak edges in the output only if they are connected to strong edges (Saad *et al.* 2007). As a result, the method is more robust to noise, and more likely to detect true weak edges as shown in Figure 7.

3.3 Singular value decomposition

Singular Value Decomposition (SVD) is a factorization technique for rectangular matrices largely used in signal processing and pattern recognition. The method is applied to extract all of the images into a data set that can be as the input for neural network training and testing processes. The purpose of singular value decomposition is to reduce a dataset containing a large number of values to a dataset containing significantly fewer values, but which still contains a large fraction of the variability present in the original data.

A non-square data matrix A of size $m \times n$ with $m > n$ can be factorized into three matrices U, S, and V using singular value decomposition as shown in equation above. Here U is an $m \times m$ matrix, S is a $m \times n$ matrix and V is an $n \times n$ matrix. S is the diagonal matrix containing all of the non-negative singular values of the original data matrix listed in descending order. U and V are orthogonal square matrices representing the left and right singular vectors for the data matrix. U represents the row space and the transpose of V represents the column space (Cao 2007).

$$A = USV^T \tag{1}$$

where matrix U is an $m \times m$ orthogonal matrix

$$U = [u_1, u_2, ... u_r, u_{r+1}, ..., u_m] \tag{2}$$

Column vectors i $\mathbf{u}$, for i = 1, 2, …, m, form an orthogonal set:

$$u_i^T u_j = \delta_{ij} = \begin{Bmatrix} 1,,,i=j \\ 0,,,i \neq j \end{Bmatrix} \tag{3}$$

And matrix V is an $n \times n$ orthogonal matrix

$$V = [v_1, v_2, ... v_r, v_{r+1}, ..., v_n] \tag{4}$$

Column vectors i **v** for i = 1, 2, …, n, form an orthogonal set:

$$v_i^T v_j = \delta_{ij} = \begin{Bmatrix} 1,,,i=j \\ 0,,,i \neq j \end{Bmatrix} \tag{5}$$

Here, S is an $m \times n$ diagonal matrix with singular values (SV) on the diagonal. The matrix S can be showed in Equation 6.

$$s = \begin{bmatrix} \sigma_1 & 0 & \cdots & 0 & 0 & \cdots & 0 \\ 0 & \sigma_2 & \cdots & 0 & 0 & \cdots & 0 \\ \vdots & \vdots & \ddots & \vdots & \vdots & \ddots & \vdots \\ 0 & 0 & \cdots & \sigma_r & 0 & \cdots & 0 \\ 0 & 0 & \cdots & 0 & \sigma_{r+1} & \cdots & 0 \\ \vdots & \vdots & \ddots & \vdots & \vdots & \ddots & \vdots \\ 0 & 0 & \cdots & 0 & 0 & \cdots & \sigma_n \\ 0 & 0 & \cdots & 0 & 0 & \cdots & 0 \end{bmatrix} \tag{6}$$

For i =1, 2, …, n , σ_i are called Singular Values (SV) of matrix A. It can be proved that:

$$\begin{aligned} &\sigma_1 \geq \sigma_2 \geq ... \geq \sigma_r > 0, \\ &\sigma_{r+1} = \sigma_{r+2} = ... = \sigma_N = 0 \end{aligned} \tag{7}$$

For i =1, 2, …, n , σ_i are called Singular Values (SV) of matrix A. The v_i's and u_i's are called right and left singular-vectors of A (Cao 2007)

3.4 Multilayered perceptron network and Levenberg-Marquardt training algorithm

There are many different types of new training algorithms have been proposed. Traditionally we selected Levenberg-Marquardt (LM) training algorithm as because it is the fastest training speed on the same precision basis. According to Saodah *et al.* 2010, it shown that the LM learning algorithm has performed higher classification accuracy as compared to the other traditional learning algorithms. The LM method is an approximation of the Gauss-Newton technique, which generally provides faster learning rate than the back propagation that is based on the steepest decent technique. The learning is equivalent to finding a multidimensional function that provides a best fit to the training data, with the criterion for "best fit" being measured in some statistical sense. The recognition performance of the MLP network will highly depend on the structure of the network and the training algorithm. In the current study, the LM algorithm has been selected to train the network. It has been shown that the algorithm has much better learning rate than the famous back propagation algorithm (Hagan and Menhaj 1994). The MLP with one single hidden layer, or also called as the Single Layer Feedforward Network (SLFN) network consists of three separate layers is shown in Figure 8. The input layer is the set of source nodes. The second layer is a hidden layer of high dimension. The output layer gives the response of the network to the activation patterns applied to the input layer (Mashor 2000).

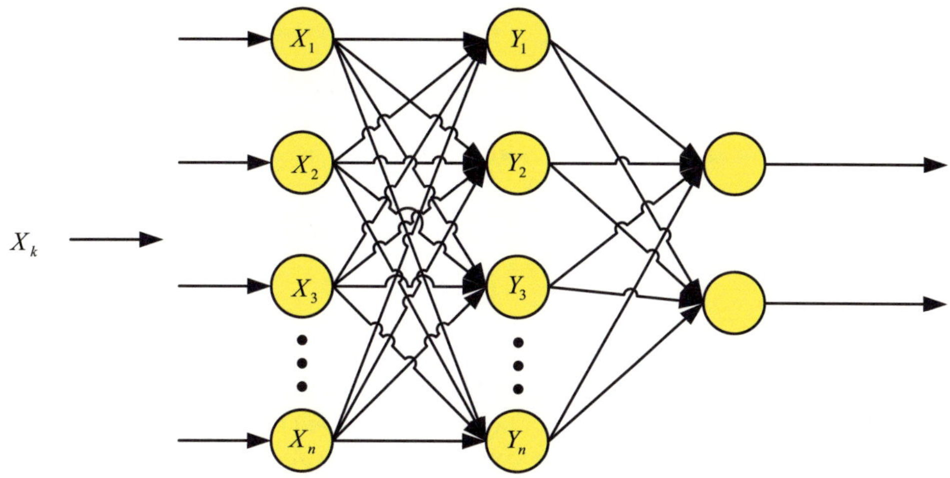

Fig. 8. Architecture of a SLFN network

The number of nodes in the input, hidden and output layers will determined the network structure. Furthermore, the hidden and output nodes have activation function that will also influence the network performance. The best network structure is normally problem dependent, hence structure analysis has to be carried out to identify the optimum structure. In the current study, the numbers of input and output nodes were fixed at 48 and 3 respectively, since the images have been divided into 48 segments and the target outputs are 3 classes of images. Therefore, only the number of hidden nodes and activation functions need to be determined. The percentage of classification performance will be used to judge the network performance to perform vehicle recognition. For this analysis the vehicle images without noise were used to determine the structure of the network. The analysis is used to determine number of hidden node, learning rate and sufficient training of epoch (Mashor 2000) & (Mashor 2004).

The Levenberg-Marquardt algorithm was designed to approach second-order training speed without having to compute the Hessian matrix. When the performance function has the form of a sum of squares (as is typical in training feedforward networks), then the Hessian matrix is based on :

$$H = J^T J \tag{8}$$

And the gradient can be computed as:

$$g = J^T e \tag{9}$$

where J is the Jacobian matrix that contains the first derivatives of the network errors with respect to the weights and biases, and e is a vector of network errors. The Jacobian matrix can be computed through a standard back propagation technique that is much less complex than computing the Hessian matrix. The Levenberg-Marquardt algorithm uses this approximation, μ to the Hessian matrix in the following Newton-like update according to Equation 10:

$$X_{k+1} = X_k - [J^T J + \mu I]^{-1} J^T e \tag{10}$$

A sigmoid function which is given by (11), is a mathematical function that produces a sigmoid curve as S shape and smoothes the transition between the input, t and the output $P(t)$. It is a real-valued and differentiable, having either a non-negative or non-positive first derivative and exactly one inflection point.

$$P(t) = \frac{1}{1 - e^{-t}} \qquad 11)$$

3.5 ELM based training algorithm

Liang *et al.* (2006) has showing the ability of the SLFN network to fix the network connection at one layer with the weights between input neurons and hidden neurons. The same goes to the output neurons where there is fix network connection with weights between hidden neurons and output neurons. However, the algorithm was unable to adjust the weights on both layers simultaneously since there is no gain provided. Based on this work, Huang *et al.* (2006) have proposed a new learning algorithm referred to as Extreme Learning Machine (ELM). ELM is a learning algorithm that is derived based on some continuous probability density function. Consequently the ELM is designed to be randomly chooses and fixes the weights between input neurons and hidden neurons, and then analytically determines the weights between hidden neurons and output neurons of the SLFN.

For N arbitrary distinct samples (x_i, t_i), where $x_i = [x_{i1}, x_{i2}, \ldots\ldots, x_{in}]^T \in R^n$ and $t_i = [t_{i1}, t_{i2}, \ldots\ldots\ldots, t_{i3}]^T \in R^m$, standard SLFNs with N hidden nodes and activation function $g(x)$ are mathematically modelled as:

$$\sum_{i=1}^{\bar{N}} \beta_i g_i(x_j) = \sum_{i=1}^{\bar{N}} \beta_i g(w_i . x_j + b_i) = o_j, \text{ j=1,.......,N,} \tag{12}$$

where $w_i = [w_{i1}, w_{i2}, \ldots\ldots, w_{in}]^T$ is the weight vector connecting the ith hidden node and the input nodes, $\beta_i = [\beta_{i1}, \beta_{i2}, \ldots, \beta_{im}]^T$ is the weight vector connecting the ith hidden node and the ouput nodes, and b_i is the threshold of the ith hidden node. $w_i \cdot x_i$ denotes the inner product of w_j and x_j.

The above N equations can be written compactly as:

$$H\beta = T , \tag{13}$$

Where

$$H\left(w_1,\ldots,w_{\tilde{N}},b_1,\ldots,b_{\tilde{N}},x_1,\ldots,x_n\right)=\begin{bmatrix} g(w_1\cdot x_1+b_1) & \cdots & g(w_{\tilde{N}}\cdot x_1+b_{\tilde{N}}) \\ \vdots & \ddots & \vdots \\ g(w_1\cdot x_N+b_1 & \cdots & g(w_{\tilde{N}}\cdot x_N+b_{\tilde{N}} \end{bmatrix}_{Nx\tilde{N}}, \quad (14)$$

$$\beta=\begin{bmatrix} \beta_1^T \\ \vdots \\ \beta_{\tilde{N}}^T \end{bmatrix} \text{ and } \mathrm{T}=\begin{bmatrix} t_1^T \\ \vdots \\ t_{\tilde{N}}^T \end{bmatrix} \quad (15)$$

Usually H is called the hidden layer output matrix of the neural network and the ith column of H represented the ith hidden node output with respect to inputs $x_1; x_2; \ldots; x_N$.

3.6 ELM learning algorithm

In order to train the arbitrary function of neural network with zero training error, Baum (1988) had presented several constructions of SLFNs with sufficient hidden neurons. However, in practice, the number of hidden neurons required to achieve a proper generalization performance on novel patterns is much less. And the resulting training error might not approach to zero but can be minimized by solving the following problem:

$$\min_{\mathrm{w_i,b_i,\beta}} H\left(w_1,\ldots,w_{\tilde{N}},b_1,\ldots,b_{\tilde{N}}\right)\beta-T^2, \quad (16)$$

Where

$$T=\begin{bmatrix} t_1^T \\ \vdots \\ t_N^T \end{bmatrix}_{Nxm} \quad (17)$$

The ELM randomly assigns and fixes the input weights w_i and biases b_i based on some continuous probability distribution function in the case of learning a structured function, only leaving output weights β_i to be adjusted according to:

$$\min_{\beta} H\beta-T^2 \quad (18)$$

The above problem is well established and known as a linear system optimization problem. It is a unique least-squares solution with minimum norm and is given by:

$$\hat{\beta}=HT \quad (19)$$

where ***H*** is the Moore-Penrose generalized inverse of the matrix **H**. As analyzed by Bartlett (1998) and Huang (2006), the generalization performance of a SLFN tends to be better with smaller magnitude of output weights. From this sense, the solution produced by the ELM in (19) not only achieves the minimum square training error but also the best generalization performance on novel patterns. Huang *et al.* (2004) summarize ELM as the follows:

ELM Algorithm: Given a training set $\aleph = \left\{ \left((x_k, t_k) | \, x_k \epsilon R^m, k = 1, \ldots\ldots, N \right) \right\}$, an activation function $g(x)$, and the number of hidden neurons $\tilde{N}$,

i. Randomly assign input weights **w***i* and biases *bi* according to some continuous probability density function.
ii. Calculate the hidden layer output matrix **H**.
iii. Calculate the output weights β_i: $\hat{\beta}$ = **H T**.

All the input data are scaled so that they have ranges between −1 to 1. In general, the SLFN trained by the ELM network starts by randomly choose the input weights which linking the input nodes to the hidden nodesand the hidden neurons' biases, After the input weights and the hidden layer biases are chosen arbitrarily, the SLFNs can be simply considered as a linear system and the output weights which linking the hidden layer to the output layer of the SLFNs can be determined analytically through the generalized inverse operation of the hidden layer output matrices (Wang & Huang, 2005, Huang *et al.* 2006).

4. Results and discussion

This section explains the series of experiments conducted and also presents some preliminary results to compare the effectiveness between the LM training algorithm and ELM training algorithm. The experiment was accomplished by using 48 geometrical features extracted from image data set as input variables to the SLFN-ELM and SLFN-LM network. As mentioned earlier, the SVD method was applied to extract all of the images into a data set that implemented as an input for neural network training and testing processes. The three (3) outputs are classed as lorry, bus or motorcycle for classification purposes. The input variables were taken from 3 sets images of motorcycle, bus and lorry. The data inputs for training and testing consist of 215 samples. For training data set are 96 sets of data and used in training process and the other used in testing process.

	'Lorry'	**'Bus'**	**'Motorcycle'**	Total
Training	49	14	33	96
Testing	52	19	48	119
Total	101	33	81	215

Table 1. Description of dataset

Table 1 summarizes the description of the dataset. The SLFN-ELM network was analysed from 1-100 hidden nodes to find the best performance network. A total of 50 trials was conducted for each hidden nodes to find optimal initialization weight. The SLFN-LM network was analysed from 1 to 100 hidden nodes to find the best performance network. However, for the SLFN trained by the LM training algorithm, a total of 10 trials was conducted since the training algorithm takes a very long time to train SLFNs using back propagation (BP) learning algorithm. The simulation for all networks was conducted in Matlab R2008b using a laptop with Intel Core2Duo 2.4 GHz CPU procesor and 4G of RAM. Table 2 tabulates the classification performance of the SLFN-ELM and SLFN-ELM. The comparison is done based on the classification accuracy, training time and optimum structure of each network.

4.1 SLFN-ELM classification performance evaluation

The relationship between the classification performance and number of hidden nodes for SLFN-ELM network is presented in Figure 9. The training and testing results of SLFN network demonstrated that the training phase with ELM algorithm are perform in very fast time to achieve the maximum accuracy after hidden nodes 30. The slope of accuracy against number of hidden nodes rises quickly starting from hidden nodes 6. The accuracy of training with ELM achieves 77.0833% and testing 74.083% at hidden nodes 6. The training and testing accuracy are seemed similar in between hidden nodes 15 to 27. The ELM is able to achieve 100% training accuracy after hidden nodes 77 however the testing accuracy is rather out performed less than 90%.

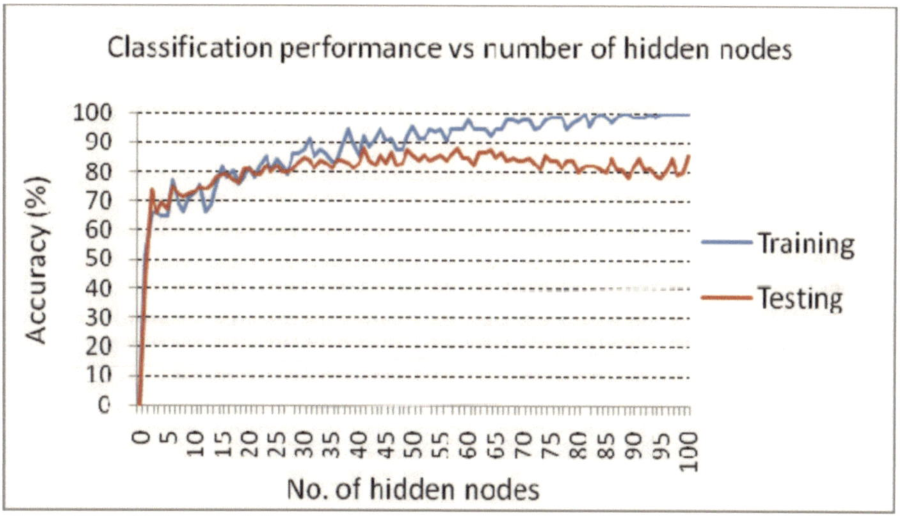

Fig. 9. Performance of the SLFN network trained by Extreme Learning Machine algorithm.

4.2 SLFN-LM classification performance evaluation

The relationship between the classification performance and number of hidden nodes for SLFN-LM network is presented as shown in Figure 10. The training and testing results are plotted in blue and red colour verified that the training phases with LM algorithm has performed timely fast to achieve the maximum accuracy after the second hidden nodes. The slope of accuracy against number of hidden nodes rises quickly starting from the first hidden nodes. The accuracy of training with ELM achieves 77.0833% and testing 75.6303% at first hidden nodes. The training and testing accuracy are seemed similar in between hidden nodes 16, 53 and 85. The LM algorithm is unable to achieve 100% training accuracy but generally it has a slight advantage in testing accuracy where its performance is similar to

ELM. This is showing that testing accuracy for LM algorithm and ELM algorithm having the same performances.

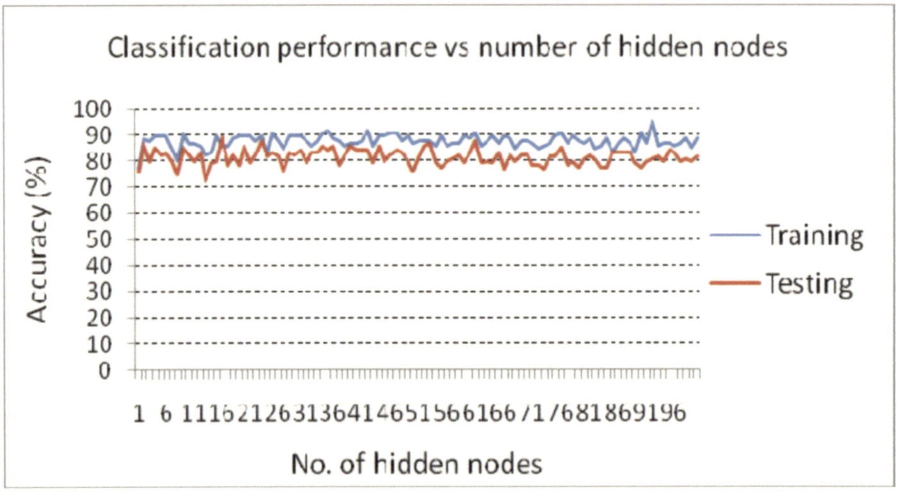

Fig. 10. Performance of the SLFN network trained by Levenberg-Marquardt algorithm

4.3 The best performance of SLFN-ELM and SLFN-LM network

The best classification performance for the SLFN-ELM and the SLFN-LM networks is analysed in section 4.1 and 4.2. The best network for the SLFN-ELM and the SLFN-LM is show in the Table 2. The best network for the SLFN-ELM is at hidden nodes 41 with testing accuracy of 88.253% although the training accuracy for the SLFN-ELM network achieves 100% training accuracy at certain hidden nodes. The best network for SLFN-LM is at hidden nodes 16 with testing accuracy of 89.0756%. These results show that SLFN-LM has possibly a slight difference of a better performance against SLFN-ELM network in term of classification accuracy. The result for training accuracy is better for SLFN-ELM network because the network can achieve 100% accuracy. However the training accuracy is not a significant criterion for classification comparison. This could be due to over-fitting problem, stopping criteria, learning rate, learning epochs and local minima.

Classifier	Accuracy (%)		Training time (s)		Hidden nodes
	Training	Testing	(seconds)	Speedup	
SLFN-ELM	92.7083	88.2353	0.0156	2426.4	41
SLFN-LM	84.375	89.0756	37852	1	16

Table 2. Classification Performance for the SLFN network using the ELM and LM training algorithm

The training time (s) for training SLFN-ELM and SLFN-LM network specify that the SLFN-ELM network is extremely fast and incomparable to the SLFN-LM network. As observed from Table 2, SLFN-ELM classifier can run 2426.4 times faster than SLFN-LM in the case when best classification performances are obtained for both SLFN-ELM and SLFN-LM.

SLFN-ELM network having a tendency to have better classification performance and can be implemented easily in the vehicle recognition system for classification purposes.

4.4 Classification performance for each vehicle using the SLFN-ELM networks

Classification performance for each vehicle using the SLFN-ELM networks is shown in Figure 11. The performance of training and testing in the scale percentage of accuracy is plotted to emphasize the problems of the network in order to recognise each vehicle precisely. From the result, it can be verify that the SLFN-ELM network are able to classify correctly up to 94.74% in percentage of testing accuracy to recognize the bus. Even as the network are only able to classify correctly up to 79.17% for lorries. These results indicate that the SLFN-ELM network is already achieving the convergence despite the fact that one of the testing accuracy of the vehicle achieves the possible maximum accuracy. As observed from Figure 11, the SLFN-ELM can classify a bus better than a lorry because the features of bus are more constant compare to lorry. In this study the type of vehicle car is excluded in order to reduce the complexity of the programming algorithm and to speed up the training and testing time for both classifier network. Furthermore the results of classification performance for vehicles with constant shape such as busses and motorcycles have achieve the accuracy of 94.74% and 94.23% respectively for correct classification in the testing phase.

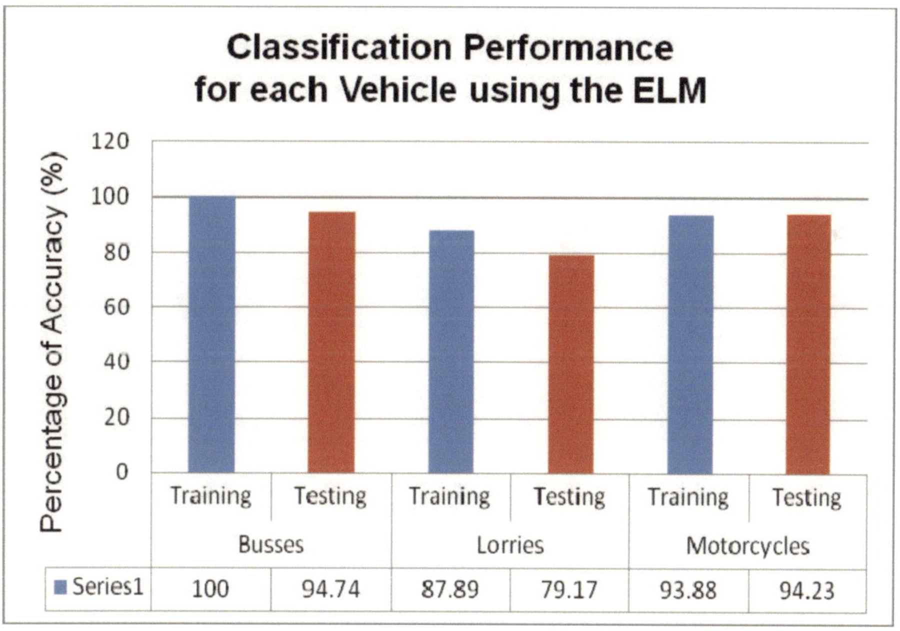

Fig. 11. Classification Performance for each Vehicle using SLFN network trained by ELM training algorithm.

4.5 Classification performance for each vehicle using SLFN-LM networks

Classification performance for each vehicle using SLFN-LM networks is shown in Figure 12. From the result, it can be prove that the SLFN-LM network are also able to classify busses, lorries and motorcycles correctly up to 94.83%, 79.23% and 94.08% respectively in percentage of testing accuracy. These results also indicate that the SLFN-LM network is already achieving the convergence despite the fact that two of the testing accuracy of the vehicle achieves the possible maximum accuracy. As observed from Figure 12, SLFN-LM also can classify a bus better than a lorry because the features of bus are more constant compare to lorry. In this study the vehicle type car is also excluded in order to reduce the complexity of the programming algorithm and to speed up the training and testing time for both classifier network. Further more the result of classification performance for vehicle with constant shape such as busses and motorcycles have achieve 94.83% and 94.08% respectively for correct classification in testing.

5. Conclusion

In this study, we have evaluated the performance of two main neural network learning algorithm, namely LM and ELM on classification of vehicle type with three classes. The results of this study demonstrate that the ELM needs extremely less training time as compared to conventional LM classifiers. The classification accuracy of ELM is slightly similar to the LM but the ELM is achievable with high accuracy performance. Also, there is significant improvement can be achieved in the testing accuracy for both classifiers by improved the significant features of data input.

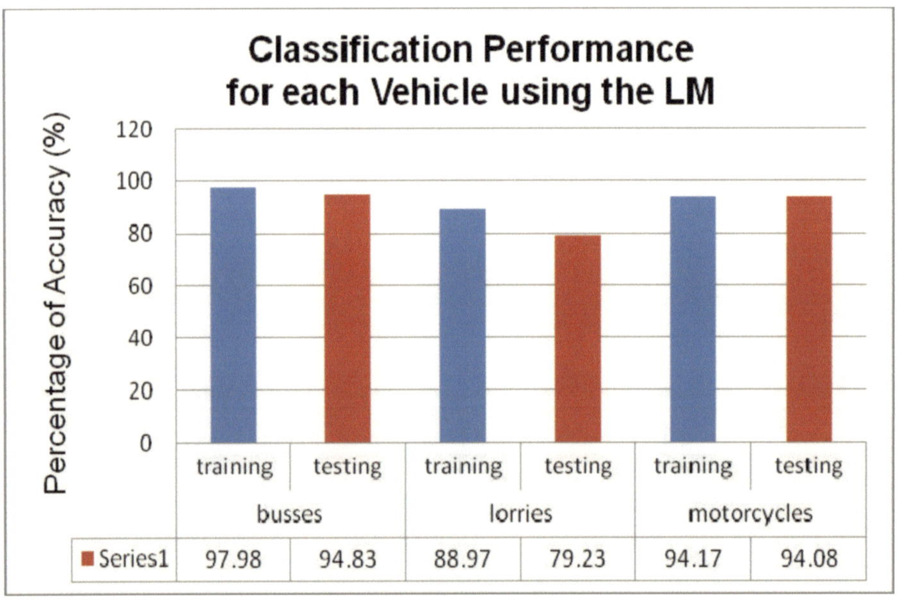

Fig. 12. Classification Performance for each Vehicle using SLFN network trained by the LM training algorithm.

6. References

Barlett, P, L. (1998). The Sample Complexity of Pattern Classification with Neural Networks: the Size of the Weights is more Important than the Size of Network, *IEEE Trans. Inf. Theory,* Vol., 44 No., 2 , (1998), 525 - 536

Baum, E, B. (1988). On the Capabilities of Multilayer Perceptrons, Journal of Complexity, Vol. 4, 193-215, 1988

Cao, L. (2007) Singular Value Decomposition Applied to Digital Image Processing, Student Trade Show and Project Reports, Arizona State University, Division of Computing Studies, Arizona State University Polytechnic Campus, Mesa, Arizona 85215, (May 2007)

Huang, G, -B.; Zhu, Q, -Y. & Siew, C, -K. (2006), Extreme Learning Machine: Theory and Applications, *Neurocomputing,* Vol. 70, (May 2006), 489-501

Hagan, M.T. and Menhaj, M. (1994). "Training Feedback Networks with the Marquardt Algorithm", *IEEE Trans. on Neural Networks,* Vol. 5, Issue 6, No. 6, pp. 989-993. ISSN: 1045-9227

Huang, G, -B. & Siew, C, -K. (2004). Extreme Learning Machine with Randomly Assigned RBF Kernels, *International Journal of Information Technology,* Vol. 11, No.1, (2004) 16-24

Huang, G, -B. & Siew, C, -K. (2004). Extreme Learning Machine: RBF Network Case, *Proceeding of the Eighth International Conference on Control, Automation, Robotics and Vision (ICARCV 2004),* Kunming, China, Dec 2004

Liang, N, -Y.; Saratchandran, P.; Huang, G, -B. & Sundarajan, N. (2006). Classification of Mental Tasks from EEG Signals Using Extreme Learning Machine, *International Journal of Neural System,* Vol.16, No.1, (2006) 29-38

Mashor M.Y. (2000). "Performance Comparison Between Back Propagation, RPE And MRPE Algorithms For Training MLP Networks", *International Journal of the Computer, the Internet and Management,* Vol. 8, No.3, 2000

Mashor, M.Y. (2004). „Performance comparison between HMLP, MLP and RBF networks with application to on-line system identification", *2004 IEEE Conference on Cybernetics and Intelligent Systems.* Singapore, Dec 2004

Omar, S.; Saad, Z.; Osman, M.K. and Isa, I. (2010), Improved Classification Performance for Multiple Multilayer Perceptron (MMLP) Network Using Voting Technique, *Proceeding of IEEE,* Fourth Asia Modelling Symposium (AMS 2010), Sabah, Malaysia, 2010.

Saad, Z.; Alias, M, F.; Mat Isa, N, A.; Zamli, K, Z. & Sulaiman, S, A. (2007), Application of Image Processing Technique to Determine Normal Sperm, *Proceedings of the International Conference on Robotics, Vision, Information and Signal Processing ROVISP 2007,* Penang, Malaysia, Nov 2007

Verma, B. and Ghosh, R. (2002). A Novel Evolutionary Neural Learning Algorithm, *Proceedings of the 2002 Congress on Evolutionary Computation,* pp. 1884-89, Honolulu, Hawaii, USA, 2002.

Wang, D. & Huang, G, -B. (2005). Protein Sequence Classification Using Extreme Learning Machine, *Proceeding of International Joint Conference on Neural Networks,* Montreal, Canada , Aug 2005

Yeu, C, -W, T.; Lim, M, -H.; Huang, G, -B.; Agarwal, A. & Ong, Y, -S. (2006). A New Machine Paradigm for Terrain Reconstruction, *IEEE Geoscience and Remote Sensing Letters,* Vol. 3, No.3, (Jul 2006) 382-386

Zhang, R.; Huang, G, -B.; Sundararajan, N. & Saratchandran, P. (2007). MultiCategory classification Using an Extreme Learning Machine for Microarray Gene Expression Expression Cancer Diagnosis, *IEEE/ACM Transactions on Computational Biology and Bioinformatics,* Vol. 4, No.3, (Jul 2007) 485-495

Zhu, Q, -Y.; Qin, A, K.; Suganthan, P, N. & Huang, G, -B. (2005). Evolutionary Extreme Learning Machine, *The Journal of the Pattern Recognition Society,* Vol. 38, (Mar 2005) 1759-1763

10

Hierarchical Bayesian Image Models

Daniel Oberhoff
Fraunhofer FIT-LIFE
Germany

1. Introduction

Despite many years of research object recognition remains a hard task for automated systems. In contrast, the tasks in object recognition come very easily to us humans. This has inspired much work in trying to replicate the human abilities by modeling one or more aspects of the human visual system based on the vast amount of research that has been carried out on it and related systems (i.e. visual systems of animals that share much of the brain structure with us, like cats, mice, and monkeys). Bayesian statistics has proven to be a very powerful too in the design, control, and use of such systems. Also it provides a strong mathematical toolset to combine the vast amount of research that has been carried out in the field of image analysis in particular and pattern recognition in general. In this chapter I will introduce Bayesian image models that are constructed in a hierarchical fashion strongly motivated by the human visual system. To do this I briefly review both Bayesian statistics and relevant neurophysiological and psychophysical findings on the human visual system. Then I proceed to introduce the principle of a Bayesian hierarchical image model of such a system. I then proceed to explain the construction of such systems for various applications and highlight the power but also the problems that these systems possess. In the course of this we will demonstrate the capabilities of some of those systems on artificial and real world tasks and wrap up with a conclusion.

2. Generative Bayesian image modeling

The underlying inspiration behind Bayesian image models is to understand the nature of the images. This puts them into the class of *generative* Bayesian models contrasing them with *discriminative* models: A generative seeks to explain the image, usually by introducing some *lattent* or *hidden* variables. A discriminative model on the other side seeks to explain only the dependency of one or more output variables on the image, in the case of object recognition the class and possibly the location of the object. While it seems natural to choose a discriminative model when seeking for an object recognition tool, there are many reasons against this. The basic problem is, that the dependency between data and labels is usually very complex. Consequently the model has to be very complex to capture this dependency. With such a complex model then it becomes hard to even find the right region of the solution space. The reason why this is so hard is because without understanding the structure of the images it is hard to infer anything from them. And understanding the structure of the images is exactly what a discriminative cost function does not reward [1]. Consequently our model should seek

[1] It does of course reward it indirectly if it helps the discriminative task, but in that case it does so very indirectly, making learning algorithms that optimize the cost function in small steps very ineffective.

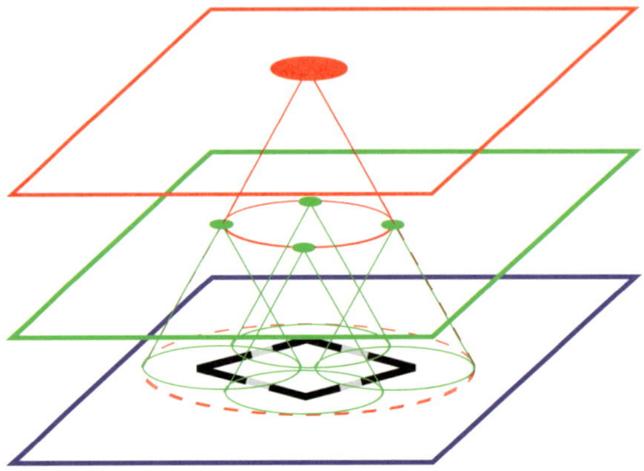

Fig. 1. Illustration of the structure of the hierarchical image model.

to understand the structure of the images first. This is then exactly what a generative model is made for: It tries to understand how the images are made, i.e. how they are *generated*. Since every image is different a generative model will use some internal representation of the image that describes it, but in a more understandable and compact way. This is so because it encodes a probability distribution over all possible images. Since out of all possible pixel configurations, assuming our image representation is pixels, only a relatively small subset actually appears. Knowing this distribution will allow it to be encoded much more compactly than by the pixels directly. This internal representation should then be a much better input to a classifier than the pixels themselves. Going one step further one may also use the complete generative model as a discriminative one, since the composition of a generative model and a classifier is effectively just another, more complex classifier. But starting with a generative model allows the use of learning algorithms that learn to explain the structure of the images. After having done that one can switch to the discriminative cost function to do a *local* search in parameter space to optimize the discriminative performance.

In the following I take an understanding of Bayesian probability formulations as a prerequisite, and also make extensive use of *graphical models* to formulate and depict the various model components. A detailed explanation of these techniques can be found, for example, in Bishop (2006). I also make sporadic use of an extension to the classical graphical model formulation called *gates* which have been ontroduced recently by Tom Minka and John Winn Minka & Winn (2008) and are very useful in the context of models wich are conditioned on discrete latent variables as is the case with the models I introduce in the following sections.

2.1 The hierarchical image model

The hierarchical image model is inspired by observations of the function of the human brain and the brain of animals such as cats and monkeys, which are very similar in regard to low- and mid-level vision processing. An important finding in this respect is the fact that visual processing takes place in a step-by-step fashion: The visual information travels through a series of localized cortical areas before it leads to any form of higher level cognition or motor action. The neurons in these areas which encode and process the information show increasingly complex response patterns to visual stimuli, and also become responsive to larger and larger regions of the observed images; one says they have increasingly large *receptive fields* (see, for example, Chalupa & Werner (2003) for more detailed reviews).

The most straight-forward interpretation of this is that what the brain does is break down

the difficult task of analyzing the visual information into a series of much smaller tasks in the spirit of *the divide and conquer* paradigm. Another important finding is, that neurons that respond to stimuli in neighboring regions of the perceived image will also be neighbors in the respective cortical areas. These two findings then lead to a topology of information processing roughly sketched in figure 1.
Going from this abstraction to a Bayesian model the activations and the input become random variables and the connections between layers are modeled using probability distributions.

2.1.1 Categorical layer

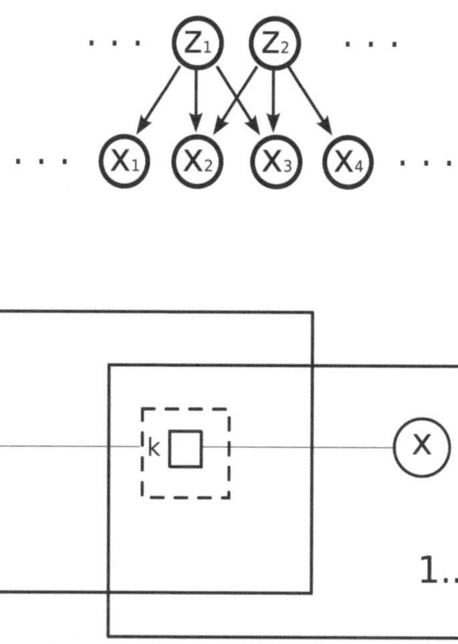

Fig. 2. The categorical model where each component of the data is modeled by one or more parents which are categorical variables selecting a different factor for each setting, parameterized by seperate parameter sets. The predictive distribution is the product of the predictive distributions of all parents.

The central operation of the hierarchical image model is the convergent encoding of variables on one layer into variables on the next layer. In this chapter we limit this choice to the *naive Bayes mixture model*: A mixture model models the probability distribution of an observed variable (which may be of any dimensionality) conditioned on a categorical latent variable $\mathbf{z}$ which can take one out of K values. Thus effectively there is a separate probability distribution over the data for each state of $\mathbf{z}$, each with the same functional form, but with different parameters. Adopting a vectorial notation for $\mathbf{z}$ with only one non-zero entry which is one (a *one-out-of-k-vector*) , the functional form of the mixture model becomes:

$$p(x \mid \mathbf{z}) = \prod_k p(x \mid \Theta_k)^{z_k} \tag{2.1}$$

where Θ_k are the parameters for each state of $\mathbf{z}$. Note that if the $p(x \mid \Theta_k)$ are from the exponential family then so is $p(x \mid \mathbf{z})$, since its logarithm is the sum of the logarithms of $p(x \mid \Theta_k)$, multiplied by the corresponding components of $\mathbf{z}$. The functional forms of $p(x \mid \Theta_k)$ I use in the applications are the *normal* or *Gaussian* distribution over unbounded real continuous variables:

$$p(x \mid \mu, \tau) = \frac{\tau}{\sqrt{2\pi}} e^{\tau(x-\mu)^2} \tag{2.2}$$

and the *multinomial* distribution over categorical variables (in one-out-of-k vector notation):

$$p(\mathbf{x} \mid ß) = \prod_k \pi_k^{x_k} \tag{2.3}$$

both of which are from the exponential family. I construct multivariate versions of these distributions by taking the product of univariate distributions of the same form but with separate parameters. Such a multivariate distributions built from the product of univariate distributions is called a *naive Bayes* model. The term *naive* refers to the implicit assumption that the input variables are conditionally independent given the latent variable and thus the covariances between input variables vanish. While this indeed is a naive assumption it simplifies inference considerably, and has been used with great success in many applications. Given a mixture model the distribution over the latent variable given a data instance is (using Bayes' law):

$$p(\mathbf{z} \mid x) = \frac{p(x \mid \Theta_k)}{\sum_k p(x \mid \Theta_k)} \tag{2.4}$$

where the denominator is the probability of the data $p(x)$ given the model. Thus using a mixture model and Bayes law the data can be encoded as a multinomial distribution by comparing the likelihood of several data models, which is a nice example how complex models can be constructed from simpler ones.
Out of these receptive field models we build a layer of the hierarchical model by arranging the receptive fields on a regular grid such that they cover the input space. The lowest level input space are feature vectors from low-level image processing, arranged in a two dimensional grid corresponding to the feature position in the image, or in the simplest case the image itself or some local image features such as gabor energy or optical flow. The latent variables of the models encoding each receptive field are then arranged in the same fashion as the receptive fields themselves, resulting in a two dimensional map of random variables. This map can then be used as feature map for the next level. In the simplest case neighboring receptive fields to not overlap, such that each input feature is modeled by a single model. If however neighboring receptive fields do overlap it has to be decided how the models are combined to model the individual input features. The simplest way to do this is to take the product of the predictive distributions of the individual models, corresponding to the situation in figure 2. Note that this leads to the *explaining away* effect Wellman & Henrion (1993), since each variable has multiple explanatory causes, which become correlated when the variable is observed. When applying this model I choose to ignore this additional correlation, and let each parent model the receptive field assigned to it independently. This could also be interpreted as replicating the receptive fields for each parent, and modeling each version independently.
In the next section I discuss a modification which offers an alternative to this rather crude treatment that avoids multiple explanations of the same variable altogether.

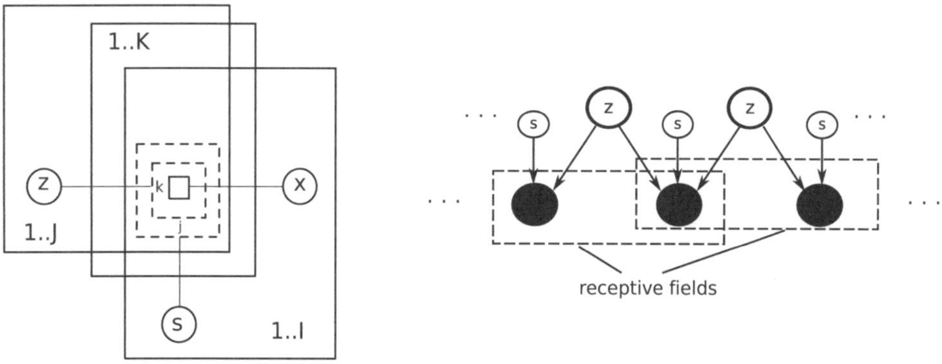

Fig. 3. The factor graph of the gated categorical layer model in gate/plate-notation *gated* left and in the form of a directed graph *right*. The switch variables s select a single parent per datapoint. This effectively induces a segmentation and avoids explaining away effects since no two parents have to explain the same datapoint.

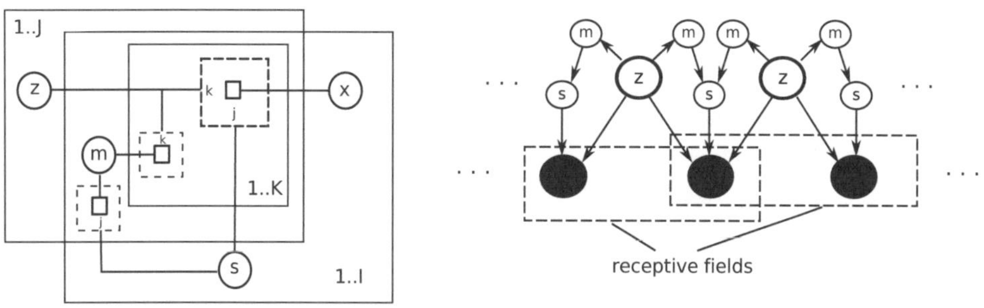

Fig. 4. The factor graph of the gated categorical layer model with additional dependencies between the latent variables and the gates (mediated via the maskbits m) in gate/plate-notation *gated* left and in the form of a directed graph *right*.

2.1.2 Gated categorical layer

To avoid explaining away I introduce additional auxiliary "switch" variables s for each input feature. The state of these variable then selects which of the models converging on this feature is responsible for explaining it. This setup is shown in figure 3. The joint distribution for a layer with gated mixture models is:

$$p(x,z,s,\Theta) = \prod_{ijk} \left[p(x_i \mid \Theta_{ijk})^{s_{ij}z_{jk}} \right] p(\Theta)p(s)p(z) \tag{2.5}$$

Besides eliminating explaining away this modification also allows a more natural modeling of occlusion of objects in a complex scene, since an object border (where the background becomes visible) can be modeled directly by a border in the field of the switch variables. This allows the model to model different objects by different internal clusters, instead of having to deal with a multitude of foreground-background combinations within receptive fields.

The switch variables can be embedded in an MRF where the pairwise potentials are chosen to increase the probability that two neighboring gates assign the corresponding data points to the same parent. This increases the probability that contiguous regions of input features are assigned to the same receptive field. If I view this setting as modulating the shape of the receptive fields the MRF can be seen as increasing the likelihood that receptive fields stay contiguous and don't fall apart into disconnected pieces. To guide the choice of the coupling factor I look towards the two-dimensional Ising Model in physics, which in probabilistic terms is a two-dimensional MRF of binary variables with positive fixed coupling between nearest neighbors. In this model a phase transition between a totally random (corresponding to no effective influence of the MRF on the gate settings) and a totally ordered (corresponding to a completely dominating influence of the MRF) state occurs at a coupling factor of around 1.56 (e to the inverse of the critical temperature as derived by Lars Onsager in 1944 Onsager (1944)). Note that this result had been derived for a four-way connected lattice and the fact that the coupled bits are part of multinomial distributions may further change this value, still Onsager's result is helpful as a rough guide.

A problem with the gated model is that information about object contours is not explicitly represented in the model. This means there is no distinction made between wether an object ends and thus the background becomes visible, or it is occluded by another object, as both induce the same kind of borders in the gate field. This can be fixed by making the shape of the receptive fields variable, thus introducing a dependency between the latent variables and the gates. I mediate this dependency via a mask bit $m_i j$ for each connection between a latent variable z_j and an input x_i: If this bit is off the latent variable is effectively disconnected from the corresponding input, meaning it will not try to generate it, and thus is not available for competition for the gate variable. The receptive field shape is encoded in the dependency between the state of the latent variable and a mask bit. This dependency is naturally parametrized by a binomial distribution over the mask bit conditioned on the state of the latent variable. The graphical model for this is shown in figure 4. The joint probability of the model becomes:

$$p(x,z,s,\Theta) = \prod_{ijk} \left[p(x_i \mid \Theta_{ijk})^{s_{ij}} \mu_{ijk}^{m_{ij}} (1-\mu_{ijk})^{1-m_{ij}} \right]^{z_{jk}} \prod_{ij} \left(\frac{m_{ij}}{\sum_{j'} m_{ij'}} \right)^{s_{ij}} p(\Theta) \tag{2.6}$$

3. Related work

The attempt to model the neural structure of mammalian brains for image processing approaches has been reflected inseveral schemes for learning and recognition of image patterns. Probably the first such network, called"Neocognitron", was suggested by Kunihiko Fukushima in 1980 Fukushima (1980). Neocognitron consists of a series ofS- and C-layers (mimicking simple and complex cell types, respectively) with shared weights for a set of local receptivefields and inhibitory and excitatory sub-populations of units with interactions resembling neural mechanisms.Neocognitron learns through a combination of winner-take-all competition and reinforcement learning, autonomously formsclasses for presented characters, and correctly classifies some slightly distorted and noisy versions of thesecharacters. In 1989 Yan LeCun et al. LeCun et al. (1989), introduced a similar but much more powerful network for writtencharacter recognition that generated local feature descriptors through back-propagation. A later version of thisnetwork, now called "LeNet", has been shown to act as an efficient framework for nonlinear-dimensionality reduction ofimage-sets Hadsell et al. (2006). "LeNet" is similar in architecture to Neocognitron, but does not learn autonomously andrequires labels to initiate the back-propagation. The latter is not biologically justified and computationallyexpensive.

In 2003 Riesenhuber and Poggio Serre et al. (2005) suggested a computational model for object recognition in the visualcortex with a similar layout called "hmax", in which they put emphasis on the correspondence between model componentsand cortical areas.

"hmax" employs Gaussian radial basis functions to model the selectivity of simple cells, and anonlinear max-function, pooling input from a local population of simple cells, to model functionality of complex cells. Learning in "hmax" is constrained to the tuning of simple cells to random snapshots of local input activity whilepresenting objects of interest. Despite of these simplifications, "hmax" and optimizations thereof where successfullyapplied to the modeling of V4 and IT neuron responses and also used as an input stage to a classifier for object andface recognition yielding very good performance Mutch & Lowe (2006); Serre et al. (2005).

Another approach that focuses very much on the neural details of neural adaptation and learning and does not use weightsharing is found in "VisNet", presented by Deco and Rolls in 2002 Rolls & Deco (2002). The most interesting ingredient totheir model is the fact that it can learn the shift invariance of the feature detectors autonomously through a temporallearning rule called the *trace rule*.

The system we present here is essentially an extension of "hmax", but with a deeper hierarchy and an unsupervisedlearning strategy employed on multiple levels of this hierarchy. This strategy, based on a biologically inspiredcombination of competition and Hebbian update, learns small but informative codebooks after as little as 2 presentationsof the training views. This is in contrast to other codebook optimization approaches which perform gradient descend inan error functionWersing & Korner (2003), which require many steps involving the whole training set. While we put a strongemphasis on a biologically plausible architecture and learning rule, we do not choose to model cortical dynamics indetail. Instead, we utilize biological concepts which help creating a system that performs competitively in terms ofrecognition performance as well as computational load.

The group of T.L. Dean et. al. Dean (2006) have done some groundwork on hierarchical graphical models for computer vision. Theirwork provides great inspiration and technical background, but it has not to our knowledge been applied to real videodata, nor have they tried to do sequence learning.

The most advanced model comparable to the one presented here, has been constructed in the group of Hinton et. al. Hinton (2007).The drawback of their approach is that they use gradient descent learning in combination with sampling methods, andtypically require on the order of thousands of iterations over the data to converge, which seems prohibitive for largevideo sequences.

4. Estimation of the hidden variables

Given an image model we need a way to perform some form of algorithmic inference to find out about the states of the hidden variables and finally the posterior distribution of the presence of an object in the image. In the following we thus review here the two most important algorithms for performing inference in a graphical Bayesian model.

4.1 Belief propagation

Belief propagation is an algorithm that is based on the work of Judea Pearl in the early eighties Pearl (1982). It has the nice property that its computational cost is linear in the size of the model while actually being exact in the case of tree shaped model graphs, where it is effectively an application of the *dynamic programming* paradigm Eddy (2004) to the marginalization problem stated in equation **??**: Consider the factor graphical model in figure 5, *left*. In order to determine the marginal distribution over x we need to marginalize out all

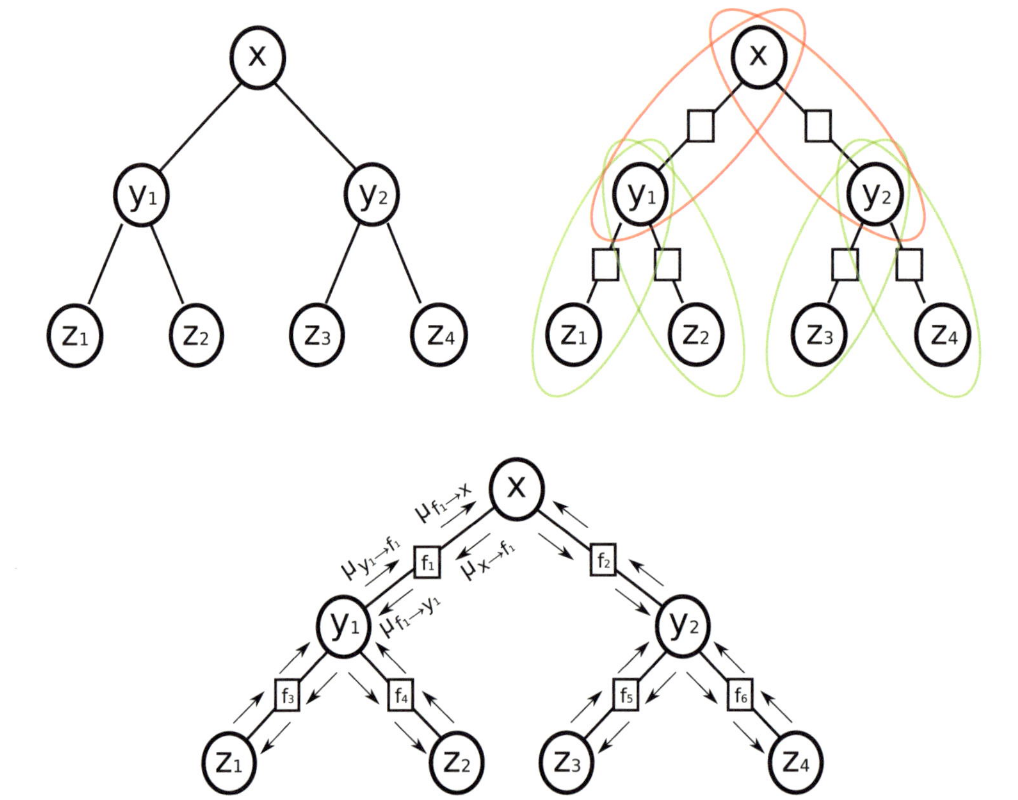

Fig. 5. The undirected dependency graph (*left*) and the corresponding factor graph (*right*) of a probabilistic model for which *belief propagation* is exact.

the other variables:

$$p(x) = \sum_{y_1,y_2,z_1,z_2,z_3,z_4} p(x, y_1, y_2, z_1, z_2, z_3, z_4). \tag{4.1}$$

We can do better than that by exploiting the factorization given by the factor graph in figure 5, *right*:

$$p(x) = \sum_{y_1,y_2,z_1,z_2,z_3,z_4} p(x,y_1)p(x,y_2)p(y_1,z_1)p(y_1,z_2)p(y_2,z_3)p(y_2,z_4) \tag{4.2}$$

$$= \left[\sum_{y_1} p(x,y_1)\left(\sum_{z_1} p(y_1,z_1)\right)\left(\sum_{z_2} p(y_1,z_2)\right)\right]$$
$$\left[\sum_{y_2} p(x,y_2)\left(\sum_{z_3} p(y_2,z_3)\right)\left(\sum_{z_4} p(y_2,z_4)\right)\right] \tag{4.3}$$

where equation 4.3 is simply the result of rearranging terms by exploiting the associativity of the real numbers. One can see that the sum decomposes into a hierarchy of sums and products that reflects the structure of the factor graph (to make this more clear I have colored the terms for the lowest level of the tree green and for the upper level red, corresponding to the colored ellipses in figure 5, *right*). I will now quickly review the general algorithm in the form found

in Bishop (2006), chapter 8 where, due to the characteristic alternation of sums and products, it is called the *sum-product algorithm*:
Consider a variable x in a graphical model. In order to find its marginal distribution we need to marginalize its adjacent factors with respect to everything else and then take the product of those marginals:

$$p(x) = \prod_{s \in neighbors(x)} \sum_{X_s} F_s(x, X_s) \tag{4.4}$$

$$= \prod_{s \in neighbors(x)} \mu_{f_s \to x}(x) \tag{4.5}$$

where $F_s(x, X_s)$ denotes the effective factor generated by the whole subtree of the graph connected to x via factor f_s and X_s denotes the set of variables in this subtree. Equation 4.4 implicitly defines the *messages* $\mu_{f_s \to x}(x)$ from the factor f_s to the variable x. To complete the algorithm we decompose the effective factor $F_s(x, X_s)$ by moving one step further away from x in the graph:

$$F_s(x, X_s) = f(x, x_1, \ldots, x_M) \prod_{m=1}^{M} G_m(x_m, X_{sm}) \tag{4.6}$$

where the x_m are the variables adjacent to the factor f_s except for out root variable x and the X_{sm} are the remaining variables in the subtree beyond x_m. The $G_m(x_m, X_{sm})$ are the contributions by the factors adjacent to x_m except for f_s:

$$G_m(x_m, X_{sm}) = \prod_{l \in neighbors(x_m) \setminus f_s} F_l(x_m, X_{ml}). \tag{4.7}$$

Now by substituting this into the definition of $\mu_{f_s \to x}(x)$ we get:

$$\mu_{f_s \to x}(x) = \sum_{X_s} f(x, x_1, \ldots, x_M) \prod_{m=1}^{M} G_m(x_m, X_{sm}) \tag{4.8}$$

$$= \sum_{\{x_1, \ldots, x_m\}} f(x, x_1, \ldots, x_M) \prod_{m=1}^{M} \sum_{X_{sm}} G_m(x_m, X_{sm}) \tag{4.9}$$

$$= \sum_{\{x_1, \ldots, x_m\}} f(x, x_1, \ldots, x_M) \prod_{m=1}^{M} \mu_{x_m \to f_s}(x_m) \tag{4.10}$$

which defines $\mu_{x_m \to f_s}(x_m)$. By substituting equation into this definition we can close the recursion:

$$\mu_{x_m \to f_s}(x_m) = \sum_{X_{sm}} G_m(x_m, X_{sm}) \tag{4.11}$$

$$= \prod_{l \in neighbors(x_m) \setminus f_s} \mu_{f_l \to x_m}(x_m) \tag{4.12}$$

where the last step again involves the rearrangement of some terms using associativity. Effectively thus calculating the marginals involves two kinds of messages. All of these messages can then be determined by initializing them with one, and then updating each one in turn. To avoid unnecessary calculations one starts at some arbitrary node, updates messages moving away from this node until all the leaves are reached, and then updates messages going all the way back to the starting node.

4.2 Sampling

An alternative way of calculating expectations under a distribution over unknown variables is by sampling methods, since sampling from a distribution and averaging over the samples is often easier than performing the required integrals directly. The advantage of sampling methods is that they can often be applied when the methods discussed above are either infeasible or yield very poor approximations. Their drawback is that often a very large amount of samples is required to gain any reasonable amount of information, and for the samples to become de-correlated form the initial conditions and from each other, which would make them useless, or decrease the actual amount of information they convey about the actual distribution of interest. Sampling can also be useful to understand the distribution the model encodes by analyzing a set of samples generated from it.

In the hierarchical image model connections between variables are local, and thus relatively sparse. Correlations between variables that are not directly connected can be expected to be relatively weak. In such a case Gibbs sampling is an appropriate sampling strategy:

- Pick a variable at random or up to a certain specified order.
- Calculate the distribution of this variable given the states of its neighbors.
- Assign this variable to a random sample from this distribution.

We use this form of sampling for the gated categorical layer because belief propagation becomes infeasible due to the large number of messages that would have to be stored and updated.

5. Learning

In order to solve our task we need algorithms to optimize our models for given cost functions. As discussed in section 2 we want to have algorithms both for optimizing the generative model, as well as for optimizing the discrimination performance. In the following I will review one algorithm for the generative learning tasks and one for the discriminative task.

5.1 Variational Bayesian expectation maximization

In the following I will review a fully Bayesian method of estimating the model paramters. This method has become known under the name of *Variational Bayesian Expectation Maximization* or (VBEM) Attias (1999) and can be seen as a generalization over more classical expectation maximization approaches such as maximum likelihood (ML) or maximum *a posteriori* Dempster et al. (1977).

5.1.1 Conjugate exponential models

Since I wish to learn the exact form of the model distribution from the data I am concerned with encoding knowledge about the parameters given the data. The most natural approach from a Bayesian standpoint is to encode this knowledge in a parameter distribution. To choose the form of this distribution I further note, that a major motivation for the approach I have chosen is the ability to learn unsupervised. Thus I will be interested in the parameter posterior after seeing the data, which is proportional to the product of the parameter prior and the data likelihood

$$p(\Theta \mid \mathbf{x}) \propto p(\Theta) \prod_i p(x_i \mid \Theta) \tag{5.1}$$

If I further allow continuous updating of the posterior, i.e. using the posterior from the data seen so far as prior for the following data, it becomes desirable that the functional form of the posterior be the same as that of the prior. Given that $p(x \mid \Theta)$ is from the exponential family a prior of the form

$$p(\theta|\eta,\nu) = g(\theta)^{\eta} h(\eta,\nu) e^{\phi(\theta)^T \nu} \tag{5.2}$$

will lead to a posterior of the same form with parameters

$$\eta' = \eta + N \tag{5.3}$$

$$\nu' = \nu + \sum_{n=1}^{N} u(x_n) \tag{5.4}$$

where N is the number of data points. The prior thus encodes a set of previous observations (or pseudo-observations if no data has actually been seen) where η plays the role of a counting variable and ν accumulates the observations sufficient statistics. Such distributions exist for many of the exponential family distributions. They are commonly referred to as the distributions' *conjugate* prior. A comprehensive list of conjugate priors for commonly used distributions can be found in Fink (1995) and a table of the distributions I use in this thesis together with some important properties can be found in the Appendix.
If all parameters of a probabilistic model are equipped with conjugate priors they are called *conjugate exponential* (CE). The probabilistic image models I construct in this thesis are built from conjugate exponential model components and also in composition always remain conjugate exponential.

5.1.2 Bayesian posterior approximation

Given a parameter prior and some data we wish to infer the posterior parameter distribution and the marginal data likelihood. This becomes intractable in the presence of hidden variables, as one would have to infer about both simultaneously:

$$p(\Theta,\mathbf{Z},\mathbf{X}) = p(\Theta,\mathbf{Z} \mid \mathbf{X})p(\mathbf{X}) \tag{5.5}$$

$$= p(\mathbf{X} \mid \Theta,\mathbf{Z})p(\mathbf{Z} \mid \Theta)p(\Theta). \tag{5.6}$$

To attack this problem one begins by introducing an approximate distribution $q(\Theta,\mathbf{Z})$ and decomposes the log-marginal probability of the data into a the expectation given the approximation and an approximation error term:

$$\ln p(\mathbf{X}) = \mathcal{L}(q) + \mathrm{KL}\,(q \parallel p) \tag{5.7}$$

$$\mathcal{L}(q) = \int\int q(\Theta,\mathbf{Z}) \ln\left(\frac{p(\Theta,\mathbf{Z},\mathbf{X})}{q(\Theta,\mathbf{Z})}\right) d\mathbf{Z}d\Theta \tag{5.8}$$

$$\mathrm{KL}\,(q \parallel p) = -\int\int q(\Theta,\mathbf{Z}) \ln\left(\frac{p(\Theta,\mathbf{Z} \mid \mathbf{X})}{q(\Theta,\mathbf{Z})}\right) d\mathbf{Z}d\Theta \tag{5.9}$$

where $\mathcal{L}(q)$ is a lower bound since the error term, given by the Kullbach-Leibler divergence between the approximation and the true posterior, is always positive. Thus I can minimize the error indirectly by maximizing the lower bound. We now turn our attention to approximations $q(\Theta,\mathbf{Z})$ which factorize between the parameters and the hidden variables:

$$q(\Theta,\mathbf{Z}) = q(\Theta)q(\mathbf{Z}). \tag{5.10}$$

In this case the lower bound decomposes into a sum of negative Kullbach-Leibler divergences:

$$\mathcal{L}(q) = -\mathrm{KL}\left(q(\Theta) \parallel p(\Theta, \mathbf{Z}, \mathbf{X})\right) - \mathrm{KL}\left(q(\mathbf{Z}) \parallel p(\Theta, \mathbf{Z}, \mathbf{X})\right) \tag{5.11}$$

and we get an EM-algorithm by optimizing each one in turn while keeping the other one fixed. Note that not further assumptions about the nature of the approximations entered the derivation. For example in one of the experiments I resort to sampling to approximate the hidden variable distribution $q(\mathbf{Z})$, which does not change the validity of the optimization, even though it might affect its quality.

When the parameter posterior approximation $q(\Theta)$ has the form of a Dirac delta function, then the variational optimization yields the maximum likelihood and maximum a posteriori variants described above. The difference between the two then lies in the choice of paramter prior, which in the case of ML is implicitly uniform [2]

In the more interesting case that the prior is conjugate to the model, i.e. the model is conjugate exponential, the true posterior has the same form as the prior. Naturally the approximation is then chosen to also have the same form as the prior. In this case the first KL in equation 5.11 can be reduced to zero by setting:

$$q(\Theta) = e^{\langle \ln p(\Theta, \mathbf{Z}, \mathbf{X}) \rangle_{q(\mathbf{Z})} 3}. \tag{5.12}$$

Since $q(\Theta)$ is conjugate to $p(\Theta, \mathbf{Z}, \mathbf{X})$ this amounts to collecting the expected sufficient statistics and the prior:

$$p(\Theta) \propto g(\Theta)^{\eta} e^{\phi(\Theta)^T \nu} \tag{5.13}$$

$$q(\Theta) \propto g(\Theta)^{\eta'} e^{\phi'(\Theta)^T \nu'} \tag{5.14}$$

$$\nu' = \nu + \sum_{i=1}^{N} \langle u(\mathbf{Z}, \mathbf{X}) \rangle \tag{5.15}$$

$$\eta' = \eta + N. \tag{5.16}$$

5.2 Stochastic gradient descent

To optimize the discriminative performance of the model I turn to direct optimization via gradient descent. Effectively this means that I train a discriminative model that has the same structure as the generative model, and is initialized with the paramters learned by the generative model (see Lasserre et al. (2006) for a detailed discussion of this approach). That is we take the gradient of a cost function that is high when the performance is good and low otherwise, and take a step in the direction of the gradient. If the cost function is sufficiently smooth this will lead us at least to a local optimum once the gradient vanishes and the descent algorithm converges. In deep models like the hierarchical image models one can make use of dynamic programming to vastly reduce the computational effort. To see this consider taking the gradient with respect to a parameter attached to a factor at the far end of the network. Using the chain rule we find this gradient by propagating the gradient with respect to the network output by propagating it through the Jacobians of the factor along every possible path between the output and this factor, and summing up the contributions of each path. Now considering we want the gradient with respect to the parameters of all factors we see

[2] A uniform prior can often not be normalized, which is then known as an *improper prior*. Nevertheless using an improper prior yields a valid posterior, up to normalization of course.

that many of the partial results can be reused. We thus propagate step by step in parallel form the output to the input, and simply store the partial results which are the gradients with respect to the factors along the way.
The proper way of performing gradient descent would be to average the gradient over the whole training set for each step. In the case of image data the amount of data becomes large very quickly. So instead I apply the gradient averaged over one image immediately after the image was presented to the network. This way of using derivatives of part of the training set is referred to as *stochastic gradient descent* (see e.g. LeCun et al. (1998) for a more detailed discussion). Averaging overr images also reduces the dominance of larger images in the gradient, which helps reducing training set bias when images of one class are much larger than images of the other classes.
In the context of this model the classification is performed by a naive Bayes classifier operating on the representation established by the highest layer of the hierarchical model. Discriminative training of this setup can be interpreted as training a non-linear logistic regression classifier with the model itself as the kernel function. As error function I consequently use the cross-entropy error which leads to an error derivative linear in the distance between predicted and actual class probabilities (see e.g. Bishop (1995) for an extended treatment of the appropriate choice of error function).
Since the error landscape will most probably not be very isotropic, that is the gradients will have widely varying magnitudes in different regions of the parameter space, we employ a momentum term that will speed up movements in directions which are consistent in consecutive evaluations, while slowing down directions which are not. While this is a very simple technique and more sophisticated techniques exist, it is easy to implement and presents little numerical difficulty. Also it can readily deal with consistent directions which are diagonal to several dimensions, which is not the case for adaptive learning rate algorithms such as the widely used diagonal Hessian Levenberg-Marquardt algorithm.

5.3 Weight sharing

To decrease the number of parameters and to exploit the fact that the presence of patterns in the image is roughly independent of the position in the image I tie parameters of the multiple receptive fields in a layer together. For learning this means that the statistics from the individual receptive fields (or the gradients in gradient descent) are summed together. This also allows the model to adapt to varying image geometry by adjusting the number of receptive fields. This effectively makes the model a kind of a *convolutional model* since the scanning of the image (or a higher layer output) is reminiscent of a convolution operation, or would be if neighboring receptive fields would overlap maximally.

5.4 Training set bias

When the training set is strongly biased, i.e. data from one class is much more ubiqutous than data from the other classes, the generative model will assign more detail to this class than to the others, since the ststistics of this class have more wight in the parameter update step of VBEM learning (see section 6.2 for empiric observation of this effect on real data). To avoid this I reweigh the statistics of the classes in the update step such that the all classes are approximately weighed equally.

5.5 Transformation invariance

To be robust against shifts and scalings in the training set we can use Bayesian marginalization to estimate the optimal shift and scale for each training image. This is done by introducing an additional selector variable that has one possible setting for every allowed shift and scale:

$$p(x \mid \Theta, \mathbf{s}) = \prod_{i,j,l} p(\mathcal{T}_{ij}(x) \mid \Theta)^{s_{ijl}} \tag{5.17}$$

$$p(x \mid \Theta) = \sum_{i,j,l} p(s_{ijl}) p(\mathcal{T}_{ij}(x) \mid \Theta) \tag{5.18}$$

where $\mathcal{T}_{ijk}$ denotes the image transformation, i and j enumerate the allowed shifts, and l enumerates the allowed scales while now s is a selector variable which is one only for one specific scale and shift. The marginalization over shifts may seem a large computational effort at first, but it can be sped up considerably by using some tricks. If a one layer hierarchy is used then the operation on the image at some point amounts to a convolution:

$$p(x \mid \Theta) = e^{\sum_{i'j'} u(x_{i-i'j-j'}) \phi(\Theta_{ij})} \tag{5.19}$$

where $i'j'$ span the receptive field. This operation can be sped up by utilizing the convolution theorem and a the Fast Fourier Transform (FFT). If a two layer hierarchy is used then we can restrict the shifts to multiples of the displacements of neighboring receptive fields of the lower layer. Then we only have to compute lower layer responses once, and can perform the marginalization on the layers outputs, since all receptive fields have the same parameters. To avoid missing information about the intermediate shifts we can also lay out the lowest level receptive field densely (which again allows evaluation of the lowest layer using the FFT), and perform pooling to reduce the resolution using the probabilistic logical or:

$$p(z_1 or z_2 \ldots or z_n) = 1 - \prod_i (1 - p(z_i)) \tag{5.20}$$

Since this yields distributions over bit-vectors instead of one-out-of-k vectors we then use a multivariate binomial as the emission model for the next layer.

5.6 Feature selection

In the detection example it may be beneficial to operate only on a subset of the receptive field. For one this makes it possible to deal with non-rectengular object shapes. It also makes it possible to supress regions of the object model which are not reliable for detection. In effect this is somewath similar to the mask bits in the segmenting graphical model. Only that in this case the parts that are masked out remain masked out and are not modelled by any other part of the model. This contradiscts the generative learning scheme, so that this kind of mask has to be learned discriminatively. I define the detection based on the model likelihood like this:

$$p(object \mid \mathbf{l}) \equiv \frac{1}{1 + e^{-(\mathbf{wl} - w_0)}} \tag{5.21}$$

where $\mathbf{l}$ is the vector of log-likelihoods from the individual receptive field positions, $\mathbf{w}$ is a vector of weights for each position, and w_0 is a constant offset. To learn the weight vector $\mathbf{w}$ I parameterize each weight using a logistic function to keep the wieghts in the range $[0, 1]$:

$$w_i \equiv \frac{1}{1 + e^{-v_i}}. \tag{5.22}$$

6. Experiments

6.1 Occlusion modeling

I demonstrate the ability of the model to separate objects that have a constant shape but occlude each other in various configurations on a toy dataset consisting of an artificially generated RGB image sequence in which three geometric shapes of red green and blue color move randomly over a black background, which occasionally occlude each other, examples are shown in figure 6. The parametric form of the emission models $p(x_i \mid \Theta_{kij})$ is a diagonal Gaussian distribution with a normal-gamma prior. Furthermore I put a truncated stick breaking prior distribution on the latent variables, thus the latent variables together with the conditional distributions over variables in their receptive fields approximate a Gaussian Dirichlet Process Mixture Model (DPMM), a non-parametric model which has the ability to find the needed number of components itself, and does not need random initialization in this kind of training procedure, as would be the case of a symmetric dirichlet prior. To speed up training I update the posterior after each image and decay it by a factor of $e^{-1/\tau}$ with τ equal to ten times the training batch size, which makes the posterior an average over an exponentially decaying window with an effective time window of ten training epochs. To slow down the training at the beginning and avoid premature sharpening of the posterior on the first few images I initialize the stick breaking and normal-gamma posteriors uniformly with a number of pseudo-counts corresponding to again ten training epochs. The topology is such that neighboring receptive fields overlap maximally, i.e. are only shifted by one pixel relative to each other. The animated figures have a size of 8x8 pixels, and the receptive fields are fifteen pixels square, thus each pixel is connected to 255 latent variables. Since each input appears at each possible position in one of the receptive fields it is contained in the model should be able to train a shift invariant representation of them.
To highlight the effects of the introduction of the gate MRF as well and the mask bits I train three different models:

model	gate MRF	mask bits
1	-	-
2	x	-
3	x	x

Table 1. Overview over the four model configurations analyzed. A cross means the corresponding feature is active in this configuration, a dash means it is not active.

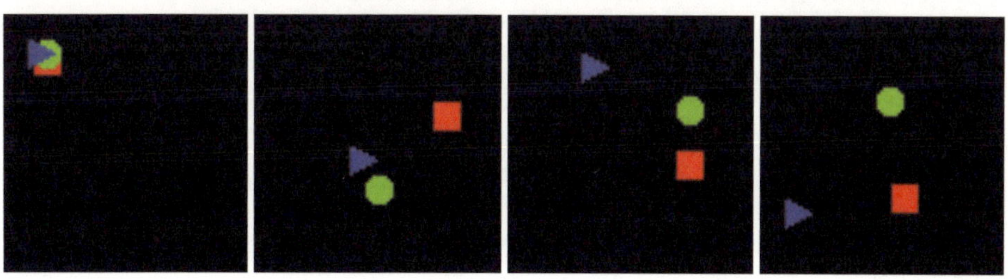

Fig. 6. Four example frames from the toy sequence. The full sequence is one hundred frames long, Each frame has a size of 80x80 pixels.

All three models are able to reconstruct their inputs from the latent variables with high confidence, but the way the input is encoded is very different. The learned receptive field

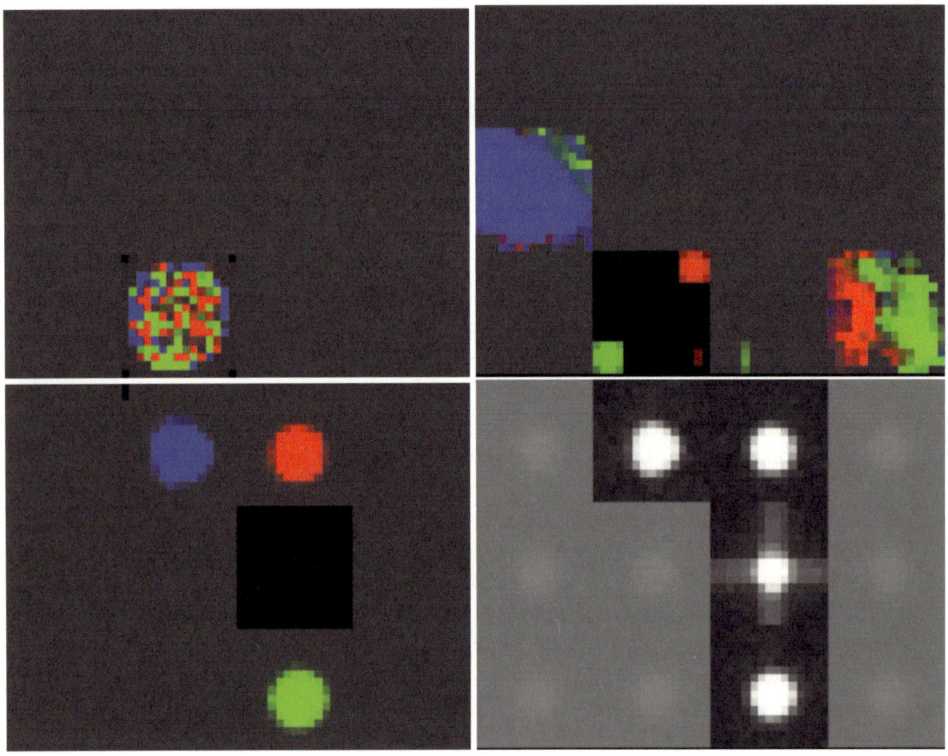

Fig. 7. Results of training the three model configurations. *upper left:* Receptive fields learned by the model with no embedded gate-MRF. No structure has been learned such that the model has to reconstruct the image pixel by pixel. *upper right:* Receptive fields learned by the model with embedded gate-MRF but no mask bits. There is more structure in the receptive fields than with no gate-MRF, but the model fails to separate the objects from each other.*lower left and right:* Receptive fields and mask bit distributions learned by the model with gate-MRF and mask bits. This model has learned a superpixel-decomposition of the image, i.e. the receptive fields and masks represent blobs of the three colors and black (the cross-shape superimposed on the mask for the black receptive field is due to border effects).

model	$\langle H(gates \mid object) \rangle$ [bits]	normalized mutual information
1	5.78	0
2	2.58	0.26
3	2.23	0.99

Table 2. Overview over the three model configurations analyzed. A cross means the corresponding feature is active in this configuration, a dash means it is not active.

together with the learned mask distribution, where applicable, are shown in figure 7. The simplest model with no gate MRF and no mask bits actually only learns a single receptive field containing pixels of all four colors. Thus all latent variables have the same setting and the gates assume settings effectively picking a pixel of the right color by selecting a latent variable with the receptive field aligned in the right way and each latent variable only models a few pixels, often only one, and each shape is modeled by many latent variables, thus no object concept is formed. When I introduce the gate MRF, enforcing smoothness in the gate field,

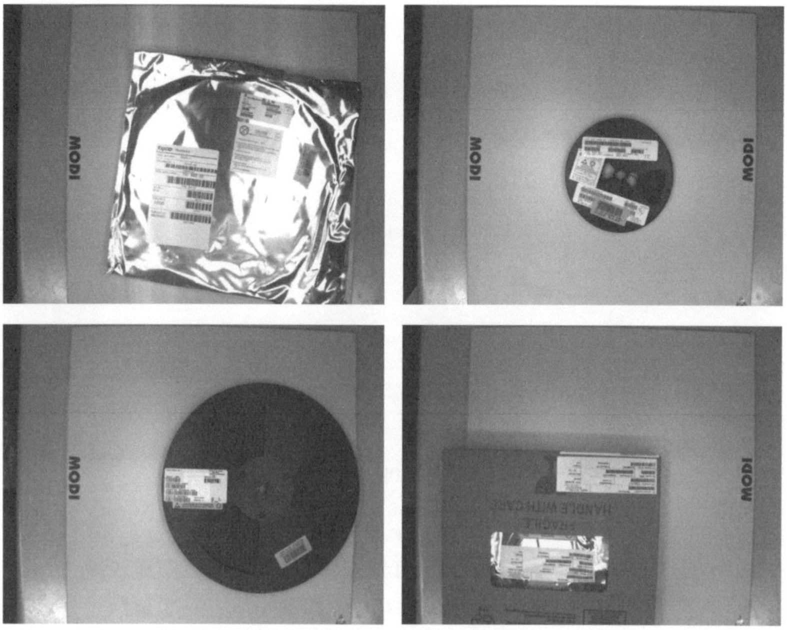

Fig. 8. Four examples of the training images used for the barcode localization task.

several receptive fields are learned and some smoothness in them emerges, but the model fails to fully separate the four objects from each others and the receptive fields still contain several colors. When the mask bits are introduced conditioned on the latent variables the model learns a super-pixel representation of the image: Four receptive fields with medium sized blobs of a each color or black emerge, and the blob-shape is encoded in the conditional mask bit distribution. While this is not quite what was hoped for the resulting code is a reasonable representation of the data, as can be seen by evaluating the average gating entropy per object, which I define by the entropy of the multinomial distribution over parents for the objects induced by the gates, and the normalized mutual information between the object identity and the latent variables, summarized in table 2 for all three experiments: Using the gate MRF and the variable receptive field shape each object can be encoded by around two bits with high fidelity.

6.2 Code tag localization

Here I apply the model to the task of locating code tags in images of items in a logistics context. The goal is to automatically identify the items by the tags placed on them from a camera image. Examples of such images are shown in figure 8. Labels for this task where generated automatically by the slow lookup procedure and hand-corrected to yield a dataset of 380 labeled images. The localization serves as a first step. In the second step the located tags are looked up in a separately maintained database. Since this step is quite slow, especially when the database is large, accurate localization is crucial.

For this task I preprocess the images by extracting two kinds of features:

- local Gabor wavelet decomposition in two scales and eight orientations
- on-center off-surround filters serving as local brightness indicators, implemented by heavily compressing the output of a local bandpass filter

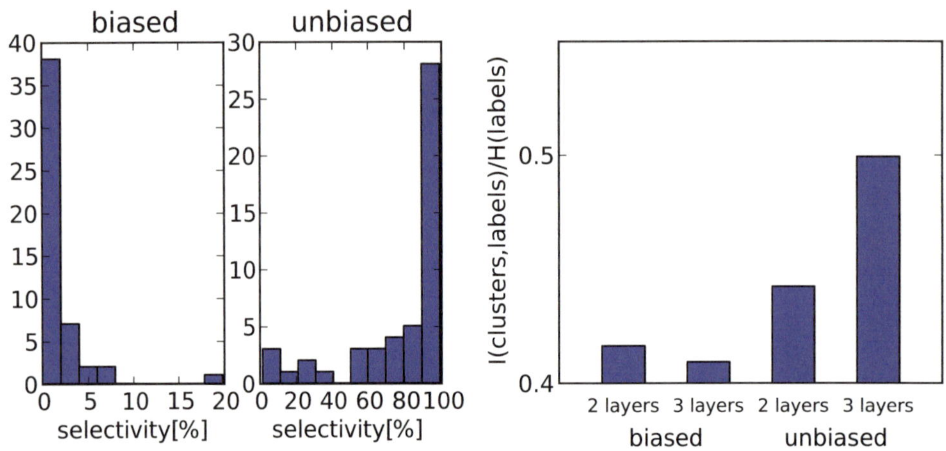

Fig. 9. *left and middle:*Histogram of cluster selectivities towards the code tags on the second layer for different bias conditions, illustrating the effect of training set bias. On the left side the trainig set bias was left uncorrected, such that background data was effectivey weighed ten times more than the targets. On the right this bias was removed by reweighing the M-step statistics so that both classes where weighed equally. The x-axis in each case shows the percentage of code tag patches relative to all input patterns assigned to a certain cluster. *right:*Mutual information between the output layer states and the labels for different settings, normalized w.r.t. to the label entropy. When the bias in the labels is removed via reweighing the additional layer helps the network in extracting the relevant information.

The resolution of these features is reduced by local maximum-pooling in each feature channel and non-overlapping two by two windows. These features are then concatenated for each location and fed into a three layer hierarchical network. This network learns to represent all of the images, not only the target regions, due to the generative nature of the model. Since during the learning stage of the hierarchy the labels are not used a strong bias in the dataset can cause a poor representation of the underrepresented class. In this example the code tags occupy only relatively small regions of the images and thus run into danger of being under-represented. To highlight the effect of training set bias I analyze the selectivity of cluster labels on the second layer for one or the other class. In figure 9 histograms of this selectivity are shown with a naive learning strategy, and one where the statistics used to update the parameters during the VBM-step where reweighed to remove the bias. As can be seen the naive strategy leaves only few, poorly selective clusters. In this case even discriminative post training can not be expected to yield very good results. On the other hand when the bias is removed the selectivity becomes more biased towards the target class (the code tags in this example). This can be understood by noting that most of the background is relatively simple, and can thus be represented by few clusters. The right-most plot in the same figure further highlights the benefit of de-biasing by showing the mutual information of cluster labels on the second and third layer with the target labels. As can be seen with the bias the second layer representation is so poor, that the third layer fails to build a better representation of the target class than the second layer. In the un-biased case this effect is gone and the third layer succeeds in improving the representation. For classification the hierarchy is trained layer by layer on eighty percent of the images. then the output of the third layer is fed into a naive Bayes classifier to learn a mapping to the target labels. The whole setup is illustrated in figure 10. The resulting system is then fine tuned using discriminative gradient descent. Figure shows the receiver operator

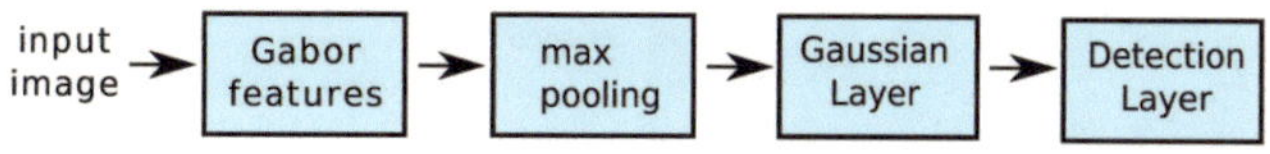

Fig. 10. Processing chain for the code tag localization task.

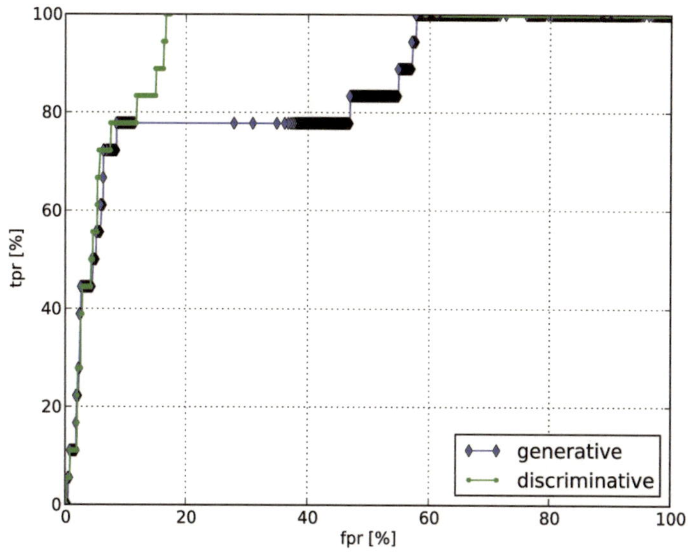

Fig. 11. ROC curves of the code tag detector in the biased and unbiased setting after generative and discriminative training.

Fig. 12. Positive examples from the INRIA pedestrians database used for training the pedestrian detector.

characteristic (ROC) curves for the remaining twenty percent of the images after generative and discriminative training.

6.3 Pedestrian detection

Pedestrian detection is an important application for object detection algorithms. As low level features I use the histograms of oriented gradients as established in Dalal & Triggs (2005), and also the training set introduced in this publication[4] (see figures 12 and 13 for examples). I use a cell-size of six pixels, a block size of 3 cells, and a block-overlap of one cell. These features are used as the input features for a classifier based on the hierarchical image model (see figure 14): These features are first fed into a 3-layer network. The lowest layer of this network has

[4] `http://pascal.inrialpes.fr/data/human/`

Fig. 13. Negative examples from the INRIA pedestrians database used for training the pedestrian detector.

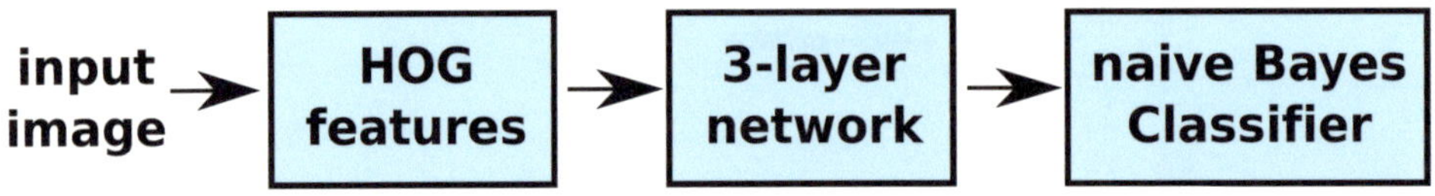

Fig. 14. Processing chain for pedestrian detection. The features are those suggested in Dalal & Triggs (2005).

receptive fields covering two by two blocks, i.e. four blocks total, with neighboring fields overlapping by one block. The next layer has receptive fields of four by four units. The top layer finally has seven by two receptive fields to cover a whole pedestrian (which in this dataset are standardized to 64x128 pixels). The receptive fields of the last layer overlap maximally to achieve relatively dense scanning for pedestrians in the input image.
Each layer of the network is trained generatively on the training set (see) to convergence using VBEM before the next layer is trained. During this training the negative examples are weighed less than the positive examples by a factor of two hundred to avoid too detailed learning of the negative data. The resulting top layer cluster labels for each input window are then fed into a naive Bayes classifier to learn a mapping to the class labels (i.e. pedestrian/non-pedestrian). Subsequently the classifier and the hierarchical network are refined discriminatively using gradient descent.
In figure I show the resulting precision-recall-curve of this setup on the test set after generative training and after the subsequent discriminative refinement. The results are comparable to those of kernelized R-HOG as presented in Dalal & Triggs (2005), though somewhat weaker in the high precision regime. The discriminative training increases the recall but further looses precision. It would be worth investigating how this precision loss may be prevented in a deep hierarchy such as this for applications that need it.

6.4 Locating faces

Here I demonstrate how the hierarchical model can be used to locate faces in images. As training I use a relatively small dataset in which the faces appear isolated against a blank wall. Furthermore during training I do not tell the model the location of the faces in the image. As training data I use the frontal views of the faces in the CBCL faces training dataset[5] shown in figure 16. Obviously this is a very small dataset, so correctly modeling parameter uncertainty is important to avoid overfitting. I train a two layer model. The lowest layer consists of a simple categorical layer with a Gaussian emission model. This layer operates on Gabor features with a bandwidth of one octave at eight orientations and two scales, where the finest scale has a wavelength of five pixels which are max-pooled by a factor of four [6].

[5] `http://cbcl.mit.edu/software-datasets/heisele/facerecognition-database.html`

[6] By "max-pooling" I mean downsampling where the max instead of the mean operation is used to summarize the input pixels flowing into one output pixel.

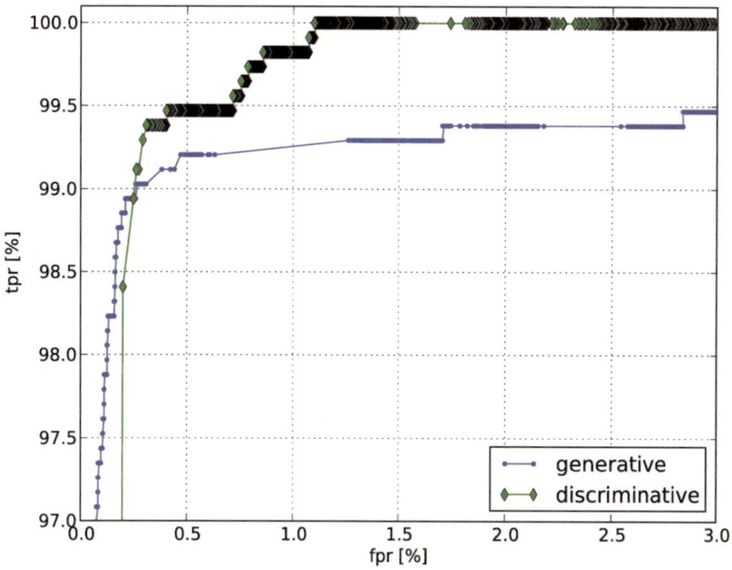

Fig. 15. ROC characteristics of the pedestrian detector after generative training and after discriminiative optimization .

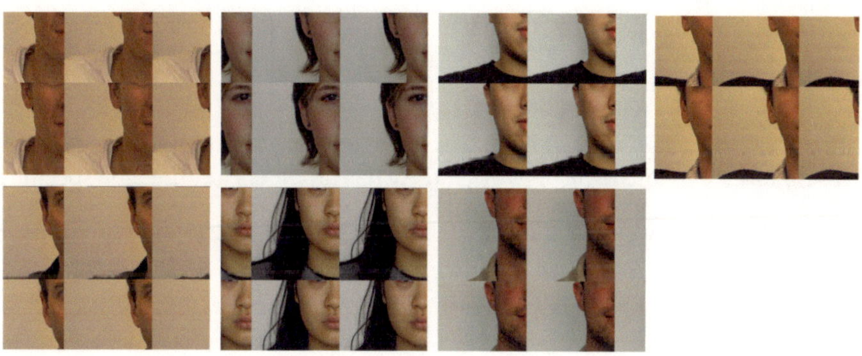

Fig. 16. Positive examples from the CBCL faces database used for training the face model.

The layer has a receptive field size of four by four with halve-overlapping receptive fields. I then use shift and scale-invariant VBEM training as described in section 5.5 to learn a single multivariate multinomial representation of a frontal face, using the output of the first layer as input. To improve this model I use conjugate gradients to do feature selection as described in section 5.6, using ten percent of the clutter images from the Caltech 256 dataset [7] as negative examples. To test the model I use it to locate the faces in the first one hundred images from the Caltech faces database [8] which shows frontal views of faces in complex environments and different lighting conditions. After feature selection the model correctly locates all but seven of the faces (see figure 19), six of which are from the same person, who seems to be badly

[7] http://www.vision.caltech.edu/Image_Datasets/Caltech256/

[8] http://www.vision.caltech.edu/Image_datasets/faces/faces.tar

Fig. 17. Some of the negative examples from the Caltech256 database used for training feature selection.

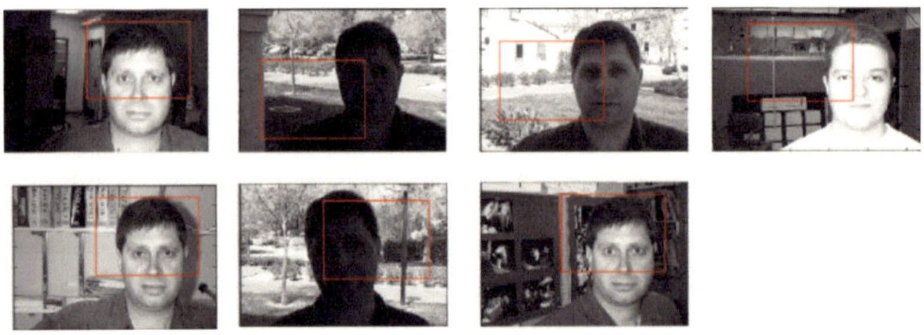

Fig. 18. The seven failures when locating faces in the first one hundred images from the Caltech fasesdataset.Obviouslythe network mostly has problems locating one specific person.

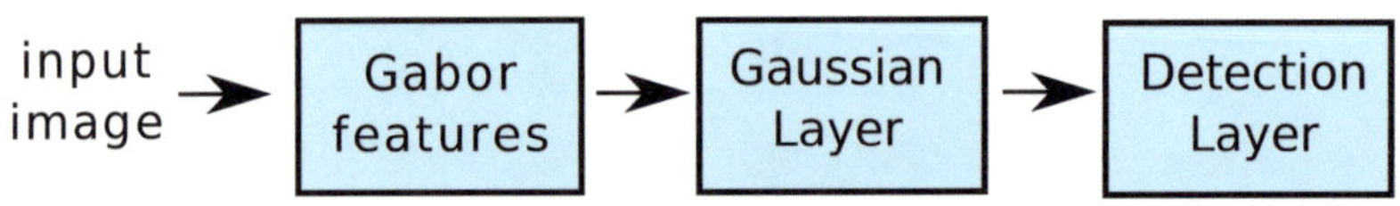

Fig. 19. The seven failures when locating faces in the first one hundred images from the Caltech fasesdataset.Obviouslythe network mostly has problems locating one specific person.

represented by the training set. Without feature selection the localization rate drops to about eighty percent.

7. Conclusion

In conclusion I introduced the Bayesian hierarchical image model for learning of statistics of arbitrary images. I have explained the motivation and basic ideas behind the generative modeling approach. I have reviewed Bayesian inference techniques and how they are applied to this model. I have explained how Bayesian techniques can be used to learn such a model with robustness to overfitting, while discrimiantive gradient descent can be used to fine tune the classification performance. I have also introduced an extension to the basic model that leading to a better representation of images by introducing automatic segmentation into the model.

In the experiments I have shown the performance of the model in various tasks. To present the behavior of the segmentation I have turned to a toy example where the details of the model behavior could be readily analyzed. The basic model in turn has been applied to several real world examples. There I showed the importance of managing training set bias by reweighing the learning statistics. The ability to do this is a consequence of the truly Bayesian treatment of the learning process. Also the results on the competitive INRIA pedestrian detection dataset shows that this approach is a valid competitor for more classical approaches such as support vector machines.

Interesting directions from here would be the analysis and possible improvement of transformation invariance, and the application of the segmentation extension to real world problems.

8. References

Attias, H. (1999). Inferring parameters and structure of latent variable models by variational bayes, *Proceedings of Fifteenth Conference on Uncertainty in Artificial Intelligence*.

Bishop, C. M. (2006). *Pattern Recognition and Machine Learning*, Springer-Verlag.

Bishop, C. M. (1995). *Neural Networks for Pattern Recognition*, Oxford University Press, 1995.

Chalupa, L. M. & Werner, J. S. (eds) (2003). *The Visual Neurosciences*, MIT Press.

Dalal, N. & Triggs, B. (2005). Histograms of oriented gradients for human detection, *in* C. Schmid, S. Soatto & C. Tomasi (eds), *International Conference on Computer Vision & Pattern Recognition*, Vol. 2, INRIA Rhône-Alpes, ZIRST-655, av. de l'Europe, Montbonnot-38334, pp. 886–893.
URL: *http://lear.inrialpes.fr/pubs/2005/DT05*

Dean, T. (2006). Scalable inference in hierarchical generative models, *Proceedings of the Ninth International Symposium on Artificial Intelligence and Mathematics*.

Dempster, A., Laird, N. & Rubin, D. (1977). Maximum likelihood from incomplete data via the em algorithm, *Journal of the Royal Statistical Society, Series B* 39(1): 1–38.

Eddy, S. R. (2004). What is dynamic programming?, *Nature Biotechnology* (22): 909–910.

Fink, D. (1995). A compendium of conjugate priors. in progress report: Extension and enhancement of methods for setting data quality objectives., *Technical report*, Cornell University.

Fukushima, K. (1980). Neocognitron: A self-organizing neural network model for a mechanism of pattern recognition unaffected by shift in position, *Biol. Cyb.* V36(4): 193–202.
URL: *http://dx.doi.org/10.1007/BF00344251*

Hadsell, R., Chopra, S. & LeCun, Y. (2006). Dimensionality reduction by learning an invariant mapping, *Proc. CVPR*, IEEE Press.

Hinton, G. E. (2007). Learning multiple layers of representation, *TRENDS in Cognitive Sciences* 11: 428.

J. M. Winn, C. M. B. (2005). Variational message passing, *J. Mach. L. Res.* 6: 558–590.

Lasserre, J., Lasserre, J., Bishop, C. & Minka, T. (2006). Principled hybrids of generative and discriminative models, *in* C. Bishop (ed.), *Proc. IEEE Computer Society Conference on Computer Vision and Pattern Recognition*, Vol. 1, pp. 87–94.

LeCun, Y., Bottou, L., Orr, G. B. & Mueller, K.-R. (1998). Efficient backprop, *Lecture Notes in Computer Science* 1524: 9–??
URL: *citeseer.ist.psu.edu/lecun98efficient.html*

LeCun, Y., Jackel, L. D., Boser, B., Denker, J. S., Graf, H. P., Guyon, I., Henderson, D., Howard, R. E. & Hubbard, W. (1989). Handwritten digit recognition: Applications of neural net chips and automatic learning, *IEEE Comm.* pp. 41–46. invited paper.

Minka, T. & Winn, J. (2008). Gates: A graphical notation for mixture models, *Technical Report MSR-TR-2008-185*, Microsoft Research.

Mutch, J. & Lowe, D. G. (2006). Multiclass object recognition with sparse, localized features, *Proc. CVPR* pp. 11–18.

Onsager, L. (1944). Crystal statistics. i. a two-dimensional model with an order-disorder transition, *Phys. Rev.* 65(3-4): 117–149.

Pearl, J. (1982). Reverend bayes on inference engines: A distributed hierarchical approach.

Rolls, E. T. & Deco, G. (2002). *The Computational Neuroscience of Vision*, Oxford University Press.

Serre, T., Kouh, M., Cadieu, C., Knoblich, U. & G. Kreiman, T. P. (2005). A theory of object recognition: Computations and circuits in the feedforward path of the ventral stream in primate visual cortex, *CBCL Memo 259*.

Wellman, M. P. & Henrion, M. (1993). Explaining "explaining away", *Pattern Analysis and Machine Intelligence, IEEE Transactions on* 15: 287–292.

Wersing, H. & Korner, E. (2003). Learning Optimized Features for Hierarchical Models of Invariant Object Recognition, *Neural Comp.* 15(7): 1559–1588.
URL: *http://neco.mitpress.org/cgi/content/abstract/15/7/1559*

11

Mean Pattern Estimation of Images Using Large Diffeomorphic Deformations

Jérémie Bigot and Sébastien Gadat
Institut de Mathématiques de Toulouse, Université Paul Sabatier (Toulouse)
France

1. Introduction

This work deals with the problem of estimating the statistical object called " mean" concerning a situation where one observe noisy images which are also corrupted through a deformation process. The difficulty of this statistical problem arises from the nature of the space in which the object to estimate are living. A popular approach in image processing is Grenander's pattern theory described in Grenander (1993) and Grenander & Miller (2007) where natural images are viewed as points in an infinite dimensional manifold and the variations of the images are modelled by the action of deformation groups on the manifold.
In the last decade, the construction of deformation groups to model the geometric variability of images, and the study of the properties of such deformation groups has been an active field of research: one may refer for instance to the works of Beg et al. (2005), Joshi et al (2004), Miller & Younes (2001) or Trouvé & Younes (2005b). But to the best of our knowledge, few results on statistical estimation using such deformations groups are available. In this setting, there has been recently a growing interest on the problem of defining an empirical mean of a set of random images using deformation groups and non-Euclidean distances. A first attempt in this direction is the statistical framework based on penalized maximum likelihood proposed in Glasbey & Mardia (2001). Computation of empirical Fréchet mean of biomedical images is discussed in Joshi et al (2004). More recently, Allassonière et al. (2007), Allassonière et al. (2009) and Ma et al. (2008) have proposed a statistical approach using Bayesian modelling and random deformation models to approximate the mean and main geometric modes of variations of 2D or 3D images in the framework of small deformations.
Starting from Bigot et al. (2009), we focus in this text on the problem of estimating a mean pattern in shape invariant models for images using random diffeomorphic deformations in two-dimensions. The main goal of this paper is to show that the framework proposed in Bigot et al. (2009) leads to the definition of an empirical Fréchet mean associated to a new dissimilarity measure between images. We study both theoretical and numerical aspects of such an empirical mean pattern. In this extended abstract, we present the main ideas of such an approach. We also give a numerical example of mean pattern estimation from a set of faces to illustrate the methodology.
Our work will be organised as follows. We first define the mathematical objects used and then model our situation of noisy and warped images with random large deformations. We aim to solve theoretically the problem of estimating the mean pattern of a set of images and state

some convergence results among some general assumptions. At last, we propose an algorithm to approach the theoretical estimator and illustrate our method on real datasets.

2. Statistical deformable framework and statement of the mean pattern estimation problem

We first describe our random model of deformations on 2-dimensional images but note that this model can be extended to higher dimensions with very minor modifications. Thus, the following paragraphs are organised as follow, we first recall in paragraph 2.1.1 the classical model of large deformation introduced in the works of Younes, (2004). Next, we describe precisely the parametric decomposition of our diffeomorphism (paragraph 2.1.3) and then explain how one can use our method to generate random large deformations with localised effects.
At last, this section ends with the paragraph 2.2 and the description of the statistical model we consider for randomly warped image corrupted by additive noise.

2.1 Mathematical model of large deformation

2.1.1 Definition

For sake of simplicity, images are considered to be functions from a compact set denoted Ω which will be set equal to Ω in the sequel. Moreover, we deal in this work with grey levelled thus the generic notation for images I will be $I : \Omega \mapsto \mathbb{R}$. The first task is to define a suitable notion of deformation of the domain Ω. For this, we will adopt the large deformation model governed by diffeomorphic flows of differential equation introduced in Trouvé & Younes (2005a). These deformations denoted Φ will later be combined with some pattern of reference $I^\star$ to produce our noisy and wrapped images $I^\star \circ \Phi + \epsilon$.
Let us first describe precisely our model to generate diffeomorphisms Φ of Ω.
We first consider any smooth vector field v from Ω to $\mathbb{R}^2$ with a vanishing assumption on the boundary of Ω:

$$\forall x \in \partial\Omega \qquad v(x) = 0. \tag{1}$$

Now, we consider the set of applications $(\Phi_v^t)_{t\in[0;1]}$ from Ω to Ω, solution of the ordinary differential equation

$$\begin{cases} \forall x \in \Omega & \Phi_v^0(x) = x, \\ \forall x \in \Omega \quad \forall t \in [0;1] & \frac{d\Phi_v^t(x)}{dt} = v(\Phi_v^t(x)). \end{cases} \tag{2}$$

A remarkable mathematical point for the ordinary differential equation (2) is that it builds a set of diffeomorphisms on Ω, Φ_v^t for any $t \in [0;1]$.
As we want to have a deformation which remains in Ω, we have imposed that $\Phi^1_{v|\partial\Omega} = Id$, meaning that our diffeomorphism is the identity at the boundaries of Ω. Note that in the above definition, v is an homogeneous vector field (it does not depend on time t) which means that the differential equation is time-homogeneous and v is also a smooth ($C^\infty(\Omega)$) function.
The solution at time $t = 1$ denoted by Φ_v^1 of the above ordinary differential equation is a diffeomorphic transformation of Ω generated by the vector field v, which will be used to model image deformations. One can easily check that the vanishing conditions (1) on the vector field v imply that $\Phi_v^1(\Omega) = \Omega$ and that Φ_v^t is a diffeomorphism for all time $t \in [0,1]$. Thus Φ_v^1 is a convenient object to generate diffeomorphisms. Indeed, to compute the inverse diffeomorphisms of Φ_v^t, it is enough to revert the time in equation (2). One may refer to Younes, (2004) for further details on this construction.

2.1.2 One dimensional example

To illustrate the simple construction based on the choice of the vector field v and the obtained diffeomorphism Φ_v^1, we consider a first simple example in one-dimension (i.e. for $v : [0,1] \to \mathbb{R}$ which generates a diffeomorphism of the interval $[0,1]$). In Figure 1, we display two vector fields that have the same support on $[0,1]$ but different amplitudes, and we plot the corresponding deformation Φ_v^1.

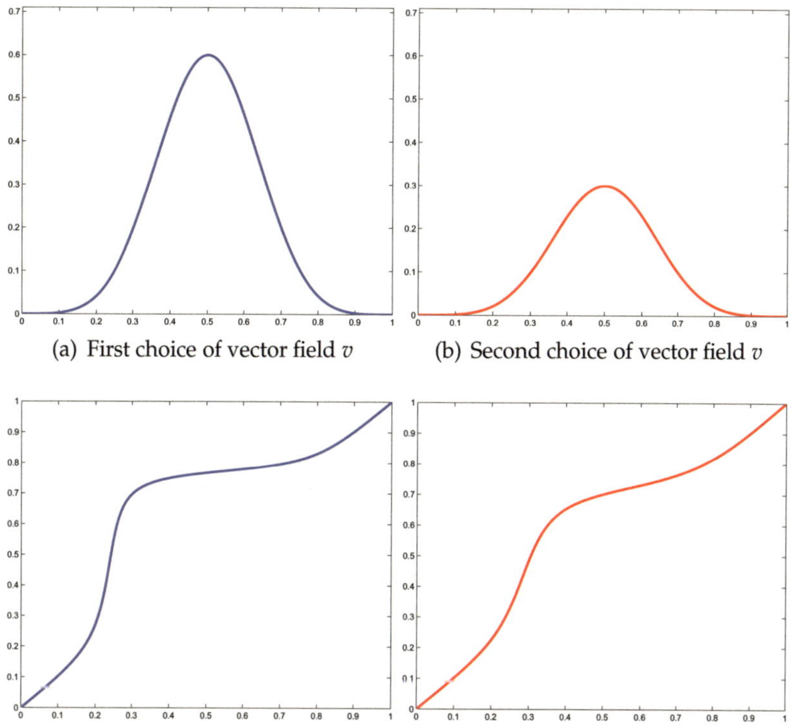

(a) First choice of vector field v (b) Second choice of vector field v

(c) Diffeomorphism Φ_v^1 obtained with blue vector field v (d) Diffeomorphism Φ_v^1 obtained with red vector field v

Fig. 1. Some numerical examples of two choices for the vector field v and the obtained diffeomophisms through ordinary differential equation (2).

Note that the deformations require the prior choice of a vector field v. One can see that the amount of deformations, measured as the local distance between Φ_v^1 and the identity, depends on the amplitude of the vector field. In the intervals where v is zero, then the deformation is locally equals to the identity as pointed in Figure 1. Hence, this simple remark asserts that local deformations will be generated by choosing compactly supported vector fields which will be decomposed in localized basis functions.

2.1.3 Building the vector field v in 2D

Parametric decomposition

Consider an integer K and some linearly independent functions $e_k : \mathbb{R}^2 \to \mathbb{R}^2$ whose choices will be discussed later on. We have chosen to use vector fields v that can be decomposed on the family of functions $e_k = (e_k^1, e_k^2)$. The deformations are generated as follows. Let

(a_k^1, a_k^2), $k = 1, \dots, K$ be coefficients in $[-A, A]$ for a given real $A > 0$. Then, we define a vector field v_a as

$$\forall x \in \Omega \qquad v_a(x) = \begin{pmatrix} \sum_{k=1}^{K} a_k^1 e_k^1(x) \\ \sum_{k=1}^{K} a_k^2 e_k^2(x) \end{pmatrix}. \tag{3}$$

Finally, one has just to run the previously defined O.D.E (2) to produce a deformation, Φ_{v_a} with a parametric representation.

Choice of e_k and numerical example

The amount of variability for diffeomorphisms Φ_{v_a} is thus related to the choice of K and basis functions e_k used to decompose the vector field v. In order to get a smooth bijection of Ω, the e_k should be at least differentiable. Such functions are built as follows. First, we choose a set of one-dimensional B-splines functions (of degree at least 2) whose supports are included in $[0; 1]$. To form two-dimensional B-splines, the common way is to use tensor products for each dimension. Recall that to define B-splines, one has to fix a set of control points and to define their degree. Further details are provided in de Boor (1978) and we will fix these parameters in the section dealing with experiments. B-splines functions are compactly supported with a local effect on the knots positions. This local influence is very useful for some problems in image warping where the deformation must be the identity on large parts of the images together with a very local and sharp effect at some other locations. The choice of the knots and the B-spline functions allows one to control the support of the vector field and therefore to define a priori the areas of the images that should be transformed.
In Figure 2, we display an example of a basis $e_k^1 = e_k^2, k = 1, \dots, K$ for vector fields generated by the tensor product of 2 one-dimensional B-splines (hence $K = 4$). An example of deformation of the classical Lena image is shown in Figure 2 with two different sets coefficients a_k sampled from a uniform distribution on $[-A, A]$ (corresponding to different values for the amplitude A, a small and a large one). The amount of deformation depends on the amplitude of A, while the choice of the B-spline functions allows one to localize the deformation.

2.1.4 Random generation of large diffeomorphisms

Given any e_k and following our last construction, one can remark that it is enough to consider a random distribution on coefficients a to generate a large class of random diffeomorphisms. In our simulations, we take for P_A the uniform distribution on $[-A, A]$ i.e. $a_k^i \sim \mathcal{U}_{[-A,A]}$, $i = 1, 2$. However, it should mentioned that in the sequel, P_A can be any distribution on $\mathbb{R}$ provided it has a compact support. The compact support assumption for P_A is mainly used to simplify the theoretical proofs for the consistency of our estimator.

2.2 Random image warping model with additive noise

We fix discretization of Ω as a square grid of $N = N_1 \times N_2$ pixels. Given any image of reference $I^\star$ and a vector field v defined on Ω, we generate a diffeomorphism through or ordinary differential equation and we can define the general warping model by:

Definition 1 (Noisy random deformation of image). *Fix an integer K and a real $A > 0$, we define a noisy random deformation of the mean template $I^\star$ as*

$$I_{\varepsilon,a}(p) = I^\star \circ \Phi_{v_a}^1(p) + \varepsilon(p),\ p \in \Omega,$$

where a is sampled from a distribution $P_A^{\otimes 2K}$ and ε is an additive noise independent from the coefficients a. The new image $I_{\varepsilon,a}$ is generated by deforming the template $I^\star$ (using the composition rule $\circ$) and by adding a white noise at each pixel of the image.

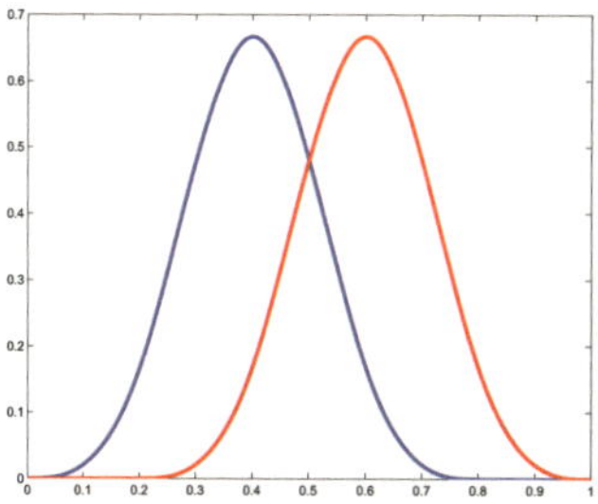

(a) Choice of 1D B-splines

(b) Original image of Lena

(c) Small deformation of Lena with a random uniform sampling of coefficients a (small value of A)

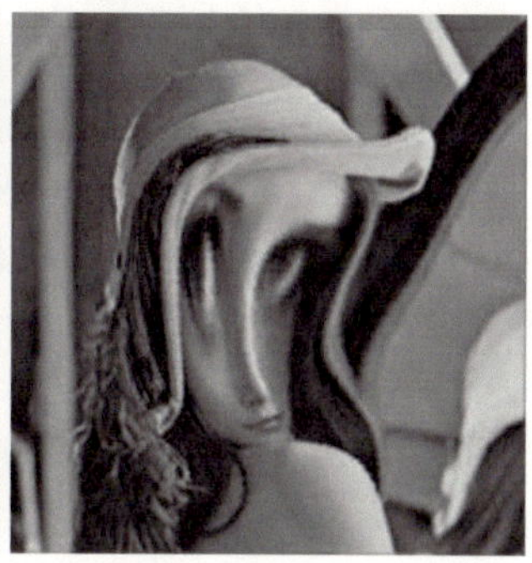

(d) Small deformation of Lena with a random uniform sampling of coefficients a (large value of A)

Fig. 2. Some numerical examples of two choices for the vector field v and the obtained diffeomophisms through ordinary differential equation (2).

Remark 1. *In our theoretical approach, we consider the pixels p as a discretization of the set Ω since our applications will be set up in this framework. However, it may be possible to handle this model in a continuous setting using the continuous white noise model. This model involves the use of an measure integration over Ω instead of sums over the pixels p of the image and we refer to Candes & Donoho (2000) for further details. Finally, remark that the image $I^\star$ is considered as a function of the whole square Ω, giving sense to $I^\star \circ \Phi_u^1(p), \forall p \in \Omega$.*

For notation convenience, we will denote Φ_a the diffeomorphism obtained at time $t = 1$ with the ordinary differential equation (2) based on the vector field v_a, $\Phi_a = \Phi_{v_a}^1$.

2.3 Statement of the problem and mathematical assumption

Using this definition of randomly warped image with additive noise, we consider now a set of n noisy images that are random deformations of the same unknown template $I^\star$ as follows:

$$\forall p \in \Omega \qquad I_{a^i,\varepsilon^i}(p) = I^\star \circ \Phi_{a^i}^1(p) + \varepsilon^i(p),\ i = 1, \ldots, n. \tag{4}$$

where ε^i are i.i.d unknown observation noise and a^i are i.i.d unknown coefficients sampled as $P_A^{\otimes K \times n}$. **Our goal is as well to estimate the mean template image $I^\star$ as to infer some several**

applications of this estimation to image processing.

One may directly realize that this problem is not so easy since the space where the denoised versions of I_{a^i,ε^i} are leaving is not a classical euclidean space such as $\mathbb{R}^d$ since the diffeomorphisms that generate the image changes from one sample i to another one i'. For instance, consider 10 handwritten realisations of the digit "two", a simple arithmetic mean does not yield satisfactory results as pointed in Figure 3.

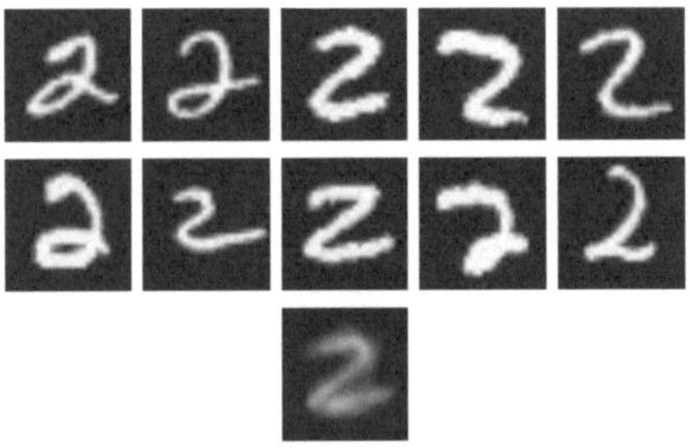

Fig. 3. Naive mean (two first rows) of a set of 10 images (Mnist database, 28×28 pixels images, see LeCun et al. (1998) for more details on this data set) and naive arithmetic mean of these images.

For our theoretical study, we will need some mathematical assumptions:

A1 There exists a constant C such that

$$|\varepsilon| < C.$$

A2

$$I^{\star}\text{is L-Lipschitz.}$$

Assumption **A1** means that the level of noise is bounded which seems reasonable since we generally observe gray-level images which take values on a finite discrete set.

Assumption **A2** is more questionable since a direct consequence is that $I^{\star}$ is continuous, which seems impossible for natural models of images with structural discontinuities (think of the space of bounded variation (BV) functions for instance). However, one can view $I^{\star}$ as a map from all points in Ω rather than just a function defined on the pixels. On Ω, it is more likely to suppose that $I^{\star}$ is the result of the convolution of $\mathcal{C}^{\infty}$-filters with captors measurements, which yields a smooth differentiable map on Ω. One may see for instance the work of Faugeras & Hermosillo (2002) for further comments on this assumption.

3. Statistical estimation of a mean pattern

3.1 The statistical problem

Consider a set of n noisy images $I_1, \ldots I_n$ that are independent realizations from the model (4) with the same original pattern $I^{\star}$. We first aim at constructing an estimate of this pattern of reference $I^{\star}$. We are looking at an algorithm that becomes sharper and sharper around the true pattern $I^{\star}$ when the number of observations n goes to $+\infty$. Without any convex structure on the images, averaging directly the observations is likely to blur the n images without yielding a sharp "mean shape". Indeed, computing the arithmetic mean of a set of images to estimate the mean pattern does not make sense as the space of deformed images $I^{\star} \circ$

Φ^1_v and the space of diffeomorphisms are not vectorial spaces. This is illustrated in the former paragraph in Figure 3. To have a consistent estimation of $I^\star$, one needs to solve an inverse problem as stated in the works of Biscay & Mora (2001) and Huilling (1998) derived from the random deformable model (4) since it is needed to remove the random warping effect (and consequently invert each diffeomorphism $\Phi^1_{a^i}$ which are unknown) before removing the noise ε^i on each image. Thus, recovering $I^\star$ is not an obvious task which requires some sophisticated statistical tools. A short description is provided in the next paragraph.

3.2 Presentation of M-estimation techniques

We will consider an optimisation problem (minimize an energy in our case) whose solution is the pattern $I^\star$ we are looking for and we will use some classical M-estimation techniques. Intuitively the ideas underlying M-estimation in statistics (see van der Waart (1998)) can be understood by considering the following simple example provided for a better understanding.

Example 1. *Let $X_1, \dots X_n \sim_{i.i.d.} P$ and $\alpha^* = \mathbb{E}_P[X_1]$. The simplest way to estimate α^* is $\hat{\alpha_n} = \frac{1}{n}(X_1 + \cdots + X_n)$. If for some real α, we define F_n and F the functions as*

$$F_n(\alpha) = \sum_{i=1}^{n} (X_i - \alpha)^2 \quad \text{and} \quad F(\alpha) = \mathbb{E}_P[(X - \alpha)^2],$$

then one can easily check that $\hat{\alpha}_n$ is the minimum of F_n and that $\alpha^\star$ is the minimum of F. Of course, F is unknown since it depends on the unknown law P, but a stochastic approximation of F is provided by F_n as soon as one observe $X_1, \dots X_n$. Moreover, one can remark that $F_n(\alpha) \to F(\alpha)$ almost surely (a.s.) as $n \to \infty$.
Thus, a simple way to obtain an estimate of $\alpha^\star = \arg\min F$ is to remark that the minimum of F_n should concentrates itself around the minimum of F as n is going to $+\infty$. Mathematically, this is equivalent to establish some results like:

$$F_n \longmapsto_{n \to \infty} F \longrightarrow \arg\min F_n \longmapsto_{n \to \infty} \arg\min F.$$

In our framework, estimating the pattern I^* involves finding a best image that minimizes an energy for the best transformation which aligns the observations onto the candidate. So we will therefore define an estimator of $I^\star$ as a minimum of an empirical contrast function F_n (based on the observations $I_1, \dots I_n$) which converges, under mild assumptions, toward a minimum of some contrast F.

3.3 A new contrast function for estimating a mean pattern

We start this paragraph with some notations.

Definition 2 (Contrast function). *Denote by $\mathcal{Z} = \{Z : \Omega \to \mathbb{R}\}$ a set of images uniformly bounded (e.g. by the maximum gray-level). Then, define $\mathcal{V}_A$ as the set of vector fields given by (3). An element v_a in $\mathcal{V}$ can thus be written as*

$$v_a = \left(\sum_{k=1}^{K} a^1_k e^1_k, \sum_{k=1}^{K} a^2_k e^2_k \right), \text{ for some } a^i_k \in [-A, A].$$

If we denote N the number of pixels, we define the function f as

$$f(a, \varepsilon, Z) = \min_{v \in \mathcal{V}_A} \sum_{p=1}^{N} \left(I_{a,\varepsilon}(p) - Z \circ \Phi^1_v(p) \right)^2, \tag{5}$$

where I is a given image of $\mathcal{Z}$, the vector field $v_a \in \mathcal{V}_A$.
In the expression of f, one can remark that a varies in a compact set (finite number of bounded coefficients) and consequently the definition of f makes sense. Intuitively, f must be understood as the optimal (minimum) cost to align the image Z onto the noisy randomly warped image $I_{a,\varepsilon}$ using a diffeomorphic transformation.
For sake of simplicity, we introduce a notation that corresponds to a discretize semi-norm over the pixels:

$$\left| I_{a,\varepsilon} - Z \circ \Phi_v^1 \right|_{\mathfrak{P}}^2 = \sum_{p=1}^{N} \left(I_{a,\varepsilon}(p) - Z \circ \Phi_v^1(p) \right)^2 .$$

At last, we define the mean contrast function F given by

$$F(Z) = \int_{[-A;A]^{2K} \times \mathbb{R}^N} f(a,\varepsilon,Z) dP(a,\varepsilon) = \mathbb{E} f(a,\varepsilon,Z)$$

where $dP(a,\varepsilon)$ is the tensorial product measure on a and ε.

$F(Z)$ must be understood as follows: it measures "on average" how far an image Z is from the image $I_{a,\varepsilon}$ generated from our random warping model using an optimal alignment of Z onto $I_{a,\varepsilon}$. Note that we only observe realizations $I_1, \ldots I_n$ that have been generated with the parameters $a^1, \ldots a^n$ and $\varepsilon^1, \ldots \varepsilon^n$.
However, our goal is to estimate a mean pattern image $Z^\star$ (possibly not unique) which corresponds to the minimum of the contrast function F when $I^\star$ (and of course $dP(a,\varepsilon)$) is unknown. As pointed before, M-estimation will enable is to replace virtually the $\mathbb{E}_{P(a,\varepsilon)}$ by a finite sum $\sum_{i=1}^n$ which depends on the observations and that mimic the former expectation. To estimate $Z^\star$, it is therefore natural to define the following empirical mean contrast:

Definition 3 (Empirical mean contrast). *We define the measure $\mathbb{P}_n$ and the empirical contrast F_n as*

$$\mathbb{P}_n(a,\varepsilon) = \frac{1}{n} \sum_{i=1}^{n} \delta_{a^i,\varepsilon^i} \text{ and } F_n(Z) = \int f(a,\varepsilon,Z) d\mathbb{P}_n(a,\varepsilon).$$

Note that even if we do not observe the deformation parameters a^i and the noise ε^i, it is nevertheless possible to optimize $F_n(Z)$ with respect to Z since it can be written as:

$$F_n(Z) = \frac{1}{n} \sum_{i=1}^{n} \min_{v_i \in \mathcal{V}_A} \left| I_i - Z \circ \Phi_{v_i}^1 \right|_{\mathfrak{P}}^2 .$$

Moreover, note that in the above equation *it is not required* to specify the law P_A or the law of the additive noise to compute the criterion $F_n(Z)$. We then introduce quite naturally a sequence of sets of estimators

$$\hat{Q}_n = \arg\min_{Z \in \mathcal{Z}} F_n(Z) \tag{6}$$

and we will theoretically compare the asymptotic behavior of these sets with the deterministic one

$$Q_0 = \arg\min_{Z \in \mathcal{Z}} F(Z). \tag{7}$$

In a second time, we will infer in section 3.5 an algorithm to estimate a mean pattern in the set $\hat{Q}_n$. This algorithm consists in a recursive procedure to solve (6). Note that both sets $\hat{Q}_n$ and Q_0 are not necessarily restricted to a singleton.

3.4 Convergence of the estimator

We first state a useful theoretical tool of M-estimation that can be found in Theorem 6.3 of Biscay & Mora (2001). We will use this result to establish the convergence of (6) toward (7). For each integer n, we denote $\hat{Z}_n$ any sequence of images belonging to $\hat{Q}_n$.

Proposition 1. *For any image Z, assume that $F_n(Z) \rightarrow F(Z)$ a.s. and that the following two conditions hold*

(C1)The set $\{f(\cdot,\cdot,Z) : Z \in \mathcal{Z}\}$ is an equicontinuous family of functions at each point of $\mathcal{X} = [-A;A]^{2K} \times \mathbb{R}^N$.

(C2)There is a continuous function $\phi : \mathcal{X} \rightarrow \mathbb{R}^+$ such that $\int_{\mathcal{X}} \phi(a,\varepsilon)dP(a,\varepsilon) < +\infty$, and for all $(a,\varepsilon) \in \mathcal{X}$ and $Z \in \mathcal{Z}$, $|f(a,\varepsilon,Z)| \leq \phi(a,\varepsilon)$.

Then

$$\hat{Q}_\infty \subset Q_0 \text{ a.s.}, \tag{8}$$

where $\hat{Q}_\infty$ is defined as the set of accumulation points of the $\hat{Z}_n$, i.e the limits of convergent subsequences $\hat{Z}_{n_k}$ of minimizers $\hat{Z}_n \in \hat{Q}_n$.

The following theorem whose proof can be found in Bigot et al. (2009) gives sufficient conditions to ensure the convergence of the M-estimator in the sense of equation (8).

Theorem 1. *Assume that conditions* **A1** *and* **A2** *hold, then the M-estimator defined through $\hat{Q}_n$ is consistent: any accumulation point of $\hat{Q}_n$ converges to Q_0 almost surely.*

This theorem ensures that the M-estimator, when constrained to live in a fixed compact set of images, converges to a minimizer $Z^\star$ of the limit contrast function $F(Z)$.
Remark that Theorem 1 only proves the consistency of our estimator when the observed images comes from the distribution defined through $I_{a,\varepsilon}$, $(a,\varepsilon) \sim dP(a,\varepsilon)$. This assumption is obviously quite unrealistic, since in practice the observed images generally come from a distribution that is different from the model (4). In Section 4, we therefore address the problem of studying the consistency of our procedure when the observed images $I_i, i = 1,\dots,n$ are an i.i.d. sample from an unknown distribution on $\mathbb{R}^N$ (see Theorem 2).

3.5 Robustness and penalized estimation

Penalized approach

First, remark that the limite of $\hat{Z}_n$ denoted $Z^\star$ may be equal to the correct pattern $I^\star$ if the observations are generated following the distribution $I_{a,\varepsilon}$, $(a,\varepsilon) \sim dP(a,\varepsilon)$. We address in this paragraph what happens when observations do not follow the law of $I_{a,\varepsilon}$.
In such situation, the minimum Z^* may be very different from the original image I^*, leading to unconsistant estimate as $n \rightarrow \infty$. This behaviour is well known in statistics (one may refer to van de Geer (2000) for instance for further details). The loss function has often to be balanced by a penalty which regularizes the matching criterion. In a Bayesian framework, this penalized point of view can be interpreted as a special choice of a prior distribution, e.g Allassonière et al. (2007). In nonparametric statistics, this regularization often takes the form of a penalized criterion which enforces the estimator to belong to a specific space satisfying appropriate regularity conditions.

Image decomposition

It may not be a good thing to just minimize L^2 distance between image and the true warped pattern as the L^2 norm on the euclidean space may not traduce the variability between all the images. Thus, it may be a good point to use another space for images than the set of real vector of size N since this canonical space may not traduce important features of image analysis (edges, textures, etc.) .
In our framework, we point out that choosing to expand the images $Z \in \mathcal{Z}$ into a set of basis functions $(\psi_\lambda)_{\lambda \in \Lambda}$, that are well suited for image processing (e.g. a wavelet basis), is by itself a way to incorporate regularization on $\hat{Z}_n$. Here, the set Λ can be finite or not. More precisely, any image Z can be parametrized by $Z = Z_\theta = \sum_{\lambda \in \Lambda} \theta_\lambda \psi_\lambda$. The estimation of a mean pattern involves the estimation of the coefficients of this image in the basis ψ_l, $\lambda \in \Lambda$. Thus, the penalization term on the image will involve the parameter θ since the basis $(\psi_\lambda)_\lambda$ will remain fixed. This yield the definition of pen_1 as

$$\text{pen}_1(\theta) = \sum_{\lambda \in \Lambda} |\theta_\lambda|.$$

Cost of diffeomorphism

Indeed, the variability may be described in a different way due to the action of the deformations for instance. Thus, in our setting, we may be interested in defining a distance between images that mostly depends on the amount of deformation required to transform the first one to the second with a regular deformation action. A good way to set up such distance is certainly to penalize the energy F with a term $|D^{(m)}\Phi_v^1|$ where m is a derivative of the diffeomorphism. Since each diffeomorphism is parametrized by a finite set of coefficients $(a_k^i)_{i,k}$, the second penalization term of the deformation will concern the unknown a.
Further, we impose regularity on the transformations by adding a penalty term to the matching criterion to exclude unlikely large deformations. The penalty must control both the deformations to avoid too large deformations (see for instance Amit et al. (1991)) and also the images to add a smoothness constraint for the reference image. For this, for Γ a symetric positive definite matrix, define the penalization of the deformation as:

$$\text{pen}_2(v) = \sum_{i=1}^{2} \sum_{k,k'=1}^{K} a_k^i \Gamma_{k,k'} a_{k'}^i.$$

Comments on pen_1 and pen_2

The first penalization term is somewhat classical and corresponds to soft-thresholding estimators, it has been widely used in various context, see for instance the work of Antoniadis & Fan (2001) , and it enables to incorportate some sparsity constraint on the set $\mathcal{Z}$.
For the deformation parameters, the choice $\text{pen}_2(v_a)$ means that we incorporate spatial dependencies using a given matrix Γ. We thus do not assume anymore that all deformations have the same weight, as it was done in the original definition of $F_n(Z)$. Obviously, other choices of penalty can be studied for practical applications and we provide in the sequel consistency results for general penalties. Two parameters λ_1 and λ_2 balance the contribution of the loss function and the penalties. High values of these parameters stress the regularity constraint for the estimator and the deformations.

Finally, we obtain the following estimator $\hat{Z}_n = \sum_{\lambda \in \Lambda} \hat{\theta}_\lambda \psi_\lambda$, with

$$\hat{\theta}_n = \arg\min_{\theta \in \mathbb{R}^\Lambda} \frac{1}{n} \sum_{i=1}^{n} \min_{v_i \in \mathcal{V}_A} \left(\left| I_i - Z_\theta \circ \Phi^1_{v_i} \right|^2_{\mathrm{P}} + \lambda_1 \mathrm{pen}_1(v_i) \right)$$
$$+ \lambda_2 \mathrm{pen}_2(\theta).$$

The effects of adding such extra terms can also be studied from a theoretical point of view. If the smoothing parameters λ_1 and λ_2 are held fixed (they do not depend on n) then it is possible to study the converge of $\hat{\theta}_n$ as n grows to infinity under appropriate conditions on the penalty terms and the set Λ.
More precisely, we address now the problem of studying the consistency of our M-estimator when the observed images (viewed as random vectors in $\mathbb{R}^N$) come from an *unknown* distribution P, that does not necessarily correspond to the model (4). For sake of simplicity we use the notation $\tilde{f}$ introduced in Equation (5), but within a penalized framework with unknown P, the dependency on ε disappears, and $\tilde{f}$ is now defined as

$$\tilde{f}(I, Z_\theta) = \min_{v \in \mathcal{V}_A} \left[\|I - Z_\theta \circ \Phi^1_v\|^2_{\mathcal{P}} + \lambda_1 \mathrm{pen}_1(v) \right] + \lambda_2 \mathrm{pen}_2(\theta), \tag{9}$$

where $\lambda_1, \lambda_2 \in \mathbb{R}^+$, $\mathrm{pen}_1(v) := \mathrm{pen}_1(a) : \mathbb{R}^{2K} \to \mathbb{R}^+$, and $\mathrm{pen}_2(\theta) : \mathbb{R}^\Lambda \to \mathbb{R}^+$. For any θ that "parametrizes" the image Z_θ in the basis $(\psi_\lambda)_{\lambda \in \Lambda}$, let $\tilde{F}$ denote the general contrast function

$$\tilde{F}(Z_\theta) = \int \tilde{f}(I, Z_\theta) dP(I), \tag{10}$$

and $\tilde{F}_n$ the empirical one defined as

$$\tilde{F}_n(Z_\theta) = \frac{1}{n} \sum_{i=1}^{n} \tilde{f}(I_i, Z_\theta).$$

The following theorem, whose proof is deferred to the Appendix, provides sufficient conditions to ensure the consistency of our estimator in the simple case when $\tilde{F}(Z_\theta)$ has a unique minimum at Z_{θ^*} for $\theta \in \Theta$, where $\Theta \subset \mathbb{R}^\Lambda$ is a compact set, and Λ is finite.

Theorem 2. *Assume that Λ is finite, that the set of vector fields $v = v_a \in \mathcal{V}$ is indexed by parameters a which belong to a compact subset of $\mathbb{R}^{2K}$, that $a \mapsto \mathrm{pen}_1(v_a)$ and $\theta \mapsto \mathrm{pen}_2(\theta)$ are continuous. Moreover, assume that $\tilde{F}(Z_\theta)$ has a unique minimum at Z_{θ^*} for $\theta \in \Theta$, where $\Theta \subset \mathbb{R}^\Lambda$ is a compact set. Finally, assume that the basis $(\psi_\lambda)_{\lambda \in \Lambda}$ and the set Θ are such that there exists two positive constants M_1 and M_2 which satisfy for any $\theta \in \Theta$*

$$M_1 \sup_{\lambda \in \Lambda} |\theta_\lambda| \leq \sup_{x \in [0,1]^2} |Z_\theta(x)| \leq M_2 \sup_{\lambda \in \Lambda} |\theta_\lambda|. \tag{11}$$

Then, if P satisfies the following moment condition,

$$\int \|I\|^2_{\infty,N} dP(I) < \infty,$$

where $\|I\|_{\infty,N} = \max_{p=1,\ldots,N} |I(p)|$, the M-estimator defined by $\hat{Z}_n = Z_{\hat{\theta}_n}$ where

$$\hat{\theta}_n = \arg\min_{\theta \in \Theta} \tilde{F}_n(Z_\theta)$$

is consistent for the supremum norm of functions defined on $[0,1]^2$ i.e.

$$\lim_{n \to \infty} \|\hat{Z}_n - Z_{\theta^*}\|_\infty = 0 \quad a.s.$$

4. Experiments and conclusion

4.1 Numerical implementation

Different strategies are discussed in Bigot et al. (2009) to minimize the criterion $\tilde{F}_n(Z_\theta)$. In the numerical experiments proposed in this text, we took the identity matrix for Γ in the formulation of pen_2. We have also chosen to simply expand the images in the pixel basis and have taken $\lambda_1 = 0$ (i.e. no penalization on the space of discrete images viewed as vectors in $\mathbb{R}^N$).

Our estimation procedure obviously depends on the choice of the basis functions $e_k = (e_k^1, e_k^2)$ that generate the vector fields. In the following, we have chosen to use tensor products of one-dimensional B-spline organized in a multiscale fashion. Let $s = 3$ be the order of the B-spline and and $J = 3$. For each scale $j = 0, \ldots, J-1$, we denote by $\phi_{j,\ell}, \ell = 0, \ldots, 2^j - 1$ the 2^j the B-spline functions obtained by taking $2^j + s$ knots points equispaced on $[0,1]$ (see de Boor (1978)). This gives a set of functions organized in a multiscale fashion as shown in Figure 4. Note that as j increases the support of the B-spline decreases which makes them more localized.

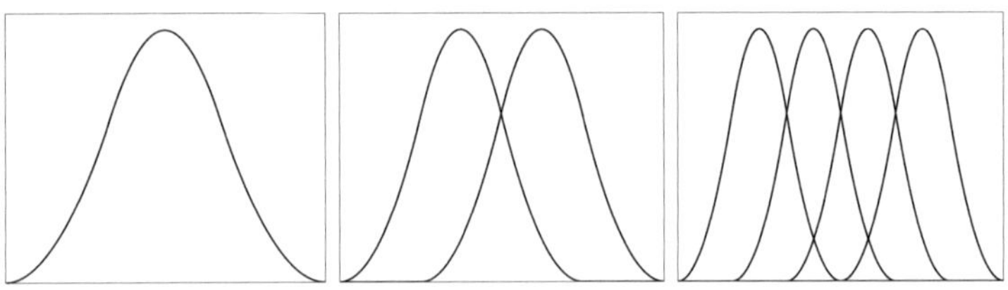

Fig. 4. An example of multiscale B-splines $\phi_{j,\ell}, \ell = 0, \ldots, 2^j - 1$ with $J = 3$ and $s = 3$, ordered left to right, $j = 0, 1, 2$.

For $j = 0, \ldots, J-1$, we then generate a multiscale basis $\phi_{j,\ell_1,\ell_2} : [0,1]^2 \to \mathbb{R}$, $\ell_1, \ell_2 = 0, \ldots, J-1$ by taking tensor products the $\phi_{j,\ell}$'s i.e.

$$\phi_{j,\ell_1,\ell_2}(x_1, x_2) = \phi_{j,\ell_1}(x_1)\phi_{j,\ell_2}(x_2).$$

Then, we take $e_k = e_{j,\ell_1,\ell_2} = (\phi_{j,\ell_1,\ell_2}, \phi_{j,\ell_1,\ell_2}) : [0,1]^2 \to \mathbb{R}^2$. This makes a total of $K = \sum_{j=0}^{J-1} 2^{2j} = \frac{2^{2J}-1}{3} = 21$.

Following these choices, one can then use the iterative algorithm based on gradient descent described in Bigot et al. (2009) to find a mean image.

4.2 Mnist database

First we return to the example shown previously in Figure 3 on handwritten digits (Mnist database). As these images are not very noisy, it is reasonable to set $\lambda_1 = 0$ and thus to not use a penalty on the space of images onto which the optimization is done. A value of $\lambda_2 = 10$ to penalize the deformations gave good results.

In Figure 5, we display the naive arithmetic mean Z_{naive} and the mean $\hat{Z}_n$ by minimizing $\tilde{F}_n(Z_\theta)$ obtained from $n = 20$ images of the digits "2". The result obtained with $\hat{Z}_n$ is very satisfactory and is clearly a better representative of the typical shape of the digits "2" in this database then the naive arithmetic mean. Indeed, $\hat{Z}_n$ has sharper edges than the naive mean which is very blurred.

In Figure 6 we finally display the comparison between the naive mean and the mean image $\hat{Z}_n$, for all digits between 0 and 9 with 20 images for each digit. One can see that our approach yields significant improvements. In particular it gives mean digits with sharp edges.

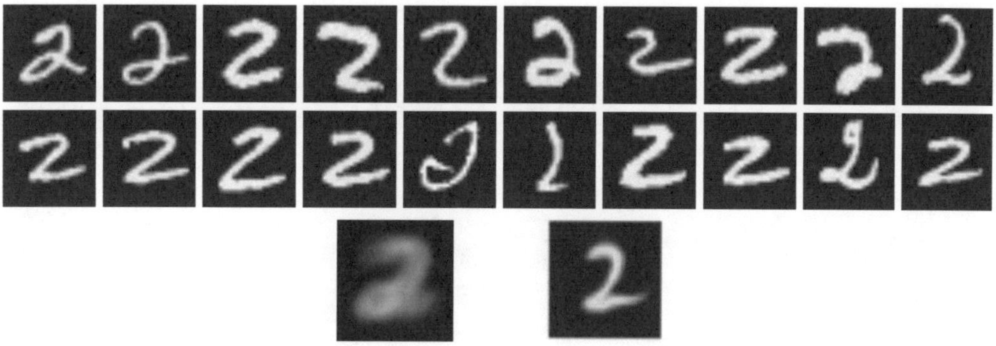

Fig. 5. Naive arithmetic mean (lower left image), mean image $\hat{Z}_n$ (lower right image) based on 20 images of the digit "2" (upper rows).

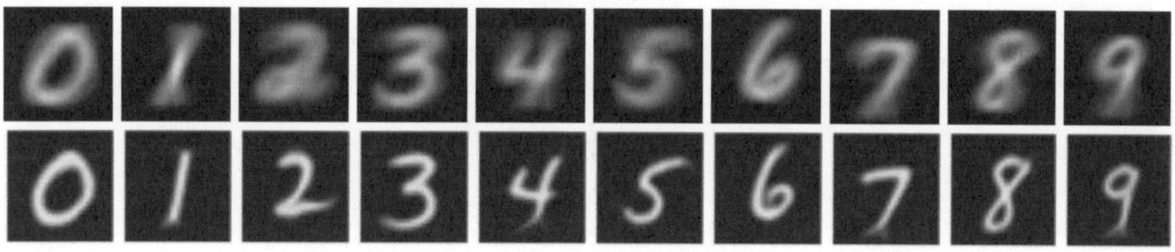

Fig. 6. Naive arithmetic mean (first row), mean image $\hat{Z}_n$ (second row) based on 20 images from the mnist database.

4.3 Olivetti faces database

Let us now consider a problem of faces averaging. These images are taken taken from the Olivetti face database Samaria & Harter (1994) and their size is $N_1 = 98$ by $N_2 = 112$ pixels. We consider 8 subjects taken from this database. For each subject, $n = 9$ images of the same person have been taken with varying lighting and facial expression. Figure 7 and Figure 8 show the faces used in our simulations.

In Figure 9 and Figure 10 we present the mean images obtained with $\lambda_2 = 1000$, and compare them with the corresponding naive mean. Note that these images are not very noisy, so it is reasonable to set $\lambda_1 = 0$. Obviously our method clearly improves the results given by the naive arithmetic mean. It yields satisfactory average faces especially in the middle of the images.

4.4 Conclusion and perspectives

We have built a very general model of random diffeomorphisms to warp images. This construction relies mainly on the choice of the basis functions e_k for generating the deformations. The choice of the e_k's is relatively large since one is only restricted to take functions with a sufficient number of derivatives that vanish at the boundaries of $[0,1]^2$. Moreover, our estimation procedure does not require the choice of a priori distributions for the random coefficients a_k^i. Other applications of this approach may be developed to obtain some clustering algorithms (K-means adaptation for unsupervised classification) using the energy introduced in this paper. Hence, this model is very flexible as many parameterizations can be chosen. We have only focused on the estimation of the mean pattern of a set of images, but one would like to build other statistics like principal modes of variations of the

Fig. 7. $n = 9$ samples of the Olivetti database for 4 subjects.

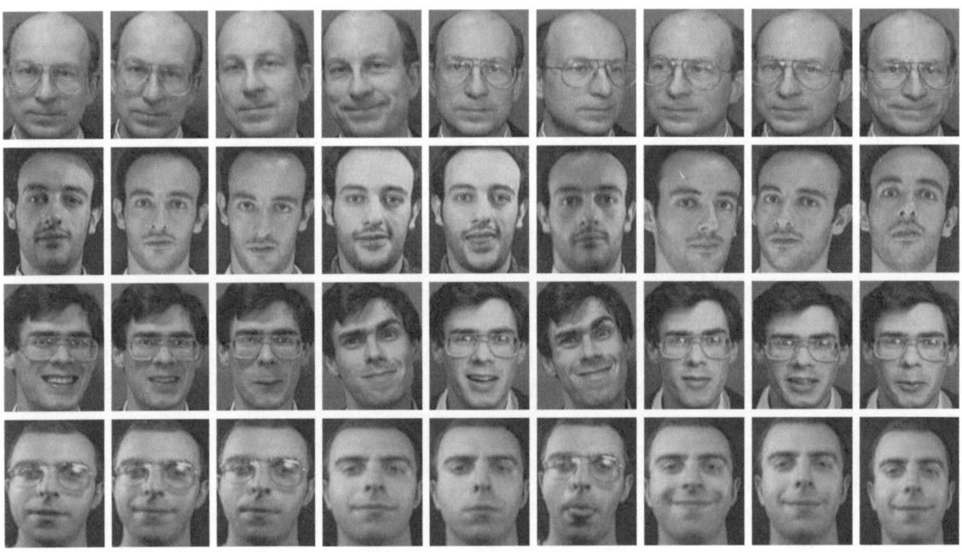

Fig. 8. $n = 9$ samples of the Olivetti database for 4 subjects.

learned distribution of the images or the deformations. Building statistics going beyond the simple mean of set of images within the setting of our model is very challenging for future investigation.

Fig. 9. Example of face averaging for 4 subjects from the Olivetti database. First row: naive arithmetic mean, second row: mean image $\hat{Z}_n$.

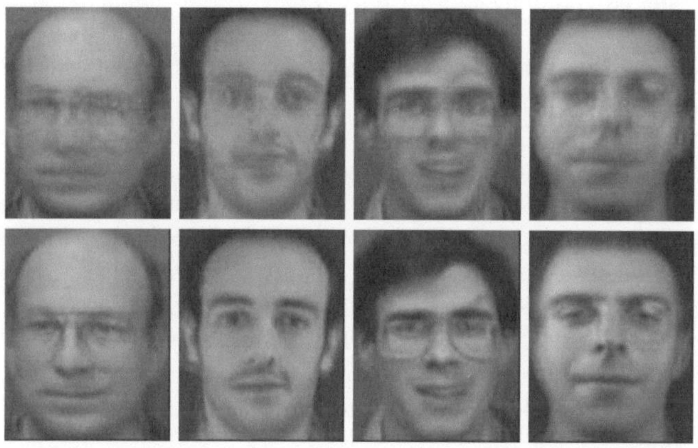

Fig. 10. Example of face averaging for 4 subjects from the Olivetti database. First row: naive arithmetic mean, second row: mean image $\hat{Z}_n$.

5. References

Allassonière, S.; Amit, Y. & Trouvé, A. (2007). Toward a coherent statistical framework for dense deformable template estimation, *Journal of the Statistical Royal Society (B)*, Vol. 69, 3-29.

Allassonière, S.; Kuhn, E. & Trouvé, A. (2009). Bayesian Deformable Models building via stochastic approximation algorithm: a convergence study, *Bernoulli*.

Amit, Y.; Grenander, U. & Piccioni, M. (1991). Structural Image Restoration through deformable template, *Journal of the American Statistical Association*, Vol. 86, 376-387.

Antoniadis, A. & Fan, J. (2001). Regularization of Wavelet Approximations, *Journal of the American Statistical Association*, Vol. 96, 939-967.

Beg, M.; Miller, M.; Trouvé, A. & Younes, L. (2005). Computing Large Deformation Metric Mappings via Geodesic Flows of Diffeomorphisms, *Int. J. Comput. Vision*, Vol. 61, No 2, 139-157.

Bigot, J.; Gadat, S. & Loubes, J.-M. (2009). Statistical M-Estimation and Consistency in large deformable models for Image Warping, *Journal of Mathematical Imaging and Vision*, Vol. 34, No. 3, 270-290.

Biscay, R. & Mora, C. (2001). Metric sample spaces of continuous geometric curves and estimation of their centroids, *Mathematische Nachrichten*, Vol. 229, 15–49.

de Boor, C. (1978). *A practical guide to splines*, Applied Mathematical Sciences, Springer-Verlag, New York, pp. 368.

Candes, E. & Donoho, D. (2000). Recovering Edges in Ill-Posed Inverse Problems: Optimality of Curvelet Frames, *Annals of Statistics*, Vol. 30, 784-842.

Faugeras, O. & Hermosillo, G. (2002). Well-posedness of eight problems of multi-modal statistical image-matching, *Biomedical Imaging*, Vol. 15, No. 23, 1-64.

Glasbey, C. & Mardia, K. (2001). A penalized likelihood approach to image warping, *Journal of the Statistical Royal Society (B)*, Vol. 63, No. 3, 465-514.

Grenander, U. (1993). *General pattern theory - A mathematical study of regular structures*, Clarendon Press.

Grenander, U. & Miller, M. (2007). *Pattern Theory: From Representation to Inference*, Oxford Univ. Press.

Huilling, L. (1998). On the consitency of Procrustean mean Shapes, *Advances in Applied Probability*, Vol. 30, 53-63.

Joshi S.; Davis B.; Jomier M. & Gerig G. (2004). Unbiased diffeomorphic atlas construction for computational anatomy, *Neuroimage*, vol. 23, 151-160.

Le Cun, Y.; Bottou, L.; Bengio, Y. & Haffner, P. (1998). Gradient-based learning applied to document recognition, *Proceedings of the IEEE*, Vol. 86, No. 11, 2278-2324.

Ma, J.; Miller, M.; Trouvé, A. & Younes, L. (2008).Bayesian Template Estimation in Computational Anatomy, *NeuroImage*, Vol. 42, No. 1, 252-26.

Miller M. & Younes L. (2001). Group Actions, Homeomorphisms, And Matching: A General Framework,*International Journal of Computer Vision*, vol. 41, 61-84.

Samaria, F.S. & Harter, A. (1994). Parameterisation of a Stochastic Model for Human Face Identification, *WACV94*, 138-142.

Trouvé, A. & Younes, L. (2005a). Local geometry of deformable templates, *SIAM Journal on Mathematical Analysis*, Vol. 37, No. 1, 17-59.

Trouvé, A. & Younes, L. (2005b). Metamorphoses Through Lie Group Action, *Foundations of Computational Mathematics*, Vol. 5, No 2, 173-198.

van de Geer, S. (2000). *Applications of empirical process theory*, Cambridge Series in Statistical and Probabilistic Mathematics, Cambridge University Press, Cambridge, xii+286.

van der Waart, A. (1998). *Asymptotic statistics*, Cambridge Series in Statistical and Probabilistic Mathematics 03, Cambridge Univ. Press , New-York, pp. 460.

Younes, L. (2004). *Invariance, déformations et reconnaissance de formes*, Mathematics & Applications, Springer-Verlag, Berlin, pp. xviii+248.

12

Scene Recognition through Visual Attention and Image Features: A Comparison between SIFT and SURF Approaches

Fernando López-García[1], Xosé Ramón Fdez-Vidal[2], Xosé Manuel Pardo[2] and Raquel Dosil[2]
[1]*Universidad Politécnica de Valencia*
[2]*Universidade de Santiago de Compostela*
Spain

1. Introduction

In this work we study how we can use a novel model of spatial saliency (visual attention) combined with image features to significantly accelerate a scene recognition application and, at the same time, preserve recognition performance. To do so, we use a mobile robot-like application where scene recognition is carried out through the use of image features to characterize the different scenarios, and the Nearest Neighbor rule to carry out the classification. SIFT and SURF are two recent and competitive alternatives to image local featuring that we compare through extensive experimental work. Results from the experiments show that SIFT features perform significantly better than SURF features achieving important reductions in the size of the database of prototypes without significant losses in recognition performance, and thus, accelerating scene recognition. Also, from the experiments it is concluded that SURF features are less distinctive when using very large databases of interest points, as it occurs in the present case.

Visual attention is the process by which the Human Visual System (HVS) is able to select from a given scene regions of interest that contain salient information, and thus, reduce the amount of information to be processed (Treisman, 1980; Koch, 1985). In the last decade, several computational models biologically motivated have been released to implement visual attention in image and video processing (Itti, 2000; García-Díaz, 2008). Visual attention has also been used to improve object recognition and scene analysis (Bonaiuto, 2005; Walther, 2005). In this chapter, we study the utility of using a novel model of spatial saliency to improve a scene recognition application by reducing the amount of prototypes needed to carry out the classification task. The application is based on mobile robot-like video sequences taken in indoor facilities formed by several rooms and halls. The aim is to recognize the different scenarios in order to provide the mobile robot system with general location data.

The visual attention approach is a novel model of bottom-up saliency that uses local phase information of the input data where the statistic information of second order is deleted to achieve a Retinoptical map of saliency. The proposed approach joints computational mechanisms of the two hypotheses largely accepted in early vision: first, the *efficient coding*

(Barlow, 1961; Attneave, 1954), which postulates that the mission of the first stages of the visual processing chain is to reduce the redundancy or predictability in the incoming data; and second, in the visual cortex relevant attributes of the image are early detected using local phase or energy analysis, such as edges of objects. At those points where these features are located there is an alignment of the local phase of the Fourier harmonics (Phase Congruency). The model of local energy to detect features (Morrone & Burr, 1988; Morrone & Owens, 1987; Kovesi, 1999) is based on this idea and demonstrated its suitability for perceptual appearance and image segmentation. Nevertheless, it is not able to prioritize the features with regards to the visual saliency. This fact is illustrated in Figure 1, where the input image is formed by bars that increment its orientation in steps of 10° from left to right and top to bottom, except for the central bar that breaks this periodicity creating a pop-out effect for the HVS.

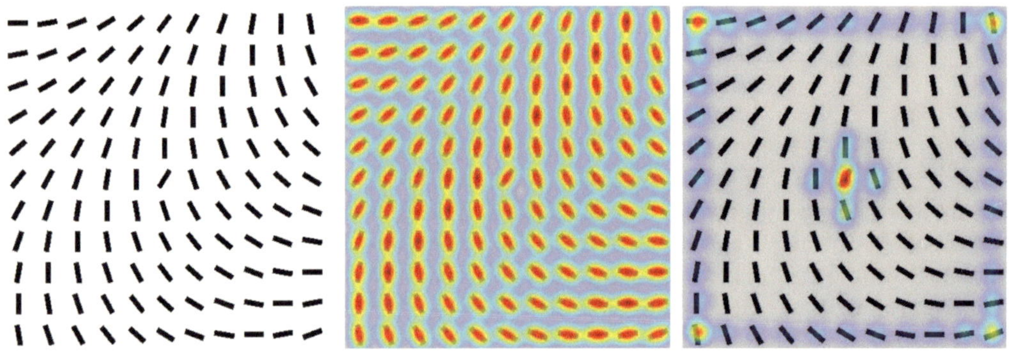

a) Original Image. b) Salience from PC. c) Salience from our model.

Fig. 1. Saliency maps of the original image; (a) from Phase Congruency (b) and the proposed model (c).

In Fig. 1b we see the map of saliency achieved using Kovesi's model (Kovesi, 1999) based on Phase Congruency (PC). It provides approximately equal weight to all features clearing away the pop-out effect. We think the reason for that is the high redundancy in images which implies correlations and thus Gaussianism in chromatic and spatial components. It is known that to handle information about phase structure is equivalent to use non-Gaussian information in data distribution (Hyvärinen et al., 2009). Thus, to focus in the information that does not depend on covariances (local phase) it is necessary to reduce redundancy, that is, to decorrelate the data. One way is through data whitening. Redundancy in RGB color components is deleted through PCA and spatial redundancy is avoided using an strategy of filter-based whitening in frequency domain. In Fig. 1c it is shown that this hypothesis works making possible to prioritize the salience of visual features from local phase.

Scene recognition is performed using SIFT (Lowe, 2004) and SURF (Bay, 2008) for image featuring (two different approaches that we compare) and the Nearest Neighbor rule for classification. SIFT features are distinctive image features that are invariant to image scale and rotation, and partially invariant to change in illumination and 3D viewpoint. They are fast to compute and robust to disruptions due to occlusion, clutter or noise. SIFT features have proven to be useful in many object recognition applications and currently they are considered the state-of-the art for general purpose and real-world object learning and recognition, together with SURF features. SURF is a robust image descriptor used in

computer vision tasks like object recognition or 3D reconstruction. The standard version of SURF is several times faster than SIFT and it is claimed by its authors to be more robust against different image transformations than SIFT. However, the results of our experimental work showed that SIFT features perform significantly better than SURF features. In combination with saliency maps, SIFT features lead to drastic reductions in the number of interest points introduced in the database of prototypes (used in 1-NN classification), also achieving very good performance in scene recognition. Thus, since the computing costs of classification are significantly reduced the scene recognition is accelerated.
The chapter is developed as follows. Next Section presents the model of spatial saliency. An overview of the image featuring methods is provided in Section 3. Section 4 deals with the scene recognition application. Experimental work and results are presented in Section 5. Finally, Section 6 is devoted to conclusions.

2. Model of spatial saliency

Figure 2 shows a general flow diagram of the saliency model. Following we describe each stage of the model.

2.1 Early stage

The goal of this initial stage is to delete the statistical information of second order in color components (RGB) and spatial components (between pixels of each color component), through different whitening processes.
The aim of the initial step in this stage is to provide the model with a color space that contains a mechanism, biologically inspired, called *short-term adaptation* (Simoncelli & Olshausen, 2001; Barlow & Foldiak, 1989), which main goal is to achieve a final synchronization in the adaptive process that promotes the most useful aspects for later processing. For that, the color RGB image is decomposed into three channels maximally decorrelated using Principal Component Analysis (PCA). Nevertheless, we are not interested in reducing the color space dimension, thus, we use a transformed space of the original dimension (3 color components). The first component corresponds to opponents channel B/W and the remaining two correspond to opponents similar to R/G and Y/B. However, the space, unlike the opponents space CIE-Lab, is adapted to the specific statistic of the incoming image.
In a second step, the goal is to eliminate the spatial redundancy among the pixels in each color channel. In this case, we use a filter-based strategic in frequency domain called Spectral Whitening (SW). It is consequence of the Wiener-Khinchin theorem: "for a stochastic process, *the average power spectrum is the Fourier Transform of the autocorrelation function*". Thus, a whitened image should have a flat power spectrum. This can be easily achieved using an adaptive filter in the frequency domain that normalizes the spectrum of the transformed Fourier corresponding to the incoming image I(x,y) in the following way:

$$n\left(\omega_x,\omega_y\right)=\frac{\Im\left[I(x,y)\right]}{\left\|\Im\left[I(x,y)\right]\right\|}=\frac{f\left(\omega_x,\omega_y\right)}{\left\|f\left(\omega_x,\omega_y\right)\right\|} \tag{1.1}$$

where $\Im[\cdot]$ is the transformed Fourier and $\omega_s=\sqrt{\omega_x^2+\omega_y^2}$ is the spatial frequency. Physically, SW is a redistribution of the spectrum energy that will achieve an enhancement

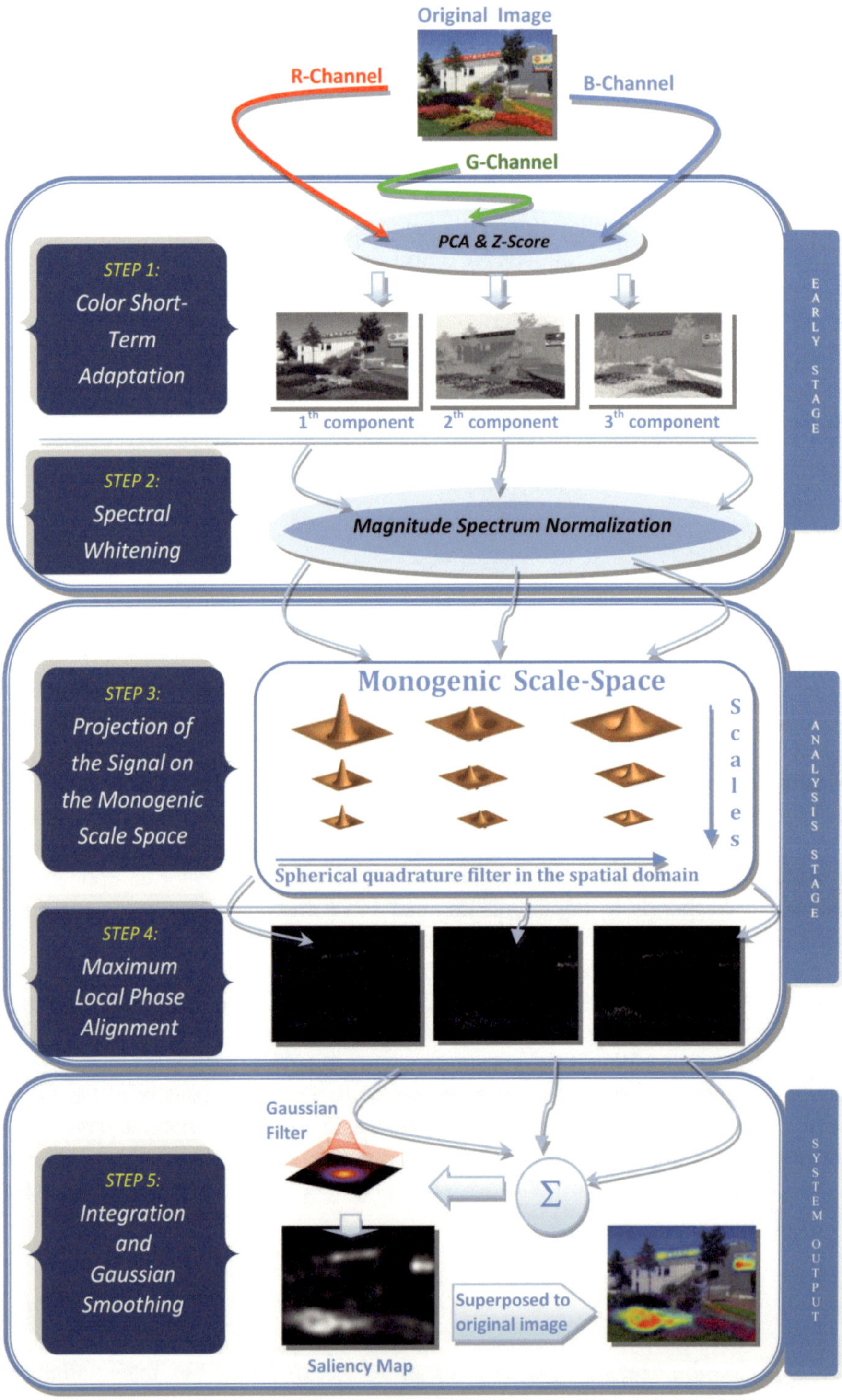

Fig. 2. General diagram showing how the data flows through the model.

of the less redundant patterns. This whitening method was previously used in the saliency model proposed by Guo et al. (Guo et al., 2008) which is based on global phase analysis.

2.2 Analysis stage

In this stage, it is analyzed the maximum alignment of the local phase of each pixel in each whitened color channel weighted by the strength of the visual features in the analyzed scale. Classical methodology to estimate the amplitude and phase in a 1D signal is the Analytic Signal. However, the 2D version was achieved partially using a quadrature phase bank filter (Gabor like filters), until the introduction of the Monogenic Signal by Felsberg & Sommer (Felsberg & Sommer, 2001). Our model uses this last methodology that achieves a new 2D analytic signal from the Riesz's transform, which is the 2D isotropic extension of Hilbert's transform. Its representation in Fourier's domain is a set of two simple filters in phase-quadrature that are not selective neither in scale nor orientation:

$$\left(H_1\left(\omega_x,\omega_y\right),H_2\left(\omega_x,\omega_y\right)\right)=\left(\frac{\omega_x}{\sqrt{\omega_x^2+\omega_y^2}}i,\frac{\omega_y}{\sqrt{\omega_x^2+\omega_y^2}}i\right) \quad (1.2)$$

The Monogenic Signal is a vector function of three components formed by the original signal and two components achieved by convolving it with the filters of Riez's transform, that is:

$$\vec{f}_M\left(x,y\right)=\left[f(x,y),f(x,y)*h_1\left(x,y\right),f(x,y)*h_2\left(x,y\right)\right] \quad (1.3)$$

where $h_1(x,y)$ and $h_2(x,y)$ are the representations in the spatial domain of $H_1(\omega_x,\omega_y)$ and $H_2(\omega_x,\omega_y)$ respectively. Because filters H_1 and H_2 are oriented in frequency domain but are not selective in scale, commonly a Gaussian like band-pass filter is used to build scaled versions of Riez's filters. In our case, we used the following log-Gauss filter:

$$G_s\left(\omega_x,\omega_y\right)=e^{-\left(\frac{\log\left(\omega/\omega_o\right)^2}{2\left(\log\left(k/\omega_o\right)\right)^2}\right)} \quad (1.4)$$

where $\omega=(\omega_x,\omega_y)$ is the spatial frequency, $\omega_o=(\omega_{ox},\omega_{oy})$ is the central frequency of the filter and k is the parameter that governs the bandwidth of the filter. If $g_s(x,y)$ is the spatial representation of previous filter, the monogenic space of scales is built as follows:

$$\begin{aligned}\vec{f}_{M,s}\left(x,y\right)&=\left[f(x,y)*g_s\left(x,y\right),f(x,y)*g_s\left(x,y\right)*h_1\left(x,y\right),f(x,y)*g_s\left(x,y\right)*h_2\left(x,y\right)\right]=\\&=\left[f_s(x,y),h_{1,s}(x,y),h_{2,s}(x,y)\right]\end{aligned} \quad (1.5)$$

The chosen bank of filters is formed by three scales (s=3) which central wavelengths were distributed in 1 octave from the minimum wavelength (assigned to $\lambda_1=8$ pixels), that is $\lambda_i=\{8, 16, 32\}$ pixels. The k parameter was fixed to achieve a bandwidth of 2 octaves in each filter in order to obtain a good spectral coverage in the bank of filters. A simple implementation of the monogenic signal, in the frequency domain, can be found in (Kovesi, 2000).

Once it is achieved the monogenic decomposition, the importance of each visual feature is measured by maximizing in each pixel of the image and for all the scales, the level of local phase alignment of the Fourier Harmonics, weighted by the strength of the visual structure in each scale (measured as local energy $\left\| f_{M,i}(x,y) \right\|$). We call this measure Weighted Maximum Phase Alignment (WMAP), and is the following:

$$WMPA(x,y) = \mathrm{w}_{\mathrm{fdn}} \cdot \max_{i=1}^{s} \left\{ \left\| \vec{f}_{M,i}(x,y) \right\| \cdot \cos\theta_i \right\} =$$

$$= \mathrm{w}_{\mathrm{fdn}} \cdot \max_{i=1}^{s} \left\{ \vec{f}_{M,i}(x,y) \bullet \left(\frac{\vec{E}_{local}(x,y)}{\left\| \vec{E}_{local}(x,y) \right\|} \right) \right\} = \tag{1.6}$$

$$= \mathrm{w}_{\mathrm{fdn}} \cdot \max_{i=1}^{s} \left\{ \left(f_i(x,y), h_{1,i}(x,y), h_{2,i}(x,y) \right) \cdot \left(\frac{\left(\sum_{i=1}^{s} f_i(x,y), \sum_{i=1}^{s} h_{1,i}(x,y), \sum_{i=1}^{s} h_{2,i}(x,y) \right)}{\left(\sqrt{\left(\sum_{i=1}^{s} f_i(x,y) \right)^2 + \left(\sum_{i=1}^{s} h_{1,i}(x,y) \right)^2 + \left(\sum_{i=1}^{s} h(x,y) \right)^2} \right)} \right) \right\}$$

where $\vec{f}_{M,i}(x,y)$ is the monogenic signal for the i-*th* scale and θ_i is the angle between vectors $\vec{f}_{M,i}(x,y)$ and $\vec{E}_{local}$. This angle measures the deviation of the local phase in the monogenic signal at the i-*th* scale respect to the local energy vector in pixel (x,y).

We are only interested on those pixels where local phase is congruent for the most of the used scales. Thus, our measure must incorporate a factor that penalizes too narrow frequency distributions. Factor $\mathrm{w}_{\mathrm{fdn}}$ is achieved as it was proposed by Kovesi (Kovesi, 1999) for his measure of local Phase Congruency (PC).

2.3 Output stage

The final stage of the model has the aim of achieving a Retinoptic measure of the salience of each pixel in the image. For that, we integrate in each pixel the WMPA(x,y) measures of each color channel:

$$Saliency(x,y) = \sum_{c=1}^{3} WMAP(x,y) \tag{1.7}$$

Finally, a smoothing is introduced by a Gaussian filter and also a normalization in order to make easy to interpret the saliency map as a probability function to receive attention.

2.4 Computational complexity

The computational efficiency of the model is low due to the load introduced by the PCA analysis, which grows lineally with the number of pixels in the image (N) and cubically with the number of components (color channels), $O(M^3+N\,M^2)$. The number of components is low and constant, M=3, thus, the asymptotic complexity depends on N. The computational complexity of the model depends on the FFT (Fast Fourier Transform) complexity performed in filtering processing. This complexity is O(N log(N)). On the other hand, the computational timing of the model is low, by example, for an image of 512x384 pixels using an Intel Core2 Quad processor at 2.4 GHz and 4Gb of RAM memory, the algorithm takes 0.91 seconds. We have to take into account that the algorithm is scientific software programmed in MATLAB.

3. Image features

SIFT and SURF belong to a set of methods aimed to detect and describe local features in images. Among these methods we can found (Mikolajczyk, 2005): shape context, steerable filters, PCA-SIFT, differential invariants, spin images, complex filters, moment invariants and gradient location and orientation histograms (GLOH). Nevertheless, SIFT and SURF have captured recent attention of researchers working on applications like object recognition, robot mapping and navigation, image stitching, 3D modeling, video tracking, etc, being its comparison a current issue in literature (Bauer, 2007).
With regards to SIFT features, we used the Lowe´s algorithm (Lowe, 2004) which works as follows. To identify the interest points (keypoints), scale space extrema are found in a difference-of-Gaussian (DoG) function convolved with the image. The extremas are found by comparing each point with its neighbors in the current image and adjacent scales. Points are selected as candidate keypoint locations if they are the maximum or minimum value in their neighborhood. Then image gradients and orientations, at each pixel of the Gaussian convolved image at each scale, are computed. For each key location an orientation, determined by the peak of a histogram of previously computed neighborhood orientations, is assigned. Once the orientation, scale, and location of the keypoints have been computed, invariance to these values is achieved by computing the keypoint local feature descriptors relative to them. Local feature descriptors are 128-dimensional vectors obtained from the pre-computed image orientations and gradients around the keypoints.
SURF features (Bay, 2008) are based on sums of 2D Haar wavelet responses and make a very efficient use of integral images to speed-up the process. As basic image descriptors they use a Haar wavelet approximation of the determinant of Hessian blob detector. There are two versions: the standard version which uses a descriptor vector of 64 components (SURF-64), and the extended version which uses 128 components (SURF-128). SURF are robust image features partly inspired by SIFT, being the standard version of SURF several times faster than SIFT. SURF features provide significantly less keypoints than SIFT, approximately the half of them (see Figure 3).

Fig. 3. SIFT (left) and SURF (right) keypoints computed for the same frame.

4. Scene recognition application

Scene recognition is related with the recognition of general scenarios rather than local objects. This approach is useful in many applications such as mobile robot navigation, image retrieval, extraction of contextual information for object recognition, and even to provide access to tourist information using camera phones. In our case, we are interested in recognize a set of different scenarios which are part of university facilities formed by four class rooms and three halls. The final aim is to provide general location data useful for the navigation of a mobile robot system. Scene recognition is commonly performed using generic image features that try to collect enough information to be able to distinguish among the different scenarios. For this purpose we used SIFT and SURF alternatives.

To compute the SIFT features we used the original code by Lowe (http://people.cs.ubc.ca/lowe/keypoints/). We also used the original code for SURF features by Bay et al (http://www.vision.ee.ethz.ch/~surf/). To carry out the classification task we used the 1-NN rule, which is a simple classification approach but fast to compute and robust. For the 1-NN approach, we need to build previously a database of prototypes that will collect the recognition knowledge of the classifier. These prototypes are a set of labelled SIFT/SURF keypoints obtained from the training frames. The class of the keypoints computed for a specific training frame will be that previously assigned to this frame in an off-line supervised labeling process. The database is then incorporated into the 1-NN classifier, which uses the Euclidean distance to select the closest prototype to the test SIFT/SURF keypoint being classified. The class of every test keypoint will be assigned to the class of the closest prototype in the database, and finally, the class of the entire test frame will be that of the majority of its keypoints.

5. Experiments and results

The experimental work consisted in a set of experiments carried out using four video sequences taken in a robot-navigation manner. These video sequences were grabbed in an university area covering several rooms and halls. Sequences were taken at 5 fps collecting a total number of 2,174 frames (7:15 minutes) for the first sequence, 1,986 frames for the second (6:37 minutes), 1,816 frames for the third (6:03 minutes) and 1,753 frames for the fourth (5:50 minutes). First and third sequences were taken in a specific order of halls and rooms: hall-1, room-1, hall-1, room-2, hall-1, room-3, hall-1, hall-2, hall-3, room-4, hall-3, hall-2, hall-1. The second and fourth sequences were grabbed following the opposite order to collect all possible viewpoints of the robot navigation through the facilities. In all the experiments, we used the first and second sequences for training and the third and fourth for testing.

In the first experiment we computed the SIFT keypoints for all the frames of the training video sequences. Then, we labelled these keypoints with the corresponding frame class: room-1, room-2, room-3, room-4, hall-1, hall-2 or hall-3. The whole set of labelled keypoints formed itself the database of prototypes to be used by the 1-NN classifier. For each frame of the testing sequences their corresponding SIFT keypoints were computed and classified. The final class for the frame was set to the majority class among its keypoints. Very good performance was achieved, 95.25% of correct classification of frames. However, an important drawback was the computational cost of classification, which was high despite the fact that 1-NN is known as a low cost classifier. This was due to the very large size of the database of prototypes formed by 1,170,215 samples. In the next experiment, we followed the previous steps but using SURF features instead of SIFT. In this case, recognition results were very bad achieving only 28.24% of recognition performance with SURF-128 features, and 25.05% using SURF-64. In both SURF cases the size of the database of prototypes was of 415, 845.

Although there are well known techniques for NN classifiers to optimize the database of prototypes (e.g. feature selection, feature extraction, condensing, editing) and also for the acceleration of the classification computation (e.g. kd-trees), at this point we are interested in the utility of using the saliency maps derived from the visual attention approach. The idea is to achieve significant reductions of the original database by selecting in each training frame only those keypoints that are included within the saliency map computed for this frame. Also, in the testing frames only those keypoints lying within the saliency maps will be considered for classification. Once the database is reduced in this way, optimizing techniques could be used to achieve even further improvements.

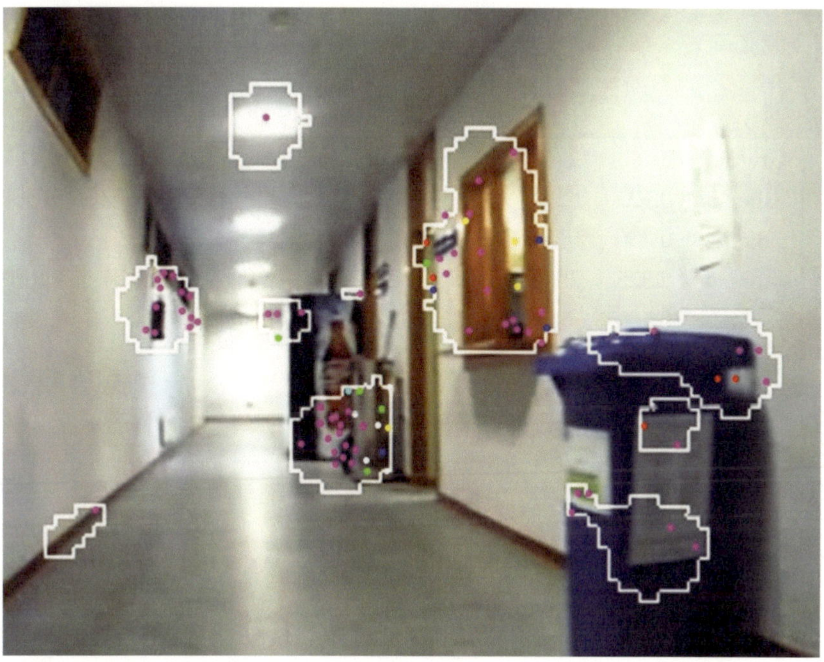

Fig. 4. Saliency regions at threshold 0.250 and corresponding SIFT keypoins.

In next experiments we carried out the idea showed in previous paragraph, although we wanted to explore more in-depth the possibilities of saliency maps. As it was commented, saliency measures are set in a range between 0 and 1, thus, we can choose different levels of saliency by simply using thresholds. We will be the least restrictive if we choose a saliency > 0.0, and more restrictive if we choose higher levels (e.g. 0.125, 0.250, etc). We planned to use eigth different saliency levels: 0.125, 0.250, 0.375, 0.500, 0.625, 0.750 and 0.875. For each saliency level we carried out the scene recognition experiment (see Figure 4) achieving the percentage of recognition performance, and the size of the database of prototypes. Results using SIFT and SURF features are shown in Tables 1, 2 and 3 and Figures 5, 6 and 7.

	Recognition %	Database Size	Database Size %
Original	95.25	1,170,215	100.0
Saliency > 0.125	95.25	779,995	66.65
Saliency > 0.250	94.72	462,486	39.52
Saliency > 0.375	93.45	273,908	23.41
Saliency > 0.500	92.21	157,388	13.45
Saliency > 0.650	89.30	86,161	7.36
Saliency > 0.750	83.31	42,418	3.62
Saliency > 0.875	56.03	15,894	1.36

Table 1. Results achieved using original frames and saliency maps with SIFT features.

	Recognition %	Database Size	Database Size %
Original	28.24	415,845	100.0
Saliency > 0.125	33.51	273,775	65.84
Saliency > 0.250	86.56	157,394	37.85
Saliency > 0.375	32.01	88,059	21.18
Saliency > 0.500	66.55	47,767	11.49
Saliency > 0.650	67.06	24,338	5.85
Saliency > 0.750	35.27	11,040	2.65
Saliency > 0.875	18.33	3,971	0.95

Table 2. Results achieved using original frames and saliency maps with SURF-128 features.

	Recognition %	Database Size	Database Size %
Original	25.05	415,845	100.0
Saliency > 0.125	27.74	273,775	65.84
Saliency > 0.250	51.50	157,394	37.85
Saliency > 0.375	25.64	88,059	21.18
Saliency > 0.500	28.97	47,767	11.49
Saliency > 0.650	67.33	24,338	5.85
Saliency > 0.750	34.89	11,040	2.65
Saliency > 0.875	19.22	3,971	0.95

Table 3. Results achieved using original frames and saliency maps with SURF-64 features.

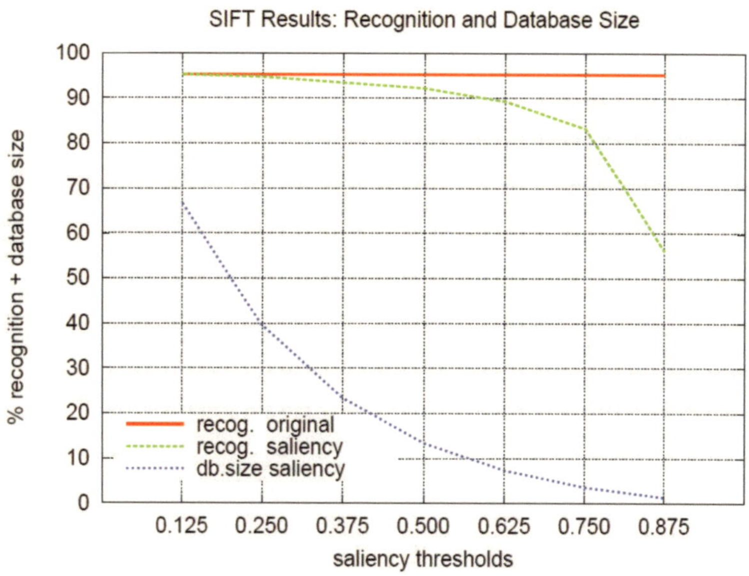

Fig. 5. Graphical results of recognition and database size using SIFT features.

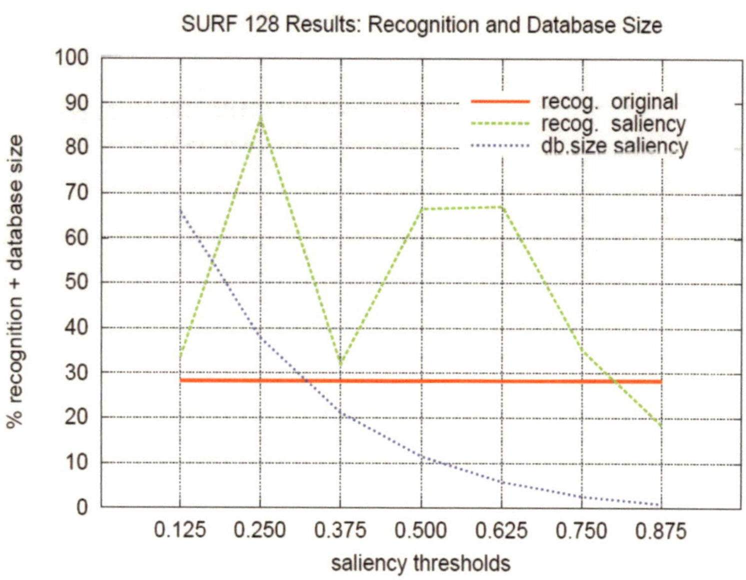

Fig. 6. Graphical results of recognition and database size using SURF-128 features.

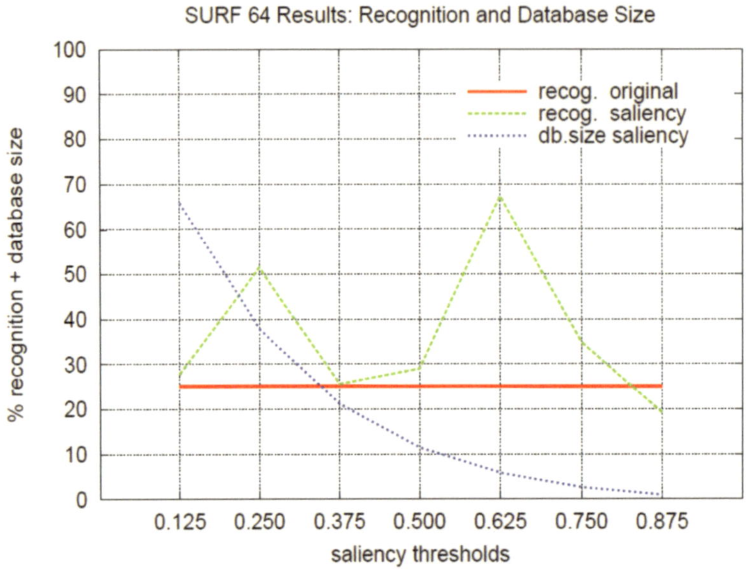

Fig. 7. Graphical results of recognition and database size using SURF-64 features.

Experimental results show that although SURF features collect significantly less interest points than SIFT features (approximately the half of them) their performance is not adequate for the scene recognition application. However, SURF features have proven to be adequate, and faster than SIFT features, in other applications (Bay, 2008). Another interesting result is that recognition performance of SURF features shows an irregular behavior with the saliency thresholds, in both cases, SURF-64 and SURF-128. A maximum peak of 86.56% is reached at saliency level 0.250 in SURF-128, while recognition results provided by SURF-64 features are worse. When using no saliency maps and even with some less restrictive thresholds, recognition results of SURF features are very bad. This means that SURF features loose distinctiveness as more interest points are used. This fact does not occur in SIFT features, thus, SIFT features present more distinctiveness than SURF features in very large databases of interest points. The best results are achieved using SIFT features, which combined with saliency maps can reduce the amount of prototypes in the database up to one order of magnitude, while the recognition performance is held, e.g. saliency level 0.500 in Table 1 and Figure 5. In this case, the performance drops to 92.21% (only 3.04 points from 95.25%) while the database size is drastically reduced from 1,170,215 to 157,388 prototypes.

6. Conclusions

In this work, scene recognition is carried out using a novel biologically inspired approach to visual attention in combination with local image features. SIFT and SURF approaches to image featuring are compared. Experimental results show that despite SURF features imply the use of less interest points the best performance corresponds by far to SIFT features. The SIFT method achieves a 95.25% of performance on scene recognition in the best case, while the SURF method only reaches 86.56%. Another important result is achieved when we use the saliency maps from the visual attention approach in combination with SIFT features. In this case, the database of prototypes, used in the classification task of scene recognition, can be drastically reduced (up to one order of magnitude) with a slightly drop in recognition performance. Thus, the scene recognition application can be significantly speeded-up. In addition, the experiments show that SURF features are less distinctive than SIFT features when we use very large databases of interest points.

7. Acknowledgements

Work supported by the Ministry of Education and Science of the Spanish Government (AVISTA-TIN2006-08447) and the Government of Galicia (PGIDIT07PXIB206028PR).

8. References

Attneave, F. (1954). Informational aspects of visual perception. *Psychological Review*, Vol. 61, No. 3, pp. 183-193, ISSN 0033-295X (print), ISSN 1939-1471 (online).

Bauer, J.; Sünderhauf, N. & Protzel, P. (2007). Comparing Several Implementations of Two Recently Published Feature Detectors. *Proceedings of The International Conference on Intelligent and Autonomous Systems*, (IAV), Toulouse, France.

Barlow, H.B. (1961). Possible principles underlying the transformation of sensory messages. *Sensory Communication*, pp. 217-234.

Barlow, H.B. & Foldiak, P. (1989). Adaptation and decorrelation in the cortex. In *The Computing Neuron*, pp. 54-72, Addison-Wesley, ISBN 0-201-18348-X.

Bay, H.; Ess, A.; Tuytelaars, T. & Gool, L. V. (2008). Speeded-Up Robust Features (SURF). *Computer Vision and Image Understanding*, Vol. 110, No. 3, pp. 346-359, ISSN 1077-3142.

Bonaiuto, J. J. & Itti, L. (2005). Combining Attention and Recognition for Rapid Scene Analysis, *Proceedings of the 2005 IEEE Computer Society Conference on Computer Vision and Pattern Recognition (CVPR05)*, pp. 90-90, ISBN 978-88-89884-09-6, San Diego (USA), June 2005, IEEE Computer Society.

Felsberg, M. & Sommer, G. (2001). The Monogenic Signal. *IEEE Transactions on Signal Processing*, Vol. 49, No. 12, pp. 3136-3144, ISSN 1053-587X.

García-Díaz, A.; Fdez-Vidal, X. R.; Dosil, R. and Pardo, X. M. (2008). Local Energy Variability as a Generic Measure of Bottom-Up Salience, In: *Pattern Recognition Techniques, Technology and Applications*, Peng-Yeng Yin (Ed.), pp. 1–24 (Chapter 1), In-Teh, ISBN 978-953-7619-24-4,Vienna.

Guo, C.L.; Ma, Q. & Zhang, L.M. (2008). Spatio-Temporal Saliency Detection Using Phase Spectrum of Quaternion Fourier Transform. In: *Proceedings of IEEE Conference on Computer Vision and Pattern Recognition 2008 (CVPR'2008)*, Nº 220, IEEE, pp. 1-8. ISBN 9781424422425.

Hyvärinen, A.; Hurri, J. & Hoyer, P.O. (2009). Natural Image Statistics. A probabilistic approach to early computational vision. Springer. ISBN 978-1-84882-491-1.

Itti, L. & Koch, C. (2000). A Saliency-based Search Mechanism for Overt and Covert Shifts of Visual Attention. *Vision Research*, Vol. 40, pp. 1489–1506, ISSN 0042-6989.

Koch, C. & Ullman, S. (1985). Shifts in Selective Visual Attention: Towards the Underlying Neural Circuitry. *Human Neurobiology*, Vol. 4, No. 4, pp. 219-227, ISSN 0721-9075.

Kovesi, P.D. (1999). Image features from phase congruency. Videre: *Journal of Computer Vision Research*. MIT Press. Vol. 1, No. 3.
Available from: http://mitpress.mit.edu/e-journals/Videre/001/v13.html

Kovesi, P.D. (2000). MATLAB and Octave Functions for Computer Vision and Image Processing. School of Computer Science & Software Engineering, The University of Western Australia.
Available from: http://www.csse.uwa.edu.au/~pk/research/matlabfns/

Lowe, D. G. (2004). Distinctive Image Features from Scale-invariant Keypoints. *International Journal of Computer Vision*, Vol. 60, No. 2, pp. 91–110, ISSN 0920-5691 (print), ISSN 1573-1405 (online).

Mikolajczyk, K. & Schmid, C. (2005). A Performance Evaluation of Local Descriptors. *IEEE Transactions on Pattern Analysis and Machine Intelligence*, Vol. 27, No. 10, pp. 1615-1630, ISSN 0162-8828.

Morrone, M.C. & Burr, D.C. (1988). Feature detection in human vision: A phase-dependent energy model. *Proceedings of the Royal Society of London B: Biological Sciences*, Vol. 235, No. 1280 , pp. 221–245, ISSN 1471-2954.

Morrone, M.C. & Owens, R. (1987). Feature detection from local energy. *Pattern Recognition Letters*, Vol. 6, No. 5, pp. 303–313, ISSN 0167-8655.

Simoncelli, E.P. & Olshausen, B.A. (2001). Natural image statistics and neural representation. *Annual Review of Neuroscience*, Vol. 24, No. 1, pp. 1193-1216, ISSN 0147-006X.

Treisman, A. & Gelade, G. (1980). A Feature Integration Theory of Attention. *Cognitive Psychologhy*, Vol. 12, pp. 97–136, ISSN 0010-0285.

Walther, D.; Rutishauser, U.; Koch, C. & Perona, P. (2005). Selective Visual Attention Enables Learning and Recognition of Multiple Objects in Cluttered Scenes. *Computer Vision and Image Understanding*, Vol. 100, pp. 1-63, ISSN 1077-3142.

13

Object Recognition using Isolumes

Rory C. Flemmer, Huub H. C. Bakker and Claire L. Flemmer
Massey University, Palmerston North
New Zealand

1. Introduction

1.1 The need for object recognition

Workers in artificial vision (AV) would say that their basic aim is to be able to take any picture and recognise the objects present and their orientations. They would say that the problem is difficult and that there are many sub-specialties and that they are working in one of them. What is the point of the endeavour? Well, it's going of be of benefit to mankind - for security or autonomous robots. But we would reply that Rottweilers are pretty good at security and are totally incompetent at recognising objects in pictures. It is therefore clear that the skill of recognising objects in pictures is not required for an agent to go about its business in the real world. Of course, CCD images seem rather like pictures when they are presented on a computer monitor but, in fact, they supply very different information from that gathered by a biological vision system operating in the real world. Visual systems in the biosphere have been around for over half a billion years (Valentine et al. 1999, Levi-Setti, 1993 and Conway-Morris, 1998) and most segment objects by motion - many animals cannot see stationary prey. In addition, the more sophisticated ones use stereopsis and information from parallax (consider the way a chicken moves its head as it examines something). It is only once we rise up the evolutionary chain to the best of the primates that the huge library of experience contained in the cortex can be used to offer a syntax of vision. If we were to rank the accomplishments of artificial vision against those of biological vision, we would have to place its current proficiency considerably below that of a cockroach or a spider - and these humble creatures function quite adequately in the world.

It is the glory of modern science and human connectivity that it is able to reduce and distribute problems to many workers and then aggregate the results of their efforts. In the case of AV this has resulted in the subspecialties having a life of their own with their own techniques, vocabulary and journals. It is not within the purview of such specialist researchers to take an integrated view of the whole endeavour and to ponder its aims and terms of reference. We, however, are striving to produce an autonomous, intelligent robot. This ineluctably requires vision capability of a high order. We are therefore forced to consider ways and means to accomplish this. Accordingly, we examined the voluminous literature and sought among the technologies of object recognition to find a working method. We sought in vain. Nobody can do a robust and adequate job of finding objects in an image.

From any elementary book on human vision (for instance, Gregory 1978), it is immediately obvious that the strategies used by biological visual systems as they deal with objects in three space, bear little relation to the problem of examining a static and complex two dimensional image. Furthermore, the problem of examining a complex two dimensional image is very, very hard - you have to have a top-end primate brain to do it. It is not surprising therefore that sixty years of AV, aimed almost exclusively at the picture problem have produced but modest accomplishments.

But we still want to build an embodied artificial intelligence and therefore we have to have vision.

1.2 Why do existing techniques not deliver?

One of the subspecialties of vision is segmentation of the image into discrete objects. This is appropriate because researchers tacitly, perhaps even subconsciously, agree that vision is all about objects. We go a lot further and have argued (Flemmer, 2009) that life and intelligence are about nothing other than objects. Unfortunately AV is not generally able to segment objects in a picture - once again, it takes an advanced primate brain to do this. However, the spider and the cockroach, with their modest intellectual machinery, have this problem handled without breaking a sweat. We can readily imagine how they might segment by movement or parallax. Of course these techniques do not work on a two dimensional image. Given a segmented image, the task of delineating the outlines of objects obviously becomes very much simpler.

It seems therefore that, if we consider the AV problem from the point of view of an agent going about its business in three-space, with stereo cameras, it will be somewhat easier, if for no other reason than that the segmentation problem becomes tractable in most situations. However, we are still faced with the task of making sense of a segmented portion of an image. There are no workable technologies to handle this, even when it is segmented and even when we can reduce it to a fairly simple image by considering only the extent of a particular object.

Can current AV analyse a fairly simple picture? It seemed to researchers in the 1980's (for example, Rosenfeld, 1987), when they had had twenty years to explore AV, that the way forward was, firstly, to find the outline of an object (its cartoon, derived from an edge-follower, together with some help from segmentation techniques) and then to recognise the object from the shape of the cartoon. They ascribed their lack of success to the poverty of their computers compared with the human brain (Ballard and Brown, 1982). Comparisons with cockroach brains were not reported. In the intervening thirty years, computers have improved 30,000 - fold (Hutcheson, 2005) and we have had the best and the brightest minds considering the problem. But in a recent review of object recognition, Da Fontura Costa and Cesar, 2009, note that "computer vision systems created thus far have met with limited success". In particular, they observe that edge-followers do not robustly yield edges, independent of lighting conditions, noise, occlusions and distortions.

For thirty years, a benchmark for edge followers has been the image of Lenna, a 1972 Playboy centrefold, shown below (Fig. 1) in modest quantities (Hutchinson, 2001).

Nor all our piety nor wit can satisfactorily find the edges of the sunny side of Lenna (Fig. 1a), despite decades of extremely close attention by graduate students. Even less can we find the edges of her reflection in the mirror (Fig. 1b) and even if we could, we could not reasonably conclude that the resulting cartoon was that of a comely maiden, although our own examination of Fig. 1b might suggest this. It is hard to see how the paradigm of edge detection and cartoon recognition could work in this case - and it is not an extraordinarily

(a) (b)

Fig. 1. (a) Image of Lenna (b) Reflection of Lenna

difficult image. A more compelling indictment is the sober fact that the scheme has failed to solve the problem despite fifty years of earnest endeavour and millions of person-hours. It is suggested (for example see Ballard and Brown, 1982 and Da Fontura et al, 2009) that the impasse can only be resolved by introducing a visual syntax to guide us in finding edges, i.e., we need a human cortex to help. This seems technically difficult.

Lately some progress has been made using Scale Invariant Feature Transforms (SIFTs). The notion is that objects have certain idiosyncrasies which, if they were scaled and rotated, would always show up in different images of the same object, if viewed from roughly the same perspective. This technique suffers from the intrinsic problem that a polka dot mug is not seen as similar to a tartan mug. Nonetheless, the technique has produced some very respectable object recognition (Brown and Lowe, 2007) although it cannot be regarded as an overarching solution.

Other techniques are reported in a comprehensive review (Da Fontura Costa and Cesar, 2009) but we judge that none of them springs forward, fully formed, to solve our problem and none is as important in the literature as cartoon creation followed by attempted recognition (Drew et al., 2009).

1.3 How do we go forward?

Let us accept that edge-followers, despite being a very mature technology, do not work to a level which allows robust object recognition. We view level sets as a subset of edge-followers (Osher and Fedkiw, 2003, and Sethian, 1999). Let us accept also that SIFTs and other techniques do not provide an immediate prospect of competent unsupervised AV.

In this chapter, we offer an avenue that might prove useful. This is the concept of iso-luminal contours - or isolumes. We have deployed this concept and elaborated it to be a method that has had some success in unsupervised object recognition. Despite the modest dimensions of our efforts and of our success, we hope that, given some attention from the massive intellectual resources of the AV community, this scheme might lead to robust unsupervised object recognition.

1.4 How will we know whether our scheme is satisfactory? Choosing a database

It is customary to test object recognition methods against image databases such as the Caltech-101 database (Amores et al., 2007), the COIL-100 database (Scheneider et al., 2005), the MIT-CSAIL database (Gao et al., 2007), the ETH-80 dataset (Dhua and Cutzu, 2006), the MPEG7 database (Belongie et al., 2002) and the Corel stock photography collection (Lew et al., 2006). This has the merit that, aside from the progenitors, the authors are viewed as comparing against a fixed standard. But our requirement is not merely the 'solution' of the object recognition problem but actually to deploy a technology for the use of an artificial intelligence. What, then, is an appropriate photographic database? Clearly it is the succession of images captured by the cameras as the robot goes about its daily round. Since this is not yet available, we have created a database (which is accessible at the URL in the appendix). This database differs from others in that it caters for our specific requirements; namely that we have specific and exact images which are our gold images. We seek to judge whether they are present or not in the other database images. This is rather different from most databases which might have, for instance, a succession of cars, all slightly different.

Our database contained two gold exemplars and 100 brass images. The gold exemplars are shown in Fig. 2. Some of the 100 brass images contain gold images, some occluded, some frank, at varying orientations and scales.

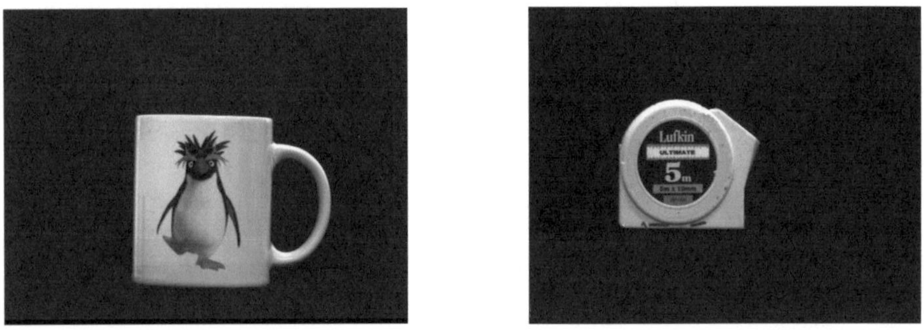

(a) (b)

Fig. 2. Two gold images used for testing; (a) a mug and (b) a measuring tape.

A selection from the brass image database is shown in Fig. 3.

2. Isolumes

Imagine that a monochrome image were placed flat on the desk (Fig. 4a). Imagine that the grey level at each i-, j-position in the image were plotted as a height above the table (Fig. 4b). This means that we can view the image as a topography. We can then connect points of equal grey level to form contours as land surveyors do with points of equal altitude. We call these contours 'isolumes'. An isolume is outlined in yellow in Fig. 4a and its corresponding representation in Fig. 4b.

2.1 Representation of objects

When we take an electronic snapshot of an object, we will see it from one definite viewpoint. But an object looks different from different perspectives, as it is rotated. To handle this, we propose recording each object as twenty views, each along the axis of a regular icosahedron (a regular polyhedron with 20 identical equilateral triangular faces). Thus each object is represented in our database by twenty 'gold' views. Such views will be 41.6 degrees apart and it is assumed that an object can be recognised provided that it is not rotated by more

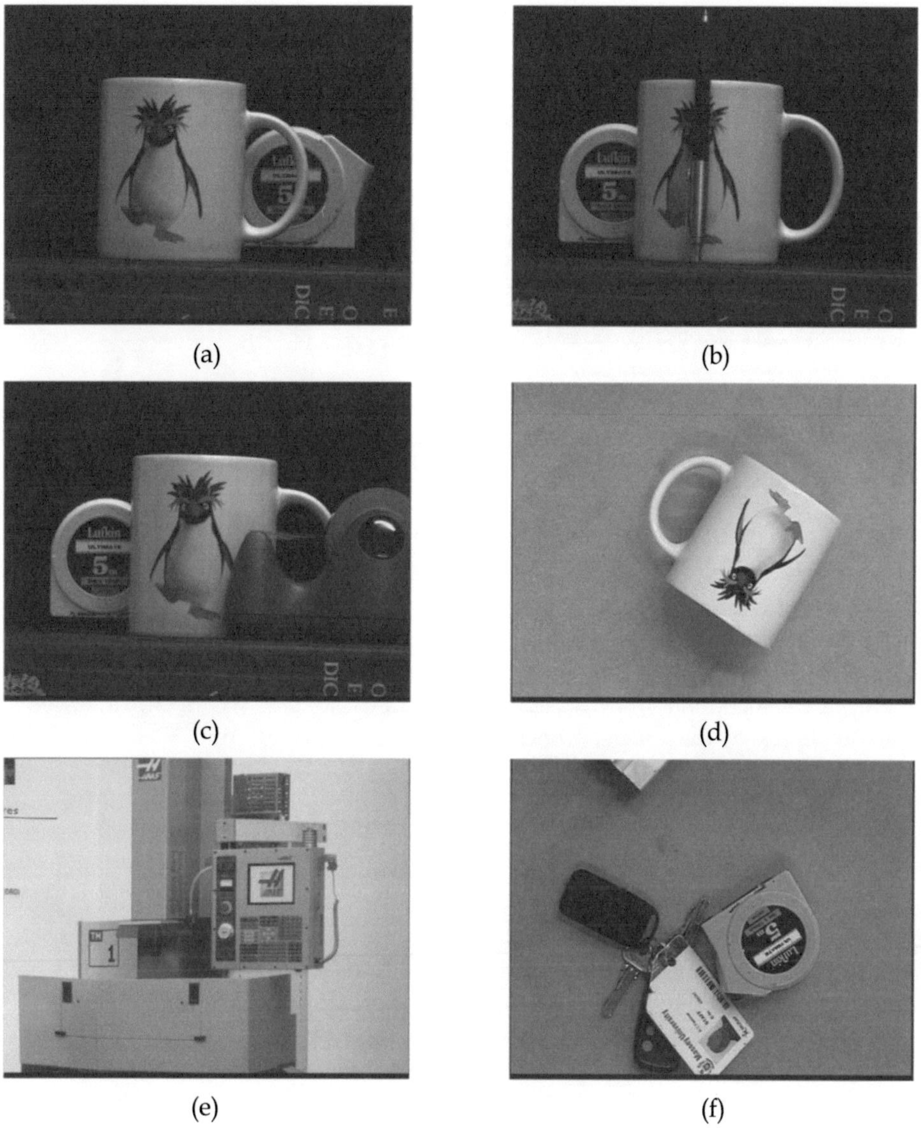

Fig. 3. (a) to (f) Six examples of images in the brass dataset

than 21 degrees away from its archival image. (We confirm this fact experimentally in due course.) With how many objects might we have to contend in our database? Educated people recognise of the order of 45,000 words (Bryson, 1990). By conducting an assay of the Oxford Dictionary, we find that about a third of these are nouns, so let us say there are 15,000 objects in our ken. An objection arises in that 'car' encompasses many models, with new ones added every year. In order to deal with this, we will need to invoke the concept of universals - which has plagued philosophers from Plato onwards. We will set this aside for the moment and consider that our library contains only specific objects and each object is recorded as twenty views. Thus 'Ford Focus 2009' and 'Ford Focus 2010' are, for the present, two distinct objects. We will return to the problem of universals later.

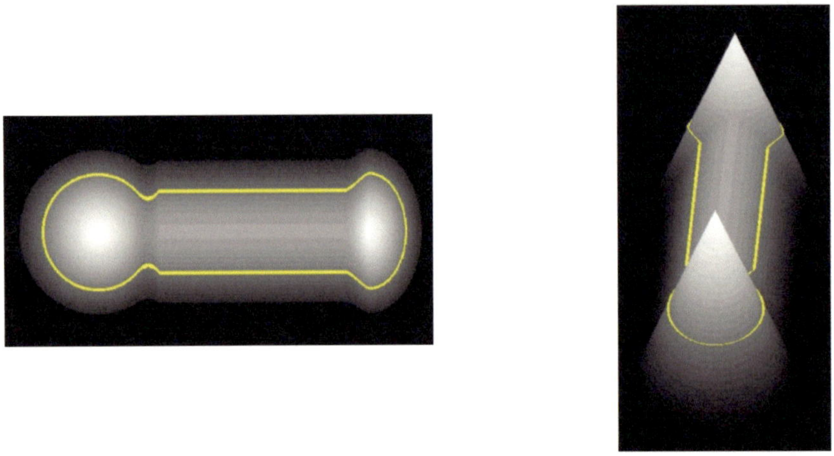

(a) (b)

Fig. 4. (a) A single isolume shown in yellow and (b) its height representation

2.2 Extraction of Isolumes from an image

In principle we can extract an isolume for every grey level in the image. In practice, it is wiser to establish the range of grey levels present in the image and then acquire isolumes at some grey level increment (not necessarily constant) so that we obtain a lesser set of isolumes to represent the image. Depending on the image, we find it convenient to use perhaps forty grey levels and we will get something like five or ten isolumes for each of these. We find, experimentally that these numbers yield a good description of the image. It turns out that we have the further requirement that we have to extract the isolumes to sub-pixel accuracy; an accuracy of 0.1 pixels is barely good enough. Before analysing the image, we introduced some Gaussian blurring so that the very sharp cliffs of the topography are given a gentler slope. Consequently, the isolumes are spaced out a little and present as a broader line. Fig. 5 shows a complex image and the isolumes of the image in blue. Intuitively it seems that they capture the sense of the image very adequately.

Where many of them coincide, they present as a solid line on the image and we would consider such a line to be an 'edge' in the traditional sense of image analysis. In fact, we could select only those multiply coincident contours and consider them as edges.

Our isolume extraction process can be viewed by examining the C# code which can be downloaded from the URL in the appendix. Undoubtedly, those who follow will do it faster and better but this code is adequate for our immediate needs. Fig. 6 shows the process which has the following steps:

1. Create arrays for RoseI(24) and RoseJ(24). These arrays specify a set of vectors such that (RoseI(0),RoseJ(0)) points along the positive I axis, with length 4, i.e. RoseI(0) = 4, RoseJ(0) = 0. For the index equal to 6, the vector points along positive J. This device permits a step to be taken from a current point in any of 24 directions by setting the index.
2. Specify grey level.
3. Create a Boolean Incidence Array of the same dimensions as the image. Call it StartPoints(). Step through the image at intervals of 5 pixels in I and J. Set the element to be true if the image grey level is close enough to the specified grey level.

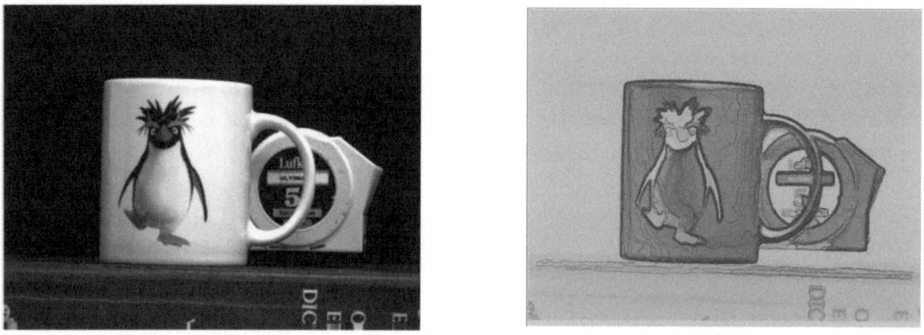

(a) (b)

Fig. 5. (a) Image (b) Isolumes of the image

4. Create a second such integer array to store the index value of a point on an isolume, IsolumeIndex. Call the array IsolumePoints().
5. Top of Loop
6. Search through the Incidence Array until a True element is found. Set this element False and start tracing the isolume at this set of coordinates.
7. Search in a circle around this point using the vector (RoseI(k), RoseJ(k)) for k = 0 to 23, to find that pixel which is closest to the specified grey level. In general there will be two such points. Choose between these points such that, as the isolume progresses from the initial point to the second point, bright is on the right. This rubric simplifies the isolume structure.
8. Interpolate between neighbours to this pixel to provide values of the isolume coordinates to sub-pixel accuracy (better than 0.1 pixel).
9. Use of the RoseI/RoseJ stratagem provides points on the isolume at intervals of about four pixels. Interpolate linearly to provide another point in the middle. Record each point as IsolumeX(IsolumeIndex) and IsolumeY(IsolumeIndex).
10. Set these two elements to the appropriate value of the IsolumeIndex in the IsolumePoints() array. Later, this will allow a very rapid search for the case where the isolume crosses itself.
11. Check that the isolume is not circling around and crossing itself. This can be done by scanning a 6x6 block of entries in the IsolumePoints() array, centred on the new point and demanding that any value found not be more than four points different from the IsolumeIndex, i.e. ignore the neck of the snake but be alert for its body.
12. If the current point is approaching a point which has already been seen on the snake or else is stepping out of the picture, then go to the start point and complete the isolume in the other direction.
13. Go to the top of the loop (step 5).

2.3 Manipulation of raw Isolumes

Once we have the isolumes, we elect to plot them (Fig. 7) as local curvature versus distance along the isolume and call this plot the fingerprint of the isolume. As we will see later, we fit a local circle to the isolume and use the reciprocal of its radius as the curvature. Consider Fig. 7 where the isolume defining the outer edge of a mug is plotted with these coordinates. Such a plot provides three distinct features; there are lobes, which present as bumps (and are marked with asterisks on the fingerprint), lines which present as portions of zero curvature (marked with lines on the fingerprint) and arcs, which have constant, non-zero curvature (and are marked with an arc on the fingerprint). Observe that the area under a lobe represents the amount of rotation of the isolume and is scale and rotation invariant. Also note that the order of the features as they appear on the plot is independent of scale and rotation, although it might be reversed.

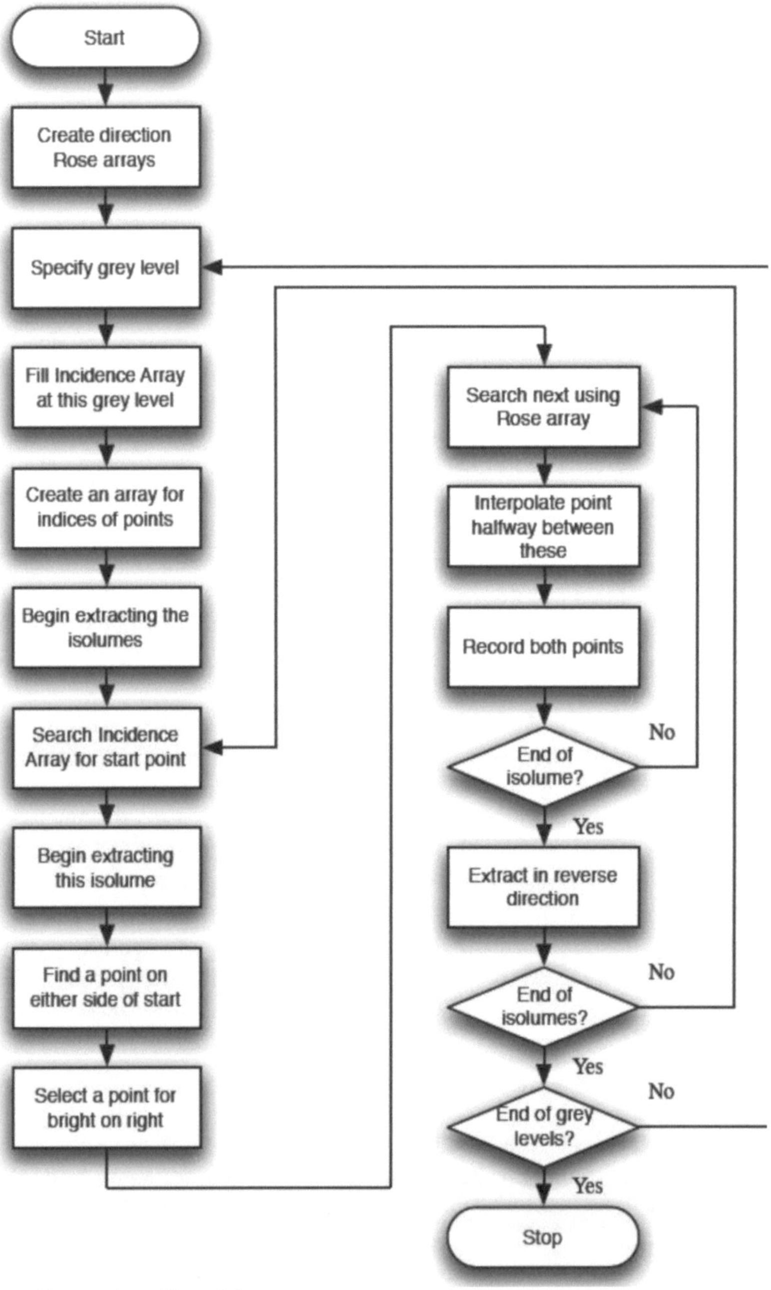

Fig. 6. Isolume Extraction Algorithm

But, before we can get to the elegant representation of the fingerprint (Fig. 7c), we have to manipulate the data quite carefully. A plot using the raw data is shown in Fig. 7b. If the data is simply averaged with five-point Gaussian smoothing, information is lost as everything is smoothed. We found that what was required was a filter that had a varying frequency response, depending on the signal. After considerable experimentation, we introduced two innovations. Firstly, in order to get the local curvature of the line, C, defined by:

$$C = d\psi/ds \quad (1)$$

Fig. 7. (a) Isolume at outer edge of mug, shown in blue, starting at lower left and proceeding clockwise

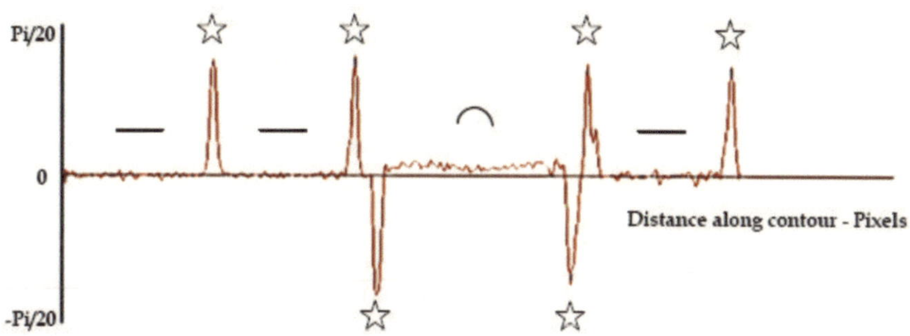

Fig. 7. (b) Unsmoothed fingerprint of the isolume in (a)

Key: Lobe ☆ Line — Arc ⌒

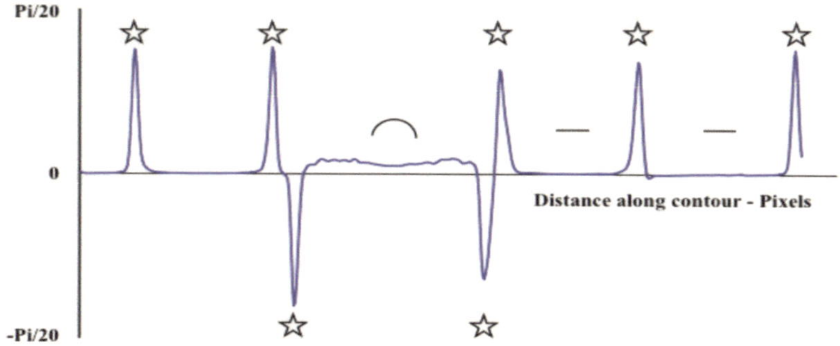

Fig. 7. (c) Dynamically smoothed fingerprint

where ψ is the angle of the local tangent to the curve and s is a measure of distance along the curve, we recognise that curvature is defined as the reciprocal of the radius of curvature. This naturally implies that it is the reciprocal of the radius of an arc which locally approximates the curve. It is then a very rapid calculation to fit a circle to three points on the data, spanning the central point at which the curvature is sought.

The second innovation was to vary the symmetrical distance between the central point and the two on either side from which the circle was computed. This distance has to be short where the isolume is turning rapidly such as the portion where it turns the corner at the top left hand corner of the mug in Fig. 7a, i.e. it is necessary to fit a small circle to capture the sharp rotation. However, as the isolume goes up the vertical side of the mug, it needs to be very large otherwise any imperfection in the isolume (arising from noise) gives rise to spurious values for the curvature. In this section of the fingerprint, it is clear that there should be no deviation from the straight line, i.e. we want a very large radius. We therefore wrote a routine to specify this distance between the centre point and the two outliers on the circle. We fitted a best-fit line to seven consecutive points, centred on the point in question. We then moved away from the central point and found empirically the distance, Span, for which the best fit line diverged from the isolume by an amount equal to (Span/10 + 0.5) pixels. It must be recognised that the coordinates defining each point of the isolume are precise to a fraction of a pixel but, as small differences are sought to determine curvature, this leads to large errors. Fitting a circle over appropriate distances ameliorates the difficulty. However, it should be recognised that the fingerprint Fig. 7c is not a perfectly accurate representation of the curvature at each point; it has lost something in the smoothing. But, since it is consistent and its distortion is not excessive, it is still useable.

Once curvature of all points on the isolume has been determined, the data are all manipulated to give a set of points at one-pixel intervals with curvature, position coordinates and a precise distance from the beginning of the isolume associated with each point.

2.4 Extraction of features

The three types of features (lobes, lines and arcs) in the isolume fingerprint have certain characteristics. The extraction of each feature and a description of the characteristics are discussed below.

2.4.1 Extraction of lobes

The extraction of lobes follows the flowchart shown in Fig. 8. The smoothed fingerprint of the isolume is scanned to find groups of points with large curvature, C, and the local maximum curvature, C_{max}, representing the apex of the lobe. The area, A, under the lobe corresponds to the angle through which the isolume contour has turned as it passes along the lobe. Referring to the isolume around the outside of the mug in Fig. 7a, the first lobe corresponds to the turn of the contour at the top left edge through 90 degrees (1.57 radians) and this is the area under the first lobe in Fig. 7c. The second and third lobes would have similar areas, although the third lobe would be negative (an anticlockwise rotation through 90 degrees).

In addition to the area, we have defined, for lobes, two further characteristics, namely skewness (S) and kurtosis (K). Skewness is a dimensionless measure of the symmetry of the lobe about its centre and quantifies the extent to which the lobe is skewed to the right or left.

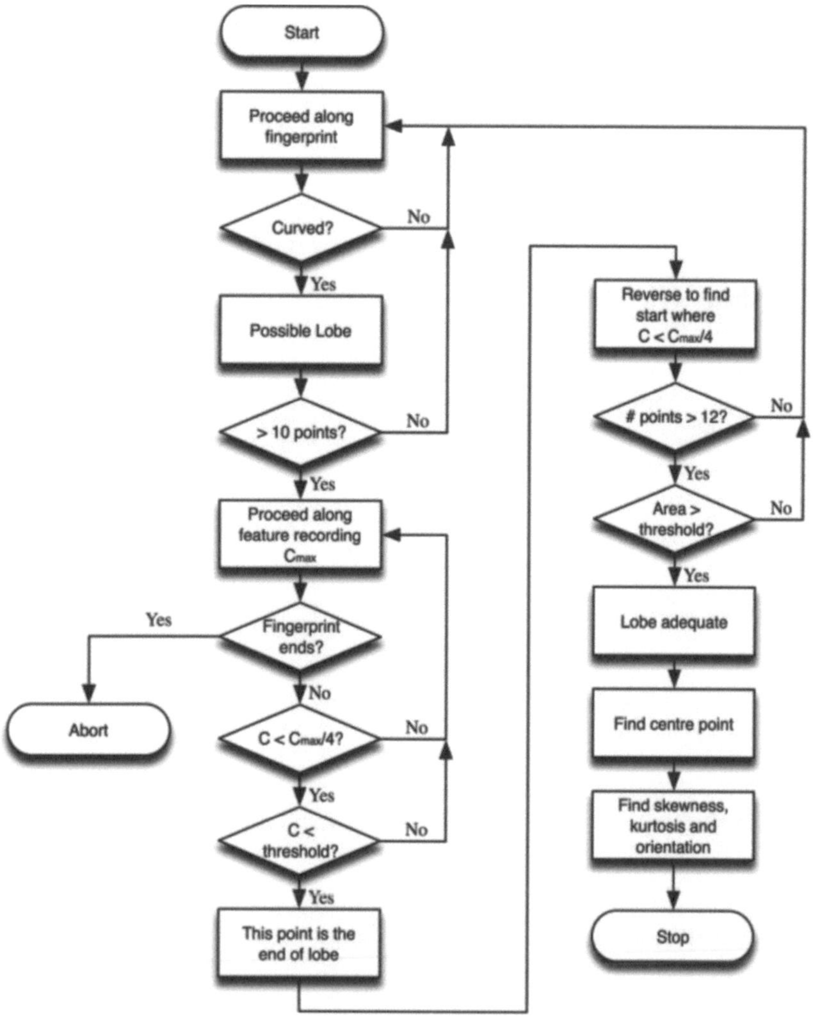

Fig. 8. Flowchart showing extraction of lobes and determination of lobe characteristics

It is defined as:

$$S = (C_G - M)/L \tag{2}$$

Where C_G is the centre of gravity of the lobe (in pixels), M is the mean of the greatest and least pixel values of the lobe, and L is the length of the lobe in pixels. For a symmetric lobe, $C_G = M$, so its skewness value is zero.

Kurtosis measures the extent to which the lobe is sharply peaked or flattened.

Let the lobe have curvature, C_i at the ith pixel and let C_{max} be the maximum curvature of the lobe. Then the normalized curvature at the ith point, c_i is:

$$c_i = C_i / C_{max} \tag{3}$$

The lobe starts at i_{start} and ends at i_{end}. Compute distance, W, such that W is the smaller of C_G-i_{start} and i_{end}–C_G. W is then the maximum interval of i, symmetrical about C_G, which is contained within the pixel values of the lobe. Set $n = 2W+1$. Then compute a dimensionless second moment of area, M_1, about the centroid, summed over all i from C_G-W to C_G+W as:

$$M_1 = \{\Sigma c_i(C_G - i)^2\}/n^2 \tag{4}$$

Let c_{ave} be the average of c_i for the interval and compute M_2 over the same interval as M_1, where:

$$M_2 = \{\Sigma c_{ave}(C_G - i)^2\}/n^2 \tag{5}$$

Kurtosis, K, is defined as:

$$K = M_1/M_2 \tag{6}$$

Note that kurtosis is non-dimensional and that if c_i were constant over the interval (i.e. the fingerprint were linear as it followed a uniformly circular arc), then $c_i = c_{ave}$ and $M_1 = M_2$ and the lobe would have $K = 1$.
Fig. 9 shows two examples of lobes and their area, skewness and kurtosis values.

Fig. 9. Two lobes: Left lobe A = 0.82 radians, S = 0.05, K = 0.53
Right lobe A = 0.82 radians, S = -0.70, K = 0.32

2.4.2 Extraction of lines

Lines are represented in the fingerprint by portions of the fingerprint where divergences of curvature from zero are small. In real fingerprints, there will generally be some divergence and we need to decide what can be tolerated. Our strategy is to walk along the fingerprint until a suitable number of points is encountered that have very small curvatures, indicating that we are now on a line. Then we walk along the line and record a bad vote for every point whose absolute curvature is larger than some threshold. The votes would be incremented as bad points as they are sequentially encountered. However, as soon as an acceptable point (with curvature less than the threshold) is encountered, this sum of bad points is set to zero. When the bad point vote exceeds some threshold, the line is declared to be terminated and, provided that there are enough 'good' points (i.e. the line is an acceptable length), its centre point is recorded, its length is recorded and its orientation relative to the i-axis, in radians, is recorded.

2.4.3 Extraction of arcs

This is similar to the extraction of lines except that there are provisions ensuring that the values within the arc do not differ from each other by more than some normalised threshold.

2.4.4 Data management

Shrink-wrapped code was developed to examine an image, extract its data and to represent it as indexed isolumes containing sequentially indexed features, be they lobes, lines or arcs. (This code is accessible from the URL given in the appendix). By this artifice, the data of an image is compressed down to something of the order of 20 Kbytes. An alternative approach is to work solely from the features. Generally a particular feature is represented in several isolumes and it is of value to obtain a smaller list of super-features, each such super-feature being the average of its contributors - from several different isolumes. Each super-feature has data covering its exact position on the image and its properties, which would include its type (whether lobe, line or arc) and further appropriate specifications. A brass image (refer to section 1.4) might have 60 super-features, a gold image perhaps 45. The attributes derived for each feature are listed in Table 1.

Feature	Properties
Lobe	Area, Skewness , Kurtosis, Orientation, X_{centre}, Y_{centre}
Line	Orientation, X_{centre}, Y_{centre}
Arc	Radius, X_{centre}, Y_{centre}, $X_{arc\ centre}$, $Y_{arc\ centre}$

Table 1. Feature Properties

3. Object Recognition: the problem defined

The object recognition problem is now patent. We 'know' up to 15,000 objects. For each object, we have 20 views, each seen from one of the axes of an icosahedron. This gives up to 300,000 views (or gold images) as our knowledge base. As we take an arbitrary view (a brass image) of any particular object, we can at most be twenty one degrees away from one of our cardinal views and we expect to be able still to recognise any object, even with some small difference in orientation.

Our intent is to deploy AV to run, unsupervised in an autonomous robot. The robot will acquire information during the looking process that will isolate objects one from another and from the background. It will look at some portion of its world and perform stereopsis in order to get a measure of distance to points in its view. It assumes that objects are sui generic in distance. This is to say that the dimensions of the object are small compared with the distance to the object from the eye. This is generally so, with exceptions such as when objects are brought very close to the camera. The robot's artificial intelligence (AI) categorises areas in its view as to distance and when it finds that a set of points is of similar distance, distinct from the background, it assumes that they represent an object. It might also be guided by coherent movement of the points against the background as a result of the camera moving or the object moving. With this information, it isolates some portion of its field of view. This is now termed the 'brass' view, possibly containing an object. It then enquires whether any one of the 300,000 object views is present. These 300,000 views contain of the order of 100 isolumes each. If we condense multiply represented features down, we will have something like 100 super-features per view, i.e., 30,000,000 super-features. This is not intractably large but neither is it a simple problem because we do not have an ordering principle. Further, much of the data is non-digital in the sense that the area of a lobe is an imprecise number which may be slightly different every time we measure it in a different

image. Therefore the technique of hashing which is of such power in many database searches is not readily available to us.
We have tried three approaches to the problem.

4. First approach – Matching of features

Note that we are here working exclusively with super-features - those features which are multiply represented in different isolumes at a point. This approach requires an initial search through the 300,000 views of the gold image database to produce a list of views which have features in common with the brass view. The resultant list will be ordered in terms of feature commonality. It is hoped to reduce the candidates by a factor of 10,000 in a coarse separation. With this reduced list, we can then enquire sequentially, as to the probability that each view on the list is actually a match with the brass image.

4.1 Coarse search

Mining of data from the database relies upon choosing a suitable key or index that can be used to extract useful candidate records very quickly from tens of millions. Speed of retrieving records is as important as the requirement that not too many possible matches be missed. We search only for matches of lobes on the basis of Area, Skewness and Kurtosis (ASK). Lines and arcs are not considered in the first instance because they are not as well defined as lobes.
Searching a database for records that contain the correct values of these discriminators to within a suitable interval is inefficient because hashing and binary searches are not possible. A better approach would be to sort them into bins and search for a coding representing membership of a particular bin. A search through the database for candidate features now amounts to looking up an index for matching bin numbers. This can reduce the search time by orders of magnitude.
The choice of the width of the bins is important since bins that are too narrow will result in measurement errors placing discriminators in the wrong bin. Conversely, bins that are too wide will decrease discrimination. The optimum size appears to be the same as the expected maximum measurement error. Where the measurement error is a percentage of the measurement rather than a fixed number this will naturally lead to the bin sizes increasing with the size of the discriminator; the log of the bin width will be a constant. We refer to these as log bins.
With log bins there is an infinite number of bins between any given value and zero. One 'catch-all' bin can be included to span the range 0 to the smallest log bin with the rest of the bins spanning the range to the largest bin.
There is a further concern however. Regardless of the size of the bin, it is possible for the discriminator to be placed in the wrong bin because it is too near the bin's edge and there is variation in the measurement from one image to the next. This can be overcome by considering membership to include not only the given bin but also the measurement's nearest neighbour bin. This will suggest that, with the bin no narrower than the measurement error, a search of the database will turn up most relevant candidates.
Database search engines are capable of concatenating search indices, so that all three discriminators can be searched simultaneously. Unfortunately, including the nearest-neighbour bin requires eight separate searches be undertaken, one for each of the eight possible combinations of two possible values (one bin and its nearest neighbour) of the three discriminators. Because the search is definite, it is fast, notwithstanding the extra bins.

Generally an object seen in a brass image will be rotated, in the plane of the image, relative to the gold image. Therefore two other relationships can be used. These involve the individual angles and distances between features in a group. (Recall that each lobe has an orientation angle relative to the image.)

If we plot all the lobes of our database in ASK space, we might expect them to cluster, with the population density declining with distance from the centroid of the cluster. We can determine the variance of this distance over a large population and by using a cutoff, in our initial search, we concentrate on lobes which are far from the centroid, i.e. abnormal; they will offer greater discrimination.

With these ideas in mind, we applied the following process:

- Find candidate views
- Discriminate geometrically
- Perform a more careful discrimination on the small number of remaining candidate views by:
  - clustering
  - iterative correspondence

4.2 Find candidate views

We find a list of candidate gold views by searching for the features of the brass image in the gold image library. We use only lobes and choose only those brass lobes which are abnormal (as defined above). This involves searching a database of up to thirty million gold features for matches to 25-75 brass lobes. We use only lobes because they have more discriminators than lines or arcs.

The resulting list of candidate views is ranked according to the number of lobes which match between gold and brass. The gold view which has the greatest number of matching brass lobes is at the top. Now we have to ask whether this best view actually matches the brass view. If not, we will consider the second best gold view and so on.

The first step is to produce a matched list of gold and brass lobes. Conceive of a list of gold lobes on the left, matched with brass lobes on the right. This is made up by taking the first gold lobe and then scanning the brass lobes to find the best match. A best brass match will have discriminators that best match the gold lobe. If they don't match well enough, then we will discard this gold lobe. Once we have the pared down list, we need to find out how many of these matches are in fact 'true.' Does the gold lobe really correspond to the brass lobe as we look at the images? Of course the comparison algorithms can't 'look' at the picture to see matches but at the end of the procedure, we can determine how well it functions by examining the images ourselves.

4.3 Geometric discrimination

The objects in the two images will generally be rotated with respect to each other by an angle, θ, and have a dilation factor, δ, i.e. the gold object will be bigger or smaller than the brass object. For those gold features which are in the brass view, they should all be on the same object and therefore they should all be turned through θ. In fact, the difference in orientation between the brass and gold feature should be equal to the rotation angle, within our measurement uncertainty limits. This can be seen in Fig. 10 where θ is the difference between the orientation of feature, f1, in the gold image and f1' in the brass image and also between f2 and f2'. The orientation of the features is shown by the arrows.

The angle between features can then be tested, i.e. the angle of the line joining a given pair of features in the image. For each connecting line the difference in angles should be θ, the rotation angle.

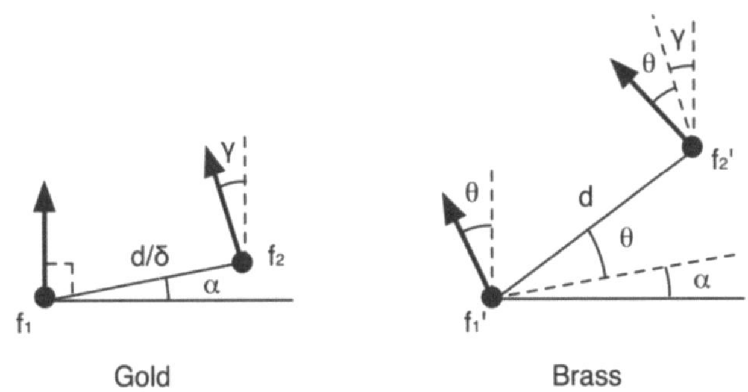

Fig. 10. Relationship between features in gold and brass images.

In a similar fashion we can calculate the ratio of distances between any given two features in the brass image and the distance between corresponding features in the gold image. The ratio should be the dilation factor.

Lobes have an orientation and a position in the image. Lines and arcs, even though not as well defined, can still be used because we can get the shortest distance between a line and a lobe or arc and we can use the line orientation. Arcs do not have an orientation but the radius can be used as an initial filter and the angle and distance to other features can be used.

Having calculated our measure of geometrical similarity for a given gold/brass pair of features, the task is now to eliminate the mismatched feature pairs. Recall our two lists. On the left is a list of gold features; on the right a list of brass features. We assume that the first gold feature corresponds to the first brass feature etc. This is on the basis of discriminator matching. But some of them will not correspond; the feature referred to in the left list will not be the same part of the object as that in the right list. We have considered two different methods to deal with this; clustering and iterative correspondence.

4.3.1 Clustering

Clustering accepts all the table pairings and then discards those pairs which do not correspond. Consider the rotation angle, θ, as the difference in orientations of brass and gold feature of each pair. If the gold view matches the brass view, and the pairs we have chosen are mostly correct, we should find that many of them have a constant difference in orientation equal to θ. We can find this angle and eliminate bad pairing by iteratively removing outliers from the cluster. The average of all the differences in orientation is found and assumed to be θ. The deviations in differences are taken from this and the feature pair with the largest deviation is struck out. The process is then repeated until the largest deviation falls within acceptable limits or we run out of feature pairs.

We can then look at the line features in both views, although lines were not included in our matched lists. By their nature, the orientation of lines is far more precise than that of other features. All possible line/line matches are examined and those that are sufficiently close to θ are used. These are then clustered in the same way to achieve a better estimate of the rotation angle, θ.

Now we can perform the same clustering operation on the dilation factor by considering the ratio of inter-feature distances between the gold image and the brass image.

This method is quick but suffers from the fact that we cannot improve on our initial matching of the two lists. We can progressively discard bad matches and we will generally fail when we don't have enough matches left. Alternatively, if the gold and brass views agree, we will see it because we end up with a reasonable number of matches.

4.4 Iterative correspondence

To overcome the deficit of poor initial matching, we could consider all possible matchings. For 75 features in each image (i.e. the brass image and the gold image) there are of the order of 75^{75} possible combinations, a number not to be seriously considered. (Note that 75^{75} = 10^{140}. This is huge compared with the 10^{79} electrons in the universe.)

There is a more efficient process. Choose the first gold feature as the pole feature and then sequentially attempt to match each brass feature with it. If the discriminators match to acceptable accuracy, consider the next available gold feature as the second feature. Run through the remaining brass features until a match is found in terms of discriminators. Now test geometrically to see whether the rotation of the second pair matches the rotation of the first pair. If it does, seek a third pair and apply tests for rotation plus dilation. Proceed in this way until a match cannot be found for some n^{th} feature of the gold list. In that case, revise the $(n-1)^{th}$ feature and proceed. In principle, this would entail the same number of possible combinations but in practice, when a certain initial match is discarded, this discards all the possible consequences and the method becomes quite quick.

Furthermore, since the geometry tests are all symmetric we need only test half of these possibilities. And, finally, the order in which the pairs are tested is not important. If a set of feature pairs, abc, is a successful combination, then so will acb or cba. This reduces enormously the potential combinations to be searched.

There is one exception to this, which is the choice of the first pair-pair combination. This is used to determine the initial estimates of rotation angle and the scale factor. Since the geometry tests are passed or failed on a tolerance figure, we choose to assume (with some claim to validity) that any truly matching features will adequately represent scale and rotation.

As the number of successfully-tested feature pairs increases, so do the number of combinations to be tested at each next step but, beyond a certain level, the possibility of the brass and gold images not matching becomes insignificant. Early testing has suggested that limiting the number of tests to 3 times the number of feature pairs squared is quite sufficient ($3 \times 75^2 = 16{,}875$).

All the feature pairs that remain have passed scrutiny. Their number will be the most robust indicator of whether the objects in the two images are the same.

4.5 Implementation

The coarse search of section 4.2 was implemented in MySQL, interrogated from C#.

A speed test was conducted by filling the gold database with three million features and performing searches. The characteristics of the features were randomly assigned. A brass image with 81 features was used. These 81 features were then searched for in the RAM-resident gold database of three million features. The ASK search key was employed, using eight searches to handle the binning problem of ASK. In a mid-line 2007 desktop computer the search took about 100ms. This implies something like one second to search the known universe of thirty million features, which is quite satisfactory because this time will halve every two years as computers improve.

4.6 Results: Object recognition based on matching of features

It was found that iterative correspondence was better than clustering. The results for object recognition based on matching of features with Iterative Correspondence are shown in Table 2a for the mug and Table 2b for the measuring tape.

Table 2a shows that the mug was recognized in all 14 of the brass images where it was unoccluded but that recognition success dropped rapidly the more the mug was occluded by other objects. 'False negatives' are the number of brass images which contained the mug but which the technique failed to recognize as the mug. 'False positives' refer to those brass images which did not contain the mug although the technique erroneously found a mug. In fact, there were no false positives. 100% occlusion means that the object is not present in the brass image.

Table 2b shows the results for the measuring tape.

Occlusion (%)	0	<25	<50	>50	100	Total
Images	14	13	5	2	66	**100**
Successful	14	8	1	1	66	**90**
False negative	0	5	4	1	0	**10**
False positive			0			

Table 2a. Results – object recognition based on matching of features for the mug by Iterative Correspondence

Occlusion (%)	0	<25	<50	>50	100	Total
Images	28	4	7	0	61	**100**
Successful	21	3	2	0	61	**87**
False negative	7	1	5	0	0	**13**
False positive			0			

Table 2b. Results – object recognition based on matching of features for the measuring tape by Iterative Correspondence

5. Second approach – Triples

5.1 Introduction

As one searches the database for features only, much of the geometric information inherent in an image is not considered since the features do not contain any information about their relationship to other features. This is considered to be a flaw in the previous approach where the geometric information has to be considered afterward. To rectify this, the concept of *triples* is introduced. As suggested by the name, these are triplets of features. The triples are created as every possible combination of three features.

The total number of triples created with n features is given by n(n-1)(n-2) /6. If n is 20 this results in 1,140 triples but, since this increases with order 3 as n increases, a practical limit is reached fairly quickly. At 40 features we have 9,880 triples, which is approaching the reasonable limit for an image. While this is a large number it should be remembered that gold images do not need to have as many features/triples—since the object will be in relative isolation—and will, therefore, pose a smaller burden on the database.
Each triple can now be considered as a triangle on the image with a feature at each vertex. This leads to a number of intrinsic geometric properties that are scale and orientation independent. This is delightful since it allows us to analyse any image for similar triples without regard to the size or orientation. We can extract several measures from each feature.

5.2 Triple orientation

The orientation of a triple can be uniquely defined in many ways. We choose to define the axis of the triple as that directed line that bisects the shortest side of the triangle formed from the three features and passes through the opposite vertex (Fig. 11).
This provides the most accurate measure of orientation. The vertex thus bisected is called the *top* of the triangle and is considered to be the 1st feature in the triple. The 2nd and 3rd features have the median and largest sides opposite them respectively (Fig. 11).
While the triple orientation is not a rotation-independent parameter it is very useful to us in deriving the following parameters that are rotation-independent, as well as providing a useful parameter to use later in discovering the rotation angle between the images.

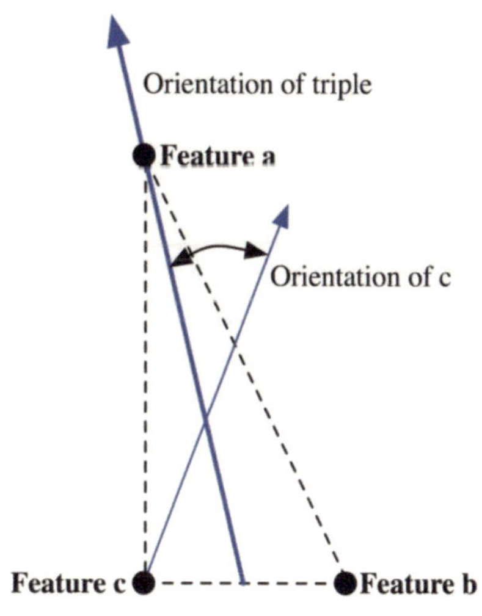

Fig. 11. Triangle formed from three features in an image. The triple orientation is given by the line bisecting the shortest side and passing through the opposite vertex. Feature orientations are given relative to this line.

5.3 Maximum and minimum distances

If one takes the longest and shortest sides of the triangle and divides them by the average length of the three sides one will have two numbers that are scale independent and which code for the shape of the triangle.

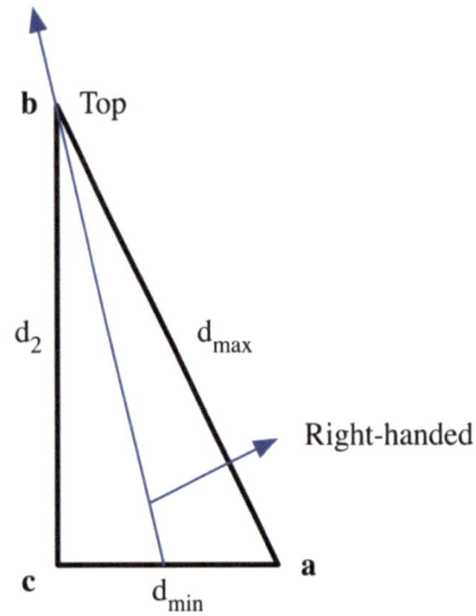

Fig. 12. Triple showing the definition of the top vertex and handedness.

5.4 Maximum and minimum angles

Since the internal angles of a triangle will sum to 180° we can describe the shape of the triangle with only two angles. These are chosen as the largest and smallest angles. They have the important property that, like the shape of the triangle, they are scale- and rotation-independent.

These two angles have an advantage over using the distances in that, for a flat triangle, the shape is highly sensitive to the distances but not to the angles.

5.5 Triple handedness

The parameters of the triple already mentioned will constrain it completely, apart from its chirality; it will appear identical to its mirror image. To break this symmetry we can define a *handedness* for the triple as the side of the orientation vector on which the longest side lies when the orientation vector points directly upwards. If the longest side is then on the right, it is a right-handed triple (see Fig. 12).

5.6 Maximum and minimum relative orientations

The relative orientations of the three features at the vertices of the triangle provide orientation- and scale-independent parameters. In this work the relative orientations are defined with respect to the orientation of the triple, i.e. the relative orientations are the clockwise angle between the triple's orientation and the feature's orientation.

Note that all three are independent of the shape of the triple's triangle.

5.7 Disambiguation

Since triples are to be matched with regard to their shape, it is important that there should be no possibility of ambiguity. For instance, were two lengths of a triple similar to each other, it is possible that in some images, one would be measured as the longer and in other images the reverse might occur. Accordingly, only those triples are accepted for comparison where there is a difference of at least 10% in the three lengths. Although this discards some triples, those remaining are always unambiguous.

5.8 Comparison strategies

We assume that we have done a coarse match, as described in section 4.2 and have winnowed our 300,000 views down to a small number, ordered in terms of probability. Our task is once again to hold up a gold view against a brass view and to determine whether they are the same. There may be about 10,000 triples in the gold view and perhaps 20,000 in the brass view. Depending on the makeup of the triple, i.e. lobe-lobe-lobe or lobe-line-arc etc., the triple will have up to 16 discriminators associated with it. To compare them sequentially and for each discriminator implies up to 3,200,000,000 tests. Many of these are comparisons for matching within a threshold rather than simple checks for equality. Consequently, on the face of it, this method will be computationally very intense.

On further consideration, we see that, if we order the tests in order of discrimination, we will quickly cut down possibilities. Experimentally we found that, if the test for equality of largest angle between triples was run first, this cut out 19 out of 20 contenders and as we followed this by other stern discriminators, the total fell very rapidly. Secondly we note that such an overall comparison can readily be done with parallel processing. Since this technology is being progressively deployed, the problem will become steadily more tractable. Currently, it is completely feasible to deploy the problem on an NVIDIA processor with 256 parallel cores and it is unlikely that this will be the high water mark for hardware. Thirdly, it is possible to sort the triples on the basis of a discriminator and to perform a binary search to the upper and lower limits of acceptance of this discriminator and then do a detailed comparison for those triples within these limits. In this way, 20,000 tests can be reduced to about 100. So, although this method is computationally intensive, this need not be its death knell.

As a first step, we can produce a list of triples which satisfy the sixteen discriminators for lobe-lobe-lobe triples (and the somewhat smaller number for other triples). But these matches are not necessarily true so we need to introduce further geometrical information to eliminate bad matches. For this the angle of rotation between the images and the dilation are needed. We used the method of clustering described above in 4.3.1. At the end of this procedure we are left with only those triples that have been matched with regard to all the discriminators and have the same orientation and size relative to the gold image.

5.9 Global application

We applied this technique to all the triples in the gold image and ran them against all the triples in the brass image, without regard to the time taken for the comparison. Our results seemed to indicate that performance was dominated by threshold settings in the comparison of discriminators; there were just too many possible solutions and inevitably each gold triple would match too many spurious brass triples. Avenues for advance were still open in that tests for orientation and dilation could narrow down the huge list of possible matches. But we elected to abandon this approach in favour of a more selective criterion.

5.10 Matching of isolumes using triples

By the nature of the process by which they are generated, isolumes provide strong organisation of all the features in the image; those features which appear on an isolume have an enduring relationship with each other. If, therefore we only compare all the triples on a gold isolume against all the triples on each successive brass isolume, we can expect to reduce

the number of possible combinations. We would expect the ratio of matches for matching isolumes to be very much larger than for unmatching isolumes. In this enterprise, we are not using aggregated super-isolumes but merely individual isolumes.
First, we perform the coarse search of 4.2. This results in a short list of gold views which might match our brass view. We then hold up each gold view against the brass view to see if it matches. In this process, we run the triples of the first isolume against the triples of each brass isolume and so on through the list of brass isolumes. Then we do this for the second gold isolume etc.

5.11 Results

The results for object recognition based on feature triples (discussed in section 5.10.) are shown in Table 3(a) for the mug and Table 3(b) for the measuring tape.

Occlusion (%)	0	<25	<50	>50	100	Total
Images	14	13	5	2	66	**100**
Successful	14	10	2	1	63	**90**
False negative	0	3	3	1	0	**7**
False positive			3			**3**

Table 3(a). Results for object recognition based on feature triples for the mug.

Occlusion (%)	0	<25	<50	>50	100	Total
Images	28	4	7	0	61	**100**
Successful	28	2	7	0	60	**97**
False negative	0	2	0	0	0	**2**
False positive			1			**1**

Table 3(b). Results for object recognition based on feature triples for the measuring tape.

5.12 Discussion

It can be seen from a comparison of the totals in Tables 2 and 3 that the introduction of triples has significantly increased the ability of the system to identify the gold objects, at a cost in false positives. In particular, the recognition of the unoccluded tape has been raised to 100% (compared with 75% for object recognition based on feature matching) as well as raising the recognition of the occluded tape from 45% (5 out of 11 images) to 82% (9 out of 11 images).
On this basis, and remembering that these results are for a fairly small library, this method has shown the potential to be used for generalised object recognition.

6. Third approach – Isolume matching

6.1 Introduction

Analysis of an image produces a number of isolumes and a set of features threaded on the isolumes. The first approach, enumeration, viewed the body of data as being the features, each with attendant descriptors, but essentially unrelated to each other until a match had been suggested. At this point it was feasible to introduce geometrical relationships between features in order to confirm the match. The second approach, triples, introduced arbitrary matchings of three features and embodied the geometrical relationships between them. This approach produced a very large number of triples which had to be compared. The new scheme, Isolume Matching, seeks to reduce the scale of the search by using the intrinsic ordering of the features by the isolume. Their order on the isolume is fundamental information and can be used advantageously.

With this in mind, we looked at the efficacy of matching contours on the basis of the order and properties of the features. It is immediately apparent that the possible scope of this work is large because we might aim at producing a robust search that would not stumble if a feature were missing either in the gold or the brass isolume. It would also tolerate a spurious feature in either isolume. But, at the outset, we consider a simple search that demands only that two isolumes be deemed to be matched when the order of the features is identical and corresponding properties match to within some threshold. Again, we are certain that later workers will massively refine our crude first efforts - provided that we show them to have merit.

We are operating, after the coarse search of section 4.2, on a candidate gold view and the question is whether this matches the current brass view. Typically the gold view will have up to 100 isolumes, each with ten or twenty features. The brass image will probably have slightly more isolumes, say 150. It is necessary to compare each gold isolume with each brass isolume - 15,000 comparisons. We do not demand that the isolumes should match over their entire lengths. It is probable that a match over quite a small number of features will be significant. Each feature must match a number of attributes that will depend on the feature. Lobes must match four attributes, including type.

Given the level of precision of these attributes we estimate that we can distinguish an unknown lobe against a known lobe to a discrimination of one part in 480. This opinion derives from discrimination to a factor of 3, based on feature type (lobe, line, arc), a discrimination of 10 based on area, 4 based on skewness and 4 based on kurtosis. These crude factors derive from our perception of the accuracy of the measurements. Lobes generally outnumber other features in most images by about 2:1. Lines provide a discrimination of one in three - solely on type. Arcs provide the same discrimination. We estimate that when we obtain five consecutive matching features, this generally provides a possible discrimination of the order of one part in a billion (say, three lobes and two non-lobes, i.e. 480x480x480x3x3). Of course this takes no account of the distribution of properties and, in practice our discrimination will be much less efficacious. But, once we have the crude match, it is likely to be true and, it is profitable to go to a more careful match where we can look into the geometrical relations between the five features. This latter, time-intensive comparison will only occur for very well-screened candidates.

6.2 Structure of the search

The logical structure of the search is simplified by introducing the concept of a cardinal feature. This has a different value for gold and brass. Call them $G_{Cardinal}$ and $B_{Cardinal}$. Then write a function called Compare(, , ,), which compares two features, one gold and one brass. The argument list of the function includes the values of the cardinal numbers and also includes D_{Gold} and D_{Brass}. These latter numbers indicate by how much we want to increment the cardinal value. For instance, an argument list of Compare($G_{Cardinal}$=1,$B_{Cardinal}$=5 ,D_{Gold} = 1,D_{Brass} = -1) would imply that on the isolumes in question, we were comparing feature number $G_{Cardinal} + D_{Gold} = 2$ on the gold isolume with feature number $B_{Cardinal} + D_{Brass} = 4$ on the brass isolume. This shorthand makes it very easy to keep track of five sequential comparisons in a nested IF structure. Clearly, as we lay feature number $G_{Cardinal}$ opposite feature number $B_{Cardinal}$, we can then sequentially compare these and the next four features by setting D_{Gold} and D_{Brass} from 0 through 4. Such a nested structure is simple to program. It is also relatively easy to check for the case where the order is reversed, in which case the values D_{Brass} would have opposite sign. As we become more sophisticated, this structure will lend itself to considering occluded and spurious features in either the gold or brass isolume. For the moment, we elect to use a five-feature check. The optimal value for this number must be determined by experiment in the fullness of time.

For the search, we set up two loops, running each gold isolume against each brass isolume. This is shown in Fig. 13.

Within each such confrontation between isolumes, we run sequentially through all the features of the gold isolume, setting each feature as $G_{Cardinal}$. For each of these features, run through all the brass isolume features setting each as $B_{Cardinal}$ and then running forward for up to five features. The test will almost always fail after one or two features and we can increment $B_{Cardinal}$ until we reach the end of the isolume. If it fails after one forward test, it attempts to match them in reverse order. If we get five matches, we do a 'Compare-in-Detail' test.

6.3 Compare-in-Detail

Assume that we have five sequentially matching features. We can then do further tests;

- Find the distances from the first non-line feature to each following non-line feature. Sum them and divide each of the above distances by this sum. The resulting numbers will be Scale- and rotation-invariant. Compare them severally with their brass equivalents. Then find that non-line feature that is farthest from the first non-line feature determined above. From this remote feature, find a set of distances to each non-line feature and normalise them using the above sum. Compare the equivalent values for brass and gold. This has the effect of taking a cross-bearing and demanding that all non-line features are in the same geometrical relationship to each other for gold and brass.
- For any arcs, normalise the radius with respect to this sum and compare between gold and brass.
- For lines, determine the angle of rotation between successive lines among the line features and demand that these angles be the same for gold and brass. This test will generally discriminate against mirror images.

After the initial match of five features and following it by the above protocol, the level of specificity is very precise and we can declare that the two portions of isolume do indeed match.

6.4 Evaluation of the method

We ran gold views of a mug and a tape against the hundred images of our database. For a particular gold view matched against a brass view, we ran perhaps 100 gold isolumes against

```
Hits = 0
For Gtrace = 1 To # gold isolumes
For gCardinal = 1 To # lobes this isolume
  For Btrace = 1 To # brass isolumes
    For bCardinal = 1 To #lobes this isolume
      If Compare(gCardinal, bCardinal, 0, 0) Then
        If Compare(gCardinal, bCardinal, 1, 1) Then
          If Compare(gCardinal, bCardinal, 2, 2) Then
            If Compare(gCardinal, bCardinal, 3, 3) Then
              If Compare(gCardinal, bCardinal, 4, 4) Then
                If CompareInDetailForward(gCardinal, bCardinal) Then
                  Hits = Hits + 1
                  Goto BailOut
                End If
              End If
            End If
          End If
        Else
          If Compare(gCardinal, bCardinal, 1, -1) Then
            If Compare(gCardinal, bCardinal, 2, -2) Then
              If Compare(gCardinal, bCardinal, 3, -3) Then
                If Compare(gCardinal, bCardinal, 4, -4) Then
                  If CompareInDetailBack(gCardinal, bCardinal) Then
                    Hits = Hits + 1
                    Goto BailOut
                  End If
                End If
              End If
            End If
          End If
        End If
      End If
    Next bCardinal
  Next Btrace
Next gCardinal
BailOut:
Next Gtrace
```

Fig. 13. Algorithm for Comparing Isolumes

perhaps 150 brass isolumes. If we found a match between five sequential features in the two isolumes we were comparing, we then did a 'Compare-in-Detail' test and perhaps declared that the isolumes matched. We then moved on to the next gold isolume. This has the effect that, when we recognise an object, the search is quicker than when we do not. At the end of the matching process, we are left with a fraction of all the gold isolumes which had counterparts in the brass image. Note that we only demand a match over five features and, when we have this, we look no further. Even without optimizing the code, the comparison of a gold view against a brass view took under a second. It seems that on a 2010 mid-range desktop computer, we can compare a gold with a brass image in under 50 milliseconds.

It might be that the crude fraction determined above could be improved by expressing it as the number of five-feature sequences matched between the two images as a fraction of the number of five-feature sequences available in the gold image. We used only the first, crude, comparison strategy because we found, experimentally that it gave us a sharp discrimination. Since we are only looking at a small part of the isolume we could expect that the lower, rectangular portion of the mug would look like the lower, rectangular portion of a tape or, indeed, like the lower, rectangular portion of any rectangular object. Thus, when we ask, is the tape a mug, we will get a non-zero result because it is in fact a bit like a mug. However, if we ask, is an actual mug a mug, we will get a much more vehement result because there will be so many more isolumes that will match. The results are presented in Table 4.

Occlusion (%)	0	<25	<50	>50	100	Total
Images	14	13	5	2	66	**100**
Successful	14	6	2	1	66	**89**
False negative	0	7	3	1	0	**11**
False positive			0			0

Table 4(a). Results for object recognition based on Isolume Matching for the mug.

Occlusion (%)	0	<25	<50	>50	100	Total
Images	28	3	7	0	62	**100**
Successful	25	3	2	0	62	**92**
False negative	3	0	5	0	0	**8**
False positive			0			0

Table 4(b). Results for object recognition based on Isolume Matching for the measuring tape.

7. Evaluation of the three methods

Examination of Tables 2, 3 and 4 allows a crude comparison of the three methods. All of the methods provide clear and unambiguous recognition of unoccluded objects, with very few false positives. In fact, on the basis of the tables, there is little to choose between them. Their performance for occluded objects is also similar.

In terms of computational burden, the third method has a clear advantage. It also has the advantage of being conceptually more akin to the human recognition process. Finally, it seems to have more room for improvement than the others. We have deployed a very crude application and found very good results. Clearly, as we extend the application, as we have already done for the other two methods, we can expect a performance improvement. The isolume matching method also lends itself to very elegant general searches of the whole database. We will not discuss this here but we can envisage very much more precise and quicker general searches than the coarse feature search discussed in section 4.2.

The tables of results were produced in order to provide a sense of the performance of the three methods for comparison. The tables make the statement that a particular object was or was not recognised in an image. But the biological experience does not deal in such certainties. All perceptions should be considered as probabilities. In fact, it is logically impossible in the biosphere to ascribe certainty to any event or condition because of the solipsistic argument. "But", you argue, "I am as sure as I need to be that this computer screen is on my desk." That is true, but if you were permitted just one glance, lasting a fraction of a second (this corresponds to the conditions which led to the above tables, where we are comparing one glance with a reality defined by the gold view), into a strange office, you could not make that assertion; it is only after you had verified the assumption two or three times that you could make the statement, and believe it, whether it were true or not. This is the human condition. And it must be the condition of a robot operating in the same circumstances.

As we set about producing vision for our embodied intelligence, we would be wise to structure our determination of reality in a similar way. We therefore need, not a decision as to whether the object is present in the picture, but a probability. This probability can only be determined by extensive experience of the method, predicting and comparing with reality. Consider that we examined a brass image and found 50% of the isolumes of a gold image to be present. In another brass image we might find 75% of them to be present. On this basis, we would certainly not be able to assign probabilities to the two findings. We would need to operate in the world and find the actual probabilities of independently-verified existence and then form a non-linear calculus in order to relate proportion of isolumes recognised with probability of existence. Even then, some objects might be more definitely recognised than others so that this functionality would have to be dependent on the object. Fortunately, we do not need to explore this concept at this stage.

As we consider using our method, the unavoidable problem occurs that certain objects are intrinsically similar and, as we deal with the variation within a universal classification, we can expect positive responses from many similar objects. It is our observation that we can be guided by the question we have asked the database, in the following sense. Not unlike the human perceptual system, we will operate essentially on the basis of perceptual hypotheses. Thus, guided by our coarse search, we always ask, "Is this gold view present in this brass image?" And we will get an answer couched in the form of the proportion of isolumes of the exemplar which we have recognised. But a lower value might be the result either of partial occlusion or else divergence in appearance between the object in the brass image and our exemplar. This uncertainty might be resolved by a further exploration. Imagine that there is a mug but no tape in the brass image. When we ask if a mug is present we get a matched isolume proportion of ξ. When we ask whether a tape is present, we will generally get a much lower but non-zero value for ξ. This is because both mug and tape have a rectangular lower section. Clearly, when we have explored all the probable options of what objects might be present, we will be either secure in our uncertainty or else have a clear judgement as to which possible object has an overwhelming ξ.

8. The Problem of Universals

8.1 The metaphysical problem stated

Plato (about 350 BC) was concerned with the theory of forms and presented his allegory of the cave where denizens could see only the shadows of objects. He argued that we see only imperfect forms of the ideal unchanging forms; these alone are true knowledge. Thus the cup which we see, in all its varieties, is a corrupt exemplar of a perfect cup. We can see how Christian doctrine was not averse to this view. Diogenes of Sinope offered the refreshing observation that "I've seen Plato's cups and table, but not his cupness and tableness" (Hicks, 1925). Philosophers over the ages have weighed into this delightful debate which is not susceptible to proof but can be thoroughly discussed.

8.2 Universals in the world of AV

We argued above that there are some 15,000 nouns which might be known to educated persons. One of these is 'cup' but clearly there is a huge variation of objects - from tea cup to D-cup, all of which fall under the universal of cup. How shall we deal with this problem which, on the face of it, is very difficult? We hesitate to appear to be wiser than Plato, but can nevertheless offer a simple solution;

If we advance the proposition that all exemplars of a universal can be transformed into each other by simple physical distortion, our problem becomes really quite easy. Consider the tea cup which we can deform quite easily by barreling the sides and reducing the base, into a bra cup. If we couldn't do this, the English language, in all its whimsy, would not have called both of them 'cup'. This is a fairly profound philosophical statement that the ideal of cupness resides in our perceptions and we are prepared to use it on those objects which satisfy our criteria for 'cupness'. The fact that the D-cup does not have a handle and yet retains 'cupness' implies that the presence of a handle is not important. We think this puts us on the side of Plato, rather than Diogenes.

8.3 Application of universals to our method

Consider the universal 'car'. As we view cars from a distance and are not concerned, for instance, with their differing hood ornaments, we see a considerable similarity among them; enough for us to ascribe a universal name to them. This universal is not ascribed on the basis of function but of shape. We can see that, by a fairly clear and simple process of distortion, we can morph an SUV (sport utility vehicle) into a sedan into a sports car.

As we consider one of our twenty cardinal views of a car, we immediately perceive that there is a need to standardise these views so that all views from the top of the car are the same, whatever car it is. We can readily agree on the three Cartesian axes within which we would embed all cars, probably choosing the road surface as one of them. In fact, we seem predisposed mentally to assign cardinal axes to objects which have symmetries. There may even be a deep-seated inclination to view their structure in terms of quadripedal symmetry. We see the clear advantages, to our AV calculus, of viewing objects in this way. Let us say that we have the same view of two different cars. We assume that, based on our agreed cardinal axes, these are the same views. Then, we contend that the one view can be changed into the other by a process of topologically simple distortion. Further, following the conception of Minkowski, our space is locally 'flat'. This is to say that the transformations do not have areas of locally intense distortion but, rather, provide little local change but progressively larger change with distance. By analogy, local space-time is flat, but over cosmological distance, curvature is significant.

This is fortunate because it allows our method of object recognition by matching isolumes to handle universals. As we test for similarity between a gold (sedan) isolume and a brass (SUV) isolume, we see that we are considering five nearest neighbour features. These tend to be close together and over this short span, the distortion is small. Therefore the angles and distances are not significantly changed and we will tend to record the concordance between the two isolumes and therefore the similarity between the sedan and the SUV. The proportion of isolumes confirmed will decrease as the views become more dissimilar.

We have merely hinted at the way in which the problem of universals can be handled but it seems that the way forward will fall within our compass.

8.4 Flexible Objects: The hand problem

8.4.1 The problem stated

As we consider an image of a hand, composed as it is of, sixteen independently moveable sections, we are struck by how difficult it would be, visually, to decipher the complex structure. This is an extreme example of the general problem of articulated objects (artus L. = joint). This extends by infinitesimal degrees to the problem of flexible objects such as a shark or a hosepipe.

8.4.2 The problem resolved

Mature consideration shows that the joint problem does not fall within the bailiwick of artificial vision because there cannot be any single image of a hand which can show the operation of a joint.

The way in which a joint operates can only be seen from a succession of images and only through the lens of an artificial intelligence apparatus which can make sense of all the constituent parts of the hand and what they are doing in the course of time. How then shall we recognise a static hand? This is an important problem in artificial vision and its gravity is demonstrated by the fact that primates have nerves in the optic bundle which fire only when they see their own hand. Clearly hands spend a lot of time within our field of vision and need to be managed. As a solution, we propose the following;

Consider that the fingers of the hand tend to move in concert as it changes its posture progressively from clenched to splayed. If we declared a clenched fist to be an object, a splayed hand to be another and perhaps two other objects at intermediate conditions, then we could interpolate between these conditions by the direct application of our method. When the hand is adopting strenuous postures such as American Sign Language, we must perforce analyse it as a succession of sixteen objects, each of which is known to us.

The notion of flexible mating between objects (as between the first and second digits of the forefinger) must be grist for the mill of a prepositional calculus - which does not fall within the scope of this chapter.

9. Conclusion

We have outlined a method which, we think, will be adequate for our needs as we proceed to develop an embodied artificial intelligence. The method seems to have no antecedent in the literature and uses concepts which have not been previously considered. We favour the approach of isolume recognition rather than comparison of features or triple matching. It seems that the performance level on our limited dataset is good and that the computational burden is not intractable.

Our work shines a dim light on what might be a broad, sunny upland, rich in promise and new concepts.

10. References

Amores, J.; Sebe, N. & Radeva, P. (2007). Context-based object-class recognition and retrieval by generalized correlograms, *IEEE Transactions on Pattern Analysis and Machine Intelligence*, Vol. 29, No. 10, pp. 1818-1833.

Ballard, D. & Brown, C. (1982). *Computer Vision*, 1st Edition, Prentice Hall, ISBN 0131653164, Eaglewood Cliffs, New Jersey, USA.

Brown, M. & Lowe, D. (2007). Automatic panoramic image stitching using invariant features, *International Journal of Computer Vision*, Vol. 74, No. 1, pp. 59-73.

Bryson, B. (1990). *The mother tongue: English and how it got that way*, Harper Collins, ISBN 0-380-71543-0, New York, USA.

Conway-Morris, S. (1998). *The crucible of creation*, Oxford University Press, ISBN 0-19-850256-7, Oxford, England.

Da Fontura Costa, L. & Cesar, R. (2009). *Shape Classification and Analysis Theory and Practice*, 2nd Ed., A. Laplante (Editor), Taylor and Francis Group, ISBN 13:978-0-8493-7929-1, Florida, USA.

Dhua, A. & Cutzu, F. (2006). Hierarchical, generic to specific multi-class object recognition, *Proceedings of the 18th International Conference on Pattern Recognition (ICPR'06)*, Vol. 1, pp. 783-788, 0-7695-2521-0/06, Hong Kong, August 2006.

Drew, M.; Lee, T. & Rova, A. (2009). Shape retrieval with eigen-CSS search, *Image and Vision Computing*, Vol. 27, pp. 748-755.

Flemmer, R. (2009). A scheme for an embodied artificial intelligence, Conference Special Session Keynote Address, *Proceedings of the 4th International Conference on Autonomous Robots and Agents (ICARA)*, pp. 1-9, Wellington, New Zealand, February 2009.

Gao, J.; Xie, Z. & Wu, X. (2007). Generic object recognition with regional statistical models and layer joint boosting, *Pattern Recognition Letters*, Vol. 28, pp. 2227-2237.

Gregory, R. (1978). *Eye and brain*, 3rd edition, World University Library, McGraw-Hill, ISBN: 0-07-024665-3, New York, USA.

Hicks, R. (1925). *The lives and opinions of eminent philosophers by Diogenes Laertius*, Translation, W. Heinemann, London, England.

Hutcheson, G. (2005). Moore's Law: the history and economics of an observation that changed the world, *The Electrochemical Society Interface*, Vol. 14, No.1, pp. 17-21.

Hutchinson, J. (2001). Culture, communication and an information age madonna, *IEEE Professional Communication Society Newsletter*, Vol. 45, No. 3, pp. 1-6.

Levi-Setti, R. (1993). *Trilobites*, University of Chicago Press, ISBN 0-226-47451-8, Chicago, Illinois, USA.

Lew, M.; Sebe, N.; Djeraba, C. & Jain, R., (2006). Content-based multimedia information retrieval: state of the art and challenges, *ACM Transactions on Multimedia Computing, Communications and Applications*, Vol. 2, No. 1, pp. 1-19.

Osher, S. & Fedkiw, R. (2003). *Level set methods and dynamic implicit surfaces*, Antman, S.; Marsden, J. & Sirovich, L. (Editors), Springer, ISBN 978-0-387-95482-0, , New York, USA.

Rosenfeld, A. (1987). *Readings in computer vision: issues, problems, principles and paradigms*, Fischler, M. & Firschein, O. (Editors), Morgan Kauffmann Reading Series, ISBN 0-934613-33-8, pp. 3-12, San Francisco, California, USA.

Valentine, J.; Jablonski, D. & Ersin, D. (1999). Fossils, molecules and embryos: new perspectives on the Cambrian explosion, *Development*, Vol. 126, No. 5, pp 851-859.

14

Small Object Recognition Techniques Based on Structured Template Matching for High-Resolution Satellite Images

Toshio Modegi[1], Tomoaki Inazawa[2], Tsugio Chiba[2] and Chiaki Kobayashi[3]
[1]*Media Technology Research Center, Dai Nippon Printing Co., Ltd.*
[2]*Infoserve Inc.*
[3]*Earth Remote Sensing Data Analysis Center*
Japan

1. Introduction

We are developing infrastructure tools of wide-area monitoring for disaster damaged areas or traffic conditions, using earth observation satellite images. In these days, resolution of optical sensors installed in earth observation satellites has been highly improved. In case of the panchromatic image captured by the QuickBird (DigitalGlobe, 2008), the ground-level resolution is about 0.6 [m], which makes possible to recognize each automobile on roads or parking lots.

The previous satellite image analysis works have been mainly focused on area segmentation and classification problems (Giovanni Poggi et al., 2005), and object recognition targets have been limited to large objects such as traffic roads or buildings (Qi Ming Qin et al., 2005), using high-resolution panchromatic satellite images. Whereas, there have been a lot of works on recognizing automobiles in aerial images including the paper (Tao Zhao et al., 2001), however, there have been almost any works trying to recognize such small objects as automobiles in satellite images excluding (So Hee Jeon et al., 2005). This previous work (So Hee Jeon et al., 2005) has been applying template matching methods to recognizing small objects but its recognition rate has been very poor because of insufficient pixel information for pattern matching.

In the previous paper (Modegi T., 2008), we proposed an interactive high-precision template matching tool for satellite images, but it took amount of calculation times and object searching area was limited and far from practical uses. In order to overcome this problem, we apply a structured identification approach similar to the work (Qu Jishuang et al., 2003). In this paper, we propose a three-layered structured template matching method, which enables recognizing small objects such as automobiles in satellite images at very little calculation load. The first layer is focusing on extracting candidate areas, which have metallic-reflection optical characteristics, where any types of transportation objects are included. The second layer is identification and removal of excessively extracted candidate areas such as roads and buildings, which have the similar optical characteristics but do not include our targets. The third layer is identifying each automobile object within the focusing area using our proposing conceptual templates (Modegi T., 2008), which are learned patterns based on user's operations, based on our improved high-speed template-matching algorithm. The following sections describe specific algorithms of each layer.

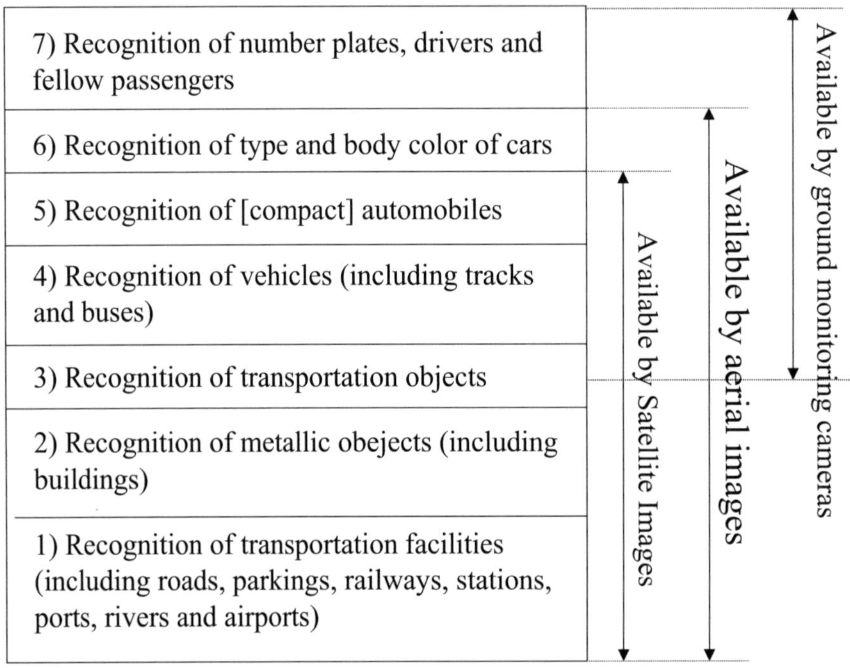

Fig. 1. 7-layered structured recognition model for automobiles on the ground.

2. Proposing structured template matching method

Figure 1 shows our proposing structured recognition model for automobiles on the ground (Modegi T., 2009), which resembles 7-layered communication protocols called as OSI (Open System Interconnection) designed by the ISO (International Standard Organization). The highest recognition level has been already operated by the Japanese police, known as "N-System", by installing a lot of monitoring cameras along highways. The current available high-resolution earth observation satellites cover up to the fifth level in Fig.1.

Figure 2 shows our proposing structured template matching method for recognizing small objects in satellite images. The first matching is called as a micro-template matching, and it extracts candidate areas thoroughly including target small objects by non-linear heuristic filtering with micro-block templates. This candidate means pixel blocks indicating metallic reflection characteristics, which any types of transport objects including automobiles have in common. This process can be made at very little calculation load and also decrease the following third matching calculation load.

The second matching is called as a clustered micro-template matching, and it removes excessively matched relatively large candidate areas, which do not include target small objects with multiple 8-neighbored connected micro-block templates called as a clustered micro-template. This process also can be made at very little calculation load and decrease more the following third matching calculation load.

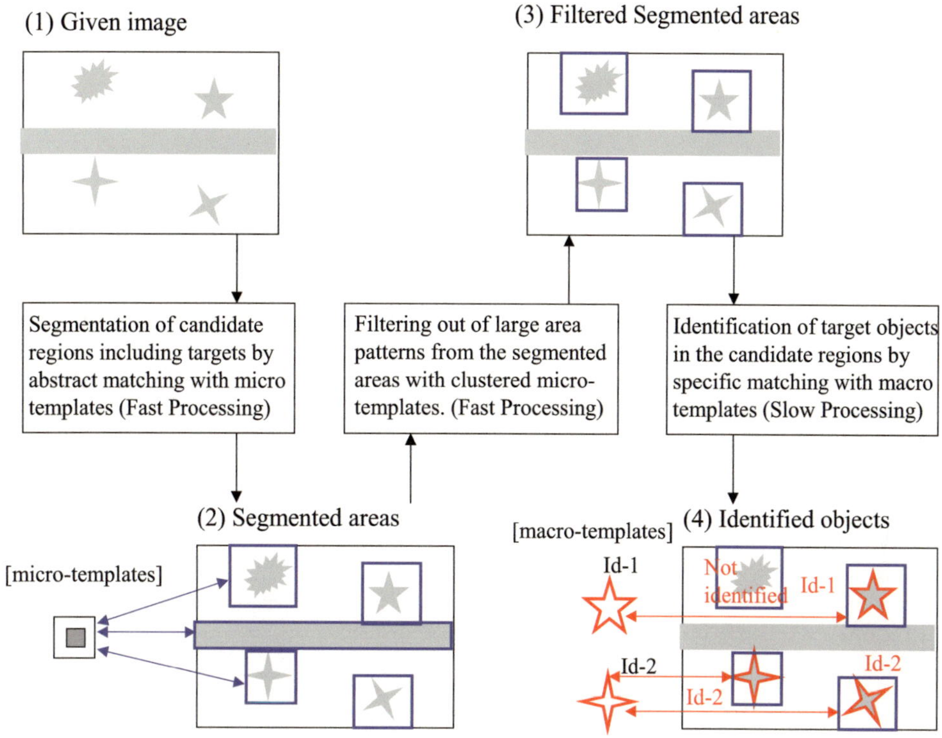

Fig. 2. Concept of structured template matching method for recognizing small objects in satellite images.

The third matching is called as a macro-template matching whose size is almost the same as the target object, and it identifies each object in the segmented candidate areas by the pixel-value correlation based pattern matching shown in the paper (Modegi T., 2008). This process needs a lot of calculation times but its calculation areas will be shrunken by the first and second matching processes.

3. Algorithms of proposing template matching methods

3.1 Micro-template matching

The Figure 3 shows a concept of micro-template matching, which defines binary mask value $M(x,y)$ for given 256 gray-scale image $I(x,y)$ ($0 \leq x \leq N_x-1$, $0 \leq y \leq N_y-1$). This process determines whether optical reflection values of each pixel block have metallic characteristics or not, by a heuristic filtering process. In other words, we determine each tiny area as shown in Fig.3 would be a part of transportation materials which we are searching. As this determination logic, we can use our following described heuristic rules defined between some pixels in the micro-template.

In case of 4 × 4 pixel micro-template shown in Fig. 3, we separate 2 × 2 inside pixels V_{ik} (k=1,4) from the other 12 outside pixels V_{ok} (k=1,12). Using these pixel values, we calculate the following 7 statistical parameters: the minimum value of outside pixels V_{omin}, the maximum value of outside pixels V_{omax}, the minimum value of inside pixels V_{imin} , the maximum value of inside pixels V_{imax}, the average value of outside pixels V_{oave}, the average value of inside pixels V_{iave}, the standard deviation value of outside pixels V_{dir}.

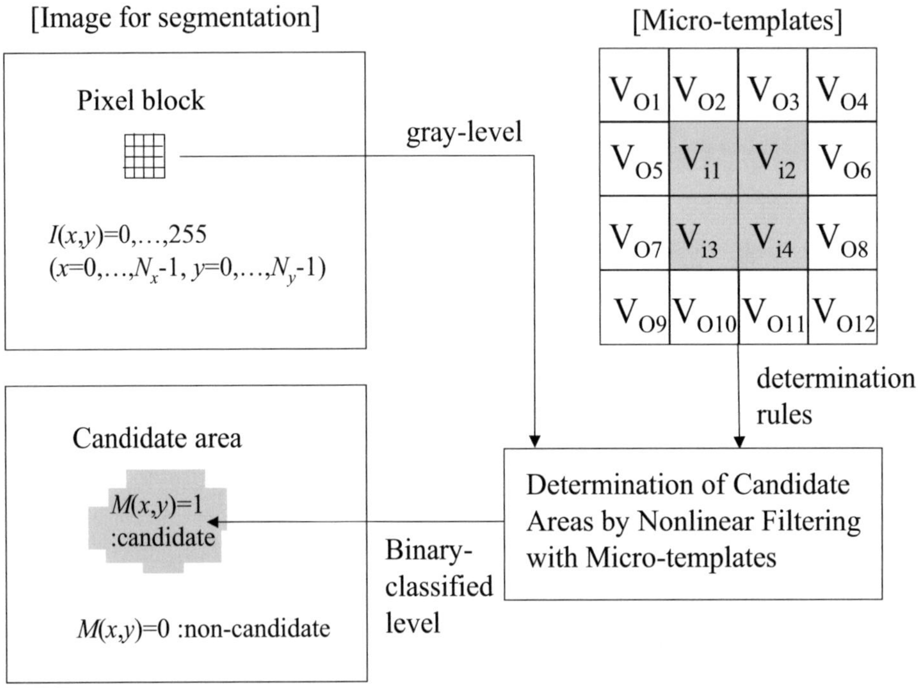

Fig. 3. Concept of micro-template matching for extracting candidate areas.

$$\begin{aligned}
V_{omin} &= Min_{k=1}^{12}\,[V_{ok}]\,,\\
V_{omax} &= Max_{k=1}^{12}\,[V_{ok}]\,,\\
V_{imin} &= Min_{k=1}^{4}\,[V_{ik}]\,,\\
V_{imax} &= Max_{k=1}^{4}\,[V_{ik}]\,,\\
V_{oave} &= (\textstyle\sum_{k=1}^{12} V_{ok})/12\,,\\
V_{iave} &= (\textstyle\sum_{k=1}^{4} V_{ik})/4\,,\\
V_{dir} &= \{\textstyle\sum_{k=1}^{12} (V_{ok}-V_{oave})^2/12\,\}^{1/2}\,.
\end{aligned} \tag{1}$$

We apply the above template to its nearest 4 × 4 pixel block values of each pixel of given satellite panchromatic image $I(x,y)$, and determine it would be included in candidate areas or not by the following rules. We have to consider both two kinds of candidate patterns, one is the inside part is brighter than the outside and the other is its negative pattern. In order to determine some pixel (x,y) included in candidate $M(x,y)$=1, the following 5 conditions should be satisfied using the 7 predetermined slice levels: S_{aoi}, S_{doi}, S_{omin}, S_{omax}, S_{imin}, S_{imax}, and S_{dir}.

These 7 kinds of slice levels can be defined interactively by indicating areas where target objects are definitely included on the image displayed screen. For each pixel in our indicated areas, we calculate the 7 statistical parameters based on the equation (1), and using either the minimum or maximum statistical parameters, we can define each of the slice levels as the following.

$$
\begin{aligned}
&1)\ |V_{oave} - V_{iave}| > S_{aoi}.\\
&(2)\ V_{omax} - V_{imin} > S_{doi},\ \text{if } V_{omax} - V_{imin} > V_{imax} - V_{omin}.\\
&\text{Or, } V_{imax} - V_{omin} > S_{doi},\ \text{if } V_{imax} - V_{omin} > V_{omax} - V_{imin}.\\
&3)\ V_{oave} > S_{omin} \text{ and } V_{oave} < S_{omax}.\\
&4)\ V_{iave} < S_{imin},\ \text{if } V_{oave} > V_{iave}.\\
&\text{Or, } V_{iave} > S_{imax},\ \text{if } V_{iave} > V_{oave}.\\
&5)\ V_{dir} > S_{dir}.
\end{aligned}
\tag{2}
$$

$$
\begin{aligned}
&1)\ S_{aoi} = \mathrm{MIN}[\,|V_{oave} - V_{iave}|\,] \bullet 0.9.\\
&2)\ S_{doi} = \mathrm{MIN}[S_1, S_2] \bullet 0.9.\\
&S_1 = V_{omax} - V_{imin},\ \text{if } V_{omax} - V_{imin} > V_{imax} - V_{omin}.\\
&S_2 = V_{imax} - V_{omin},\ \text{if } V_{imax} - V_{omin} > V_{omax} - V_{imin}.\\
&3)\ S_{omin} = \mathrm{MIN}[V_{oave}] \bullet 0.9,\\
&S_{omax} = MAX[V_{oave}] \bullet 1.1.\\
&4)\ S_{imin} = MAX[V_{iave}] \bullet 1.1,\ \text{if } V_{oave} > V_{iave}.\\
&S_{imax} = MIN[V_{iave}] \bullet 0.9,\ \text{if } V_{iave} > V_{oave}.\\
&5)\ S_{dir} = \mathrm{MIN}[V_{dir}] \bullet 0.9.
\end{aligned}
\tag{3}
$$

In case of the pixel value of given monochrome image is between 0 and 255, we give typically these slice levels as S_{aoi}=15, S_{doi}=80, S_{omin}=100, S_{omax}=160, S_{imin}=35, S_{imax}=245, and S_{dir}=10 .

3.2 Clustered micro-template matching

In the first micro-template matching, all of metallic reflection characteristic areas are selected as candidates, but these characteristics are not limited to transportation materials. In general, edge parts of buildings and roads are the same characteristics and selected as candidates. Ironically these non-transport areas are larger than our target transport objects, and increase searching load of the next object identification processes. Therefore, in this section we provide an identifying and removing process of excessively selected candidate areas.

In general, incorrectly selected candidate areas such as edge parts of buildings and roads are long slender shape, which can be detected as multiple 8-neighbor connected micro-template blocks called as a clustered micro-template. However, some large areas such as parking lots may include target objects. Therefore, we have to distinguish these patterns from correctly selected large areas where multiple target objects are located closely, with their pixel value characteristics in the detected clustered area.

Figure 4 shows an algorithm of recognizing these incorrectly selected areas to be removed.

Fig.4-(1) shows 8 × 8 pixel parts of selected candidate areas, where painted pixels are determined as candidates based on the equation (2). On this image, we will search long candidate pixel clusters, whose height or width is larger than S_N-pixel length. In order to find these clusters, we will track 8-neighbored connected candidate pixels from the top-left pixel shown in Fig.4-(2) and Fig.4-(3). Supposing the previous candidate pixel $[i, j]$, in the horizontal direction we will find next candidate pixel from the three pixels $[i+1, j-1]$, $[i+1, j]$ and $[i+1, j+1]$ as shown in Fig.4-(2). Similarly, in the vertical direction we will find next candidate pixel from the three pixels $[i-1, j+1]$, $[i, j+1]$ and $[i+1, j+1]$ as shown in Fig.4-(3).

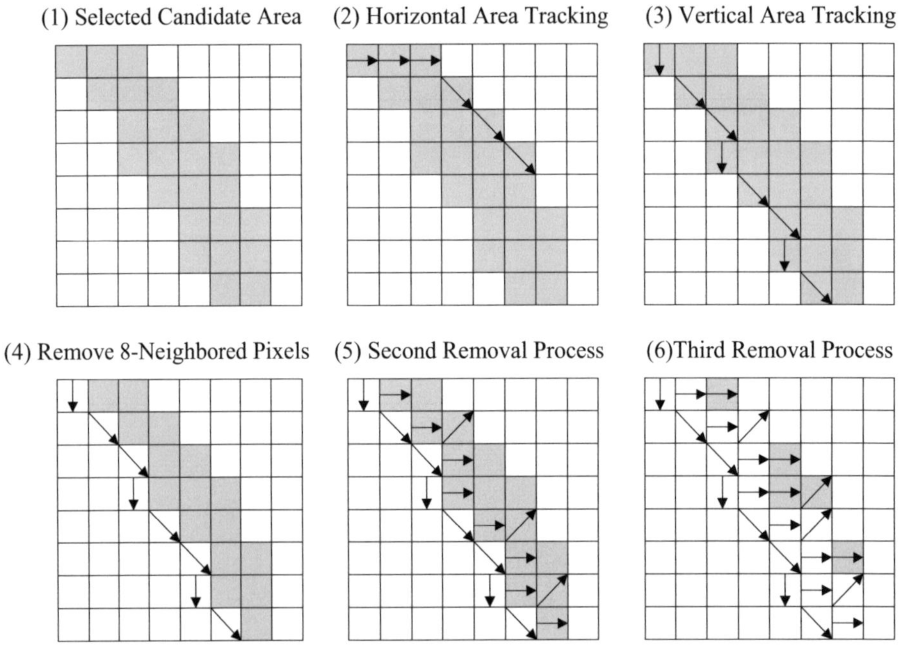

Fig. 4. Algorithm of clustered micro-template matching for removing excessively selected large candidate areas.

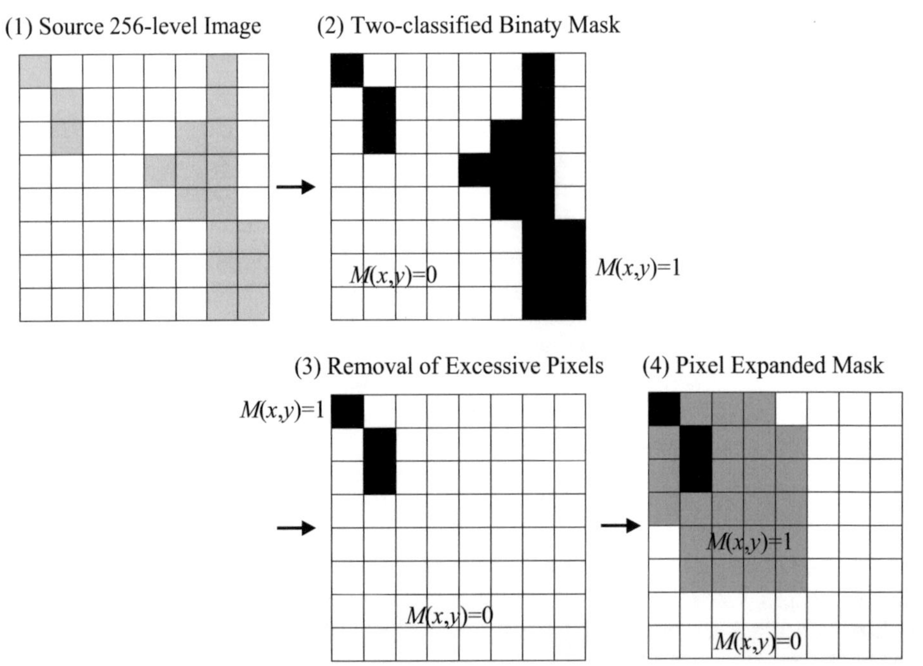

Fig. 5. Example of both micro-template matching and clustered micro-template matching processes.

In the either horizontal or vertical direction, if we can find successfully a S_N-pixel length cluster, we will calculate the minimum, maximum and average pixel value of this cluster as C_{min}, C_{max} and C_{ave}. Defining two slice levels as S_{cave} and S_{cmax}, if the following conditions are satisfied, we will extend the cluster by finding another 8-neighbored connected candidate pixels around previously found clustered pixels. Typically, we give to these slice levels as S_N =13, S_{cave}=50 and S_{cmax}=50, in case of the pixel value of given monochrome image is between 0 and 255.

$$C_{ave}>S_{cave} \text{ and } C_{max}-C_{min}>S_{cmax} . \tag{4}$$

Then we will reset all of tracked pixels in the extended cluster to non-candidate pixels as $M(x,y)=0$, whereas each of left candidate pixels $[x,y]$ will be extended to 4 × 4 candidate pixel block as $M(x+i,y+j)=1$ for $0\le i\le 3$ and $0\le j\le 3$.

Figure 4-(3) shows in the vertical direction we have found a 8-pixel length cluster (S_N =8), then we will reset all of tracked pixels in the cluster to non-candidate pixels as shown in Fig.4-(4). Furthermore, we extend removing areas around the removed cluster. Fig.4-(5) shows its second extended removed cluster, and Fig.4-(6) shows its third extended removed cluster.

Figure 5 shows a series of both micro-template matching and clustered micro-template matching processes. In Fig.5-(2), we found a small 3-pixel area and a large 15-pixel area with a micro-template. Then the larger area has been removed as $M(x,y)=0$ with a clustered micro-template as shown in Fig.5-(3). Finally, we extend each of left 3 candidate pixels to 4 × 4 candidate pixel block. Therefore, the size of final candidate area $M(x,y)=1$ becomes 27-pixel size.

3.3 Macro-template matching

As a final process, we identify each target object within the selected candidate areas using macro-template whose size is almost the same as that of searching objects. In order to execute this process efficiently, we propose using conceptual templates.

Figure 6 shows a concept of our proposing macro-template matching. The upper two objects have different shape, size and color each other. If these two objects are captured by a camera with some light sources, we can obtain tremendous kinds of images including 4 images shown in the middle part of Fig.6. In order to identify these objects, we have to prepare amounts of templates, at least two kinds of templates in this example. Our proposing macro-template matching makes possible identify the objects on these various kinds of captured images with small amounts of templates called as conceptual templates.

Our proposing macro-template matching process consists of two kinds of matching processes, the angle-independent and angle-dependent processes, based on the previous work (Modegi T., 2008). The first angle-independent process is mainly comparing a gray-level histogram of each determining block with that of a template. If the first matching process is successful, the second angle dependent process will be made. This is mainly comparing a normalized correlation coefficient of each determining block with those of several angle rotated image blocks of a template. If one of rotated image is fitted, the determining block will be identified as that template pattern.

Figure 7 shows how to define templates in our proposing macro-template matching algorithm. A template image $I_t(a,x,y)$ is originally an extracted block of pixels in some sample image, which is not necessarily this working image for search $I(x,y)$. Then this image

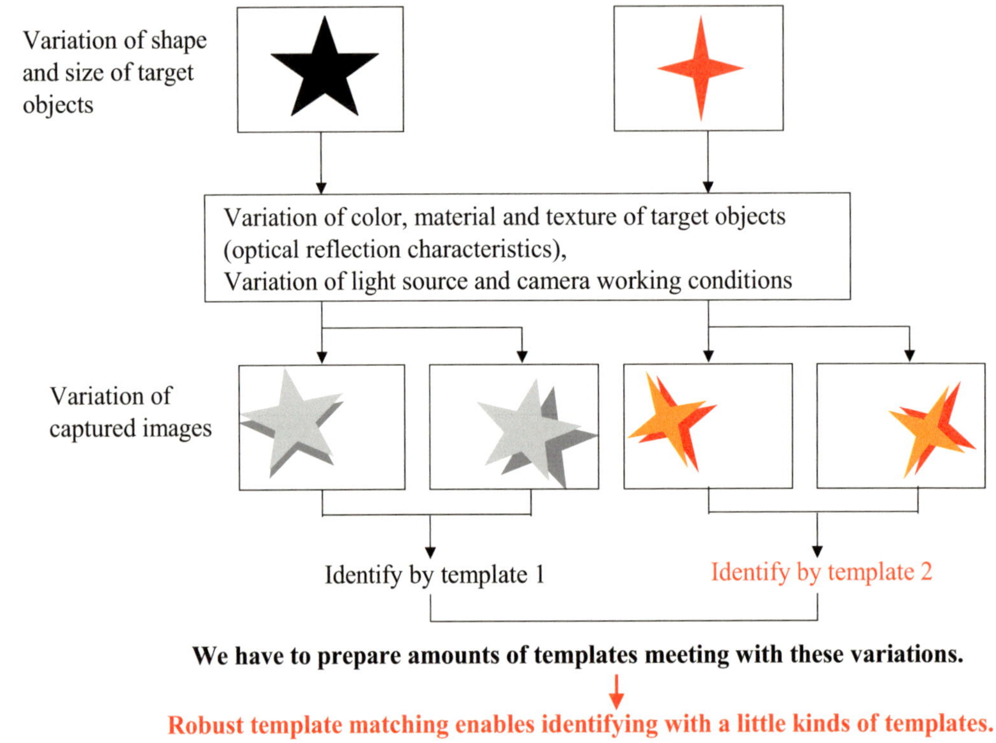

Fig. 6. Concept of our proposing template matching using conceptual templates.

is rotated to 8 kinds of angle for angle-dependent matching, and 8 kinds of template images are defined. In each defined $N \times N$ pixel template $I_t(a,x,y)$, two kinds of quadangle-shape outlines are defined for making mask image data $M_t(a,x,y)$. The inner outlines indicate the actual outline pattern of a target and the nearest patterns outside these inner outlines will be considered for another closely located object identification. The common area of the inner areas in all of angles shown the bottom of Fig.7 is used for the angle-independent template matching as the following algorithm (b) and (c), whereas the outer outlined area is used for the angle-dependent template matching as the following algorithm (d) and (e).

The following describes a specific algorithm of our proposing macro-template matching.

a. Check the inside pixels of inner mask are candidate. If $D_{can} \geq N^2/2$, proceed to the next.

$$D_{can}= \sum_{y=0}^{N-1} \sum_{x=0}^{N-1} M(x+X,y+Y) \bullet M_t(0,x,y)/3 . \tag{5}$$

b. Calculate a 16-step brightness histogram value difference D_{his} between the angle-0 template $H_t(v)$ (v=0,..,15) and its corresponding working image $H(v)$, based on $I_t(0,x,y)/16$ and $I(x+X,y+Y)/16$, where $M_t(0,x,y) \geq 3$, $x=0,\ldots,N-1$ and $y=0,\ldots,N-1$.

$$D_{his}=1000 \bullet \sum_{v=0}^{15} |H(v)-H_t(v)| / \sum_{v=0}^{15} \{H(v)+H_t(v)\} . \tag{6}$$

c. Calculate a dispersion value difference D_{dis} between the angle-0 template and its corresponding working image, where $M_t(0,x,y) \geq 3$.

$$
\begin{aligned}
C &= \textstyle\sum_{y=0}^{N-1}\sum_{x=0}^{N-1} M_t(0,x,y)/3\,.\\
I_{ave} &= \textstyle\sum_{y=0}^{N-1}\sum_{x=0}^{N-1} I(x+X,y+Y)\bullet M_t(0,x,y)/3/C\,.\\
I_{tave} &= \textstyle\sum_{y=0}^{N-1}\sum_{x=0}^{N-1} I_t(0,x,y)\bullet M_t(0,x,y)/3/C\,.\\
I_{dis} &= \textstyle\sum_{y=0}^{N-1}\sum_{x=0}^{N-1} |I(x+X,y+Y)-I_{ave}|\bullet M_t(0,x,y)/3/C\,.\\
I_{tdis} &= \textstyle\sum_{y=0}^{N-1}\sum_{x=0}^{N-1} |I_t(0,x,y)-I_{tave}|\bullet M_t(0,x,y)/3/C\,.\\
D_{dis} &= 1000\bullet|I_{dis}-I_{tdis}|/(I_{dis}+I_{tdis})\,.
\end{aligned} \tag{7}
$$

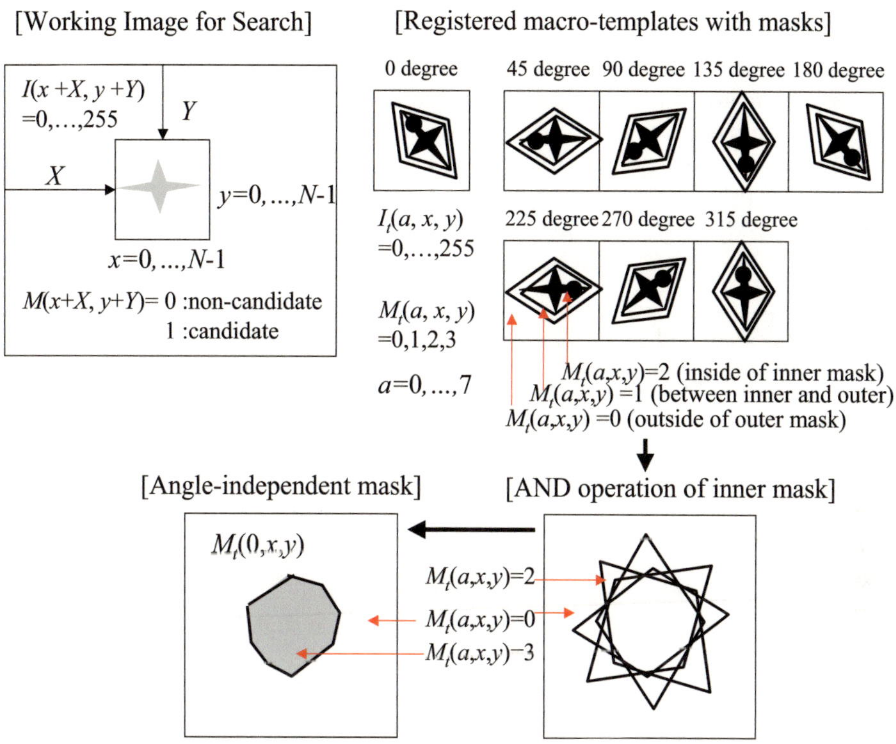

Fig. 7. Template definitions of our proposing macro-template matching algorithm.

d. Calculate a pixel value difference summation $D_{sub}(a)$ between all angles (a=0,…,7) of template and its corresponding working image, where $M_t(a,x,y)\geq 1$.

$$
\begin{aligned}
D_{sub}(a) = &\textstyle\sum_{y=0}^{N-1}\sum_{x=0}^{N-1} |I(x+X,y+Y)-I_t(a,x,y)|\\
&\bullet M_t(a,x,y)\\
&/\textstyle\sum_{y=0}^{N-1}\sum_{x=0}^{N-1} \{I(x+X,y+Y)+I_t(a,x,y)\}\bullet M_t(a,x,y).
\end{aligned} \tag{8}
$$

e. Calculate a normalized correlation coefficient value $D_{cor}(a)$ between all angles (a=0,…,7) of the template and its corresponding working image, where $M_t(a,x,y)\geq 1$. Determine the fitted angle a_{max} which makes the value of $D_{cor}(a_{max})$ be the maximum.

$$
\begin{aligned}
C &= \sum_{y=0}^{N-1}\sum_{x=0}^{N-1} M_t(a,x,y)\,. \\
I_{ave}(a) &= \sum_{y=0}^{N-1}\sum_{x=0}^{N-1} I(x+X,y+Y)\bullet M_t(a,x,y)/C\,. \\
I_{tave}(a) &= \sum_{y=0}^{N-1}\sum_{x=0}^{N-1} I_t(a,x,y)\bullet M_t(a,x,y)/C\,. \\
D_{cor}(a) &= 1000\bullet \sum_{y=0}^{N-1}\sum_{x=0}^{N-1}\{I(x+X,y+Y)-I_{ave}(a)\} \\
&\quad \bullet\{I_t(a,x,y)-I_{tave}(a)\}\bullet M_t(a,x,y) \\
&\quad /[\sum_{y=0}^{N-1}\sum_{x=0}^{N-1}\{I(x+X,y+Y)-I_{ave}(a)\}^2\bullet M_t(a,x,y) \\
&\quad \bullet \sum_{y=0}^{N-1}\sum_{x=0}^{N-1}\{I_t(a,x,y)-I_{tave}(a)\}^2\bullet M_t(a,x,y)]^{1/2}\,.
\end{aligned} \tag{9}
$$

Figure 8 shows a construction of total macro-template matching processes for identifying each small object included in candidate areas. The first and second processes are based on our proposing template matching processes, which calculate 4 kinds of matching parameters D_{his}, D_{dis}, $D_{sub}(a_{max})$ and $D_{cor}(a_{max})$ with the fitted angle parameter a_{max} for some position. The first process (1) finds a matching position (X_c,Y_c) where all of matching parameters are satisfied with the predefined matching conditions as $D_{his}\leq S_{his}$, $D_{dis}\leq S_{dis}$, $D_{sub}(a_{max})\leq S_{sub}$ and $D_{cor}(a_{max})\geq S_{cor}$. The second process (2) corrects the matching position to the

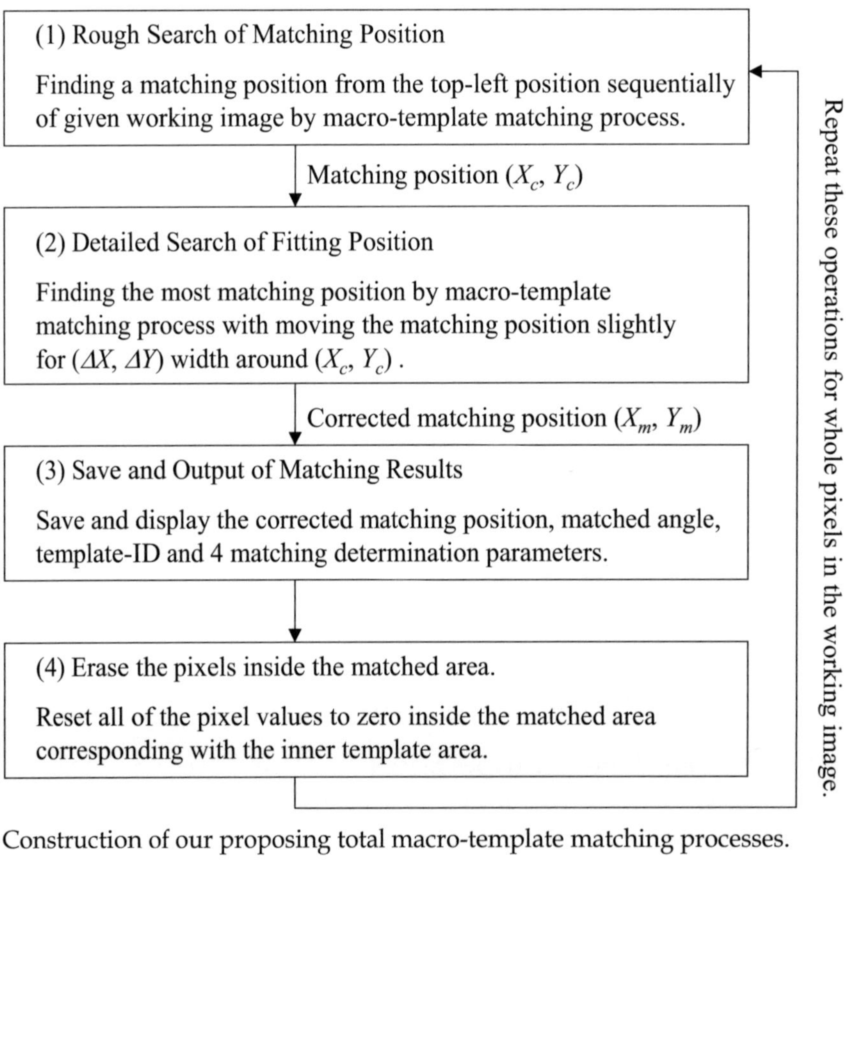

Fig. 8. Construction of our proposing total macro-template matching processes.

most fitted position (X_m, Y_m) where D_{his}, D_{dis} and $D_{sub}(a_{max})$ to be the minimum, and $D_{cor}(a_{max})$ to be the maximum. The third process (3) saves and displays this matched position (X_m, Y_m), matching parameters and the matched angle parameter. The fourth process clears values of the pixel block to zero, corresponding with this matched area where $M_t(x,y) \geq 2$, in the working image $I(x,y)$. This process prevents picking up the already matched area in duplicate.

Figure 9 shows interactive definition processes of macro-template matching conditions: 4 kinds of slice levels as S_{his}, S_{dis}, S_{sub} and S_{cor}, and conceptual updated templates. The first process (1) defines a position (X_c, Y_c) to be matched interactively by a user where the target area should be identified as an object. The second process (2) corrects the defined position to the most fitted position (X_m, Y_m), where D_{his}, D_{dis} and $D_{sub}(a_{max})$ will be the minimum and $D_{cor}(a_{max})$ will be the maximum. The third process calculates 4 kinds of slice levels as: $S_{his}=D_{his}\bullet 1.1$, $S_{dis}=D_{dis}\bullet 1.1$, $S_{sub}=D_{sub}\bullet 1.1$ and $S_{cor}=D_{cor}\bullet 0.9$. The fourth process updates the template image $I_t(x,y)$ by mixing it with the matched pixel block in the working image $I(x,y)$ in order half of pixels to become those of the working image as shown in Fig.10. This process makes the template match with more types of patterns and become a more conceptual pattern.

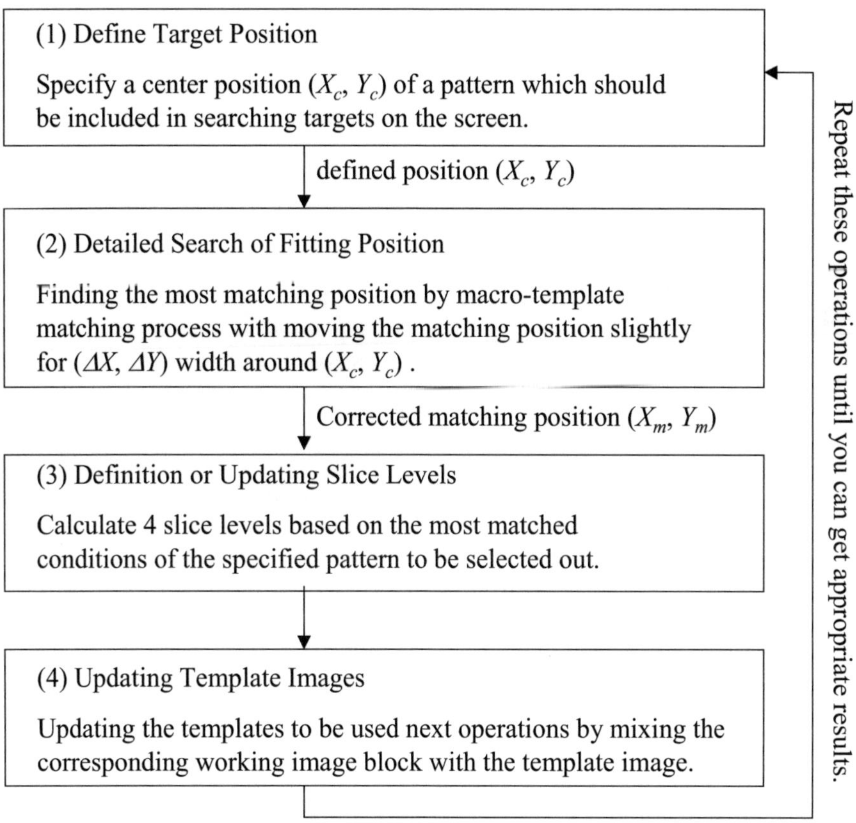

Fig. 9. Interactive definition processes of macro-template matching conditions.

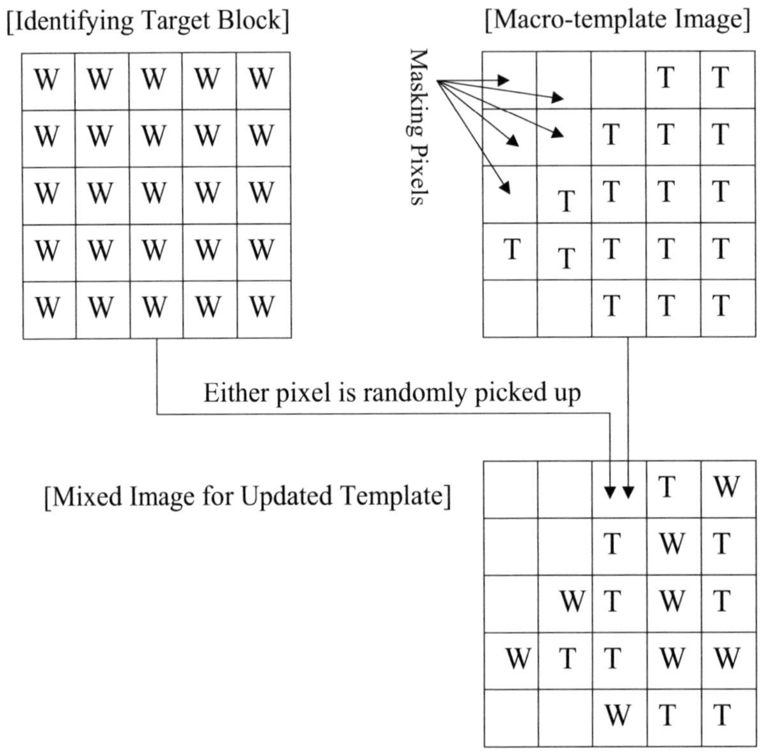

Fig. 10. Updating process of template images.

4. Experimental results

The Figure 11 shows an example of experimental results using a QuickBird (DigitalGlobe, 2008) panchromatic 11-bit monochrome 13032 x 13028 pixel satellite image Fig. 11-(a) shows 664 x 655 trimmed area after the first segmentation process has been made with a 4 x 4 pixel micro-template. Extracted candidate areas are indicated in red. Fig.11-(b) shows modified area after the clustered template-matching process has been made. The large candidate areas such as roads, which do not include automobiles, have been removed from the candidate. Fig.11-(c) shows the three-time zoomed area 591 x 468 (a parking lot image) of the center-left 197 x 156 after the third identification process has been made with 52 x 52 pixels, 4 kinds of angle macro-templates, whose initial definition and updated patterns are shown in Fig.12. Then the slice levels are defined as: S_{his}=603, S_{dis}=600, S_{sub}=130 and S_{cor}=412.

Fig. 11. Example of automobile recognition experiments by our proposing template matching using a 0.6 [m]-resolution QuickBird panchromatic image (13032 x 13028 pixels).

In this final stage, 61 automobile objects out of 85 automobiles in this picture could be correctly identified, whereas 19 objects out of 558 non-target patterns were excessively identified. This incorrect identification rate has been improved, compared with that of without a micro-template matching or a clustered micro-template matching as shown in Table 1, which shows identification precision rates in three kinds of experiments whether adding a micro-template matching or a clustered micro-template matching. However, correct identification rate has been slightly worse, which should be improved in the future.

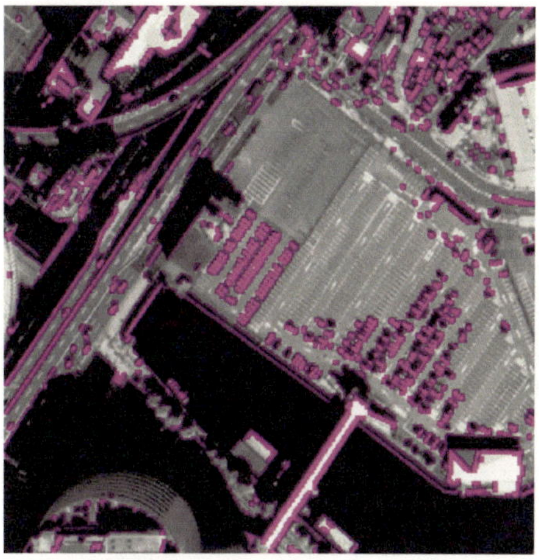

(a) Candidate areas painted in red by micro-template matching (664 x 655 pixels).

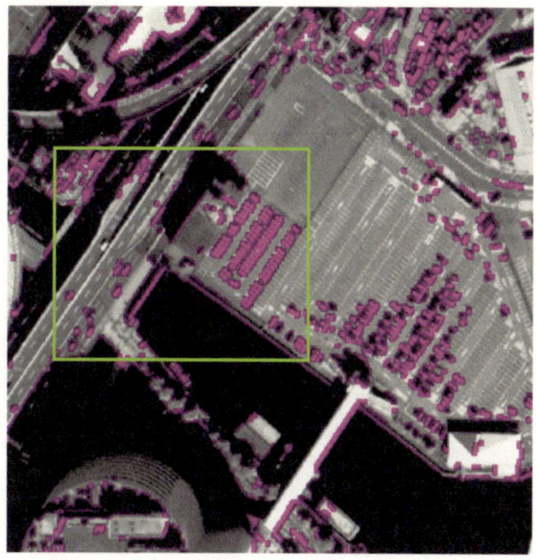

(b) Large area patterns such as roads are filtered out from the candidate areas by a clustered micro-template matching.

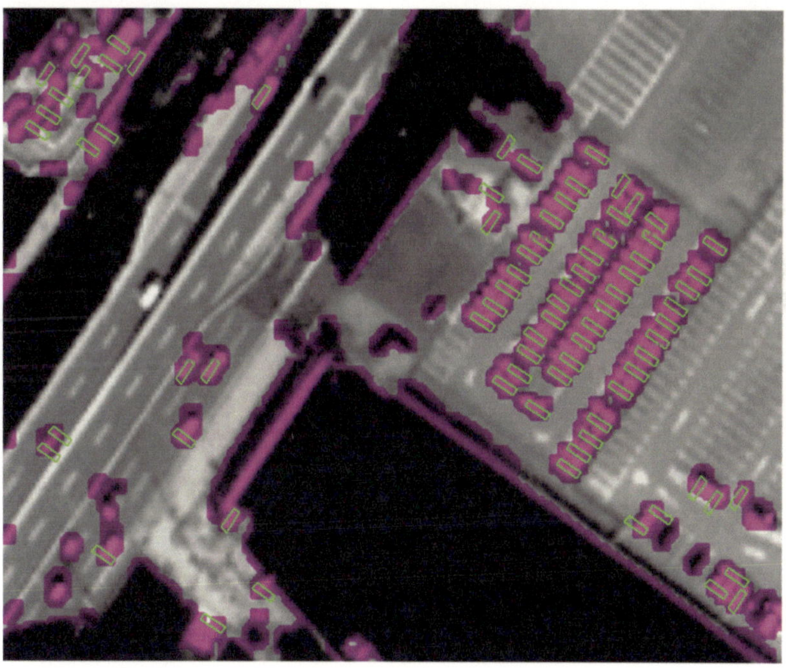

(c) Identified examples of automobile objects by macro-template matching, outlined in green (197 x 156).

Fig. 11. (Continued) Example of automobile recognition experiments by our proposing template matching using a 0.6 [m]-resolution QuickBird panchromatic image (13032 x 13028 pixels).

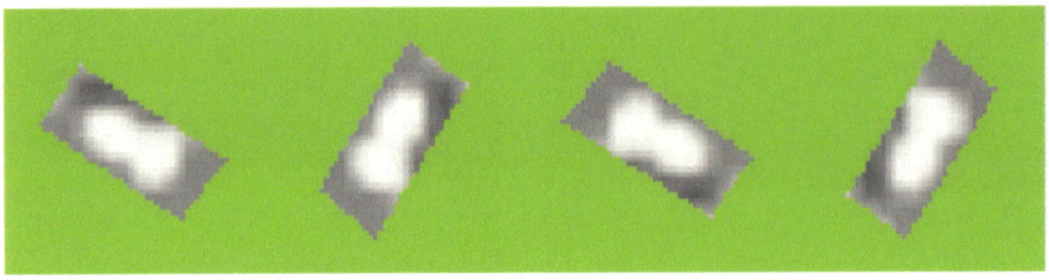

(a) Initial macro-template images 4 kinds of angle (52 × 52)

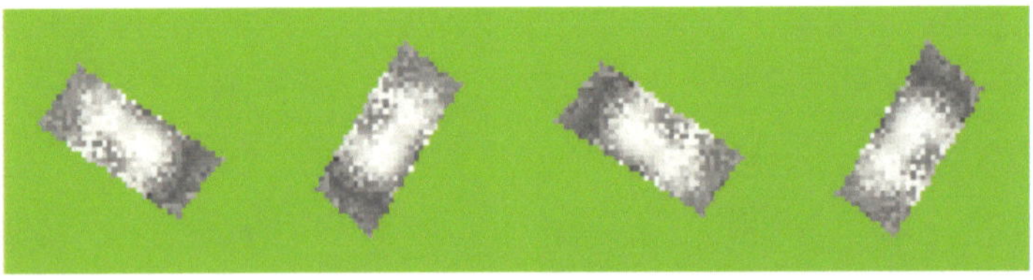

(b) Updated macro-template images used for matching (52 × 52)

Fig. 12. Template definition and updated macro-template image examples (52×52).

Method	true patterns sensitivity (false negative)	false patterns specificity (false positive)
(1) Macro-template matching only	63 74.1% (22/85)	39 93.0% (39/558)
(2) Micro-template matching & Macro-template matching	62 72.9% (23/85)	22 96.0% (22/558)
(3) Micro-template matching with Clustered micro-templates & Macro-template matching	61 71.7% (24/85)	19 96.5% (19/558)

Table 1. Automobile pattern recognition precision results in three kinds of template matching experiments.

5. Texture analysis application of our proposed method

Our proposing micro-template matching method can be extended to indentify the other kinds of objects or areas other than transportation objects. For example, we are trying to extract rice field areas in several kinds of satellite images including low-resolution SAR images by designing micro templates for detecting some spatial frequency feature patterns. In this section, we present an application of our proposing micro-template matching method to texture analysis of satellite images.

5.1 Proposing texture analysis method

Our proposing texture analysis method proposed is based on the micro-template matching method proposed in this paper. This makes binary determinations whether the target pixel $I(x,y)$ is included in metallic texture areas or not, using micro-templates defined with multiple binary determination rules around nearest $N \times N$ pixel blocks. Applying the micro-tmeplates around the target pixel $I(x,y)$ (=0—255), we can create a binary image $B(x,y)$ (=0 or 1) which indicates metallic areas. In this paper, we propose extending this micro-template to the filter matrices $M(x,y)$ (= –1 or +1) which have spatial frequency analysis functions as shown in Fig.13 and Fig.14.

For $N \times N$ block pixels (N=8) around the pixel $I(x,y)$ in given source image data, we calculate the following 4 parameters, and determine $B(x,y)$ (=0 or 1) whether the target pixel should have predefined texture characteristics or not, by all of the calculated parameter values are included in predefined ranges or not. More specifically, we define 8 kinds of slice values as L_{dis}, H_{dis}, L_{f1}, H_{f1}, L_{f2}, H_{f2}, L_{f4}, H_{f4}; if $L_{dis} \leq D_{dis} \leq H_{dis}$, $L_{f1} \leq F_1 \leq H_{f1}$, $L_{f2} \leq F_2 \leq H_{f2}$, and $L_{f4} \leq F_4 \leq H_{f4}$, we set as $B(x,y)$=1 (x=1,8; y=1,8).

(1) Pixel Dispersion Value: D_{dis}

$$
\begin{aligned}
&I_{ave}\text{: Average values of } N \times N \text{ block pixels,}\\
&\{\textstyle\sum_{y=1}^{8}\sum_{x=1}^{8} I(x,y)\}/64 \\
&D_{dis}=\{\textstyle\sum_{y=1}^{8}\sum_{x=1}^{8} (I(x,y)-I_{ave})^2\}^{1/2}/8.
\end{aligned}
\tag{10}
$$

(2) First Spatial Frequency Components: F_1

We defined 4 kinds of matrices from (1-1-1) to (1-1-4) shown in Fig.13 as $M_{x11}(x,y)$ to $M_{x14}(x,y)$, and 4 kinds of matrices from (1-2-1) to (1-2-4) as $M_{y11}(x,y)$ to $M_{y14}(x,y)$. Using these matrices, we calculate the following F_{x1i} and F_{y1i} (i=1,4), define the maximum values F_{x1} to F_{y1} among each of 4 values F_{x1i} and F_{y1i} (i=1,4), and define a square root average value of these two as F_1.

$$
\begin{aligned}
&F_{x1i}=|\textstyle\sum_{y=1}^{8}\sum_{x=1}^{8} \{I(x,y)-I_{ave}\}\cdot M_{x1i}(x,y)|/64,\ (i=1,4)\\
&F_{y1i}=|\textstyle\sum_{y=1}^{8}\sum_{x=1}^{8} \{I(x,y)-I_{ave}\}\cdot M_{y1i}(x,y)|/64,\ (i=1,4)\\
&F_{x1}=\mathrm{MAX}_{i=1,4}F_{x1i}\\
&F_{y1}=\mathrm{MAX}_{i=1,4}F_{y1i}\\
&F_1=(F_x{}^2+F_y{}^2)^{1/2}.
\end{aligned}
\tag{11}
$$

(3) Second Spatial Frequency Components: F_2

We defined 2 matrices (2-1-1) and (2-1-2) shown in Fig.14 as $M_{x21}(x,y)$ and $M_{x22}(x,y)$, and 2 matrices (2-2-1) and (2-2-2) as $M_{y21}(x,y)$ and $M_{y22}(x,y)$. Using these matrices, we calculate the following F_{x2i} and F_{y2i} (i=1,2), define the maximum values F_{x2} to F_{y2} among each of 2 values F_{x2i} and F_{y2i} (i=1,2), and define a square root average value of these two as F_2.

-1	-1	-1	-1	+1	+1	+1	+1
-1	-1	-1	-1	+1	+1	+1	+1
-1	-1	-1	-1	+1	+1	+1	+1
-1	-1	-1	-1	+1	+1	+1	+1
-1	-1	-1	-1	+1	+1	+1	+1
-1	-1	-1	-1	+1	+1	+1	+1
-1	-1	-1	-1	+1	+1	+1	+1
-1	-1	-1	-1	+1	+1	+1	+1

(1-1-1) Horizontal First Spatial Frequency Components

+1	-1	-1	-1	-1	+1	+1	+1
+1	-1	-1	-1	-1	+1	+1	+1
+1	-1	-1	-1	-1	+1	+1	+1
+1	-1	-1	-1	-1	+1	+1	+1
+1	-1	-1	-1	-1	+1	+1	+1
+1	-1	-1	-1	-1	+1	+1	+1
+1	-1	-1	-1	-1	+1	+1	+1
+1	-1	-1	-1	-1	+1	+1	+1

(1-1-2) Horizontal First Spatial Frequency Components

+1	+1	-1	-1	-1	-1	+1	+1
+1	+1	-1	-1	-1	-1	+1	+1
+1	+1	-1	-1	-1	-1	+1	+1
+1	+1	-1	-1	-1	-1	+1	+1
+1	+1	-1	-1	-1	-1	+1	+1
+1	+1	-1	-1	-1	-1	+1	+1
+1	+1	-1	-1	-1	-1	+1	+1
+1	+1	-1	-1	-1	-1	+1	+1

(1-1-3) Horizontal First Spatial Frequency Components

+1	+1	+1	-1	-1	-1	-1	+1
+1	+1	+1	-1	-1	-1	-1	+1
+1	+1	+1	-1	-1	-1	-1	+1
+1	+1	+1	-1	-1	-1	-1	+1
+1	+1	+1	-1	-1	-1	-1	+1
+1	+1	+1	-1	-1	-1	-1	+1
+1	+1	+1	-1	-1	-1	-1	+1
+1	+1	+1	-1	-1	-1	-1	+1

(1-1-4) Horizontal First Spatial Frequency Components

-1	-1	-1	-1	-1	-1	-1	-1
-1	-1	-1	-1	-1	-1	-1	-1
-1	-1	-1	-1	-1	-1	-1	-1
-1	-1	-1	-1	-1	-1	-1	-1
+1	+1	+1	+1	+1	+1	+1	+1
+1	+1	+1	+1	+1	+1	+1	+1
+1	+1	+1	+1	+1	+1	+1	+1
+1	+1	+1	+1	+1	+1	+1	+1

(1-2-1) Vertical First Spatial Frequency Components

+1	+1	+1	+1	+1	+1	+1	+1
-1	-1	-1	-1	-1	-1	-1	-1
-1	-1	-1	-1	-1	-1	-1	-1
-1	-1	-1	-1	-1	-1	-1	-1
-1	-1	-1	-1	-1	-1	-1	-1
+1	+1	+1	+1	+1	+1	+1	+1
+1	+1	+1	+1	+1	+1	+1	+1
+1	+1	+1	+1	+1	+1	+1	+1

(1-2-2) Vertical First Spatial Frequency Components

+1	+1	+1	+1	+1	+1	+1	+1
+1	+1	+1	+1	+1	+1	+1	+1
-1	-1	-1	-1	-1	-1	-1	-1
-1	-1	-1	-1	-1	-1	-1	-1
-1	-1	-1	-1	-1	-1	-1	-1
-1	-1	-1	-1	-1	-1	-1	-1
+1	+1	+1	+1	+1	+1	+1	+1
+1	+1	+1	+1	+1	+1	+1	+1

(1-2-3) Vertical First Spatial Frequency Components

+1	+1	+1	+1	+1	+1	+1	+1
+1	+1	+1	+1	+1	+1	+1	+1
+1	+1	+1	+1	+1	+1	+1	+1
-1	-1	-1	-1	-1	-1	-1	-1
-1	-1	-1	-1	-1	-1	-1	-1
-1	-1	-1	-1	-1	-1	-1	-1
-1	-1	-1	-1	-1	-1	-1	-1
+1	+1	+1	+1	+1	+1	+1	+1

(1-2-4) Vertical First Spatial Frequency Components

Fig. 13. Proposing filter matrices for texture analysis (1).

-1	-1	+1	+1	-1	-1	+1	+1
-1	-1	+1	+1	-1	-1	+1	+1
-1	-1	+1	+1	-1	-1	+1	+1
-1	-1	+1	+1	-1	-1	+1	+1
-1	-1	+1	+1	-1	-1	+1	+1
-1	-1	+1	+1	-1	-1	+1	+1
-1	-1	+1	+1	-1	-1	+1	+1
-1	-1	+1	+1	-1	-1	+1	+1

(2-1-1) Horizontal Second Spatial Frequency Components

+1	-1	-1	+1	+1	-1	-1	+1
+1	-1	-1	+1	+1	-1	-1	+1
+1	-1	-1	+1	+1	-1	-1	+1
+1	-1	-1	+1	+1	-1	-1	+1
+1	-1	-1	+1	+1	-1	-1	+1
+1	-1	-1	+1	+1	-1	-1	+1
+1	-1	-1	+1	+1	-1	-1	+1
+1	-1	-1	+1	+1	-1	-1	+1

(2-1-2) Horizontal Second Spatial Frequency Components

-1	-1	-1	-1	-1	-1	-1	-1
-1	-1	-1	-1	-1	-1	-1	-1
+1	+1	+1	+1	+1	+1	+1	+1
+1	+1	+1	+1	+1	+1	+1	+1
-1	-1	-1	-1	-1	-1	-1	-1
-1	-1	-1	-1	-1	-1	-1	-1
+1	+1	+1	+1	+1	+1	+1	+1
+1	+1	+1	+1	+1	+1	+1	+1

(2-2-1) Vertical Second Spatial Frequency Components

+1	+1	+1	+1	+1	+1	+1	+1
-1	-1	-1	-1	-1	-1	-1	-1
-1	-1	-1	-1	-1	-1	-1	-1
+1	+1	+1	+1	+1	+1	+1	+1
+1	+1	+1	+1	+1	+1	+1	+1
-1	-1	-1	-1	-1	-1	-1	-1
-1	-1	-1	-1	-1	-1	-1	-1
+1	+1	+1	+1	+1	+1	+1	+1

(2-2-2) Vertical Second Spatial Frequency Components

-1	+1	-1	+1	-1	+1	-1	+1
-1	+1	-1	+1	-1	+1	-1	+1
-1	+1	-1	+1	-1	+1	-1	+1
-1	+1	-1	+1	-1	+1	-1	+1
-1	+1	-1	+1	-1	+1	-1	+1
-1	+1	-1	+1	-1	+1	-1	+1
-1	+1	-1	+1	-1	+1	-1	+1
-1	+1	-1	+1	-1	+1	-1	+1

(3-1) Horizontal Fourth Spatial Frequency Components

-1	-1	-1	-1	-1	-1	-1	-1
+1	+1	+1	+1	+1	+1	+1	+1
-1	-1	-1	-1	-1	-1	-1	-1
+1	+1	+1	+1	+1	+1	+1	+1
-1	-1	-1	-1	-1	-1	-1	-1
+1	+1	+1	+1	+1	+1	+1	+1
-1	-1	-1	-1	-1	-1	-1	-1
+1	+1	+1	+1	+1	+1	+1	+1

(3-2) Vertical Fourth Spatial Frequency Components

Fig. 14. Proposing filter matrices for texture analysis (2).

$$F_{x2i}=|\sum_{y=1}^{8}\sum_{x=1}^{8}\{I(x,y)-I_{ave}\}^{\bullet}M_{x2i}(x,y)|/64,\ (i=1,2)$$
$$F_{y2i}=|\sum_{y=1}^{8}\sum_{x=1}^{8}\{I(x,y)-I_{ave}\}^{\bullet}M_{y2i}(x,y)|/64,\ (i=1,2)$$
$$F_{x2}=\mathrm{MAX}_{i=1,2}F_{x2i} \quad (12)$$
$$F_{y2}=\mathrm{MAX}_{i=1,2}F_{y2i}$$
$$F_2=(F_{x2}^2+F_{y2}^2)^{1/2}.$$

(4) Fourth Spatial Frequency Components: F_4

We defined 2 matrices (3-1) and (3-2) shown in Fig.14 as $M_{x4}(x,y)$ and $M_{y4}(x,y)$. Using these matrices, we calculate the following F_{x4i} and F_{y4}, and define a square root average value of these two as F_4.

$$F_{x4}=|\sum_{y=1}^{8}\sum_{x=1}^{8}\{I(x,y)-I_{ave}\}^{\bullet}M_{x4}(x,y)|/64$$
$$F_{y4}=|\sum_{y=1}^{8}\sum_{x=1}^{8}\{I(x,y)-I_{ave}\}^{\bullet}M_{y4}(x,y)|/64 \quad (13)$$
$$F_4=(F_{x4}^2+F_{y4}^2)^{1/2}.$$

Then we describe how to define 8 kinds of slice values as L_{dis}, H_{dis}, L_{f1}, H_{f1}, L_{f2}, H_{f2}, L_{f4}, H_{f4} interactively. We indicate one of target texture areas to be extracted, area-O, and also indicate two reverse feature areas not to be extracted: area-A and area-B. We calculate average values of 4 parameters D_{dis}, F_1, F_2, F_4 based on the equations described above for each of three selected areas. We define average values in the area-A as A_{dis}, A_{f1}, A_{f2}, A_{f4}, average values in the area-B as B_{dis}, B_{f1}, B_{f2}, B_{f4}, average values in the area-O as O_{dis}, O_{f1}, O_{f2}, O_{f4}. In case of $A_{dis}<B_{dis}$, we can set the values as follows:

$$\text{If } A_{dis}<O_{dis}<B_{dis} \text{ then } L_{dis}=(A_{dis}+O_{dis})/2,$$
$$H_{dis}=(B_{dis}+O_{dis})/2.$$
$$\text{If } A_{dis}<B_{dis}<O_{dis} \text{ then } L_{dis}=(B_{dis}+O_{dis})/2,\ H_{dis}=\infty. \quad (14)$$
$$\text{If } O_{dis}<A_{dis}<B_{dis} \text{ then } L_{dis}=0,\ H_{dis}=(A_{dis}+O_{dis})/2.$$

In case of $A_{dis}>B_{dis}$, we can apply the above by changing values of A_{dis} and B_{dis}.

5.2 Example of rice field area extraction

Applying the previously described texture analysis method to several feature areas in satellite images, we have obtained the specific average values of 4 parameters D_{dis}, F_1, F_2, F_4. As experiment images, we used two kinds of QuickBird (DigitalGlobe, 2008) panchromatic images (urban area:13032×13028 pixels, rural area:29195×34498 pixels), we have extracted 252×182 pixel area and 1676×1563 pixels area from each image and converted depth of brightness level from 11-bits to 8-bits. We selected three areas from the first image, which were a road area without cars existed, a parking area without cars existed and a parking area with multiple cars parked in parallel. And we also selected three areas form the second image, which were a town and housing area, a rice field area and a river area. For each of these selected 6 areas, we calculated average values of 4 parameters D_{dis}, F_1, F_2, F_4, as plotted in Fig.15.

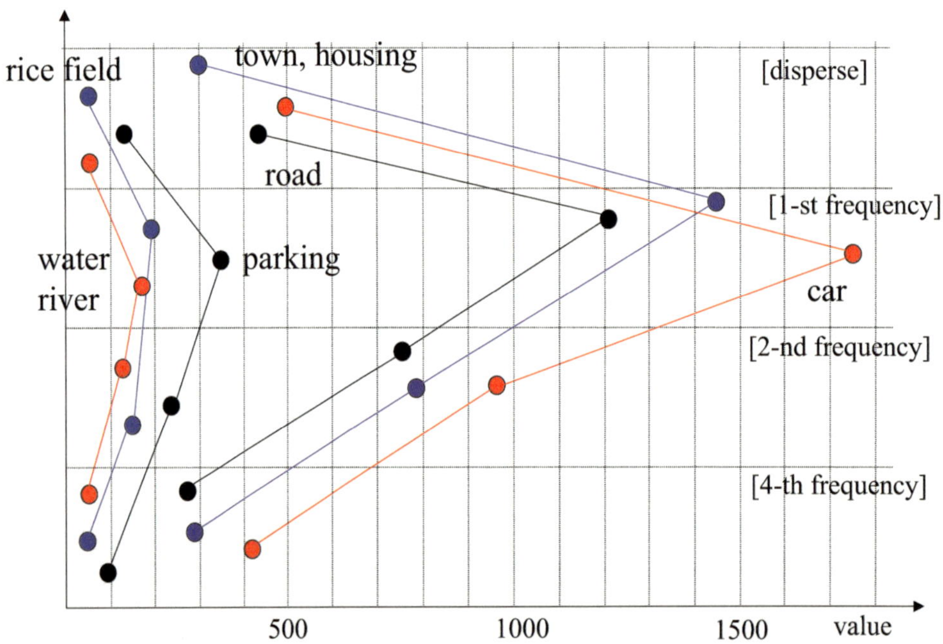

Fig. 15. Specific parameter values of texture analysys in 6 kinds of areas in QuickBird (DigitalGlobe, 2008) satellite images.

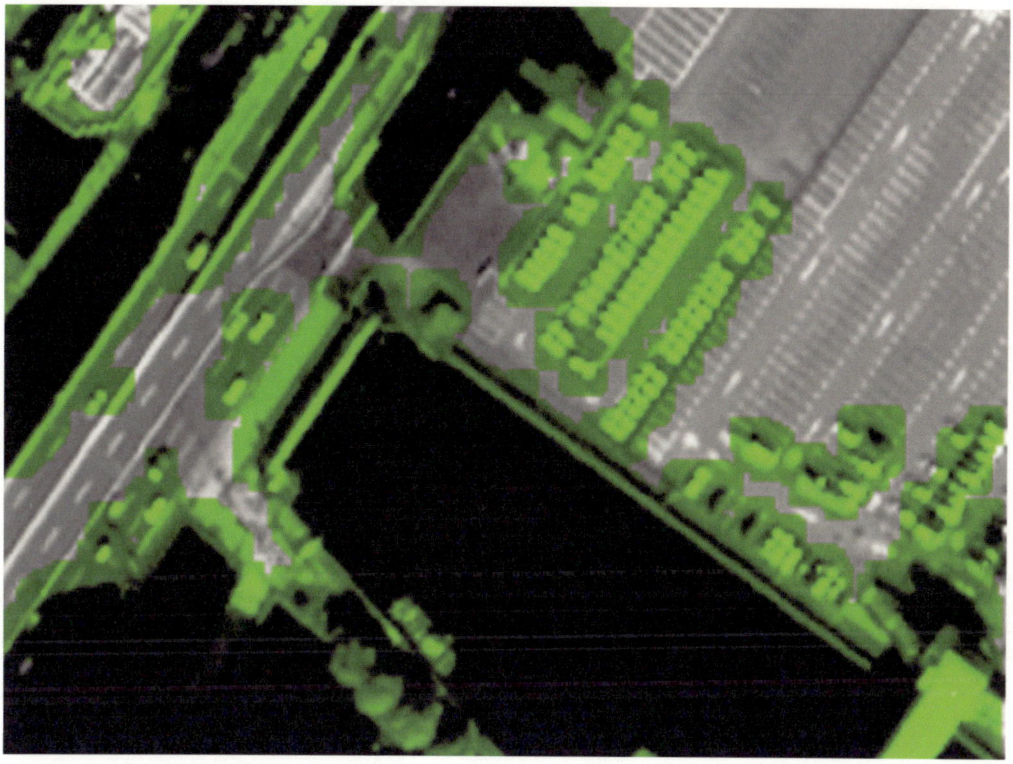

Fig. 16. Example of automobile extraction experiment from road and parking areas in QuickBird (DigitalGlobe, 2008) image.

(1) Original panchromatic image(1676×1563 pixels).

(2) Extraction of rice field areas and river areas.

(3) Removing the river areas from the image (2).

Fig. 17. Three kinds of texture separation experiments of rice field areas, river areas, town and housing areas in QuickBird (DigitalGlobe, 2008) image.

In Fig.15, We have divided the vertical direction to four parts, and plotted 4 average parameters for each of the 6 selected areas plotted from the top to bottom parts: pixel dispersion values, first spatial frequency components, second spatial frequency components, and fourth spatial frequency components. The horizontal dimension is 100-time integer values of calculated values by the equation (1) to (4). For example, Figure 16 shows a result of extraction experiment for the first urban area image, setting slice values as L_{dis}=520, H_{dis}=10000, L_{f1}=2200, H_{f1}=10000, L_{f2}=770, H_{f2}=10000, L_{f4}=300, H_{f4}=10000.
As shown in Fig.15, parameter values of the rice field area and the river area are nearer compared with the values of the town and housing area. This indicates, it is difficult to separate the two areas of the rice field area and the river area than separating them from the town and housing area. Therefore, we have made separation experiments of these 3 kinds of texture in the same image, as shown in Fig.17.
Using the source image Fig.17-(1), the result of extraction is shown in Fig.17-(2), setting parameters as L_{dis}=0, H_{dis}=96, L_{f1}=0, H_{f1}=396, L_{f2}=0, H_{f2}=280, L_{f4}=0, H_{f4}=96. Then from the processed image Fig.17-(2), the result of extraction is shown in Fig.17-(3), setting parameters as L_{dis}=21, H_{dis}=96, L_{f1}=0, H_{f1}=396, L_{f2}=80, H_{f2}=280, L_{f4}=0, H_{f4}=96. We can almost separate the rice filed areas from the river areas except the several edge parts of river areas are incorrectly extracted.

6. Conclusions

In this paper, we have proposed a three-layered structured template matching method for decreasing calculation loads and improving identification precisions against the conventional template-matching algorithm. The first layer called as a micro-template matching is focusing on extracting candidate areas, which have metallic-reflection optical characteristics, where any types of transportation objects are included. The second layer called as a clustered micro-template matching is identification and removal of excessively extracted candidate areas such as roads and buildings, which have the similar optical characteristics but do not include our targets. The third layer called as macro-template matching is identifying each automobile object within the focusing area using our proposing conceptual templates, which are learned patterns based on user's operations, based on our improved high-speed template-matching algorithm. In our experiments using our proposed method, we could extract about 70% automobile objects correctly in a single scene of a QuickBird panchromatic image.
Moreover, we have proposed giving a texture analysis function to the first micro-template matching process, by adding independent spatial frequency component as parameters. The previously proposed micro-template matching has been using only a mixed parameter of pixel dispersion value and first spatial frequency component in this proposing texture analysis. It has been difficult to distinguish similar texture characteristic areas shown in such as Fig.17-(2) and Fig.17-(3). We have found overcoming this problem by giving independent spatial frequency component parameters separating from pixel dispersion parameters and adding the second spatial frequency component parameter. As future works, we are going to evaluate functions of the other first and fourth spatial frequency components in several kinds of satellite images, and redesign matrices size or analysis parameters.
We suppose our proposing technology creates new industrial applications and business opportunities of high-cost earth observation satellite images such as a wide-area traffic monitoring, which compensates for the blind areas of the conventional terrestrial traffic

monitoring. Especially, this is effective for planning of city constructions and next-generation traffic networks.

7. References

Tao Zhao & Nevatia R. (2001). Car detection in low resolution aerial image, *Proceedings of Eighth IEEE International Conference on Computer Vision ICCV 2001*, Vol.1, pp. 710-717, ISBN 0-7695-1143-0, Vancouver, BC, July 2001, IEEE, NJ US

Qu Jishuang; Wang Chao & Wang Zhengzhi (2003). Structure-context based fuzzy neural network approach for automatic target detection, *Proceedings of IEEE International Conference on Geoscience and Remote Sensing Symposium IGARSS '03*, Vol.2, pp. 767-769, ISBN 0-7803-7929-2, July 2003, IEEE, NJ US

So Hee Jeon ; Kiwon Lee & Byung-Doo Kwon (2005). Application of template matching method to traffic feature detection using KOMPSAT EOC imagery, *Proceedings of IEEE International Geoscience and Remote Sensing Symposium (IGRSS'05)*, pp. 441-443, ISBN 0-7803-9050-4, conference location, July 2005, IEEE, NJ US

Qi-Ming Qin; Si-Jin Chen; Wen-Jun Wang; De-Zhi Chen & Lin Wang (2005). The building recognition of high resolution satellite remote sensing image based on wavelet analysis, *Proceedings of IEEE International Conference on Machine Learning and Cybernetics*, Vol.7, pp. 4533-4538, ISBN 0-7803-9091-1, August 2005, IEEE, NJ US

Giovanni Poggi; Giuseppe Scarpa & Josiane B. Zerubia (2005). Supervised segmentation of remote sensing images based on a tree-structured MRF model, *IEEE Transactions on Geoscience and Remote Sensing*, Vol.43, No.8, (August 2005) pp. 1901-1911, ISSN 0196-2892

DigitalGlobe (2008). QuickBird Sattellite Images by DigitalGlobe, provided by Hitachi Software Engineering Co.,Ltd. (http://www.hitachisoft.jp/products/hgiis/index.html) 2008, Japan.

Modegi T. (2008). Development of Pattern Searching Tool for Satellite Images Using Conceptual Template Patterns, *Proceedings of the 70-th Information Processing Society of Japan*, Demo-2, pp. 1-2, Tukuba Japan, March 2008, IPSJ, Tokyo Japan

Modegi T. (2009). Target Detection Tool for High Resolution Images: "TD-HRS", Enable to Recognize Vehicle Objects in Satellite Images, *Proceedings of the 71-th Information Processing Society of Japan*, Demo-4, pp. 1-2, Kusatsu Japan, March 2009, IPSJ, Tokyo Japan

15

Hybrid Optical Neural Network-Type Filters for Multiple Objects Recognition within Cluttered Scenes

Ioannis Kypraios
School of Engineering & Design, University of Sussex, Falmer, Brighton, BN1 9QT U.K.

1. Introduction

A robust invariant pattern detection and classification system needs to be able to recognise the object under any usual *a priori* defined distortions such as translation, scaling and in-plane and out-of-plane rotation (Wood, 1996) (see Fig. 1). Ideally, the system should be able to recognise (detect and classify) any complex scene of objects even within background clutter noise. This problem is a very complex and difficult one. Here, we will consider only non-deformable (*solid*) objects (Forsyth & Ponce, 2003). In effect, they maintain their form independent of any of the distortions just described. Early studies (Casasent & Psaltis, 1976) in trying to solve the invariant pattern recognition problem include the system based on a modified logarithmic Mellin transform (Grace & Spann, 1991; Sheng & Arsenault, 1986; Sheng & Lejeune, 1991). Other work (Mersereau & Morris, 1986) has focused on a system based on a circular harmonic filter (Hsu et al., 1982; Hsu & Arsenault, 1982, 1984) illuminated with white light illumination. (Jensen et al., 1987) have described an optical image pattern recognition system based on log-polar mapping (Bryngdahl, 1974; Cederquist & Tai, 1984) of a Fourier transformed input pattern to convert in-plane rotation and scale changes into shift properties. The system's implementation by a correlator has allowed translation invariance of the input pattern. Although, the real-time practical use of these systems has been superseded, useful concepts for future implementation of filters can be extracted from this work.

In literature, broadly, two main categories of pattern recognition systems exist. The first category consists of linear combinatorial-type filters (LCFs) (Stamos, 2001). Proper image analysis in the frequency domain is done with the help of Fourier Transformation (FT) (Lynn & Fuerst, 1998; Proakis & Manolakis, 1988). The second category consists of pure neural modelling approaches. (Wood, 1996) has given a brief but clear review of invariant pattern recognition methods. His survey has divided the methods into two main categories of solving the invariant pattern recognition problem. The first category has two distinct phases of separately calculating the features of the training set pattern to be invariant to certain distortions and then classifying the extracted features. The second one, instead of having two separate phases, has a single phase which parameterises the desired invariances and then adapts them. (Wood, 1996) has also described the integral transforms, which fall under the first category of feature extractors. They are based on Fourier analysis, such as the multidimensional Fourier transform, Fourier-Mellin transform, triple correlation (Delopoulos et al., 1994) and others. Part of the first category is also the group of algebraic invariants, such as Zernike moments (Khotanzad & Hong, 1990; Perantonis & Lisboa, 1992), generalised moments (Shvedov et al., 1979) and others. Wood has given examples of the second category, the main representative of this category being based on artificial neural network (NNET) architectures. He has presented the weight-sharing neural networks (LeCun, 1989; LeCun et al. 1990), the high-order neural networks (Giles & Maxwell, 1987; Kanaoka et al. 1992; Perantonis & Lisboa, 1992; Spirkovska & Reid, 1992), the time-delay neural networks (TDNN) (Bottou et al., 1990; Simard & LeCun, 1992; Waibel et al., 1989) and others. Finally, he has included a third category or the miscellaneous group where it consists of the methods which cannot strictly be categorised under either the feature-extraction feature-classification approach or the parameterised approach. Such methods are image normalisation pre-processing (Yuceer & Oflazer, 1993) methods for achieving invariance to certain distortions. (Dobnikar et al., 1992) have compared the invariant pattern classification (IPC) neural network architecture versus the Fourier transform (FT) method. They used for their comparison black-and-white images. They have proven the generalisation properties and fault-tolerant abilities to input patterns of the artificial neural network architectures.

An alternative approach for the solution of the invariant pattern recognition problem has been well demonstrated previously with the Hybrid Optical Neural Network (HONN) filter. HONN filter combines the digital design of a filter by artificial neural network techniques with an optical correlator-type implementation of the resulting combinatorial correlator type filter. There are two main design blocks in the HONN filter, the NNET block and the optical correlator-type block. The input images pass first through the NNET block. The extracted images from the NNET block's output are used in the composite image synthesis of the correlator-type block where we have chosen to be of the combinatorial-type.

In order to keep consistency between the different mathematical symbols of NNET architectures and optical correlators we have applied similar notation rules throughout this chapter. We denote the variable names and functions by non-italic letters, the names of the vectors by italic lower case letters and the matrices by italic upper case. The frequency domain vectors, matrices, variable names and functions are represented by bold letters and the space domain vectors, matrices, variables and functions by plain letters.

Section 2 describes briefly the design and implementation of the general HONN filter. Section 3 describes how the design of the general HONN filter can be altered to accommodate multiple objects recognition of the same and of different class. Section 4 describes the design and implementations of the unconstrained-HONN (U-HONN), the constrained-HONN (C-HONN), and the modified-HONN (M-HONN) filters for multiple objects recognition. Section 5 consists of the comparative analysis of U-HONN, C-HONN and M-HONN filters for multiple objects recognition. Section 6 concludes.

2. General hybrid optical neural network filter

The main motivation for the initial design and implementation of the HONN filter was to achieve the performance advantages of both NNET architectures (Kypraios et al. 2004a) and the optically implemented correlators (Bahri et Kumar, 1988). NNET architectures exhibit non-linear superposition abilities (Kypraios et al., 2002) of the training set pattern images and generalisation abilities (Beale & Jackson, 1990) over the whole set of the whole set of the

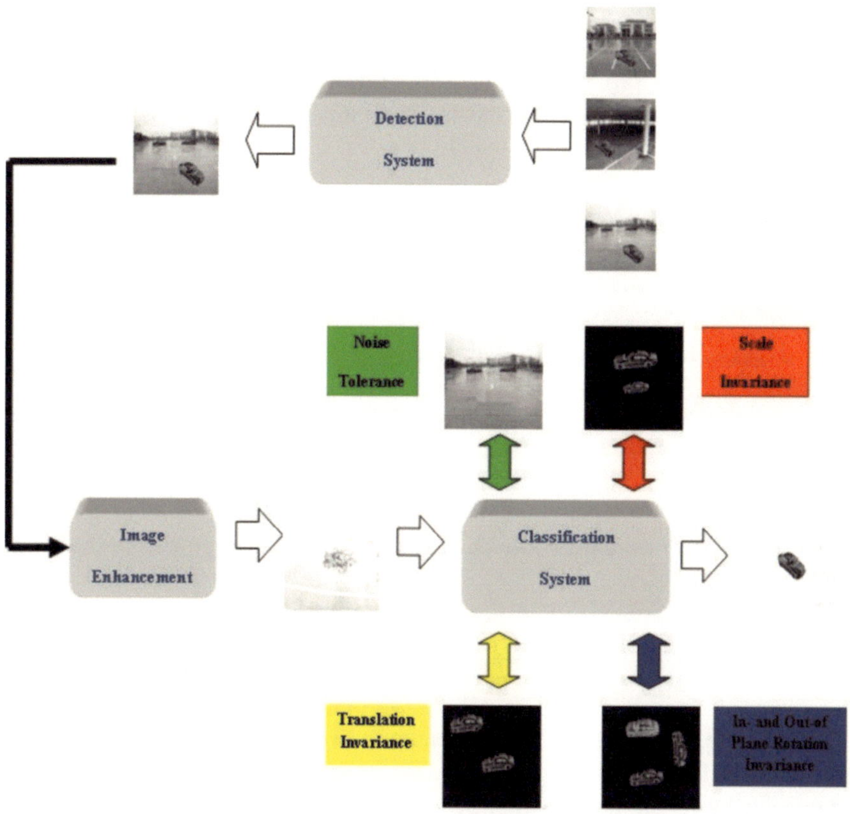

Fig. 1. A robust invariant pattern detection and classification system

input images. Optical correlators allow high speed implementation of the algorithms described. In effect, the HONN filter combines the digital design of a filter by NNET techniques with an optical correlator-type implementation of the resulting combinatorial correlator type filter (Kumar, 1992). Briefly, the original input images pass first through the NNET block and, then, the extracted images from the NNET block's output are used to form a combinatorial-type filter. Thus the output of the combinatorial-type correlator block is a composite image of the HONN filter's output. To test the HONN filter we correlate the filter with an input image.

Let $h(k,l)$ denote the composite image of the combinatorial-type correlator, such as synthetic discriminant function (SDF) filter, and $x_i(k,l)$ denote the training set images, where $i=1,2,\cdots,N$ and N is the number of the training images used in the synthesis of the combinatorial-type correlator. The basic filter's transfer function, from the weighed linear combination of x_i is given by:

$$h(k,l)=\sum_{i=1}^{N}\alpha_i\, x_i(k,l) \tag{1}$$

where the coefficients $\alpha_i(i=1,2,\cdots,N)$ are to set the constraints on the peak given by **c**. The α_i values are determined from:

$$\alpha = R^{-1}c \tag{2}$$

where α is the vector of the coefficients $\alpha_i(i=1,2,\cdots,N)$, $\boldsymbol{R}$ is the correlation matrix of t_i and $\boldsymbol{c}$ is the peak constraint vector. The elements of this are usually set to zeros for false-class objects and to ones for true-class objects.
Let's assume that an image s is the input vector to an NNET's hidden neuron (node), $t_{p\kappa}$ represent the target output for a pattern p on node κ and $o_{p\kappa}$ represent the calculated output at that node. The weight from node ι to node κ is represented by $w_{\iota\kappa}$. The activation of each node κ, for pattern p, can be written as:

$$net_{p\kappa} = \sum\left(w_{\iota\kappa}o_{p\kappa} + b_\iota\right) \tag{3}$$

i.e. it is the weighted sum of the calculated output from the node ι to node κ. b_ι represents the bias vector of unit ι. We train a specifically configured NNET architecture with N training set images. The network has N neurons in the hidden layer, i.e. equal to the number of training images. There is a single neuron at the output layer to separate two different object classes. From eqn. (3) the net input of each of the neurons in the hidden layer is now given by:

$$net_{x_i} = \sum_{\iota=1}^{m\times n} w_\iota^{x_i} s_\iota^{x_i} \tag{4}$$

where *net* is the net input of each of the hidden neurons. $w_\iota^{x_i}$ are the input weights from the input layer to the hidden neurons for the training image x_i of size [mxn] in matrix form or of size [1x(mxn)] in vector form. Similarity, for the training image x_N of size [mxn] in matrix form ([1x(mxn)] in vector form) the net input, net_{x_N} is given by:

$$net_{x_N} = \sum_{i=1}^{mxn} w_\iota^{x_N} s_\iota^{x_N} \tag{5}$$

From eqns. (1), and (3) and (5) there is a direct analogy between the combinatorial-type filter synthesis procedure and the combination of all the layers' weighted input vectors.
Two possible and equivalent specially configured designs (Kypraios et al. 2004a) of NNET architectures can form the basis of the combinatorial-type filter synthesis. In both of the designs each neuron of the hidden layer is trained with only one of the training set images. In effect, $neuron_1$ with the training image x_1, $neuron_2$ with the training image x_2 and so on, ending with $neuron_N$ with the training image x_N. In the first design the number of the input sources is kept constant whereas in the second design the number of the input sources is equal to the number of the training images. In effect the number of the input weights increases proportionally to the size of the training set:

$$N_{iw} = N\times[m\times n] \tag{6}$$

where N_{iw} is the number of the input weights, N, is the size of the training set equal to the number of the training images and [mxn] is the size of the image of the training set. The latter design would allow parallel implementation, since all the training images could be

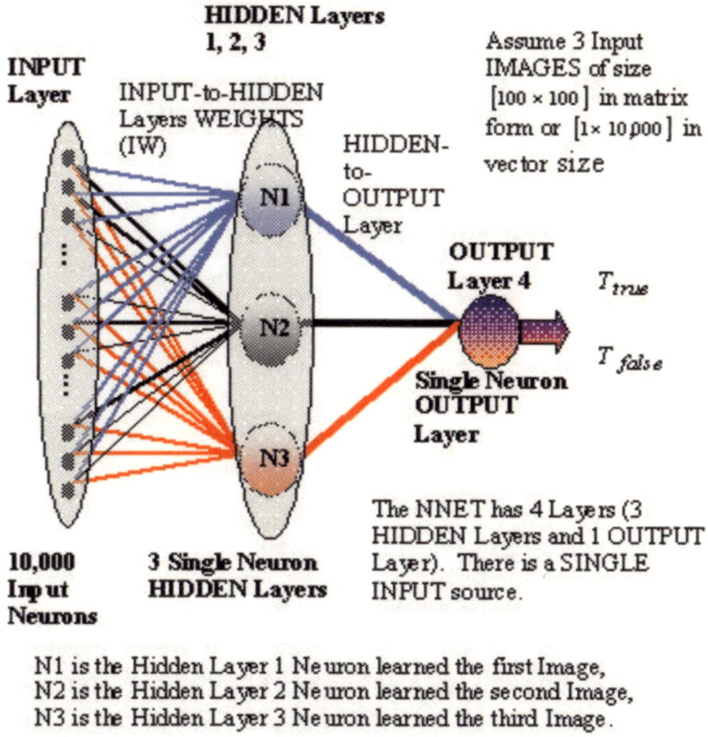

Fig. 2. Custom design of NNET block at general-HONN filter

input through the NNET in parallel due to the parallel input sources. However, to allow easier implementation, we chose the former design of the NNET.

Hence, assume there are three training images of a car, size [100x100] ([1x(100x100)] in vector form), of different angle of view, to pass through the NNET. The chosen first design (see Fig. 2) uses one input source used for all the training images. Then, the input source consists of 10,000 i.e. [1x(100x100)] input neurons equal to the size of each training image (in vector form). Each layer needs, by definition, to have the same input connections to each of its hidden neurons. However, Fig. 2 is referred to as of four-layered architecture since there are three hidden layers (shown here aligned under each other) and one output layer. The input layer does not contain neurons with activation functions and so is omitted in the numbering of the layers. Each of the hidden layers consist of only one hidden neuron. Though the network initially is fully connected to the input layer during the training stage, only one hidden layer is connected for each training image presented through the NNET. Fig. 2 is thus not a contiguous four-layered architecture during training which is why the distinction is made.

In the chosen configured NNET architecture design, the initial values of the input weights, the layer weights and the biases are based on the Nguyen-Widrow (Nguyen & Widrow, 1989, 1990) initialisation algorithm. The transfer function of the hidden layers is set as the Log-Sigmoidal function. When a new training image is presented to the NNET we leave connected the input weights of only one of the hidden neurons. In order not to upset any previous learning of the rest of the hidden layer neurons we do not alter their weights when the new image is input to the NNET. It is emphasised that there is no separate feature extraction stage (Casasent et al., 1998; Talukder & Casasent, 1999) applied to the training set image. To achieve faster learning we used a modified steepest descent (Hagan et al., 1996) back propagation algorithm based on heuristic techniques. The adaptive training algorithm updates the weights and bias values according to the gradient descent momentum and an adaptive learning rate (Hagan et al., 1996):

$$\Delta w(i,i+1) = \mu \times \Delta w(i-1,i) + \lambda \times \mu \times \frac{\Delta P_f}{\Delta w(i+1,i)} \tag{7}$$

$$\Delta b(i,i+1) = \mu \times \Delta b(i-1,i) + \lambda \times \mu \times \frac{\Delta P_f}{\Delta b(i+1,i)} \tag{8}$$

$$\lambda = \left\{ \begin{array}{ll} \lambda = \lambda + \varepsilon & \text{if } \Delta P_f < 0 \\ \lambda = no\ change & \text{if } 0 < \Delta P_f \ \&\& \ \Delta P_f > \max(P_f) \\ \lambda = \lambda - \varepsilon & \text{if } \Delta P_f > \max(P_f) \end{array} \right\} \tag{9}$$

where now variable i is the iteration index of the network and is updated every time all the training set images pass through the NNET. Δw is the update function of the input and layer weights, Δb is the update function of the biases of the layers and μ is the momentum constant. The momentum allows the network to respond not only to the local gradient, but also to recent trends in the error surface. It functions like a low-pass filter by removing the small features in the error surface which allows NNET not to get stuck in a shallow local minimum, but to slide through such a minimum. P_f is the performance function usually set as being the mean square error (mse) and ΔP_f is the derivative of the performance function. The learning rate is indicated with the letter λ. It adapts iteratively based on the derivative of the performance function ΔP_f. In effect, if there is a decrease in the ΔP_f, then the learning rate is increased by the constant ε. If ΔP_f increases but the derivative does not take a value higher than the maximum allowed value of the performance function, $\max(P_f)$ then the learning rate does not change. If ΔP_f increases more than $\max(P_f)$, then the learning rate decreases by the constant ε. The layer weights remain connected with all the hidden layers for all the training set and throughout all the training session.

3. Multiple objects recognition

All the HONN-type filters can accommodate multiple objects of the same class to be recognised within an input cluttered image due to the shift invariance properties inherited by its correlator unit. In the general HONN filter (see Fig. 3) all the input images first pass through the NNET unit. Each training image is multiplied (element wise) with the corresponding weight connections (mask). Then, the training set images after being transformed (masked) through the NNET unit by being multiplied with the mask, pass through the correlator unit where they are correlated with the masked test set images. The

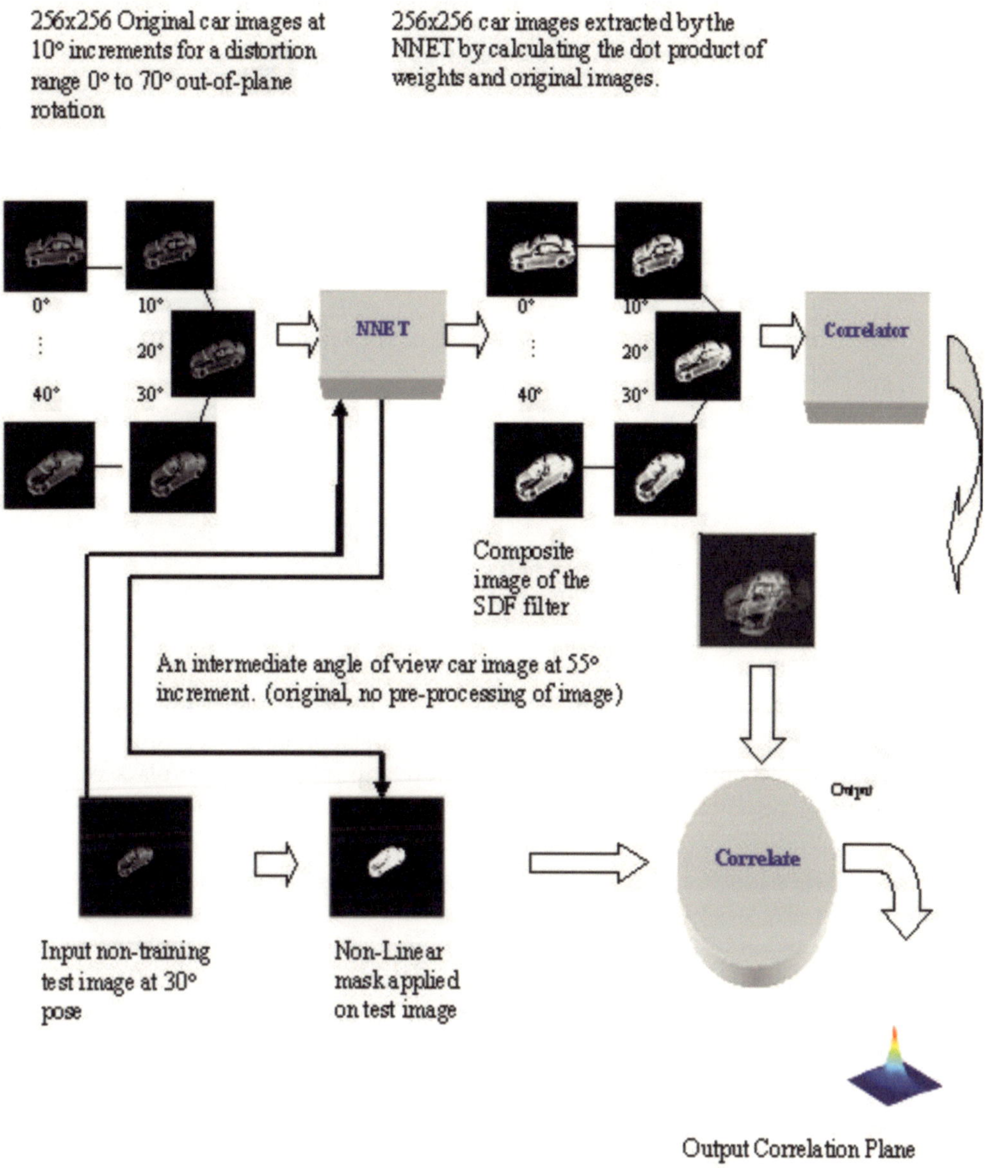

Fig. 3. Block diagram of the general-HONN filter

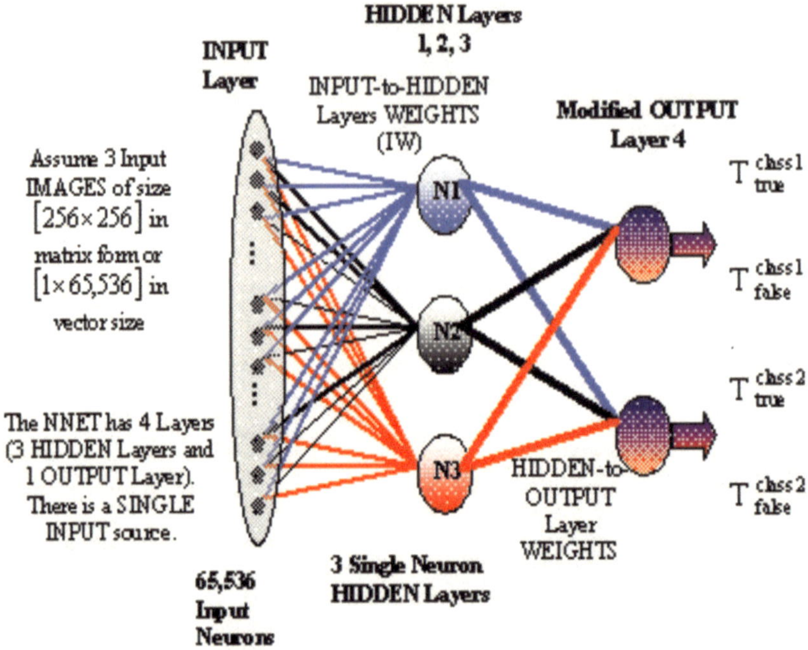

Fig. 4. Modified NNET block architecture for enabling multiple objects recognition of the same and of different classes

cross-correlation of each masked test set image with the transformed training set images (reference kernel) returns an output correlation plane peak value for each cross-correlation step. In effect, the maximum peak height values of the output correlation plane correspond to the recognised true-class objects.

3.1 Modified NNET block architecture for multiple objects of different classes recognition

Fig. 4 shows the modified NNET block architecture for accommodating multiple objects for more than one class recognition. In all the HONN-type filters presented here, i.e. Unconstrained-, Constrained-, and Modified-HONN filters, NNET is implemented as a feedforward multi-layer architecture trained with a backpropagation algorithm (Beale & Jackson, 1990). It has a single input source of input neurons equal to the size of the training image or video frame in vector form. In effect, for the training image or frame $x_{i=1...N}$ of size $[m\times n]$, there are $[m\times n]$ input neurons in the single input source. The input weights are fully connected from the input layer to the hidden layers. There are N_{iw} input weights proportional to the size of the training set. The number of the hidden layers, N_l is equal to the number of the images or video frames of the training set N:

$$N=1,2,3,\cdots,i \text{ and } N_l=N \tag{10}$$

We have set to each hidden layer to contain a single neuron. The layer weights are fully connected to the output layer. Now, the number of the layer weights N_{lw} is given by:

$$N_{lw} = N \times N_{opn} \text{ and } N_{opn} = N_{classes} \tag{11}$$

where N_{opn} is the number of the output neurons and $N_{classes}$ is the number of the different classes. In effect, we have augmented the output layer by adding more output neurons, one for each different class. On Fig. 4 we assume $N_{classes} = 2$. Thus:

$$N_{opn} = N_{classes} = 2 \text{ so, there are } N_{lw} = N \times 2 \tag{12}$$

and

$$N_{class1_{lw}} = N \text{ and } N_{class2_{lw}} = N \tag{13}$$

where $N_{class1_{lw}}$ and $N_{class2_{lw}}$ are the layer weights corresponding to object class 1 and object class 2, respectively. There are bias connections to each one of the hidden layers:

$$N_b = N \tag{14}$$

where N_b is the number of the bias connections. There are $N_{targetw}$ target connections form the N_{opn} output neurons of the output layer:

$$N_{targetw} = N_{opn} \tag{15}$$

Thus, for $N_{classes} = 2$ there are N transformed images being created for class 1 and N transformed images being created for class 2. Then, both sets of transformed images are used for the synthesis of the filter's composite image.

4. Unconstrained-, Constrained-, and Modified-HONN filters for multiple objects recognition

Next, we describe the implementation of the unconstrained-hybrid optical neural network (U-HONN), the constrained-hybrid optical neural network (C-HONN), and the modified-hybrid optical neural network (M-HONN) filters for multiple objects recognition of the same and of different classes.

4.1 Unconstrained-HONN filter for multiple objects recognition

In general, unconstrained linear combinatorial-type filters (Mahalanobis et al., 1994; Mahalanobis & Kumar, 1997; Zhou & Chao, 1999) produce broader correlation peaks but offer better distortion tolerance. However, they are not explicitly optimised to provide good quality discrimination ability between classes. LCFs, such as the SDF filter (Sudharsanan et al., 1990) set hard constraints on the correlation peak height values of the training images. During the synthesis of the filter, peak height constraints are applied at the origin. In effect, all the training set images, when correlated with an LCF, are set to produce certain pre-specified peak values, but there is no information provided for the test image correlation peak height values of the training images. In the unconstrained correlation filter synthesis

(Mahalanobis et al., 1994; Mahalanobis & Kumar, 1997; Zhou & Chao, 1999) there are no hard constraints on the correlation peak heights. Thus, the assumption made is that by removing the hard constraints the number of possible solutions the filter can draw on increases by allowing the correlation peak height values to move freely to any value, so improving its performance.

Assume we have now $N_{classes}$ objects of different classes in the input image. Then, if do not set hard constraints on the correlation peak heights generated by the HONN filter, and add the transformed images $S_i^{class}(m,n)$, of size each $[m \times n]$, of each class, without any hard constraint weights at the origin, then we can synthesise the U-HONN filter (Kypraios et al., 2004b), which its transfer function is given by:

$$U-HONN = \sum_{i=1\ldots N_{classes}\times N}^{N_{classes}\times N} S_i^{class}(m,n) \tag{16}$$

or in the frequency domain eqn. (16) is re-written as:

$$U-HONN = \sum_{i=1\ldots N_{classes}\times N}^{N_{classes}\times N} S_i^{class}(u,v) \tag{17}$$

where $S_i^{class}(u,v)$ is the frequency domain transformed input image i of each class (with (*u*, *v*) the frequency components of the image), N is the number of the input images, the image index $i = 1\ldots(N_{classes} \times N)$, i.e. there are N transformed images of each of the $N_{classes}$ in the filter's synthesis, and index $N_{classes} = class1, class2, \ldots, classK$ (K any non-zero positive integer number, $K \in \Im^{+}$.

The non-linear U-HONN filter is inherently shift invariant and may be employed as an optical correlator-type filter. It may be used as a space domain function in a joint transform correlator architecture or be Fourier transformed and used as a Fourier domain filter in a 4-f Vander Lugt (Vander Lugt, 1964) type optical correlator.

4.2 Constrained-HONN filter for multiple objects recognition

Following a similar technique used for constraining an LCF we can constrain the correlation peaks at the centre of the correlation plane of the general HONN filter. The transfer function of the produced C-HONN filter (Kypraios et al., 2004a), now for multiple objects of the same and of different class, is given by:

$$C-HONN = \sum_{i=1\ldots N_{classes}\times N}^{N_{classes}\times N} \alpha_i \cdot S_i^{class}(m,n) \tag{18}$$

or in the frequency domain eqn. (18) is re-written as:

$$C-HONN = \sum_{i=1\ldots N_{classes}\times N}^{N_{classes}\times N} \alpha_i \cdot S_i^{class}(u,v) \tag{19}$$

where $S_i^{class}(u,v)$ is the frequency domain transformed input image i of each class (with (*u*, *v*) the frequency components of the image), N is the number of the input images, the image index $i = 1\ldots(N_{classes} \times N)$, i.e. there are N transformed images of each of the $N_{classes}$ in the filter's synthesis, and index $N_{classes} = class1, class2, \ldots, classK$ (K any non-zero positive integer number, $K \in \Im^{+}$. Now, the transformed images $S_i^{class}(m,n)$, of size each $[m \times n]$, of each class, are multiplied with the hard constraint weights $\alpha_{i=1 \ldots N_{classes} \times N}$ set on the correlation peak heights of the N input images at the centre of the correlation plane.

The C-HONN filter is composed of a non-linear space domain superposition of the training set images. The multiplying coefficient becomes a function of the input weights and the layer weights, rather than a simple linear multiplying constant as used in a conventional LCF synthesis. Thus, the non-linear C-HONN filter is inherently shift invariant and it may be employed in an optical correlator as would a linear superposition LCF, such as the SDF-type filters. As for the U-HONN filter, it may be used as a space domain function in a joint transform correlator architecture or be Fourier transformed and used as Fourier domain filter in a 4-f Vander Lugt (Vander Lugt, 1964) type optical correlator.

4.3 Modified-HONN filter for multiple objects recognition

The following observations are made for the general HONN filter. Though the LCFs contain no information on non-reference objects in the training set used during their synthesis, the NNET includes information for reference and non-reference images of the true-class object. That is due to the NNET interpolating non-linearly between the reference images (Kypraios et al., 2002) included in the training set and forcing all the non-reference images to follow the activation graph. Moreover, the NNET generalises between all the reference and non-reference images. Motivated by these observations, we apply an optical mask to the filter's input (see Fig. 5). The mask is built by the weight connections of the reference images of the true-class object and is applied to all the tested images:

$$\Gamma_c = W^{x_c} \cdot L^{x_c}$$

$$= \begin{bmatrix} w_{11}^{x_c} & w_{12}^{x_c} & \cdots & w_{1n-1}^{x_c} & w_{1n}^{x_c} \\ w_{21}^{x_c} & w_{22}^{x_c} & \cdots & w_{2n-1}^{x_c} & w_{2n}^{x_c} \\ \vdots & & & & \\ w_{m1}^{x_c} & w_{m2}^{x_c} & \cdots & w_{mn-1}^{x_c} & w_{mn}^{x_c} \end{bmatrix} \cdot \begin{bmatrix} l_{11}^{x_c} & \cdots & l_{1q}^{x_c} \\ l_{21}^{x_c} & \cdots & l_{2q}^{x_c} \\ \vdots & & \\ l_{n1}^{x_c} & \cdots & l_{nq}^{x_c} \end{bmatrix}$$

$$= \begin{bmatrix} w_{11}^{x_c} \cdot l_{11}^{x_c} + w_{12}^{x_c} \cdot l_{21}^{x_c} + \cdots + w_{1n}^{x_c} \cdot l_{n1}^{x_c} & \cdots\cdots & w_{11}^{x_c} \cdot l_{1q}^{x_c} + w_{12}^{x_c} \cdot l_{2q}^{x_c} + \cdots + w_{1n}^{x_c} \cdot l_{nq}^{x_c} \\ w_{21}^{x_c} \cdot l_{11}^{x_c} + w_{22}^{x_c} \cdot l_{21}^{x_c} + \cdots + w_{2n}^{x_c} \cdot l_{n1}^{x_c} & \cdots\cdots & w_{21}^{x_c} \cdot l_{1q}^{x_c} + w_{22}^{x_c} \cdot l_{2q}^{x_c} + \cdots + w_{2n}^{x_c} \cdot l_{nq}^{x_c} \\ \vdots & & \\ w_{m1}^{x_c} \cdot l_{11}^{x_c} + w_{m2}^{x_c} \cdot l_{21}^{x_c} + \cdots + w_{mn}^{x_c} \cdot l_{n1}^{x_c} & \cdots\cdots & w_{m1}^{x_c} \cdot l_{1q}^{x_c} + w_{m2}^{x_c} \cdot l_{2q}^{x_c} + \cdots + w_{mn}^{x_c} \cdot l_{nq}^{x_c} \end{bmatrix} \quad (20)$$

where W^{x_c} and L^{x_c} are the matrices of the input and layer weights. $W_{mn}^{x_c}$ are the input weights from the input neuron of the input vector element at row m and column n to the associated hidden layer for the training image $x_c(m,n)$. $l_{nq}^{x_c}$ are the hidden layer weights from the hidden neuron n to the associated output neuron q. Now, instead of multiplying each training image with the corresponding weight connections as for the C-HONN filter, we keep constant the weight connection values, setting them to be equal with a randomly chosen image included in the training set $x_c(m,n)$. The matrix Γ_c is used to build the optical mask for M-HONN.

The transfer function of the M-HONN filter (Kypraios et al., 2008, 2009) for multiple object recognition of different class objects is written as follows:

$$M-HONN = \sum_{i=1\ldots N_{classes}\times N}^{N_{classes}\times N} \alpha_i \cdot S_i^{class}(m,n)$$

$$=\alpha_1 \cdot \left(\Gamma_c^{class} \cdot X_1(m,n)\right) + \alpha_2 \cdot \left(\Gamma_c^{class} \cdot X_2(m,n)\right) + \cdots + \alpha_N \cdot \left(\Gamma_c^{class} \cdot X_N(m,n)\right) \quad (21)$$

or in the frequency domain eqn. (21) is re-written as:

$$M-HONN = \sum_{i=1\ldots N_{classes}\times N}^{N_{classes}\times N} \alpha_i \cdot S_i^{class}(u,v) \quad (22)$$

where $S_i^{class}(u,v)$ is the frequency domain transformed input image i of each class (with ***u, v)*** the frequency components of the image), N is the number of the input images, the image index $i=1\ldots(N_{classes}\times N)$, i.e. there are N transformed images of each of the $N_{classes}$ in the filter's synthesis, and index $N_{classes} = class\,1, class\,2, \ldots, class\,K$ (K any non-zero positive integer number, $K \in \Im^+$. The transformed images $S_i^{class}(m,n)$ are calculated from the dot product of Γ_c^{class} for each class, which corresponds to an output neuron of the augmented NNET, with the corresponding training image $X_i(m,n)$.

Thus, the filter is composed of a non-linear space domain superposition of the training set images (similarly, it can be formed from video frames of the training set images). As for all the HONN-type filters, the multiplying coefficients now become a non-linear function of the input weights and the layer weights, rather than a simple linear multiplying constant as used in a constrained linear combinatorial-type filter synthesis procedure. The non-linear M-HONN filter is inherently shift invariant and it may be employed in an optical correlator as would a linear superposition LCF, such as the SDF-type filters. It may be used as a space domain function in a joint transform correlator architecture or be Fourier transformed and used as Fourier domain filter in a 4-f Vander Lugt (Vander Lugt, 1964) type optical correlator.

5. Comparative analysis of HONN-type filters

It was confirmed experimentally that by choosing different values of the target classification levels for the true-class T_{true}^{class} and false-class T_{true}^{false} objects i.e. the output layer's neuron's target output for the true-class object and the corresponding false-class object, and for each of the different object classes, respectively of the NNET (see Fig. 4), the U-HONN, C-HONN, and M-HONN filters', for multiple objects recognition, behaviour can be varied to suit different application requirements. Hence, by increasing the absolute distance of the target classification levels between the different object classes and between each object class and

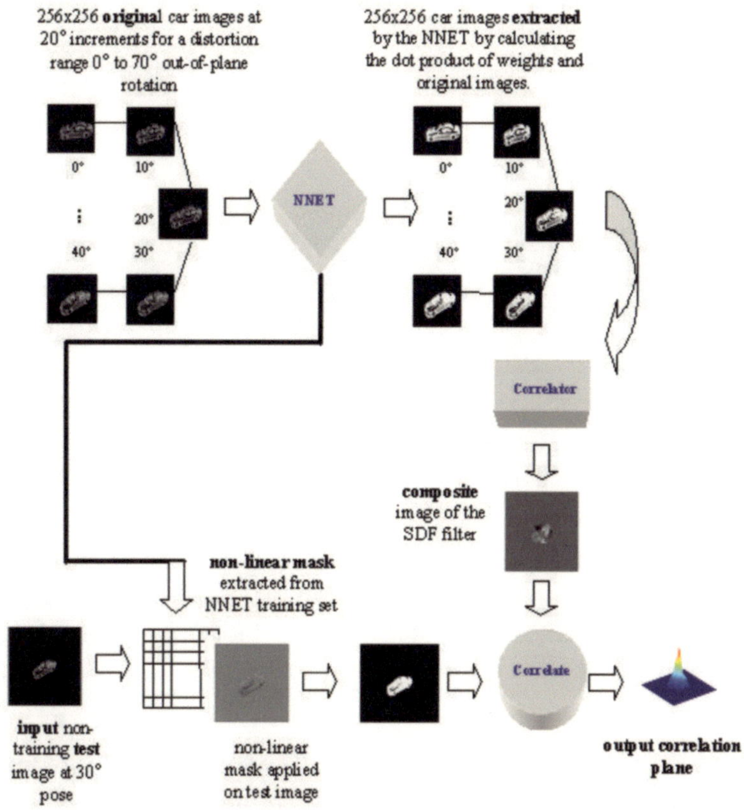

Fig. 5. Block diagram of the M-HONN filter

each corresponding false-class i.e. $\Delta T^{class}_{true} = \left|T^{class1}_{false} - T^{class2}_{false}\right|$ and $\Delta T^{class}_{true} = \left|T^{class1}_{true} - T^{class2}_{true}\right|$ the filters exhibited generally sharp peaks and good clutter suppression but are more sensitive to intra-class distortions i.e. they behave more like a high-pass biased filter, whereas by decreasing the absolute distance of the target classification levels between the different object classes and between each object class and each corresponding false-class the filters exhibited relatively good intra-class distortion invariance but producing broad correlation peaks i.e. they behave more like a minimum variance synthetic discriminant function (MVSDF) filter (Kumar, 1986). It is noted that though U-HONN, C-HONN and M-HONN filters behaviour can be varied by increasing or decreasing the absolute distance of the target classification levels between the different object classes and between each object class and each corresponding false-class, however even for the same training and test set images and for the same target classification levels the individual morphology of each filter's output correlation plane differs based on its individual transfer function characteristics. Therefore, next we will study comparatively the characteristics of its filter for multiple objects recognition within cluttered scenes. Thus, we have kept the same target classification levels for all the filters and all the conducted simulations to be able to extract useful comparison conclusions. It must be noted, again, the selected target classification levels are not optimised for each individual filter form, but rather we are aiming to set values that can allow reasonable performance for all of the filters, U-HONN, C-HONN and M-HONN.

(a) (b)

Fig. 6. (a) Test set image data, and (b) training set background car park scenes

Obviously, the optimised target classification levels achieve best performance when set individually for each of U-HONN, C-HONN and M-HONN filters (Kypraios, 2009; Kypraios et al. 2004a, 2004b, 2008, 2009).

5.1 Test data

For the conducted simulations for comparing the U-HONN, C-HONN and M-HONN filters' performance within cluttered scenes we used different image data sets. The first data set consists of an S-type Jaguar car model at 10° increments of out-of-plane rotation at an elevation angle of approximately 45°. A second image data set consists of images of a Mazda Efini RX-7 Police car model at 45° elevation angle. A third image data set consists of typical empty car park scenes (background scene images). A fourth image data set (cluttered scenes) consists of the background images of typical car parks and the images of the S-type car model and the MazdaRX-7 car model added in the background scene (see Fig. 6). All the image data sequences used in the training sets and test sets were used in grey-scale bitmap format. All the image data sequences used in the training sets and test sets were of size [256x256]. All the input video frames prior being processed by the NNET are concatenated row-by-row in to a vector form, i.e. [1x(256x256)]. Normally this size of input image data is practically impossible to be processed in real-time, since to be implemented by enough input and layer weights for 256x256 pixels input images would require in input weights:

$$N \times \left[1x\left(256 \times 256 \right) \right] \tag{23}$$

So, assume (see Fig. 4) N=10 images or video frames to be processed through any neural network architecture would require in input weights:

$$10 \times \left[1x\left(256 \times 256 \right) \right] = 655{,}360 \tag{24}$$

which is more than half-a-million input weight connections! Hence, it only becomes possible to overcome this problem by using the novel selective weight connection architecture.

Additionally, the heuristic training algorithm with momentum and an adaptive learning rate employed into the NNET training stage speeds up the learning phase and reduces the memory size needed to fully complete the training stage. Here, it worth mentioning that the video frame sequences for all the test series were processed by a Dual Core CPU at 2.4 GHz with 4GB RAM in few a msec.

5.2 Simulation results of C-HONN for multiple objects recognition

The training set consisted of true-class 1 object of the Jaguar S-type for a distortion range over 20° to 70° at 10° increments. At least one Mazda Efini RX-7 car image has been added in the training set to be of true-class 2 object. At least one background image of a typical car park scene has been included in the training set of the NNET block to fall inside the false-class. For the C-HONN filter we constrained in the correlator-type block the true-class 1 object images (Jaguar S-type) to unit peak-height output correlation value, the true-class 2 object images (Mazda Efini RX-7) to half-a-unit peak-height output correlation value, and all the false-class images (background scenes) to zero peak-height output correlation value. The test set consisted of a non-training in-class true-class 1 object at an intermediate car pose (non-training) and a non-training in-class true-class 2 object at an intermediate car pose (non-training) inserted in an unknown (non-training) background scene. During the true-classes objects' insertion additional Gaussian noise is added in the test set image, too. For our application purposes and for enabling us to extract useful comparison conclusions we have set in the NNET block the true-class 1 object target classification levels $T_{true}^{class1} = +40$ and the true-class 2 object target classification levels $T_{true}^{class2} = +20$. All the false-class images and all the background images with the car park scenes were set to $T_{false}^{class1} = -1$ for false-class 1 and to $T_{false}^{class2} = -1$ for false-class 2.

Several simulations with different test sets were conducted. For the purpose of this study indicatively we show one of the results recorded. Thus, Fig. 7 (a) shows the normalised, to the maximum correlation peak intensity value, isometric correlation plane for the used test set image. Fig. 7 (b) shows the position of a tracking box on top of the detected area at the output correlation plane of the true-class objects. Also, in Table 1, we have recorded the peak-to-correlation energy ratio (PCE) value, the peak-to-secondary-peak ratio (PSPR) value and the discrimination ability percentage (%) of recognising the different true-class objects for the shown output correlation plane. From the complete series of the recorded results, it is apparent that the C-HONN filter is able to detect and classify correctly both true-class objects, class 1 of Jaguar S-type and class 2 of Mazda Efini RX-7 at non-training intermediate out-of-plane rotation angles, and suppress background clutter scene. From Fig. 7 (a) and Table 1, C-HONN filter gave sharp correlation peaks with good correlation peak-height values. Note that the PSPR values should not be confused with the discrimination ability of the filter. PSPR values indicate the maximum peak-height value in comparison to the sidelobes and not to the overall output correlation plane for the test set image. Thus, the discrimination ability % value (also indicates the filter's inter-class separation ability) which C-HONN filter gave for the shown isometric correlation plane, and for separating class 1 and class 2 objects was 36.5616% (column 3 of Table 1). Though the LCFs offer no information for non-reference objects of the training set in their synthesis, the NNET block of all the HONN-type filters offers information for reference (trained) and non-reference

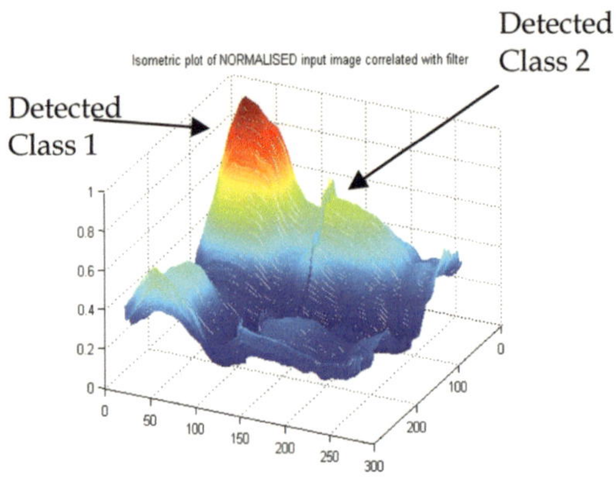

(a)

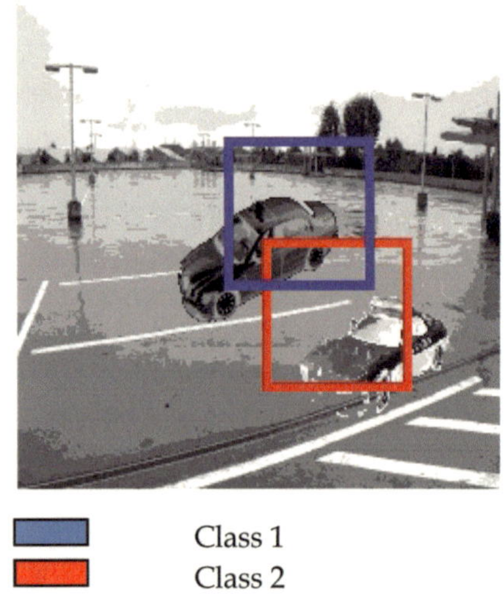

(b)

Fig. 7. (a) Normalised, to the maximum correlation peak intensity value, isometric output correlation plane of the C-HONN filter for a test set image, and (b) tracking boxes on top of the detected of the true-class objects areas at the output correlation plane; class 1of Jaguar S-type is shown with blue colour and class 2 of Mazda Efini RX-7 is shown with the red colour

(non-training) images of the true-class objects. Consequently, LCFs, such as SDF-type filters, depend solely on the information built inside the composite image formed from the reference images. However, the C-HONN filter for multiple objects recognition was able to generalise enough within the cluttered images and successfully recognise the true-class objects even at non-reference (non-training) out-of-plane rotation angles and within non-reference background car park scene.

5.3 Simulation results of U-HONN for multiple objects recognition

We used the same training and test data sets as for the C-HONN filter for multiple objects recognition. However, we created two slightly different training sets, one with at least one non-training background image included and a second one with no background images included. During the U-HONN filter for multiple objects recognition's synthesis of its composite image this time we set no hard constraints on the correlation peak-height values. For our application purposes and for enabling us to extract useful comparison conclusions

PCE	PSPR	Discrimination Ability %
0.0054	0.2458	36.5616

Table 1. C-HONN filter for multiple objects recognition within cluttered scenes performance assessment values

we have kept the same, as for the C-HONN filter for multiple objects recognition, target classification levels in the NNET block i.e. true-class 1 object target classification level $T_{true}^{class1} = +40$ and the true-class 2 object target classification level $T_{true}^{class2} = +20$. All the false-class images and all the background images with the car park scenes were set to $T_{false}^{class1} = -1$ for false-class 1 and to $T_{false}^{class2} = -1$ for false-class 2.

Several simulations with different test sets were conducted. For the purpose of this study indicatively we show one of the results recorded. Thus, Fig. 8 (a) shows the normalised, to the maximum correlation peak intensity value, isometric correlation plane for the used test set image with at least one background non-reference car park scene included in the training set, Fig. 8 (b) shows the normalised, to the maximum correlation peak intensity value, isometric correlation plane for the used test set image with no background car park scene included in the training set, and Fig. 9 shows the position of a tracking box on top of the detected area at the output correlation plane of the true-class objects for the isometric correlation plane shown in Fig. 8 (a). In Table 2 we have recorded the PCE values, the PSPR values and the discrimination ability % of recognising the different true-class objects for both shown output correlation planes in Fig. 8 (a) and Fig. 8 (b). From the complete series of the recorded results, it is apparent that the U-HONN filter is able to detect and classify correctly both true-class objects, class 1 of Jaguar S-type and class 2 of Mazda Efini RX-7 at non-training intermediate out-of-plane rotation angles, and suppress background clutter scene. But, when there was at least one non-reference background scene included in the U-HONN filter's synthesis then it increased the detected false-class areas at the output correlation plane (see Fig. 8 (b)). Thus, as it was expected from U-HONN filter for multiple objects recognition's design and transfer function (see eqns. (16) and (17)), the resulted solutions from correlating the test set image with the U-HONN filter's transfer function are increasing in comparison with the C-HONN filter since there are no hard constraints imposed on the correlation peak-heights for U-HONN filter. However, by including a false-class non-reference background image in the filter's synthesis, it produces more unwanted false-class peaks in comparison to having not included any background images. From Fig. 7 and Fig. 8 (a) (for background images included in the training set), and from Table 1 and Table 2 U-HONN filter for multiple objects recognition produces higher PSPR with smaller sidelobes values i.e. sharper correlation peaks, but C-HONN filter for multiple objects recognition produces higher correlation peak-height values with broader sidelobes (smaller PSPR values). The discrimination ability % value U-HONN filter gave for Fig. 8 (a) shown isometric correlation plane, and for separating class 1 and class 2 objects was 12.0242% and for Fig. 8 (b) was approximately 2% (column 3 of Table 2), which for both isometric plots it is less than the discrimination ability % value that C-HONN filter gave. In effect, U-HONN filter for multiple objects recognition it maximises the correlation peak-heights (including the false-class ones in the case of Fig. 8 (a) plot) at the output correlation plane in expense of broadening the sidelobes and, thus, decreasing its discrimination ability %, for the test set images to recognise the true-class objects in the cluttered scenes. Consequently, for U-HONN, broader sidelobes means better intra-class ability and better distortion range, i.e. it is able to maintain high correlation peak-heights for recognising intermediate non-reference out-of-plane rotation angles of the true-class objects with less correlation peak-height value decrease (drop) than C-HONN filter. Again, as for the C-HONN filter for multiple objects recognition, the U-HONN filter for multiple objects recognition was able to generalise

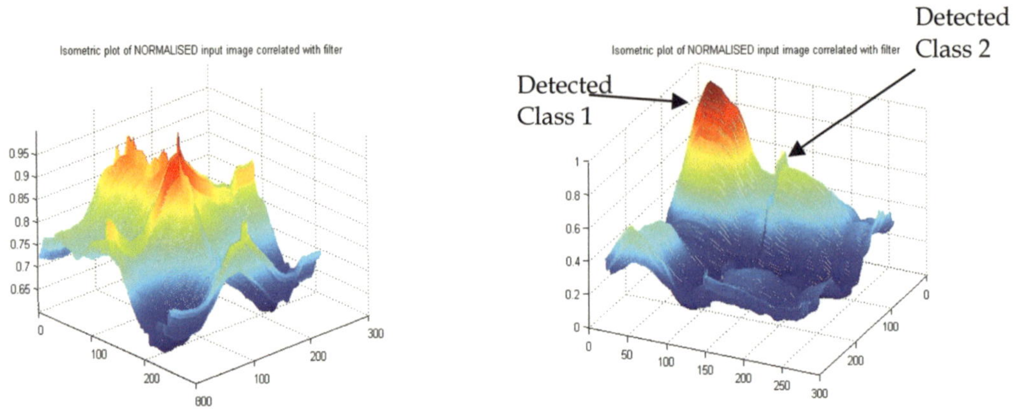

(a) (b)

Fig. 8. (a) Normalised, to the maximum correlation peak intensity value, isometric output correlation plane of the U-HONN filter for a test set image with at least one background non-reference car park scene included in the training set, and (b) normalised, to the maximum correlation peak intensity value, isometric correlation plane for the used test set image with no background car park scene included in the training set

enough within the cluttered images and successfully recognise the true-class objects even at non-reference (non-training) out-of-plane rotation angles and within non-reference background car park scene.

5.4 Simulation results of M-HONN for multiple objects recognition

We used the same training and test data sets as for the C-HONN filter for multiple objects recognition. As for the C-HONN filter for multiple objects recognition, we constrained in the correlator-type block of the M-HONN filter for multiple objects recognition the true-class 1 object images (Jaguar S-type) to unit peak-height output correlation value, the true-class 2 object images (Mazda Efini RX-7) to half-a-unit peak-height output correlation value, and all the false-class images (background scenes) to zero peak-height output correlation value. For our application purposes and for enabling us to extract useful comparison conclusions we have kept the same, as for the C-HONN filter for multiple objects recognition, target classification levels in the NNET block i.e. true-class 1 object target classification level $T_{true}^{class1} = +40$ and the true-class 2 object target classification level $T_{true}^{class2} = +20$. All the false-class images and all the background images with the car park scenes were set to $T_{false}^{class1} = -1$ for false-class 1 and to $T_{false}^{class2} = -1$ for false-class 2.

Several simulations with different test sets were conducted. For the purpose of this study indicatively we show one of the results recorded. Fig. 10 (a) shows the normalised, to the maximum correlation peak intensity value, isometric correlation plane for the used test set image and Fig. 10 (b) shows the position of a tracking box on top of the detected area at the output correlation plane of the true-class objects. In Table 3 the PSPR value is recorded for the test set image. From the complete series of the recorded results, it is apparent that the M-HONN filter is able to detect and classify correctly both true-class objects, class 1 of Jaguar

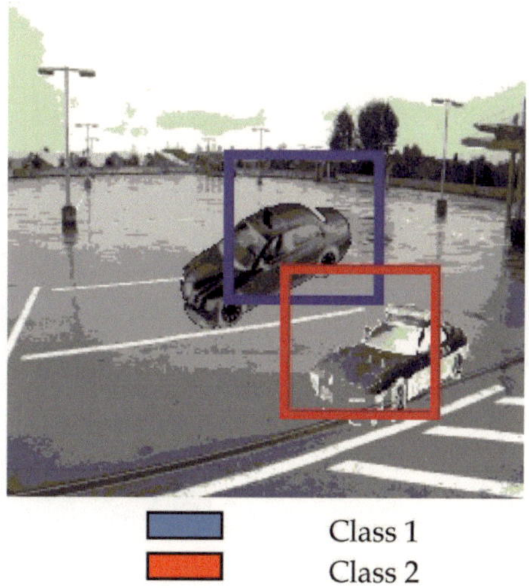

Fig. 9. Tracking boxes on top of the detected areas of the true-class objects at the output correlation plane of U-HONN filter for multiple objects recognition; class 1of Jaguar S-type is shown with blue colour and class 2 of Mazda Efini RX-7 is shown with the red colour

U-HONN for multiple objects	PCE	PSPR	Discrimination Ability %
Train Set with Backgorund Images included	0.0020	0.9522	12.0242
Train Set with NO Backgorund Images included	**0.0044**	**0.0840**	**approx. 2.0**

Table 2. U-HONN filter for multiple objects recognition within cluttered scenes performance assessment values

S-type and class 2 of Mazda Efini RX-7 at non-training intermediate out-of-plane rotation angles, and suppress background clutter scene. From the isometric plots shown in Fig. 7, Fig. 8 (b), Fig. 9 and Fig. 10, and from Table 1, Table 2 and Table 3 it is found that the M-HONN filter for multiple objects recognition produces higher PSPR values and i.e. sharper peaks than the C-HONN and U-HONN filters for multiple objects recognition. However, from the full series of the conducted tests it is recorded that the M-HONN filter for multiple objects recognition produces a higher drop for the non-training intermediate car poses within the background clutter than the C-HONN and U-HONN filters for multiple objects recognition (Kypraios, 2009; Kypraios et al. 2008). In effect, the M-HONN filter for multiple objects recognition confirms its design expectation of producing optimum performance (sharper peak-heights) within cluttered scenes than U-HONN and C-HONN filters for multiple objects recognition in expense of a drop in its intra-class (non-training images of intermediate out-of-plane rotation angles of true-class objects) distortion tolerance.

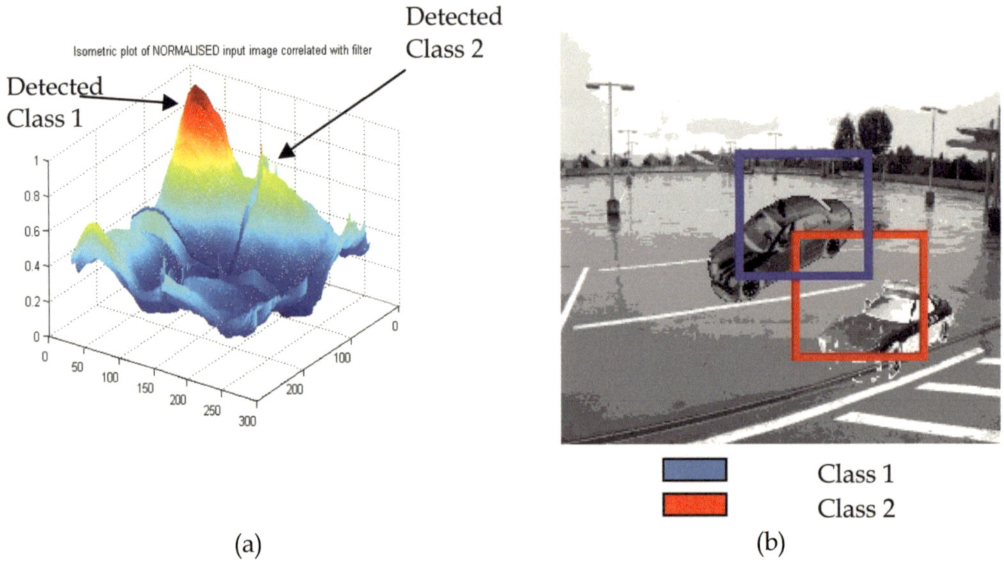

Fig. 10. (a) Normalised, to the maximum correlation peak intensity value, isometric output correlation plane of the M-HONN filter for a test set image, and (b) tracking boxes on op of the detected of the true-class objects areas at the output correlation plane; class 1of Jaguar S-type is shown with blue colour and class 2 of Mazda Efini RX-7 is shown with the red colour

PCE	PSPR	Discrimination Ability %
0.0050	0.3026	20.4320

Table 3. M-HONN filter for multiple objects recognition within cluttered scenes performance assessment values

M-HONN filter for multiple objects recognition gave for the shown isometric correlation plane in Fig. 10, and for separating class 1 and class 2, the discrimination ability % value of 20.4320% (column 3 of Table 3). Thus, C-HONN filter for multiple objects recognition exhibits higher discrimination ability than the M-HONN filter for multiple objects recognition. Still, the M-HONN filter is able to separate adequately the different classes of objects. Again, as for the U-HONN and C-HONN filters for multiple objects recognition, the M-HONN filter for multiple objects recognition was able to generalise enough within the cluttered images and successfully recognise the true-class objects even at non-reference (non-training) out-of-plane rotation angles and within non-reference (unknown) background car park scene.

6. Conclusion

We have compared with each other the performance of the U-HONN, C-HONN and M-HONN filters for multiple objects recognition. We have described how the U-HONN, C-

HONN and M-HONN filters can accommodate the recognition of multiple objects of the same or of different classes. Due to the shift invariance properties inherited by its correlator unit the filter can accommodate multiple objects of the same class to be detected within an input cluttered image. Also, the architecture of the NNET block of the general-HONN filter allows the recognition of multiple objects of different classes within the input cluttered image by augmenting the output layer of the unit. U-HONN, C-HONN and M-HONN filters for multiple objects recognition may be used as a space domain function in a joint transform correlator architecture or be Fourier transformed and used as a Fourier domain filter in a 4-f Vander Lugt-type optical correlator. It was confirmed experimentally that by increasing or decreasing the absolute distance of the target classification levels between the different object classes and between each object class and each corresponding false-class i.e. $\Delta T_{true}^{class} = \left|T_{false}^{class1} - T_{false}^{class2}\right|$ and $\Delta T_{true}^{class} = \left|T_{true}^{class1} - T_{true}^{class2}\right|$, the U-HONN, C-HONN, and M-HONN filters, for multiple objects recognition, behaviour can be varied to behave from more like a high-pass biased filter to more like a MVSDF filter for serving the different application requirements. However, even for the same training and test set images and for the same target classification levels the individual morphology of each filter's output correlation plane differs based on its individual transfer function characteristics. Therefore, for all the conducted tests the target classification levels for all the filters have been kept the same in order to be able to extract useful comparison conclusions. It must be noted the target classification levels are chosen to values which can allow good performance for all the filters and for keeping the same values. Obviously, best performance can be achieved by setting the values individually for each of U-HONN, C-HONN and M-HONN filters but not to the same target classification levels.

U-HONN, C-HONN and M-HONN filters for multiple objects recognition exhibit simultaneously shift and out-of-plane rotation invariances with a single pass over the data, i.e. there is not needed more than one filter to be trained for shift invariance and separately another one for out-of-plane rotation invariance. Additionally, they exhibit good tolerance-to-clutter performance without disturbing the other simultaneously exhibit properties of out-of-plane rotation and shift invariances. In general, the HONN-type filters are shown experimentally to be performing better than the LCFs. U-HONN, C-HONN and M-HONN filters are proven to recognize correctly the multiple true-class objects of the same or of different classes within non-reference (unknown i.e. not previously trained) background scenes. U-HONN filter for multiple objects recognition exhibits better distortion range, i.e. it maintains good correlation peak height for recognising intermediate non-reference out-of-plane rotation angles of the true-class objects, and higher peak-heights but in expense of broader sidelobes in recognising the true-class objects within the cluttered scene than the C-HONN and M-HONN filters. M-HONN filter design is optimised for producing best performance in recognising objects within cluttered scenes. Hence, it was found that it gave sharper peaks than the U-HONN and C-HONN filters for recognising the true-class objects of the different classes within the unknown car park scene. However, C-HONN filter for multiple objects recognition produces more controlled peak-heights and better discrimination ability between the true-class objects of different classes within the cluttered scenes than the U-HONN and M-HONN filters for multiple objects recognition. U-HONN, C-HONN and M-HONN filters for multiple objects recognition can be employed, amongst the many application areas, in image content-based Internet search engines. The simultaneous properties of U-HONN, C-HONN and M-HONN filters of shift and out-of-plane rotation invariances, can reduce the number of stored images for each object class and, consequently reduce the time needed for an Internet image-to-image search engine (content-based search engine) to search the complete data set of matched images. Moreover, the accommodation of multiple objects recognition of the same and of different classes with the same single filter and with a single pass over the training and test data reduces the training times instead of training several filters for the different object classes.

7. References

Wood, J. (1996). Invariant Pattern Recognition: A Review. *Pattern Recognition,* Vol.29, No.1, pp. 1-17

Forsyth, D. A. & Ponce, J. (2003). *Computer Vision –A Modern Approach,* Prentice Hall International, Inc. (Pearson Education, Inc.),ISBN-10 0130851981, ISBN-13 978-0130851987

Sheng, Y., & Arsenault, H. H. (1986). Experiments on Pattern Recognition Using Invariant Fourier-Mellin Descriptors, *Journal of Optical Society of America A (Optics and Image Science),* Vol.3, pp. 771-776

Sheng, Y., & Lejeune, C. (1991). Invariant Pattern Recognition Using Fourier-Mellin Transforms and Neural Networks, *Journal of Optics,* Vol.22, pp. 223-228

Grace, A., & Spann, M. (1991). A Comparison Between Fourier-Mellin Descriptors and Moment Based Features For Invariant Object Recognition Using Neural Networks, *Pattern Recognition Letters,* Vol.12, pp. 635-643

Casasent, D. & Psaltis D. (1976). Position, Rotation and Scale Invariant Optical Correlation, *Applied Optics,* Vol.15, No.7, pp. 1795-1799

Mersereau, K. & Morris, G. (1986). Scale, Rotation, and Shift Invariant Image Recognition, *Applied Optics,* Vol.25, No.14, pp. 2338-2342

Hsu, Y. N., Arsenault, H. H. & April, G. (1982). Optical Pattern Recognition Using Circular Harmonic Expansion, *Applied Optics,* Vol. 21, pp. 4012

Hsu, Y. N. & Arsenault H. H. (1984). Pattern Discrimination By Multiple Circular Harmonic Components, *Applied Optics,* Vol.23, pp. 841

Jensen, A. S., Lindvold, L. & Rasmussen, E. (1987). Transformation of Image Positions, Rotations and Sizes Into Shift Parameters, *Applied Optics,* Vol.26, No.9, pp. 1775-1781

Bryngdahl, O. (1974). Geometrical Transformations In Optics, *Journal of Optical Society of America,* Vol.64, pp. 1092

Cederquist, J. & Tai, A. M. (1984). Computer-Generated Holograms For Geometric Transformations, *Applied Optics,* Vol.23, pp. 3099

Stamos, E. (2001). *Algorithms for Designing Filters for Optical Pattern Recognition,* D.Phil. Thesis, Department of Electronic and Electrical Engineering, University College London

Lynn, P. A. & Fuerst, W. (1998). *Introductory Digital Signal Processing- with Computer Applications,* John Wiley & Sons Ltd.

Proakis, J. G. & Manolakis, D. G. (1988). *Introduction to Digital Signal Processing,* Prentice Hall International Paperback Editions

Delopoulos, A., Tirakis, A. & Kollias, S. (1994). Invariant Image Classification Using Triple-Correlation-Based Neural Networks, *IEEE Transactions on Neural Networks,* Vol.5, No.3, pp. 392-408

Perantonis, S. & Lisboa, P. (1992). Translation, Rotation and Scale Invariant Pattern Recognition by High-Order Neural Networks and Moment Classifiers, *IEEE Transactions on Neural Networks,* Vol.3, No.2, pp. 241-251

Khotanzad, A. & Hong, H. (1990). Invariant Image Recognition by Zernike Moments, *IEEE Transactions on Pattern Analysis and Machine Intelligence,* Vol. 12, pp. 489-497

Shvedov, A., Schmidt, A. & Yakubovich, V. (1979). Invariant Systems of Features in Pattern Recognition, *Automation Remote Control,* Vol. 40, pp. 131-142

LeCun, Y. (1989). Generalisation and Network Design Strategies, *Connectionism in Perspective,* Pfeirer, R., Schreter, Z., Fogelman-Soulié, F. & Steels, L., Elsevier Science, Amsterdam

LeCun, Y., Boser, B., Denker, J. S., Henderson, D., Howard, R. E., Hubbard, W., Jackel, L. D. (1990). Handwritten Digit Recognition with a Backpropagation Network, *Advances in Neural Information Processing Systems,* Touretzky, D., Morgan Kaufmann, Vol.2, pp. 396-404

Spirkovska, L. & Reid, M. (1992). Robust Position, Scale and Rotation Invariant Object Recognition Using Higher-Order Neural Networks, *Pattern Recognition,* Vol.25, pp. 975-985

Giles, C. L. & Maxwell, T. (1987). Learning, Invariance and Generalisation in Higher-Order Neural Networks, *Applied Optics,* Vol.26, pp. 4972-4978

Kanaoka, T., Chellapa, R., Yoshitaka, M. & Tomita, S. (1992). A Higher-Order Neural Network for Distortion Invariant Pattern Recognition, *Pattern Recognition Letters,* Vol.13, pp. 837-841

Waibel, A., Hanazawa, T., Hinton, G , Shikano, K. & Lang, K. (1989). Phoneme Recognition Using Time-Delay Neural Networks, *IEEE Transactions on Acoustics, Speech Signal Processing,* Vol.37, No.3, pp. 328-339

Bottou, L., Fogelman- Soulié, F., Blanchet, P. & Lienard, J. S. (1990). Speaker Independent Isolated Digit Recognition : Multilayer Perceptrons vs Dynamic Time Warping, *Neural Networks,* Vol.3, pp. 453-465

Simard, P. & LeCun, Y. (1992). Reverse TDNN : An Architecture for Trajectory Generation, *Advances in Neural Information Processing Systems,* Moody, J., Hanson, S. & Lipmann, R., Morgan Kauffmann, Vol.4, pp. 579-588

Yuceer, C. & Oflazer, K. (1993). A Rotation, Scaling and Translation Invariant Pattern Classification System, *Pattern Recognition,* Vol.26, No.5, pp. 687-710

Kypraios, I., Young, R. C. D., Birch, P. M. & Chatwin, C. R. (2004a). Object Recognition Within Cluttered Scenes Employing a Hybrid Optical Neural Network Filter, *Optical Engineering Special Issue on Trends in Pattern Recognition,* Vol.43, pp. 1839-1850

Bahri, Z. & Kumar, B. V. K. (1988). Generalized Synthetic Discriminant Functions, *Journal of Optical Society of America,* Vol.5, No.4, pp. 562-571

Kypraios, I., Young, R. C. D., Chatwin C. R. (2002). An Investigation of the Non-Linear Properties of Correlation Filter Synthesis and Neural Network Design, *Asian Journal of Physics,* Vol.11, No.3, pp. 313-344

Beale, R. & Jackson, T. (1990). *Neural Computing : An Introduction,* Institute of Physics Publishing, Hilger, ISBN 0852742622, 9780852742624, Bristol, Philadelphia

Kumar, B. V. K. (1992). Tutorial Survey of Composite Filter Designs for Optical Correlators, *Applied Optics,* Vol.31, No.23, 4773-4801

Nguyen, D. & Widrow, B. (1989). The Truck Backer-Upper: An Example of Self-Learning in Neural Networks, *Proceedings of the IEEE International Joint Conference on Neural Networks,* Vol.2, pp. 357-363

Nguyen, D. & Widrow, B. (1990). Improving the Learning Speed of 2-Layer Neural Networks by Choosing Initial Values of the Adaptive Weights, *Proceedings of the IEEE International Joint Conference on Neural Networks,* Vol.3, pp. 21-26

Casasent, D., Neiberg, L. M. & Sipe, M. A. (1998). Feature Space Trajectory Distorted Object Representation for Classification and Pose Estimation, *Optical Engineering,* Vol.37, No.3, pp. 914-923

Talukder, A. & Casasent, D. (1999). Non-Linear Features for Product Inspection, *Optical Pattern Recognition X, Proceedings of SPIE,* Vol.3715, pp. 32-43

Hagan, M. T., Demuth, H. B. & Beale, M. H. (1996). *Neural Network Design,* PWS Publishing, ISBN 0-9717321-0-8, Boston, MA

Sudharsanan, S. I., Mahalanobis, A. & Sundareshan, M. K. (1990). A Unified Framework for the Synthesis of Synthetic Discriminant Functions with Reduced Noise Variance and Sharp Correlation Structure, *Optical Engineering,* Vol.29, pp. 1021-1028

Mahalanobis, A., Kumar, B. V. K., Song, S., Sims, S. R. F. & Epperson, J. F. (1994). Unconstrained Correlation Filters, *Applied Optics,* Vol.33, No.17, pp. 3751-3759

Zhou, H. & Chao, T. H. (1999). MACH Filter Synthesising for Detecting Targets in Cluttered Environment for Gray-Scale Optical Correlator, *Optical Pattern Recognition X, Proceedings of SPIE,* Vol.3715, pp. 394-398

Mahalanobis, A. & Kumar, B. V. K. (1997). Optimality of the Maximum Average Correlation Height Filter for Detection of Targets in Noise, *Optical Engineering,* Vol.36, No.10, pp. 2642-2648

Kypraios, I., Young, R. C. D. & Chatwin, C. R. (2004b). Performance assessment of Unconstrained Hybrid Optical Neural Network filter for Object Recognition Tasks in Clutter, *Optical Pattern Recognition XV, Proceedings of SPIE,* Vol.5437, pp. 51-62

Vander Lugt, A. (1964). Signal Detection By Complex Spatial Filtering, *IEEE Transactions on Information Theory,* Vol.10, pp. 139-145

Kypraios, I., Lei, P. W., Birch, P. M., Young, R. C. D. & Chatwin C. R. (2008). Performance Assessment of the Modified-Hybrid Optical Neural Network Filter, *Applied Optics,* Vol.47, No.18, pp. 3378-3389

Kypraios, I., Young, R. C. D. & Chatwin, C. R. (2009). Modified-Hybrid Optical Neural Network Filter for Multiple Objects Recognition within Cluttered Scenes, *Optics and Photonics for Information Processing III, Proceedings SPIE,* Vol.7442, pp. 74420P-74420P-12

Kumar, B. V. K. (1986). Minimum Variance Synthetic Discriminant Functions, *Journal Optics Society America A,* Vol.3, pp. 1579-1584

Kypraios, I. (2009). A Comparative Analysis of the Hybrid Optical Neural Network-type Filters Performance within Cluttered Scenes, *51st International Symposium ELMAR, IEEE Region 8/IEEE Croatia/EURASIP,* Vol.1, pp. 71-77

16

Super-Resolution Object Recognition Approach for Complex Edged Objects by UWB Radar

Rahmi Salman and Ingolf Willms
Fachgebiet Nachrichtentechnische Systeme,
Universität Duisburg-Essen, 47057 Duisburg
Germany

1. Introduction

Technical investigation, research and development in the wide field of security technology have been increased in recent years. Robotics as a great deal of this progress aims at advanced mobile security robots that can measure their surrounding environment accurately and provide various sensing applications. These robots will gain a steady increasing importance in private homes, industry and military. Such robots equipped with Ultra Wideband (UWB) Radar are promising for near field, non-contacting and non-destructive sensing technologies. Compared to optical or infrared systems UWB Radar does not need a visual LOS condition which makes it suitable for smoke and dust filled emergency scenarios. In contrast to common CW-Radar, due to the wide frequency band which corresponds to a high resolution in time domain, UWB Radar is possible to separate multiple reflections of multipath propagation in sub-centimetre range. Because of the presence of low frequencies UWB Radar systems are able to penetrate dielectric materials to perform subsurface imaging. Hence, UWB has superior advantages compared to classical near-field sensing technologies which make it an ideal candidate for security robots.

The object recognition (OR) method proposed in this work is part of a super-resolution Radar imaging system by backscattered UWB signals on the basis of a reference data set. The purpose of this method is detection, recognition and classification of unknown objects.

2. System setup and system design

Radar imaging is an active remote sensing technique meaning that the scene to be imaged is illuminated by a wave transmitted by the Radar system. The receiver of the system measures the variation of the electromagnetic field intensity over time collecting echoes which contain geometrical feature information of the area in the antennas footprint. The goal of the data processing is to generate a visual image of the target from the received electro-magnetic field. To get proper and sufficient information it is necessary to scan the scene, i.e. move the sensors along a certain trajectory and record UWB pulses. In case of UWB Radar, the measured pulse approximates the channel impulse response either directly or after post-processing. Plotting the measured channel impulse responses in a 2D Radarmatrix with the time-of-flight or the distance versus the antenna position leads to a so called radargram with the amplitude indicating the intensity of the received field. The radargram is a convenient way of illustrating results of measurements and is the preferred method of displaying Radar data for further post-processing.

2.1 Objects under test and reference alphabet

The investigated objects and the reference alphabet derived from these consist of simple canonical and some polygonal complex objects in the form of beams with no variance in the 3rd dimension. In figure 1 the used 12 objects are shown.

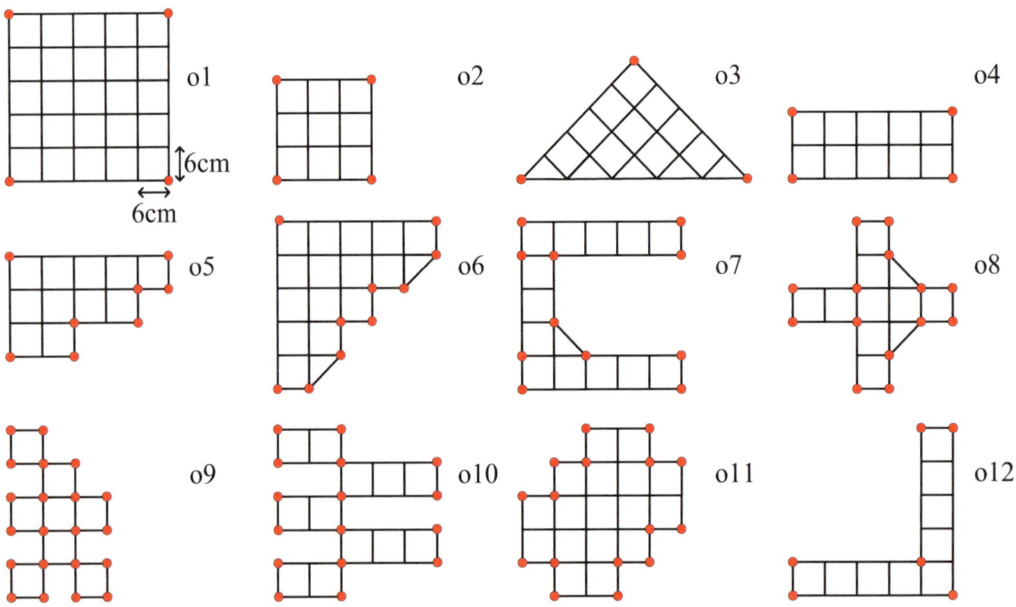

Fig. 1. Cross-section of the used 12 objects and the reference alphabet (abstracted objects consisting only discrete values equal red dots)

The reference alphabet is extracted out of a priori known dimensions of each object and consists of discrete values which are marked in figure 1 with red dots. For this purpose every edge and corner of each object is marked as a pixel with a value of 1 in a 1000 x 1000 pixel grid according to 1 mm distance between two neighboured pixels. Straight segments of the object are neither sampled nor set in any other way as a pixel at first. Hence, in the rest of the reference image pixels are set to 0 yielding to binary reference images by means of the subsequent recognition process is performed.

2.2 Simulated and measured radar data

The performance investigations of the introduced OR algorithm are carried out based on simulated Radar data obtained by Ray Tracing. To enable a quantitative proving of the effectiveness of the proposed OR algorithm, the geometric structures of each massive object were modelled by polygons and fed into the aforementioned simulation tool, which is described in its basics in (Geng & Wiesbeck, 1998; Schultze et al., 2008). The similarity between these simulations and real measurements is significantly high which could be verified in (Salman et al., 2008). In each of the 12 investigated scenarios one of the objects of

figure 1 was located in the middle of a room of 10x10 m^2 size and a height of 4 m. In these scenarios a quasi-monostatic antenna configuration (one antenna above the other) was moved around each object on a circular track with a radius of 1 m and at a constant level above the floor. Here, the antennas perform a scan with a 1 degree grid resulting in 360 impulse responses of a corresponding radargram. A frequency band between 2.5 and 12.5 GHz with 1601 frequency points was used. This corresponds to a frequency resolution of 6.25 MHz and thus to an unambiguous range of 48 m or 160 ns which is sufficient for most of indoor scenarios. Also antenna characteristics have been taken into account in the simulations. Here, two double-ridged horn antennas are applied. These antennas have approximately 20° opening angle (3 dB less than maximum beyond this angle). Their patterns have been measured in an anechoic chamber for all frequencies in the considered frequency band and were convoluted with the simulated channel impulse responses.
Nevertheless, experimental validations were started to complement these investigations and therefore objects o2 - o7 were built in same dimensions and scanned with same track and same antennas which were analyzed by the Ray Tracer. The used sensor system consists of a UWB Maximum Length Binary Sequence (M-Sequence) Radar system for data acquisition. Compared to pulse Radar, the energy of the transmitted waveform is spread equally over time when using an M-sequence Radar thus eliminating the power spikes of short pulses. This provides reduction of complexity and costs for the analogue electronics in the Radar device which do not need to handle high-power short-time signals thus allowing for a cheaper hardware implementation. The block diagram of an M-sequence Radar is given in figure 2.

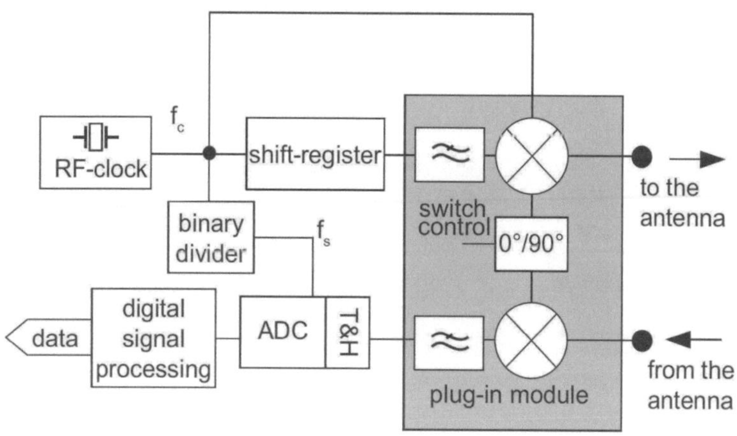

Fig. 2. Basic structure of an M-Sequence Radar with attached IQ Up/Down-converter

The shift register generates periodically (using a ring-register) the binary M-sequence with the clock frequency f_c which is the stimulus signal. The M-sequence is a special binary pseudo random code which has a very short triangular auto-correlation function. Due to Nyquist the range of the frequency spectrum is DC - $f_c/2$ meaning that the width of the pulse is adjustable directly by the clock frequency. This signal is sent to the Tx port of the device. The Tx port can either be connected directly to the transmit antenna for baseband transmission (DC - 4.5 GHz) or an additional IQ up-converter can be used which modulates the waveform to a carrier frequency of 9 GHz for passband transmission. The reflected signal is received by the receive antenna, downconverted to baseband (if the IQ up-converter is employed) and sampled. In most wideband RF-systems, the data gathering is based on sub-sampling in order to reduce the data throughput, this is also the case with the M-sequence Radar. Usually the sampling time control is a challenging task but this is not the case for M-sequence sub-sampling, since a simple binary divider does this job in a very stable way by keeping an absolute linear (equivalent) time base of the captured signal. The divided pulse directly pushes the ADC and the track and hold circuit (T&H). The T&H captures the wideband input signal and provides it to the ADC which can work at a suitable low sampling rate f_s. In order to increase the signal to noise ratio, it is of advantage to apply synchronous averaging in the digital domain. More detailed information can be found in (Sachs et al., 2005).

2.2 Sensor track

The emulation of the free movement of a mobile robot platform is provided by two symmetric arrangements of linear rails. Each of them has 2 degrees of freedom in the movement plane. On each of them there is a rotating platform actuated by another step-motor. These platforms serve as mounting points for either antennas or targets. With this setup the circular scan was performed with the antennas fixed and the target rotating around its own axis on the rotor platform. This emulated the case where a robot is moving on a circle around a target. The setup of the measurement configuration with its essential devices is sketched in figure 3 for a better overview.

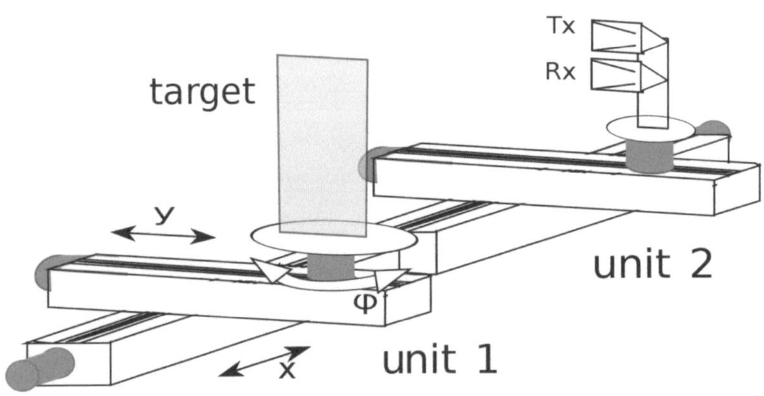

Fig. 3. Layout of the measurement setup with its main devices for experimental validations

Figure 4 shows an example of a simulation-based radargram of object o3 with a triangular cross section. Each object has a specific radar cross section that is strongly angle of radiation dependent. For the purpose of comparison Figure 5 shows the radargram of a real object with same dimensions measured by aforementioned M-Sequence Radar in the passband, i.e 4.5 GHz - 13 GHz. On the left side of both figures 4 and 5 each radargram is determined by a circular track with the object positioned in the centre and the sensors at 1m distance. This is expectedly ideal in the simulated case as both sides of the equal-sided triangular at 45° and 135° cause a specular reflection. However, in the measured radargram of figure 5 a misalignment of the object is noticeable. There is a translative shift of approximately 2 cm to the centre of rotation which has absolutely no influence onto the whole post-processing at all. As far as the position of the sensors is known, the track can be arbitrarily.

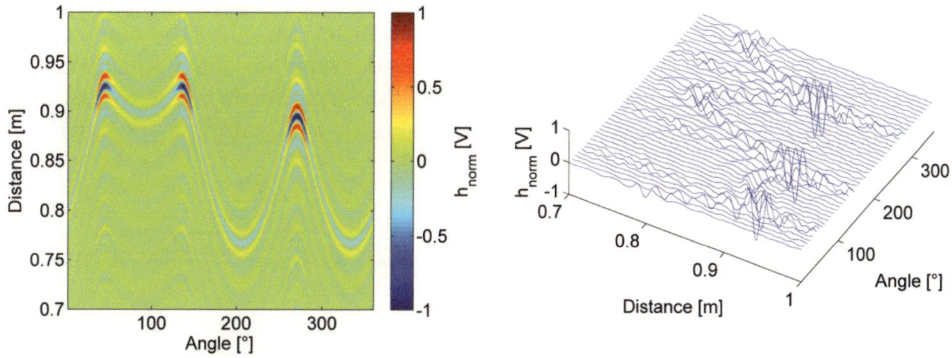

Fig. 4. Radargram of simulated object o3 (left) and every 8th pulse of same Radar data (right)

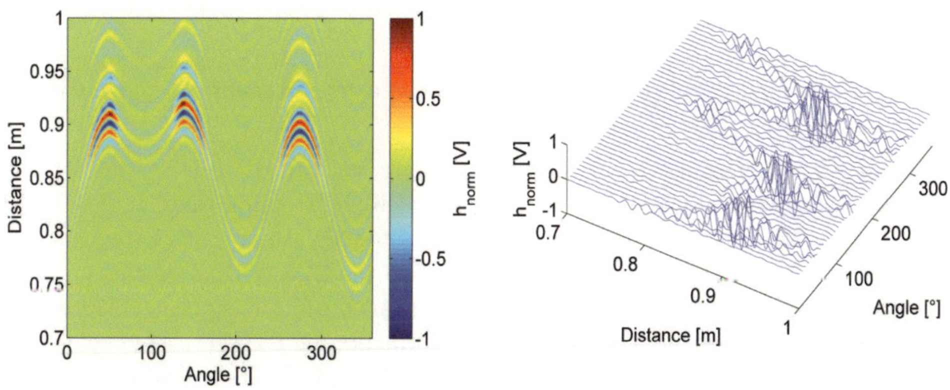

Fig. 5. Measured radargram of object o3 (left) and every 8th pulse of same Radar data (right)

Also for other objects the similarity between simulations and measurements is significantly high. Thus, the performance of the UWB Ray Tracer is verified and serves as basis for further investigations.

2.3 Pre-processing of measured data

Before any algorithm for object reconstruction can be applied, a number of signal processing steps have to be applied onto the raw-data of the M-Sequence Radar device. The raw-data must be up-sampled and up-converted, if the IQ-converter is attached. The signal is provided in the equivalent complex baseband (ECB), as it is usual in high frequency hardware realizations to avoid the effort of high sampling rates. Furthermore, calibration and interpolation is necessary to provide processing-ready data for subsequent algorithms like the imaging and the OR.

In the measured scenario the reference signal is obtained without the object. A reference pulse is needed for the subtraction of the background reflections (clutter) and antenna crosstalk from the raw signals. The antenna crosstalk is not negligible because the antennas are mounted one above the other at a distance of 12 cm which causes moderate coupling. Moreover, the influence of the microwave devices (e.g. RF switches, RF cables etc.) is compensated by calibration. The interpolation is performed in frequency domain by Fourier transforming the time domain signal. Zero padding and the Hamming window in the frequency domain are applied. After inverse Fourier transforming the time domain signal has finer quantization steps and therewith an improved resolution and a smoother signal form. The Hamming window suppresses sidelobes in the time domain which would appear if a rectangular window was used. Both pre-processing steps are applied and depicted in figure 6.

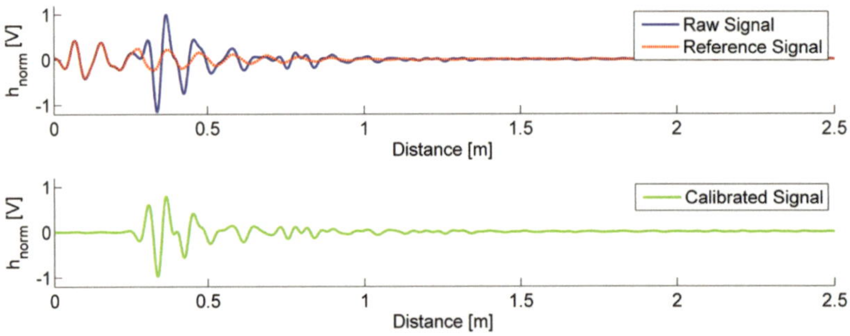

Fig. 6. Interpolated raw signal with antenna crosstalk (above) and calibrated signal after removing the reference signal (below)

Both system signals, i.e. in baseband and passband, are real-valued, as it is usual for every real physically transmitted signal. However, to avoid high sampling rates, as it would be necessary due to Nyquist to sample at least 2 times of the highest appearing frequency, the representation of the passband signal is performed in the ECB. This is essential, because such high frequency digital oscillators are either not available or too expensive. Moreover, it is possible to separate the signal carrier and its information by the complex envelope. The ECB is known to be the down converted version of its analytical Signal in the passband. Let $s_{PB}(t)$ be a real valued passband signal, e.g. the Radar signal with attached up/down converter, then

$$s_{PB}^{+}(t) = s_{PB}(t) + j \cdot \hat{s}_{PB}(t) \tag{1}$$

is the analytical signal, with

$$\hat{s}(t) = H\{s(t)\} = f^{-1}\{-j \cdot \mathrm{sgn}(\omega) f\{s(t)\}(\omega)\}(t) \tag{2}$$

being the Hilbert transform of s(t) expressed by the Fourier transform. Here $f\{\bullet\}$ is the Fourier transform and $H\{\bullet\}$ the Hilbert transform. Obviously, an analytical signal is a signal whose imaginary part is the Hilbert transform of its real part. The ECB signal $s_{ECB}(t)$ can be expressed as

$$s_{ECB}(t) = s_{PB}^{+}(t) e^{-j2\pi f_0 t}. \tag{3}$$

Here, f_0 is the carrier frequency. In the spectrum it leads to

$$S_{ECB}(\omega) = S^{+}_{PB}(\omega + \omega_0). \tag{4}$$

3. Highly accurate wavefront detection

To achieve super-resolution of the Radar system, wavefronts have to be detected accurately and, in case of multiple reflections, overlapping pulses must be separated by a suitable algorithm. A wavefront is a curve within the radargram where each point on the curve indicates the distance at which a reflective feature of the object, visible from the sensor setup, is located. A reflective feature can either be a smooth, large (in comparison to the smallest wavelength) plane or edges and corners, which cause scattering and retroreflection, respectively. Based on the speed of light value these wavefronts are used to determine the distance between the reflecting point and the sensor. In this work, these distances are used in subsequent algorithms to extract a Radar image and to enable the OR. The highly accurate wavefront detection becomes a challenging task when it deals with multi-scattering conditions. This is the case when complicated objects have surface variations less than a wavelength or have many concave and convex edges like the objects o5 - o12. Distortion is caused by richly interfered signals scattered from multiple scattering centres of the object surface. This results in constructive and destructive interference which leads to deformation of the pulse. In this section two algorithms shall be introduced in detail which have proven to be robust and efficient, i.e. a correlation based method and an optimization problem solved by a genetic algorithm.

In both algorithms, again a reference pulse is needed. The double-ridged horn antennas used in this work have 20° opening angle to the left and right, respectively. The amplitude of the transfer function within this area, and therewith the attenuation, is marginal and negligible. Since the cross-range resolution is proportional to the wavelength and inverse proportional to the aperture, measurements in the passband are chosen to provide lower wavelengths and therewith finer resolution. A set of reference pulses is shown in figure 7 which were obtained as reflection against a cylinder (diameter 9 cm) and a large metal plate, respectively. For the purpose of comparison, they are normalised in amplitude and delay.

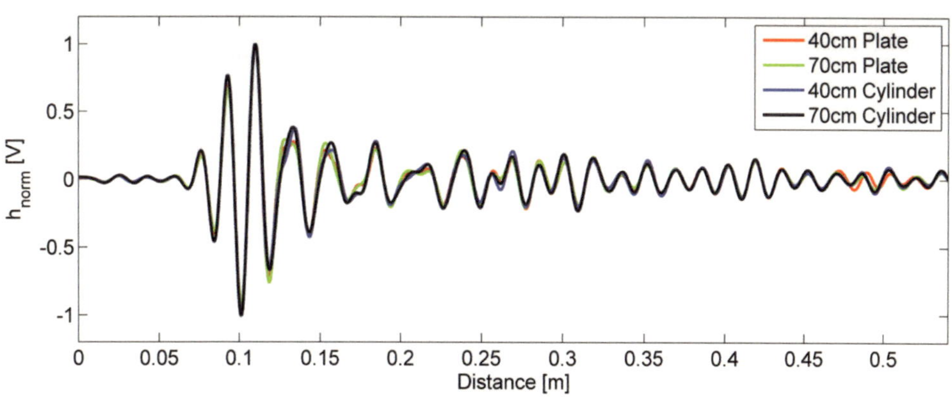

Fig. 7. A set of reference pulses taken at different distances against a plate and cylinder with normalised amplitude and delay

Once a wavefront has been detected in a signal under test, the distance has to be extracted accurately. A distinctive part of the reference pulse has to be marked as the location or moment respectively, when the reflection takes place at the objects surface. Assume $ref(\mathrm{t})$ to be the reference pulse then usually $\max\{|ref(\mathrm{t})|\}$ is set to be the point, or moment respectively, in which the reflection actually takes place. This point has the maximum instantaneous energy detected by the sensor which corresponds with the reflection. However, an adaption to the Radar data can be necessary with a change of the sign of the reference pulse. This depends on the sign of the maximum amplitude of the radar data which was within these investigations negative. For further processing it makes sense to shift the reference pulse such that $\max\{|ref(\mathrm{t})|\}$ is in the origin of the time-axis. This leads to the reference pulse used in this work and is shown in figure 8.

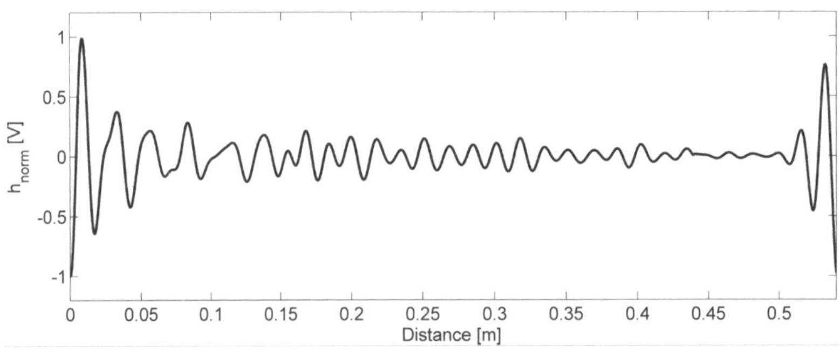

Fig. 8. calibrated and normalised reference pulse used in this work

3.1 Correlation based wavefront detection – the matched filter principle

The basic idea of this algorithm, first introduced in (Hantscher et al., 2007) is to locate echoes iteratively by evaluating the normalized cross-correlation function of the signal under test with an offline determined reference pulse. The maximum of this cross-correlation function indicates the shift with which the reference pulse has highest similarity within the signal under test. Once a wavefront is extracted, the algorithm recursively subtracts scattered pulses to resolve multiple echoes. This step is iterated on the resulting signal until a termination condition is fulfilled. The termination condition is determined heuristically, e.g. when a certain difference in the signal power before and after subtraction is reached, or simply when a fixed number of wavefronts are of interest or, as it was the case within this work, when the normalized correlation coefficient which equals 0 for orthogonal signals and 1 for identical ones, is less a threshold, e.g. 0.5 . The correlation coefficient for the 1st wavefront (i=1) is

$$ccf_{\mathrm{echo,i}}(\mathrm{t_d}) = \frac{\sum_{\mathrm{k=1}}^{\mathrm{K}} s_{\mathrm{i}}(\mathrm{t_k}) \cdot ref(\mathrm{t_k}\text{-}\mathrm{t_d})}{\sqrt{\sum_{\mathrm{k=1}}^{\mathrm{K}} \left(s_{\mathrm{i}}(\mathrm{t_k})\right)^2} \cdot \sqrt{\sum_{\mathrm{k=1}}^{\mathrm{K}} \left(ref(\mathrm{t_k})\right)^2}} \qquad (7)$$

with time samples $\mathrm{t_k}$, the mean-value free reference signal $ref(\mathrm{t_k})$ and mean-value free signal under test $s_{\mathrm{i}}(\mathrm{t_k})$. $ccf_{\mathrm{echo,1}}(\mathrm{t_d})$ is proportional to the cross correlation function and represents the correlation coefficient for each time delay t_d normalized by the RMS values of $s_i(t_k)$ and $ref(t_k)$. The normalization avoids the problem of higher signal energies resulting in higher correlation values. The parameter

$$\Delta t_{echo,i} = \arg\max_{t_d}\left(\left|ccf_{echo,i}(t_d)\right|\right) \tag{8}$$

contains the time difference between the first detected reflection and the calibrated reference pulse, i.e. the moment at which the reference signal matches best the signal under test. Actually, because of the calibration of the reference pulse in figure 8 $\Delta t_{echo,i}$ equals the round trip time, or in combination with the velocity of light, the distance from the sensors to the reflecting centre. In order to investigate the signal under test for further reflections, the earlier detected wavefront has to be removed coherently since it covers other reflections. A scaling factor

$$s_f = \frac{s(\Delta t_{echo,i})}{ref(t_k\text{-}\Delta t_{echo,i})} \tag{9}$$

is estimated by taking the ratio of the amplitudes of the detected wavefront and the reference pulse at the point of maximum correlation. This scaling factor gives an estimation with which amplitude the reference signal has to be removed from the signal under test. This substraction operation provides the new signal under test

$$s_{i+1}(t_k) = s_i(t_k) - s_f \cdot ref(t_k\text{-}\Delta t_{echo,i}), \tag{10}$$

which then will be analysed for further wavefronts. Similarly, further wavefronts are extracted iteratively by repeating equation (7) and the adjacent ones. This strategy can be considered as the matched filter principle with the reference pulse as the impulse response of the pulse shaping filter of the transmitter as well as the one of the receiver. This parameter estimation scheme maximizes the signal-to-noise power ratio.

3.2 Wavefront detection by a genetic algorithm

The correlation based wavefront detection works excellent for single simple shaped objects (e.g. o1-o4) or several simple objects which are separated by distances of several wavelengths. The small computation effort satisfies real time conditions and the range resolution is in sub centimetre range. Under these assumptions interference is negligible and waveforms are not distorted very much. However, for complex shaped objects which cause multiple reflections, wavefronts can interfere with each other. Especially when the overlap range is within a pulsewidth, constructive and/or destructive interference are hardly separable.

For scenarios with multiple scattering conditions a genetic optimization algorithm (GA) for modelling the impulse response has proven to be very efficient. Hence, the pulse separation task is formulated as a multidimensional optimization problem and extracts even interfering pulses. Because of multimodality and complexity analytical approaches are not appropriate in every case. Here, GA has been proven to be a powerful tool by applying a heuristic search (Johnson & Rahmat-Sammi, 1997). The GA used in this paper is similar to (Hantscher & Diskus, 2009). The main difference is that the sensors in this work have no angle dependence, because they have narrow main lobes resulting in an aperture with negligible incident angle.

The basic idea of the GA is that the signal under test $s(\mathrm{t_k})$ with time samples $\mathrm{t_k}$ and index k is assumed to be described by a superposition of shifted and weighted reference pulses $ref(\mathrm{t_k})$. The set of reference pulses which vary by different parameters weight w_g and delay d_g of the gth wavefront, shall approximate $s(\mathrm{t_k})$ best with every meaningful combination of both parameters. A meaningful quality criterion can e.g. be the least square value. In contrast to the correlation based algorithm, the number of wavefronts G has to be presumed and was set to 3 within these investigations. The block diagram of the GA process is shown in figure 9.

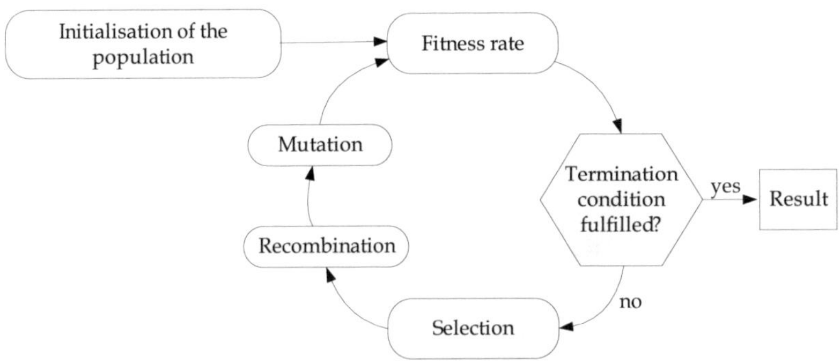

Fig. 9. Block diagram of the used GA for wavefront detection

Firstly, the GA starts for every signal under test with an initialisation of a population of N individuals. Each individual resembles a potential solution of the optimisation problem. Here, every individual comprise the parameters weight w_g and delay d_g to provide a potential solution

$$c(\mathrm{t_k}) = \sum_{g=1}^{G} w_g \cdot ref(\mathrm{t_k} - d_g). \tag{11}$$

The parameters w_g and d_g are assigned uniformly distributed in the initialisation of the population. For example d_g should be close to the area where the object is supposed to be and w_g should be in relation to used power levels. The number of individuals is chosen to be N = 200. Figure 10 shows an assembly of such a population for a better overview.

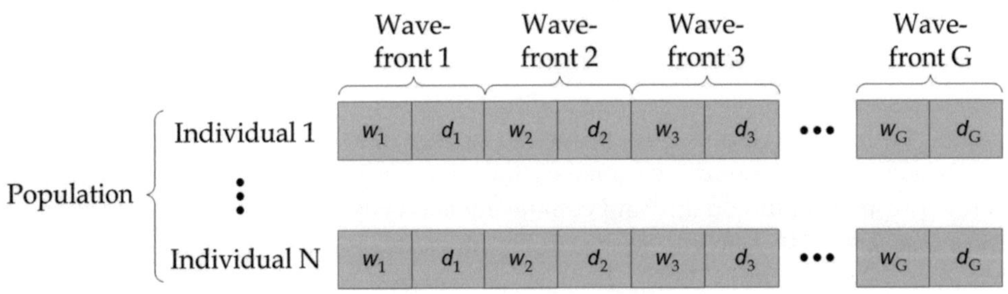

Fig. 10. A population of N individuals with G wavefronts

In the next step the quality of the approximation is determined by means of a fitness function, i.e. the difference between of the signal under test and each individual in the least square sense

$$F = \sqrt{\frac{1}{K}\sum_{k=1}^{K}\left(s(t_k) - c(t_k)\right)^2} = \sqrt{\frac{1}{K}\sum_{k=1}^{K}\left[\left(s(t_k) - \sum_i w_i \cdot ref(t_k\text{-}d_i)\right)\right]^2} . \tag{12}$$

$$\rightarrow \min \qquad \rightarrow \min$$

After having calculated the fitness of each individual, it is decided whether the termination condition of the GA is fulfilled. In (Hantscher & Diskus, 2009) the difference between the fitness of the best and the fitness of the worst is less than a threshold, of e.g. 2%. However, numerous simulations and measurements show that this strategy can break the GA off too early or hung up in an infinite loop. To take a constant number of iterations has proven more efficient. If the termination condition is not fulfilled the next step "selection" is applied. Before the recombination can be carried out, the required individuals have to be chosen here. The worst N/2 individuals are removed from the population and the remaining N/2 individuals are selected for the recombination. The remaining individuals form randomly N/4 sets of parents and each produce 2 children by a so called one-point crossover. This results again in a population of N individuals. The one-point crossover works as follows. Every set of parents is split after a random set of parameter into two parts. Then, all parameter beyond that cut are swapped within both parents resulting in two new individuals called children. This procedure is repeated with every set of parents. Figure 11 shows the principle of the one-point crossover.

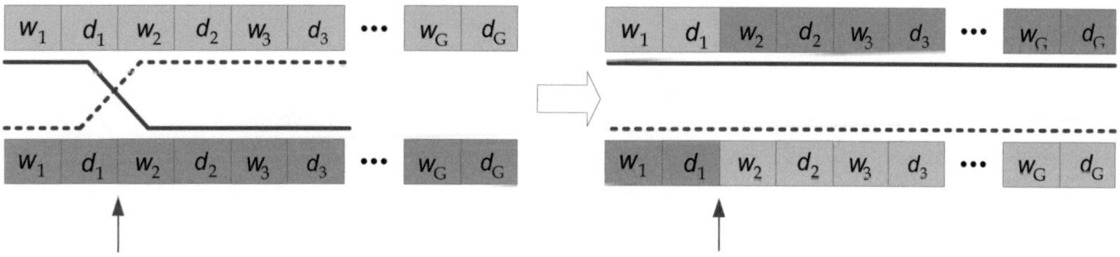

Fig. 11. Operation of the one-point crossover method

Finally, the mutation operation is applied onto the new population. The algorithm is guarded against getting stuck in a local minimum by changing the parameters w_g and d_g slightly. To the delay d_g a normally distributed random number with a mean of 0 is added and the weight w_g is multiplied with a normally distributed random number with a mean of 1. Both standard deviations should be chosen adaptively. At the beginning of iterations a high standard deviation secures the genetic deviation, whereas a low standard deviation at the end causes a fine tuning of the solutions. Finally, the GA calculates again the fitness of each individual and starts another iteration until the determination condition is fulfilled (maximum number of iterations). The result is the individual with lowest mean square error with which the signal under test can be reconstructed in an approximated type.

The number of wavefronts G was set to 3 within these investigations which satisfied resolution assumptions. Even for signals with only one wavefront, the remaining two wavefronts were located around the actual one because of the fitness conditions. Hence, a simple filter which connects two nearby wavefronts was sufficient to complete the GA results.

In the following a couple of results for both wavefront detection algorithms are shown. Figure 12 deals with object o5. The radargrams and additionally the detected wavefronts are depicted. The threshold for the correlation coefficient was set to 0.4 .

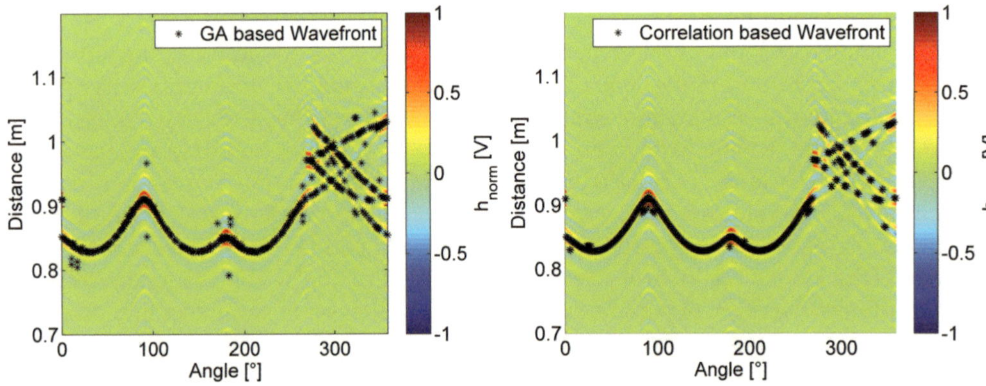

Fig. 12. Detected wavefronts by both algorithms for object o5

To demonstrate the quality of estimating the wavefront the 289th impulse response of figure 12 was reconstructed by superpositioning the weighted and shifted wavefronts of both algorithms.

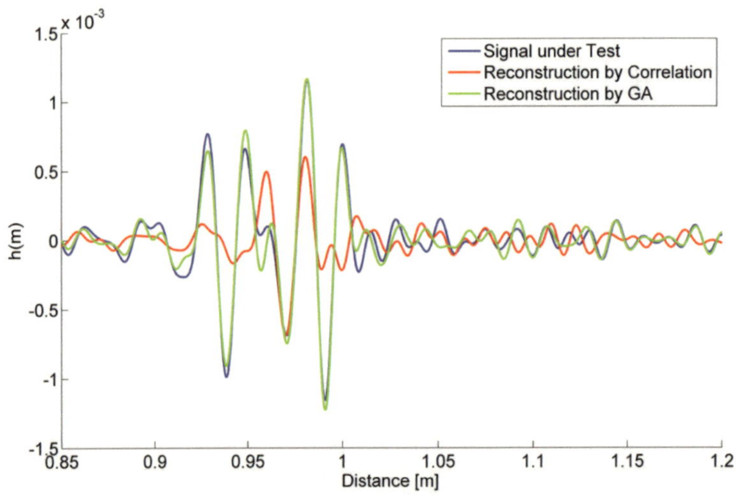

Fig. 13. Reconstruction of a signal under test with both wavefront detection algorithms

Obviously, and this is what was proven with numerous simulations and measurements with numerous objects, the GA performs more efficient under multi scattering conditions than the correlation algorithm. However, if the object is most probably a simple one without edges, corners and high variations, then the correlation algorithm should be preferred because of time saving. But normally, a Radar image is performed for unknown objects and in this cases the GA provides more precise wavefront detections.

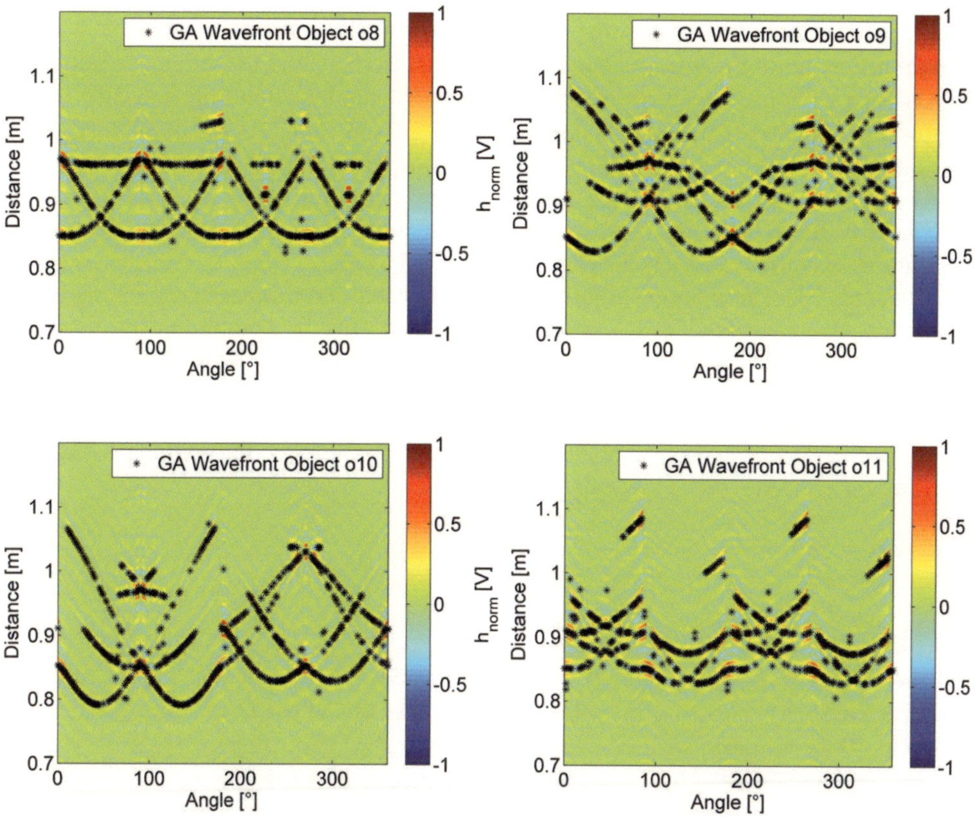

Fig. 14. Examples of some radargrams including detected wavefronts with the GA

4. Super resolution UWB imaging

A large variety of imaging algorithms was designed, mostly based on migration techniques (Hantscher et al., 2006; Zetik et al., 2005), Synthetic Aperture techniques (McIntosh et al., 2002) which are related close to the migrations, time-reversal algorithms (Liu et al., 2007) and other optimization algorithms (Massa et al., 2005). However, these algorithms are inappropriate for emergency scenarios because of the immense computational load excluding real-time conditions. Even though, these obtained images have inadequate image resolution and need further processing to extract an object contour. In contrary, it was shown that the inverse boundary scattering transform (IBST) which is given by

$$\begin{cases} x(x_w) = x_w - z_w \cdot dz_w / dx_w \\ z(x_w) = z_w \cdot \sqrt{1-(dz_w / dx_w)^2} \end{cases} \tag{13}$$

and IBST inspired algorithms are a simpler and more computationally efficient UWB imaging algorithm which determines the direction of Radar responses based on changes of the round-trip times (RTT) and thus performs a direct imaging. Here, x and z are the coordinates of the final radar image which contains the shape of the object. The variable z_w represents the distance of the wavefront to the antenna position x_w. Therefore, the IBST requires only the knowledge of the round-trip times of the wavefronts at every antenna position. Since the introduction of the original IBST in 2004 (Sakamoto & Sato, 2004) there has been significant research effort for improvements by extending it to 3-D, bistatic configurations and non-planar tracks (Helbig et al., 2008) for imaging the outer surface of a target and even for medium penetrating in-wall imaging (Janson et al., 2009).
However, IBST utilizes the derivative of the received data and hence is sensitive to noise. Moreover it is hard to apply for complex objects with multi-scattering behaviour and discontinuous wavefronts, as it is the case for objects o5 – o12.
In (Kidera et al., 2008) an imaging algorithm was proposed that utilizes fuzzy estimation for the direction of arrival (DOA). It extracts a direct mapping by combining the measured distance of the wavefront with its DOA. Moreover it realizes a stable imaging of even complex objects and requires neither preprocessing like clustering or connecting discontinuous wavefronts, nor any derivatives. The angular estimation of the DOA relies on the convergence of nearby wavefronts to the wavefront under test if the antenna positions of those nearby wavefronts move towards the regarding one. A membership function

$$f(\theta, X_i, Z_i) = e^{-\frac{\{\theta - \theta(X_i, Z_i)\}^2}{2\sigma_\theta^2}}, \tag{14}$$

is utilized where $\theta(X_i, Z_i)$ is defined as the angle between the intersection point of the regarded wavefront circle with the neighbouring wavefront of the ith antenna position and the x-axis. This is performed for all possible $\theta = 0°...359°$ and for $i = 1...N$ with N neighbouring wavefronts which intersect the wavefront circle of the regarded one. The angular estimation of the wavefront under test is calculated by

$$\theta_{opt} = \arg\max_{\theta} \left\{ s(X_i, Z_i) f(\theta, X_i, Z_i) e^{-\frac{\{X - X_i\}^2}{2\sigma_x^2}} \right\}, \tag{15}$$

where $s(X_i, Z_i)$ is the signal amplitude of the ith antenna position and σ_x and σ_θ are empirically determined constants. The crucial parameters of this algorithm are σ_x and σ_θ which can be considered to be the standard deviation of the exponential terms having Gaussian curvature. Hence, σ_x and σ_θ determine the width of this Gaussian curvature and therewith its focus. However, depending on the chosen value of σ_x and σ_θ more or less influence of wavefronts of neighbouring antenna positions can be taken into account which results either in images of rather smooth and straight planes or, in contrast, highlight edges and corners. Figure 15 shows the case in which the edges are highlighted by the algorithm.

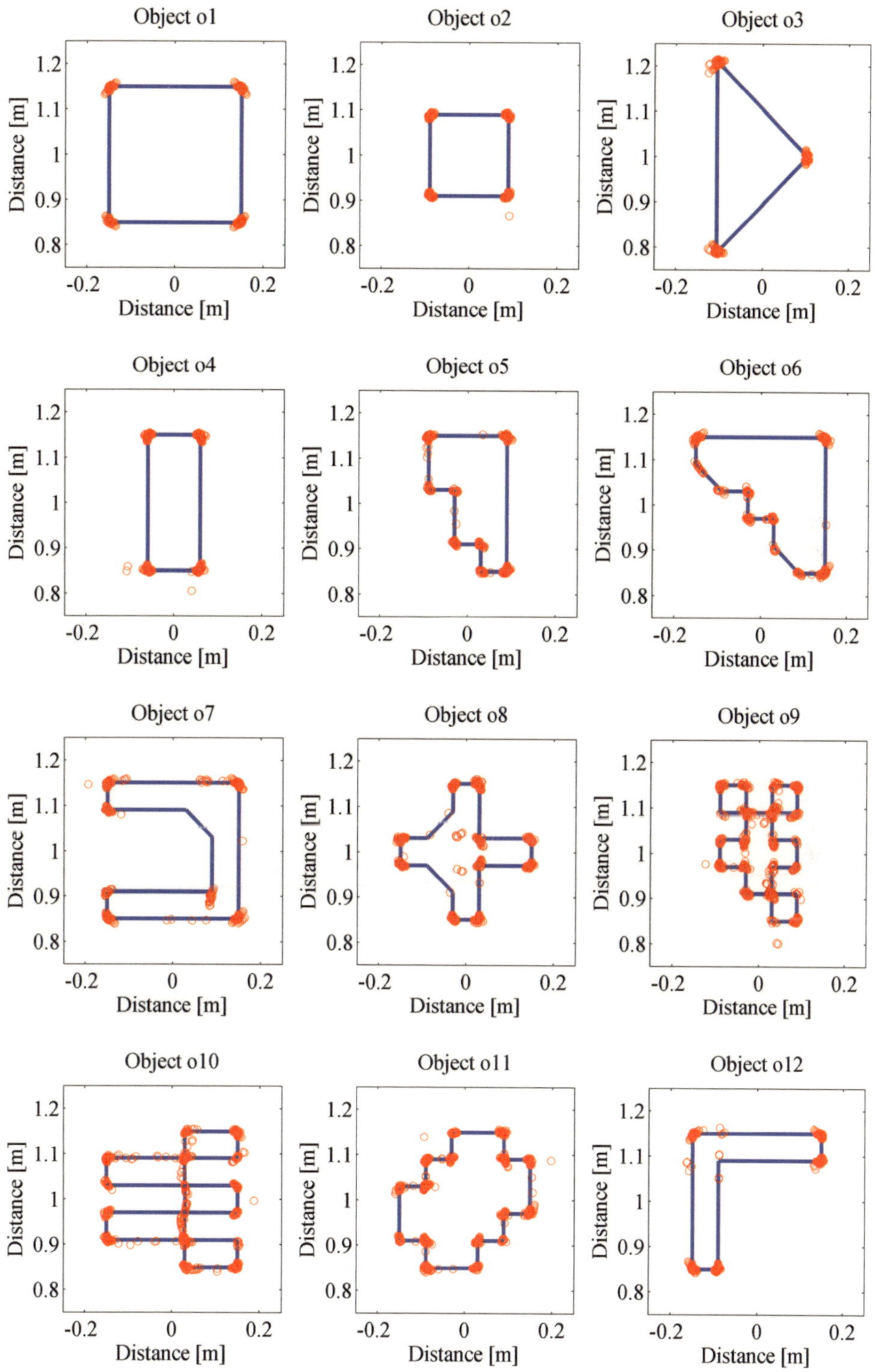

Fig. 15. Raw images determined by the imaging algorithm and the object contour

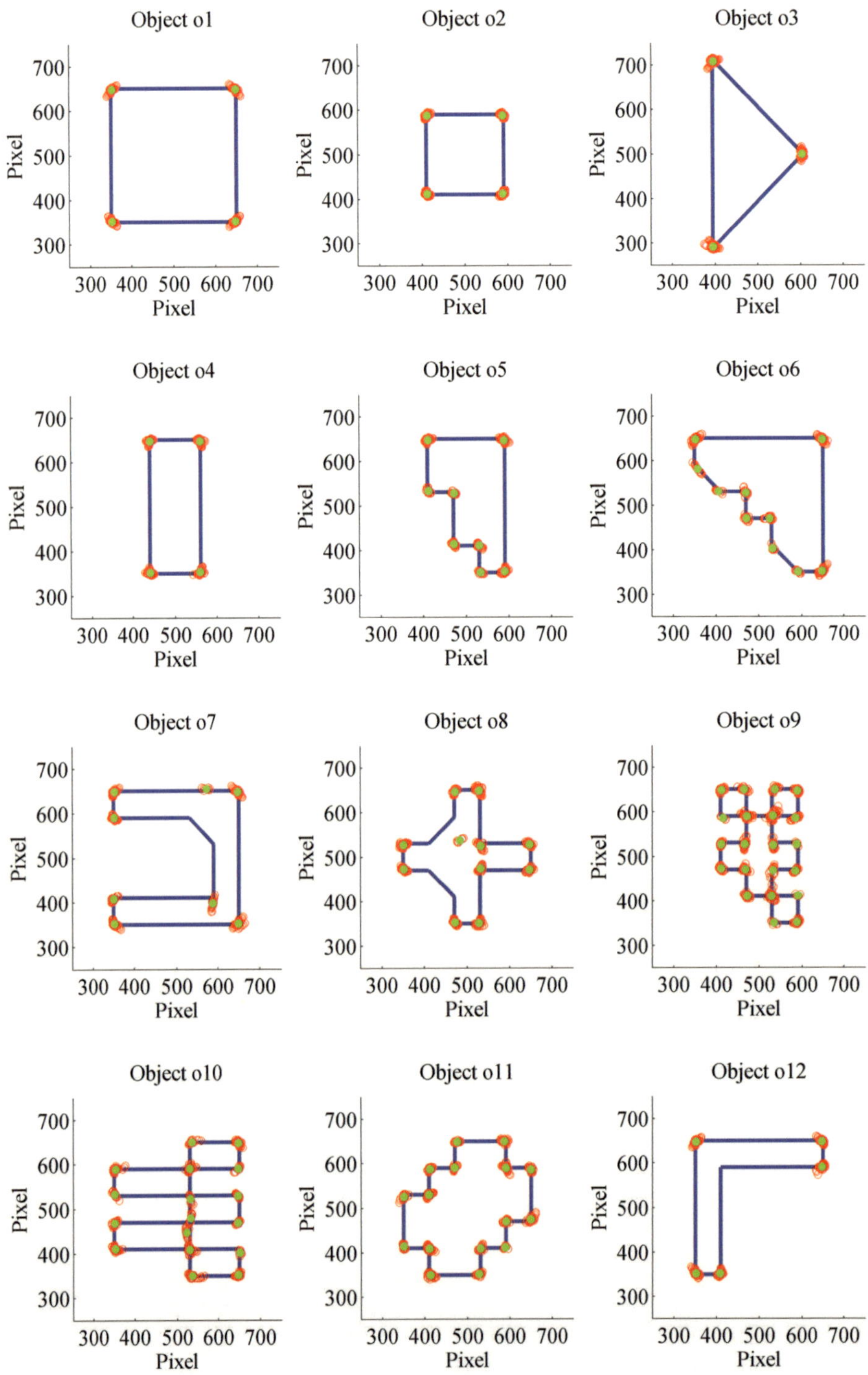

Fig. 16. Clustered and filtered images ready for the OR processing

4.1 Post processing of raw images

In order to perform the OR the UWB image has to be adapted to the reference alphabet of chapter 2.1. Hence, the values of the imaging parameters σ_x and σ_θ are chosen with a low value and a post processing in terms of filtering and clustering is applied. At first, a clustering is performed to merge image pixels of one edge or corner to one cluster. In case the image consists of K image pixels with Cartesian coordinate $P_j(x,y)$ for the j-th pixels, then every pixel for which

$$\left|P_m - P_n\right| \leq 1\text{cm} \qquad \forall \text{m}=\text{n}=[1;\text{K}] \tag{16}$$

holds, are merged to one cluster. A filtering is performed by deleting clusters with less then 4 pixels to avoid isolated image pixels. For every remaining cluster the centre of mass is calculated which is the representative of the corresponding edge or corner. Thus, the pixel at the centre of mass of every cluster is set a value of 1. The remaining pixels are set to 0. Both post processing steps are applied onto the raw images, the results are shown in figure 16.

5. Object recognition algorithm

5.1 Moment based feature

The image moments are calculated by the invariant moment algorithm (Chen, 1993). Based on 5 central moments $\mu_{p,q}$ 7 other moments φ_i can be determined which are invariant to translation, rotation and scaling. Here, shape parameters of the object are extracted based on the objects geometry and its distribution of pixels. The invariant moments are determined for every object both of the reference alphabet and the post processed images.

5.2 Texture based feature

The texture feature consists of polar Fourier descriptors (FD). The parameterization of the boundary line is not any more expressed by a path length p, instead the angle Φ between the radius from the center of mass to a point on the boundary and the x-axis is used. However, the straight segments between corners and edges have to be sampled equiangular for the recognition process with polar Fourier descriptors. Therefore the pixel with the value of 1 of each reference image are connected in ascending angular order. These connections are afterwards sampled equiangular resulting in a series of 360 values which equal 360 radii. The resulting polar signature with a one degree grid is used and a Fourier Transformation is applied onto the resulting N = 360 real valued series. The obtained coefficients are known as the polar FD of the object boundary. The resulting N wave number coefficients run from 0 to N-1, or respectively due to Nyquist from -N/2 to N/2-1. In contrast to classical FD the polar FD are translation and rotation invariant if the absolute values of the coefficients are regarded. However, the 0-th coefficients of the polar FD represent the mean radius. Hence, the polar FD can be made scale invariant by normalizing all coefficients with reference to the 0-th one. In this work this is not done, because o1 and o2 both are squares just with different dimension and shall be treated as 2 different objects.

5.3 Geometrical features

Geometrical features are obtained both for the reference alphabet and the images of the object under test. The translation and rotation invariant geometrical features are:

- Total mass of the image
- Eccentricity
- Bounding circle
- Form factor

The total mass is the sum of the pixels belonging to the object. In case of binary images it is the sum of all pixel-values in the image. The eccentricity is based on 2nd order moments and ranges from 0 to 1. It is a measure for the circularity of an object. The bounding circle is defined as the circumference of the circle which is just large enough to contain all object pixels. The form factor is the relation between the bounding circle and the total mass of the image and is a measure for the compactness of the image.

5.4 Combined object recognition

Each image under test is compared against every 12 reference images by a MSE classifier applied to all six features. Hence, every object under test has six 1 by 12 error-vectors $\vec{e}_{\mathrm{i}}\ \ \forall\, \mathrm{i}=1\ldots6$ with MSE values for each of the 12 compared combinations and for all 6 features. For reasons of expressing a recognition rate in probabilities all $\vec{e}_{\mathrm{i}}$ of every object are mapped to a probability vector

$$\vec{p}_{\mathrm{i}}(j)=\mathrm{e}^{-\frac{\vec{e}_{\mathrm{i}}(j)^2}{0.1\mathrm{std}(\vec{e}_{\mathrm{i}})^2}} \qquad \forall j=1\ldots12 \wedge \mathrm{i}=1\ldots6 \tag{17}$$

with std(.) as the standard deviation. To achieve a cumulative probability of 1 per object and per feature, each $\vec{p}_{\mathrm{i}}$ is normalized to

$$\vec{p}_{\mathrm{norm,i}}(j)=\frac{\vec{p}_{\mathrm{i}}(j)}{\sum_{m=1}^{12}\vec{p}_{\mathrm{i}}(m)} \qquad \forall j=1\ldots12 \wedge \mathrm{i}=1\ldots6. \tag{18}$$

Then, after multiplicative combination of every feature with

$$\arg\max_j\left\{\prod_{\mathrm{i}=1}^{6}\vec{p}_{\mathrm{norm,i}}(j)\right\} \qquad \forall j=1\ldots12, \tag{19}$$

a joint OR probability can perform a recognition of the jth reference object for the object under test.

6. Results and conclusion

In this chapter a robust UWB OR algorithm is presented which is based on super-resolution UWB imaging. Geometrical features are extracted and used in a joint maximum probability algorithm. After combining geometrical features with the moment invariant algorithm and the Fourier descriptors, both OR algorithms can recognize all 12 objects correctly. In every case the probability for the 1st failure (or the 2nd probable object) was significantly smaller than the correct decision.

7. Acknowledgement

The authors thank the Deutsche Forschungsgemeinschaft (DFG) for the support of the work as part of the "Cooperative Localisation and Object Recognition in Autonomous UWB Sensor Networks" (CoLOR) project within the UKoLoS priority program.

8. References

Chen, C. C. (1993). Improved moment invariants for shape discrimination, *Pattern Recognition Journal,* Vol. 26, No. 5, 1993, pp. 683-686.

Geng, N. & Wiesbeck, W. (1998). *Planungsmethoden für die Mobilkommunikation,* Springer Verlag, ISBN 3540647783, Berlin, 1998.

Hantscher, S.; Reisenzahn, R. & Diskus, C. (2006). Analysis of Imaging Radar Algorithms for the Identification of Targets by Their Surface Shape, *IEEE International Conference on Ultra-Wideband, ICUWB 2006,* Waltham, USA, Oct. 2006.

Hantscher, S.; Etzlinger, B.; Reisenzahn, A. & Diskus, C. G. (2007). A Wavefront Extraction Algorithm for High-Resolution Pulse Based Radar Systems, *IEEE International Conference on Ultra-Wideband, ICUWB 2007,* Singapore, Sep. 2007.

Hantscher, S & Diskus, C. G. (2009). Pulse-Based Radar Imaging Using a Genetic Optimization Approach for Echo Separation. *IEEE Sensors Journal.*Vol. 9, No. 3, March 2009, pp. 271–276.

Helbig, M.; Hein, M.A.; Schwarz, U. & Sachs, J. (2008). Preliminary investigations of chest surface identification algorithms for breast cancer detection", *IEEE International Conference on Ultra-Wideband, ICUWB 2008,* Hannover, Germany, Sept. 2008.

Janson, M.; Salman, R.; Schultze, Th.; Willms, I.; Zwick, T. & Wiesbeck, W. 2009. Hybrid ray racing/FDTD UWB model for object recognition. *Frequenz Journal of RF-Engineering and Telecommunications*, Vol. 63, No. 9/10, Sept./Oct. 2009, pp. 217-220.

Johnson, J. M. & Rahmat-Sammi, Y. (1997). Genetic Algorithm in Engineering Electromagnetics. *IEEE Antennas and Propagation Magazine.* Vol. 39, No. 4, Aug. 1997, pp. 7 - 25.

Kidera, S.; Sakamoto, T. & Sato, T. (2008). High-Speed UWB Radar Imaging Algorithm for Complex Target Boundary without Wavefront Connections. *XXIX General Assembly of the International Union of Radio Science (URSI)*, Chicago, Illinois, USA, Aug. 2008.

Liu, D.; Krolik, J. & Carin, L. (2007). Electromagnetic target detection in uncertain media: Time-reversal and minimum-variance algorithms. *IEEE Transactions on Geoscience and Remote Sensing.* Vol. 45, No. 4, April 2007, pp. 934-944.

Massa, A.; Franceschini, D.; Franceschini, G.; Pastorino, M.; Raffetto, M. & Donelli, M. (2005). Parallel GA-based approach for microwave imaging applications. *IEEE Transactions on Antennas and Propagation.* Vol. 53, No. 10, Oct. 2008, pp. 3118-3127.

McIntosh, J.S.; Hutchins, D.A.; Billson, D.R.; Noble, R.A.; Davies, R.R.; Koker, L. (2002). SAFT Imaging Using Immersed Capacitive Micromachined Ultrasonic Transducers, *International Ultrasonics Symposium,* Munich, Germany, Oct. 2002.

Sachs, J.; Kmec, M.; Zetik, R.; Peyerl, P.; Rauschenbach, P. (2005). Ultra Wideband Radar Assembly Kit. *IEEE international Geoscience and Remote sensing Symposium, IGARS 2005,* Seoul, Korea, July 2005.

Sakamoto, T. & Sato T. (2004). A target shape estimation algorithm for pulse radar systems based on boundary scattering transform. *IEICE Transactions on Communications*. Vol. E87-B, No.5, May 2004 , pp.1357-1365.

Salman, R.; Schultze, Th. & Willms, I. (2010). Performance Enhancement of UWB Material Characterisation and Object Recognition for Security Robots. *Journal of Electrical and Computer Engineering*. Vol. 2010, Article ID 314695, 6 pages, 2010.

Schultze, Th.; Porebska, M.; Wiesbeck, W. & Willms, I. (2008). Onsets for the Recognition of Objects and Image Refinement using UWB Radar, *German Microwave Conference, GEMIC 2008*, Hamburg-Harburg, Germany, March 2008.

Zetik, R.; Sachs, J. & Thomä, R. (2005). Imaging of Propagation Environment by Channel Sounding, *XXVIIIth General Assembly of URSI*, New Delhi, India, Oct. 2005.

Part 3

Object Registration and Recognition in 3-D Domain

17

3D Object Registration and Recognition using Range Images

Erdem Akagündüz and İlkay Ulusoy
Middle East Technical University
Turkey

1. Introduction

In recent years, retrieving semantic information from digital cameras, for instance object recognition, has become one of the hottest topics of computer vision. Since the boundaries of this problem range from recognizing objects in a range image to estimating the pose of an object from an image sequence, a variety of studies exist in the literature. Before remembering the previous approaches on the subject, it is better to refer to the definitions of the elementary attributes of the fundamental step in object recognition, feature extraction, which are repeatability under orientation, scaling, sampling and noise.

Orientation invariance in computer vision is the ability, which enables a method to extract the same features from the original and the rotated (oriented) version of an image (2D or range image etc.). Since any movement in the scene or camera introduces considerable rotation in the signal, this is a basic ability which is usually satisfied in recent object recognition approaches. The critical setback for orientation invariance is the self occlusion caused by the orientation of the object with respect to the camera. Many recent studies solve this problem by partial matching algorithms, which also enable pose estimation in scenes with diverse rotation.

The ability to extract features independent of their scale, namely scale invariance, is another important ability for a method. For 2D images, it is both related to object's size and pixel resolution. Thus scale invariance in 2D also correlates with invariance under sampling, which, as it name implies, is the ability to extract similar features from similar signals with different sampling rates. However, since range images encapsulate metric information independent of the resolution they have, the notion of scale and sampling invariance is interpreted in a different manner for them. This different notion is discussed in the succeeding sections.

Finally, the very basic ability of a computer vision system is its robustness to noise. Noise exists in various forms depending on the scene and sensor attributes. Since a very basic operation in image processing literature, unlimited number of approaches exits. However, methods using scale-space of signals have proven to be most robust under different types of noise.

1.1 Previous work

The state of the art challenges in 3D object recognition systems are scale invariance and robustness to occlusion. These two issues are usually the main reasons from which the real world recognition problems inherit their complexity. For object recognition from range images, the literature neither satisfactorily discusses these issues, nor has yet proposed a sufficient solution.

Range images, which have been usually processed as 2D images, carry both the 3D metric and geometric information of objects in the scene. Several local or global 3D point features and 3D descriptors were derived from these sampled surfaces and used for 3D object recognition, 3D object category recognition, 3D surface matching and 3D registration. Some of these features are SIFT (Lowe, 2004) (as directly applied to 2D rendered range images), 2.5D SIFT (Lo & Siebert, 2009), multi-scale features (Li & Guskov, 2007; Pauly et al., 2003), spin images (Johnson & Hebert, 1999), 3D point signatures (Chua & Jarvis, 1997), 3D shape context (Frome et al, 2004), surface depth, normal and curvature histograms (Hetzel et al., 2001), 3D point fingerprints (Sun & Abidi, 2001), or extended Gaussian images (Horn, 1984).

3D descriptors or histograms generally define the whole or a part of an object, using different properties of the surfaces such as curvatures, normal directions, distances to a base point etc. They are very powerful in representing a surface patch for recognition purpose. However when they are globally defined, they are brittle against occlusions. On the other hand, local descriptors are defined around feature points. However, detecting feature points and estimating the effect region of the local descriptor around a feature point are serious problems. Using fixed sized local descriptors obtained from random points on the surface (Johnson & Hebert, 1999) is one of the earlier approaches.

3D feature points are salient points that are extracted from the range image surfaces. If they are sufficiently repeatable, stable and invariant to scale and orientation, a sparse and robust representation of the sampled surface can be obtained. In addition, if the scales of the features are known, then effect regions can be defined around their center. Thus, multi-scale features obtained using the scale-space of the input surface are very advantageous for scale invariance and robustness to occlusions.

Until recently, very few studies have been reported on the invariance limits of scale in 3D feature extraction. Reference (Li & Guskov, 2007) extracts multi-scale salient features using only two scale levels of the surface normals and analyzes its performance on object recognition for the Stuttgart range image database. Reference (Pauly et al., 2003) extracts multi-scale features which are classified based on surface variation estimation using covariance analysis of local neighborhoods, in order to construct line features. Reference (Lo & Siebert, 2009) define the 2.5D SIFT, the direct implementation of SIFT (Lowe, 2004) framework on range images, however they present their comparison with simple match matrices and avoid giving a comparison of recognition capabilities. All of these methods (Lowe, 2004; Li & Guskov, 2007; Pauly et al., 2003) construct a scale space of the surface using difference of Gaussians (DoG) and seek for the maxima within this scale space, while neither of them attempts to test the scale invariance limits of their methods on scale varying database.

1.2 The notion of scale for range images

Traditionally scale concept in computer vision relates to object's pixel dimension in the image, which correlates to both sensor resolution and object's actual size. Accordingly the scale invariance definition in 2D image processing is the ability to extract features independent of both size and sampling. For this reason solely object size is usually unknown or obtained only proportional to scene or other objects. However for range images, the metric size of the object is acquired independent of sensor resolution. Thus, the range image encapsulates both the object's metric size and its sampling information. This is the reason why the concept of scale invariance for range images is different than its conventional definition in 2D.

In this approach we define the scale invariance concept for range images as extracting the features independent of the scale or sampling of the object together with a metric size parameter. This enables us to match similar objects of different size and also indicate the scale ratio between them. For this reason we resample the range scans such that the average of the distances between neighboring points is a constant value. When curvature values are calculated at a constant scale/sampling ratio, they become invariant of resolution. If a scale-space definition is used they become scale invariant as well. Thus, the thresholds used for classifying curvature classification become universal. In this study all range images are re-sampled to an average value of 0.5 mm/sample ratio before the features are extracted.

1.3 Scale-space approach

Scale invariance concept is strongly related to the scale-space concept. As thoroughly examined in (Lindeberg, 1994) feature's actual scale or metric size can be obtained from the scale-space of that signal. The nuance between scale invariance and scale information in feature extraction lies in the definition of scale-space. Scale invariance may be satisfied with very simple methods, however if features with scale information is required, a definition of scale-space of the signal is needed. Reader should refer to (Lindeberg, 1994) for a detailed analysis of scale-space concept in computer vision. A scale space of range images are depicted in Figure 1.

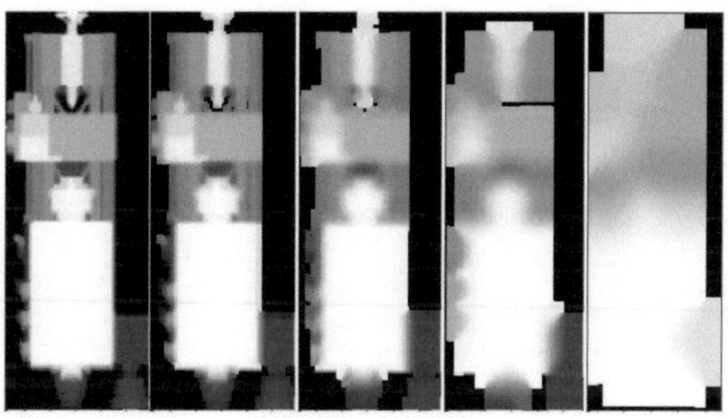

Fig. 1. The scale levels of a range image (Hetzel et al., 2001) constructed by pyramiding are depicted. The black regions are the invalid points.

Among many methods to construct a scale-space for a signal, pyramiding is one of the most preferred. While constructing a pyramid for a range image, the invalid points must be processed carefully. Invalid points are either background or simply unknown since they could not been acquired properly by the scanner. For most 3D data processing methods, these invalid points are simply ignored and calculations are carried out using only the valid points. However if a pyramid of a 3D range image, which contains a group of invalid points, is to be constructed; these invalid points should be handled properly. When constructing a pyramid for a 2D intensity image, the pyramiding operator is convolved throughout the image with no exceptions. However for a depth image, including invalid points; it is possible that one might experience difficulties in boundary regions where valid and invalid points are next to each other. In these occasions, the segments of the pyramiding filter, which corresponds to invalid points, should be omitted. This way the true shape of the object may be preserved in higher scales. In Figure 1, the scale space of a surface is constructed using Gaussian pyramiding [Burt & Adelson, 1984]. Around the valid point boundaries the smoothing filter avoids blending with invalid points. This way, sharp boundaries of an object can be preserved.

2. 3D feature extraction

In this section, curvature types used to extract features from 3D surfaces are summarized. Different curvatures classification types are reminded.

2.1 Curvature classification

In literature, there are different types of surface curvatures which are used to classify surface patches. We commence by the very basic curvatures, the principle curvatures, from which other curvature values are obtained.

2.1.1 Principle curvatures

In differential geometry, the two principal curvatures at a given point of a surface measure how the surface bends by different amounts in different directions at that point. At each point p of a differentiable surface in 3D Euclidean space one may choose a unique unit normal vector. A normal plane at p is one that contains the normal, and will therefore also contain a unique direction tangent to the surface and cut the surface in a plane curve. This curve will in general have different curvatures for different normal planes at p. The principal curvatures at p, denoted κ_1 and κ_2, are the maximum and minimum values of this curvature. Figure 2 depicts these curvatures and their normal planes.

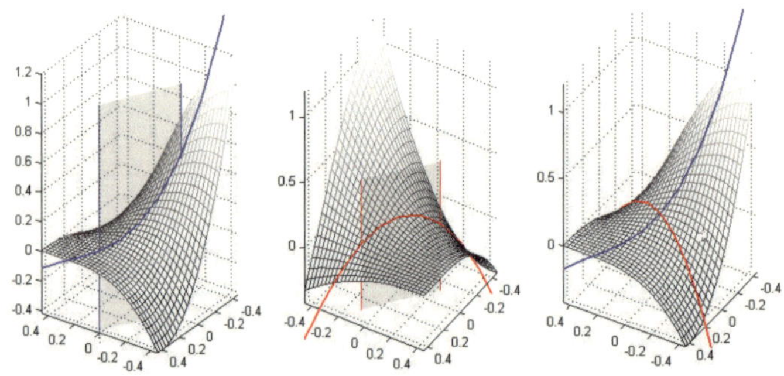

Fig. 2. The normal plane with the maximum curvature is seen. b) The normal plane with the minimum curvature is seen c) $\kappa_1 = 1.56$ and $\kappa_2 = -2.37$. The surface is a patch from a monkey saddle: $z(x,y) = x^3 - 3 \cdot x \cdot y^2$.

The principal curvature values and the principle directions of the curvatures are calculated by taking the eigenvalue decomposition of the Hessian Matrix which is defined as:

$$\mathbf{H} = \begin{bmatrix} \frac{\partial^2 \mathbf{X}}{\partial u^2} & \frac{\partial^2 \mathbf{X}}{\partial uv} \\ \frac{\partial^2 \mathbf{X}}{\partial uv} & \frac{\partial^2 \mathbf{X}}{\partial v^2} \end{bmatrix} \tag{1}$$

The eigenvalues of this symmetric matrix give the principal curvatures κ_1 and κ_2, where the eigenvectors give the principle curvature directions. Surface points can be classified according to their principal curvature values at that point. A point on a surface is classified as:
Elliptic: ($\kappa_1 \bullet \kappa_2 > 0$) if both principal curvatures have the same sign. The surface is locally convex or concave.
Umbilic: ($\kappa_1 = \kappa_2$) if both principal curvatures are equal and every tangent vector can be considered a principal direction (and *Flat-Umbilic* if $\kappa_1 = \kappa_2 = 0$).
Hyperbolic: ($\kappa_1 \bullet \kappa_2 < 0$) if the principal curvatures have opposite signs. The surface will be locally saddle shaped.
Parabolic: ($\kappa_1 = 0$, $\kappa_2 \neq 0$) if one of the principal curvatures is zero. Parabolic points generally lie in a curve separating elliptical and hyperbolic regions.
This is the basic classification for surfaces according to their principal curvatures. Mean (H) and Gaussian (K) curvatures, shape index (S) and curvedness (C) can also be calculated using the principal curvatures and more essential classifications can be performed using these values.

2.1.2 Mean and gaussian curvatures

Using principal curvatures, Mean (H) and Gaussian (K) Curvatures are calculated as:

$$H = (\kappa_1 + \kappa_2)/2 \, , K = \kappa_1 \cdot \kappa_2 \tag{2}$$

H is the average of the maximum and the minimum curvature at a point, thus it gives a general idea on how much the point is bent. K is the multiplication of the principal curvatures and its sign indicates whether the surface is locally elliptic or hyperbolic. Using HK values, the regions are defined as in Table 1.

	K>0	K=0	K<0
H<0	Convex (Elliptic or Umbilic)	Ridge (Convex Parabolic)	Saddle Ridge (Hyperbolic)
H=0	(Not possible)	Planar (Flat-Umbilic)	Minimal (Hyperbolic)
H>0	Concave (Elliptic or Umbilic)	Valley (Concave Parabolic)	Saddle Valley (Hyperbolic)

Table 1. Shape Classification in HK curvature space.

2.1 Shape index and curvedness

(Koenderink & Doorn, 1992) defines an alternative curvature representation using the principal curvatures. This approach defines two measures: the shape index (S) and the curvedness (C). Shape index (S) defines the shape type and curvedness (C) decides if the shape is locally planar or not.

$$S = 2/\pi \cdot \arctan\left(\kappa_1 + \kappa_2 / \kappa_1 - \kappa_2\right) \ (\kappa_1 > \kappa_2), \ C = \sqrt{\kappa_1^2 + \kappa_2^2 / 2} \tag{3}$$

The shape index value of a point is independent of the scaling of that shape. However C is not scale or resolution invariant. Both S and C are orientation invariant. (Koenderink &

Doorn, 1992) uses S value in order to classify a point. S values changes between [-1,+1] where -1 defines cup shapes (convex elliptical) and + 1 defines cap shapes (concave elliptical). They define constant shape index values in order to define shape types. These values are given in Table 2 below. However their original classification does not differentiate hyperbolic regions into three different types (yellow-orange-red regions, i.e. saddle valley, hyperbola and saddle ridge). For this reason another constant shape index value may be defined (3/16) for this purpose. The Curvedness (C) values are used to understand if the region is planar or not. For planar regions C value is very close to zero (i.e. below the zero threshold C_{zero}) (Table 2).

Convex (Elliptic)	$S \in [+5/8,1] \cap C > C_{zero}$
Convex (Parabolic)	$S \in [+3/8,+5/8] \cap C > C_{zero}$
Saddle Ridge	$S \in [+3/16,+3/8] \cap C > C_{zero}$
Planar	$C < C_{zero}$
Hyperbola	$S \in [-3/16,+3/16] \cap C > C_{zero}$
Concave (Elliptic)	$S \in [-1,-5/8] \cap C > C_{zero}$
Concave (Parabolic)	$S \in [-5/8,-3/8] \cap C > C_{zero}$
Saddle Valley	$S \in [-3/16,+3/16] \cap C > C_{zero}$

Table 2. Shape Index and Curvedness Classification

2.2 Curvature scale-spaces

The curvature values are calculated using surface gradients. Thus they give basic information on surface behavior. In order to calculate surface gradients analytically, explicit surface functions may be used. However in real world applications, the 3D surfaces are digitized into sampled points and there's no global explicit function of the surface. Hence, the surface gradients are calculated within a neighborhood of sampled points. For this reason the calculated curvatures are local approximations, which are valid on a certain scale. Therefore the curvatures are calculated for each scale level, so that curvature scale-spaces are obtained.

In Figure 3, H, K, S and C curvature scale spaces of the range image given in Figure 1 are depicted. Figure 3.a shows the scale-space of H values. The concave regions which have positive H values, are painted in red, where convex regions with negative H values are painted in blue. For both regions the magnitude of the curvature is demonstrated by color intensity. As seen from the figure, the convex region denoted by number 1 is designated as a peak in higher scales since this element is relative large for the given resolution of the 3D scan. Similarly in Figure 3.b, K values obtained from different scales of the surface are depicted. The parabolic regions with positive K values are painted in red, where the hyperbolic regions with negative K values are painted in blue. In Figure 3.c, the shape index values obtained from different scale levels of the surface are examined. Since shape index value is capable of classifying the surface into the fundamental surface types (except planes), the scale-space of the shape index values clearly demonstrate the scale coordinates of the surface features (colors correspond to Table 2). As seen from this figure, the convex region denoted by number 1 is designated as a peak in higher scales and is not existent in lower scales. Finally in Figure 3.d, C values obtained from different scale levels are examined.

Curvedness values can be used to detect planar regions, since regions having sufficiently small curvedness values are defined as planes. In Figure 3.d, the gray level intensities designate C values, where zero C value corresponds to black. In this figure, the region denoted by numbers 1, 2, 3 and 4 in different scale levels corresponds to a planar region on the surface and it is designated as plane in the first four scale levels in C scale-space. However in the fifth C scale-space level is it not designated as plane, since in this scale, the region is designated as pit (Figure 3.a and 3.c).

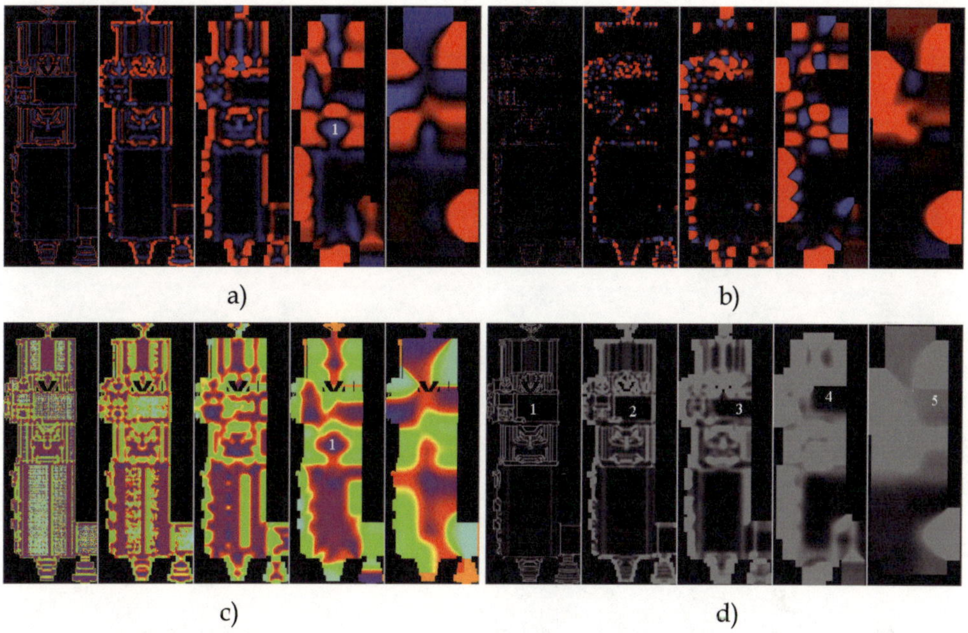

Fig. 3. Curvature scale-spaces: a) Mean Curvature (H), b) Gaussian Curvature (K), c) Shape Index (S), d) Curvedness (C).

2.3 Extraction of scale invariant features

Most curvature oriented methods find salient points on the range image which are defined around a local patch. If the size of this effective local region is kept constant, only the features which are smaller than this size of the local region can be extracted over the surface. In other words, if principal curvature values of a point are calculated using the neighboring points around a radius of d mm, only the features which have sizes smaller than $\pi \cdot d^2$ mm^2 could be extracted. Thus, if the method uses a constant radius of locality when extracting the features, there is no notion of scale invariance. Even though shape index value is invariant to scale, if the principal curvatures are calculated at a constant scale level, the feature's scale is still ambiguous, unknown and incomparable.

The only method to overcome this fact is to search for the features at different scale levels of the surface. For this purpose, a scale space of the surface should be constructed and curvature values should be calculated at all levels of this scale-space. When moved through this scale-space, smaller features vanish and larger features which were not obvious at smaller scales become visible towards the higher scales.

There are different methods to construct a scale-space of a surface. In this study, we use the Gaussian Pyramid approach [6] because image size decreases exponentially with the scale level and hence also the amount of computation required to process the data. First, HK (or SC) values are calculated and pixels are classified based on surface types separately for each pyramid layer using Table 1. The regions are classified to eight different types, namely peak, saddle ridge, convex cylinder, pit, saddle valley, concave cylinder, plane and hyperbolic, similar to [1]. Then each layer is expanded by up-sampling to a fixed size. Finally, by putting each classified curvature scale level on top of each other, a scale-space of the classified features is obtained. We call this scale space as UVS space where U and V are used for surface dimensions and S is used for scale (Figure 4). The method for constructing a UVS space is detailed in [7].

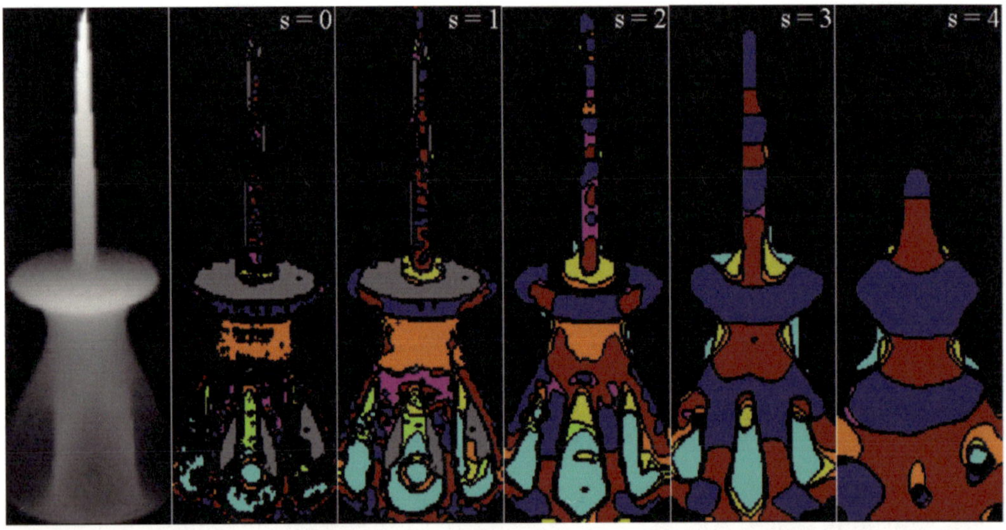

Fig. 4. Labeled layers of UVS space constructed by HK (or SC) values where S is increasing from left to right. The original surface level is indicated by "S=0". Labels are given by colors. *(peak: blue, saddle ridge: red, convex cylinder: purple, pit: cyan, saddle valley: yellow, concave cylinder: green, hyperbolic: orange, plane: gray.)*

In order to extract the features from curvature scale spaces, the following procedure is applied. Inside the classified scale-space, each connected component of the same type of voxels is found and considered as a feature element on the surface. The total number of voxels inside the connected component represents the feature's volume (v_i) and the centre of mass of the connected component is the positional centre of the feature ($\mathbf{x}_i$). Since a connected component may have different number of elements in different scales, a weighted average of the scale value is calculated for each connected component as the actual scale of that feature (s_i). Although each connected component has different numbers of elements in each different scale level, it has the biggest number of elements on the scale which is closest to its actual scale. The area (A) of the connected component at this layer is used to calculate the radius (r_i) (4), which also defines the size of that fundamental element.

$$r = \sqrt{A / 4 \cdot \pi} \tag{4}$$

Finally, for each feature element extracted from the surface, the following attributes are obtained: the type (t_i), the positional centre of mass ($\mathbf{x}_i$), the scale (s_i), the size (r_i) and the volume (v_i) (Figure 5).

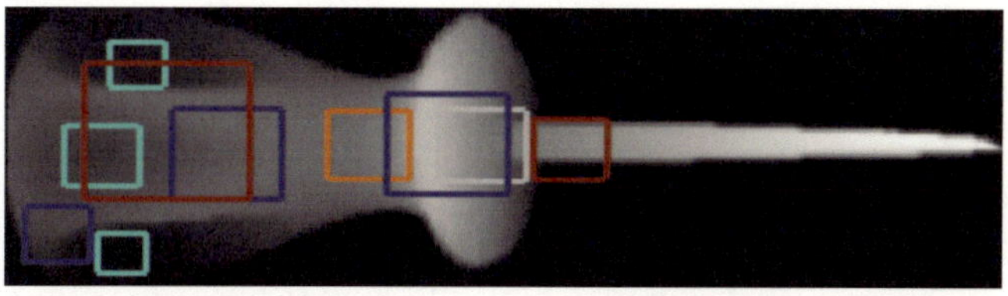

Fig. 5. Ten largest extracted features are shown as squares where the feature center ($\mathbf{x}_i$) is given by the square center, the feature size (r_i) is given by the square size and the feature type is given by its color.

2.3.1 Scale-space localization

As mentioned in the previous sections, the location and the scale of a feature are estimated by computing the weighted average of the curvature values of the elements (voxels) covered by the connected component defining that feature in the UVS volume. In this section, we would like to show that this kind of localization is very precise.

A weight value is assigned to each voxel inside the connected component using the second norm of the absolute differences of the curvature values from the applied threshold values (if HK curvature scale-space is to be constructed):

$$w_{i,j} = \left(\left(\mathbf{H_{i,j}} - \epsilon_\mathbf{H}\right)^2 + \left(\mathbf{K_{i,j}} - \epsilon_\mathbf{K}\right)^2\right)^{\frac{1}{2}} \tag{5}$$

The localization of the features in the UVS volume and on the surface is crucial. This localization should be robust to noise and any type of transformations. For example in (Lowe, 2004), the SIFT descriptor is sought in a scale space of different octaves, where all local maxima (or minima) are selected as features. Instead of using the weighted averages, a similar approach to (Lowe, 2004) may be applied to our method, where a single maximum for each connected component is found in the UVS space. However, as it is seen in Figure 6,

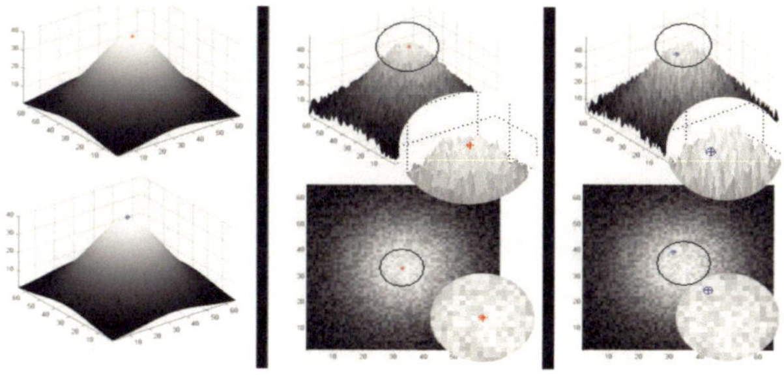

Fig. 6. Localization of the peak feature using both methods a) For the ideal surface both methods localize the peak feature correctly (top: weighted average, bottom: single maximum). b) For the noisy surface, the feature is still correctly localized using weighted averages. c) The localization fails under noise when the single maximum method is used.

this approach will fail under noise or in complex scenes. Imagine that we have a simple surface with a single peak and its noisy version. When the center of the peaky feature is sought over the surface with noise, it is seen that a local maximum value inside a connected component may divert the center from its original position (Figure 6.c) although the surface is smoothed in higher scales. In return for this, our method localizes the features correctly (Figure 6.b) and is robust to noise.

2.3.2 Importance of scale-space search

As mentioned before, the main motivation and contribution in this study is the scale-space search of curvature values. In order to show the significance of scale space search, the feature extraction results with and without scale-space search are depicted in this subsection.

When the scale-space search is omitted, the curvatures are found only at the given resolution. Even though scale/sampling ratio is controlled (usually it is not controlled since this ratio changes even when the distance between the 3D scanner and the object changes), the types and the sizes of the features are detected wrong when only the given resolution is considered. In Figure 7, the extracted features of the original screwdriver object and its scaled version (by 0.8), both with and without scale-space search, are depicted. The features extracted from the original and the scaled versions of the screwdriver object using only the given resolution are usually mislabeled (Figure 7.a,b). For example, only some planar features are located on the handle of the object and the actual shape of the handle could not be extracted. Thus, most surface structures are generally labeled as planes when only the given resolution is considered. Since the original resolutions of 3D images are very high, even inside a peaky region, a point may be considered as a plane because the neighboring points are very close to each other. As a result, many small planar regions are detected in large concave areas. Thus, only when a scale space search is performed, the real types and sizes of the surface features could be extracted (Figure 7.c,d).

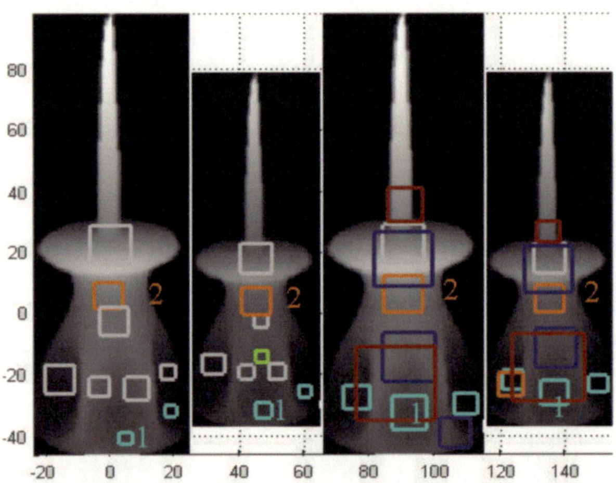

a) b) c) d)

Fig. 7. Ten largest features extracted using a) original image without scale-space search, b) scaled image (by 0.8) without scale-space search, c) original image with scale-space search, d) scaled image (by 0.8) with scale-space search.

Second of all, the feature sizes can only be correctly extracted if scale-space search is used. Since Figure 7.d is 0.8 times resized version of Figure 7.c, the radius of a feature found in Figure 7.d is also 0.8 times smaller than the radius of the corresponding feature found in Figure 7.c. However, this property of robustness under scaling can not be observed when only the given resolution is used for feature detection. Although most features are correspondent in Figures 7.a and 7.b, their radii are faulty. The shape in Figure 7.b is smaller than the one in Figure 7.a by a ratio of 0.8, however the radii of the features numbered as 1 and 2 in Figure 7.b are larger than the radii of the corresponding features in Figure 7.a. Thus it is clearly seen that in order to extract features with their size properties, scale-space search is a must.

3. Topological model

In this section, using the feature elements extracted from the UVS space, a global 3D surface representation is constructed. A scale and orientation invariant representation is proposed, where the spatial topology of the object is given as a graph structure which carries the relative information among the features over the 3D surface. The relativity is not only in terms of spatial information but in terms of orientation and scaling as well.

As explained in the previous subsection, for each feature element the following attributes are obtained: the type (t_i), the volume (v_i), the positional centre of mass ($\mathbf{x}_i$), the orientation vector ($\mathbf{n}_i$), the scale (s_i) and the size (r_i). If each feature is referred as a node in a topology graph where the nodes carry the feature element's attributes and the links between the nodes carry some relative information; a topological representation may be obtained.

In order to make this representation orientation and scale invariant, the links between the nodes must carry "relative" or in other words "normalized" information. An example of this type of relation could be the length between two nodes normalized using a scale invariant measure specific for that topology. The relative 3D direction between two nodes might also be used. Furthermore scale difference between the nodes would carry scale invariant information. These relative link attributes can be listed such as:

Normalized distance from Node A to B ($|\mathbf{x}_B - \mathbf{x}_A|/r_A$ or $|\mathbf{x}_B - \mathbf{x}_A|/2^s$): The distance between two nodes can be normalized using the scale or the size of a base node (A) in the topology. Thus this relation stays invariant under scaling and orientation of the source signal.

Link Vectors or Link Angles $(\mathbf{x}_B - \mathbf{x}_A)/|\mathbf{x}_B - \mathbf{x}_A|$: The unit vector from a node (B) to a specific base node (A) in the topology will also remain invariant under scale. However this link vector will be variant under orientation. In order to make this information both scale and orientation invariant, the angles between these unit vectors might be used. For an n-node topology there would be n-1 unit vectors. For any two these unit vectors, an angle can be calculated. This angle will be invariant of both scale and orientation. For n-1 number of unit vectors, we would obtain C(n-1,2) number of angles, which is also equal to (n-1)·(n-2)/2. The angle can be calculated as:

$$\alpha_{BAC} = \alpha_{CAB} = \cos^{-1}\left(\left[(\vec{\mathbf{x}}_B - \vec{\mathbf{x}}_A)/\left|\vec{\mathbf{x}}_B - \vec{\mathbf{x}}_A\right|\right]^{\mathrm{T}} \cdot \left[(\vec{\mathbf{x}}_C - \vec{\mathbf{x}}_A)/\left|\vec{\mathbf{x}}_C - \vec{\mathbf{x}}_A\right|\right]\right) \tag{6}$$

Normal Vector Difference ($\mathbf{n}_B - \mathbf{n}_A$): The difference vector between the unit normal vector of node B ($\mathbf{n}_B$) and unit normal vector of the specific base node A ($\mathbf{n}_A$) will stay invariant of orientation and scale.

Feature Scale Difference and Size Ratio (s_A-s_B or r_A/r_B): As explained in (Lindeberg, 1994), the scale difference between two nodes is invariant to scaling. The ratio of the size of a node (B) (which is strongly related to scale of that feature) to the size a specific base node (A) will stay invariant of scaling as well.

Imagine we have a four-node topology with nodes A, B, C and D. Assume that node A is defined as the base node of the topology. Then the following vector will be scale and orientation invariant:

$$\boldsymbol{\lambda}_i = [\ t_A, t_B, t_C, t_D, \frac{|\vec{\mathbf{x}}_B - \vec{\mathbf{x}}_A|}{r_{A(or\,2^{s_A})}}, \frac{|\vec{\mathbf{x}}_C - \vec{\mathbf{x}}_A|}{r_A}, \frac{|\vec{\mathbf{x}}_D - \vec{\mathbf{x}}_A|}{r_A}, \alpha_{BAC}, \alpha_{BAD}, \alpha_{DAC} \cdots$$
$$\ldots \vec{\mathbf{n}}_B - \vec{\mathbf{n}}_A, \vec{\mathbf{n}}_C - \vec{\mathbf{n}}_A, \vec{\mathbf{n}}_D - \vec{\mathbf{n}}_A, r_B/r_A\,(or\, s_B - s_A), r_C/r_A, r_D/r_A\ ] \tag{7}$$

This feature vector $\boldsymbol{\lambda}_i$ has 16 elements (as scalars or vectors). For an n-node topology, the number of elements in this vector will be $n+3\cdot(n-1)+(n-1)\cdot(n-2)/2$. This four-node relation may also be shown on a topological chart as shown in Figure 8. Node A is called the base node because the link relations are calculated relative to this node.

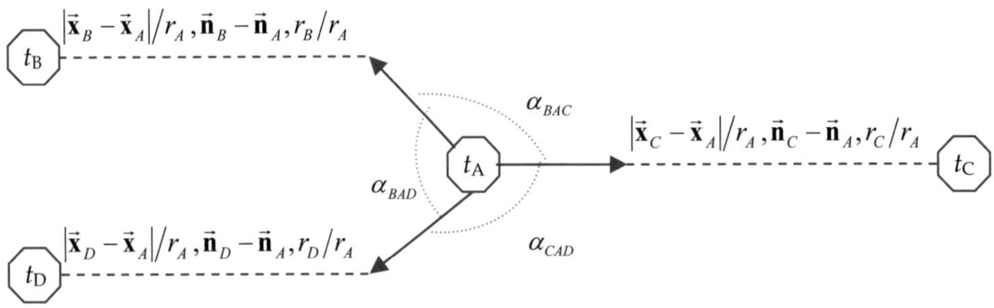

Fig. 8. Four-node, scale and orientation invariant feature vector is shown in a topological chart.

This vector is orientation and scale invariant since all relations are defined relative to node A. However for some applications, orientation and/or scale invariance may not be desired. For example, if the metric size of the object to be recognized is known, then scale invariance is unnecessary. Similarly if the orientation of the object relative to the sensor device is fixed, then orientation invariance capability of a recognition system will be redundant. For this reason orientation and/or scale dependent versions of this vector may be defined.

$$\boldsymbol{\lambda}_i = [\ t_A, t_B, t_C, t_D, |\vec{\mathbf{x}}_B - \vec{\mathbf{x}}_A|, |\vec{\mathbf{x}}_C - \vec{\mathbf{x}}_A|, |\vec{\mathbf{x}}_D - \vec{\mathbf{x}}_A|, \alpha_{BAC}, \alpha_{BAD}, \alpha_{DAC} \cdots$$
$$\ldots \vec{\mathbf{n}}_B - \vec{\mathbf{n}}_A, \vec{\mathbf{n}}_C - \vec{\mathbf{n}}_A, \vec{\mathbf{n}}_D - \vec{\mathbf{n}}_A, r_A, r_B, r_C, r_D, \ldots\ ] \tag{8}$$

Equation (8) is an example of an orientation invariant but not scale invariant feature vector representing a four-node topology, since the link lengths and feature sizes are not normalized according to the base node A. On the other hand the feature vector in Equation (9) is scale invariant but not orientation invariant because the feature normal vectors and link vectors are not normalized according to node A.

Using one of (7), (8) or (9), a feature vector $\boldsymbol{\lambda}_i$ among n-nodes may be obtained. However excessive number of nodes might be (actually are usually) extracted from a range image.

$$\lambda_i = [\ t_A, t_B, t_C, t_D, \frac{|\vec{\mathbf{x}}_B - \vec{\mathbf{x}}_A|}{r_A}, \frac{|\vec{\mathbf{x}}_C - \vec{\mathbf{x}}_A|}{r_A}, \frac{|\vec{\mathbf{x}}_D - \vec{\mathbf{x}}_A|}{r_A}, \ldots$$
$$\ldots \frac{(\vec{\mathbf{x}}_B - \vec{\mathbf{x}}_A)}{|\vec{\mathbf{x}}_B - \vec{\mathbf{x}}_A|}, \frac{(\vec{\mathbf{x}}_C - \vec{\mathbf{x}}_A)}{|\vec{\mathbf{x}}_C - \vec{\mathbf{x}}_A|}, \frac{(\vec{\mathbf{x}}_D - \vec{\mathbf{x}}_A)}{|\vec{\mathbf{x}}_D - \vec{\mathbf{x}}_A|},\ \vec{\mathbf{n}}_A, \vec{\mathbf{n}}_B, \vec{\mathbf{n}}_C, \vec{\mathbf{n}}_D, . r_B/r_A, r_C/r_A, r_D/r_A\ ] \tag{9}$$

Therefore, many n-node combinations may be obtained from a range image and these different n-node feature vectors represents different parts of the 3D surface. The algorithm to obtain a complete set of feature vectors which represents the whole 3D surface is given below:

- Extract all feature elements from the surface:

Node[1]: (t_1), (v_1), (x_1), (n_1), (s_1), (r_1)
Node[2]: (t_2), (v_2), (x_2), (n_2), (s_2), (r_2)
Node[3]: (t_3), (v_3), (x_3), (n_3), (s_3), (r_3)
Node[4]: …

- Select M nodes with M largest radii (r_i) OR volume (v_i).
- Order these selected M largest nodes according to the criteria below:
- Order them according to their type.
- If there is more than one occurrence of a type, order them according to their radius (r_i) OR volume (v_i).
- For the ordered M nodes do the following:
- Select node group size n: (2<n<M)
- Obtain all possible (k number of) combinations of node groups of n among the M ordered nodes: k=C(M,n)
- Among each n-node combination, keep the order of the nodes according to the previous step.
- For all k combinations,
- Select the first feature as the base node.
- Extract the feature vectors λ_i using one of (7), (8) or (9).
- Then stack these row vectors in a feature matrix $\Lambda = [\lambda^T\ \lambda_2^T\ \lambda_3^T \ldots \lambda_k^T]T$.

This feature matrix Λ will be a scale and/or orientation representation depending on the equation used to calculate the feature vectors.

4. Experimental work

In this section, some experiments using proposed method is demonstrated. The transform invariant n-node topology is used to register and recognize range images.

4.1 3D object registration

Surface registration is an intermediate but crucial step within the computer vision systems workflow. The goal of registration is to find the Euclidian motion between a set of range images of a given object taken from different positions in order to represent them all with respect to a reference frame. Registration in general can be divided into two: coarse registration and fine registration (Salvi et al, 2006). In coarse registration, the main goal is to compute an initial estimation of the grid motion between two clouds of 3D points using correspondences between both surfaces. In fine registration, the goal is to obtain the most accurate solution as possible. Needless to say that the latter method usually uses the output of the former one as an initial estimate so as to represent all range image points with respect to a common reference system. Then it refines the transformation matrix by minimizing the distance between the temporal correspondences, known as closest points. For a wide literature survey on registration of range images reader may refer to (Salvi et al, 2006).

In this study, we perform coarse registration using the proposed scale invariant features. The homogenous transformation, which includes 3D rotation, translation and scaling between two range images, is estimated. However different from previous approaches not single features are matched as correspondences, instead the triples that were used to recognize object categories are used.

4.1.1 Triple correspondences

In the previous sections, n-node topologies of scale invariant features were constructed. Using these n-node topologies, transform invariant object recognition was performed and analyzed. The topology set included n=3 number of nodes, namely triplets. Only a general consensus between all matched triplets would give the true transformation and prove that the matched triplets are actually true features that represent the objects. For this purpose using the extracted triplets in the previous subsection, a coarse registration is carried out using "random sample consensus" (RANSAC) method.

4.1.2 RANSAC using triplets

RANSAC is an abbreviation for "RANdom SAmple Consensus". It is an iterative method to estimate parameters of a mathematical model from a set of observed data which contains outliers. It is a non-deterministic algorithm in the sense that it produces a reasonable result only with a certain probability, with this probability increasing as more iterations are allowed. The algorithm was first published by (Fischler & Bolles, 1981).

A basic assumption is that the data consists of "inliers", i.e., data whose distribution can be explained by some set of model parameters, and "outliers" which are data that do not fit the model. In addition to this, the data can be subject to noise. The outliers can come, e.g., from extreme values of the noise or from erroneous measurements or incorrect hypotheses about the interpretation of data. RANSAC also assumes that, given a (usually small) set of inliers, there exists a procedure which can estimate the parameters of a model that optimally explains or fits this data.

The RANSAC algorithm is often used in computer vision, e.g., to simultaneously solve the correspondence problem and estimate the fundamental matrix related to a pair of stereo cameras.

For our case, very similar to solving the correspondence problem in stereo images, the method is used to estimate the homogeneous transformation between to range images. Instead of using candidate point matches, candidate triplet matches are used. As explained in the previous section, the triplets are matched by some well-defined similarity measures. In order to eliminate the false matches, and obtained the transformation only between the true triplet matches, RANSAC is run.

RANSAC also requires a similarity measure to test for the homogenous transformation between two triplet matches. However for RANSAC, different from the similarity measures used to find candidate matches, only the spatial information is used. In other words, at any iteration of RANSAC, if there is candidate transformation, the absolute Euclidian difference between the first triplet and the transformed second triplet is used. The output of the

RANSAC is a homogenous transformation vector, which defines the transformation between any two corresponding points on the registered range images, such that:

$$\overline{\mathbf{P}} = \mathbf{A} \cdot \mathbf{P} = \begin{bmatrix} \overline{P}_x \\ \overline{P}_x \\ \overline{P}_x \\ \overline{s}_p \end{bmatrix} = \left[\begin{array}{c|c} \mathbf{R}_{3x3} & \mathbf{T}_{3x1} \\ \hline \mathbf{0}_{1x3} & S \end{array} \right] \cdot \begin{bmatrix} P_x \\ P_y \\ P_z \\ s_p \end{bmatrix} = \begin{bmatrix} \mathbf{R} \cdot \mathbf{P} + s\mathbf{T} \\ S \cdot s_p \end{bmatrix} \quad (10)$$

4.1.3 Results

In this subsection some experiments on registration using the proposed feature are presented. The first experiment is the simplest case, where there is only in-plane rotation between two artificial surfaces. There's 135° in-plane rotation between the surfaces. The result of RANSAC is given below together with the ideal transformation matrix. The results prove a quite successful coarse registration. In Figure 9, the matched features can also be seen. Colors designate different feature types.

RANSAC result is: $\left[\begin{array}{ccc|c} -0.6627 & 0.6479 & -0.1149 & 43.1966 \\ -0.6896 & -0.6807 & 0.0394 & 156.433 \\ 0.0342 & 0.1096 & 0.9344 & -5.0095 \\ \hline 0 & 0 & 0 & 1.0772 \end{array} \right]$,

and the ideal result is: $\left[\begin{array}{ccc|c} -0.7071 & 0.7071 & 0 & 45 \\ -0.7071 & -0.7071 & 0 & 155 \\ 0 & 0 & 1 & -5 \\ \hline 0 & 0 & 0 & 1 \end{array} \right]$

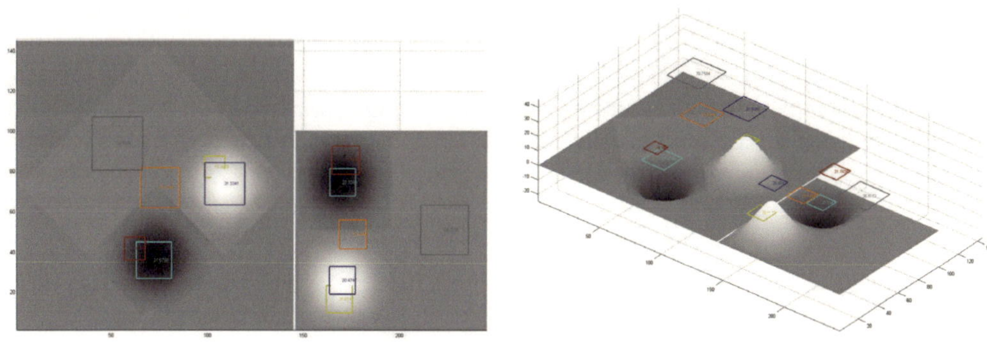

Fig. 9. Matched features from the registered artificial range images.

The same experiment was also performed on range images from the Stuttgart database. Since these images are not captured with controlled rotation, we have chosen two images with rotation on a single axis. The result is given below together with the ideal transformation matrix. In Figure 10, the matched features can also be seen. Colors designate different feature types.

RANSAC result is: $$\begin{bmatrix} 0.8616 & -0.0265 & 0.2065 & 0.06336 \\ -0.0032 & 0.9691 & -0.0105 & -0.4065 \\ -0.1914 & 0.0068 & 0.8159 & 8.8006 \\ \hline 0 & 0 & 0 & 1.0042 \end{bmatrix},$$

and the ideal result is ($\alpha \approx 30^o$): $$\begin{bmatrix} \cos(\sim\alpha) & 0 & \sin(\sim\alpha) & 0 \\ 0 & 1 & 0 & 0 \\ \sin(\sim\alpha) & 0 & \cos(\sim\alpha) & T_z \\ \hline 0 & 0 & 0 & 1 \end{bmatrix}.$$

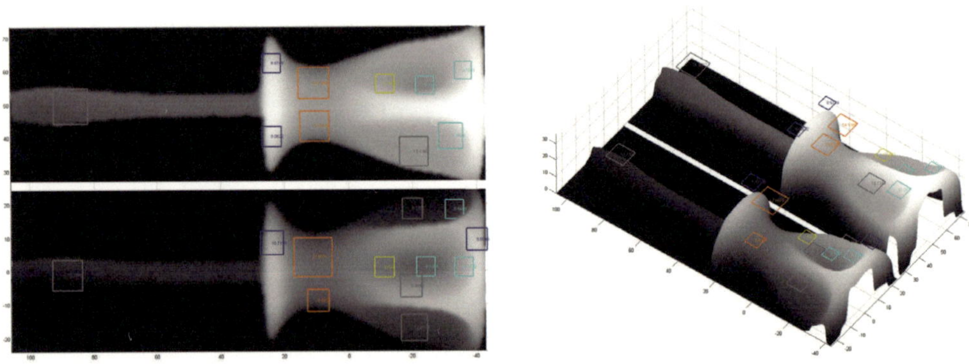

Fig. 10. Matched features from the registered range images from Stuttgart Database

Since the extracted features are scale invariant (and so as the triplets), it is possible to register scaled versions of range images and calculated the scaling ratio between to objects. For this purpose using the %25 scaled versions of the Stuttgart database objects (vs. the originals), registration is performed. The result of RANSAC is given below together with the ideal transformation matrix. The results on scaled range images demonstrate successful scale invariant coarse registration. In Figure 11, the matched features can also be seen. Colors, as usual, designate different feature types.

RANSAC result is: $$\begin{bmatrix} 0.9442 & -0.0143 & -0.0623 & 0.6810 \\ 0.0349 & 0.9899 & -0.0204 & 0.4130 \\ 0.0519 & -0.0067 & 0.9449 & 0.6304 \\ \hline 0 & 0 & 0 & 0.4955 \end{bmatrix},$$

and the ideal result is: $$\begin{bmatrix} 1 & 0 & 0 & 0 \\ 0 & 1 & 0 & 0 \\ 0 & 0 & 1 & 0 \\ \hline 0 & 0 & 0 & \mathbf{0.5} \end{bmatrix}.$$

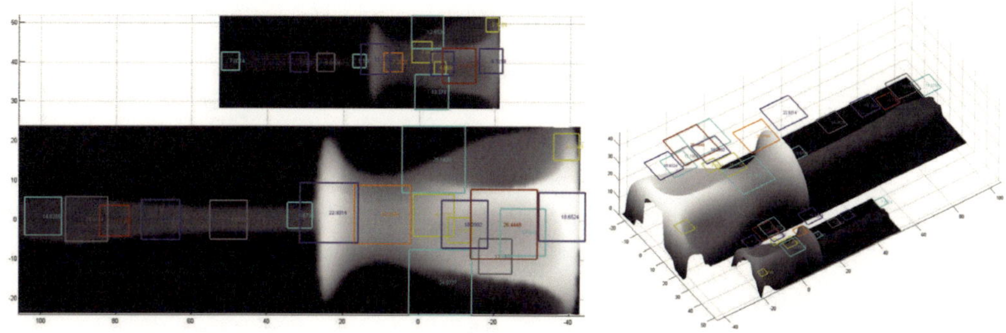

Fig. 11. Matched features from the registered range images from Stuttgart Database. The surfaces are scaled versions of the same range image.

4.1 3D object recognition

In order to prove the importance of scale-space search for scale-invariant object recognition, we have created 0.5 times scaled versions (i.e. 0.25 times scaled in area) of eight objects from Stuttgart range image database. We have used original 258 images of each object as training images and 258 scaled images for testing. 3D geometric hashing is used as the recognition method. A feature vector is constructed using the ten largest feature elements as in Figure 5. By obtaining all possible triplets among these 10 features (totally C(10,3) = 120 triplets for each range image) the feature vector is built. In order to make this feature vector scale and orientation invariant; equation (9) is used.

In this study, these feature vectors are used in a geometric hashing method for object recognition purpose. The main reason behind using geometric hashing is that it allows partial matching of small topologies in a general topology so that the recognition process becomes robust to noise, rotation and even occlusion. In our hashing method, indexing is done by the types of the triplets and each entry includes the feature vector of the triplet besides the code of the pose and the object. At the preprocessing stage of hashing, for each range image in the training set of category of object (for example range images of bunny taken from various angles), the feature vectors are calculated. This database construction stage can be computed offline. For various range image training sets belonging to different objects, this operation is completed. Consequently at the recognition stage, features of the test model (i.e. the model to be recognized) are extracted and then related hash table indexes are obtained. By comparing the hash table entries using a similarity measure between the feature vectors, matching features are found. Corresponding to the indexes in the training sets, matched model's vote is incremented by one for a particular training set. Finally, the database model which receives the greatest number of votes is taken as the match of the test object.

Using the scale-space search, %96.56 average recognition success is obtained. When the scale space search is omitted, the success falls dramatically to %59.54. It is clearly seen that scale-space search is a must, if scaled versions of the objects are to be recognized. In Figure 6, the results are depicted as confusion matrices. The left-most column indicates the scaled test images, and the upper-most row indicates the original training images. Each value in the diagonal cells indicates the percentage success of recognizing a scaled version of an object using the features obtained from the originally sized range image (Figure 12).

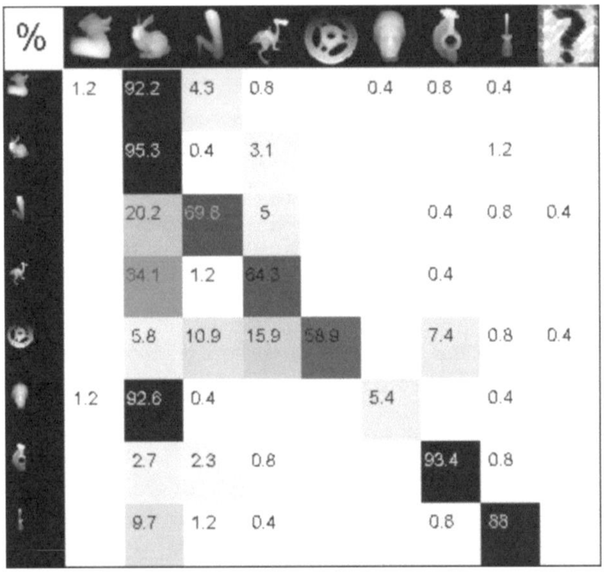

a)

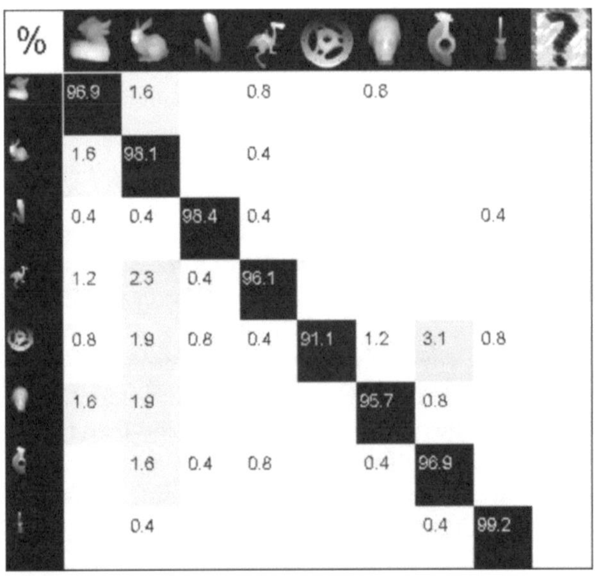

b)

Fig. 12. a) Result for the test, in which the scale-space search is omitted, is shown. The average success dramatically falls to %59.54 when the scale-space search is omitted. b) Result for the test with scale-space search is shown. The average recognition success is %96.56. It is clearly seen that scale-space search is a must, if scaled versions of objects are to be recognized.

5. Conclusions

Understanding the notion of scale invariance for 3D surfaces is crucial to extract scale invariant features with their scale information. For this reason, a scale (size and resolution) and orientation invariant 3D feature detection method is proposed in this study. The method extracts the size of the feature independent of the sampling, scale or the orientation of the objects. For this purpose a scale-space search of HK curvatures is developed.

It is clearly seen in various experiments that scale-space search is a must if utter scale and orientation invariance is intended. With only the given resolution of the surface, the feature extraction method is always dependent on the sampling rate or the thresholds used. For a feature detection system to be independent of any property of the source signal, the features must be sought within a scale-space.

In addition, when scale-space is used, the size of a feature, which defines the effective extent of the detected interest region, can be obtained. By this way, scale and orientation invariant points and their effective sizes can be provided for local region based descriptors such as spin image or splash representation.

The use of scale-space also brings robustness to noise. Since scale-space levels are created using Gaussian filters, within the higher levels of the scale-space, any level of noise disappears and large features can be extracted very clearly although the surfaces are noisy.

When the scale invariant feature extraction is used for 3D object recognition, the resulting recognition performance is much better than when feature extraction is done only for the given scale.

Results show that, the extracted features can be used for coarse registration of range images. The registration inherits the scale, sampling and orientation invariant nature of the features, and rotated and scaled versions of objects can be successfully matched. The scale ratio between the matched objects can be obtained.

In addition recognition in a scale varying database can be performed if scale invariant features are used. Objects of different size from a huge database, are efficiently recognized using sparse feature vectors.

As a feature study, the features may be applied to time-of-flight (TOF) camera images and robust implementations may be developed for real-time robotics applications.

6. References

Burt, P. & Adelson, E. (1983) The Laplacian Pyramid as a Compact Image Code. *IEEE Transactions on Communications*, Vol. 31, No. 4, Apr 1983, pp. 532-540.

Chua, C. S. & Jarvis, R. (1997) Point Signatures: a new representation for 3D object recognition. *Int. J. of Computer Vision*, Vol.25 , No.1, October 1997, pages: 63 - 85

Fischer, M.A. & Bolles, R. (1981) Random sample consensus: a paradigm for model fitting with applications to image analysis and automated cartography. *Communications of the ACM*, Vol.24, No.6, June 1981, pp.381-395.

Frome, A.; Huber D.; Kolluri, R.; Bülow, T.; Malik, T. (2004) Recognizing objects in range data using regional point descriptors. *Proceeedings of European Conf. on Computer Vision ECCV 2004*, vol 3, pp. 224-237

Hetzel, G.; Leibe, B.; Levi, P. & Schiele, B.(2001) 3D Object Recognition from Range Images using Local Feature Histograms. *Proceedings of International Conference on Computer Vision and Pattern Recognition (CVPR'01)*, vol.2, pp. 394-399

Horn, B.K.P. (1984) Extended Gaussian Images. *Proceedings of the IEEE*, Vol.72, No.2, December 1984, pp. 1671-1686,

Johnson, E. & Hebert, M. (1999) Using Spin Images for efficient object recognition in cluttered 3D scenes. *IEEE Transactions on Pattern Analysis and Machine Intelligence*, Vol. 21, No. 5: 433-449.

Koenderink J. & Doorn, A. J. (1992). Surface shape and curvature scale, *Image Vision and Computing*, Vol. 10, No. 8, October 1992, pp. 557–565.

Li, X. J. & Guskov, I. (2007) 3D Object recognition from range images using pyramid matching", *Proceedings of ICCV'07 Workshop on 3D Representation for Recognition (3dRR-07)*, pp. 1-6

Lindeberg, T. (1994). *Scale-Space Theory in Computer Vision*. Kluwer Academic Publishers,Norwell, MA, USA

Lo , T.W.R. & Siebert, J.P. (2009). Local feature extraction and matching on range images 2.5D SIFT. *J. Computer Vision and Image Understanding*, Vol. 113, No. 12, December 2009, pages 1235-1250.

Lowe, D. G. (2004). Distinctive Image Features from Scale-invariant Keypoints. *Int. J. Computer Vision*, vol. 60, no. 2, pp. 91-110

Pauly, M.; Keiser,R. & Gross M. (2003). Multi-scale Feature Extraction on Point-Sampled Surfaces. *Proceedings of EUROGRAPHICS'03*, Vol. 22, No. 3.

Salvi, J; Matabosch, C.; Fofi, D & Forest, J. (2006) A review of recent range image registration methods with accuracy evaluation. *Image Vision and Computing*, Vol. 25, No.5, May 2007, pp. 578-596.

Sun, Y. & Abidi, M. A. (2001) Surface Matching by 3D Points Fingerprint. *Proceeding of Eighth International Conference on Computer Vision (ICCV'01)*, Vol. 2, pp.263.

18

Fibre Bundle Models and 3D Object Recognition

Fangxing Li[1], Linyu Peng[2] and Huafei Sun[3]
[1,3]*Beijing Institute of Technology*
[2]*University of Surrey*
[1,3]*China P. R.*
[2]*UK*

1. Introduction

Surface modeling is a fundamental issue in 3D images, shape synthesis and recognition. Recently, a surface model called the fibre bundle model is proposed (Chao et al., 2000; Chao & Kim, 2004; Chao et al., 2004; Chao & Li, 2005; Suzuki & Chao, 2002). The fibre bundle model becomes powerful in its full generality however still needs much information, the information of these two curves at all points, which are roughly equivalent to the information of pointwise representation itself. On the other hand, to apply such a surface model efficiently in shape generation and representation, one needs to know the geometrical quantities of the model.

Object recognition techniques using 3D image data are expected to play an important role in recognition-synthesis image coding of 3D moving pictures or animations in virtual environments and image communications. Currently used 3D free object representations seem insufficient in the sense that, for models such as generalized cylinders or super-quadratics, it is usually difficult to find the invariant features, especially to find the complete set of invariants, which is defined as the smallest number of invariants in order to uniquely determine and reproduce the shapes (Chao & Ishii, 1999; Chao & Suzuki, 2002; Chao et al., 1999; Kawano et al., 2002; Sano et al., 2001).

From the view of differential geometry and Riemannian geometry, the authors obtained the geometric structures about fibre bundle models (Li et al., 2008, 1; 2). Meanwhile, an algorithm of 3D object recognition using the linear Lie algebra models is presented, including a convenient recognition method for the objects which are symmetrical about some axis (Li et al., 2009).

2. Fibre bundle model and its geometry

2.1 Fibre bundle model of surfaces

A surface $F = \{F(u,v)\}$ is called a fibre bundle on a given base curve $b = \{b(v), v \in \mathbb{R}\}$, if locally (i.e. at a neighborhood of any point) F is a direct product of b and another curve called a fibre curve. More specifically, as shown in Fig. 1, there is a projection map $\pi : F \to b$, such that for a point $x \in b$, there is a curve $f_x = \{f_x(u), u \in \mathbb{R}\}$ on F

$$f_x := \pi^{-1}(x) \subset F, \tag{1}$$

which is called a fibre at the base point x. For any $x \in b$, there is a neighborhood of x in $b : U_x \in b$ such that

$$\pi^{-1}(U_x) \cong U_x \times f_x. \tag{2}$$

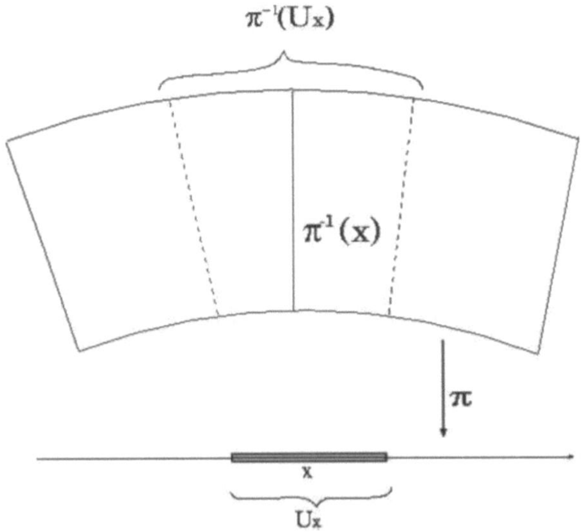

Fig. 1. Fibre bundle model of surfaces.

The fibre bundle model can represent any surface F, e.g. generalized cylinders and ruled surfaces are special cases of this model.
On the other hand, the fibre bundle model is a local direction product, which means the fibre curves could be very different at each base point. Such a nontrivial fibre bundle thus can represent arbitrary complicated surface.

2.2 Fibre bundle model of 1-parameter lie groups of linear lie algebra and its geometry

Let the fibre curve of the fibre bundle model be a 1-parameter Lie group

$$g_v = \{g_v(u) = e^{Au}b(v), u \in \mathbb{R}\}, \tag{3}$$

where A is a 3×3 matrix called the representation matrix of the fibre curve. Therefore, the surface is defined as

$$F = \{x(u,v) = e^{Au}b(v), u, v \in \mathbb{R}\}. \tag{4}$$

The points $b(v)$ on the base curve b are initial points of integral flows of 1-parameter Lie groups g_v.
The Lie algebra of this fibre bundle (roughly can be regarded as its tangent vector field) is a linear Lie algebra

$$L := \frac{\partial x}{\partial u} = x_u = Ae^{Au}b(v) = Ax. \tag{5}$$

A major advantage of this model is that the Lie algebras of fibre curves are uniquely determined by a complete set of invariants I under Euclidean transformation

$$I = \{\sigma_1, \sigma_2, \sigma_3, \phi_1, \phi_2, \phi_3\}, \tag{6}$$

where $\{\sigma_i\}$ are the singular values of A, assuming the singular value decomposition of $A^R = R^T A R, R \in SO_3(\mathbb{R})$ is $A^R = U^T \Lambda V, \Lambda = diag\{\sigma_i\}$. $\{\phi_i\}$ are the Euler angles of $VU^T \in SO_3(\mathbb{R})$. Here, a complete set of invariants is the minimal set of invariants which can uniquely determine the curve. Thus, information to describe the fibre-bundle surface model is the base curve and the six invariants of the linear Lie algebra, i.e. of the representation matrix A.

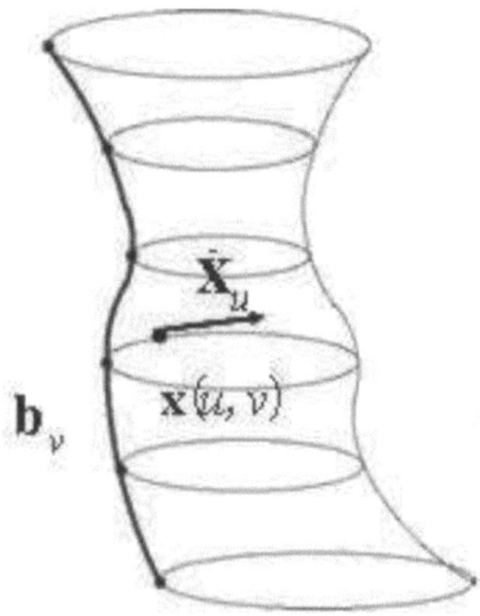

Fig. 2. Fibre bundle of 1-parameter groups of linear Lie algebra.

Lemma 2.1 For any $n \times n$ matrix $A = (a_{ij})$ where $a_{ij} \in \mathbb{R}$ and any $u \in \mathbb{R}$, one has

1. $\frac{\mathrm{d}}{\mathrm{d}u}(e^{Au}) = Ae^{Au} = e^{Au}A$;
2. $\det(e^{Au}) = e^{\mathrm{tr}(Au)} = e^{\mathrm{tr}(A)u}$, where $\mathrm{tr}(A)$ is the trace of A;
3. when $AB = BA$, $e^{A+B} = e^A e^B = e^B e^A$;
4. $(e^A)^T = e^{A^T}$.

Lemma 2.2 $A \in so_3(\mathbb{R}) = \{B | B^T = -B\}$, then $e^{Au} \in SO_3(\mathbb{R}) = \{B | B^T B = I, |B| = 1\}$, where $u \in \mathbb{R}$.

Proof. If $A \in so_3(\mathbb{R})$, we can get that $A^T = -A$ and $\mathrm{tr}(A) = 0$. Then from Lemma 2.1, we get $(e^{Au})^T e^{Au} = e^{A^T u} e^{Au} = e^{(A^T + A)u} = I$ and $\det(e^{Au}) = e^{\mathrm{tr}(A)u} = 1$. Therefore, $e^{Au} \in SO_3(\mathbb{R})$.

Theorem 2.1 For the fibre bundle surface defined by

$$F := \{x(u,v) = e^{Au} b(v), u, v \in \mathbb{R}\}, \tag{7}$$

where $A \in so_3(\mathbb{R})$, and $b(v)$ is a two order differentiable vector, the Gaussian curvature K and the mean curvature H of the fibre bundle surface are given by

$$K = \frac{\det(Ab, b', A^2 b) \det(Ab, b', b'') - (\det(Ab, b', Ab'))^2}{(|Ab|^2 |b'|^2 - ((Ab) \cdot b')^2)^2} \tag{8}$$

and

$$H = \frac{1}{2}\frac{|b'|^2\det(Ab,b',A^2b) - 2((Ab)\cdot b')\det(Ab,b',Ab') + |Ab|^2\det(Ab,b',b'')}{(|Ab|^2|b'|^2 - ((Ab)\cdot b')^2)^{\frac{3}{2}}}, \tag{9}$$

respectively, where $(\cdot)$ denotes the inner product of vectors and det the determinant of an $n \times n$ matrix, respectively.
Proof. Firstly, from the Lemmas we can get

$$x_u = Ae^{Au}b, x_v = e^{Au}b'$$

and

$$x_{uu} = e^{Au}A^2b, x_{uv} = x_{vu} = e^{Au}Ab', x_{vv} = e^{Au}b''.$$

Then we can get

$$E = (x_u \cdot x_u) = |Ab|^2, F = (x_u \cdot x_v) = ((Ab)\cdot b'), G = (x_v \cdot x_v) = |b'|^2,$$

$$|\, x_u \times x_v \,|^2 = (x_u \cdot x_u)(x_v \cdot x_v) - (x_u \cdot x_v)^2 = |Ab|^2|b'|^2 - ((Ab)\cdot b')^2$$

and

$$L = \frac{(x_u, x_v, x_{uu})}{|x_u \times x_v|} = \frac{\det(Ab,b',A^2b))}{\sqrt{|Ab|^2|b'|^2 - ((Ab)\cdot b')^2}},$$

$$M = \frac{(x_u, x_v, x_{uv})}{|x_u \times x_v|} = \frac{\det(Ab,b',Ab')}{\sqrt{|Ab|^2|b'|^2 - ((Ab)\cdot b')^2}},$$

$$N = \frac{(x_u, x_v, x_{vv})}{|x_u \times x_v|} = \frac{\det(Ab,b',b'')}{\sqrt{|Ab|^2|b'|^2 - ((Ab)\cdot b')^2}}.$$

Therefore the Gaussian curvature is given by

$$\begin{aligned} K &= \frac{LN - M^2}{EG - F^2} \\ &= \frac{\det(Ab,b',A^2b)\det(Ab,b',b'') - (\det(Ab,b',Ab'))^2}{(|Ab|^2|b'|^2 - ((Ab)\cdot b')^2)^2} \end{aligned}$$

and the mean curvature is given by

$$\begin{aligned} H &= \frac{1}{2}\frac{LG - 2MF + NE}{EG - F^2} \\ &= \frac{1}{2}\frac{|b'|^2\det(Ab,b',A^2b) - 2((Ab)\cdot b')\det(Ab,b',Ab') + |Ab|^2\det(Ab,b',b'')}{(|Ab|^2|b'|^2 - ((Ab)\cdot b')^2)^{\frac{3}{2}}}. \end{aligned}$$

Example 2.1 Taking $b(v) = (0, \sin(v), \cos(v))^T$, $A = \begin{pmatrix} 0 & -1 & 0 \\ 1 & 0 & 0 \\ 0 & 0 & 0 \end{pmatrix}$, from Lemma 2.2, we know that $e^{Au} \in SO_3(\mathbb{R})$, then we can get $x(u,v) = e^{Au}b(v)$. Thus, we can get

$$\begin{aligned} &b' = (0, \cos(v), -\sin(v))^T, b'' = (0, -\sin(v), -\cos(v))^T, \\ &Ab = (-\sin(v), 0, 0)^T, Ab' = (-\cos(v), 0, 0)^T, A^2b = (0, -\sin(v), 0)^T. \end{aligned}$$

Then the Gaussian curvature is given by

$$K = 1$$

and the mean curvature is

$$H = \begin{cases} 1, & \sin(v) \geq 0 \\ -1, & \sin(v) < 0 \end{cases}.$$

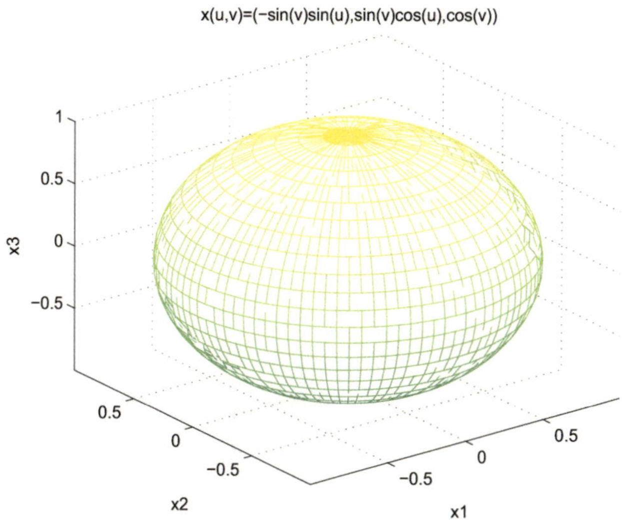

Fig. 3. The figure of $x(u,v)$ in Example 2.1.

Example 2.2 Taking $b(v) = (1,1,v)^T$, $A = \begin{pmatrix} 0 & -1 & 0 \\ 1 & 0 & 0 \\ 0 & 0 & 0 \end{pmatrix}$, we get $x(u,v) = e^{Au}b(v)$. Therefore we can get

$$b' = (0,0,1)^T, b'' = (0,0,0)^T,$$
$$Ab = (-1,1,0)^T, Ab' = (0,0,0)^T, A^2b = (-1,-1,0)^T.$$

Then the Gaussian curvature is given by

$$K = 0$$

and the mean curvature is

$$H = -\frac{\sqrt{2}}{4}.$$

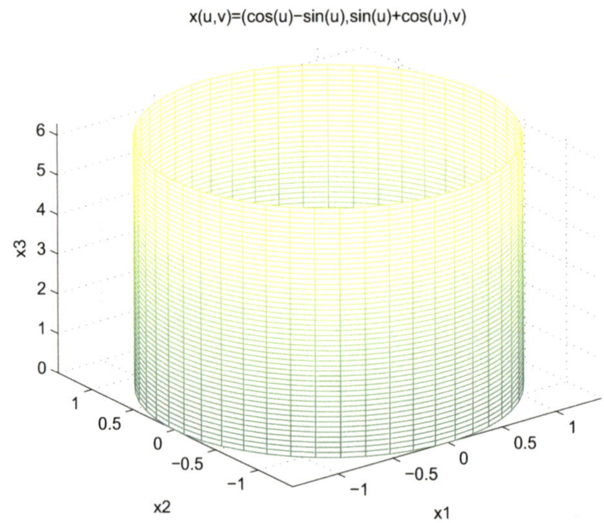

Fig. 4. The figure of $x(u,v)$ in Example 2.2.

Example 2.3 Taking $b(v) = (\cos^3(v), \sin^3(v), v)^T$, $A = \begin{pmatrix} 0 & -1 & 0 \\ 1 & 0 & 0 \\ 0 & 0 & 0 \end{pmatrix}$, we get $x(u,v) = e^{Au}b(v)$.

Hence

$$\begin{aligned}
&b' = (-3\cos^2(v)\sin(v), 3\sin^2(v)\cos(v), 1)^T,\\
&b'' = (-3\cos^3(v) + 6\sin^2(v)\cos(v), -3\sin^3(v) + 6\sin(v)\cos^2(v), 0)^T,\\
&Ab = (-\sin^3(v), \cos^3(v), 0)^T, Ab' = (-3\sin^2(v)\cos(v), -3\cos^2(v)\sin(v), 0)^T,\\
&A^2b = (-\cos^3(v), -\sin^3(v), 0)^T.
\end{aligned}$$

Then the Gaussian curvature is given by

$$K = \frac{48 - 96\sin^2(2v) + 36\sin^4(2v)}{(4 + 6\sin^2(2v) - 9\sin^4(2v))^2}$$

and the mean curvature is given by

$$H = \frac{18\sin^2(2v) - 16}{(4 + 6\sin^2(2v) - 9\sin^4(2v))^{3/2}}.$$

We can see that

$$K = \begin{cases} -12, \sin(2v) = 1 \\ 3, \sin(2v) = 0 \\ 0, \sin(2v) = \frac{\sqrt{6}}{3} \end{cases}.$$

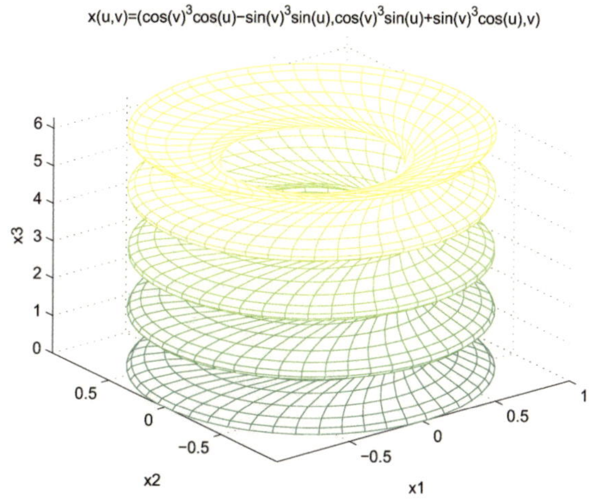

Fig. 5. The figure of $x(u, v)$ in Example 2.3.

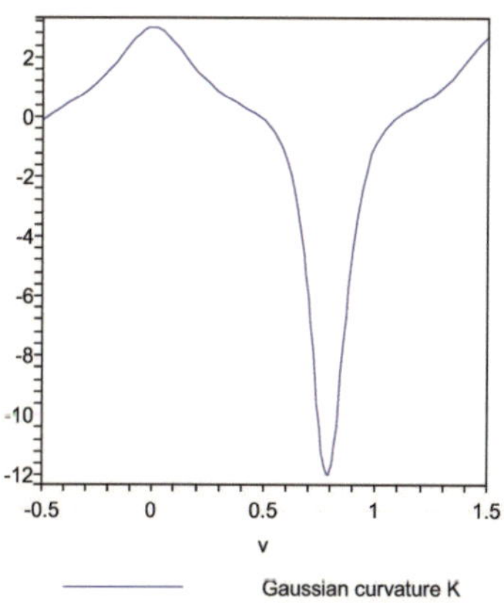

(a) The Gaussian curvature K.

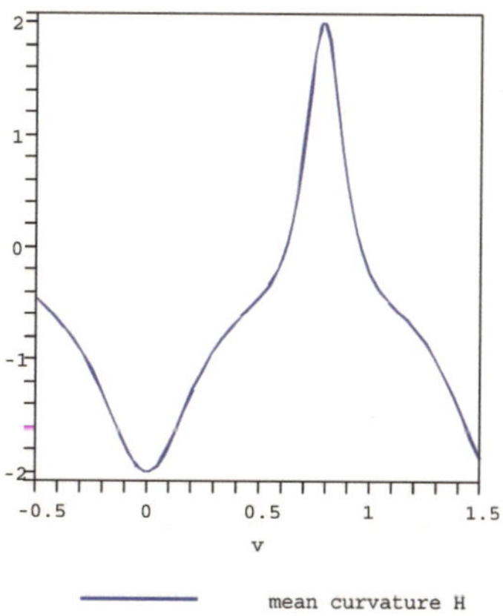

(b) The mean curvature H.

Fig. 6. Curvatures of $x(u, v)$ in Example 2.3.

2.3 Fibre bundle model of 1-parameter lie groups of Hamiltonian lie algebra and its geometry

Consider a spatial curve on a surface M as

$$x(t) := \begin{pmatrix} x_1(t) \\ x_2(t) \\ x_3(t) \end{pmatrix} \in M \subset \mathbb{R}^3 \tag{10}$$

and a state vector as $y(t) = (y_1(t), y_2(t), \cdots, y_6(t))^T \in \mathbb{R}^6$

$$y(t) := \begin{pmatrix} \dot{x}(t) \\ x(t) \end{pmatrix} \in M \otimes T_x M, \tag{11}$$

where T_xM is the tangent space of M at point x. A Hamiltonian Lie algebra of tangent vector fields is defined by the infinitesimal generator

$$\begin{pmatrix} \ddot{x}(t) \\ \dot{x}(t) \end{pmatrix} = \begin{pmatrix} A & B \\ C & D \end{pmatrix} \begin{pmatrix} \dot{x}(t) \\ x(t) \end{pmatrix} \tag{12}$$

or $\dot{y} = Hy$, where $H := \begin{pmatrix} A & B \\ C & D \end{pmatrix}$ is called a representation matrix.

For a special fibre bundle model of 1-parameter Lie groups of Hamiltonian Lie algebra defined by

$$F := \{y(u,v) = e^{Hu}b(v), u, v \in \mathbb{R}\},$$

which is an embedded surface of $\mathbb{R}^6$, where $e^{Hu} \in SO_6(\mathbb{R})$ and $b(v)$ is a two order differentiable vector, one can get the following

Theorem 2.2 The Gaussian curvature $K(u,v)$ of the model is given by

$$\begin{aligned} K(u,v) = & \frac{1}{\det(g_{ij})}((Hb \cdot Hb'') + |Hb'|^2) \\ & + \frac{(Hb \cdot Hb')}{\det^2(g_{ij})}((Hb \cdot b')(Hb \cdot b'') + (Hb \cdot b')(Hb' \cdot b') \\ & - (Hb \cdot Hb')|b'|^2 - (b' \cdot b'')|Hb|^2), \end{aligned} \tag{13}$$

where $(\cdot)$ denotes the inner product of vectors and det the determinant of an $n \times n$ matrix, respectively.

Proof. Using Lemma 2.1, we can get

$$x_u = He^{Hu}b, \;\; x_v = e^{Hu}b'$$

and

$$x_{uu} = H^2e^{Hu}b, \;\; x_{uv} = x_{vu} = He^{Hu}b', \;\; x_{vv} = e^{Hu}b''.$$

Then from $g_{ij} = (x_i \cdot x_j)$, we can get the Riemannian metric as

$$(g_{ij}) = \begin{pmatrix} |Hb|^2 & (Hb \cdot b') \\ (Hb \cdot b') & |b'|^2 \end{pmatrix}.$$

The determinant and inverse of (g_{ij}) are respectively given by

$$\det(g_{ij}) = |Hb|^2|b'|^2 - (Hb \cdot b')^2$$

and

$$(g^{ij}) = \frac{1}{\det(g_{ij})} \begin{pmatrix} |b'|^2 & -(Hb \cdot b') \\ -(Hb \cdot b') & |Hb|^2 \end{pmatrix}.$$

From

$$\Gamma^k_{ij} = \frac{1}{2}g^{kl}\left(\partial_j g_{li} + \partial_i g_{lj} - \partial_l g_{ij}\right),$$

one can get

$$\Gamma_{11}^{1} = \frac{1}{\det(g_{ij})}(Hb \cdot b')(Hb \cdot Hb'),\ \Gamma_{11}^{2} = -\frac{1}{\det(g_{ij})}(Hb \cdot Hb')|Hb|^2,$$

$$\Gamma_{12}^{1} = \Gamma_{21}^{1} = \frac{1}{\det(g_{ij})}(Hb \cdot Hb')|b'|^2,\ \Gamma_{21}^{2} = \Gamma_{12}^{2} = \frac{1}{\det(g_{ij})}(Hb \cdot b')(Hb \cdot Hb'),$$

$$\Gamma_{22}^{1} = \frac{1}{\det(g_{ij})}(((Hb' \cdot b') + (Hb \cdot b''))|b'|^2 - (Hb \cdot b')(b' \cdot b'')),$$

$$\Gamma_{22}^{2} = -\frac{1}{\det(g_{ij})}(((Hb' \cdot b') + (Hb \cdot b''))(Hb \cdot b') - (b' \cdot b'')|Hb|^2).$$

Using

$$R_{ijkl} = R_{ikl}^{h} g_{hj},$$

where

$$R_{ikl}^{h} = \partial_k \Gamma_{il}^{h} - \partial_l \Gamma_{ik}^{h} + \Gamma_{il}^{j} \Gamma_{jk}^{h} - \Gamma_{ik}^{j} \Gamma_{jl}^{h},$$

we can get the nonzero component of the curvature tensors

$$\begin{aligned} R(u,v,u,v) =& (Hb \cdot Hb'') + |Hb'|^2 \\ &+ \frac{(Hb \cdot Hb')}{\det(g_{ij})}((Hb \cdot b')(Hb \cdot b'') + (Hb \cdot b')(Hb' \cdot b') \\ &- (Hb \cdot Hb')|b'|^2 - (b' \cdot b'')|Hb|^2). \end{aligned}$$

Then from the definition of the Gaussian curvature

$$K(u,v) = \frac{R(u,v,u,v)}{\det(g_{ij})},$$

one can the the conclusion directly.

In all of the following examples, $A = \begin{pmatrix} 0 & 1 & 0 \\ -1 & 0 & 0 \\ 0 & 0 & 0 \end{pmatrix}$, $B = \begin{pmatrix} 0 & 1 & 0 \\ 1 & 0 & 1 \\ 0 & 1 & 0 \end{pmatrix}$, $C = -B$ and $D = -A^T$, then $H = \begin{pmatrix} A & B \\ C & D \end{pmatrix}$.

Example 2.4 Taking $b(v) = (v,1,1,2,3,4)^T$, therefore, $b'(v) = (1,0,0,0,0,0)^T, b''(v) = (0,0,0,0,0,0)^T$. We can get

$$K = \frac{109}{(2v^2 - 6v + 59)^2} > 0.$$

Example 2.5 Taking $b(v) = (\cos v, \sin v, 0, 1, 1, 0)^T$, then $b'(v) = (-\sin v, \cos v, 0, 0, 0, 0)^T, b''(v) = (-\cos v, -\sin v, 0, 0, 0, 0)^T$. We can get

$$K = -\frac{2\sqrt{2}+1}{144} < 0.$$

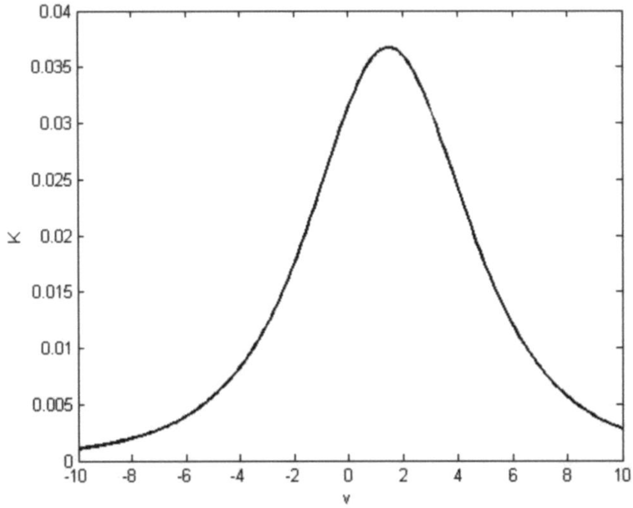

Fig. 7. Gaussian curvature of the surface in Example 2.4.

Example 2.6 Taking $b(v) = (v, 0, a, -a, 0, a)^T$, since $b'(v) = (1, 0, 0, 0, 0, 0)^T, b''(v) = (0, 0, 0, 0, 0, 0)^T$. We can get

$$K = 0.$$

3. 3D object recognition based on fibre bundle models

Recall the fibre bundle model in (4) as

$$F = \{x(u, v) = e^{Au} b(v), u, v \in \mathbb{R}\}, \tag{14}$$

where A is the representation matrix of the fibre curve. The base curve $b(v)$ can also be described by a voluntariness initial point $x_0 \in \mathbb{R}$ and its representation matrix B given by

$$b(v) = e^{Bv} x_0. \tag{15}$$

And its tangent vector field is also a tangent vector field shown as

$$\frac{\partial x}{\partial v} := Be^{Bv} x_0 = Bb(v). \tag{16}$$

Therefore, the information to describe the fibre bundle model is the base curve and the invariants of the linear Lie algebra, i.e., the representation matrix A or representation matrix A, B and the initial point x_0.

3.1 Simulations with known representation matrixes and the initial points

Next simulation results of shape synthesis using the proposed models are shown together with the invariants of representation matrix A or representation matrixes A, B and the initial point x_0.

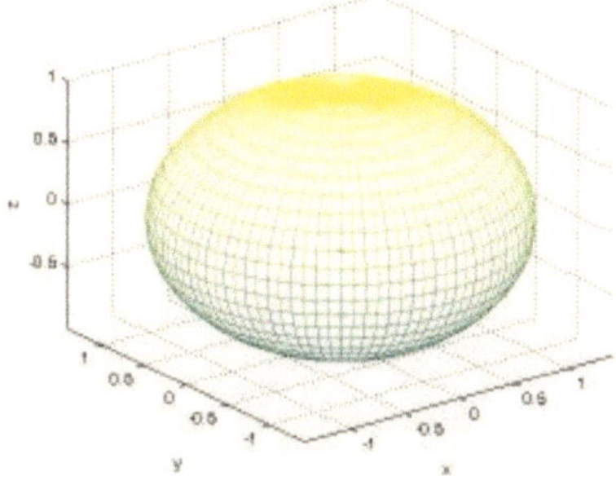

(a) Base curve $(\sin v, \sin v, \cos v)^T$.

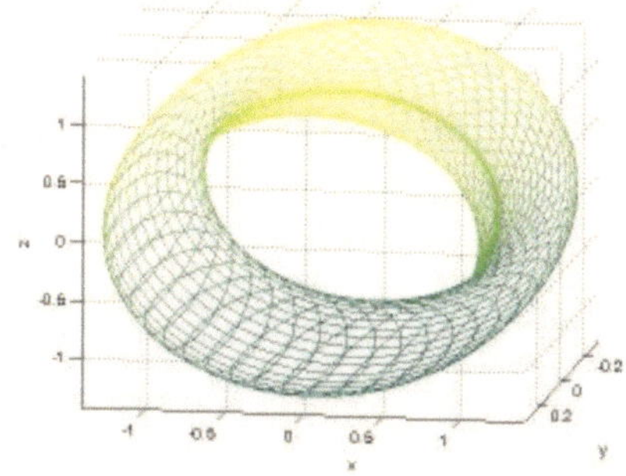

(b) Base curve $(\cos^3 v, \sin v \cos^3 v, 1)^T$.

Fig. 8. Simulations with representation matrixes A and base curves $b(v)$. The representation matrixes A are $\begin{pmatrix} 0 & 1 & 0 \\ -1 & 0 & 0 \\ 0 & 0 & 0 \end{pmatrix}$ and $\begin{pmatrix} 0 & 0 & -1 \\ 0 & 0 & 0 \\ 1 & 0 & 0 \end{pmatrix}$ in (a) and (b), respectively.

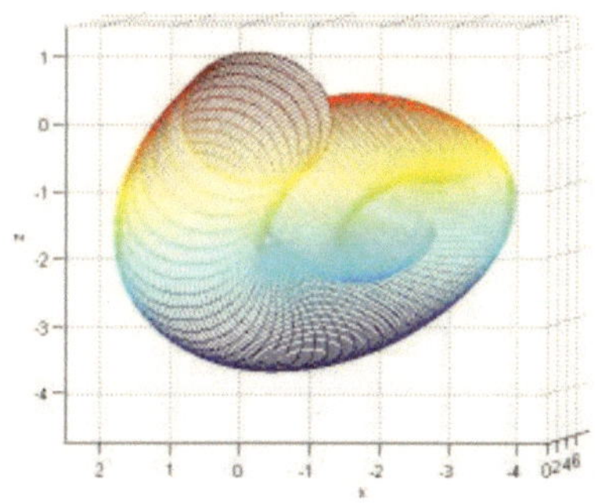

(a) With initial point $(1,1,0)^T$.

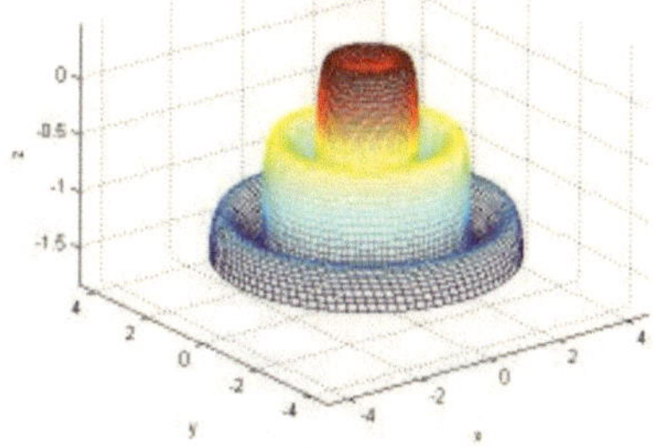

(b) With initial point $(0,1,0)^T$.

Fig. 9. Simulations with representation matrixes A, B and initial points x_0. In (a), the representation matrixes are $A = \begin{pmatrix} 2 & 1.5 & 2 \\ -2 & -1.5 & -2 \\ -3 & -1.5 & -1 \end{pmatrix}$, and $B = \begin{pmatrix} 0 & 0 & 2 \\ -2 & 0 & 2 \\ 2 & 0 & 0 \end{pmatrix}$. And in (b), $A = \begin{pmatrix} 0 & -1 & 0 \\ 1 & 0 & 0 \\ 0 & 0 & 0 \end{pmatrix}$, $B = \begin{pmatrix} 0 & -1 & -1 \\ 2 & 1 & -2 \\ 2 & 2 & -1 \end{pmatrix}$.

3.2 Algorithm of 3D object recognition

Here we introduce an algorithm to obtain the invariants of a linear Lie algebra model from local image data of 3D objects as follows.

1. Take more than $N > 9$ position vectors $\{x_i\}_{i=1}^N$ on the object. Calculate the normal vectors at all positions $\{n_i\}_{i=1}^N$ from geometric relation, and normalize them.
2. From the position and normal vectors to build the following equations in entries of the representation matrix A under a rotation, where A stems from normalization

$$L := \frac{\partial x}{\partial u} = x_u = Ae^{Au}b(v) = Ax.$$

According to that the tangent vector field perpendicular to the normal vectors, we can get that n_i perpendiculars to $\frac{\partial x}{\partial u}|_{x_i} = Ax|_{x_i}$, then we can get

$$n_i^T A x_i,$$

namely,

$$n_i^T \begin{pmatrix} a & b & c \\ d & e & f \\ g & h & i \end{pmatrix} x_i.$$

3. From linear system, we get the components of fibre representation matrix A.
4. Just liking the fibre representation matrix extraction, we can take more than nine position vectors y_i and the corresponding normal vectors to build this equation to solve the coefficient of the base curve representation matrix B.
5. Given a discretional initialization point x_0 and using the obtained representation matrix A and B to restore the primary 3D objects.

When we give the fibre representation matrix $A = \begin{pmatrix} 0 & -1 & 0 \\ 1 & 0 & 0 \\ 0 & 0 & 0 \end{pmatrix}$, then we can use Taylor series to calculate its linear Lie algebra

$$\exp(Au) = \begin{pmatrix} \cos u & -\sin u & 0 \\ \sin u & \cos u & 0 \\ 0 & 0 & 1 \end{pmatrix}. \tag{17}$$

So if we know the initialization point x_0 and the base curve representation matrix B, we can use this representation matrix A to express a form symmetry about an axis without solve the representation matrix A. That can help us easy to express a large number of shapes of 3D objects. (Fig. 8 and Fig. 9)

3.3 Practicality recognition

Next we consider the recognition of two objects, the sphere and vase. Our target sphere is shown in Fig. 10.

Firstly we give a base curve data (easy to confirm) and take more than nine position vectors from the sphere to recognize the object. Here we take data number as 30. From the algorithm, we can get the representation matrix as

$$A = \begin{pmatrix} -0.01 & 1 & -0.0043 \\ -0.9825 & -0.0032 & 0.0204 \\ 0.0202 & 0.0013 & -0.0001 \end{pmatrix}. \tag{18}$$

For the target vase shown in Fig. 12, we have to consider it as three parts, capsule, middle part and bottom, and do the simulations, respectively.

The target vase is a form symmetry about an axis, as presented we can use matrix $A = \begin{pmatrix} 0 & -1 & 0 \\ 1 & 0 & 0 \\ 0 & 0 & 0 \end{pmatrix}$ as the fibre representation matrix, then we only need to extract the base curve representation matrix B.

Fig. 10. Recognize target sphere.

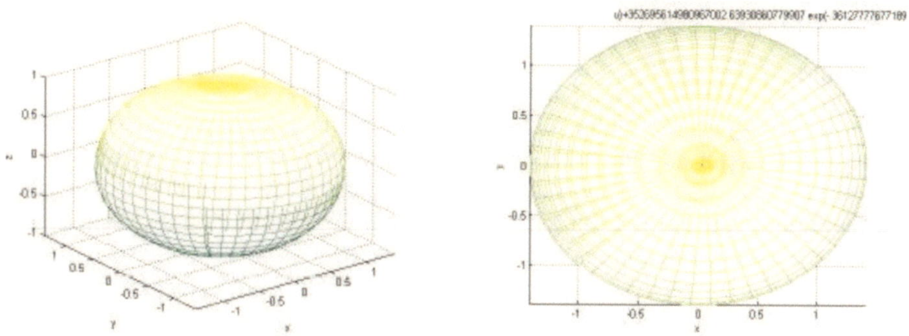

(a) Recognition result (date number 30). (b) Recognition result (view from the top).

Fig. 11. Recognition for a sphere.

For all the simulations in Fig. 13, the initial points are the same as $x_0 = (1, -1, 0)^T$. Meanwhile, from the algorithm, we obtain the base curve representation matrixes B in (a), (b) and (c) as $\begin{pmatrix} -6.0859 & 1 & -0.0689 \\ 0.7695 & -0.0865 & 0.0066 \\ -1.8276 & 0.3112 & -0.0212 \end{pmatrix}$, $\begin{pmatrix} -6.5247 & 1 & 0.2672 \\ -3.9099 & 0.6090 & 0.1608 \\ -0.6605 & 0.1122 & 0.0277 \end{pmatrix}$ and $\begin{pmatrix} -0.3293 & 1 & -0.0442 \\ -3.8194 & 3.0828 & -0.3170 \\ 13.1096 & -5.3890 & 0.8316 \end{pmatrix}$, respectively.

By the way, all the recognition results are exactly calculated and restored under strong noisy environments.

Fig. 12. Recognize target vase.

4. Conclusion

As we know, differential geometry and Riemannian geometry are powerful in applications in kinds of fields, and many methods and subjects are proposed, e.g. geometric mechanics, human face recognition using the method of manifold and geometry in statistics. In this chapter, we show the beauty of the geometry of the fibre bundle models of 1-parameter Lie groups of linear Lie algebra and Hamiltonian Lie algebra.

Fibre bundle model is effective in its representation for objects. Any object can represent as the form of a fibre bundle model, theoretically. Nevertheless, in practice, it's a challenging task for one to get the parameters of a special object. When the representation matrixes and the initial points are given, one can obtain beautiful photos for 3D objects. However, once one have the object, how to recognize it, namely, how to realize it in one's computer is the special challenging but the most important work. We propose an algorithm for 3D object recognition mainly based on the geometric relationship of the positions and normal vectors. The recognition results of sphere and vase demonstrate the algorithm perfectly.

5. Acknowledgements

This work is partially supported by the National Natural Science Foundations of China, No. 10871218, No. 10932002.

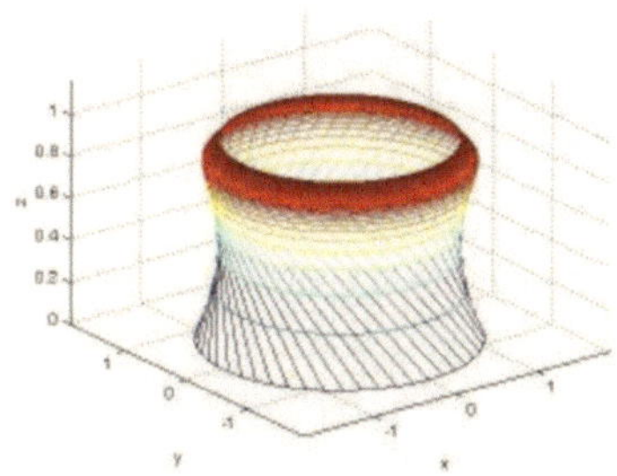

(a) Capsule recognition result.

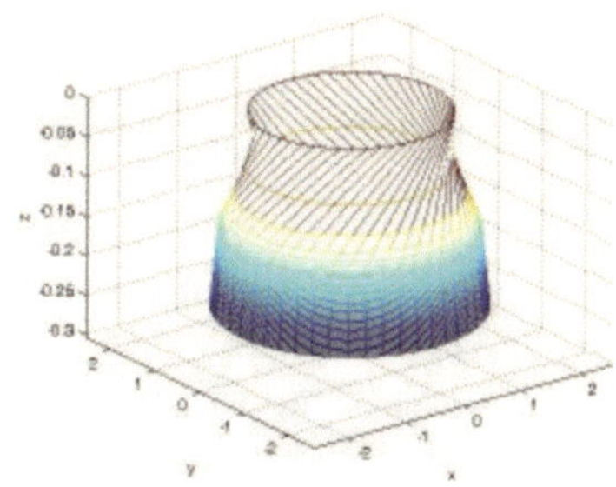

(b) Middle part of the vase's recognition result.

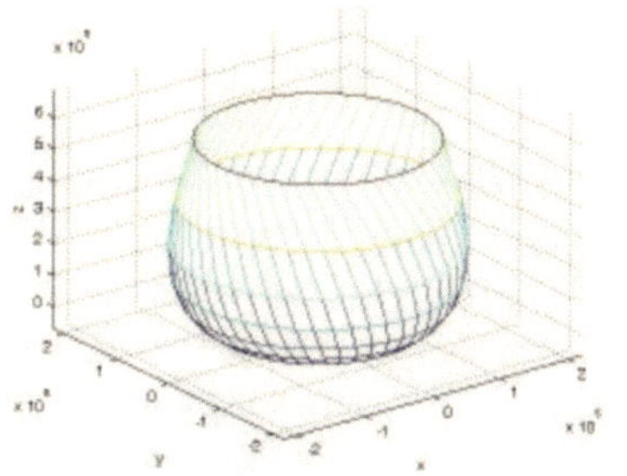

(c) Bottom of the vase's recognition result.

Fig. 13. Recognition for a vase.

6. References

Chao, J. & Ishii, S. (1999). Invariant Recognition and Segmentation of 3D Object Using Lie Algebra Models, *Proceedings of International Conference on Image Processing*, Vol.1: 550-554.

Chao, J., Karasudani, A. & Minowa, K. (2000). Invariant Representation and Recognition of Objects Using Linear Lie Algebra of Tangent or Normal Vector Fields, *IEICE Japan Trans.(D-II)*, J83-D-II(9): 1870-1878.

Chao, J. & Kim, J. (2004). A Fibre Bundle Model of Surfaces and its Generalization, *Proceedings of the 17th International Conference on Pattern Recognition*, Vol.1: 560-563.

Chao, J., Kim, J. & Nagakura, A. (2004). A New Surface Model Based on a Fibre-bundle of 1-Parameter Groups, *IEEE International Conference on Multimedia and Expo*, Vol.1: 129-132.

Chao, J. & Li, F. (2005). A Surface Model Based on a Fibre Bundle of 1-Parameter Groups of Hamiltonian Lie Algebra, *IEEE International Conference on Image Processing*, Vol.1: 1021-1024.

Chao, J. & Suzuki, M. (2002). Invariant Extraction and Segmentation of 3D Objects Using Linear Lie Algebre Model, *Proceedings of International Conference on Image Processing*, Vol.1: 205-208.

Chao, J., Ura, K. & Honma, G. (1999). Generation of 3D Objects Using Lie Algebra Models Based on Curvature Analysis and Comparison with B-spline Fitting, *Proceedings of International Conference on Image Processing*, Vol.4: 366-370.

Chern, S.S., Chen, W. & Lam, K.S. (1999). *Lectures on Differential Geometry*, Series on University Mathematics, Vol.1, World Scientific Publishing Company.

Hall, B.C. (2003). *Lie Groups, Lie Algebras, and Representations: An Elementary Introduction*, Springer-Verlag, New York.

Kawano, S., Makino, M., Ishii, S. & Chao, J. (2002). Meshing Technology with Quality Assurance for Curved Surfaces Defined by Linear Lie Algebra, *Systems and Computers in Japan*, Vol.33(No.10): 64-73.

Li, F., Peng, L. & Sun, H. (2008). On Fibre Bundle Surfaces and Their Curvatures, *Journal of Beijing Institute of Technology*, Vol.17(No.4): 451-454.

Li, F., Wu, P., Peng, L. & Sun, H. (2008). Surface Model Based on a Fibre Bundle of Hamiltonian Lie Algebra and Gaussian Curvature, *Science & Technology Review*, Vol.26(No.8): 37-39.

Li, F., Wu, P., Sun, H. & Peng, L. (2009). 3D Object Recognition Based on Linear Lie Algebra Model, *Journal of Beijing Institute of Technology*, Vol.18(No.1): 46-50.

Olver, P.J. (1986). *Applications of Lie Groups to Differential Equations*, Springer-Verlag.

Petersen, P. (2006). *Riemannian Geometry (Second Edition)*, Springer.

Sano, H., Makino, M. & Chao, J. (2001). An Adaptive High Quality Mesh Generation for Surface Defined by Linear Lie Algebra, *Japan Society for Simulation Technology*, Vol.20: 251-258.

Suzuki, M. & Chao, J. (2002). Invariant Extraction and Segmentation of 3D Objects with Linear Lie Albegra Model, *IEICE Japan Trans. on Information Systems(D)*, E85-D(8): 1306-1313.

19

Experiences in Recognizing Free-Shaped Objects from Partial Views by Using Weighted Cone Curvatures

Carlos Cerrada[1], Santiago Salamanca[2], Antonio Adan[3], Jose Antonio Cerrada[1] and Miguel Adan[3]
[1]*Universidad Nacional de Educacion a Distancia,*
[2]*Univeridad de Extremadura and* [3]*Universidad de Castilla-LaMancha*
Spain

1. Introduction

The *recognition* problem tries to identify an object, called unknown or *scene* object, from a set of objects in an object database, generally called *models*. The problem of *positioning* or *alignment* solves the localization of an object in a scene with respect to a reference system linked to the model of this object. One of the most common ways of solving this problem is *matching* the unknown object on the corresponding object in the object database. Although conceptually recognition and positioning are two different problems, in practice, especially when only part of the object is available (i.e. partial view), they are closely related. If we can align the unknown object precisely on one of the different objects in the database, we will have solved not only positioning but also recognition.

In a general sense, an object recognition system finds objects in the real world from an image of the world, using object models which are known a priori. There is a wide variety of approaches that propose different solutions to recognize 3D objects. Most of them use representation models based on geometrical features where the solution depends on the feature matching procedure. The method we present in this work is concerned with the case when only range data from a partial view of a given free-shaped object is available. Recognition must be carried out by matching this range data of the partial view with of all the possible views of every complete object in the stored object database. The resolution of the problem is of real practical interest since it can be used in tasks with industrial robots, mobile robot navigation, visual inspection, etc.

Regarding the kind of models used in the different approaches there are two fundamental 3D representation categories: object-based representation and view-centred representation. The first tries to generate the model according to the appearance of the object from different points of view, while the second creates models based on representative characteristics of the objects. More detailed information on them will be included in next section.

The structure of this chapter is as follows. Section 2 shows a short survey of recent and more important works that could be considered closer to our work. Section 3 is devoted to make a general description of the stages in which the proposed method is decomposed. The first stage and the WCC feature, which is the key of our method, are studied in detail in section

4. Some explanations of the two remaining stages are stated in section 5. Then, the main experimental results of the method are analyzed in section 6, making special emphasis in the high reduction rates achieved in the first stage. Section 7 states the conclusions of this work.

2. State of the art in 3D recognition methods

As it has been stated in the introduction, 3D recognition methods are highly dependent on the type of chosen representation to model the considered objects. Anyway, all the existing representation approaches belong to one of the two mentioned categories: view-centred representation and object-based representation.

In view-centred representations each object is described in terms of several intensity images taken from different points of view. They try to generate the object model according to the appearance of the object from diverse viewing directions. Representation techniques using aspect graphs or others using silhouettes, and mainly those methods based on principal components, belong to this category. Examples of the last one can be found in (Campbell & Flynn, 1999) of in (Skocaj & Leonardis, 2001).

Another view-based object recognition strategy is described in (Serratosa et al, 2003). They use a *Function-Described Graph (FDG)* that gives a compact representation of a set of attributed graphs corresponding to several views of polyhedral objects. Then the recognition process can be accomplished by comparison between each model and the graph of the unclassified object.

In the work of (Cyr & Kimia, 2004) the similarity between two views of the 3D object is quantified by a metric that measures the distance between their corresponding 2D projected shapes. A slightly different approach is proposed by (Liu et al., 2003), where the so called *Directional Histogram Model* is defined and evaluated for those objects that have been completely reconstructed.

Object-based representations try to model the object surface or the object volume by using significant geometric features referred to a local coordinate system. Representations in this category can be included in four major groups: curves and contours, axial, volumetric and surface representations respectively. The method proposed in this work can be included in the last group and, consequently, a more detailed analysis of the related techniques in this group is exposed next.

(Chua & Jarvis, 1997) code surroundings information at a point of the surface through a feature called *Point Signature*. Point signature encodes information on a 3D contour of a point P of the surface. The contour is obtained by intersecting the surface of the object with a sphere cantered on P. The information extracted consists on distances of the contour to a reference plane fixed to it. So, a parametric curve is computed for every P and it is called point signature. An index table, where each bin contains the list of indexes whose minimum and maximum point signature values are common, is used for making correspondences.

(Johnson & Hebert, 1999) have been working with polygonal and regular meshes to compare two objects through *Spin Image* concept. Spin image representation encodes information not for a contour but for a region around a point P. Two geometrical values (α, β) are defined for the points of a region and a 2D histogram, with α and β as coordinates, is finally constructed.

In (Yamani & Farag, 2002) a representation that stores surface curvature information from certain points produces images, called *Surface Signatures*, at these points. As a result of that, a standard Euclidean distance to match objects is presented. Surface signature representation has several common points with spin image. In this case, surface curvature information is extracted to produce 2D images called surface signature where 2D coordinates correspond to other geometrical parameters related to local curvature.

The two last mentioned methods are halfway between the two basic categories since they do not capture the appearance of the object from each point of view, but provide just a characteristic measurement of the object. This is also our case since our basis will be different measurements on the meshes or on the range data of the objects, calculated from different points of view. In this particular direction is addressed the problem in (Adan & Adan, 2004) where a shape similarity measure is introduced and applied. Nevertheless, this solution does not solve satisfactorily the object recognition problem from real partial views, which is the main purpose of our method.

3. Overall method: Functioning principle

The method presented in this work obtains effective database reduction by applying sequentially different global characteristics calculated on the spherical meshes and the range data of partial views (Fig. 1).

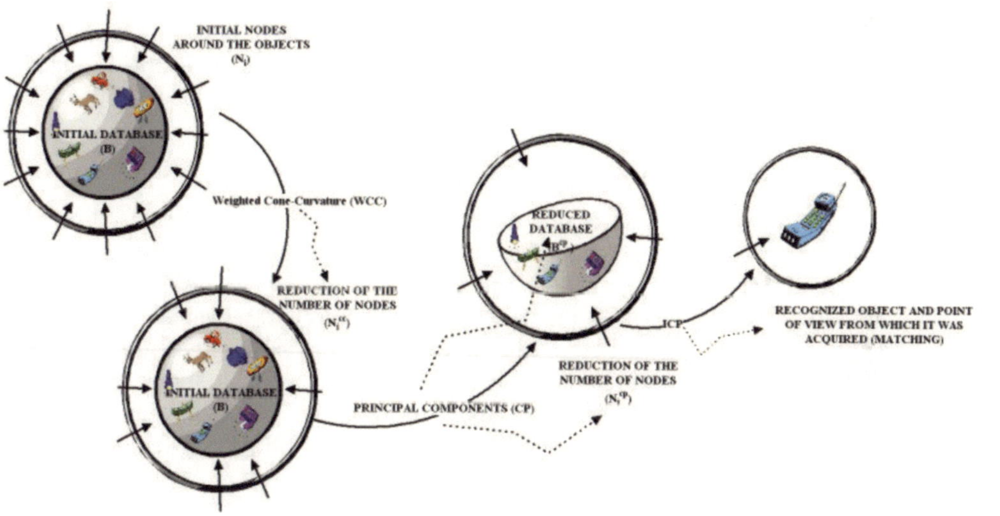

Fig. 1. Scheme of the different stages of the method for object recognition from partial views: graphical representation.

In the first stage we use a new invariant that we call *Weighted Cone-Curvature (WCC)* to determine a first approximation to the possible axes of vision from which this partial view has been acquired. Discretization of the vision space is obtained by circumscribing a spherical mesh around the model of the complete object. Each node in this mesh, together with the origin of coordinates, defines the initial axes of vision around this model. Therefore, determining the possible axes of vision from which the partial view has been acquired is equivalent to selecting a set of nodes on the mesh and rejecting the others. It is important to bear in mind that with this reduction what we are doing implicitly is a reduction of the possible rotations that could be applied on the partial view to match it on the model of the complete object.

We will call the nodes obtained after this first step $\mathbf{N}_i^{cc} \subset \mathbf{N}_i$, where $\mathbf{N}_i$ are the initial nodes of the spherical mesh circumscribed in the *i*-th object of the database. As is deduced from the explanation, in this stage the number of models in the object database is not reduced.
Another invariant based on the principal components (eigen values + eigen vectors) of the partial view and complete object range data will be applied in a second stage on the selected nodes. After this features comparison a list for each of the objects in the database will be created with the $\mathbf{N}_i^{cc}$ nodes ordered according to the error existing in the eigen values comparison. This ordering in turn means that it is possible to identify which object has the greatest probability of matching the partial view. At the end of this second stage a reduction of the models in the object database is obtained together with the reduction of the nodes determined in the previous stage. If we call the initial object database **B**, the base obtained after comparing the eigen values will be $\mathbf{B}^{pc} \subset \mathbf{B}$, and the nodes for each object $\mathbf{N}_i^{pc} \subset \mathbf{N}_i^{cc}$.
The eigen vectors will allow a first approximation to be done to the rotation existing between the partial view and each one of the objects of $\mathbf{B}^{pc}$, which will be used in the last stage when the *Iterative Closest Point (ICP)* algorithm (Besl and Mckay, 1992) is applied. This allows the matching to be done between the range data, and the convergence error of the algorithm will indicate the object to which the partial view belongs.
The last two stages of the method are based on conventional techniques, whereas the first one represents a novel way of dealing with this problem. Therefore, only this key stage of the applied method will be explained with more detail in next section.

4. First stage: Robust determination of the point of view

This is the most important phase of our approach because of its novelty. As it has been mentioned, the purpose of this stage in the overall recognition method is the estimation of the possible points of view from which the given partial view of the object has been acquired are estimated. For this task the new characteristic WCC, which is computed from the partial spherical model, is proposed. The specific partial modelling technique applied is not going to be explained in detail here, and a deeper analysis can be found in (Salamanca et al., 2000). Nevertheless, some preliminary concepts must be introduced to present and explain the power of this feature. First of all it must be said that the WCC feature is derived from the previous concept of *Cone-Curvature (CC)* defined in (Adan & Adan, 2004). But CC concept was originally introduced to represent complete models of objects and it is not directly applicable to partial modeling. Therefore, before establishing a WCC definition it is necessary to introduce the CC concept, and previous to it some spherical modeling basics should be expressed.
CC concept is an invariant feature defined on *Modeling Wave Models (MWM)* (Adan et al., 2000). These MWM were originally defined to represent complete models of objects. The surface representation of a complete object is defined over a mesh T_I of h nodes, being h=*ord*(T_I), with 3-connectivity relationship derived from the tessellation of the unit sphere. Then T_I is deformed in a controlled manner until it fits the available range data of the complete object surface. This new mesh adjusted to the object surface is called T_M. It has exactly the same number h of nodes of the original tessellated sphere and is composed of hexagonal or pentagonal patches. Then, several geometric features can be extracted from T_M and mapped into T_I. In this way, models for all considered objects have the same number of nodes and equal mesh topology.

Let us call generically T to any of these meshes coming from the standard tessellated unit sphere. To make easier the features mapping and the subsequent searching algorithms, some others topological substructures can be defined around the standard mesh T. For example, any node N of the total h can be considered as *Initial Focus* of a new topological structure call *Modeling Wave Set (MWS)*. This MWS is built from another simpler structure called *Modeling Wave (MW)*. And the last one is composed by a collection of samples of other simpler structure called *Wave Front* (denoted as F).

In practical, given any initial focus N, its associated MW structure organizes the rest of the nodes of the mesh in disjointed subsets following a new relationship. Each subset contains a group of nodes spatially disposed over the sphere as a closed quasi-circle, resulting in subsets that look like concentric rings on the sphere. Since this organization resembles the shape of a wave, the name of Modeling Wave has been chosen to call it. With similar reasoning, each of the disjointed ring-shaped subsets is known as Wave Front, and initial node N is called Focus. Of course, the MW structure remains in T across the deformation and fitting process, as it can be seen in Fig. 2.

From the previous ideas it can be deduced that any node of T may be focus and can generate its own MW. Therefore h different MWs can be generated in a model, being the set formed by these h MWs what constitutes the Modeling Wave Set.

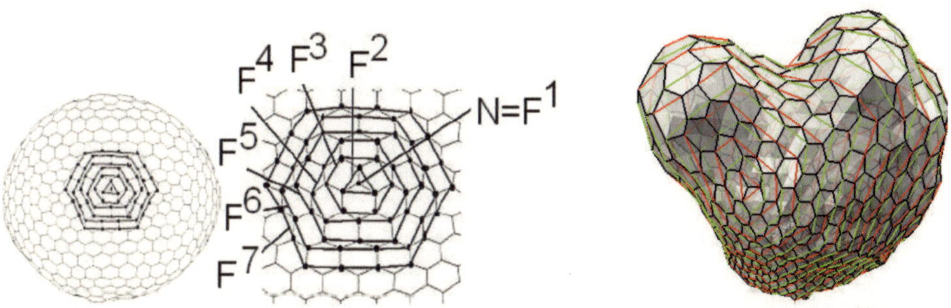

Fig. 2. Left, the first seven consecutive WFs drawn over the standard unit sphere T_I. Right, fitted T_M mesh (corresponding to a complete object) with several WFs plotted on it.

These substructures can be formally defined as follows:

Definition 1. Let N be any node of the tessellated sphere T, and let us call it Initial Focus. Let F^j be the j-th Wave Front associated to the Initial Focus N, with j = 1 ... q-1. The consecutive Wave Fronts verify the following construction law:

$$F^1 = \{N\} \tag{1}$$

$$\vdots$$

$$F^{j+1} = V(F^j) - \bigcup_{m=1}^{j-1} F^m \qquad \forall j = 1,\cdots,q-1 \tag{2}$$

where V represents the three-neighbour local relationship imposed by T.

Definition 2. *Let MW^N be the Modeling Wave with Initial focus N. MW^N is a partition of the tessellated sphere T integrated by the q consecutive Wave Fronts associated to the Initial Focus N, i.e., $MW^N = \{F^1, F^2, \ldots, F^q\}$.*

It is important to notice that each node of the standard mesh together with its origin of coordinates configures a different viewing direction. Therefore, each viewing direction has associated a Modeling Wave. Fig. 3 shows two MWs on the tessellated sphere and the axes of vision defined by the focus and the origin of coordinates in both cases.

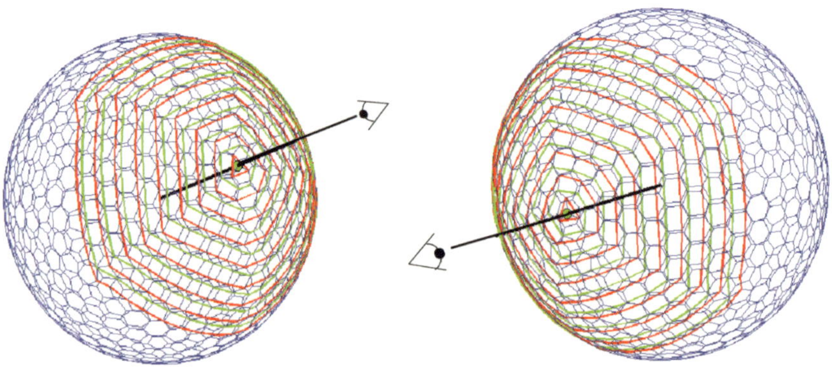

Fig. 3. Representation of two Modeling Waves on the tessellated sphere. Each MW is associated to a different point of view

Definition 3. *We call Modeling Wave Set associated to T to the integration of all the Modeling Waves that can be built from the nodes of T, i.e.,* $MWS = \{MW^1, MW^2, \ldots, MW^h\}$*, where* MW^i, $i = 1 \ldots h$*, is the Modeling Wave with the i-th node of T as Initial Focus.*

In order to adapt the MWS representation to partial data we have developed a partial MWS modeling procedure. Two half-spheres can be defined along the viewing direction; one in front, called $T_{1/2}$, and the other one at the back. The process is based on deforming the first one half-sphere $T_{1/2}$, while the second one is rejected. An approximation stage of $T_{1/2}$ to the normalized object data points and a posterior local regularization stage are performed in order to get the deformed mesh to be as uniform as possible. The result is a set of nodes, denoted generically as T' instead of T, fixed to the surface data as much as possible. Fig. 4 illustrates some aspects of this procedure, but a more detailed explanation can be found at (Salamanca et al., 2000).

Notice that now the number of nodes of each partial model is usually different to each other and it is less than the number of nodes in the standard unit sphere, i.e. $h' = ord\ (T') \neq h$. Contrary to complete model, the Modeling Wave structure appears broken in the partial models. Consequently when part of the surface of an object is available we just adapt the method taking the set of complete Wave Fronts that appears in the partial model corresponding to the partial view. In fact, spherical features of an object must now be calculated from its partial spherical model T', which has been created from the range data of a given partial view. After the mentioned mesh adjustment process, the obtained T' mesh also has hexagonal or pentagonal patches. Each of the nodes of this mesh has a connectivity of 3 except for those nodes that are in the contour with connectivity less than 3. Fig. 5 shows the intensity image of an object and the obtained spherical model for a partial view of the object acquired from a given point of view. Partial mesh has now much less nodes than the standard unit sphere. Contour nodes are drawn in red in the right half of Fig.5.

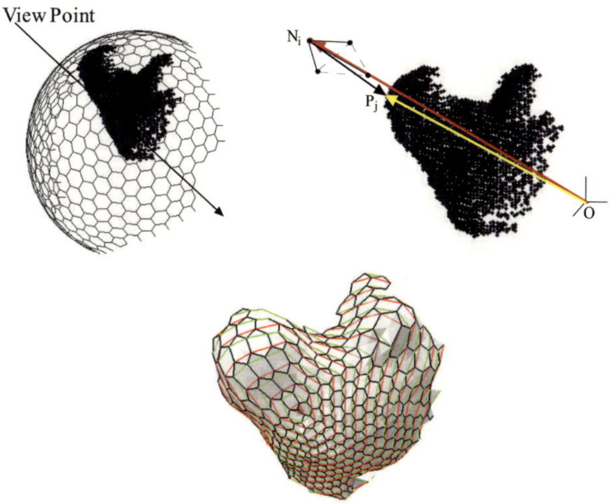

Fig. 4. Partial view modeling. Left above, $T_{1/2}$ associated to normalized object data points. Right above, approximation process. Bellow, partial model showing some broken WFs

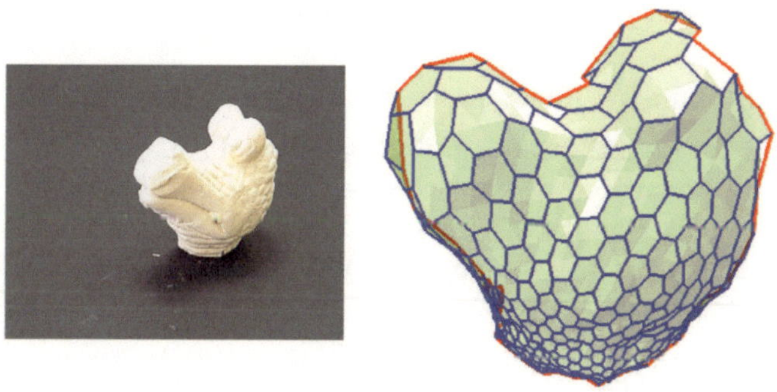

Fig. 5. Intensity image of an object and spherical model for a partial view of the object.

4.1 Cone-Curvature. Concept, definitions and properties

Once the modeling structure has been created is time to compute discrete values of some three-dimensional object features and storing them conveniently in the MWS structure. So, it is possible to map global and local features of T_M over T_I considering 3-connectivity, like discrete curvature measurements (Hebert et al., 1995), colour features, distance to the origin of coordinates, etc. In this case, Cone-Curvature (CC) represents an intuitive feature based on the MW structure taking into account the location of the WFs inside the model T_M. In the following formal definition of CC we will use generically T' to call to the spherical mesh because this definition is applicable both to complete and partial meshes.

Definition 4. *Let N be Initial Focus on T'. We call j-th Cone Curvature α^j of N to the angle of the cone with vertex N whose surface is fitted to the j-th Wave Front of the Modeling Wave associated to N. Formally:*

$$\alpha^j = sign(F^j) * \left| \frac{\pi}{2} - \frac{1}{t_j} \sum_{i=1}^{t_j} \gamma_i^j \right| \tag{3}$$

$$\gamma^j{}_i = \angle C^j N N_i \ , N_i \in F^j$$

where t_j is the number of nodes of F^j and C^j is the barycentre of F^j. The range of CC values is [$-\pi/2$, $\pi/2$], being the sign assigned taking into account the relative location of O, C^j, and N, where O is the origin of the coordinate system fixed to T' (see Fig. 6).

Given a focus N, there exists a set of wave fronts, q, which define the CCs for this focus $\{\alpha^1, \alpha^2, \alpha^3, \ldots \alpha^q\}$ that provide complete information about the curvature of the surroundings of N. Finally, q, which we call *Front Order*, can have values from 2 (case q = 1 does not make sense) to the maximum number of fronts that the object has. As we want to work with partial models, the maximum order corresponds to the higher complete Wave Front.

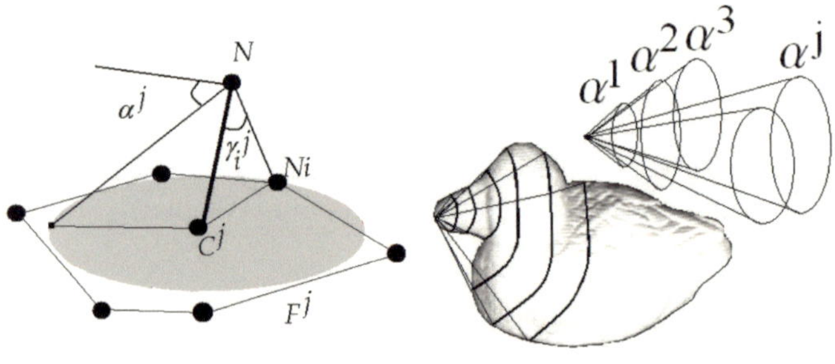

Fig. 6. Left, definition of the CC. Right, visualization of the CC for a node N

Next we will analyze several meaningful properties of CC on MWS models. These properties can be summarized as: uniqueness, invariance to affine transformations (translation, rotation and scaling), robustness and adaptability.

Fig. 7 plots a set of CCs $\{\alpha^1, \alpha^2, \alpha^3, \ldots \alpha^q\}$ q = 18, for different nodes of a mesh model. In this case the locations of the nodes correspond to different areas in the mesh. Note that their CC

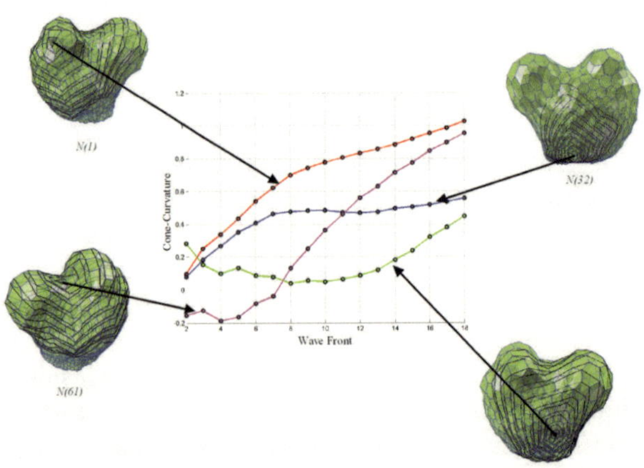

Fig. 7. Representation of CC ($\{\alpha^1, \alpha^2, \alpha^3, \ldots \alpha^q\}$, q = 18), for the nodes $N(1)$, $N(7)$, $N(32)$ and $N(61)$ of T_M.

distributions are very distant. Consequently different zones of an object can be represented and recognized by a CC vector.

In Fig. 8 the mesh T' has been coloured to represent the values of the CCs for different orders (2, 8, 14 and 16). As it can be seen, there exists continuity in the colours of the mesh in both cases: for the same order (i.e. between the nodes of a same mesh) and for different orders (i.e. between the nodes of the different meshes). On the other hand, the change in colour (equivalent to the change in the CC) is much less in the lower orders. This means that high orders give poorer information than lower orders.

In order to demonstrate that CC is invariant to affine transformations Fig. 9 shows the CCs after carrying out a set of random rotations, translations and scaling. Models and CC graphs for five cases can be seen in it. Note that CC vectors suffer a little variation in all cases.

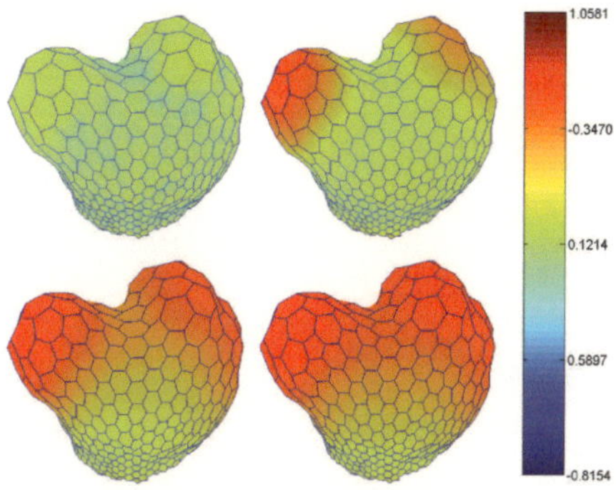

Fig. 8. Representation in colour of the cone-curvatures in each mesh node for orders 2, 8, 14 and 16 (left to right and from top to bottom). A bar is also shown where the colours for the maximum, mean and minimum cone-curvatures of the object can be seen.

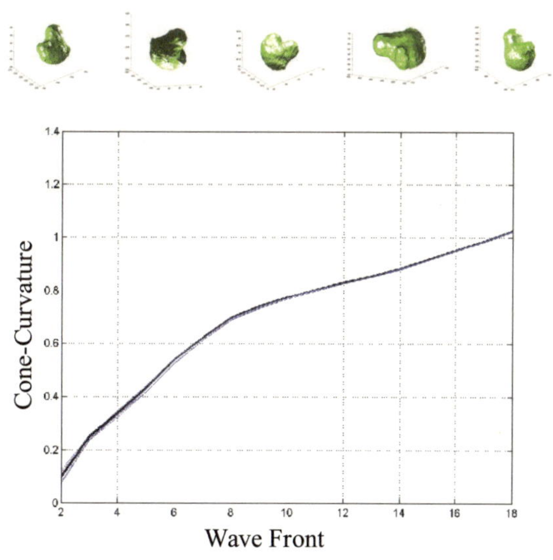

Fig. 9. CCs for five free-form models obtained from rotation, translation and scaling of the original range data. The invariance existing in this measurement can be seen.

Next property is concerning to the robustness of the CCs. In this case, a random noise has been generated for each node proportional to the inter-node mean distance. Fig. 10 shows the meshes and cone-curvatures for 0%, 5%, 10%, 25%, 50% and 100% of noise. The colour used for drawing the meshes is the same colour as in the graphs of the CCs. In all these graphs it can be seen that CCs remains invariant for normal noise levels.

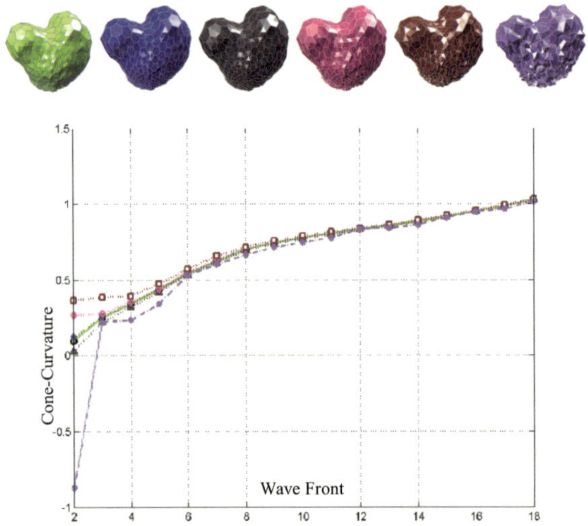

Fig. 10. Representation of CCs with different levels of noise in the mesh (0%, 5%, 10%, 25%, 50% y 100%). The colour used of the meshes is the same as in the representation of CC.

Finally CC concept is flexible or adaptable in the next sense. As it has been said in previous paragraphs the CC values depend on the depth level over the MW structure. So, different combinations with respect to different criteria could be chosen for exploring an object (model) through its CC. For instance, we can consider a wide range of criteria: explorations for only one WF for low levels, for medium levels and for high levels. On the other hand we can choose explorations using contiguous/discontiguous Wave Fronts throughout the whole MW structure. This means that, using the object model and following different criteria, a wide variety of parts of the object (or depth levels) can be chosen in order to recognize an object. This property is obviously the key for performing further recognition approaches in partial and occluded scenes as will be discussed in the next section.

4.2 Weighted Cone-Curvature (WCC)

In order to apply the CCs to the recognition of partial views several factors have to be considered in advance:

1. The number of complete wave fronts in a partial view is variable.
2. The number of wave fronts can vary between a partial model and its corresponding complete model.
3. The mean length of the internode distance is different for the partial model and the complete model in the same object.

These questions imply that one-to-one comparison between the CCs of the same order between the partial and total models could be inefficient. Therefore, we have used a more compact information from the CCs which reduces the dimensionality, replacing each CC vector $\{\alpha^1, \alpha^2, \alpha^3, \ldots \alpha^q\}$ with a scalar that summarizes the information of q CCs. Thus each node of a model has a single value associate and, consequently, an object is characterized by h values, h being the number of nodes of the corresponding model. We call this feature Weighted Cone-Curvature (WCC).

To evaluate quantitatively if the proposed reduction is possible, the correlation existing between the CCs was calculated. This is shown in gray scale in Fig. 11 (white for high values and black for low values), and it has been calculated as the mean value of all the correlation coefficients of the meshes in the database. From analysis of the figure, and as we had envisaged, it can be concluded that there is a high correlation between fronts of near orders, which increases as this order increases.

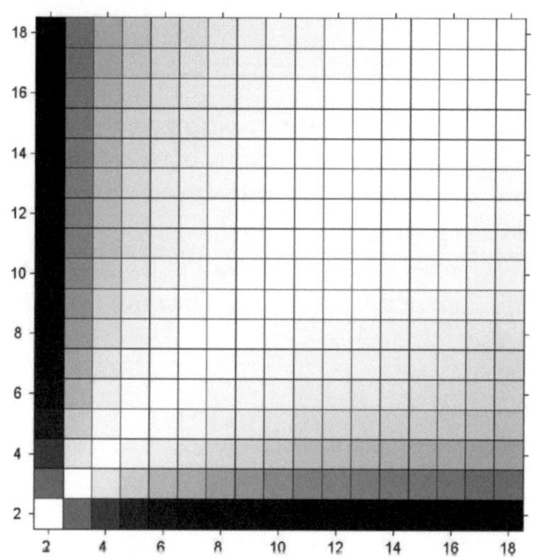

Fig. 11. Illustration of the correlation existing between the Cone-Curvatures of the wave fronts of orders 2 to 18 in the database.

If we denote the WCC for each $N' \in T'$ as c^w, the linear combination will be:

$$c^w = \sum_{j=1}^{q} v^j \alpha^j \tag{4}$$

where v^j are the coordinates of the eigen vector associated with the eigen value of greater value of the covariance matrix for the q initial variables.

This eigen vector was determined empirically by evaluating the principal components on the Cone-Curvatures of all the mesh nodes. As regards the orders considered, we studied three possibilities:

1. Wave fronts from $q = 2$ to $q = 18$.
2. Wave fronts from $q = 4$ to $q = 18$.
3. Wave fronts from $q = 4$ to $q = 9$.

Fig. 12 represents, for the object that we are analyzing, the WCCs in the three cases, plotted over the object mesh and using a colour code to express the range from negative to positive values. We can see that the WCCs for the first and second cases are very similar.

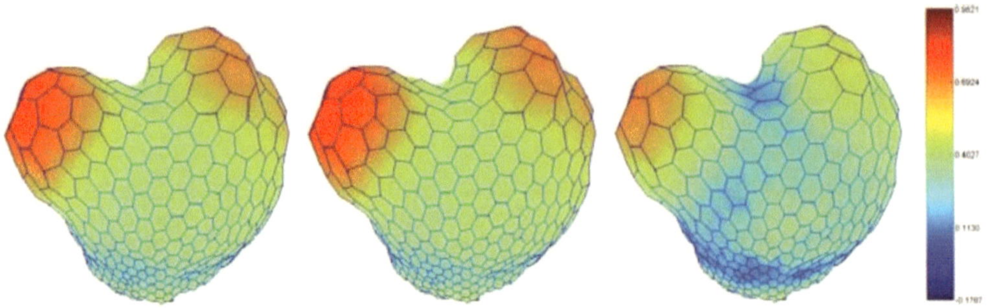

Fig. 12. Representation in colour of the WCCs of each mesh node for cases (1), (2) and (3) (left to right). A bar is shown where the colours can be seen for the maximum, mean and minimum WCCs of the object.

4.3 Application of WCC to partial views recognition

WCCs allow us to carry out a selection of regions on a complete object model that can be similar to a specific region of the scene. For this selection, an error measurement between scene and model is defined as follows:

Definition 5. *Let $N' \in T'$ be the node of the partial mesh T' which is the nearest to the axis of vision. The error or distance of comparison of weighted cone-curvatures for each $N \in T_i$, where T_i is the i-th total model of the object database is defined as:*

$$e_j(N) = \left| c^{w'}(N') - c^{w}\left(N_j\right) \right| \tag{5}$$

where the subscript j extends from 1 to the maximum number of nodes existing in T_i and $|\bullet|$ represents the absolute value.

The fact of conditioning the reduction of nodes around T_i to just one measurement of error can cause significant errors in this reduction. Therefore, in order to reinforce the reduction, for each $N \in T_i$ two errors will be measured. The first will consider the WCC's to the furthest fronts generated from N'. We will call this error deep error and give it the symbol $e_j^p(N)$. The second will consider the nearest fronts generated from N'. This time we will call the error superficial error and give it the symbol $e_j^s(N)$.

In both instances a set of errors equal to the number of nodes existing in T_i is obtained, and from these errors the nodes $\mathbf{N}_i^{cc}$ of the mesh that will be passed to the next stage of the algorithm will be determined. If we call $\mathbf{N}^p$ to the set of nodes of T_i with less e_i^p values, and $\mathbf{N}^s$ to the set of nodes of T_i with less e_i^s values, $\mathbf{N}_i^{cc}$ will be:

$$\mathbf{N}_i^{cc} = \mathbf{N}^p \cup \mathbf{N}^s \tag{6}$$

5. Principal components and ICP stages

In this section the last two stages of the recognition algorithm will be commented on for matching the partial views on complete models. These are the principal components and ICP stages. In the principal components stage the method proposed is based on calculating the principal components on the range data that we employed to obtain the model T' used in the previous stage. If we call these data **X**, the principal components are defined as the eigen values and eigen vectors $\{(\lambda_i, \vec{e}_i) \quad i = 1, \cdots, m\}$ of the covariance matrix.

The eigen values are invariant to rotations and displacements and the eigen vectors to displacements. The eigen vectors conform a reference system linked to the data. This means that the eigen values can be used to evaluate what part of the range data of the complete model correspond to the scene, and the eigen vectors to calculate a first approximation to the transformation of the partial data to be matched on the total data. This approximation will only reflect the rotation sub matrix of the total transformation, since the origins of the two frames will coincide.

To apply this technique it is necessary to evaluate, before the recognition process, all the possibly existing partial views on the range data of the complete object. For this, the space of the possible points of view existing around the object was discretized, and a method was developed for generating *virtual partial views (VPV)* based on the z-buffer algorithm. From each of these VPV their principal components will be calculated and used in the matching stage as explained earlier.

Comparison of the eigen values gives information about the possible areas where the partial view can be matched, but this information is global and, as we have said, only gives information about the rotation.

Thus it will be necessary to do a final calculation stage to refine the matching and to calculate the definitive transformation. For this we will use the ICP algorithm on a number of possible candidates marked in the eigen value comparison stage. The ICP must start from an approximation to the initial transformation, which in our case corresponds to the transformation given in the matching of the eigen vectors. The ending error in the ICP algorithm will measure the exactness of the definitive transformation and the correctness of the area where the view will be matched.

The comparison of the eigen values of the partial view and the virtual partial views is done by measuring an index of error given in the following expression:

$$e_i^{pc}(N) = \left\| \Lambda_i^v(N) - \Lambda^r \right\| \tag{7}$$

where $N \in \mathrm{N}_i^{cc}$ is the node from where we generated the VPV, $\Lambda_i^v(N)$ is the vector formed by the eigen values of the VPV generated from the node N of the i-th object of the object database (*i*=*1,..., K*), $\Lambda^r = \{\lambda_1^r, \lambda_2^r, \lambda_3^r\}$ is the vector formed by the eigen values of the real partial view and $\| \bullet \|$ is the Euclidean distance.

After the error has been calculated for all the $\mathbf{N}_i^{cc}$ nodes and all the objects in the object database, we obtain a list of these errors, e_i^{pc} (*i*=*1,..., K*), ordered from least to great. If we compare the first error (least error for a set object) in all the lists, an ordering of the different objects in the object database will be obtained. Thus in the last stage we can apply the ICP algorithm on a subset of the object database, just $\mathbf{B}^{pc}$, and for each of the objects using the transformations associated with the subset of nodes that have produced these errors.

For the resolution of the ICP it is necessary to determine an approximation to the transformation matrix R_1, between the partial view and the object in the object database. It is determined by applying the Horn method (Horn, 1988). This is calculated bearing in mind that the eigen vectors are orthonormal, and therefore:

$$R_1 = E^r(E_i^v(N))^{-1} = E^r(E_i^v(N))^T \quad (8)$$

where $E_i^v(N)$ are the eigen vectors of the VPV generated from $N \in \mathbf{N}^{pc}$ of the i-th model of the object database $\mathbf{B}^{pc}$, and E^r are the eigen vectors of the partial view.

6. Experimental results

The method presented in this work has been tested over a set of 20 objects. Range data of these objects have been acquired by means of a range sensor which provides an average resolution of approximately 1 mm. Real size of the used objects goes from 5 to 10 cm. height and there are both polyhedral shaped and free form objects (see Fig. 13). MWS models have been built by deforming a tessellated sphere with h=1280 nodes.

Fig. 13. Image of the objects used in the test of the algorithm.

The recognition was done for three partial views per object, except in one of them where after the determination of its partial model it was seen that it did not have enough wave fronts to be able to compare the weighted cone-curvatures. This means that recognition was done on a total of 59 partial models. The success rate has been the 90%, what demonstrates the validity of the method. The average computation time invested by the whole process was 90 seconds, programmed over a Pentium 4 at 2.4 GHz. computer under Matlab environment. A more detailed analysis of these results is next.

As it has been explained, in the first stage the weighted cone-curvatures of the partial model were compared for a node with a maximum number of wave fronts. From this comparison $\mathbf{N}_i^{cc}$ was determined (equation (6)). In the considered experiments, the maximum value of the number of nodes that form the sets $\mathbf{N}^p$ (deep search) and $\mathbf{N}^s$ (superficial search) was 32 each. Since the mesh used to obtain the complete model T_i was 1280, the minimum reduction of the space search in this stage was 95%. The reduction can be even bigger as long as there are nodes coinciding in $\mathbf{N}^p$ and $\mathbf{N}^s$. This step was carried out for all the objects of the initial database **B** and took an average of 7.95 seconds.

Concerning the second stage, it started from these nodes and the eigen values were compared, which allowed us to achieve the first reduction of the database ($\mathbf{B}^{pc}$ database). Reduction of the nodes obtained in the previous stage is also accomplished ($\mathbf{N}_i^{pc}$ set). It was determined experimentally that $\mathbf{B}^{pc}$ consists of approximately 35% of the objects of **B** and $\mathbf{N}_i^{pc}$ of approximately 8% of the nodes of $\mathbf{N}^{cc}$ per object, which represent very satisfactory reduction rates of the stage. This process spent around 1 sec.

Finally, the ICP algorithm was applied on seven objects (the mentioned 35% remaining in the $\mathbf{B}^{pc}$ database) and three nodes (corresponding to the mentioned 8%) for each $\mathbf{N}_i^{pc}$ object. As it can be deduced, most of the time invested by the algorithm was practically consumed in this stage.

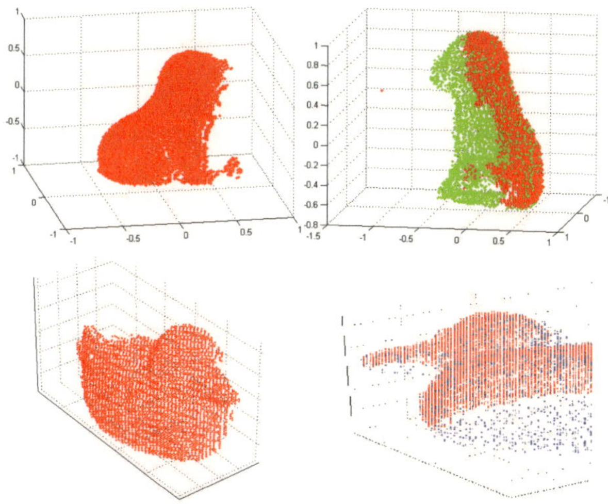

Fig. 14. Results obtained with several scenes of free-form objects without auto-occlusion

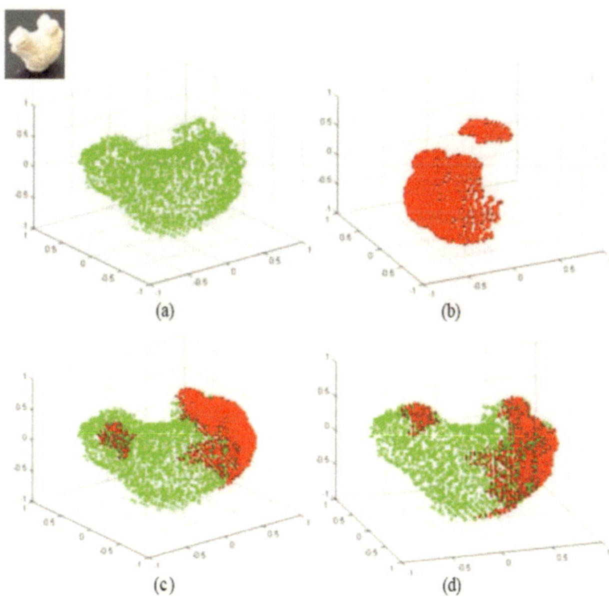

Fig. 15. Details of the process in a case of auto-occlusion. In (a) we can see the range data of the complete object, in (b) the range data of the scene which we want to recognize, and the result before (c) and after (d) ICP application.

Fig. 14 shows the results obtained with several scenes consisting of free-form objects. In these examples scene range data is superimposed to the complete object. Fig. 15 illustrates details of this process in a case of auto-occlusion. Part (a) presents the range data of the complete object, part (b) corresponds to range data of the scene, part (c) shows both range data superimposed after the raw transformation obtained in the principal components stage is applied and part (d) contains the final results after ICP algorithm application. Some plots have been rotated to enhance data visualization.
Complementary tests of this recognition procedure have been carried out in slightly different environments, for example in (Salamanca et al., 2007). Nevertheless, no significant performance differences can be extracted from the analysis of the obtained results in all these cases.

7. Conclusions

This work has described the experiences with a method for the recognition of free-form objects from their partial views. The method is divided into three stages: Weighted Cone-Curvatures stage, Principal Components stage, and ICP stage, being the first one the most effective from the recognition point of view. Due to this fact and to the originality of the handled features, this stage has been described in more detail in the chapter.
A new feature called Weighted Cone-Curvature is used in the first stage. This feature is measured on the spherical model built from the object range data. Its definition and application have been extended from the originally designed case of complete objects to the more specific case when only partial viewing of the objects are available. By the way, and as it has been stated, this has been the main objective of the present work. The basics of spherical modeling have been included, as well as the method for computing the WCC in complete and partial objects models. From the analysis of the WCC feature it has been demonstrated that it exhibits very adequate properties for applying in recognition and positioning tasks. These characteristics allow achieving important reductions in the number of nodes that define the possible axes of vision from which the partial view has been acquired. In fact, the experiments presented in this work have shown that the reduction rate is, as minimum, of 95%, what means in practice a very significant reduction.
In the last two stages of the algorithm the definitive candidate is searched looking for the best matching of the partial view with the candidates of the previous stages. In the first of these two stages, the eigen values of the Principal Components of the partial view are compared with those Principal Components virtually extracted from the complete models just in the directions determined in the WCCs stage. By means of this stage we reduce again the nodes that define the possible axes of vision and the original database. We also calculate, from the eigen vectors of the Principal Components, a first approximation to the transformation matrix between the partial view and the complete object. Finally, in the second of these two stages, the ICP algorithm is applied and the selected candidate is chosen as a function of the convergence error. The fine transformation matrix is also estimated at this point.
The validity of the full method was proven with the recognition of 59 partial views in an object database of 20 objects, both polyhedral and free-shaped. The global success rate was 90%.
In contrast, two minor limitations of the algorithm can be mentioned. In first place, the use of spherical models restricts the applicability of the method since it does not allow coping with objects with genus different to zero. Even more, the spherical modeling technique by

itself is extremely complex. On the second hand, the time of execution of the algorithm is high, which means that its application in real time systems is not possible. At this concern it must be said that the algorithm it has been completely programmed in Matlab, what means a significant slowing down in execution time. Nevertheless, all the algorithms using representations like ours that have been mentioned in the introduction present this limitation.

8. Acknowledgements

The research described in this work has been supported by the Spanish CICYT through the grants DPI2008-05444 and DPI2009-14024-C02-01. It also belongs to the activities carried out in the frame of the RoboCity2030-II excellence research network of the CAM (ref. S2009/DPI-1559).

9. References

Adan, A.; Cerrada, C. & Feliu, V. (2000). Modeling wave set: Definition and application of a new topological organization of 3D object modelling. *Computer Vision and Image Understanding*, Vol. 79, No. 2, (August 2000) 281–307, ISSN 1077-3142

Adan, A. & Adan, M. (2004). A flexible similarity measure for 3D shapes recognition. *IEEE Transactions on Pattern Analysis and Machine Intelligence*, Vol. 26, No. 11, (November 2004) 1507–1520, ISSN 0162-8828

Besl, P.J. & McKay, N.D. (1992). A method for registration of 3-D shapes. *IEEE Transactions on Pattern Analysis and Machine Intelligence*, Vol. 14, No. 2, (February 1992) 239–256, ISSN 0162-8828

Campbell, R.J. & Flynn, P. J. (1999). Eigenshapes for 3D object recognition in range data, *Proceedings of the IEEE Conference on Computer Vision and Pattern Recognition*, Vol. 2, pp. 2505–2510, Fort Collins, Colorado, USA, June 1999, IEEE Computer Society

Chua, C. S. & Jarvis, R. (1997). Point signatures: A new representation for 3D object recognition. *International Journal of Computer Vision*, Vol. 25, No. 1, (October 1997) 63–85, ISSN 0920-5691

Cyr, C.M. & Kimia, B.B. (2004). A similarity-based aspect-graph approach to 3D object recognition. *International Journal of Computer Vision*, Vol. 57, No. 1, (April 2004) 5–22, ISSN 0920-5691

Hebert, M.; Ikeuchi, K. & Delingette, H. (1995). A spherical representation for recognition of free-form surfaces. *IEEE Transactions on Pattern Analysis and Machine Intelligence*, Vol. 17, No. 7, (July 1995) 681–690, ISSN 0162-8828

Horn, Berthold K.P. (1988). Closed form solutions of absolute orientation using orthonormal matrices. *Journal of the Optical Society of America A*, Vol. 5, No. 7, (July 1988) 1127–1135, ISSN 1084-7529

Johnson, A.E. & Hebert, M. (1999). Using spin images for efficient object recognition in cluttered 3D scenes. *IEEE Transactions on Pattern Analysis and Machine Intelligence*, Vol. 21, No. 5, (May 1999) 433–449, ISSN 0162-8828

Liu, X; Sun, R.; Kang, S. B. & Shum, H.Y. (2003). Directional histogram for three-dimensional shape similarity, *Proceedings of the IEEE Conference on Computer Vision and Pattern Recognition*, Vol. I, pp. 813–820, Los Alamitos, California, USA, June 2003, IEEE Computer Society

Salamanca, S.; Cerrada, C. & Adan, A. (2000). HWM: a new spherical representation structure for modeling partial views of an object. *Proceedings of the International Conference on Pattern Recognition (ICPR'2000)*, Vol. 3, pp. 770–773, Barcelona, Spain, September 2000, IEEE Computer Society

Salamanca, S.; Adan, A., Cerrada, C., Adan, M.; Merchan, P. & Perez, E. (2007). Reconocimiento de objetos de forma libre a partir de datos de rango de una vista parcial usando cono curvaturas ponderadas. *Revista Iberoamericana de Automatica e Informatica Industrial*, Vol. 4, No. 1, (Enero 2007) 95–106, ISSN 1697-7912

Serratosa, F.; Alquezar, R. & Sanfeliu, A. (2003) Function-described graphs for modelling objects represented by sets of attributed graphs. *Pattern Recognition*, Vol. 36, No. 3, (March 2003) 781–798, ISSN 0031-3203

Skocaj, D. & Leonardis, A. (2001). Robust recognition and pose determination of 3-D objects using range image in eigenspace approach, *Proceedings of 3rd International Conference on 3D Digital Imaging and Modeling (3DIM 2001)*, pp. 171–178, Quebec City, Canada, May-June 2001, IEEE Computer Society

Yamany, S. & Farag, A. (2002). Surfacing signatures: An orientation independent free-form surface representation scheme for the purpose of objects registration and matching. *IEEE Transactions on Pattern Analysis and Machine Intelligence*, Vol. 24, No. 8, (August 2002) 1105–1120, ISSN 0162-8828